T0207011

Facebook Nation

Newton Lee

Facebook Nation

Total Information Awareness

Third Edition

 Springer

Newton Lee
Institute for Education, Research, and Scholarships
Los Angeles, CA, USA

ISBN 978-1-0716-1869-1   ISBN 978-1-0716-1867-7   (eBook)
https://doi.org/10.1007/978-1-0716-1867-7

This Springer imprint is published by the registered company Springer Science+Business Media, LLC
part of Springer Nature.
The registered company address is: 1 New York Plaza, New York, NY 10004, U.S.A.

To peace, love, and freedom

Acknowledgements

The author wishes to thank the following contributing authors for writing some of the book chapters:

Julien Carbonnell, University of Cergy-Pontoise
Mats Danielson, Stockholm University
Love Ekenberg, International Institute of Applied Systems Analysis
Alex Houg, BlitzMetrics
Inessa Lee, Institute for Education, Research, and Scholarships
Adriana Mihai, University of Bucharest
Emily Temple-Wood, WikiProject Women Scientists
Dennis Yu, BlitzMetrics

About the Book

This book explores total information awareness empowered by social media. At the FBI Citizens Academy in February 2021, I asked the FBI about the January 6 Capitol riot organized on social media that led to the unprecedented ban of a sitting U.S. President by all major social networks. In March 2021, Facebook CEO Mark Zuckerberg, Google CEO Sundar Pichai, and Twitter CEO Jack Dorsey appeared before Congress to face criticism about their handling of misinformation and online extremism that culminated in the storming of Capitol Hill.

With more than three billion monthly active users, Facebook family of apps is by far the world's largest social network. Facebook as a nation is bigger than the top three most populous countries in the world: China, India, and the United States. Social media has enabled its users to inform and misinform the public, to appease and disrupt Wall Street, to mitigate and exacerbate the COVID-19 pandemic, and to unite and divide a country.

Mark Zuckerberg once said, "We exist at the intersection of technology and social issues." He should have heeded his own words. In October 2021, former Facebook manager-turned-whistleblower Frances Haugen testified at the U.S. Senate that Facebook's products "harm children, stoke division, and weaken our democracy."

This book offers discourse and practical advice on information and misinformation, cybersecurity and privacy issues, cryptocurrency and business intelligence, social media marketing and caveats, e-government and e-activism, as well as the pros and cons of total information awareness including the Edward Snowden leaks.

Contents

About the Author

Prof. Newton Lee is the founding president of the 501(c)(3) nonprofit Institute for Education, Research, and Scholarships based in Los Angeles, California and a 2021 graduate of the FBI Citizens Academy.

Lee was the founder of Disney Online Technology Forum, creator of AT&T Bell Labs' first-ever commercial artificial intelligence tool, inventor of the world's first annotated multimedia OPAC for the U.S. National Agricultural Library, developer of an AI Expert System for counterterrorism at the Institute for Defense Analyses, designer of an AI Expert System in pharmacology and drug interactions at Virginia Tech, and the longest serving editor-in-chief in the history of the Association for Computing Machinery for its publication Computers in Entertainment (2003–2018).

He graduated Summa Cum Laude from Virginia Tech with a B.S. and M.S. degree in Computer Science (specializing in Artificial Intelligence), and he earned a perfect GPA from Vincennes University with an A.S. degree in Electrical Engineering and an honorary doctorate in Computer Science.

Lee has lectured at Emily Carr University, Massachusetts Institute of Technology, Simon Fraser University, University of Southern California, Vincennes University, and Woodbury University. He has been honored with a Michigan Leading Edge Technologies Award, two community development awards from the California Junior Chamber of Commerce, and four volunteer project leadership awards from The Walt Disney Company.

Part I
Prologue

Chapter 1
From 1984 to Total Information Awareness

"Information is the oxygen of the modern age. It seeps through the walls topped by barbed wire, it wafts across the electrified borders, the Goliath of totalitarianism will be brought down by the David of the microchip."
– President Ronald Reagan (June 1989)

"One of my heroes, Edwin Land of Polaroid, said about the importance of people who could stand at the intersection of humanities and sciences, and I decided that's what I wanted to do."
– Apple and Pixar co-founder Steve Jobs (December 2009)

"We exist at the intersection of technology and social issues."
– Facebook CEO Mark Zuckerberg (September 2011)

"It's important to recognize that you can't have 100% security and also then have 100% privacy and zero inconvenience."
– President Barack Obama (June 2013)

"Understanding who you serve is always a very important problem, and it only gets harder the more people that you serve."
– Facebook CEO Mark Zuckerberg (April 2014)

"The NSA might still be watching us. But now we can watch them."
– U.S. Congressman Jim Sensenbrenner (May 2014)

"Public support and understanding are essential to the FBI's success. We can't accomplish our mission if people don't believe us and trust us; our credibility can make all the difference in whether someone comes forward with a vital piece of information that could prevent crime or a terrorist attack."
– FBI Director Christopher Wray (March 2021)

1.1 U.S. Capitol Riot on January 6, 2021

The U.S. Capitol's last breach was more than 200 years ago in August 1814 by invading British troops who set fire to the building and other landmarks during the raging war of 1812 (1). At the FBI Citizens Academy on February 23, 2021, I asked

© Springer Science+Business Media, LLC, part of Springer Nature 2021
N. Lee, *Facebook Nation*, https://doi.org/10.1007/978-1-0716-1867-7_1

the FBI about the January 6 Capitol riot organized on social media that led to the unprecedented ban of a sitting U.S. President by all major social networks. I questioned, "According to *The Washington Post*, an FBI office in Norfolk, Virginia, issued a warning on January 5th that extremists were preparing to travel to Washington to commit violence and 'war.' Now according to fbi.gov, there are more than 830 special agents in the Washington D.C. field office. What could FBI have done in response to the Capitol riot during the four-hour insurrection on January 6th?"

Previously on September 10, 2020, I had a lunch meeting with an FBI special agent to discuss COVID-19, school and community safety, domestic terrorism, and the prevention of American Civil War II. Prior to the meeting, the special agent had requested a copy of *Counterterrorism and Cybersecurity*, my second book after *Facebook Nation* in the *Total Information Awareness* trilogy. My book sings high praises of the FBI for their breakthrough investigation into the 9/11 terrorist attacks. The fact that J. Edgar Hoover and I share the same birthday on January 1st only added to my excitement when I was nominated by the special agent to join the FBI Citizens Academy (see Fig. 1.1).

Two months after my lunch meeting with the FBI, Jim Arroyo of the Oath Keepers posted in November 2020 his two-part videos on YouTube titled "The Coming Civil War?" (2) Second Civil War sounds far-fetched, but not so metaphorically. Half of the U.S. would implement abortion bans if or when the U.S. Supreme Court were to overturn Roe v. Wade which ruled (7–2) in 1973 that unduly restrictive state regulation of abortion is unconstitutional (3). Twenty-two U.S. states have active military forces known as state guards that are independent of the federal government. In December 2021, Florida governor Ron DeSantis proposed reinstating the Florida State Guard to be the defense force under his command (4).

The FBI was understandably concerned about public safety in the divisive and politically charged atmosphere nationwide, especially during and after the polarized 2020 U.S. presidential election, no matter who won. Little did we anticipate the violent attack against the 117th United States Congress at the U.S. Capitol on January 6, 2021 in an attempt to disrupt the ongoing joint session on counting the Electoral College ballots—a final step to confirm President-elect Joe Biden's victory in the 2020 presidential election over incumbent President Donald Trump.

On March 2, 2021, FBI Director Christopher Wray testified on Capitol Hill, saying "that attack, that siege was criminal behavior, plain and simple. And it's behavior that we, the FBI, view as domestic terrorism" (5). Before we examine the failed insurrection organized on social media that left five people dead, more than a hundred injured, and subsequent suicide of four capitol police officers, let us travel back in time to 1984.

1.2   President Ronald Reagan on April 3, 1984

On April 3, 1984, President Ronald Reagan signed the National Security Decision Directive (NSDD) 138: Combating Terrorism, which authorized the increase of intelligence collection directed against groups or states involved in terrorism (6) (7).

U.S. Department of Justice

Federal Bureau of Investigation

Office of the Director   *Washington, D.C. 20535-0001*

March 23, 2021

Prof. Newton Lee
Federal Bureau of Investigation
Indianapolis Division

Dear Prof. Lee:

Congratulations on your graduation from the FBI Citizens Academy program. I'm grateful for your willingness to sacrifice valuable time from your work and family to learn more about the FBI and our mission.

What you have learned will hopefully give you a unique insight into the successes of our organization as well as some of the challenges that we and our law enforcement partners face every day. We hope that you will share this knowledge with others, and serve as an FBI ambassador in your workplace and your community. By spreading the word, you help us to demystify the FBI and let people know the vital role our special agents, analysts, and professional staff play in protecting all people in the United States and Americans around the world.

Public support and understanding are essential to the FBI's success. We can't accomplish our mission if people don't believe us and trust us; our credibility can make all the difference in whether someone comes forward with a vital piece of information that could prevent crime or a terrorist attack.

Beyond serving as an ambassador for the Bureau, I would ask you to do three more things as a Citizens Academy graduate. First, continue to be a role model in your community and a leader in your chosen field. Second, please recommend your peers to us for the Citizens Academy program, so even more people can benefit from this experience. And third, please join the FBI Citizens Academy Alumni Association, which promotes safer communities through community service projects with an emphasis on the FBI's mission.

Thank you for your support. We look forward to working with you in the coming years to protect our communities and our country.

Sincerely yours,

Christopher A. Wray
Director

Fig. 1.1 A Letter from FBI Director Christopher Wray on March 23, 2021

RONALD REAGAN

January 5, 1983

Mr. Newton Lee
Rm 133
Harrison Hall Vu
Vincennes, Indiana 47591

Dear Mr. Lee:

I am grateful to you, more than I can express in a letter,
for your wonderful support of our Congressional Committee.

I know you worked extremely hard in this last election to
protect the progress we have made in rebuilding our military strength and restoring economic prosperity.

(some original text has been omitted for this excerpt)

Your faith and support have meant so much to me in the past.
I pray I can count on you again to make a generous contribution to help our Party and our nation.

Sincerely,

Ronald Reagan

RR/ces

Fig. 1.2 Excerpt of a Letter from President Ronald Reagan on January 5, 1983

I was a graduate student at Virginia Tech majoring in computer science with special-
ization in artificial intelligence (8).

A year earlier in January 1983, I received a surprise letter from the White House
sent to my alma mater Vincennes University. The 4-page letter opened with "Dear
Mr. Lee: I am grateful to you, more than I can express in a letter, for your wonderful
support of our Congressional Committee." (See Fig. 1.2) Although I was neither a
registered Republican nor Democrat at the time, I was truly delighted by the
President's letter.

In the summer of 1984, then Virginia Tech professor Dr. Timothy Lindquist
introduced me to Dr. John F. Kramer at the Institute for Defense Analyses (IDA), a
nonprofit think tank serving the U.S. Department of Defense (DoD) and the
Executive Office of the President (9). Partly motivated by President Reagan's letter,
I accepted the internship and became a research staff member at IDA. My first summer project was to assist in the drafting of the Military Standard Common APSE
(Ada Programming Support Environment) Interface Set (CAIS) (10). My second
project in the winter semester was to design a counterterrorism software program
for a multi-agency joint research effort involving the Defense Advanced Research

Projects Agency (DARPA), National Security Agency (NSA), and Federal Bureau of Investigation (FBI).

As a co-pioneer of artificial intelligence applications in counterterrorism, I helped develop a natural language parser and machine learning program to digest news and articles in search of potential terrorist threats around the globe. Employing psychology and cognitive science, the prototype system thinks like a human in constructing small-scale models of reality that it uses to anticipate events (11). The knowledge representation and data structures were based on "A Framework for Representing Knowledge" by MIT Artificial Intelligence Lab researcher Marvin Minsky (12). A similar idea was used in software by IBM and Baylor College of Medicine to digest thousands of research papers and then predict new discoveries that could help to develop new cancer drugs (13).

I joined AT&T Bell Laboratories in 1985 to further my research on artificial intelligence and expert systems. At Bell Labs, I conceived Dynamic Mental Models (DM2) as a general algorithm that combines analytical models and experiential knowledge in diagnostic problem solving, regardless of the problem domains (14). The algorithm mimics a human expert in formulating and using an internal, cognitive representation of a physical system during the process of diagnosis. In 1989, the U.S. Army Research Office studied DM2 for use in diagnostic support of complex modern weapons systems with encouraging results (15).

Inspired by Steve Jobs' revolutionary NeXT machines, I switched my focus to multimedia applications in 1989. Jobs later told Walter Isaacson in an interview, "One of my heroes, Edwin Land of Polaroid, said about the importance of people who could stand at the intersection of humanities and sciences, and I decided that's what I wanted to do" (16). Integrating artificial intelligence, expert systems, natural language processing, and hypermedia, I developed on the NeXT Computer the world's first annotated multimedia Online Public Access Catalog (OPAC) at Virginia Tech Library Systems (VTLS) and the U.S. National Agricultural Library (17).

Despite NeXT's limited commercial success, its NeXTSTEP operating system and object-oriented programming had a wide-ranging impact on the computer industry. Tim Berners-Lee at the European Organization for Nuclear Research (CERN) used a NeXT Computer in 1991 to create the first web browser and web server (18). NeXT also gained popularity at U.S. federal agencies including the Naval Research Laboratory (NRL), National Security Agency (NSA), Defense Advanced Research Projects Agency (DARPA), Central Intelligence Agency (CIA), and National Reconnaissance Office (NRO) (19).

In 1996, I switched my focus again, this time to the World Wide Web, when I joined Disney Online to build games, websites, social media, and search technology for The Walt Disney Company. Disney is an early adopter of the Internet as well as online communities. In 2000, I led a team in creating Disney Online Chat Studio and multiplayer games where children could engage in safe chats and send pre-screened messages to one another (20).

It was at Disney where I met Dr. Eric Haseltine whom I invited to my Disney Online Technology Forum in 2001 to give a talk on how a human brain reacts neurologically to stories. After the 9/11 terrorist attacks, Haseltine left his position as Executive Vice President of R&D at Walt Disney Imagineering to join the National

Security Agency (NSA) as Director of Research in 2002. From 2005 to 2007, Haseltine was Associate Director for Science and Technology at the newly established Office of the Director of National Intelligence (ODNI). In collaboration with Georgetown University researchers (21), Haseltine and his successor Steve Nixon at ODNI oversaw the development of Argus, a biosurveillance artificial intelligence program that monitors foreign news reports and other open sources looking for anything that could provide an early warning of an epidemic, nuclear accident, or environmental catastrophe (22).

1.3   Total Information Awareness

In an April 2002 statement, Dr. Tony Tether, then director of Defense Advanced Research Projects Agency (DARPA), informed the U.S. Senate Committee on Armed Services about the new establishment of the Information Awareness Office (IAO) headed by controversial ex-Navy Admiral John Poindexter, former U.S. National Security Advisor to President Ronald Reagan (See Fig. 1.3). IAO's charter was to "develop the information systems needed to find, identify, track, and understand terrorist networks and vastly improve what we know about our adversaries" (23). IAO was responsible for the Evidence Extraction and Link Discovery

Fig. 1.3 Official Seal of the Information Awareness Office (IAO)

program, Wargaming the Asymmetric Environment program, and Total Information Awareness (TIA) program.

The American public was startled on November 9, 2002 by *The New York Times* headline: "Pentagon Plans a Computer System That Would Peek at Personal Data of Americans" (24). Total Information Awareness (TIA) prompted privacy concerns that the system would provide intelligence analysts and law enforcement officials with instant access to information collected from personal emails, phone calls, credit card records, medical records, banking transactions, travel documents, and other sources without any requirement for a search warrant.

In a March 2003 statement to the U.S. House of Representatives Armed Services Committee, Tether attempted to pacify the controversy by affirming that DRAPA's Information Awareness programs, including TIA, were not developing technology to maintain dossiers on every U.S. citizen or to assemble a giant database on Americans. Instead, TIA was designed as an experimental, multi-agency prototype network that enables law enforcement to collaborate, "connect the dots," and prevent terrorist attacks (25). In spite of DRAPA's final attempt to justify TIA by renaming Total Information Awareness to Terrorism Information Awareness (26), the U.S. Congress eliminated the funding for TIA and terminated the Information Awareness Office (IAO) in August 2003 (27).

However, TIA did not end in 2003.

In February 2008, the Federal Bureau of Investigation (FBI) awarded a nearly $1 billion contract to Lockheed Martin to help create a "Next Generation Identification" (NGI) system – a massive database of people's physical characteristics including fingerprints, palm prints, scars, tattoos, iris eye patterns, facial shapes, and other biometric information (28). "It's the beginning of the surveillance society where you can be tracked anywhere, any time and all your movements, and eventually all your activities will be tracked and noted and correlated," said Barry Steinhardt, then director of the American Civil Liberties Union's Technology and Liberty Project (29).

In March 2008, a *Wall Street Journal* article reported that the National Security Agency (NSA) has been building essentially the same system as TIA. Siobhan Gorman wrote, "According to current and former intelligence officials, the spy agency now monitors huge volumes of records of domestic emails and Internet searches as well as bank transfers, credit-card transactions, travel and telephone records. ... The NSA uses its own high-powered version of social-network analysis to search for possible new patterns and links to terrorism" (30). The American Civil Liberties Union (ACLU) responded by accusing the NSA of reviving TIA to be an "Orwellian" domestic spying program (31).

Earlier in January 2008, Pulitzer Prize-winner Lawrence Wright wrote in *The New Yorker* an in-depth article about the U.S. intelligence community focusing on the Office of the Director of National Intelligence (ODNI) and the necessity for interagency communications – something that TIA was meant to facilitate. Wright observed, "The fantasy worlds that Disney creates have a surprising amount in common with the ideal universe envisaged by the intelligence community, in which environments are carefully controlled and people are closely observed, and no one seems to mind" (32).

While the Disney universe (not counting Disney+) is confined to its theme parks and certain visiting hours, social networks such as Facebook, Instagram, Twitter, and YouTube are reaching more than 3 billion people worldwide 24/7 in their workplaces, schools, homes, and even on the go with their mobile devices. The social networks are leading the way towards Total Information Awareness.

Looking back to the 60's, DARPA initiated and funded the research and development of Advanced Research Projects Agency Network (ARPANET) that went online in 1969 (33). The success of ARPANET gave rise to the global commercial Internet in the mid-1990s and the new generation of Fortune 500 companies today including Amazon.com, Google, eBay, and Facebook.

As if life comes full circle in the 21st century, the ubiquitous social networks such as Facebook, Instagram, Twitter, and YouTube are creating the technologies, infrastructures, and big data necessary for the DARPA-proposed Total Information Awareness program. Facial recognition, location tracking, ambient social apps on GPS-enabled devices, Google Street View, digital footprints, and data mining are some key elements in information awareness. In fact, the homepage of DARPA conspicuously displays social media icons for Twitter, Facebook, YouTube, Instagram, and LinkedIn (See Fig. 1.4).

On March 29, 2012, the Obama administration announced more than \$200 million in funding for "Big Data Research and Development Initiative" (34). Information Innovation Office has replaced the Information Awareness Office (35). The first wave of agency commitments includes National Science Foundation (NSF), National Institutes of Health (NIH), Department of Energy (DOE), U.S. Geological Survey, and Department of Defense (including DARPA) (36). Not to imply that DARPA intends to resurrect the Total Information Awareness program, but the

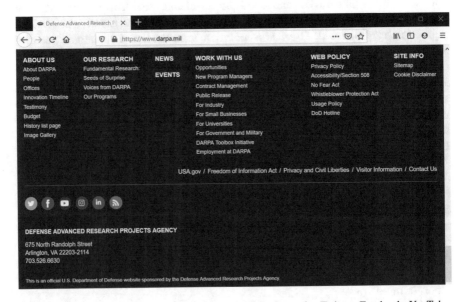

Fig. 1.4 Homepage of DARPA showing social media icons for Twitter, Facebook, YouTube, Instagram, and LinkedIn

DARPA-proposed Anomaly Detection at Multiple Scales (ADAMS) program is one of several key technologies that are directly applicable to Total Information Awareness (37).

The U.S. government has also been learning from private businesses who often share customers' data to make a profit. Letitia Long, Director of the National Geospatial-Intelligence Agency (NGA) described the shift across the post-9/11 intelligence community as the transition from a "need-to-know" atmosphere to a "need-to-share and need-to-provide" culture (38). The shift has increased the government's effectiveness in combating terrorism, but it has also opened the door to potential leakage of classified information.

1.4 Edward Snowden's NSA Leaks and PRISM

On May 20, 2013, Edward Snowden, an employee of defense contractor Booz Allen Hamilton at the National Security Agency, arrived in Hong Kong from Hawaii with four laptop computers in his possession. The computer hard drives contained some of the U.S. government's top secret programs (39).

On June 1, *Guardian* journalists Glenn Greenwald and Ewen MacAskill and documentary maker Laura Poitras flew from New York to Hong Kong to begin a week of interviews with Snowden.

On June 5, *The Guardian* published a top-secret document by the U.S. Foreign Intelligence Surveillance Court. The April 2013 court order forced Verizon to hand over the phone records of millions of Americans, including but not limited to session identifying information (e.g., originating and terminating telephone number, International Mobile Subscriber Identity (IMSI) number, and International Mobile station Equipment Identity (IMEI) number) (40).

On June 6, a second *Guardian* story unveiled the top-secret PRISM program that allows officials to collect without court orders any data including emails, chat, videos, photos, stored data, voice-over-IP, file transfers, video conferencing, logins, and online social networking details from communication providers and social networks (See Fig. 1.5). Under the PRISM program, the NSA spends about $20 million annually to access the servers of the participating companies, beginning in 2007 with Microsoft, followed by Yahoo! in 2008, Google, Facebook, and PalTalk in 2009, YouTube in 2010, Skype and AOL in 2011, and Apple in 2012. (See Fig. 1.6).

In response to the revelation of PRISM, a senior U.S. official issued a statement: "*The Guardian* and *Washington Post* articles refer to collection of communications pursuant to Section 702 of the Foreign Intelligence Surveillance Act. This law does not allow the targeting of any US citizen or of any person located within the United States" (41).

On June 7, President Barack Obama defended the NSA dragnet surveillance programs: "They help us prevent terrorist attacks. … It's important to recognize that you can't have 100% security and also then have 100% privacy and zero inconvenience" (42). A former senior U.S. intelligence official explained NSA director

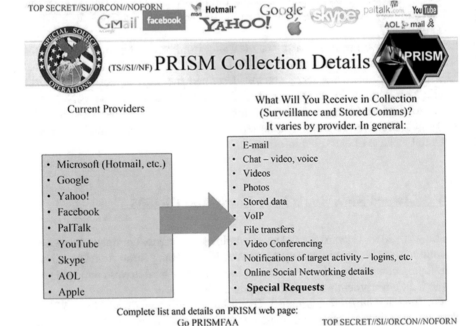

Fig. 1.5 PRISM Collection Details (Courtesy of *The Guardian*)

Gen. Keith Alexander's rationale behind the surveillance programs: "Rather than look for a single needle in the haystack, his approach was, 'Let's collect the whole haystack. Collect it all, tag it, store it. ... And whatever it is you want, you go searching for it'" (43).

The NSA released a memorandum indicating that the agency monitored a mere 1.6% of the world's Internet traffic. However, a shrewd commentator by the name "Pavel87" made the observation that "if you take away porn, advertisement, streaming video and music, you are left with the 1.6% of ACTUAL information such as email, VoIP and chats. So the NSA actually filters out 98.4% of irrelevant content and reads 100% of your actual info" (44).

Apart from Boundless Informant, MUSCULAR, PRISM, QUANTUM, Steller Wind, Tempora, Turbulence, Xkeyscore and spying on foreign countries by the NSA and British's Government Communications Headquarters (GCHQ), there is much more top-secret information that has not been made public by the journalists in the know. Snowden even "demanded" the journalists that they should consult the government before publishing (45).

The Washington Post Editorial Board opined that "the first U.S. priority should be to prevent Mr. Snowden from leaking information that harms efforts to fight terrorism and conduct legitimate intelligence operations." It did not regret what had been disclosed to the public because "documents published so far by news organizations have shed useful light on some NSA programs and raised questions that deserve debate, such as whether a government agency should build a database of Americans' phone records." However, it warned that "Mr. Snowden is reported to

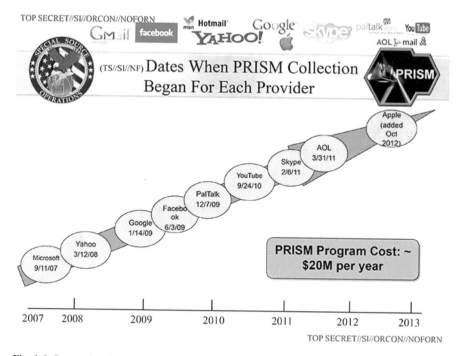

Fig. 1.6 Dates when PRISM Collection Began for each Provider (Courtesy of *The Guardian*)

have stolen many more documents, encrypted copies of which may have been given to allies such as the WikiLeaks organization" (46).

In July 2013, *The Guardian* in London destroyed the hard drives containing top-secret documents leaked by Edward Snowden after a threat of legal action by the British government. Guardian editor Alan Rusbridger said in an interview, "I explained to British authorities that there were other copies in America and Brazil so they wouldn't be achieving anything. But once it was obvious that they would be going to law I preferred to destroy our copy rather than hand it back or allow the courts to freeze our reporting. … I don't think we had Snowden's consent to hand the material back, and I didn't want to help the UK authorities to know what he had given us" (47).

In August 2013, pro-privacy email service provider Lavabit with 350,000 users including Edward Snowden was shut down by its owner Ladar Levison amid court battle. "I have been forced to make a difficult decision: to become complicit in crimes against the American people or walk away from nearly 10 years of hard work by shutting down Lavabit," Levison wrote in a statement. "After significant soul searching, I have decided to suspend operations" (48).

While Americans are equally divided on labeling Edward Snowden a hero or a traitor (49), Snowden justified his actions by saying that "I can't in good conscience allow the U.S. government to destroy privacy, Internet freedom, and basic liberties for people around the world with this massive surveillance machine they're secretly building" (50). In a May 2014 interview with Brian Williams at NBC News, Snowden said, "Being a patriot doesn't mean prioritizing service to government above all. Being a patriot means knowing when to protect your country, when to protect your Constitution, when to protect your countrymen from the violations and encroachments of adversaries. And those adversaries don't have to be foreign countries. They can be bad policies. ... When you look at the carefulness of the programs that have been disclosed... the way these have all been filtered through the most trusted journalist institutions... the way the government has had a chance to chime in on these and to make their case... How can it be said that I did not serve my government and how can it be said that this harmed the country when all three branches of government have made reforms as a result of it?" (51).

1.5 Social Networks' Responses to NSA Leaks and PRISM

WikiLeaks founder Julian Assange said in a May 2011 interview, "Facebook in particular is the most appalling spying machine that has ever been invented. Here we have the world's most comprehensive database about people: their relationships, their names, their addresses, their locations and their communications with each other, their relatives – all sitting within the United States, all accessible to US intelligence" (52).

Edward Snowden's NSA leaks in June 2013 have reinvigorated Assange's bold accusation (53). However, Facebook has vehemently denied giving the NSA and FBI "back door" access to their servers (54). Nevertheless, military and civilian technologies have interwoven into every fabric of our society. NSA's research has contributed significantly to the development of the supercomputer, the cassette tape, the microchip, quantum mathematics, nanotechnology, biometrics, and semiconductor technology (55). The algorithm that powers Roomba, a household robot vacuum cleaner, was originally developed for clearing minefields (56). Facebook co-founder and CEO Mark Zuckerberg himself said at the 2011 F8 developers conference, "We exist at the intersection of technology and social issues" (57).

On June 7, 2013, Zuckerberg responded personally to the allegedly "outrageous" press reports about PRISM (58):

"Facebook is not and has never been part of any program to give the US or any other government direct access to our servers. We have never received a blanket request or court order from any government agency asking for information or metadata in bulk, like the one Verizon reportedly received. And if we did, we would fight it aggressively. We hadn't even heard of PRISM before yesterday.

When governments ask Facebook for data, we review each request carefully to make sure they always follow the correct processes and all applicable laws, and then only provide the information if is required by law. We will continue fighting aggressively to keep your information safe and secure.

We strongly encourage all governments to be much more transparent about all programs aimed at keeping the public safe. It's the only way to protect everyone's civil liberties and create the safe and free society we all want over the long term."

Along with Facebook, Google and Apple also denied any knowledge of PRISM. Google told *The Guardian*: "Google cares deeply about the security of our users' data. We disclose user data to government in accordance with the law, and we review all such requests carefully. From time to time, people allege that we have created a government 'back door' into our systems, but Google does not have a back door for the government to access private user data" (54). Whereas Apple told CNBC: "We have never heard of PRISM. We do not provide any government agency with direct access to our servers, and any government agency requesting customer data must get a court order" (59).

For damage control as well as to bolster their public image, Apple, Facebook, Google, LinkedIn, Microsoft, and Yahoo! all have released Transparency Reports showing criminal, Foreign Intelligence Surveillance Act (FISA), and other requests for information from the U.S. government. For the six-month period from January to June 2013, Apple received FISA and law enforcement requests affecting between 2,000 and 3,000 accounts (60), Facebook between 5,000 and 5,999 accounts (61), Google between 9,000 and 9,999 accounts (62), LinkedIn under 250 accounts (63), Microsoft between 15,000 and 15,999 accounts (64), and Yahoo! between 30,000 and 30,999 accounts (65).

Facebook said that it would "push for even more transparency, so that our users around the world can understand how infrequently we are asked to provide user data on national-security grounds." However, Microsoft conceded, "What we are permitted to publish continues to fall short of what is needed to help the community understand and debate these issues" (66).

At the TechCrunch Disrupt Conference in September 2013, Yahoo! CEO Marissa Mayer gave an honest answer – a welcoming change from all the standard denial statements by most technology companies. Mayer said, "In terms of the NSA, we can't talk about those things because they are classified. Releasing classified information is treason, and you're incarcerated. … It makes more sense for us to work within the system. We file suit against the government … asking to be able to be more transparent with the numbers on the NSA requests" (67).

In October 2013, *The Washington Post* published the NSA documents about the MUSCULAR project that secretly taps into the communications links connecting Yahoo and Google data centers around the world. Figure 1.7 shows a NSA presentation on "Google Cloud Exploitation." In response, Google's chief legal officer David Drummond said, "We are outraged at the lengths to which the government seems to have gone to intercept data from our private fiber networks, and it underscores the need for urgent reform" (68).

In November 2013, German newspaper *Der Spiegel* reported on Snowden's leaks about NSA's QUANTUM program that redirects some users to fake LinkedIn and Slashdot websites to plant malware on the users' computers. LinkedIn denied any knowledge of the program and said that it "would never approve such activity" (69).

At the 2013 RSA conference, an FBI agent propositioned Wickr cofounder Nico Sell about adding a back door to her mobile app that provides military-grade encryption of text, picture, audio and video messages as well as anonymity and secure file shredding features. Sell told Meghan Kelly at *Venture Beat*, "I think he was trying to intimidate me. He just caught me really off-guard. I feel like he was mad. I mean, I said that I was doing a no-backdoor guarantee in the presentation. That was one of the major messages there" (70).

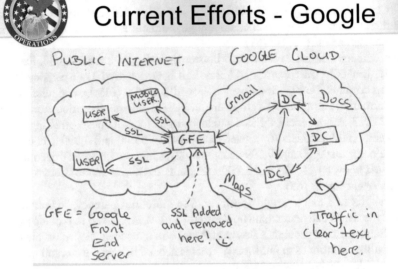

Fig. 1.7 Google Cloud Exploitation (Courtesy of *The Washington Post*)

F-Secure and some fellow companies decided to boycott the 2014 RSA conference in protest of the alleged $10 million dollar payment from the NSA to RSA for inserting a back door into its encryption products. Nico Sell questioned if those boycotters were also boycotting Google, Facebook, and Microsoft: "I bet those guys were also paid for backdoors. It's hard to boycott everybody who is paid for a backdoor" (70).

While privacy advocates, media skeptics, and conspiracy theorists continue to question the real involvement of technology companies with the NSA, Google has beefed up the security of Gmail by encrypting communications between Google's servers as well as to and from end users (71). Yahoo! has also encrypted all information that moves between its data centers and to/from its consumers (72). Microsoft has expanded encryption across its services and reassured customers that its products do not contain back doors (73). And Facebook CEO Mark Zuckerberg called President Barack Obama on March 12, 2014 to express his frustration about the government's spying and hacking programs. Zuckerberg said after the phone call, "When our engineers work tirelessly to improve security, we imagine we're protecting you against criminals, not our own government. … The U.S. government should be the champion for the Internet, not a threat. They need to be much more transparent about what they're doing, or otherwise people will believe the worst. … Unfortunately, it seems like it will take a very long time for true full reform" (74).

1.6 Reform Government Surveillance and Reset the Net

In May 2014, the U.S. House of Representatives approved a new bill to curb NSA's domestic dragnet surveillance. U.S. congressman Jim Sensenbrenner who shepherded the 2001 USA Patriot Act said, "The NSA might still be watching us, but now we can watch them" (75). Sensenbrenner criticized the PRISM program in a statement, "While I believe the Patriot Act appropriately balanced national security concerns and civil rights, I have always worried about potential abuses. Seizing phone records of millions of innocent people is excessive and un-American" (76).

The spat between American businesses and the U.S. government has now come full circle, as ex-NSA official "Chris" Inglis warned technology companies that amass vast amounts of personal information to learn from the agency's mistakes. "There's an enormous amount of data held in the private sector," said Inglis. "There might be some concerns not just on the part of the American public, but the international public" (77). Indeed, Facebook CEO Mark Zuckerberg told Farhad Manjoo of *The New York Times* in an April 2014 interview: "Understanding who you serve is always a very important problem, and it only gets harder the more people that you serve" (78).

In June 2014, a year after Snowden's NSA leaks, the Reform Government Surveillance coalition of nine technology companies published an open letter to the members of the U.S. Senate, urging them to pass a version of the USA Freedom Act that offers more transparency than the one passed by the U.S. House of Representatives (79):

Dear Members of the Senate:

It's been a year since the first headlines alleging the extent of government surveillance on the Internet.

We understand that governments have a duty to protect their citizens. But the balance in many countries has tipped too far in favor of the state and away from the rights of the individual. This undermines the freedoms we all cherish, and it must change.

Over the last year many of our companies have taken important steps, including further strengthening the security of our services and taking action to increase transparency. But the government needs to do more.

In the next few weeks, the Senate has the opportunity to demonstrate leadership and pass a version of the USA Freedom Act that would help restore the confidence of Internet users here and around the world, while keeping citizens safe.

Unfortunately, the version that just passed the House of Representatives could permit bulk collection of Internet "metadata" (e.g. who you email and who emails you), something that the Administration and Congress said they intended to end. Moreover, while the House bill permits some transparency, it is critical to our customers that the bill allows companies to provide even greater detail about the number and type of government requests they receive for customer information.

It is in the best interest of the United States to resolve these issues. Confidence in the Internet, both in the U.S. and internationally, has been badly damaged over the last year. It is time for action. As the Senate takes up this important legislation, we urge you to ensure that U.S. surveillance efforts are clearly restricted by law, proportionate to the risks, transparent, and subject to independent oversight.

Signed,

Tim Armstrong, *AOL*

Tim Cook, *Apple*
Drew Houston, *Dropbox*
Mark Zuckerberg, *Facebook*
Larry Page, *Google*
Jeff Weiner, *LinkedIn*
Dick Costolo, *Twitter*
Satya Nadella, *Microsoft*
Marissa Mayer, *Yahoo!*

On June 5, 2014, Edward Snowden came out to support the launch of "Reset the Net" – a day of action to raise public awareness of online privacy tools (80). It was organized by the nonprofit organization Fight for the Future led by co-founder Tiffiniy Cheng.

On September 2, 2020, seven years after Snowden blew the whistle, the US court of appeals for the ninth circuit concluded that "the warrantless telephone dragnet that secretly collected millions of Americans' telephone records violated the Foreign Intelligence Surveillance Act and may well have been unconstitutional" (81). The ruling was made in spite of the argument from US officials that spying had played a crucial role in fighting domestic extremism.

Is it possible to strike a balance between individual privacy and national security? The answer lies in social media where individuals and groups are willing to share information publicly, enabling government officials to collect and analyze data without warrant and constitutional violation.

References

1. **Senate Historical Office.** Burning of Washington, 1814. [Online] United States Senate. [Cited: March 1, 2021.] https://www.senate.gov/artandhistory/history/common/generic/August_Burning_Washington.htm.
2. **Arroyo, Jim.** The Coming Civil War? Parts 1 & 2. [Online] Prescott eNews, November 23, 2020. https://prescottenews.com/index.php/2020/11/23/the-coming-civil-war-parts-1-2/.
3. **Sneed, Tierney and Krishnakumar, Priya.** Overturning Roe could mean women seeking abortions have to travel hundreds of miles. CNN. [Online] October 30, 2021. https://www.cnn.com/2021/10/30/politics/roe-wade-reversal-abortion-driving-distances/index.html.
4. **Contorno, Steve.** DeSantis proposes a new civilian military force in Florida that he would control. CNN. [Online] December 3, 2021. https://www.cnn.com/2021/12/02/politics/florida-state-guard-desantis/index.html.
5. **NPR Transcripts.** FBI Director Defends Agency In Testimony, Calls Jan. 6 Attack 'Domestic Terrorism'. [Online] NPR, March 2, 2021. https://www.npr.org/transcripts/972970812.
6. **The White House.** National Security Decision Directive 138. [Online] Homeland Security Digital Library, April 3, 1984. https://fas.org/irp/offdocs/nsdd/nsdd-138.pdf.
7. **United States White House Office.** National Security Decision Directive 138: Combating Terrorism. [Online] Homeland Security Digital Library, April 26, 1984. https://www.hsdl.org/?abstract&did=440725.
8. **Virginia Tech Department of Computer Science .** Alumnus Newton Lee envisions a future with universal rights for all. [Online] Virginia Tech. [Cited: February 14, 2021.] https://cs.vt.edu/Alumni/Alumni-in-the-news/lee-alumni-profile.html.
9. **Institute for Defense Analyses.** IDA's History and Mission. [Online] IDA. [Cited: January 1, 2002.] https://www.ida.org/aboutus/historyandmission.php.

10. **Ada Joint Program Office.** Military Standard Common APSE (Ada Programming Support Environment) Interface Set (CAIS). [Online] Defense Technical Information Center, 1985. http://books.google.com/books/about/Military_Standard_Common_APSE_Ada_Progra. html?id=EjEYOAAACAAJ.

11. **Carik, Kenneth.** The Nature of Explanation. [Online] Cambridge University Press, 1943. http://www.cambridge.org/us/knowledge/isbn/item1121731/.

12. **Minsky, Marvin.** A Framework for Representing Knowledge. [Online] MIT AI Laboratory Memo 306, June 1974. http://web.media.mit.edu/~minsky/papers/Frames/frames.html.

13. **Simonite, Tom.** Software Mines Science Papers to Make New Discoveries. [Online] MIT Technology Review, November 25, 2013. http://www.technologyreview.com/news/520461/ software-mines-science-papers-to-make-new-discoveries/.

14. **Lee, Newton S.** DM2: an algorithm for diagnostic reasoning that combines analytical models and experiential knowledge. [Online] International Journal of Man-Machine Studies (Volume 28, Issue 6, pp. 643-670), June 1988. http://www.sciencedirect.com/science/article/ pii/S002073738880066X.

15. **Berwaner, Mary.** The Problem of Diagnostic Aiding. [Online] The Defense Technical Information Center, October 30, 1989. www.dtic.mil/cgi-bin/GetTRDoc?AD=ADA239200.

16. **Mackey, Maureen.** Steve Jobs: 10 Revealing Quotes from His Biography. [Online] The Fiscal Times, October 24, 2011. http://www.thefiscaltimes.com/Articles/2011/10/24/ Steve-Jobs-10-Revealing-Quotes-from-His-Biography.

17. **Lee, Newton S.** InfoStation: A multimedia access system for library automation. [Online] The Electronic Library. (Volume 8, Issue 6, pp. 415-421.), November 1990. http://www.emeraldinsight.com/journals.htm?articleid=1667862.

18. **Berners-Lee, Tim.** The WorldWideWeb browser. World Wide Web Consortium (W3C). [Online] [Cited: January 1, 2012.] http://www.w3.org/People/Berners-Lee/ WorldWideWeb.html.

19. **McCarthy, Shawn.** Next's OS finally is maturing. (NextStep Unix operating system). [Online] Government Computer News, March 6, 1995. http://business.highbeam.com/436948/ article-1G1-16723518/next-os-finally-maturing.

20. **Lee, Newton and Madej, Krystina.** Disney Stories: Getting to Digital. [Online] Springer Science+Business Media, April 27, 2012. http://www.amazon.com/ Disney-Stories-Getting-Newton-Lee/dp/1461421004.

21. **Wilson, James M. V.** Statement by James M. Wilson V, MD, Research Faculty at Georgetown University, before the Senate Homeland Security & the Federal Workforce, and the District of Columbia. [Online] The U.S. Senate, October 4, 2007. http://www.hsgac.senate.gov//imo/ media/doc/WilsonTestimony.pdf.

22. **U.S. News & World Report.** Q&A: DNI Chief Scientist Eric Haseltine. [Online] U.S. News & World Report. [Cited: November 3, 2006.] http://www.usnews.com/usnews/news/ articles/061103/3qahaseltine_print.htm.

23. **Tether, Tony.** Statement by Dr. Tony Tether, Director of Defense Advanced Research Projects Agency, submitted to the United States Senate Armed Services Committee. [Online] The U.S. Senate, April 10, 2002. http://armed-services.senate.gov/statemnt/2002/April/Tether.pdf.

24. **Markoff, John.** THREATS AND RESPONSES: INTELLIGENCE; Pentagon Plans a Computer System That Would Peek at Personal Data of Americans. [Online] The New York Times, November 9, 2002. http://www.nytimes.com/2002/11/09/us/threats-responses-intelligence-pentagon-plans-computer-system-that-would-peek.html.

25. **Tether, Tony.** Statement by Dr. Tony Tether, Director of Defense Advanced Research Projects Agency, submitted to the U.S. House of Representatives. [Online] Defense Advanced Research Projects Agency, March 27, 2003. http://www.darpa.mil/WorkArea/DownloadAsset. aspx?id=1778.

26. **Defense Advanced Research Projects Agency.** Report to Congress regarding the Terrorism Information Awareness Program. [Online] Electronic Privacy Information Center, May 20, 2003. http://epic.org/privacy/profiling/tia/may03_report.pdf.

27. **108th Congress.** House Report 108-283 – MAKING APPROPRIATIONS FOR THE DEPARTMENT OF DEFENSE FOR THE FISCAL YEAR ENDING SEPTEMBER

30, 2004, AND FOR OTHER PURPOSES. [Online] The Library of Congress, 2003. http://thomas.loc.gov/cgi-bin/cpquery/?&sid=cp108alJsu&refer=&r_n=hr283.108&db_ id=108&item=&&sid=cp108alJsu&r_n=hr283.108&dbname=cp108&&sel= TOC_309917&.

28. **FBI National Press Office.** FBI Announces Contract Award for Next Generation Identification System. [Online] Federal Bureau of Investigation, February 12, 2008. http://www.fbi.gov/news/pressrel/press-releases/fbi-announces-contract-award-for-next-generation-identification-system.

29. **Cratty, Carol.** Lockheed gets $1 billion FBI contract. [Online] CNN, February 13, 2008. http://edition.cnn.com/2008/TECH/02/13/fbi.biometrics/index.html.

30. **Gorman, Siobhan.** NSA's Domestic Spying Grows As Agency Sweeps Up Data: Terror Fight Blurs Line Over Domain; Tracking Email. [Online] The Wall Street Journal, March 10, 2008. http://online.wsj.com/article/SB120511973377523845.html.

31. **American Civil Liberties Union.** Stunning New Report on Domestic NSA Dragnet Spying Confirms ACLU Surveillance Warnings. [Online] ACLU, March 12, 2008. http://www.aclu.org/technology-and-liberty/stunning-new-report-domestic-nsa-dragnet-spying-confirms-aclu-surveillance-wa.

32. **Wright, Lawrence.** The Spymaster. Can Mike McConnell fix America's intelligence community? [Online] The New Yorker, January 21, 2008. http://www.newyorker.com/reporting/2008/01/21/080121fa_fact_wright?currentPage=all.

33. **National Science Foundation.** NSF and the Birth of the Internet. [Online] The National Science Foundation. [Cited: August 7, 2014.] http://www.nsf.gov/news/special_reports/nsf-net/home.jsp.

34. **Kalil, Tom.** Big Data is a Big Deal. [Online] The White House, March 29, 2012. http://www.whitehouse.gov/blog/2012/03/29/big-data-big-deal.

35. **Information Innovation Office.** I2O Focus Area. [Online] DARPA. [Cited: April 3, 2012.] http://www.darpa.mil/Our_Work/I2O/.

36. **Office of Science and Technology Policy, Executive Office of the President.** Obama Administration Unveils "Big Data" Initiative: Announces $200 Million In New R&D Investments. [Online] The White House, March 29, 2012. http://www.whitehouse.gov/sites/default/files/microsites/ostp/big_data_press_release.pdf.

37. **Executive Office of the President.** Big Data Across the Federal Government. [Online] The White House, March 29, 2012. http://www.whitehouse.gov/sites/default/files/microsites/ostp/big_data_fact_sheet_final_1.pdf.

38. **Young, Denise.** Letitia Long: A Global Vision. Alumna leads intelligence agency in new era of collaboration. [Online] Virginia Tech Magazine, Spring 2012. http://www.vtmag.vt.edu/spring12/letitia-long.html.

39. **Gidda, Mirren.** Edward Snowden and the NSA files – timeline. [Online] The Guardian, July 25, 2013. http://www.theguardian.com/world/2013/jun/23/edward-snowden-nsa-files-timeline.

40. **theguardian.com.** Verizon forced to hand over telephone data – full court ruling. [Online] The Guardian, June 5, 2013. http://www.theguardian.com/world/interactive/2013/jun/06/verizon-telephone-data-court-order.

41. **Greenwald, Glenn and MacAskill, Ewen.** NSA Prism program taps in to user data of Apple, Google and others. [Online] The Guardian, June 6, 2013. http://www.theguardian.com/world/2013/jun/06/us-tech-giants-nsa-data.

42. **Jackson, David.** Obama defends surveillance programs. [Online] USA Today, June 7, 2013. http://www.usatoday.com/story/news/politics/2013/06/07/obama-clapper-national-security-agency-leaks/2400405/.

43. **Nakashima, Ellen and Warrick, Joby.** For NSA chief, terrorist threat drives passion to 'collect it all'. [Online] The Washington Post, July 14, 2013. http://www.washingtonpost.com/world/national-security/for-nsa-chief-terrorist-threat-drives-passion-to-collect-it-all/2013/07/14/3d26ef80-ea49-11e2-a301-ea5a8116d211_story.html.

44. **Perez, Evan.** Documents shed light on U.S. surveillance programs. [Online] CNN, August 9, 2013. http://www.cnn.com/2013/08/09/politics/nsa-documents-scope/index.html.

45. **Ohlheiser, Abby.** Edward Snowden Would 'Like to Go Home'. [Online] The Wire, May 28, 2014. http://www.thewire.com/national/2014/05/edward-snowden-would-like-to-go-home/371784/.

46. **Editorial Board.** Plugging the leaks in the Edward Snowden case. [Online] The Washington Post, July 1, 2013. http://www.washingtonpost.com/opinions/how-to-keep-edward-snowden-from-leaking-more-nsa-secrets/2013/07/01/4e8bbe28-e278-11e2-a11e-c2ea876a8f30_story.html.

47. **Borger, Julian.** NSA files: why the Guardian in London destroyed hard drives of leaked files. [Online] The Guardian, August 20, 2013. http://www.theguardian.com/world/2013/aug/20/nsa-snowden-files-drives-destroyed-london.

48. **Poulsen, Kevin.** Snowden's e-mail provider shuts down amid court battle. [Online] August 9, 2013. http://www.cnn.com/2013/08/09/tech/web/snowden-email-lavabit/index.html.

49. **Edwards-Levy, Ariel and Freeman, Sunny.** Americans Still Can't Decide Whether Edward Snowden Is A 'Traitor' Or A 'Hero,' Poll Finds. [Online] The Huffington Post, October 30, 2013. http://www.huffingtonpost.com/2013/10/30/edward-snowden-poll_n_4175089.html.

50. **Smith, Matt.** NSA leaker comes forward, warns of agency's 'existential threat'. [Online] CNN, June 9, 2013. http://www.cnn.com/2013/06/09/politics/nsa-leak-identity/index.html.

51. **NBC News.** Inside the Mind of Edward Snowden. [Online] NBC News, May 28, 2014. http://www.nbcnews.com/feature/edward-snowden-interview/snowden-being-patriot-means-knowing-when-protect-your-country-n117151.

52. **RT News.** WikiLeaks revelations only tip of iceberg – Assange. [Online] RT News, May 2, 2011. http://www.rt.com/news/wikileaks-revelations-assange-interview/.

53. **Taylor, Chris.** Through a PRISM, Darkly: Tech World's $20 Million Nightmare. [Online] Mashable, June 6, 2013. http://mashable.com/2013/06/06/through-a-prism-darkly-techs-20-million-nightmare-is-our-fault/.

54. **Fitzpatrick, Alex.** Facebook, Google, Apple, Yahoo Make Similar PRISM Denials. [Online] Mashable, June 6, 2013. http://mashable.com/2013/06/06/facebook-google-apple-prism/#.

55. **National Security Agency.** Our History Video Transcript. [Online] National Security Agency, January 15, 2009. http://www.nsa.gov/public_info/speeches_testimonies/nsa_videos/history_of_nsa.shtml.

56. **Glass, Nick and Ponsford, Matthew.** The secret military tech inside household robot vacuum cleaner. [Online] CNN, March 31, 2014. http://www.cnn.com/2014/03/31/tech/innovation/the-secret-military-technology-roomba-vacuum/index.html.

57. **Bosker, Bianca.** Facebook's f8 Conference (LIVE BLOG): Get The Latest Facebook News. [Online] The Huffington Post, September 22, 2011. http://www.huffingtonpost.com/2011/09/22/facebook-f8-conference-live-blog-latest-news_n_975704.html.

58. **Zuckerberg, Mark.** I want to respond personally to the outrageous press reports about PRISM. [Online] Facebook, June 7, 2013. https://www.facebook.com/zuck/posts/10100828955847631.

59. **CNBC.** Apple to @CNBC. [Online] Twitter, June 6, 2013. https://twitter.com/CNBC/status/342778613264945152.

60. **Apple.** Report on Government Information Requests. [Online] Apple, November 5, 2013. https://www.apple.com/pr/pdf/131105reportongovinforequests3.pdf.

61. **Stretch, Colin.** Facebook Releases New Data About National Security Requests. [Online] Facebook Newsroom, February 3, 2014. http://newsroom.fb.com/news/2014/02/facebook-releases-new-data-about-national-security-requests/.

62. **Salgado, Richard.** Shedding some light on Foreign Intelligence Surveillance Act (FISA) requests. [Online] Google Official Blog, February 4, 2014. http://googleblog.blogspot.com/2014/02/shedding-some-light-on-foreign.html.

63. **Rottenberg, Erika.** Updated LinkedIn Transparency Report: Including Requests Related to U.S. National Security-Related Matters. [Online] LinkedIn Official Blog, February 3, 2014. http://blog.linkedin.com/2014/02/03/updated-linkedin-transparency-report-including-requests-related-to-u-s-national-security-related-matters/.

64. **Smith, Brad.** Providing additional transparency on US government requests for customer data. [Online] Microsoft TechNet, February 3, 2014. http://blogs.technet.com/b/microsoft_on_the_issues/archive/2014/02/03/providing-additional-transparency-on-us-government-requests-for-customer-data.aspx.

65. **Bell, Ron and Altschuler, Aaron.** More Transparency For U.S. National Security Requests. [Online] Yahoo, February 3, 2014. http://yahoo.tumblr.com/post/75496314481/more-transparency-for-u-s-national-security-requests.

66. **Gustin, Sam.** Tech companies jockey to seem the most transparent. [Online] CNN, June 18, 2013. http://www.cnn.com/2013/06/18/tech/web/tech-companies-data-transparent/index.html.

67. **TechCrunch.** Marissa Mayer Comments on the NSA I Disrupt SF 2013. [Online] TechCrunch, September 11, 2013. http://www.youtube.com/watch?v=gS78slU6kq8.

68. **Gellman, Barton and Soltani, Ashkan.** NSA infiltrates links to Yahoo, Google data centers worldwide, Snowden documents say. [Online] The Washiongton Post, October 30, 2013. http://www.washingtonpost.com/world/national-security/nsa-infiltrates-links-to-yahoo-google-data-centers-worldwide-snowden-documents-say/2013/10/30/e51d661e-4166-11e3-8b74-d89d714ca4dd_story.html.

69. **Neal, Ryan W.** Edward Snowden Reveals 'Quantum Insert': NSA And GCHQ Used Fake LinkedIn And Slashdot Pages To Install Spyware. [Online] International Business Times, November 11, 2013. http://www.ibtimes.com/edward-snowden-reveals-quantum-insert-nsa-gchq-used-fake-linkedin-slashdot-pages-install-spyware.

70. **Kelly, Meghan.** Wickr cofounder to give Reddit AMA on what it's like to be bullied by the FBI. [Online] Venture Beat, January 10, 2014. http://venturebeat.com/2014/01/10/nico-sell-ama/.

71. **Pagliery, Jose.** Google tries to NSA-proof Gmail. [Online] CNNMoney, March 21, 2014. http://money.cnn.com/2014/03/20/technology/security/gmail-nsa/index.html.

72. **Mayer, Marissa.** Our Commitment to Protecting Your Information. [Online] Yahoo!, November 18, 2013. http://yahoo.tumblr.com/post/67373852814/our-commitment-to-protecting-your-information.

73. **Smith, Brad.** Protecting customer data from government snooping. [Online] Microsoft Blogs, December 4, 2013. http://blogs.technet.com/b/microsoft_blog/archive/2013/12/04/protecting-customer-data-from-government-snooping.aspx.

74. **Pagliery, Jose.** Mark Zuckerberg calls Obama to complain about NSA. [Online] CNNMoney, March 14, 2014. http://money.cnn.com/2014/03/13/technology/security/mark-zuckerberg-nsa/index.html.

75. **Mascaro, Lisa.** House overwhelmingly approves bill to curb NSA domestic spying. [Online] Los Angeles Times, May 22, 2014. http://www.latimes.com/nation/politics/la-na-nsa-reforms-20140523-story.html.

76. **The New York Times Editorial Board.** President Obama's Dragnet. [Online] The New York Times, June 6, 2013. https://www.nytimes.com/2013/06/07/opinion/president-obamas-dragnet.html.

77. **Yadron, Danny.** Ex-NSA Official Inglis Warns Tech Firms: Be Transparent. [Online] The Wall Street Journal, March 5, 2014. http://online.wsj.com/news/articles/SB10001424052702304732804579421733369167364.

78. **Manjoo, Farhad.** Can Facebook Innovate? A Conversation With Mark Zuckerberg. [Online] The New York Times, April 16, 2014. http://bits.blogs.nytimes.com/2014/04/16/can-facebook-innovate-a-conversation-with-mark-zuckerberg/.

79. **Reform Government Surveillance.** Reform Government Surveillance. [Online] ReformGovernmentSurveillance.com, June 2014. https://www.reformgovernmentsurveillance.com/USAFreedomAct.

80. **Fight for the Future.** Privacy Pack. [Online] Reset the Net, June 5, 2014. https://pack.resetthenet.org/.

81. **Reuters.** NSA surveillance exposed by Snowden was illegal, court rules seven years on. [Online] The Guardian, September 3, 2020. https://www.theguardian.com/us-news/2020/sep/03/edward-snowden-nsa-surveillance-guardian-court-rules.

Part II
Privacy in the Age of Big Data

Chapter 2
Social Networks and Privacy

"In the future, everyone will be world-famous for 15 minutes."
– Andy Warhol (1968)

"You have zero privacy anyway. Get over it."
– Scott NcNealy, Sun Microsystems (January 1999)

"If you have something that you don't want anyone to know, maybe you shouldn't be doing it in the first place."
– Eric Schmidt, Google (December 2009)

"People have really gotten comfortable not only sharing more information and different kinds, but more openly and with more people. That social norm is just something that has evolved over time."
– Mark Zuckerberg, Facebook (January 2010)

"What children post online or search as part of their homework should not haunt them as they apply to colleges or for jobs. YouTube should not be turned into YouTracked."
– U.S. Representative Edward J. Markey (November 2012)

"Privacy is not dead. ... The kind privacy that is becoming more of the norm is dependent on our ability to move freely among the myriad services and apps, and to opt in selectively, both in what we use and how we choose to use them."
– Author Jack Cheng (June 2013)

"I have felt that my own communications were probably monitored, and when I want to communicate with a foreign leader privately, I type or write the letter myself, put it in the post office and mail it."
– President Jimmy Carter (March 2014)

"Would you rather have your first kiss on YouTube? Or a transcript of everything you said on your first date available on Google?"
– Forbes writer Jordan Shapiro's 9-year-old son (May 2014)

"Privacy is dead. Ownership is not dead. Everyone cares about owning their conversations and their pictures. I think that's the word we need to start using instead of privacy, because privacy has been tainted."
– Nico Sell, DEF CON and Wickr (June 2014)

© Springer Science+Business Media, LLC, part of Springer Nature 2021
N. Lee, *Facebook Nation*, https://doi.org/10.1007/978-1-0716-1867-7_2

*"A majority of Americans say they use YouTube and Facebook,
while use of Instagram, Snapchat and TikTok is especially
common among adults under 30."*
                                        – Pew Research Center (April 2021)

2.1   Zero Privacy and the Central Intelligence Agency

On May 7, 2013, the Central Intelligence Agency (CIA) selected undercover officer
Frank Archibald as the new head of its National Clandestine Service and kept his
identity secret while he remained undercover as the agency chief in Latin America.

However, within 24 hours, his name was outed on Twitter by Columbia University
journalism professor John Dinges (1) who successfully pieced together publicly available information: *The Washington Post* described the new head as "a longtime officer
who served tours in Pakistan and Africa and was recently in charge of the agency's
Latin America division, according to public records and former officials." The
Associated Press added that he "once ran the covert action that helped remove Serbian
President Slobodan Milosevic from power" (2). Prof. Dinges said in a telephone interview with *Mashable*, "It was pretty obvious who he was. It took me about five minutes
to find out. It wasn't secret, nobody leaked it; it was not a big secret" (3).

On May 9, 2013, 48 hours after the CIA appointment, one website used Intelius
to find Archibal's address, date of birth, and names of relatives. The site also posted
online photos of his house taken from Google Maps and Google Street View (4).

Half a year earlier in November 2012, CIA director David Petraeus resigned as
head of the spy agency after the FBI uncovered his private emails that confirmed his
secret extramarital affair with his biographer Paula Broadwell. CNN's John D. Sutter
asked, "When the CIA director cannot hide his activities online, what hope is there
for the rest of us?" (5).

Way back in January 1999, Scott McNealy, co-founder and CEO of Sun
Microsystems for 22 years, told a group of reporters and analysts: "You have zero
privacy anyway. Get over it" (6). A decade later in December 2009, Google's then-
CEO Eric Schmidt said, "If you have something that you don't want anyone to
know, maybe you shouldn't be doing it in the first place" (7). In defense of the NSA
surveillance programs, President Barack Obama said in June 2013, "It's important
to recognize that you can't have 100% security and also then have 100% privacy and
zero inconvenience" (8).

2.2   The Archer, Carrier Pigeons, and President Jimmy Carter

A college friend of my wife, in his twenties, graduated from a well-known university
with a Master's degree in computer science. Instead of looking for a well-paying job,
he prefers to spend most of his time living in the remote countryside without a cell

phone or Internet connection. He is a skilled archer who hunts for food in the forest. He is also a self-proclaimed magician (think Tim Kring's *Heroes*, not David Copperfield). He enjoys a life of solitude and privacy. Nevertheless, even an eccentric person like him cannot completely escape the temptation of social networks. He has a Facebook profile with a small handful of photos of himself and his handmade enchanted objects. He updates his Facebook page rarely, but when he does, his small circle of college friends would be glued to the computer screen to find out what he is up to. He has limited social interaction by offering limited glimpses into his life to a limited number of friends. As a result, he enjoys reasonably good privacy.

In the year 2012 when more than two billion people were connected online (9), an Arizona man in Phoenix distrusted technology so much that he refused to use a phone or computer altogether. In order to communicate with his business partner who lived across town in Phoenix, the Arizona man sent his messages via carrier pigeons (10). We could call it old-fashioned or paranoia. During World War II, about 250,000 pigeons were used by all branches of the U.K. military and the Special Operations Executive to deliver messages between mainland Europe and Britain (11).

Andrea Mitchell of *NBC News* interviewed President Jimmy Carter in March 2014. On the topic of privacy, Carter said, "As a matter of fact, you know, I have felt that my own communications are probably monitored. And when I want to communicate with a foreign leader privately, I type or write a letter myself, put it in the post office, and mail it" (12). Taking the president's words to heart, Google began testing in June 2014 a new super-secure email feature with end-to-end encryption. "We recognize that this sort of encryption will probably only be used for very sensitive messages or by those who need added protection," said Google product manager Stephan Somogyi (13).

The archer, the pigeon man, and President Jimmy Carter are among the few who are determined to safeguard their own privacy with strong convictions, while the overwhelming majority of people are willing to give up some part of their privacy in exchange for being connected. An old English proverb says, "If you can't beat them, join them."

Most people have families, friends, and business acquaintances that they keep in constant contact with through in-person meetings, emails, phone calls, and online social networking services such as Facebook, Instagram, and Twitter. Most people enjoy making new friends. However, social interaction inevitably raises the privacy issue. Online social networks only exacerbate privacy concerns. The risk is often outweighed by the consumer's need to communicate.

Facebook CEO and co-founder Mark Zuckerberg told a live audience in a January 2010 interview with *TechCrunch*: "Why would I want to put any information on the Internet at all? Why would I want to have a website? In the last 5 or 6 years, blogging has taken off in a huge way. There are all these different services that have people sharing more information. People have really gotten comfortable not only sharing more information and different kinds, but more openly and with more people. That social norm is just something that has evolved over time" (14).

Zuckerberg's view resonated with Robert Scoble, a former technology evangelist at Microsoft best known for his blog Scobleizer. "I make everything public on my Facebook account, and I'm not worried about privacy because the more I share about who I am and what interests me, the more Facebook can bring me content that I care about," said Scoble, "Yes, people have lost jobs because of things they have posted on Facebook, but you can also end up getting jobs and making all kinds of great connections because you've posted about your passions" (15).

2.3   The Pervasiveness of Facebook

Facebook's original mission is "to give people the power to share and make the world more open and connected" (16). But knowing that connecting people online is not enough, Facebook changed its mission in June 2017 to "give people the power to build community and bring the world closer together" (17).

Launched in February 2004 by Mark Zuckerberg, Facebook has quickly become one of the most pervasive interpersonal communication tools. One month after its official launch, Facebook expanded from Harvard to Stanford, Columbia, and Yale University. Within one year, in December 2004, Facebook reached nearly 1 million active users.

In September 2011, Facebook's chief technology officer Bret Taylor confirmed that Facebook has more than 800 million active users, 350 million of whom use Facebook on mobile devices each month (18). In February 2012, the Facebook IPO filing revealed that the company has reached 845 million users, 483 million of them use the site every day (19) and 425 million of them access Facebook on mobile devices (20). By January 2021, Facebook revised the total number of monthly active users to 3.3 billion active people across Facebook family of apps (21).

In August 2013, more than 128 million Americans – one out of three people in the United States – visited Facebook every day (22). According to a study done in May 2011, Americans spent a total of 53.5 billion minutes a month on Facebook, more than Yahoo! (17.2 billion minutes), Google (12.5 billion), AOL (11.4 billion), MSN (9.5 billion), YouTube (9.1 billion), eBay (4.5 billion), Blogger (724 million), Tumblr (624 million), and Twitter (565 million) (23).

By January 2021, Facebook has reached more than half of the U.S. adult population. Pew Research Center published the survey report "Social Media Use in 2021" which summarizes that "a majority of Americans say they use YouTube and Facebook, while use of Instagram, Snapchat and TikTok is especially common among adults under 30" (24). Figure 2.1 shows a steady increase of YouTube viewers among U.S. adults; and Facebook remains a close second with the same 69 % reach of American adults over the past 5 years.

Earlier, a 2011 research from NM Incite, a Nielsen McKinsey company, reveals no surprise that knowing someone in real life is the top reason (82%) cited for "friend-ing" someone on Facebook (25). The second main reason (60%) is to add friends of their mutual friends online. Other reasons include business networking (11%), physical attractiveness (8%), increasing friend count (7%), and friend everyone (7%). The so-called "friend collectors" send requests out of curiosity and nosiness.

Growing share of Americans say they use YouTube; Facebook remains one of the most widely used online platforms among U.S. adults

% of U.S. adults who say they ever use ...

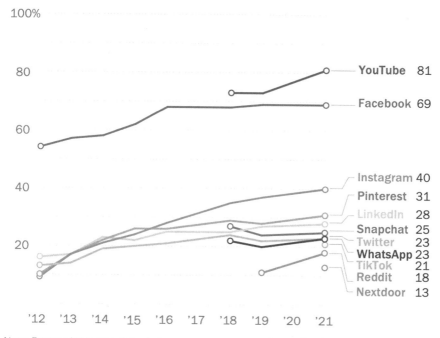

Note: Respondents who did not give an answer are not shown. Pre-2018 telephone poll data is not available for YouTube, Snapchat and WhatsApp; pre-2019 telephone poll data is not available for Reddit. Pre-2021 telephone poll data is not available for TikTok. Trend data is not available for Nextdoor.
Source: Survey of U.S. adults conducted Jan. 25-Feb. 8, 2021.
"Social Media Use in 2021"

PEW RESEARCH CENTER

Fig. 2.1 Social Media Use in 2021 (courtesy of Pew Research Center)

Many Facebook addicted users are afflicted with the oh-so itch-able question, "I wonder what so-and-so is doing now" (26). In May 2014, Facebook added an "Ask" feature to let users inquire about their Facebook friends' relationships and other personal information (27). Facebook also rolled out an audio-recognition feature that can identify what song is playing or what show or movie is on TV, making it easier for users to share what they are listening to or watching without typing (28).

Omar L. Gallaga, a reporter for *Austin American-Statesman,* admitted his Facebook addiction on CNN, "More than just a daily habit, Facebook has become the place where I get important, often surprising glimpses into the lives of the 1,365 people with whom I've chosen to connect. (That's not counting friends-of-friends, for Facebook's tentacles are ever-extended)" (29).

Most people have the unquenchable need to communicate and share information. As Mark Zuckerberg wrote in his letter for the Facebook IPO filing on February 1, 2012, "We live at a moment when the majority of people in the world have access to the internet or mobile phones –the raw tools necessary to start sharing what they're thinking, feeling and doing with whomever they want" (30).

"People don't want to be talked to, they want to be talked with," said Roy Sekoff, founding editor of *The Huffington Post* (31). However, the busy lifestyle and fast-paced society have deprived people of the face-to-face quality time among friends, families, and acquaintances. CNN producer Kiran Khalid, a self-admitted social-media addict, tried to disconnect from all electronic communications for five days in December 2011. Her conclusion was that severing her dependency on social networks removed an obstacle to real conversations (32).

26-year-old Paul Miller, a senior editor for *The Verge,* decided to leave the Internet for a year beginning on May 1, 2012 (33). "I think there are two kinds of people who live with technology constantly in their face: people who freak out when they're forcefully separated from their devices or connectivity, as if their arm has been cut off, and people who feel really chill when they're forcefully separated from their devices or connectivity, as if they've been let out of prison. I've spoken to many of both kinds as I've prepared for leaving the internet, and thankfully I fall in the latter camp" (34).

After a year of Internet hiatus, Miller came back online May 1, 2013 to find 22,000 unread emails in his inbox (35). He described the offline experience "existential and introspective" and the back-to-online experience traumatic: "I got on Facebook I didn't know how to use Facebook. I almost had a panic attack that night. … Now that I'm back on the Internet I really want to be the shining example of what it's like to actually pay attention to somebody and put away your devices" (36).

Most people simply cannot survive without their digital fixations. Facebook is the prolific communication tool that fills the void created by the lack of real face-to-face conversations. As far back as September 2005, *TechCrunch* reported that 85% of college students use Facebook to communicate with friends, both on campus and from their former high schools (37). Today, it is almost inconceivable for a university student not to have a Facebook page.

Facebook is more convenient than emails and less intrusive than phone calls. Someone may wake up at 3 in the morning, post a new photo and write some comments on Facebook. The information goes out to all their online friends. However, there is no distinction between best friends who can keep a secret, casual friends who may laugh at it, and strangers who either do not care about it or use the information for malicious purposes. "We are close, in a sense, to people who don't necessarily like us, sympathize with us or have anything in common with us," Prof. Jon

Kleinberg of Cornell University told *The New York Times*. "It's the weak ties that make the world small" (38).

2.4   Chairs Are Like Facebook

On October 4, 2012, Facebook released a new 91-second video *The Things That Connect Us* depicting chairs, doorbells, airplanes, bridges, dance floors, basketball, a great nation, and the universe (39):

> *Chairs. Chairs are made so that people can sit down and take a break. Anyone can sit on a chair, and if the chair is large enough, they can sit down together. And tell jokes. Or make up stories. Or just listen. Chairs are for people. And that is why **chairs are like Facebook**.*
>
> *Doorbells. Airplanes. Bridges. These are things people use to get together so they can open up and connect about ideas, and music, and other things people share.*
>
> *Dance floors. Basketball. A great nation. A great nation is something people build, so that they can have a place where they belong.*
>
> *The universe is vast and dark and makes us wonder if we are alone. So maybe the reason we make all of these things is to remind ourselves that we are not.*

Directed by acclaimed Mexican filmmaker Alejandro González Iñárritu, the cleverly crafted video has been described by some critics as "puzzling" and "disingenuous" (40). Nonetheless, it is not difficult to see that the video alludes to the rise of Facebook nation with over 1 billion cybercitizens in 2012 (41) and more than 3 billion monthly active users in 2021 (42). It is truly a global phenomenon since the majority of Facebook users live outside the U.S. and Canada.

"Chairs are like Facebook" — Chairs are the most basic, ubiquitous, and indispensable furniture in most parts of the world. Facebook is one of the most prevalent social networks today. However, sitting in stationary chairs puts stress on spinal disks and increases the chance of lower-back injury, resulting in $11 billion a year in workers' compensation claims (43). Unlike stationary chairs, Facebook must be quick to adapt to changes.

"We are not [alone]" — Facebook users tell jokes, make up stories, or just listen to other Facebook friends. In an interview with *Ad Age*'s Ann-Christine Diaz, Facebook's head of consumer marketing Rebecca Van Dyck linked Facebook with the innate human desire to connect. Dyck said, "We make the tools and services that allow people to feel human, get together, open up. Even if it's a small gesture, or a grand notion — we wanted to express that huge range of connectivity and how we interact with each other" (44).

On Facebook, people volunteer their personal information such as their gender, birthday, education, workplace, city of residence, interests, hobbies, photos, friends, families, schoolmates, coworkers, past histories, relationship status, likes, dislikes, and even current location. By satisfying the insatiable desire for communication with others who seem to be willing to listen, people have voluntarily sacrificed some degree of personal privacy. "Have one's cake and eat it too" does not apply to personal privacy in the world of ubiquitous social networks.

2.5   Facebook and Personal Privacy

Facebook headquarters' address is 1 Hacker Way, Menlo Park, California 94025. (21) 1 Hacker Way was apparently the second choice after 1 Social Circle (45). Both of which fit the Facebook culture and product quite nicely.

"Hacking is core to how we build at Facebook," the company said in a blog post announcing Facebook's 2012 Hacker Cup competition (46). "Whether we're building a prototype for a major product like Timeline at a Hackathon, creating a smarter search algorithm, or tearing down walls at our new headquarters, we're always hacking to find better ways to solve problems" (47).

In 2003, Mark Zuckerberg hacked into the Harvard computer network and stole private dormitory student ID photos in order to create Facemash, the predecessor to Facebook. Similar to the Hot or Not website founded in 2000 by James Hong and Jim Young, Facemash placed two photos next to each other at a time and asked users to choose the hotter person. Facemash attracted 450 visitors and more than 22,000 photo views in its first day of launch before the website was forced to shut down. Zuckerberg was charged by the Harvard administration with breach of security, violating copyrights and individual privacy (48). Zuckerberg wrote in an email to *The Harvard Crimson* in November 2003, "Issues about violating people's privacy don't seem to be surmountable. I'm not willing to risk insulting anyone" (48).

Zuckerberg, an ingenious hacker, has been known for meeting with prospective investors wearing pajamas. He remains true to himself and does not answer to anybody. "Mark and his signature hoodie: He's actually showing investors he doesn't care that much; he's going to be him," said Michael Pachter, an analyst for Wedbush Securities. "I think that's a mark of immaturity. I think that he has to realize he's bringing investors in as a new constituency right now, and I think he's got to show them the respect that they deserve because he's asking them for their money" (49).

Although Facebook became a publicly traded company in May 2012, Zuckerberg continues to hold majority control over the company. Firstly, his 23% shares of Facebook stock carry outsized voting rights that give him 31% voting power. Secondly, he has "irrevocable proxy" over the voting power of almost 56% of Facebook's shares held by other stakeholders. The U.S. Securities and Exchange Commission (SEC) asked Facebook in February 2012 to "more fully explain how the risk of Mr. Zuckerberg's control affects … the Class A common stockholders on a short-term and long-term basis" (50).

Based on Zuckerberg's history and his personal attitude towards people's privacy, it came as no surprise that Facebook was charged by the U.S. Federal Trade Commission (FTC) for failing to keep privacy promises and violating federal law – the Federal Trade Commission Act (51). The FTC eight-count complaint lists a number of instances in which Facebook allegedly made promises that it did not keep (52). The charges include the following:

1. In December 2009, Facebook changed its website so certain information that users may have designated as private – such as their Friends List – was made

public. They didn't warn users that this change was coming, or get their approval in advance.

2. Facebook represented that third-party apps installed by the users would have access only to user information that they needed to operate. In fact, the apps could access nearly all of users' personal data – data the apps didn't need.

3. Facebook told users they could restrict sharing of data to limited audiences – for example with "Friends Only." In fact, selecting "Friends Only" did not prevent their information from being shared with third-party applications their friends used.

4. Facebook had a "Verified Apps" program and claimed it certified the security of participating apps. It didn't.

5. Facebook promised users that it would not share their personal information with advertisers. It did.

6. Facebook claimed that when users deactivated or deleted their accounts, their photos and videos would be inaccessible. But Facebook allowed access to the content, even after users had deactivated or deleted their accounts.

7. Facebook claimed that it complied with the U.S.-EU Safe Harbor Framework that governs data transfer between the U.S. and the European Union. It didn't.

Without putting up a legal fight, Facebook in November 2011 agreed to the proposed settlement (53) that the company is (54):

1. barred from making misrepresentations about the privacy or security of consumers' personal information;

2. required to obtain consumers' affirmative express consent before enacting changes that override their privacy preferences;

3. required to prevent anyone from accessing a user's material more than 30 days after the user has deleted his or her account;

4. required to establish and maintain a comprehensive privacy program designed to address privacy risks associated with the development and management of new and existing products and services, and to protect the privacy and confidentiality of consumers' information; and

5. required, within 180 days, and every two years after that for the next 20 years, to obtain independent, third-party audits certifying that it has a privacy program in place that meets or exceeds the requirements of the FTC order, and to ensure that the privacy of consumers' information is protected.

Apart from the accusations from the U.S. government, several lawsuits were filed in February 2012 against Facebook for tracking its users even after they logged out of the service (55). Computer blogger Nik Cubrilovic explained, "Even if you are logged out, Facebook still knows and can track every page you visit that has Facebook integrated. The only solution is to delete every Facebook cookie in your browser, or to use a separate browser for Facebook interactions" (56). Facebook engineers have issued numerous fixes but none to the complete satisfaction of privacy advocates.

In addition, five Facebook members in California sued Facebook for publicizing their "likes" of certain advertisers on the "sponsored stories" feature without paying them or giving them a way to opt out. In May 2012, Facebook agreed to pay $10 million to charity in settling the would-be class-action lawsuit for violating users' rights to control the use of their own names, photographs, and likenesses (57). In December 2013, two Facebook users, Matthew Campbell and Michael Hurley, filed a lawsuit against Facebook for scanning "private" messages between users for links and other information that can be sold to advertisers, marketers, and data aggregators (58).

In fact, according to *The Zuckerberg Files* created and maintained by Prof. Mike Zimmer at the University of Wisconsin-Milwaukee, Facebook CEO Mark Zuckerberg has uttered the word "privacy" or "private" only 68 times in public between 2009 and early 2014. "Facebook is causing us to rethink so many things about our views on privacy and information," said Zimmer. "Looking at what Zuckerberg says can help us understand Zuckerberg's position and also why Facebook is what it is" (59).

2.6   Facebook Friends and Personal Privacy

Although Facebook has been found liable for some of the online privacy issues, many Facebook users have not been vigilant in safeguarding their own privacy. A May 2010 report by Pew Internet indicated that only two-thirds of Facebook users said they had ever changed the privacy settings to limit what they share with others online (60). A January 2012 study by *Consumer Reports Magazine* revealed, "Almost 13 million users said they had never set, or didn't know about, Facebook's privacy tools. And 28 percent shared all, or almost all, of their wall posts with an audience wider than just their friends" (61).

In November 2011, Lars Backstrom from the Facebook Data Team reported that an average user had 190 online friends (62). A Georgetown University study shows a much higher number among college students – young adults reported an average of 358 Facebook friends, with young women reporting 401 friends and young men reporting 269 friends (63). However, according to the GoodMobilePhones survey in January 2011, the average Facebook user does not know one fifth of the people listed as friends on the site (64).

To prove the point, a group of students at Millburn High School in New Jersey created a Facebook account in 2009 for a fictional new student in their school (65). They named her "Lauren" and gave her a fake profile including a picture of a random high school girl downloaded from the Internet. This "Lauren" requested to be Facebook friends with 200 of her classmates. Only two students messaged "Lauren" to question who she was. Nearly 60% of the 200 students accepted her friendship, and an additional 55 Facebook users requested "Lauren" to be their friends, even though they obviously did not know her.

In fact, of all the reasons why a Facebook user removes a friend online, 41% of the users answered, "Don't know him/her well." (25) Those unknown friends, or rather strangers – a more accurate description, have access to photos and information that are meant for only the intended audiences or trusted friends and families. A February 2012 report from Pew Internet & American Life Project indicates that less than 5% of users hide content from another user on their Facebook feed (66).

In June 2013, Alexandra Cetto and fellow researchers from the University of Regensburg in Germany launched "Friend Inspector" – a serious game aimed at 16–25 year olds to improve their privacy awareness on Facebook. The game had been downloaded over 100,000 times within five months of its launch (67).

In March 2014, Facebook started sending out "Privacy Checkups" using a cartoon dinosaur as the messenger to alert users about safeguarding their privacy (68). "Sorry to interrupt," the message reads, "you haven't changed who can see your posts lately, so we just wanted to make sure you're sharing this post with the right audience." Facebook would then ask the user to select either "Friends," "Public," or "More Option" for the new posts.

2.7 Facebook, Children, and COPPA

In a 2011 interview with the *PEOPLE* magazine, President Barack Obama and the First Lady said that they did not allow their daughters Sasha and Malia on Facebook. Their reason was, "Why would we want to have a whole bunch of people who we don't know knowing our business? That doesn't make much sense" (69). Sasha and Malia were only 10 and 13 years old at the time.

The American public, however, paints a different story about Facebook usage. More than 55% of parents help their underage children to lie to get on Facebook, violating the site's terms of service that prohibit kids under 13 from joining. A 2011 survey conducted by Harris Interactive shows that one in five parents acknowledged having a 10-year-old on Facebook, 32% of parents allowing their 11-year-olds and 55% of parents allowing their 12-year-olds to use Facebook (70). According to *Consumers Reports* in May 2011, there are at least 7.5 million children under 13 and 5 million children ages 10 and under who are actively using Facebook (71).

Perhaps parents are not the only ones to blame, because children of all ages are facing increasing peer pressure from their friends and schoolmates. "I need your advice," a mother posed a question to Danah Boyd, coauthor of *Why parents help their children lie to Facebook about age: Unintended consequences of the Children's Online Privacy Protection Act*, "My 11-year-old daughter wants to join Facebook. She says that all of her friends are on Facebook. At what age do you think I should allow her to join Facebook?" (72).

Children are also most vulnerable to advertisements. In September 2010, *The Wall Street Journal* investigated 50 popular websites aimed at teens and children and 50 most popular U.S. sites overall (73). The investigators found that popular children's websites install 30% more tracking technologies (e.g. cookies and beacons) than do the top U.S. websites (74). Although the tracking data does not include the children's names, it can include their ages, races, hobbies, online habits, posted comments, likes and dislikes, as well as their general locations such as the cities of residence.

In 1998, the U.S. Congress enacted the Children's Online Privacy Protection Act (COPPA), requiring the Federal Trade Commission (FTC) to regulate commercial websites targeted at children and web operators who have actual knowledge of a child's participation (75). COPPA requires web site owners to notify parents and obtain their consent before collecting, using, or disclosing children's personal information.

I was a senior staff engineer and senior producer at Disney Online between 1996 and 2006. Being a family-oriented company, Disney took COPPA and children's online safety very seriously. We made sure that the Disney websites were COPPA-compliant and addressed COPPA-related issues at the weekly senior staff meetings.

The first-ever Disney MMORPG game *ToonTown Online* debuted in 2003 allows players, most of whom are children, to communicate with other players in *ToonTown* via a free-form chat if and only if the players know each other outside the game world (76). A "True Friends" verification involving a six-digit secret code is required to gain access to free-form chat.

Online safety for kids is number one in the website design and business decisions at Disney Online. Moreover, Disney is highly selective in accepting advertisements to display on its websites targeted for families and children. When I was a senior producer at Disney, I worked closely with strategic partners Google, Yahoo!, and WebSideStory. I had to write special software code to filter out the inappropriate ads before any sponsored ads are displayed among the search results on the Disney websites such as Disney.com and FamilyFun.com.

In August 2007, Disney Online purchased Club Penguin with 700,000 paid users (77). By mid-2011, Club Penguin has 12 million members, essentially becoming the world's largest social network for kids (78). A combination of games, educational resources, and social networking, Club Penguin presents a fictional world made up of user-created penguins that act as avatars for the millions of kids aged 8 to 11 in more than 190 countries around the world (79).

In July 2010, Disney Online acquired social-gaming company Playdom with 42 million players (80). Less than a year later in May 2011, the Federal Trade Commission charged that Disney's Playdom violated COPPA since 2006 as children under the age of 13 were able to register for the site, share their ages and email addresses, all without parental consent. Playdom continued to violate COPPA after the merger with Disney in August 2010, resulting in a tarnished reputation and a $3 million fine (81).

"Let's be clear: Whether you are a virtual world, a social network, or any other interactive site that appeals to kids, you owe it to parents and their children to provide proper notice and get proper consent," said Jon Leibowitz, Chairman of the Federal Trade Commission. "It's the law, it's the right thing to do, and, as today's settlement [with Disney's Playdom] demonstrates, violating COPPA will not come cheap" (82).

COPPA, however, does not address the issue that addiction to social networks at an early age can be detrimental to normal child development. A 2012 Stanford University study examined the children's behaviors from a sample of nearly 3,500 girls aged 8 to 12. The researchers concluded that tween girls who spend much of their waking hours switching frantically between YouTube, Facebook, television, and text messaging are more likely to develop social problems (83). Spending too many hours online takes away the time for face-to-face personal interactions that are essential for normal mental development.

At the 119th Annual Convention of the American Psychological Association held in August 2011, Professor Larry D. Rosen at California State University, Dominguez Hills, gave a plenary talk entitled, "Poke Me: How Social Networks Can Both Help and Harm Our Kids." Rosen discussed the disturbing findings that "teens who use Facebook more often show more narcissistic tendencies while young adults who have a strong Facebook presence show more signs of other psychological disorders, including antisocial behaviors, mania and aggressive tendencies" (84).

Ironically, a May 2013 Pew Research Center report on "Teens, Social Media, and Privacy" indicated that teens' enthusiasm for Facebook was waning due to the increasing adult presence, people sharing excessively, and stressful "drama" (85). "We did see a decrease in [teenage] daily users [during the quarter], especially younger teens," Facebook chief financial officer David Ebersman admitted during a conference call with analysts in October 2013 (86).

In an effort to hang on to the coveted teen demographic, Facebook in October relaxed its privacy settings for teens to allow 13- to 17-year-olds to share photos, updates, and comments with the general public (87). Facebook defended its new policy by stating, "We take the safety of teens very seriously, so they will see an extra reminder before they can share publicly. When teens choose 'Public' in the audience selector, they'll see a reminder that the post can be seen by anyone, not just people they know, with an option to change the post's privacy" (88).

As federal regulators have been preparing to update COPPA since 2012, big companies like Apple, Disney, Facebook, Google, Microsoft, Twitter, and Viacom have all objected to portions of a federal effort to strengthen online privacy protections for children, citing the negative impact on economic growth and job creation. In response, U.S. Representative Edward J. Markey, Democrat of Massachusetts and co-chairman of the Bipartisan Congressional Privacy Caucus, said in a phone interview, "What children post online or search as part of their homework should not haunt them as they apply to colleges or for jobs. YouTube should not be turned into YouTracked" (89).

When Facebook introduced Graph Search at a press conference in January 2013, a Facebook employee stood on stage and searched for "friends of my friends who are single and living in San Francisco" (90). Facebook's Graph Search lets users search for others by common interest, location, age, and other criteria. To protect minors, information on Facebook users under 18 is hidden from the search results (91).

2.8   Netflix and Social Apps on Facebook

In September 2011, Facebook began rolling out new "Read. Watch. Listen. Want." features that let "social apps" broadcast every interaction users have with them (92). The apps are opt-in, but few users read the fine print or adjust the default settings (93). Some users might be surprised to find applications like Spotify, Kobo eBooks, Hulu, Yahoo! News, and Nike+ GPS broadcasting every song they stream, book they read, video they watch, news story they glance over, or place they visit (94).

Back in December 2007, Facebook launched Beacon, resulting in a class-action lawsuit against Facebook, Fandango, Blockbuster, Overstock, and Gamefly for violating the 1988 Video Privacy Protection Act (VPPA) that aims at preserving the confidentiality of people's movie-watching records. Facebook shut down Beacon in 2009 and agreed to pay $9.5 million to create a new foundation for promoting privacy and security (95).

Notwithstanding the fiasco of the defunct Facebook Beacon program, Netflix, with 26 million subscribers (96) and 1 billion hours of video views in June 2012 (97), allows Facebook users see what films or television content friends are watching and will let users watch as well via Facebook (98). To clear the hurdle of the Video Privacy Protection Act (VPPA), Netflix has successfully lobbied the U.S. House of Representatives in passing a measure in December 2011 to amend the VPPA, allowing Netflix to integrate with Facebook more easily (99). And in December 2012, the U.S. Senate passed a legislation allowing Netflix users to share what movies they had watched with their Facebook friends (100).

In spite of the legislative victories, Netflix was accused in 2011 of violating VPPA that requires video rental services to destroy users' personal information "as soon as practicable, but no later than one year from the date the information is no longer necessary for the purpose for which it was collected." In February 2012, Netflix settled a class-action privacy lawsuit for $9 million (101); and in May, Netflix announced that it would "decouple" former customers' movie rental history from their personal information within one year after they cancel their accounts (102).

In September 2014, Netflix added a privacy feature to let users control which shows they want to share with their Facebook friends. "Starting today, we're launching our new social recommendation feature that allows you to easily and privately recommend the shows you love to the people you care about," said Cameron Johnson, Netflix's director of production innovation (103).

With Netflix and social apps' integration with Facebook, we no longer need to call up our friends to ask what they were doing last weekend or what they are doing at the moment. Everything is on Facebook in real time. The "all-knowing" persuasive social network has diminished the necessity for real-life personal conversations. Other flourishing social apps such as the microblogging Twitter and the virtual pinboard Pinterest reinforce the popular trend of public sharing of information on the Internet (104).

2.9 Facebook Timeline and Open Graph

Not only does Facebook enable users to share current activities with one another, the social network has introduced at the 2011 F8 Conference new Timeline and Open Graph to facilitate "frictionless sharing" or "auto-share".

The new Facebook Timeline displays a user's life stories, sharing and highlighting their most memorable posts, photos, and life events (105). "No activity is too big or too small to share," said Mark Zuckerberg. "You don't have to 'Like' a movie. You just watch a movie. … We think it's an important next step to help you tell the story of your life" (106).

Indeed, "to tell the story of your life" resonates with millions of Facebook addicts. But some critics have cautioned that Facebook may be invading too much into one's personal life, as the user will be asked to add date of birth, key events, memories, personal events and feelings that happen outside of the social network (107).

To help users tell the story of their life with minimal effort, Facebook's Open Graph technology allows third-party apps and websites to tell Facebook what people are doing, and to automatically publish information to their Timelines without having to ask for permission to post content to Facebook over and over again. *Mashable* calls it "real-time serendipity" (108).

By January 2012, sixty apps had been launched with Facebook's auto-share; they include Hulu, Yahoo! News, *Wall Street Journal*, *USA Today*, *The Washington Post*, Digg, Soundcloud, Turntable.fm, Rhapsody, and Spotify (109). Apple's iTunes and Pandora, however, did not plan to participate in the Facebook Music auto-publish feature (110).

In March 2012, Facebook announced that nearly 3,000 Timeline apps have launched in the past two months (111). The apps makers include foursquare, Nike, *The Onion*, Vevo, Fandango, Viddy, Endomondo, RootMusic, Foodspotting, Pose, and Votizen. Fandango, for instance, claimed to have tens of millions of online visitors and 1.4 million Facebook fans (112). Launched on March 13, 2012, the Fandango Timeline app "Movies with Friends" allows Facebook fans to share:

1. Movies they've rated and reviewed on Fandango, from "Must Go" to "Oh No!"
2. Movies they want to see, indicated by the "I'm In!" button
3. Movie trailers, clips and celebrity interviews they have just watched
4. Articles they've read on Fandango's "Freshly Popped" blog

By using Facebook's Timeline and social apps with Open Graph, an average user is knowingly communicating with an average of 130 online friends. Unknowingly, however, many of the popular apps on Facebook have been transmitting user information such as names and their friends' names to dozens of advertising and Internet tracking companies. *The Wall Street Journal's* investigation in October 2010 uncovered that Rapleaf, a database marketing company in San Francisco, compiled and sold profiles of Facebook users based in part on their online activities (113).

Facebook has since cracked down on apps that sold user data and banned Rapleaf from data scraping on Facebook (114).

2.10   Ambient Social Apps and Digital Surveillance

Ambient social apps are the new generation of mobile apps that automatically share information about the user's whereabouts with nearby people in their social networks by broadcasting their locations at all times to friends.

Launched in March 2009, foursquare is a location-based social networking website and mobile app that allows users to check in at a venue, thereby posting their location based on the GPS hardware in the mobile device. In June 2011, foursquare had 10 million users (115). By August 2014, foursquare has grown to 50 million people worldwide with 6 billion check-ins; and over 1.9 million businesses have claimed their locations to connect with their customers (116). President Barack Obama is one of its high-profile users. "The White House is now on foursquare, which is the latest way for you to engage with the administration," Kori Schulman, Deputy Director of Outreach for the Office of Digital Strategy, wrote in *The White House Blog,* "Now you'll be able to discover tips from the White House featuring the places President Obama has visited, what he did there, plus historical information and more" (117). Foursquare has since split its main app into two separate apps, the Foursquare City Guide and Swarm (118). In 2020, Foursquare merged with Factual to access 25 million always-on users and 14 billion check-ins across 190 countries (119).

The growing popularity of foursquare has ignited a slew of new ambient social apps. Sonar, for instance, was a mobile app that analyzes Facebook, Twitter, Foursquare, and LinkedIn networks to see if any online friends are nearby physically. According to the Sonar website before it went offline in September 2013, the mobile app "bottles the 1000s of connections that you miss every day – friends, friends of friends, fellow alumni, likeminded strangers – and put them in the palm of your hand. Sonar helps you use the information you share about yourself online to connect with the person sitting next to you" (120). A screenshot displayed on the Sonar homepage shows who, among friends and friends of friends, are currently in the Museum of Modern Art and how long they have been there.

Glancee was created to be both a Facebook app and an iPhone/Android app that explores the Facebook profiles of people nearby and notifies the user when someone nearby has common friends or mutual interests (121). The Radar function on Glancee displays how close the friends are in proximity, from steps away to hundreds of yards apart. Glancee was acquired by Facebook in May 2012 and subsequently closed down (122).

Banjo started out as an ambient social app that alerts its user about friends who are nearby and pinpoints their locations on a street map. Nine months after its launch, Banjo had registered 1 million users in April 2012 (123). The Banjo website posted a story that inspired the creation of the app: "Banjo founder Damien Patton was in the Boston airport waiting for a flight to Vegas. A buddy he hadn't seen in years was waiting for a different flight just one gate over. Damien tweeted. His friend checked in. Both posted about their locations, yet they missed connecting simply because they were using different social networks" (124). In January 2014, Banjo rebranded itself as "The Live Internet" for its 6 million users to discover and experience live events in real time (125). In March 2020, Banjo signed a $20.7 million contract with Utah that granted the company access to the state's traffic, CCTV, and public safety cameras for law enforcement purposes (126). In February 2021, it was found that the company had renamed itself as safeXai to better reflect Banjo's focus on digital surveillance (127).

Highlight was a free iPhone app that enables its users to learn about each other when they are close by. Using Facebook's data, the users can see each other's names, photos, mutual friends, hobbies, interests, and anything they have chosen to share. Highlight stated in its website in 2012: "When you meet someone, Highlight helps you see what you have in common with them. And when you forget their name at a party a week later, Highlight can help you remember it" (128). Eric Eldon, Editor of *TechCrunch,* had speculated that business cards would soon be replaced by Highlight (129). However, Pinterest acquired the team behind Highlight in 2016 and shut down the app (130).

And now for something completely different (in a Monty Python-esque sense of humor), Hell Is Other People was an experiment in anti-social media. Using four-square, the site tracked your "friends" and calculated optimally distanced locations for avoiding them (131). The app creator Scott Garner wrote on his website in June 2013, "This project is partially a satire, partially a commentary on my disdain for 'social media,' and partially an exploration of my own difficulties with social anxiety" (132). Garner certainly made a good point as social media is contributing to the rise in real-world stalking.

2.11 Stalking Apps and Badoo (aka Facebook for Sex)

In May 2012, Facebook acquired Glancee and closed down its app (133). On June 25, 2012, Facebook quietly tested a new mobile feature "Find Friends Nearby" (aka "Friendshake") that allowed users to find other Facebook members nearby using the mobile web as well as iOS and Android apps (134). Facebook engineer Ryan Patterson said, "I built Find Friends Nearby with another engineer for a hackathon project. … For me, the ideal use case for this product is the one where when you're out with a group of people whom you've recently met and want to stay in contact with. Facebook search might be effective, or sharing your vanity addresses or business cards, but this tool provides a really easy way to exchange contact information with multiple people with minimal friction" (135).

However, Dave Copeland of *ReadWriteWeb* called Find Friends Nearby "Facebook's Newest Stalking App" (136). Facebook quietly pulled the feature off its website and mobile apps after a few hours of testing. A Facebook spokesperson told *Wired*, "This wasn't a formal release – this was just something that a few engineers were testing. With all tests, some get released as full products, others don't. Nothing more to say on this for now, but we'll communicate to everyone when there is something to say" (137).

Ambient social apps on GPS-enabled devices can be useful and fun, but the tools inadvertently empower stalkers as well. "Girls Around Me" is an epitome of such controversial mobile apps in 2012. At the push of a button, the app would go into radar mode and fill the map with pictures of girls in the neighborhood: girls who have checked into the nearby locations using foursquare, and who have public pictures on their Facebook profiles.

After "Girls Around Me" had been downloaded 70,000 times, foursquare cut off access to the app, rendering the app useless. A foursquare spokeswoman said, "The application was in violation of our API policy, so we reached out to the developer and shut off their API access. foursquare has a policy against aggregating information across venues, to prevent situations like this where someone would present an inappropriate overview of a series of locations" (138).

"Girls Around Me" developer had no choice but to remove the app from the iTunes Store, but the developer defended itself in a public statement, "Girls Around Me does not provide any data that is unavailable to a user when he uses his or her social network account, nor does it reveal any data that users did not share with others. The app was intended for facilitating discovering of great public venues nearby. The app was designed to make it easier for a user to step out of door and hang out in the city, find people with common interests and new places to go to" (139).

The demise of "Girls Around Me" only fueled the growing popularity of Badoo – the world's largest social network for "meeting new people" with 28.4 million monthly active users in September 2020 (140). Relatively unknown in the United States, Badoo has become a mass phenomenon in Brazil, Mexico, France, Spain, Italy, and other countries after the site launched in 2006. Inspired by the nightclub known as "Telephone Bar" in St. Petersburg, Badoo's founder Andrey Andreev created the social network to be like a nightclub on the phone (141).

The Badoo website and its mobile app enable users to meet people nearby. The app's "hook-up" feature accounts for an overwhelming 80% of usage, and a third of a million U.K. users admitted to using Badoo to find sexual partners (142). Around the world, Badoo has earned the notorious nickname "Facebook for Sex" (143).

Andreev defended his company amid controversy over heavy sexual overtones, "Badoo is not for sex, it's for adventure. If you go to a nightclub, of course you've got the opportunity to find a girl or a boy – but it's not necessarily for sex, it could be to enjoy five mojitos and nothing else. Badoo simply continues the offline lifestyle. Badoo is just a casual way to hook up with people, as you do in the street or nightclub. But we make the world work faster" (144).

Other sex apps include Bang With Friends, Pure, and Tinder. "We wanted an easy way to find sex, basically," said Pure's co-founder Roman Sidorenko (145). As more people are broadcasting their real-time location and personal information, however, privacy and personal safety are becoming an issue. There have been reports of assaults and rapes of Skout and Grindr members while the majority of crimes tied to location-based apps may go unreported (146).

Pete Cashmore, founder and CEO of Mashable.com, questions whether ambient social networking is "the scariest tech trend of 2012" (147). Paul Davison, CEO of Highlight, told CNN at the 2012 LeWeb London conference, "People freak out, they say it's creepy. And if they don't want to share, then that's fine, they don't have to. But the social benefits to this far outweigh any cost to privacy" (148).

In April 2014, Facebook (re)introduced a new mobile feature called "Nearby Friends" that enables Facebook friends to track each other in real time using location information (149). For privacy reason, users have to opt in in order to activate the feature.

2.12 Facial Recognition Apps

In October 2011, Alessandro Acquisti, professor of IT and public policy at Carnegie Mellon University's Heinz College, demonstrated a proof-of-concept iPhone application that can snap a photo of a person and within seconds display their name, date of birth and social security number (150). "To match two photos of people in the United States in real time would take four hours," said Acquisti. "That's too long to do in real time. But assuming a steady improvement in cloud computing time, we can soon get much closer to that reality than many of us believed" (151).

In June 2012, Facebook acquired Face.com – a preeminent provider of facial recognition technology on the Internet (152). Face.com wrote on its website, "Face. com builds facial recognition software that is not only highly accurate, but also works efficiently at web-scale. Our facial recognition analytics are able to identify faces well, despite difficult circumstances like poor lighting, poor focus, subjects wearing eyeglasses, facial hair, and even Halloween costumes. Face recognition isn't just for the government or in the movies – you can use it yourself in all kinds of ways, from tagging photos to social networking" (153).

Two years before Facebook's acquisition, face.com rolled out its free facial recognition API (application programming interface) in May 2010 to encourage developers to tap its facial recognition technology for use in their own websites and applications (154). By November 2011, more than 35,000 developers have built apps to detect and recognize more than 37 billion photos (155).

Some of the popular applications include "Photo Finder," "Photo Tagger," and "Celebrityfindr." "Photo Finder" is a Facebook app that scans the public photos in the user's social network and suggests tags for the photos that are currently untagged or partially tagged (156). The app recognizes people even if they are making odd facial expressions or are turned to the side. "Photo Tagger" searches through the user's photo albums or the albums of their friends, and tags people in batches (157). And "Celebrityfindr" scans Twitter and looks for photos of celebrities and lookalikes that have been posted publicly (158).

Other facial recognition software applications in a prototype stage include "HoneyBadger," "Facialytics," and "Emotional Breakdown" (159). Using face.com's technology, "HoneyBadger" sends an alert text message to the registered owner if the laptop is being used by someone else, "Facialytics" tracks a crowd's emotions over time, and "Emotional Breakdown" examines how happy or sad someone is in a photo.

In October 2013, Meitar Moscovitz (aka maymay) released "Predator Alert Tools" for OkCupid, FetLife, Facebook, and Lulu that use CreepShield's facial recognition API (160) to scan user profile pictures against the National Sex Offender Registry (161).

In December 2013, FacialNetwork.com announced the beta release of "NameTag" – the first real-time facial recognition app for Google Glass (162). The app allows Google Glass users to capture images from their live video and scan them against photos from social media, dating sites, and a database of more than 450,000 registered sex offenders.

In September 2014, the FBI launched its Next Generation Identification (NGI) system for law enforcement agencies to identify people by their faces using photos from Facebook, Google images, police, surveillance cameras, and DMV records (163). In fact, more than half of all state DMVs have already installed facial recognition systems (164).

In November 2015, Facebook added its facial recognition technology into Messenger. "We like to look at the use cases for what people are doing now and what people could be doing, and how could we make it even easier. Lots of times [artificial intelligence] can be a great tool for that," said Messenger product manager Peter Martinazzi (165).

In February 2021, TikTok—a video-sharing social networking service owned by Chinese company ByteDance—settled for $92 million in a lawsuit that alleged the company was misusing facial recognition to track and profile users for the purpose of ad targeting (166).

Insurance company Lemonade uses facial recognition technology to analyze videos submitted by their clients when they file insurance claims. The company's AI software detects signs of fraud by picking up "non-verbal cues that traditional insurers can't" (167). In May 2021 amid public relations controversy, Lemonade defended its use of artificial intelligence by clarifying that "AI that uses harmful concepts like phrenology and physiognomy has never, and will never, be used at Lemonade" (168).

2.13 Facial Recognition on Facebook, Google, and iPhone

"We wouldn't exist without Facebook," said Gil Hirsch, CEO of face.com. "By far the biggest scale for face recognition is your friends on Facebook" (169).

Indeed, by April 2009, Facebook users had uploaded over 15 billion digital photographs to the social network, making Facebook the single largest repository of photographs in the world (170). The growth rate is 220 million new photos per week. Every day, Facebook users are adding more than 100 million tags to photos on Facebook (171).

In December 2010, Facebook began to roll out its own facial recognition technology, Photo Tag Suggest, which scans users' and their friends' photos for recognizable faces, and suggests nametags for the faces by matching them with users' profile photos and other tagged photos on the social network (172). Facebook automatically opts its users into the Photo Tag Suggest service, which prompted a security firm to issue a warning in June 2011 that Facebook is eroding the online privacy of its users by stealth (173). Although Facebook users can disable "Suggest photos of me to friends" in the Facebook account's privacy settings, many people are unaware of this extra privacy setting.

When *Engadget* published an article on Facebook's facial recognition in April 2011, a commenter beneath the story quipped, "Awesome! Now I can take pictures of cute girls at the grocery store or at the park, upload them and Facebook will tell me who they are!" (174).

Lee Tien, a senior staff attorney at the Electronic Frontier Foundation, wrote in his email to *PCWorld*, "Facial recognition is especially troubling because cameras are ubiquitous and we routinely show our faces. And of course, one can take pictures of crowds, so it scales a bit better than, say, fingerprints. ... If Facebook misidentifies someone, the consequences are not the same as when a police video-camera misidentifies you as a suspect" (175).

Facebook's acquisition of face.com in June 2012 solidifies the importance of facial recognition in social networking. The move can also be viewed as Facebook's preemptive tactic against Google and Apple.

Back in September 2008, Google deployed facial recognition technology to its online photo service Picasa (176). Similarly, Apple released the "Faces" feature in iPhoto in January 2009 (177). With a reasonable success rate, Picasa and iPhone helped users label their photos with the names of subjects. As facial recognition technology began to mature, Apple added the Faces feature to its professional photography software Aperture in 2010 (178).

In December 2011, Google followed the Facebook footstep and introduced "Find My Face" as a tagging suggestion tool for its Google+ social network (179).[1] The tool has the same functionality as Facebook's Photo Tag Suggest. Unlike Facebook, which activates its Photo Tag Suggest by default, Google prompts users to opt into the service before Find My Face is activated. Moreover, if the tagger is not in the tagee's circles of friends, Google requires the tagee to approve the name tagging before it goes public. Facebook, on the contrary, does not require pre-approval for tags. Facebook allows all tags to go live before notifying the tagees, who are then allowed to remove unwanted tags.

---

[1] Google+ began to shut down on April 2, 2019. Google had disclosed two significant data leaks that could have exposed information for tens of millions of Google+ users to outside developers. (261)

Amid concerns raised by privacy advocates and U.S. Federal Trade Commission, Benjamin Petrosky, product counsel for Google+, said, "Privacy has been baked right into this feature [Find My Face]. ... We've been researching vision technologies for many years, including pattern recognition, facial detection, and facial recognition, and our approach is to treat this very carefully. We don't want to deploy a technology until it's ready and the appropriate privacy tools are in place" (180). Meanwhile, Erin Egan, Facebook's chief privacy policy officer, defended the company by claiming that it does enough to safeguard its members' privacy by notifying them when they have been tagged and allowing them to remove tags once they have been made (181).

While Prof. Alessandro Acquisti's 2011 proof-of-concept iPhone application is not yet a commercial product, face.com released a free iPhone app called Klik in March 2012 (182). When Klik detects a face, it connects to the user's Facebook account and scans all the friends' photos in order to identify the person in view. Given the limited number of Facebook friends that a user may have, facial recognition can be done in real time.

As smartphones and iPads are connected to cloud computing services over the Internet, it is a matter of time for companies to introduce new mobile applications that can run millions of face comparisons in seconds, even without tapping into the power of the supercomputers at the National Security Agency or San Diego Supercomputing Center. Google has developed a distributed computing infrastructure for training large-scale artificial neural networks to detect objects based on self-taught learning and deep learning research (183). By scanning YouTube videos, the artificial neural networks have been learning how to recognize faces of animals and people.

Privacy concerns with the growing adoption of facial recognition have prompted Adam Harvey at New York University to create *CV Dazzle*, a computer vision (CV) camouflage project that combines makeup and hair styling with face-detection thwarting designs (184). Some of the camouflage techniques include wearing oversized sunglasses, avoiding enhancers such as eye shadow and lipstick, and partially obscuring the nose-bridge area and ocular region (185).

Harvey might be overreacting, but Edward Snowden's NSA leaks have revealed that the NSA intercepts "millions of images per day" including about 55,000 "facial recognition quality images" in 2011. "The government and the private sector are both investing billions of dollars into face recognition research and development," said Jennifer Lynch at the Electronic Frontier Foundation. "The government leads the way in developing huge face recognition databases, while the private sector leads in accurately identifying people under challenging conditions" (186). In fact, Facebook's DeepFace system outperforms the FBI at facial recognition (187). Yaniv Taigman and colleagues reported that DeepFace "reaches an accuracy of 97.35% on the Labeled Faces in the Wild (LFW) dataset, reducing the error of the current state of the art by more than 27%, closely approaching human-level performance" (188) (see Fig. 2.2).

On a lighter note, animals are not concerned with privacy, and facial recognition can be quite useful. In May 2014, Finding Rover released an iOS app that uses facial

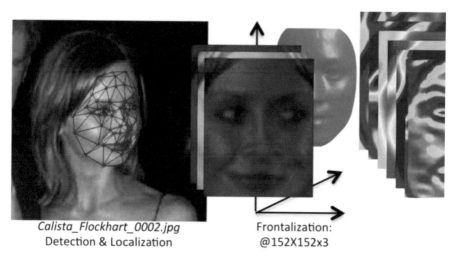

Calista_Flockhart_0002.jpg   Frontalization:
Detection & Localization   @152X152x3

Fig. 2.2 DeepFace Analysis of Calista Flockhart (Courtesy of Facebook)

recognition for dogs to help owners find their lost dogs (189). Facebook users can register their dogs for free; and if their dogs ever get lost, they can use the Finding Rover app to find the missing pets. (Not only that "every dog has its day", but also that "every dog has its data" in the digital information age.)

Although computer vision can help identify just about any objects of interest, non-facial image recognition has a much better chance of mass adoption. In April 2014, Pete Warden, founder of Jetpac, released the open-source DeepBeliefSDK and demonstrated how to build object recognition into an iOS app (190). In June 2014, Amazon's chief executive Jeff Bezos announced the new "Fire" smartphone. "The Firefly button lets you identify printed Web and email addresses, phone numbers, QR and bar codes, artwork, and over 100 million items, including songs, movies, TV shows, and products – and take action in seconds," said Bezos (191).

2.14   Virtual Passports: From Privacy to Data Use

Mark Zuckerberg told a captive audience at the 2014 F8 Conference, "'Login with Facebook'… We know a lot of people are scared of pressing this button" (192).

When Spotify, a popular music streaming service, announced in September 2011 that all new Spotify accounts would require a Facebook login, the company justified the requirement by asking the users to think of it as a virtual "passport" (193). The idea is reminiscent of Microsoft's Passport in 1999 to provide consumers a single login and wallet for communication and commerce on the Internet (194). Privacy concerns, public distrust, and software security issues contributed to the failure of Microsoft's Passport in 2004 as an Internet-wide unified-login system (195).

With the rise of social networks, Facebook has become a large-scale consumer identity provider (IdP) that allows users to access multiple websites with a single login (196). Unlike Microsoft, Facebook has succeeded in convincing media websites and users to adopt its unified-login system ("passport") such that personal information can be easily shared across the Internet. Even Microsoft's new social search network So.cl uses Facebook authentication (197).

As we know, countries issue passports. In the 2012 TEDGlobal conference, Navy Admiral James Stavridis said, "The six largest nations in the world in descending order: China, India, Facebook, the United States, Twitter, and Indonesia" (198). With over 3 billion monthly active users in 2021, Facebook as a nation has overtaken China as the largest "country" in the world (21). Facebook even offers a memorialization feature for families and friends to leave posts on the deceased's profile Walls in remembrance (199). Cybercitizens are becoming as real as citizens; and their Facebook pages are more revealing than their real-life passports.

In the Facebook nation, "power users" dominate the online space by excessively tagging photos, sending messages, "like"-ing things all the time, and obsessively "friend"-ing new people on Facebook. Power users make up between 20% to 30% of the Facebook population (200).

Approximately 81.7% of the daily users reside outside the United States and Canada (21). In the U.S., Facebook ranks No. 1 in time spent and ad impressions, and No. 2 in total internet visits (behind Google) (201). And the most popular free iPhone app of all time is Facebook (ahead of Pandora, Instagram, YouTube, and Skype) (202).

Each Facebook user is sharing personal information among an average of 130 online friends, roughly 25% of whom are strangers. 20% to 30% of the Facebook populations are considered "power users" that have between 359 and 780 online friends. Without invoking complex mathematics, we can infer from the numbers that millions of people have access to information that is not really meant to be publicly shared.

Even if a Facebook user has zero online friends, they are still sharing all of their personal information with Facebook. In fact, Facebook has quietly renamed its "Privacy Policy" to "Data Use Policy" in September 2011 to reflect more accurately what Facebook does with the data collection (203).

At the January 2012 Digital Life Design (DLD) conference in Munich, Facebook's chief operating officer Sheryl Sandberg said, "We are our real identities online" (204). Cybercitizens are becoming as real as citizens. Our online identities are more revealing than our own passports.

In light of Facebook's Timeline, social apps auto-share, facial recognition photo tagging, and violation of the Federal Trade Commission Act, a *Los Angeles Times* article in September 2011 declared, "Facebook has murdered privacy" (205).

Nevertheless, Facebook is not the only culprit.

2.15 Social Search: Google, plus Your World and Microsoft's Bing

In December 2009, Google's then CEO Eric Schmidt told CNBC's Maria Bartiromo in an interview, "If you have something that you don't want anyone to know, maybe you shouldn't be doing it in the first place, but if you really need that kind of privacy, the reality is that search engines – including Google – do retain this information for some time, and it's important, for example that we are all subject in the United States to the Patriot Act. It is possible that that information could be made available to the authorities" (206).

On January 10, 2012, Google began to roll out its most radical transformation ever with "social search" – a new search engine that understands not only content, but also people and relationships (207). Google search provides not only results from the public web, but also personal content or things shared on social networks such as Google+ and YouTube. Google Fellow Amit Singhal wrote in the Google Blog: "Search is pretty amazing at finding that one needle in a haystack of billions of webpages, images, videos, news and much more. But clearly, that isn't enough. You should also be able to find your own stuff on the web, the people you know and things they've shared with you, as well as the people you don't know but might want to … all from one search box" (208).

In January 2012, Google announced its new privacy policy, effective March 1, that replaces more than 60 different privacy polices across Google. They admitted that the company has been collecting and compiling data about its users based on their activities across Google products and services including search engine, Gmail, YouTube, and Android cell phones (209). In regard to search particularly, Google states in its policies and principles that "if you're signed into Google, we can do things like suggest search queries – or tailor your search results – based on the interests you've expressed in Google+, Gmail, and YouTube. We'll better understand which version of Pink or Jaguar you're searching for and get you those results faster" (210). Some may argue that the new Google search is way too personal, as editor Brent Rose expressed in a January 2012 *Gizmodo* article: "The fact that you can't opt-out of shared search data, and that Google will know more about you than your wife? That's a little creepy" (211).

A letter signed by 36 state attorneys general was sent to Google co-founder and CEO Larry Page. The letter reads, "On a fundamental level, the policy appears to invade consumer privacy by automatically sharing personal information consumers input into one Google product with all Google products" (212). In particular, questions were raised about whether users can opt-out of the new data sharing system either globally or on a product-by-product basis (213). Google responded that by folding more than 60 product-specific privacy policies into one, the company is explaining its privacy commitments in a simpler and more understandable manner (214).

The Electronic Frontier Foundation explained, "Search data can reveal particularly sensitive information about you, including facts about your location, interests, age, sexual orientation, religion, health concerns, and more" (215). Nick Mediati wrote in *PC World*, "This grand consolidation means that all of your Google account data will live in a single database that every Google service can access. Google Maps will have access to your Gmail data, which will have access to your YouTube history, and so on" (216). Users who log on to Google, Gmail, and YouTube cannot opt out of Google's new privacy policy (217).

Before Google plus Your World, Microsoft's search engine Bing has been collaborating with Twitter since 2009 and Facebook since 2010 to surface more personalized content in search results. Microsoft pays Twitter to obtain a real-time feed of tweets for its search engine Bing (218). Bing users have the ability to see what their friends have liked across the web, including news articles, celebrities, movies, and music (219).

The idea behind the search integration is the "Friend Effect" – a decision made when someone obtains a friend's stamp of approval (220). For example, critics may pan a movie that you are interested in, but if your friends say the movie is worth seeing anyway, you are more likely to watch that movie. A Nielsen report titled "Global Trust in Advertising and Brand Messages" has validated the "Friend Effect" by showing that an overwhelming 92% of consumers around the world trust recommendations from friends and family above all other forms of advertising (221).

In 2011, Microsoft spruced up its mobile Bing site with Facebook integration (222) and deepened the ties between Bing and Facebook by displaying the social search results along with Facebook friends' pictures, cities of residence, education, employment details, travel locations, and even shopping lists (223).

In response to Google, plus Your World, Microsoft redesigned Bing in 2012 to feature the new "Sidebar," a social search function to scour user's social networks to surface information relevant to the search queries (224). For instance, a search for "Los Angeles Chinese restaurants" will return existing posts from friends talking about a similar topic on Facebook, Twitter, and Google+.

In a 2012 interview with *The Guardian*, Google co-founder Sergey Brin complained, "all the information in [the Facebook and iPhone] apps – that data is not crawlable by web crawlers. You can't search it" (225). Indeed, all search engines have the same mission of prying into every detail in every corner of the world in order to unearth as much information as possible. However, the walled garden of Facebook and social media have been increasingly driving more referral traffic than traditional search. Tanya Corduroy, digital development director for *The Guardian,* reported in March 2012 that Facebook made up more than 30% of the newspaper's referrals compared to a mere 2% eighteen months ago (226).

Social search is shaping the future of search engines, making search results more personal, more comprehensive, and hopefully more useful. It is shifting the landscape of search engine optimization (SEO) to incorporate "Friend Effect" in addition to keywords, meta tags, cross-linking, and other traditional SEO techniques. Google co-founder Larry Page once said, "The ultimate search engine is something as smart as people – or smarter" (227).

2.16   Self-Destructing Messages

Self-destructing messages were popularized by the Mission Impossible TV series starring Peter Graves (228) and the motion pictures of the same title starring Tom Cruise (229). Like the seemingly impossible moon landing, Hollywood has repeatedly predicted the future, including self-destructing messages.

Launched in September 2011, Snapchat is a photo messaging app developed by Evan Spiegel and Robert Murphy at Stanford University. Users can send each other ephemeral photos, videos, text, and drawings (collectively known as snaps) that self-destruct after 1 to 10 seconds (230). Snapchat quickly earned a notorious reputation as a tool for sending risqué messages. In October 2013, Snapchat introduced Stories that are rolling compilations of snaps that last at most 24 hours (231).

By April 2014, over 700 million snaps are shared per day on Snapchat – more than Facebook, WhatsApp, and other social networks. Snapchat Stories have amassed 500 million views per day (232).

Although a major goal of Snapchat is to avoid the privacy pitfall of social media, it is far from foolproof. First, the recipient can take a screenshot before the time runs out. Second, "expired" Snapchats can be brought back from the dead. "As a digital forensics firm," said Richard Hickman, digital forensic examiner at Decipher Forensics. "We offer for anyone wanting to retrieve their Snapchats for an affordable price of $300–$600. Parents and law enforcement can mail us phones, and we will extract the Snapchat data, and send the phone and data back in a readable format" (233).

In May 2014, Snapchat settled charges with the Federal Trade Commission for deceiving customers about self-destructing messages. Moreover, Snapchat also uploaded entire contact lists from users' iPhones without permission. "If a company markets privacy and security as key selling points in pitching its service to consumers, it is critical that it keep those promises," said FTC Chairwoman Edith Ramirez (234).

When Snapchat repeatedly refused Facebook's acquisition offers, Facebook followed suit and released the Facebook Poke app in December 2012 (235). Essentially a Snapchat clone, Facebook Poke lets users discreetly send messages, photos, and videos that are deleted in a few seconds.

In April 2013, following the trend popularized by Snapchat and Poke, Efemr offers an app that posts time-limited messages, photos, and videos to Twitter (236). Tweets are automatically deleted after a set amount of time chosen by its user, but Efemr clarifies on its website that "due to the different time zones and third party server response time, efemr may not be able to delete tweets at the exact time chosen. There may be a delay of approximately 1 to 3 minutes" (237).

In June 2014, Facebook launched the Slingshot app to allow users exchange photos and videos without requiring Facebook accounts (238). Like WhatsApp, users signs up for Slingshot with their mobile phone number. Similar to Snapchat, photos and videos disappear from users' smartphones after they are viewed.

Apple also jumped on the self-destructing message bandwagon in June 2014 when it announced that audio and video messages within iOS 8 will automatically vanish within a few minutes. "You don't want to have to clean these up," said Greg

Joswiak, head of iOS product marketing. "Audio and video messages can take up space, so they're set to self-destruct unless you choose to keep them" (239).

In March 2017, Facebook Messenger became the third clone of Snapchat Stories when it introduced a new "Day" option for users to post photos, videos, and text that vanish after 24 hours (240).

2.17   Facebook Anonymous Login

In June 2010, chief political correspondent Declan McCullagh at *CNET* reported that "even if someone is not a Facebook user or is not logged in, Facebook's social plug-ins collect the address of the Web page being visited and the Internet address of the visitor as soon as the page is loaded – clicking on the Like button is not required. If enough sites participate, that permits Facebook to assemble a vast amount of data about Internet users' browsing habits" (241).

Four years later at the April 2014 F8 Conference, Facebook unveiled Anonymous Login that allows users to sign into apps without sharing their identities and personal information contained in their Facebook accounts (242). Circumventing privacy concerns helps to eliminate the potential barrier for many users to try out new apps – a welcome news for both app developers and users.

According to Facebook, Anonymous Login promises to be a great feature for third-party app developers (243):

- The most convenient way for people to log into your app without sharing their personal information.
- An easy way for people to try your app: Increase your conversions by helping people get started with your app quickly. They won't have to create a password or share their personal information.
- One login across every device: Just like Facebook Login, when people log in on one device, they can continue their experience across their other devices. It's the best combination of convenience and privacy.
- Fully compatible with Facebook Login: Anonymous Login is designed to work seamlessly with Facebook Login. People using your app can upgrade from Anonymous Login to Facebook Login with just a few taps.

Shortly after the introduction of Anonymous Login, Facebook announced in May 2014 that it was going to reduce the amount of automatic posts from apps to users' News Feed. In other words, Facebook gave up on automatically posting everything we do online with Instagram, Pinterest, Farmville, Spotify, RunKeeper, and other apps (244). Instead of sharing stories implicitly, users can explicitly share their Open Graph stories and have more control over when they share from the apps that they use (245)·

CNN's Doug Gross commented on Facebook's privacy stand in 2014: "Critics have questioned Facebook's commitment to privacy over the course of its 10-year history, claiming the company would prefer users share as openly as possible -- which advertisers like -- than adjust their settings to be more private. But changes in recent months suggest the social platform has decided on a different tack" (246).

To the privacy advocates, it seems that Facebook is finally heading the right direction!

2.18   Anonymous Social Apps

With Confide, Rumr, Secret, Whisper, and Yik Yak, a growing number of anonymous social apps enable people to share whatever they are thinking anonymously without worrying about consequences. As a result, there is no way to tell what posts are true or false. Some messages are brutally honest while some others may be deemed offensive. One of the posts on Whisper said, "I danced with two people at my wedding. The one I married, and the one I wish I married instead" (247) (see Fig. 2.3).

Whisper CEO Michael Heyward told *Business Insider*, "You are who you are when no one else is looking. Anonymity is a really powerful tool. But we think about it like that Spiderman' quote: 'With great power comes great responsibility.' Think about all the things you can do with a hammer. You can build something great … or you can kill someone" (248).

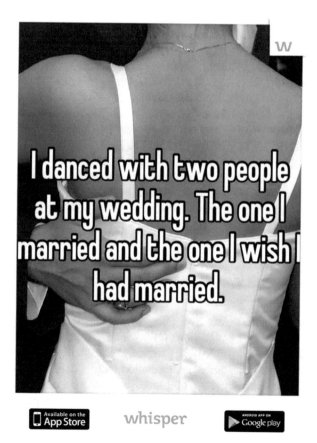

Fig. 2.3 An Anonymous Post on Whisper

In June 2014 during the intensifying conflict in Iraq, many Iraqis could not get on Facebook and Twitter, but they were able to use the Whisper app to share real-time information anonymously. Before the media could confirm the U.S. embassy's partial staff relocation, a whisper was posted online: "US embassy in Baghdad is evacuating!!! Yepppppppp!!!!" (249).

A month prior in May 2014, Secret made to the top 10 most popular downloads on the Apple App Store in Russia, Ukraine, Moldova, Latvia, and The Netherlands. Secret user registration requires no real names and no user profile, because "it's not about who you are — it's about what you say. It's not about bragging — it's about sharing, free of judgment" (250).

The anonymous social app is expanding to the United States and China. In an email to *TechCrunch*, Secret co-founder David Byttow wrote, "Secret has caught on in Russia. It climbed to the #1 social network in a number of days. They really love it. … China is a special market, and one can't expect to just put English product in China or simply translate it and call it a day. It takes a local team to build for the Chinese market. Usually this involves forming a joint-venture or some other arrangement" (251).

Inspired by Secret, Leak is a new service launched in August 2014 to allow people to send anonymous emails without using their own email addresses. "We wanted Leak to be a really positive and exciting tool," said Leak cofounder Laurent Desserrey. "It's sure that people can send negative leaks, but that is really not what the product is about. It's about saying the truth you're ashamed to say. And if it's getting negative you can block emails from Leak" (252).

Upfront Ventures' general partner Mark Suster opines that "at its best apps like Secret or Whisper can be a place where people can reach out to the community for support. They could be a place to find solace when you're lonely or problem solve when you don't know who else to turn to. But for now Secret is not that. It's something all together different. It is … Perez Hilton. TMZ. Joan Rivers. Geraldo Rivera. All rolled up into one anonymous bitchy session" (253).

In spite of the potential risk of misinformation and disinformation, anonymous social apps can be powerful tools for citizen journalists, whistleblowers, political activists, crime tippers, and other cybercitizens whose online privacy is a matter of the utmost importance.

2.19   Responses to Zero Privacy

Absolute privacy is unattainable. Everything we say can be captured and deciphered remotely by picking up the vibrations on a window, a plastic cup, or a leaf of a houseplant in the room (254) (255). Researchers at Intel and University of California, Berkeley demonstrated that private information can be extracted from encrypted HTTPS communications by searching for patterns in the data stream (256). New York artist Heather Dewey-Hagborg extracted the DNA from a strand of hair, a cigarette butt, or a chewed piece of gum from a public place, and then recreated a

3-D face in the form of a portrait sculpture that resembles the person who left the DNA behind (257).

In response to Scott McNealy's statement, "You have zero privacy anyway. Get over it" (6), *PC World* columnist Stephen Manes wrote, "He's right on the facts, wrong on the attitude. It's undeniable that the existence of enormous databases on everything from our medical histories to whether we like beef jerky may make our lives an open book, thanks to the ability of computers to manipulate that information in every conceivable way. But I suspect even McNealy might have problems with somebody publishing his family's medical records on the Web, announcing his whereabouts to the world, or disseminating misinformation about his credit history. Instead of 'getting over it,' citizens need to demand clear rules on privacy, security, and confidentiality" (258).

In light of Edward Snowden's NSA leaks, author Jack Cheng wrote on CNN, "The revelation that the government is snooping on our communications in the interest of national security is nothing new. This latest incident doesn't come as a shocker. ... Privacy is not dead. ... It is not simply a matter of sharing more or less; not merely how much but in what way and with whom. Privacy is contingent on who we're trying to keep something private from – family, friends, acquaintances, employers, strangers. ... Friends of mine will untag themselves from Facebook photos to hide more unflattering images of themselves if they are 'friends' with their employers. Some refrain from posting to Facebook things they don't want their parents to see, opting for Twitter instead, where their parents don't have accounts. Snapchat is built around a privacy-minded constraint: Mission Impossible-esque messages that self-destruct shortly after opening. ... The kind privacy that is becoming more of the norm is dependent on our ability to move freely among the myriad services and apps, and to opt in selectively, both in what we use and how we choose to use them" (259).

A security expert and longtime organizer for DEF CON, Nico Sell cofounded Wickr, a mobile app that provides military-grade encryption of text, picture, audio and video messages as well as anonymity and secure file shredding features. "Privacy is dead," Sell told Laurie Segall in a CNN interview in June 2014. "Ownership is not dead. Everyone cares about owning their conversations and their pictures. I think that's the word we need to start using instead of privacy, because privacy has been tainted" (260).

References

1. **Dinges, John.** New head of #CIA clandestine service was head of #LatinAmerica Division since ca 2011. Francis "Frank" Archibald, 57. [Online] Twitter, May 8, 2013. https://twitter.com/jdinges/statuses/332135896373661697.
2. **Stein, Jeff.** Nice Invisibility Cloak! [Online] Newsweek, October 11, 2013. http://mag.news-week.com/2013/10/11/nice-invisibility-cloak.html.
3. **Bicchierai, Lorenzo Franceschi.** Did a Professor's Tweet Reveal the Identity of CIA's New Chief Spy? [Online] Mashable, May 10, 2013. http://mashable.com/2013/05/10/new-cia-chief-spy-outed-twitter/.
4. **Cryptome.** Francis "Frank" Archibald, Jr. [Online] Cryptome, May 9, 2013. http://cryptome.org/2013-info/05/archibald/francis-archibald.htm.

5. **Sutter, John D.** What the Petraeus scandal says about digital spying and your e-mail. [Online] CNN, November 14, 2012. http://www.cnn.com/2012/11/14/tech/petraeus-email-privacy/index.html.
6. **Sprenger, Polly.** Sun on Privacy: 'Get Over It.'. [Online] Wired, January 26, 1999. http://www.wired.com/politics/law/news/1999/01/17538.
7. **Newman, Jared.** Google's Schmidt Roasted for Privacy Comments. [Online] PCWorld, December 11, 2009. http://www.pcworld.com/article/184446/googles_schmidt_roasted_for_privacy_comments.html.
8. **Jackson, David.** Obama defends surveillance programs. [Online] USA Today, June 7, 2013. http://www.usatoday.com/story/news/politics/2013/06/07/obama-clapper-national-security-agency-leaks/2400405/.
9. **Singel, Ryan.** The Internet gets a hall of fame (yes including Al Gore). [Online] CNN, April 14, 2012. http://www.cnn.com/2012/04/24/tech/web/internet-hall-of-fame/index.html.
10. **Ellis, Blake.** Craziest tax deductions: Carrier pigeons. [Online] CNNMoney, March 9, 2012. http://money.cnn.com/galleries/2012/pf/taxes/1203/gallery.wacky-tax-deductions/.
11. **Martinez, Michael.** UK spies unable to crack coded message from WWII carrier pigeon. [Online] CNN, November 24, 2012. http://www.cnn.com/2012/11/23/world/europe/uk-wwii-pigeon-mystery/index.html.
12. **Gregory, David.** Meet the Press with David Gregory. [Online] NBC News, March 23, 2014. http://www.nbcnews.com/meet-the-press/meet-press-transcript-march-23-2014-n59966.
13. **Pagliery, Jose.** Google testing super-secure email. [Online] CNNMoney, June 3, 2014. http://money.cnn.com/2014/06/03/technology/security/google-encryption/index.html.
14. **Matyszczyk, Chris.** Zuckerberg: I know that people don't want privacy. [Online] CNet, January 10, 2010. http://www.cnet.com/news/zuckerberg-i-know-that-people-dont-want-privacy/.
15. **Consumer Reports magazine editors.** Facebook & your privacy. Who sees the data you share on the biggest social network? [Online] Consumer Reports, June 2012. http://www.consumerreports.org/cro/magazine/2012/06/facebook-your-privacy/index.htm.
16. **Kelly, Heather.** Mark Zuckerberg explains why he just changed Facebook's mission. [Online] CNN Business, June 22, 2017. https://money.cnn.com/2017/06/22/technology/facebook-zuckerberg-interview/index.html.
17. **Zuckerberg, Mark.** Today at the Facebook Communities Summit we changed our mission to focus on bringing the world closer together. [Online] Facebook, June 22, 2017. https://www.facebook.com/zuck/posts/10154944663901634.
18. **Olivarez-Giles, Nathan.** Facebook F8: Redesigning and hitting 800 million users. [Online] Los Angeles Times, September 22, 2011. http://latimesblogs.latimes.com/technology/2011/09/facebook-f8-media-features.html.
19. **Tsukayama, Hayley.** Facebook's reach: 845 million and counting. [Online] The Washington Post, February 1, 2012. http://www.washingtonpost.com/business/technology/facebooks-reach-845-million-and-counting/2012/02/01/gIQAV0gwiQ_story.html.
20. **Sengupta, Somini.** Risk and Riches in User Data for Facebook. [Online] The New York Times, February 26, 2012. http://www.nytimes.com/2012/02/27/technology/for-facebook-risk-and-riches-in-user-data.html.
21. **Facebook.** Facebook Reports Fourth Quarter and Full Year 2020 Results. [Online] Facebook. [Cited: April 11, 2021.] https://investor.fb.com/investor-news/press-release-details/2021/Facebook-Reports-Fourth-Quarter-and-Full-Year-2020-Results/default.aspx.
22. **Saba, Jennifer.** Facebook reveals daily users for U.S. and UK, data aimed at advertisers. [Online] Reuters, August 14, 2013. http://in.reuters.com/article/2013/08/13/facebook-users-idINDEE97C0DC20130813.
23. **Nielsen.** Nielsen Social Media Report: Q3 2011. [Online] Nielsen, 2011. http://blog.nielsen.com/nielsenwire/social/.

24. **Auxier, Brooke and Anderson, Monica.** Social Media Use in 2021. [Online] Pew Research Center, April 7, 2021. https://www.pewresearch.org/internet/2021/04/07/social-media-use-in-2021/.

25. **NM Incite.** Friends & Frenemies: Why We Add and Remove Facebook Friends. [Online] NM Incite, December 19, 2011. http://www.nmincite.com/?p=6051.

26. **Bartz, Andrea and Ehrlich, Brenna.** Beware the Facebook 'friend collector'. [Online] CNN, December 20, 2011. http://www.cnn.com/2011/12/21/tech/social-media/netiquette-friend-collector/index.html.

27. **Gross, Doug.** Facebook wants to know if you're dating anyone. [Online] CNN, May 20, 2014. http://www.cnn.com/2014/05/20/tech/social-media/facebook-ask-relationship-status/index.html.

28. **Selekman, Aryeh.** A New, Optional Way to Share and Discover Music, TV and Movies. [Online] Facebook Newsroom, May 21, 2014. http://newsroom.fb.com/news/2014/05/a-new-optional-way-to-share-and-discover-music-tv-and-movies/.

29. **Gallaga, Omar L.** Why I won't be quitting Facebook. [Online] CNN, May 17, 2012. http://www.cnn.com/2012/05/17/tech/social-media/facebook-gallaga/index.html.

30. **Benoit, David.** Mark Zuckerberg's Letter From The Facebook Filing. [Online] The Wall Street Journal, February 1, 2012. http://blogs.wsj.com/deals/2012/02/01/mark-zuckerbergs-letter-from-the-facebook-filing/.

31. **Glenn, Devon.** AOL To Launch Huffington Post Streaming Network. [Online] Social Times, February 3, 2012. http://socialtimes.com/aol-to-launch-huffington-post-streaming-network_b89001.

32. **Khalid, Kiran.** A social-media addict tries to disconnect. [Online] CNN, December 28, 2011. http://www.cnn.com/2011/12/14/tech/social-media/khalid-social-media-unplug/index.html.

33. **Sutter, John D.** Prominent blogger: 'I'm leaving the Internet for a year'. [Online] CNN, May 2, 2012. http://www.cnn.com/2012/05/02/tech/web/paul-miller-quits-internet/index.html.

34. **Miller, Paul.** Offline: day one of life without internet. [Online] The Verge, May 2, 2012. http://www.theverge.com/2012/5/2/2994277/paul-miller-diary-offline-day-of-life-without-internet.

35. **—.** I'm still here: back online after a year without the internet. [Online] The Verge, May 1, 2013. http://www.theverge.com/2013/5/1/4279674/im-still-here-back-online-after-a-year-without-the-internet.

36. **Kelly, Heather.** Disconnected: My year without the Internet. [Online] CNN, May 10, 2013. http://www.cnn.com/2013/05/10/tech/web/paul-miller-internet-year/index.html.

37. **Arrington, Michael.** 85% of College Students use FaceBook. [Online] TechCrunch, September 7, 2005. http://techcrunch.com/2005/09/07/85-of-college-students-use-facebook/.

38. **Markoff, John and Sengupta, Somini.** Separating You and Me? 4.74 Degrees. [Online] New York Times, November 21, 2011. http://www.nytimes.com/2011/11/22/technology/between-you-and-me-4-74-degrees.html.

39. **Facebook.** The Things That Connect Us. [Online] Facebook, October 4, 2012. http://www.youtube.com/watch?v=c7SjvLceXgU.

40. **Haglund, David.** Facebook's Disingenuous New Ad. [Online] Slate, October 4, 2012. http://www.slate.com/blogs/browbeat/2012/10/04/facebook_chair_ad_why_chairs_explained_video_.html.

41. **Ortutay, Barbara.** Facebook tops 1 billion users. [Online] USA Today, October 4, 2012. http://www.usatoday.com/story/tech/2012/10/04/facebook-tops-1-billion-users/1612613/.

42. **Facebook Investor Relations.** Facebook Reports Fourth Quarter and Full Year 2020 Results. [Online] Facebook, January 27, 2021. https://investor.fb.com/investor-news/press-release-details/2021/Facebook-Reports-Fourth-Quarter-and-Full-Year-2020-Results/default.aspx.

43. **Takahashi, Corey.** New Office Chair Promotes Concept of 'Active Sitting'. [Online] The Wall Street Journal, July 21, 2007. http://online.wsj.com/article/SB869433022356380000.html.

44. **Greenfield, Rebecca.** Facebook's New Ad Finds 'Real Human Emotion' in Chairs. [Online] The Atlantic Wire, October 4, 2012. http://www.theatlanticwire.com/technology/2012/10/facebook-aims-real-human-emotion-new-ad/57596/.

45. **Protalinski, Emil.** Facebook's new headquarters is located at 1 Hacker Way. [Online] ZDNet, December 6, 2011. http://www.zdnet.com/blog/facebook/facebooks-new-headquarters-is-located-at-1-hacker-way/5831.

46. **Alves, David.** Announcing Facebook's 2012 Hacker Cup. [Online] Facebook, January 4, 2012. https://www.facebook.com/notes/facebook-engineering/announcing-facebooks-2012-hacker-cup/10150468260528920.

47. **Segall, Laurie.** Facebook seeks world champion hacker. [Online] CNNMoney, January 4, 2012. http://money.cnn.com/2012/01/04/technology/facebook_hacker_cup/index.htm.

48. **Kaplan, Katharine A.** Facemash Creator Survives Ad Board. [Online] Harvard Crimson, November 19, 2003. http://www.thecrimson.com/article/2003/11/19/facemash-creator-survives-ad-board-the/.

49. **Milian, Mark.** Zuckerberg's Hoodie a 'Mark of Immaturity,' Analyst Says. [Online] Bloomberg, May 8, 2012. http://go.bloomberg.com/tech-deals/2012-05-08-zuckerbergs-hoodie-a-mark-of-immaturity-analyst-says-2/.

50. **Schaefer, Steve.** SEC Pressed Facebook On Zynga, Instagram And Zuckerberg's Control Pre-IPO. [Online] Forbes, June 15, 2012. http://www.forbes.com/sites/steveschaefer/2012/06/15/sec-pressed-facebook-on-zynga-instagram-pre-ipo/.

51. **Federal Trade Commission.** Facebook Settles FTC Charges That It Deceived Consumers By Failing To Keep Privacy Promises. [Online] Federal Trade Commission, November 29, 2011. http://www.ftc.gov/opa/2011/11/privacysettlement.shtm.

52. **—.** FTC complaint against Facebook. [Online] Federal Trade Commission, 2011. http://www.ftc.gov/os/caselist/0923184/111129facebookcmpt.pdf.

53. **Pepitone, Julianne.** Facebook settles FTC charges over 2009 privacy breaches. [Online] CNNMoney, November 29, 2011. http://money.cnn.com/2011/11/29/technology/facebook_settlement/index.htm.

54. **Federal Trade Commission.** FTC proposed settlement. [Online] Federal Trade Commission, 2011. http://www.ftc.gov/os/caselist/0923184/111129facebookagree.pdf.

55. **Protalinski, Emil.** Facebook faces nationwide class action tracking cookie lawsuit. [Online] ZDNet, February 29, 2012. http://www.zdnet.com/blog/facebook/facebook-faces-nationwide-class-action-tracking-cookie-lawsuit/9747.

56. **Cubrilovic, Nik.** Logging out of Facebook is not enough. [Online] New Web Order, September 25, 2011. http://nikcub.appspot.com/posts/logging-out-of-facebook-is-not-enough.

57. **Levine, Dan and McBride, Sarah.** Facebook to pay $10 million to settle suit. [Online] Reuters, June 16, 2012. http://www.reuters.com/article/2012/06/16/net-us-facebook-settlement-idUSBRE85F0N120120616.

58. **Riley, Charles.** Facebook faces suit over private messages. [Online] CNNMoney, January 3, 2014. http://money.cnn.com/2014/01/03/technology/facebook-privacy-lawsuit/index.html.

59. **Pepitone, Julianne.** Zuckerberg rarely mentions the word 'privacy'. [Online] CNNMoney, January 7, 2014. http://money.cnn.com/2014/01/07/technology/social/zuckerberg-files/index.html.

60. **Madden, Mary and Smith, Aaron.** Reputation Management and Social Media. [Online] Pew Internet, May 26, 2010. http://pewinternet.org/Reports/2010/Reputation-Management/Part-2/Attitudes-and-Actions.aspx.

61. **Consumer Reports magazine editors.** Facebook & your privacy. Who sees the data you share on the biggest social network? [Online] Consumer Reports, June 2012. http://www.consumerreports.org/cro/magazine/2012/06/facebook-your-privacy/index.htm.

62. **Backstrom, Lars.** Anatomy of Facebook. [Online] Facebook, November 21, 2011. https://www.facebook.com/notes/facebook-data-team/anatomy-of-facebook/10150388519243859.

63. **Pempek, Tiffany A., Yermolayeva, Yevdokiya A. and Calvert, Sandra L.** College Students' Social Networking Experiences on Facebook. [Online] Georgetown University, May 4, 2012. http://cdmc.georgetown.edu/papers/College_Students'_Social_networking_Experiences_on_Facebook.pdf.

64. **Cohen, Jackie.** You Don't Know One-Fifth of Your Facebook Friends. [Online] All Facebook, January 13, 2011. http://www.allfacebook.com/you-dont-know-one-fifth-of-your-facebook-friends-2011-01.

65. **Podvey, Heather.** Do you really KNOW your Facebook friends? [Online] Applywise, September 2009. http://www.applywise.com/sep09_facebook.aspx.

66. **Hampton, Keith, et al.** Why most Facebook users get more than they give. [Online] Pew Research Center, February 2, 2012. http://www.pewinternet.org/Press-Releases/2012/Facebook-users.aspx.

67. **arXiv.** Can a Serious Game Improve Privacy Awareness on Facebook? [Online] MIT Technology Review., March 5, 2014. http://www.technologyreview.com/view/525376/can-a-serious-game-improve-privacy-awareness-on-facebook/.

68. **Albergotti, Reed.** Facebook's Blue Dino Wants You to Mind Your Posting. [Online] Wall Street Journal, April 1, 2014. http://blogs.wsj.com/digits/2014/04/01/facebooks-blue-dino-wants-you-to-mind-your-posting/.

69. **Westfall, Sandra Sobieraj.** President Obama Talks Facebook and TV Habits. [Online] PEOPLE Magazine, December 14, 2011. http://www.people.com/people/article/0,,20553487,00.html.

70. **Kang, Cecilia.** Parents help underage children lie to get on Facebook, survey finds. [Online] The Washington Post, November 1, 2011. http://www.washingtonpost.com/blogs/post-tech/post/parents-help-underage-children-lie-to-get-on-facebook-survey-finds/2011/11/01/gIQA-F6D1cM_blog.html.

71. **Fox, Jeffrey.** Five million Facebook users are 10 or younger. [Online] Consumer Reports, May 10, 2011. http://news.consumerreports.org/electronics/2011/05/five-million-facebook-users-are-10-or-younger.html.

72. **Boyd, Danah.** Why parents help their children lie to Facebook about age: Unintended consequences of the 'Children's Online Privacy Protection Act'. [Online] Journal of the Internet, November 7, 2011. http://www.uic.edu/htbin/cgiwrap/bin/ojs/index.php/fm/article/view/3850/3075.

73. **The Wall Street Journal.** What They Know - Kids. [Online] The Wall Street Journal Blogs, September 17, 2010. http://blogs.wsj.com/wtk-kids/.

74. **Stecklow, Steve.** On the Web, Children Face Intensive Tracking. [Online] The Wall Street Journal, September 17, 2010. http://online.wsj.com/article/SB10001424052748703904304575497903523187146.html.

75. **Federal Trade Commission.** Complying with COPPA: Frequently Asked Questions. [Online] Bureau of Consumer Protection Business Center, July 16, 2014.

76. **Mine, Mark R., Shochet, Joe and Hughston, Roger.** Building a massively multiplayer game for the million: Disney's Toontown Online. [Online] ACM Computers in Entertainment, October 2003. http://dl.acm.org/citation.cfm?doid=950566.950589.

77. **Barnes, Brooks.** Disney Acquires Web Site for Children. [Online] The New York Times, August 2, 2007. http://www.nytimes.com/2007/08/02/business/02disney.html.

78. **Choney, Suzanne.** Disney lets Club Penguin domain lapse, site goes down. [Online] MSNBC, June 21, 2011. http://technolog.msnbc.msn.com/_news/2011/06/21/6907472-disney-lets-club-penguin-domain-lapse-site-goes-down.

79. **Sniderman, Zachary.** How Disney's Club Penguin Became the Biggest Social Network for Kids. [Online] Mashable, December 13, 2011. http://mashable.com/2011/12/13/club-penguin-disney/.

80. **McCarthy, Caroline.** Disney to acquire social-gaming company Playdom. [Online] CNET, July 27, 2010. http://news.cnet.com/8301-13577_3-20011844-36.html.

81. **Reisinger, Don.** FTC: Disney's Playdom violated child protection act. [Online] CNET, May 13, 2011. http://news.cnet.com/8301-13506_3-20062566-17.html.

82. **Federal Trade Commission.** Operators of Online "Virtual Worlds" to Pay $3 Million to Settle FTC Charges That They Illegally Collected and Disclosed Children's Personal Information.

[Online] Federal Trade Commission News, May 12, 2011. http://www.ftc.gov/opa/2011/05/playdom.shtm.

83. **Milian, Mark.** Study: Multitasking hinders youth social skills. [Online] CNN, January 25, 2012. http://www.cnn.com/2012/01/25/tech/social-media/multitasking-kids/index.html.

84. **Rosen, Larry D.** Social Networking's Good and Bad Impacts on Kids. Psychologists explore myths, realities and offer guidance for parents. [Online] American Psychological Association, August 6, 2011. http://www.apa.org/news/press/releases/2011/08/social-kids.aspx.

85. **Madden, Mary, et al.** Teens, Social Media, and Privacy. [Online] Pew Research Internet Project, May 21, 2013. http://www.pewinternet.org/2013/05/21/teens-social-media-and-privacy/.

86. **Pepitone, Julianne.** Facebook admits young teens are losing interest in the site. [Online] CNNMoney, October 31, 2013. http://money.cnn.com/2013/10/30/technology/social/facebook-earnings/index.html.

87. **Kelly, Heather.** Facebook changes privacy settings for teens. [Online] CNN, October 31, 2013. http://www.cnn.com/2013/10/16/tech/social-media/facebook-teens-privacy/.

88. **Facebook.** Teens Now Start With "Friends" Privacy for New Accounts; Adding the Option to Share Publicly. [Online] Facebook Newsroom, October 16, 2013. http://newsroom.fb.com/news/2013/10/teens-now-start-with-friends-privacy-for-new-accounts-adding-the-option-to-share-publicly/.

89. **Singer, Natasha.** A Trail of Clicks, Culminating in Conflict. [Online] The New York Times, November 5, 2012. http://www.nytimes.com/2012/11/06/technology/silicon-valley-objects-to-online-privacy-rule-proposals-for-children.html.

90. **Fiegerman, Seth.** How Facebook's Graph Search could disrupt online dating. [Online] CNN, January 16, 2013. http://www.cnn.com/2013/01/16/tech/social-media/facebook-graph-search-dating/index.html.

91. **Gross, Doug.** Facebook highlights privacy protection for minors on Graph Search. [Online] CNN, February 15, 2013. http://www.cnn.com/2013/02/14/tech/social-media/facebook-graph-search-minors/index.html.

92. **Ho, Erica.** Report: Facebook Adding Read, Listened, Watched and Want Buttons. [Online] Time Magazine, September 20, 2011. http://techland.time.com/2011/09/20/report-facebook-to-launch-read-listened-watched-and-want-buttons/.

93. **MacManus, Richard.** "Read" in Facebook – It's Not a Button, So Be Careful What You Click! [Online] ReadWriteWeb, September 22, 2011. http://www.readwriteweb.com/archives/read_in_facebook_social_news_apps.php.

94. **Segall, Laurie.** Facebook's Ticker broadcasts everything you do. [Online] CNN, September 29, 2011. http://money.cnn.com/2011/09/29/technology/facebook_ticker_privacy/index.htm.

95. **Vascellaro, Jessica E.** Facebook Settles Class-Action Suit Over Beacon Service. [Online] The Wall Street Journal, September 18, 2009. http://online.wsj.com/article/SB125332446004624573.html.

96. **Netflix.** Netflix Company Facts. [Online] Netflix. [Cited: July 9, 2012.] https://signup.netflix.com/MediaCenter/Facts.

97. **Hastings, Reed.** Congrats to Ted Sarandos, and his amazing content licensing team. Netflix monthly viewing exceeded 1 billion hours for the first time ever in June. [Online] Reed Hastings, July 3, 2012. https://www.facebook.com/reed1960/posts/10150955446914584.

98. **NetFlix.** Watch this now: Netflix & Facebook. [Online] NetFlix US & Canada Blog, September 22, 2011. http://blog.netflix.com/2011/09/watch-this-now-netflix-facebook.html.

99. **Davis, Wendy.** House Clears Way for Netflix Streams on Facebook. [Online] MediaPost News, December 7, 2011. http://www.mediapost.com/publications/article/163718/house-clears-way-for-netflix-streams-on-facebook.html.

100. **Shu, Catherine.** Senate Passes Netflix-Backed Revision Of Privacy Law, Paving Way For Facebook Sharing. [Online] TechCrunch, December 20, 2012. http://techcrunch.com/2012/12/20/senate-passes-netflix-backed-revision-of-privacy-law-paving-way-for-facebook-sharing/.

101. **Davis, Wendy.** Netflix Settles Data Retention Suit For $9M. [Online] MediaPost News, February 13, 2012. http://www.mediapost.com/publications/article/167755/netflix-settles-data-retention-suit-for-9m.html.

102. —. Netflix To Revise Data Retention Practices. [Online] MediaPost News, May 30, 2012. http://www.mediapost.com/publications/article/175728/netflix-to-revise-data-retention-practices.html.

103. **Shaw, Lucas.** Netflix Gives Users Added Control Over Facebook Sharing. [Online] Bloomberg, September 2, 2014. http://www.bloomberg.com/news/2014-09-02/netflix-users-get-control-over-shows-shared-on-facebook.html.

104. **Pidaparthy, Umika.** Interest, meet Pinterest: Site helps users catalog their passions. [Online] CNN, January 26, 2012. http://www.cnn.com/2012/01/26/tech/web/pinterest-website/index.html.

105. **Facebook.** Introducing Timeline: Tell your life story with a new kind of profile. [Online] Facebook. [Cited: January 25, 2012.] http://www.facebook.com/about/timeline.

106. **Milian, Mark and Sutter, John D.** Facebook revamps site with 'Timeline' and real-time apps. [Online] CNN, September 22, 2011. http://www.cnn.com/2011/09/22/tech/social-media/facebook-announcement-f8/index.html.

107. **Peters, Nikki.** Introducing the NEW Facebook Timeline. [Online] Social Media Today, November 21, 2011. http://socialmediatoday.com/marketmesuite-app/392011/introducing-new-facebook-timeline.

108. **Parr, Ben.** Facebook Open Graph Seeks to Deliver Real-Time Serendipity. [Online] Mashable, September 22, 2011. http://mashable.com/2011/09/22/new-facebook-open-graph/.

109. **Milian, Mark.** 60 apps launch with Facebook auto-share. [Online] CNN, January 19, 2012. http://www.cnn.com/2012/01/18/tech/social-media/facebook-actions-apps/index.html.

110. —. Some apps steer clear of Facebook auto-publish tool. [Online] CNN, January 18, 2012. http://www.cnn.com/2012/01/18/tech/social-media/facebook-pandora/index.html.

111. **Baig, Edward C.** Fandango, Vevo, more launch Facebook apps. [Online] USA Today, March 12, 2012. http://content.usatoday.com/communities/livefrom/post/2012/03/facebook-3000-timeline-apps/1.

112. **Fandango.** Fandango Makes Moviegoing More Social than Ever with New Facebook Timeline App, "Movies with Friends". [Online] PRnewsire, March 13, 2012. http://www.prnewswire.com/news-releases/fandango-makes-moviegoing-more-social-than-ever-with-new-facebook-timeline-app-movies-with-friends-142449025.html.

113. **Steel, Emily and Fowler, Geoffrey A.** Facebook in Privacy Breach. [Online] The Wall Street Journal, October 8, 2010. http://online.wsj.com/article/SB10001424052702304772804575558484075236968.html.

114. **O'Neill, Nick.** Facebook Shuts Down Apps That Sold User Data, Bans Rapleaf. [Online] AllFacebook.com, October 29, 2010. http://www.allfacebook.com/facebook-shuts-down-apps-that-sold-user-data-bans-rapleaf-2010-10.

115. **Tsotsis, Alexia.** foursquare Now Officially At 10 Million Users. [Online] TechCrunch, June 20, 2011. http://techcrunch.com/2011/06/20/foursquare-now-officially-at-10-million-users/.

116. **foursquare.** foursquare by the numbers. [Online] foursquare. [Cited: August 11, 2014.] https://foursquare.com/about/.

117. **Schulman, Kori.** Take a Tip from the White House on foursquare. [Online] The White House Blog, August 15, 2011. http://www.whitehouse.gov/blog/2011/08/15/take-tip-white-house-foursquare.

118. **Etherington, Darrell and Crook, Jordan.** Foursquare Splits Into Two Apps, But Will Either Be Strong Enough To Survive? [Online] TechCrunch, May 1, 2014. https://techcrunch.com/2014/05/01/foursquare-splits-into-two-apps-but-will-either-be-strong-enough-to-survive/.

119. **Crook, Jordan and Ha, Anthony.** Foursquare merges with Factual. [Online] TechCrunch, April 6, 2020. https://techcrunch.com/2020/04/06/foursquare-merges-with-factual/.

120. **Sonar.** About Sonar. [Online] Sonar. [Cited: March 8, 2012.] http://www.sonar.me/about.

121. **Glancee.** About Glancee. [Online] Glancee, March 8, 2012. http://www.glancee.com/.
122. **Higginbotham, Stacey.** Facebook buys Glancee in another mobile play. [Online] Gigaom, May 4, 2012. http://gigaom.com/2012/05/04/facebook-buys-glancee-in-another-mobile-play/.
123. **Bryant, Martin.** Location-based social discovery app Banjo hits 1 million users in 9 months. [Online] The Next Web, April 18, 2012. http://thenextweb.com/insider/2012/04/18/location-based-social-discovery-app-banjo-hits-1-million-users-in-9-months/.
124. **Banjo.** Banjo: Our Story. [Online] Banjo. [Cited: March 8, 2012.] http://ban.jo/about/.
125. **—.** Banjo: The Live Internet. [Online] Banjo. [Cited: March 29, 2013.] http://ban.jo/.
126. **Koebler, Jason, Maiberg, Emanuel and Cox, Joseph.** This Small Company Is Turning Utah Into a Surveillance Panopticon. [Online] Vice, March 4, 2020. https://www.vice.com/en/article/k7exem/banjo-ai-company-utah-surveillance-panopticon.
127. **Stroud, Matt.** Banjo Quietly Rebranded Itself Following Report on Former CEO's KKK Past. [Online] OneZero, February 11, 2021. https://onezero.medium.com/banjo-quietly-rebranded-itself-following-report-on-former-ceos-kkk-past-11223803c19d.
128. **Highlight.** About Highlight. [Online] Highlight. [Cited: March 8, 2012.] http://highlig.ht/about.html.
129. **Eldon, Eric.** foursquare And Glancee Are Cool, But Here's Why I'm So Excited About Using Highlight At SXSW. [Online] TechCrunch, March 3, 2012. http://techcrunch.com/2012/03/03/myhighlight/.
130. **Newton, Casey.** Pinterest acquires the team behind Highlight, the breakout social app that wasn't. [Online] The Verge, July 14, 2016. https://www.theverge.com/2016/7/14/12189906/pinterest-highlight-acquisition-math-camp-shots.
131. **Waxman, Olivia B.** 'Hell Is Other People': An Anti-Social Network. [Online] TIME Magazine, June 20, 2013. http://newsfeed.time.com/2013/06/20/hell-is-other-people-an-anti-social-network/.
132. **Gaudin, Sharon.** 'Hell is Other People' is the anti-social app. [Online] Computer World, June 21, 2013. https://www.computerworld.com/article/2498130/-hell-is-other-people%2D%2Dis-the-anti-social-app.html.
133. **Tsotsis, Alexia.** Facebook Buys Location-Based Discovery App Glancee. [Online] TechCrunch, May 4, 2012. http://techcrunch.com/2012/05/04/facebook-buys-location-based-discovery-app-glancee/.
134. **Chang, Alexandra.** Facebook Quietly Releases 'Find Friends Nearby,' Then Quietly Pulls It. [Online] Wired, June 25, 2012. http://www.wired.com/gadgetlab/2012/06/facebook-quietly-releases-find-friends-nearby-then-quietly-pulls-it/.
135. **Lunden, Ingrid.** Find Friends Nearby': Facebook's New Mobile Feature For Finding People Around You [Updated]. [Online] TechCrunch, June 24, 2012. http://techcrunch.com/2012/06/24/friendshake-facebooks-new-mobile-feature-for-finding-people-nearby-and-a-highlight-killer/.
136. **Copeland, Dave.** How To Use Facebook's Newest Stalking App. [Online] ReadWriteWeb, June 25, 2012. http://www.readwriteweb.com/archives/how-to-use-facebooks-newest-stalking-app.php.
137. **Chang, Alexandra.** Facebook Quietly Releases 'Find Friends Nearby,' Then Quietly Pulls It. [Online] Wired, June 25, 2012. http://www.wired.com/gadgetlab/2012/06/facebook-quietly-releases-find-friends-nearby-then-quietly-pulls-it/.
138. **Dowell, Andrew.** Tracking Women: Now There's Not An App For That. [Online] The Wall Street Journal, March 31, 2012. http://blogs.wsj.com/digits/2012/03/31/tracking-women-now-theres-not-an-app-for-that/.
139. **Austin, Scott and Dowell, Andrew.** 'Girls Around Me' Developer Defends App After foursquare Dismissal. [Online] The Wall Street Journal, March 31, 2012. http://blogs.wsj.com/digits/2012/03/31/girls-around-me-developer-defends-app-after-foursquare-dismissal/.
140. **Au-Yeung, Angel.** Bumble, The Online Dating App Where Women Make The First Move, Files To Go Public. [Online] Forbes, January 15, 2021. https://www.forbes.com/sites/angelauyeung/2021/01/15/bumble-the-online-dating-app-where-women-make-the-first-move-files-to-go-public/.

141. **Rooney, Ben.** A Very Social Network. [Online] The Wall Street Journal, January 24, 2012. http://blogs.wsj.com/tech-europe/2012/01/24/the-very-social-network/.

142. **Editors, Huffington Post.** Badoo: Website 'Like Facebook But For Sex' Hits 130 Million Users. [Online] Huffington Post UK, December 13, 2011. http://www.huffingtonpost.co.uk/2011/12/13/badoo-facebook-sex-_n_1145909.html.

143. **Bloxham, Andy.** 'Sex social network' Badoo has 1m users in Britain. [Online] The Telegraph, December 13, 2011. http://www.telegraph.co.uk/technology/news/8952240/Sex-social-network-Badoo-has-1m-users-in-Britain.html.

144. **Rowan, David.** How Badoo built a billion-pound social network... on sex. [Online] Wired UK, April 25, 2011. http://www.wired.co.uk/magazine/archive/2011/05/features/sexual-network.

145. **Roose, Kevin.** No-Frill Thrills: The Rise of Minimalist Sex Apps. [Online] New York Magazine, August 19, 2013. http://nymag.com/daily/intelligencer/2013/08/rise-of-minimalist-sex-apps.html.

146. **Segall, Laurie.** When location apps overshare, predators follow the signal. [Online] CNNMoney, June 15, 2012. http://money.cnn.com/2012/06/15/technology/location-app-predators/index.htm.

147. **Cashmore, Pete.** The scariest tech trend of 2012? [Online] CNN, March 6, 2012. http://www.cnn.com/2012/03/01/tech/mobile/tech-trends-sxsw-cashmore/index.html.

148. **Neild, Barry.** With new mobile apps, no one's a stranger. [Online] CNN, June 20, 2012. http://www.cnn.com/2012/06/20/tech/mobile/highlight-badoo-le-web/.

149. **Kelly, Heather.** Facebook launches friend-tracking feature. [Online] CNN, April 18, 2014. http://www.cnn.com/2014/04/17/tech/mobile/facebook-nearby-friends/index.html.

150. **CNN.** Warning! 1 picture can hack your identity. [Online] CNN, October 7, 2011. http://money.cnn.com/video/technology/2011/10/05/t-ts-iphone-camera-id.cnnmoney/.

151. **Goldman, David.** Face recognition: In the future, can you remain anonymous? [Online] CNNMoney, January 13, 2012. http://money.cnn.com/2012/01/13/technology/face_recognition/index.htm.

152. **Peterson, Tim.** Facebook Gets a New Face(.com). Facial recognition startup follows Instagram buy. [Online] Adweek, June 18, 2012. http://www.adweek.com/news/technology/facebook-gets-new-facecom-141196.

153. **face.com.** About face.com and Face Recognition. [Online] face.com. [Cited: March 11, 2012.] http://face.com/about.php.

154. **Casperson, Matthew.** Face.com Opens Free Facial Recognition API. [Online] ProgrammableWeb, May 4, 2010. http://blog.programmableweb.com/2010/05/04/face-com-opens-free-facial-recognition-api/.

155. **Goldman, David.** Your face is being tracked: Find My Facemate. [Online] CNNMoney, December 13, 2011. http://money.cnn.com/galleries/2011/technology/1112/gallery.face-recognition-apps/6.html.

156. **Nicole, Kristen.** Photo Finder: 100 Invites to Auto Tag Facebook Photos. [Online] All Facebook, March 24, 2009. http://www.allfacebook.com/photo-finder-invite-2009-03.

157. **—.** Photo Tagger Automatically Tags Your Facebook Photos. [Online] All Facebook, July 21, 2009. http://www.allfacebook.com/photo-tagger-2009-07.

158. **CelebrityFindr.** Celebrity Finder. [Online] CelebrityFindr. [Cited: March 11, 2012.] http://www.celebrityfindr.com/.

159. **Segall, Laurie.** Photo hackers explore the creepy zone. [Online] CNNMoney, September 7, 2011. http://money.cnn.com/2011/09/07/technology/startups/photo_hack/index.htm.

160. **CreepShield.** CreepShield.com - Facial Recognition for Online Dating. [Online] CreepShield. [Cited: August 12, 2014.] http://www.creepshield.com/.

161. **Moscovitz, Meitar.** Maybe Days. [Online] Meitar Moscovitz, October 14, 2013. http://days.maybemaimed.com/post/64045337134/there-are-now-four-dating-websites-that-have.

162. **McGee, Jordan.** FacialNetwork.com Announces Beta Release Of "NameTag" The First Real-Time Facial Recognition App For Google Glass. [Online] Yahoo! Finance,

December 19, 2013. http://finance.yahoo.com/news/facialnetwork-com-announces-beta-release-200300439.html.

163. **Pagliery, Jose.** FBI launches a face recognition system. [Online] CNNMoney, September 16, 2014. http://money.cnn.com/2014/09/16/technology/security/fbi-facial-recognition/index.html.

164. **Bruegge, Richard Vorder.** Facial Recognition and Identification Initiatives. [Online] Federal Bureau of Investigation. [Cited: September 21, 2014.] http://biometrics.org/bc2010/presentations/DOJ/vorder_bruegge-Facial-Recognition-and-Identification-Initiatives.pdf.

165. **Wagner, Kurt.** Facebook Folds Facial Recognition Technology Into Messenger. [Online] Vox, November 9, 2015. https://www.vox.com/2015/11/9/11620460/facebook-folds-facial-recognition-technology-into-messenger.

166. **BBC.** TikTok agrees legal payout over facial recognition. [Online] BBC News, February 26, 2021. https://www.bbc.com/news/technology-56210052.

167. **Metz, Rachel.** This $5 billion insurance company likes to talk up its AI. Now it's in a mess over it. [Online] CNN Business, May 27, 2021. https://www.cnn.com/2021/05/27/tech/lemonade-ai-insurance/index.html.

168. **Team Lemonade.** Lemonade's Claim Automation. [Online] Lemonade, May 26, 2021. https://www.lemonade.com/blog/lemonades-claim-automation/.

169. **Goldman, David.** Your face is being tracked: Facebook. [Online] CNN, December 13, 2011. http://money.cnn.com/galleries/2011/technology/1112/gallery.face-recognition-apps/5.html.

170. **Vajgel, Peter.** Needle in a haystack: efficient storage of billions of photos. [Online] Facebook, April 30, 2009. http://www.facebook.com/note.php?note_id=76191543919.

171. **Mitchell, Justin.** Making Photo Tagging Easier. [Online] The Facebook Blog, December 15, 2010. http://www.facebook.com/blog/blog.php?post=467145887130.

172. **Ionescu, Daniel.** Facebook Adds Facial Recognition to Make Photo Tagging Easier. [Online] PCWorld, December 16, 2010. http://www.pcworld.com/article/213894/facebook_adds_facial_recognition_to_make_photo_tagging_easier.html.

173. **Cluley, Graham.** Facebook changes privacy settings for millions of users - facial recognition is enabled. [Online] Sophos naked security, June 7, 2011. http://nakedsecurity.sophos.com/2011/06/07/facebook-privacy-settings-facial-recognition-enabled/.

174. **Flatley, Joseph L.** Facebook planning facial recognition for picture uploads? (update: yes!). [Online] Engadget, April 5, 2011. http://www.engadget.com/2011/04/05/facebook-planning-facial-recognition-for-picture-uploads/#comments.

175. **Geuss, Megan.** Facebook Facial Recognition: Its Quiet Rise and Dangerous Future. [Online] PCWorld, April 26, 2011. http://www.pcworld.com/article/226228/facebook_facial_recognition_its_quiet_rise_and_dangerous_future.html.

176. **Shankland, Stephen.** Revamped Google Picasa site identifies photo faces. [Online] CNet, September 2, 2008. http://news.cnet.com/8301-13580_3-10026577-39.html.

177. **Lee, Nicole.** First taste of iLife '09: iPhoto's face recognition. [Online] CNet, January 30, 2009. http://news.cnet.com/8301-17938_105-10153818-1.html.

178. **Dalrymple, Jim.** Apple's Aperture 3 adds face recognition, GPS. [Online] CNet, February 9, 2010. http://news.cnet.com/8301-13579_3-10449880-37.html.

179. **Steiner, Matt.** Making photo tagging easier with Find My Face. [Online] Google+, December 8, 2011. https://plus.google.com/101560853443212199687/posts/VV45vivcFq4#101560853443212199687/posts/VV45vivcFq4.

180. **Goldman, David.** Your face is being tracked: Google. [Online] CNNMoney, December 9, 2011. http://money.cnn.com/galleries/2011/technology/1112/gallery.face-recognition-apps/4.html.

181. —. Google unveils 'Find My Face' tool. [Online] CNNMoney, December 9, 2011. http://money.cnn.com/2011/12/09/technology/google_find_my_face/index.htm.

182. —. Real-time face recognition comes to your iPhone camera. [Online] CNNMoney, March 12, 2012. http://money.cnn.com/2012/03/12/technology/iPhone-face-recognition/index.htm.

183. **Dean, Jeff and Ng, Andrew.** Using large-scale brain simulations for machine learning and A.I. [Online] Google Official Blog, June 26, 2012. http://googleblog.blogspot.com/2012/06/using-large-scale-brain-simulations-for.html.

184. **Harvey, Adam.** Camouflage from Computer Vision. [Online] CV Dazzle. [Cited: May 29, 2012.] http://cvdazzle.com/.

185. **Cheshire, Tom.** How to use camouflage to thwart facial recognition. [Online] Wired, January 4, 2012. http://www.wired.co.uk/magazine/archive/2012/01/how-to/how-to-use-camouflage-to-thwart-facial-recognition.

186. **Risen, James and Poitras, Laura.** N.S.A. Collecting Millions of Faces From Web Images. [Online] The New York Times, May 31, 2014. http://www.nytimes.com/2014/06/01/us/nsa-collecting-millions-of-faces-from-web-images.html.

187. **Brandom, Russell.** Why Facebook is beating the FBI at facial recognition. [Online] The Verge, July 7, 2014. http://www.theverge.com/2014/7/7/5878069/why-facebook-is-beating-the-fbi-at-facial-recognition.

188. **Taigman, Yaniv, et al.** DeepFace: Closing the Gap to Human-Level Performance in Face Verification. [Online] Facebook. [Cited: July 9, 2014.] https://www.facebook.com/publications/546316888800776/.

189. **Finding Rover, Inc.** Finding Rover - The app that uses facial recognition for dogs to help owners find lost dogs. Help us make sure that every lost dog is found. [Online] Finding Rover, Inc., May 9, 2014. https://itunes.apple.com/us/app/finding-rover-app-that-uses/id669691504.

190. **Warden, Pete.** How to add a brain to your smart phone. [Online] Pete Warden's Blog, April 8, 2014. http://petewarden.com/2014/04/08/how-to-add-a-brain-to-your-smart-phone/.

191. **Gross, Doug.** New Amazon phone makes it easy to buy stuff … from Amazon. [Online] CNN, June 18, 2014. http://www.cnn.com/2014/06/18/tech/mobile/amazon-fire-phone-firefly/index.html.

192. **Edwards, James.** Here's Everything Facebook Just Announced At Its Big Developer Conference. [Online] Business Insider, April 30, 2014. http://www.businessinsider.com/mark-zuckerberg-at-facebook-f8-2014-4.

193. **Van Buskirk, Eliot.** Spotify Defends Facebook Requirement as 'Good and Simple'. [Online] evolver.fm, September 26, 2011. http://evolver.fm/2011/09/26/spotify-defends-facebook-log-in-requirement-as-good-and-simple/.

194. **Microsoft.** Microsoft Passport: Streamlining Commerce and Communication on the Web. [Online] Microsoft News Center, October 11, 1999. http://www.microsoft.com/presspass/features/1999/10-11passport.mspx.

195. **ZDNet UK.** Passport failure shows the folly of Microsoft's ways. [Online] ZDNet, January 4, 2005. http://www.zdnet.co.uk/news/it-at-work/2005/01/04/passport-failure-shows-the-folly-of-microsofts-ways-39183062/.

196. **Peterson, Robyn.** Who Owns Your Identity on the Social Web? [Online] Mashable, October 21, 2011. http://mashable.com/2011/10/21/web-identity/.

197. **Microsoft Research.** About So.cl. Frequently Asked Questions. [Online] Microsoft. [Cited: May 21, 2012.] http://www.so.cl/about/faq.

198. **Stavridis, James.** A Navy Admiral's thoughts on global security. [Online] TED, June 2012. http://www.ted.com/talks/james_stavridis_how_nato_s_supreme_commander_thinks_about_global_security.

199. **Kelly, Max.** Memories of Friends Departed Endure on Facebook. [Online] The Facebook Blog, October 26, 2009. http://www.facebook.com/blog.php?post=163091042130.

200. **Hampton, Keith, et al.** Why most Facebook users get more than they give. [Online] Pew Research Center, February 3, 2012. http://pewinternet.org/Reports/2012/Facebook-users/Summary/Power-Users.aspx.

201. **Delo, Cotton.** Facebook Warns Brands that Scale in Social Won't Come for Free. [Online] Advertising Age, March 5, 2012. http://adage.com/article/digital/facebook-warns-brands-scale-social-free/233105/.

202. **Yarow, Jay.** The 25 Most Popular Free iPhone Apps Of All Time. [Online] Business Insider, May 4, 2013. http://www.businessinsider.com/ the-most-popular-free-iphone-apps-2013-5?op=1.

203. **Facebook.** Statement of Rights and Responsibilities Update. [Online] Facebook. [Cited: April 22, 2012.] http://www.facebook.com/fbsitegovernance/app_4949752878.

204. **Keen, Andrew.** Battle Lines Drawn as Data Becomes Oil of Digital Age. [Online] DLD (Digital Life Design), January 25, 2012. http://www.dld-conference.com/news/digital-business/battle-lines-drawn-as-data-becomes-oil-of-digital-age_aid_3097.html.

205. **Guynn, Jessica.** Is Facebook killing your privacy? Some say it already has. [Online] Los Angeles Time, September 26, 2011. http://latimesblogs.latimes.com/technology/2011/09/is-facebook-killing-your-privacy-.html.

206. **Newman, Jared.** Google's Schmidt Roasted for Privacy Comments. [Online] PCWorld, December 11, 2009. http://www.pcworld.com/article/184446/googles_schmidt_roasted_for_privacy_comments.html.

207. **Sutter, John D.** Google search undergoes 'most radical transformation ever'. [Online] CNN, January 10, 2012. http://www.cnn.com/2012/01/10/tech/web/google-search-plus/index.html.

208. **Singhal, Amit.** Search, plus Your World. [Online] The Official Google Blog, January 10, 2012. http://googleblog.blogspot.com/2012/01/search-plus-your-world.html.

209. **Gross, Doug.** Google seeks to clarify new privacy policy. [Online] CNN, January 27, 2012. http://www.cnn.com/2012/01/27/tech/web/google-privacy-clarified/index.html.

210. **Google Policies & Principles.** One policy, one Google experience. [Online] Google. [Cited: January 27, 2012.] http://www.google.com/policies/.

211. **Rose, Brent.** How Will Google's New Privacy Policy Affect You? [Online] Gizmodo, January 25, 2012. http://gizmodo.com/5879163/how-will-googles-new-privacy-policy-affect-you/.

212. **Gross, Doug.** Attorneys general have 'strong concerns' about Google privacy rules. [Online] CNN, February 22, 2012. http://www.cnn.com/2012/02/22/tech/web/google-privacy-attorneys-general/index.html.

213. **U.S. Congress.** Letter to Mr. Larry Page from Congress of the United States. [Online] United States Senate (Senator Ed Markey of Massachusetts), January 26, 2012. http://markey.house. gov/sites/markey.house.gov/files/documents/2012_0126.Google%20Prviacy%20Letter.pdf.

214. **Chavez, Pablo.** Changing our privacy policies, not our privacy controls. [Online] Google Public Policy Blog, January 31, 2012. http://googlepublicpolicy.blogspot.com/2012/01/changing-our-privacy-policies-not-our.html.

215. **Galperin, Eva.** How to Remove Your Google Search History Before Google's New Privacy Policy Takes Effect. [Online] Electronic Frontier Foundation, February 21, 2012. https://www.eff.org/deeplinks/2012/02/ how-remove-your-google-search-history-googles-new-privacy-policy-takes-effect.

216. **Mediati, Nick.** Google Privacy Checklist: What to Do Before Google's Privacy Policy Changes on March 1. [Online] PC World, February 28, 2012. http://www.pcworld.com/article/250950/google_privacy_checklist_what_to_do_before_googles_privacy_policy_changes_on_march_1.html.

217. **CNN Blogs.** Google's new privacy policy in effect today: 'Accept, or decline and be banished'. [Online] CNN, March 1, 2012. http://outfront.blogs.cnn.com/2012/03/01/ googles-new-privacy-policy-accept-or-decline-and-be-banished.

218. **Paul Yiu and the Bing Social Search Team.** Bing is Brining Twitter Search to You. [Online] Bing Community Search Blog, October 21, 2009. http://www.bing.com/community/site_blogs/b/search/archive/2009/10/21/bing-is-bringing-twitter-search-to-you.aspx.

219. **Ostrow, Adam.** Facebook and Bing's Plan to Make Search Social. [Online] Mashable, October 13, 2010. http://mashable.com/2010/10/13/facebook-bing-social-search/.

220. **Mehdi, Yusuf.** Facebook Friends Now Fueling Faster Decisions on Bing. [Online] Bing Community Search Blog, May 16, 2011. http://www.bing.com/community/site_blogs/b/search/archive/2011/05/16/news-announcement-may-17.aspx.

221. **The Nielsen Company.** Consumer Trust in Online, Social and Mobile Advertising Grows. [Online] Nielsen, April 10, 2012. http://blog.nielsen.com/nielsenwire/media_entertainment/consumer-trust-in-online-social-and-mobile-advertising-grows/ and http://www.nielsen.com/content/dam/corporate/us/en/reports-downloads/2012-Reports/global-trust-in-advertising-2012.pdf.

222. **Seifert, Dan.** Microsoft spruces up mobile Bing site with Facebook integration. [Online] MobileBurn.com, September 12, 2011. http://www.mobileburn.com/16588/news/microsoft-spruces-up-mobile-bing-site-with-facebook-integration.

223. **Slattery, Brennon.** Bing, Facebook Deepen Ties, Threaten Google +1. [Online] PC World, May 17, 2011. http://www.pcworld.com/article/228057/bing_facebook_deepen_ties_threaten_google_1.html.

224. **Goldman, David.** Bing fires at Google with new social search. [Online] CNNMoney, May 10, 2012. http://money.cnn.com/2012/05/10/technology/bing-redesign/index.htm.

225. **Katz, Ian.** Web freedom faces greatest threat ever, warns Google's Sergey Brin. [Online] The Guardian, April 15, 2012. http://www.guardian.co.uk/technology/2012/apr/15/web-freedom-threat-google-brin.

226. **Keen, Andrew.** Opinion: Is the social web an asteroid for the Google dinosaur? [Online] CNN, March 30, 2012. http://articles.cnn.com/2012-03-30/opinion/opinion_keen-google-social-media_1_google-maps-google-products-larry-page?_s=PM:OPINION.

227. **Keay, Andra.** Google Search – the Hidden Story – Andra Keay - ARIN 6912. [Online] University of Sydney, August 12, 2010. http://www.slideshare.net/andragy/google-search-history.

228. **IMDb.** Mission: Impossible. [Online] IMDb, 1966–1973. http://www.imdb.com/title/tt0060009/.

229. **—.** Mission: Impossible. [Online] IMDb, May 22, 1996. http://www.imdb.com/title/tt0117060/.

230. **Alba, Davey.** Snapchat Hands-on: Send Photos Set to Self-Destruct. [Online] Laptop Magazine, May 16, 2012. http://blog.laptopmag.com/hands-on-with-snapchat-send-photos-set-to-self-destruct.

231. **Hamburger, Ellis.** Snapchat's next big thing: 'Stories' that don't just disappear. [Online] The Verge, October 3, 2013. http://www.theverge.com/2013/10/3/4791934/snapchats-next-big-thing-stories-that-dont-just-disappear.

232. **—.** Real talk: the new Snapchat brilliantly mixes video and texting. [Online] The Verge, May 1, 2014. http://www.theverge.com/2014/5/1/5670260/real-talk-the-new-snapchat-makes-texting-fun-again-video-calls.

233. **Knibbs, Kate.** For a price, your 'expired' Snapchats can be brought back from the dead. [Online] Digital Trends, May 8, 2013. http://www.digitaltrends.com/social-media/you-can-find-old-snapchat-picture-data-on-your-phone-according-to-new-research/.

234. **Pagliery, Jose.** Snapchat settles FTC charges for lying about privacy. [Online] CNNMoney, May 9, 2014. http://money.cnn.com/2014/05/08/technology/security/snapchat-ftc/.

235. **Kelly, Heather.** Facebook releases Poke app for self-destructing messages. [Online] CNN, December 22, 2012. http://www.cnn.com/2012/12/21/tech/social-media/facebook-poke-app/index.html.

236. **Welch, Chris.** Give your tweets a death sentence with Efemr. [Online] The Verge, April 28, 2013. http://www.theverge.com/2013/4/28/4279214/give-your-tweets-death-sentence-efemr.

237. **efemr.** What's efemr. [Online] efemr. [Cited: June 15, 2014.] https://www.efemr.com/corporate/about.html.

238. **Oreskovic, Alexei.** Facebook launches mobile app that does not require Facebook account. [Online] Reuters, June 17, 2014. http://in.reuters.com/article/2014/06/17/facebook-slingshot-idINKBN0ES28320140617.

239. **Griggs, Brandon.** Big changes coming to iPhone messaging. [Online] CNN, June 3, 2014. http://www.cnn.com/2014/06/03/tech/mobile/apple-messages-app/index.html.

240. **Facebook Messenger's 'Day' Becomes Third Clone of Snapchat Stories. [Online]** Bloomberg, March 9, 2017. https://www.bloomberg.com/news/articles/2017-03-09/ facebook-messenger-s-day-becomes-third-clone-of-snapchat-stories.
241. **McCullagh, Declan.** Facebook 'Like' button draws privacy scrutiny. [Online] CNet, June 2, 2010. http://www.cnn.com/2010/TECH/social.media/06/02/cnet.facebook.privacy.like/.
242. **Spehar, Jeffrey.** The New Facebook Login and Graph API 2.0. [Online] Facebook, April 30, 2014. https://developers.facebook.com/blog/post/2014/04/30/the-new-facebook-login/.
243. **Facebook.** Anonymous Login. [Online] Facebook. [Cited: May 31, 2014.] https://developers. facebook.com/products/anonymous-login/.
244. **Hamburger, Ellis.** Facebook gives up on automatically posting everything you do online. [Online] The Verge, May 27, 2014. http://www.theverge.com/2014/5/27/5754862/ facebook-gives-up-on-automatically-sharing-everything-you-do-online-open-graph.
245. **Yang, Peter.** Giving people more control over when they share from apps. [Online] Facebook, May 27, 2014. https://developers.facebook.com/blog/post/2014/05/27/ more-control-with-sharing/.
246. **Gross, Doug.** Facebook is cutting back on spammy auto-posts. [Online] CNN, May 29, 2014. http://www.cnn.com/2014/05/29/tech/social-media/facebook-automatic-posts/index.html.
247. **Anonymous.** I danced with two people at my wedding. [Online] whisper, June 2013. http:// whisper.sh/whisper/04dcc79a60232a436970b838ad52f396a40cb5.
248. **Shontell, Alyson.** Secret-Sharing App Whisper Is Nearing 3 Billion Monthly Pageviews Because It Does Something Facebook Can't. [Online] Business Insider, December 16, 2013. http://www.businessinsider.com/whisper-2013-12.
249. **Segall, Laurie.** Iraqis turn to Whisper app during conflict. [Online] CNNMoney, June 16, 2014. http://money.cnn.com/2014/06/16/technology/social/whisper-app-iraq/index.html.
250. **No names or profiles.** Secret. [Online] Secret. [Cited: June 3, 2014.] https://www.secret.ly/.
251. **Lawler, Ryan.** Secret Launches In China With A 'Secret' Partner, Adds Language Preferences As It Blows Up In Russia. [Online] TechCrunch, June 2, 2014. http://techcrunch. com/2014/06/01/secret-in-china/.
252. **Bell, Karissa.** Anonymous email app launches with 'creepy' stunt. [Online] Mashable, August 5, 2014. http://www.cnn.com/2014/08/05/tech/web/leak-anonymous-email/index.html.
253. **Suster, Mark.** How do I Really Feel About Anonymous Apps Like Secret? [Online] Bothsid.es, March 15, 2014. http://www.bothsidesofthetable.com/2014/03/15/ how-do-i-really-feel-about-anonymous-apps-like-secret/.
254. **Borger, Julian.** NSA files: why the Guardian in London destroyed hard drives of leaked files. [Online] The Guardian, August 20, 2013. http://www.theguardian.com/world/2013/aug/20/ nsa-snowden-files-drives-destroyed-london.
255. **Kelly, Heather.** Eavesdropping with a camera and potted plants. [Online] CNN, August 7, 2014. http://www.cnn.com/2014/08/06/tech/innovation/visual-microphone-research/ index.html.
256. **Simonite, Tom.** Statistical Tricks Extract Sensitive Data from Encrypted Communications. [Online] MIT Technology News, June 19, 2014. http://www.technologyreview.com/ news/528336/statistical-tricks-extract-sensitive-data-from-encrypted-communications/.
257. **Angley, Natalie.** Artist creates faces from DNA left in public. [Online] CNN, September 4, 2013. http://www.cnn.com/2013/09/04/tech/innovation/dna-face-sculptures/index.html.
258. **Manes, Stephen.** Private Lives? Not Ours! [Online] PC World, April 18, 2000. http://www. pcworld.com/article/16331/private_lives_not_ours.html.
259. **Cheng, Jack.** Privacy is not dead. [Online] CNN, June 8, 2013. http://www.cnn. com/2013/06/08/opinion/cheng-privacy-snooping/index.html.
260. **Pagliery, Jose.** Secret message app Wickr moves to Wall Street. [Online] CNNMoney, June 27, 2014. http://money.cnn.com/2014/06/27/technology/security/wickr-finance/index.html.
261. **Welch, Chris.** Google begins shutting down its failed Google+ social network. [Online] The Verge, April 2, 2019. https://www.theverge.com/2019/4/2/18290637/ google-plus-shutdown-consumer-personal-account-delete.

Chapter 3
Smartphones and Privacy

"We're as surprised as anybody to see all that information flowing. It raises a lot of questions for the industry – and not [only] for Carrier IQ."

– Carrier IQ's Andrew Coward (December 2011)

"[Mobile World Congress] really should be held in Geneva, close to where Mary Shelley created Frankenstein. With our increasing addiction to our mobile phones, we are in danger of creating a monster."

– Social critic Andrew Keen (February 2012)

"Your cell phone is communicating completely digital; it's part of the Internet. The attack surfaces for adversaries to get on the Internet now include all those mobile devices. ... The mobile security situation lags. It's far behind."

– NSA Director Army Gen. Keith Alexander (July 2012)

"There are no more tables for two; tables for four are our most intimate encounters—two humans and two devices.

– Rev. Nancy Colier (March 2014)

"The vast majority of Americans – 97% – now own a cellphone of some kind. The share of Americans that own a smartphone is now 85%."

– *Pew Research Center (April 2021)*

3.1   Smartphones

Apple announced in January 2021 that it had an install base of 1 billion iPhones and a total of 1.65 billion active devices (1). In May 2021, Google announced at its (virtual) I/O Developer Conference that Android was running on 3 billion active devices, at a growth rate of about 500 million new devices every two years (2).

In September 2011—a decade prior to the 2021 Apple and Google announcements—82.2 million Americans own smartphones, 70% of which are either iPhones or Android phones (3). 64.2 million U.S. smartphone users accessed social networking sites or blogs on their mobile devices at least once in December 2011 (4). March

N. Lee, *Facebook Nation*, https://doi.org/10.1007/978-1-0716-1867-7_3

2012 marked the tipping point when a majority (50.4%) of U.S. mobile subscribers owned smartphones (5). A decade later in February 2021, the share of Americans that own a smartphone jumped to a whopping 85%. "The vast majority of Americans – 97% – now own a cellphone of some kind. The share of Americans that own a smartphone is now 85%, up from just 35% in Pew Research Center's first survey of smartphone ownership conducted in 2011" (6).

In fact, a staggering 1.4 billion smartphones were sold worldwide in 2020, and an estimated 1.5 billion smartphones would be shipped in 2021 due to 5G adoption (7). Smartphones are the most prevalent portable social networking devices among some 4 billion Internet users (8).

In June 2011, a Harris Interactive survey of 2,510 Americans aged 18 and older showed that people are so addicted to their mobile devices that a majority of them would "sneak-a-peek" at their smartphones even during work meetings by employing tactics such as "hiding their mobile device under the table or in a notebook" or "excusing themselves to go to the restroom" (9).

A U.K. study in 2012 revealed that two-thirds of people suffer from "nomophobia" – the fear of being without their phone (10). Young adults, aged 18 to 24, are more nomophobic (77%) than average. 41% of people, more men than women, have two phones or more in an effort to stay connected.

In a March 2014 article in *Psychology Today*, Rev. Nancy Colier wrote, "A friend of mine is separating from her husband because he cannot separate from his iPhone. ... There are no more tables for two; tables for four are our most intimate encounters—two humans and two devices" (11).

Technology is trying to keep up with human's demand. The tremendous growth of cell phone usage in the United States has created "spectrum crunch" – running out of the airwaves necessary to provide voice, text, and Internet services (12). To alleviate the problem, U.S. Congress authorized the Federal Communications Commission (FCC) in 2012 to hold voluntary incentive spectrum auctions for broadcast TV to turn in to the FCC spectrum that they are not using (13).

Mobile security, however, is seriously lagging behind. "Your cell phone is communicating completely digital; it's part of the Internet," said Army Gen. Keith Alexander, director of the NSA and commander of the U.S. Cyber Command. "The attack surfaces for adversaries to get on the Internet now include all those mobile devices. ... The mobile security situation lags. It's far behind" (14). Nonetheless, as security strategist Brian Contos at McAfee said, "People aren't going to go back to driving the Model T any more than they're going to go back to rotary telephones because of the risks on smartphones" (15).

3.2 Location Tracking on iPhone and iPad

In April 2011, Alasdair Allan and Pete Warden reported that iPhones and 3G iPads are regularly recording the position of the device into a hidden file called "consolidated.db" (16). The secret database file has been storing the locations (latitude-longitude coordinates) and time stamps, effectively tracking the history of movement of the iPhone and 3G iPad users for a year since iOS 4 was released in 2010. Although the data is unencrypted and unprotected on the mobile device, it is sent to Apple in an anonymous and encrypted form (17).

Apple has since learned to be more transparent and upfront with customers. On the new iPad 2 setup procedure, users can enable or disable Location Services that allow Apple's Maps, Compass, Camera, Photos, Weather, Reminders, Safari, Find My iPad, and other apps to gather and use data indicating the user's approximate location. The user location is determined using GPS along with crowdsourced Wi-Fi hotspot and cell tower locations. During the iPad 2 setup, Apple also asks the user for permission to automatically send diagnostics and usage data to Apple. Diagnostic data may include location information.

In March 2013, Apple acquired indoor-GPS company WifiSLAM which combines traditional GPS coordinates with smartphone tools such as accelerometers and compasses in order to pinpoint the user's location indoors within about 8 feet. "This accuracy will change how you interact with indoor environments," said WifiSLAM co-founder Anand Atreya. "Think about going to the supermarket. We can provide information relevant to the product right in front of you" (18). Merchants can track customers by their mobile devices' permanent media access control (MAC) addresses.

U.S. retailers including American Apparel, Family Dollar, Home Depot, and Nordstrom have experimented with indoor GPS to track customers' shopping behaviors (19). Some consumers have complained about the perceived invasion of privacy and decided to turn off their smartphones while shopping.

In June 2014, Apple announced at its Worldwide Developers Conference (WWDC) that the WiFi scanning in iOS 8 would use "random, locally administered MAC addresses" instead of permanent MAC addresses. The change will essentially stop retail analytics companies from tracking shoppers in stores using their mobile devices' MAC addresses (20). However, companies can still use iBeacon, Apple's implementation of Bluetooth Low Energy (BLE) wireless technology in iOS 7 and 8, to detect the proximity of mobile devices and send them advertisements and other information (21).

3.3   Carrier IQ

Not to be outdone by the iPhone location tracking software, the Carrier IQ software has been found on about 150 million cell phones including the iPhone, Android, BlackBerry, and Nokia phones (22). On November 28, 2011, security researcher Trevor Eckhart posted a video on YouTube detailing hidden software installed on smartphones that secretly logs keypresses, SMS messages, and browser URLs (23). Carrier IQ responded by saying "we're as surprised as anybody to see all that information flowing" (24) and went on to explain that the hidden software allows network operators to "better understand how mobile devices interact with and perform on their network" by uploading diagnostic data once per day, at a time when the device is not being used (25).

Amid the public outcry over the Carrier IQ tracking scandal, a lone columnist Matthew Miller at *ZDNet* concurred with Carrier IQ. He voiced his opinion: "A few years back I was asked if I could install software on my phone so that a company could track my usage patterns to improve services. I accepted and was paid something like $5 to $10 a month for each phone used and sending this data. ... The media has made it more malicious than it really is and I am not concerned about my phone usage at all. ... It sounds to me like the software is designed to BENEFIT consumers and is not being used to track and target you" (26).

Regardless of the real intention of Carrier IQ, the truth remains that no one wants some strangers or companies snooping around behind their back. To know a person's location over time generates a great deal of information about the person. American Civil Liberties Union (ACLU) expounded on the severity of the issue, "A person who knows all of another's travels can deduce whether he is a weekly church goer, a heavy drinker, a regular at the gym, an unfaithful husband, an outpatient receiving medical treatment, an associate of particular individuals or political groups – and not just one such fact about a person, but all such facts" (27).

Although AT&T, T-Mobile, Sprint, and Apple have said that they use the Carrier IQ software in line with their own privacy policies, the Federal Trade Commission and Federal Communications Commission have opened an investigation into the practices of Carrier IQ as possibly unfair or deceptive (28).

While secret location tracking and Carrier IQ are in the spotlight, they are just the tip of the iceberg that deserves scrutiny. As people are communicating via voice, photos, and videos on their cell phones, the phone companies are recording the metadata that travels with them, including locations, identity of the callers and receivers, amount of data transferred, and the costs of the transmissions (29). Verizon keeps such data on their servers for 12 months, Sprint for 24 months, T-Mobile for 60 months, and AT&T for 84 months (30). Most individuals have over 1 million pieces of personal information in the possession of cell phone companies over a 4-year span. This information is analyzed and sold to other companies that handle localized advertisements and offer personalized search results. According to *USA Today*, AT&T, Verizon, and BellSouth have also provided this information to the National Security Agency (NSA), which reportedly aims "to create a database of every call ever made within the nation's borders" (31).

3.4 Smartphone Data Collection Transparency

In the 2011 article titled "Your phone company is selling your personal data," CNN's David Goldman wrote that "your phone company knows where you live, what websites you visit, what apps you download, what videos you like to watch, and even where you are. Now, some have begun selling that valuable information to the highest bidder" (32). In fact, all major carriers sell their customers' smartphone data. "An interesting transformation is happening in wireless, in which consumers are no longer customers – they're the product," said Dan Hays, principal in PricewaterhouseCooper's communications and technology practice. "The trick is for operators to find out how to make money without violating their relationships and trust with their users" (33).

Under the increasing scrutiny from consumers and government officials, companies are learning to be more transparent with data collection practices (34), and giving their customers the option to opt out of their data collection. For instance, Verizon Wireless sent their customers an email on November 17, 2011 about their new privacy programs – information the phone company collects and how the phone company uses the information:

1. Mobile Usage Information:

   a. Addresses of websites you visit when using our wireless service. These data strings (or URLs) may include search terms you have used.
   b. Location of your device ("Location Information").
   c. App and device feature usage.

2. Consumer Information:

   a. Information about your use of Verizon products and services (such as data and calling features, device type, and amount).
   b. Demographic and interest categories provided to us by other companies, such as gender, age range, sports fan, frequent diner, or pet owner ("Demographics").

The information is used by Verizon Wireless and shared with other companies to create business and marketing reports, as well as to make mobile ads more relevant for the consumers. As a consolation, Verizon Wireless assures their customers, "Under these new programs, we will not share outside of Verizon any information that identifies you personally." In addition, consumers are given a chance to opt out of the new privacy programs within 45 days of receiving the email notice.

We are witnessing more transparency in business practices today. In November 2011, two U.S. shopping malls (Promenade Temecula in California and Short Pump Town Center in Virginia) announced that they would track shoppers' movements throughout the premises by monitoring the signals from their cell phones (35). The collected data monitored how the shopping crowds moved from store to store, and how long they lingered in any given shop. Consumers could opt out by turning off their cell phones. After an intervention from a U.S. Senator who raised privacy concerns, the shopping malls ceased their monitoring programs (36).

U.S. retailers including J.C. Penney and Home Depot are reportedly also considering using the same cell phone technology to track their customers (37). Meanwhile, Neiman Marcus hosted its second in-store foursquare challenge in March 2012. For a chance to win a coffee table book, participating customers checked in using the location-based social site foursquare to a Neiman Marcus location on March 31 using their smartphones (38). At Walgreens, customers checking in to the drugstore via a foursquare or Facebook mobile app would receive e-flyers and e-coupons (39).

3.5   Always On

Some may say that smartphones are liberating and convenient anytime and anywhere, but others may vehemently disagree when "anytime and anywhere" becomes "all the time and everywhere." Social critic Andrew Keen declared in a February 2012 CNN article that our mobiles have become Frankenstein's monster: "As always, Mobile World Congress, the world's largest mobile telephone extravaganza, is being held in Barcelona this year. But it really should be held in Geneva, close to where Mary Shelley created Frankenstein. That's because, with our increasing addiction to our mobile phones, we are in danger of creating a monster that we are less and less able to control. … These hardware companies will articulate the benefits of their technology in terms of personal empowerment. But the real truth behind these increasingly intelligent devices is personal disempowerment" (40).

Keen's point of view is manifested in the mobile phone users' reactions to the April 2012 release of the photo-sharing Instagram app on Android devices. With 14 million users, Instagram was awarded the 2011 iPhone App of the Year (41). A crossbreed between Facebook and Twitter, Instagram enables sharing and comments on friends' pictures as well as allows people to follow other users. When the iPhone-exclusive app was made available for Android, an insidious tweet war broke out between iPhone and Android users. *CNET* associate editor Emily Dreyfuss remarked, "Which smartphone we own has begun to inform our identities. In our gadget-filled lives, our phones have become another way for us to organize ourselves into separate groups, to label each other as 'other' and 'apart.' Our tech has come to define us" (42).

Since the $1 billion acquisition by Facebook, Instagram has hit 1 billion monthly users in December 2020 (43). To allow for user control of online privacy, Facebook launched Instagram Direct in December 2013 to let users send text, video, and photo messages to each other privately on Android and iPhone (44).

Regardless of Android or iPhone, smartphone addiction can be a nuisance in public. In March 2012, a Philadelphia bus rider named Eric was so annoyed by loud phone calls on the bus that he decided to jam the cell phone signals using an electronic jammer (45). "A lot of people are extremely loud, no sense of just privacy or anything. When it becomes a bother, that's when I screw on the antenna and flip the switch," said Eric before realizing that cell phone jamming is illegal in the United States. Apparently, many share Eric's sentiment. During the weekend after Eric appeared on NBC10 News, "cell phone jammer" became one of the top 10 searches on Google Trends (46). Jokingly perhaps, controversial CNN contributor Bob Greene suggested bringing back the phone booths, or phoneless booths to be precise, in public places around the country for people to make their private cell phone calls (47). No one believes that the idea would work. Stationary phone booths simply do not sit well with the consumer's need for mobility that makes cell phones so attractive in the first place.

3.6 Mobile Apps Privacy Invasion

Besides the carrier-installed apps on cell phones, there are plenty of utility and social media apps that users may download onto their cell phones. With an install base of over 1 million people, Path for iPhone and Android is one such free app that is "the smart journal that helps you share life with the ones you love" (48). In February 2012, Arun Thampi in Singapore discovered that Path uploaded the entire iPhone address book (names, email addresses, phone numbers, etc.) to its servers without seeking permission from the user (49). Within a couple of days, Path co-founder and CEO Dave Morin issued a public apology and released a new version of the app that asks the user for permission to upload the address book from iPhones and Android devices (50).

It turns out that Path is not alone. Twitter also acknowledged in February 2012 that when a user taps the "Find friends" feature on its smartphone app, the company downloads the user's entire address book, including email addresses and phone numbers, and keeps the data on its severs for 18 months (51). Unlike Path, Twitter did not apologize, and the company simplify clarified the language associated with Find Friends: Instead of "Scan your contacts," it would display "Upload your contacts" for iPhones and "Import your contacts" for Android devices in order to inform the users that the entire address book would be shared with Twitter.

Path and Twitter mobile apps have become emblematic of disrespect for individual privacy in the digital information age. It is conceivable that many more smartphone apps are collecting private information without the knowledge of the users. Facebook, Flickr, and other mobile apps have been accused of reading text messages and other personal information on their installed cell phones (52). LinkedIn's mobile app was caught collecting users' complete calendar event, including email addresses of people users are meeting with, meeting subject, location and meeting notes (53).

Moreover, security experts have demonstrated that Apple's iOS platform enables software developers to create mobile apps to upload all the photos, calendars, and recorded conversations on an iPhone (54). Similarly, Google's Android platform also allows developers to build mobile apps to copy or steal photos and personal data from the Android phones of unwitting users (55).

Imagine you are talking to your friend on the phone about going to Hawaii for your next vacation. After you hang up, you start getting calls from travel agencies, sunscreen pharmaceuticals, and other companies trying to sell you something useful for your upcoming trip. There are two possible reactions to this: One, you are spooked by the invasion of privacy; or two, you are delighted by the offers of coupons and promotions without having to search for them online.

3.7 Mobile Apps for Children

In September 2011, the Federal Trade Commission settled its first legal action against a mobile app developer in enforcement of the Children's Online Privacy Protection Act (56). According to the consent decree, the iOS developer was fined $50,000 and ordered to start publishing information about the kinds of data collected via their apps and how that data is shared, to get parental consent before collecting any new data, and to delete all the data they had collected so far (57).

In February 2012, the Federal Trade Commission issued a staff report showing the results of a survey of mobile apps for children (58). The survey reveals that neither the app stores nor the app developers provide adequate information for parents to determine what data is being collected from their children, how it is being shared, or who will have access to it. The report states, "[The FTC] staff was unable to determine from the promotion pages whether the apps collected any data at all – let alone the type of data collected, the purpose of the collection, and who collected or obtained access to the data. ... Although the app store developer agreements require developers to disclose the information their apps collect, the app stores do not appear to enforce these requirements. This lack of enforcement provides little incentive to app developers to provide such disclosures and leaves parents without the information they need. ... Ads running inside an app may incorporate various capabilities allowing the user to do things like directly call phone numbers or visit websites appearing in the ad" (59).

In a Fall 2013 research report by Common Sense Media, 72% of children age 8 and under have used a mobile device for some type of media activity such as playing games, watching videos, or using apps, up from 38% in 2011; and 38% of children under 2 have also used a mobile device for media, up from 10% in 2011 (60).

In June 2013, President Barack Obama announced the new ConnectED initiative to connect 99% of America's students to the Internet through high-speed broadband and high-speed wireless within 5 years (61). In response, Microsoft offered $1 billion in April 2014 to help set up public school kids with mobile devices across the country's 14,000 public school districts (62).

There will be a lot more variety of mobile apps for children, and as a result, more scrutiny as well.

3.8 Android Market and Google Play

In October 2011, the Android Market had over 200,000 free and paid apps (63) available for 190 million activated Android devices around the world (64). By December 2011, Google announced that 10 billion apps have been downloaded from the Android Market (65). As of April 2021, there were almost 3 million Android apps on Google Play (66).

With the overwhelming number of new mobile apps, Google has fallen short of ensuring that the mobile apps are tested to be free of virus and suspicious behavior (67). For example, DroidDream, a trojan rootkit exploit, was released in early March 2011 to the Android Market in the form of several free applications that were, in many cases, pirated versions of existing priced apps (68). This exploit allowed hackers to steal information such as IMEI and IMSI numbers, phone model, user ID, and service provider. Such information can be used in cloning a cell phone and using it illegally without the knowledge of the original owner. The exploit also installed a backdoor that allowed the hackers to download more code to the infected device.

In February 2012, Google revealed the use of "Bouncer" to automate the scanning of Android Market for potentially malicious software without requiring developers to go through an application approval process (69). Google reported, "The [Bouncer] service has been looking for malicious apps in Market for a while now, and between the first and second halves of 2011, we saw a 40% decrease in the number of potentially-malicious downloads from Android Market. This drop occurred at the same time that companies who market and sell anti-malware and security software have been reporting that malicious applications are on the rise" (70).

In the same report, Google also admitted, "no security approach is foolproof, and added scrutiny can often lead to important improvements" (70). Indeed, while faking an SSL certificate enabled iOS developer Arun Thampi to watch the transmitted data and thereby expose the Path app, it would be more difficult if the data was encrypted without SSL.

In March 2012, Google replaced Android Market with Google Play to offer consumers a broad spectrum of content including books (previously Google eBookstore), music (previously Google Music), movies, and mobile apps (71).

The consolidation, along with the proliferation of Android devices worldwide, seems to pay off. In Q1 2014, Google Play led the iOS App Store in downloads by approximately 45% according to App Annie Analytics (72). The growth was driven mostly by emerging markets such as Russia, Brazil, Mexico, and Turkey.

3.9   Apple's App Store

In March 2011, Apple's App Store had over 500,000 free and paid apps (73) available for more than 100 million iPhone users worldwide (74). By July 2011, the App Store had reached 15 billion downloads (75); and by December of the same year, iOS apps had generated six times the revenue of Android apps (76).

In June 2012, Apple CEO Tim Cook announced at the annual Worldwide Developers Conference, "The App Store now has 400 million accounts – the largest number of accounts with credit cards anywhere on the Internet. Some 650,000 apps are now available. ... Customers have now downloaded an astounding 30 billion apps" (77). In October 2013, Cook updated the audience at the annual iPad event that more than 1 million apps were in the App Store and over 60 billion total apps had been downloaded (78).

Despite Apple's assertion of its tight quality control over its App Store, a scam Pokemon game reached number 2 on Apple's App Store charts in February 2012 and raked in $10,000 before it was pulled (79). The 99-cent "Pokemon Yellow" game crashed as soon as it opened. The debacle called into question Apple's approval process, let alone the company's ability to ensure that the mobile apps have a privacy policy in place. The consensus in the developer community believes that "overworked Apple reviewers, with thousands of apps waiting in the approval queue, likely don't test apps too thoroughly at first. But once they gain popularity, the Apple team gives them a closer look" (80).

On February 15, 2012, Apple announced that it will start requiring mobile apps to obtain explicit permission from iPhone and iPad users before the apps can collect and store information about user's personal contacts. "Apps that collect or transmit a user's contact data without their prior permission are in violation of our guidelines," Apple spokesman Tom Neumayr told CNN (81).

In May 2013, Apple's App Store reached another milestone by hitting 50 billion downloads (82). Six years later in 2019, App Store saw a record 204 billion downloads as consumers spent over $120 billion on apps, subscriptions and other in-app purchases (83).

3.10 Facebook App Center

On May 9, 2012, Facebook unveiled Facebook App Center, a clearinghouse for social apps on the web and on smartphones. Facebook's Aaron Brady wrote in the Developer Blog, "For the over 900 million people that use Facebook, the App Center will become the new, central place to find great apps like Draw Something, Pinterest, Spotify, Battle Pirates, Viddy, and Bubble Witch Saga. … The App Center is designed to grow mobile apps that use Facebook – whether they're on iOS, Android or the mobile web" (84).

The Facebook App Center opened in June 2012 with over 600 apps (85). Featuring mobile and web apps, the App Center gives users personalized recommendations and lets them browse through the apps that their friends are using.

A Facebook app has access to plenty of user information on Facebook, which includes the user's name, profile pictures, username, user ID, networks, friend list, gender, age range, and locale as well as a user's email address and birthday on some occasions (86). This makes a malicious Facebook app much more dangerous.

Back in January 2011, Facebook had disabled a feature that gave app developers access to user's address and phone number (87). It remains to be seen whether the Facebook App Center will do a better job than the Google Android Market and Apple Store in screening their apps.

References

1. **Nellis, Stephen.** Apple sees revenue growth accelerating after setting record for iPhone sales, China strength. [Online] Reuters, January 27, 2021. https://www.reuters.com/article/us-apple-results/apple-tops-wall-street-expectations-on-record-iphone-revenue-china-sales-surge-idUSKBN29W2TD.

2. **Lardinois, Frederic.** Android now powers 3B devices. [Online] TechCrunch, May 18, 2021. https://techcrunch.com/2021/05/18/android-now-powers-3b-devices/.

3. **Chansanchai, Athima.** 70 percent of US-owned smartphones are iPhones or Androids. [Online] MSNBC, August 31, 2011. http://technolog.msnbc.msn.com/_news/2011/08/31/7538973-70-percent-of-us-owned-smartphones-are-iphones-or-androids.

4. **comScore.** comScore Releases the "2012 Mobile Future in Focus" Report. [Online] comScore Press Release, February 23, 2012. http://www.comscore.com/Press_Events/Press_Releases/2012/2/comScore_Releases_the_2012_Mobile_Future_in_Focus_Report.

5. **Nielsen.** America's New Mobile Majority: a Look at Smartphone Owners in the U.S. [Online] Nielsen Wire, May 7, 2012. http://blog.nielsen.com/nielsenwire/online_mobile/who-owns-smartphones-in-the-us/.

6. **Pew Research Center.** Mobile Fact Sheet. [Online] Pew Research Center, April 7, 2021. https://www.pewresearch.org/internet/fact-sheet/mobile/.

7. **Ivan.** Gartner: smartphone sales to grow 11% in 2021, 5G to reach 35% share. [Online] GSMArena, February 5, 2021. https://www.gsmarena.com/gartner_smartphone_sales_to_grow_11_in_2021_5g_to_account_for_35-news-47598.php.

8. **International Telecommunication Union (ITU).** Global ICT Statistics. [Online] ITU. [Cited: April 25, 2021.] https://www.itu.int/en/ITU-D/Statistics/Pages/stat/default.aspx.

9. **Qumu.** Harris Poll – Mobile Video in the Workplace. [Online] Qumu Press Release, July 11, 2011. http://www.qumu.com/news/news-releases/419-qumu-harris-survey.html.

10. **The Telegraph.** Rise in nomophobia: fear of being without a phone. [Online] The Telegraph, February 16, 2012. http://www.telegraph.co.uk/technology/news/9084075/Rise-in-nomophobia-fear-of-being-without-a-phone.html.

11. **Colier, Nancy.** Is Anyone Worth Turning Off Your Phone? [Online] Psychology Today, March 11, 2014. http://www.psychologytoday.com/blog/inviting-monkey-tea/201403/is-anyone-worth-turning-your-phone.

12. **Goldman, David.** Sorry, America: Your wireless airwaves are full. [Online] CNN, February 21, 2012. Money. http://money.cnn.com/2012/02/21/technology/spectrum_crunch/.

13. **Shapiro, Gary.** Congress Gets It on Wireless Broadband. [Online] Forbes, February 22, 2012. http://www.forbes.com/sites/garyshapiro/2012/02/22/congress-gets-it-on-wireless-broadband/.

14. **Merica, Dan.** Five things you need to know about U.S. national security. [Online] CNN, July 29, 2012. http://security.blogs.cnn.com/2012/07/29/five-things-you-need-to-know-about-u-s-national-security/.

15. **Neild, Barry.** Could hackers seize control of your car? [Online] CNN, March 2, 2012. http://www.cnn.com/2012/03/02/tech/mobile/mobile-car-hacking/index.html.

16. **Allan, Alasdair and Warden, Peter.** Got an iPhone or 3G iPad? Apple is recording your moves. [Online] O'Reilly Radar, April 20, 2011. http://radar.oreilly.com/2011/04/apple-location-tracking.html.

17. **Apple Inc.** Apple Q&A on Location Data. [Online] Apple Press Info, April 27, 2011. http://www.apple.com/pr/library/2011/04/27Apple-Q-A-on-Location-Data.html.

18. **Gross, Doug.** The growing push to track your location indoors. [Online] CNN, March 26, 2013. http://www.cnn.com/2013/03/25/tech/mobile/apple-indoor-gps/index.html.

19. **Kopytoff, Verne.** Stores Sniff Out Smartphones to Follow Shoppers. [Online] MIT Technology Review, November 12, 2013. http://www.technologyreview.com/news/520811/stores-sniff-out-smartphones-to-follow-shoppers/.

20. **Davis, Wendy.** Apple Moves To Stop Location-Tracking By Mobile Analytics Companies. [Online] Online Media Daily, June 9, 2014. http://www.mediapost.com/publications/article/227587/apple-moves-to-stop-location-tracking-by-mobile-an.html.

21. **Ranger, Steve.** What is Apple iBeacon? Here's what you need to know. [Online] ZDNet, June 10, 2014. http://www.zdnet.com/what-is-apple-ibeacon-heres-what-you-need-to-know-7000030109/.

22. **Kravets, David.** Researcher's Video Shows Secret Software on Millions of Phones Logging Everything. [Online] Wired, November 29, 2011. http://www.wired.com/threatlevel/2011/11/secret-software-logging-video/.

23. **Eckhart, Trevor.** Carrier IQ Part #2. [Online] Trevor Eckhart, November 28, 2011. http://www.youtube.com/watch?v=T17XQI_AYNo.

24. **Goldman, David.** Carrier IQ: 'We're as surprised as you'. [Online] CNN, December 2, 2011. http://money.cnn.com/2011/12/02/technology/carrier_iq/index.htm.

25. **Schroeder, Stan.** Understanding Carrier IQ: The Most Detailed Explanation So Far. [Online] Mashable, December 13, 2011. http://mashable.com/2011/12/13/understanding-carrier-iq/.

26. **Miller, Matthew.** Carrier IQ is good for you, so why get so spun up? [Online] ZDNet, December 2, 2011. http://www.zdnet.com/blog/cell-phones/carrier-iq-is-good-for-you-so-why-get-so-spun-up/6983.

27. **ACLU.** Cell Phone Location Tracking Public Records Request. [Online] American Civil Liberties Union, April 6, 2012. http://www.aclu.org/protecting-civil-liberties-digital-age/cell-phone-location-tracking-public-records-request.

28. **Horwitz, Sari.** Carrier IQ faces federal probe into allegations software tracks cellphone data. [Online] The Washington Post, December 14, 2011. http://www.washingtonpost.com/business/economy/feds-probing-carrier-iq/2011/12/14/gIQA9nCEuO_story.html.

29. **Popova, Maria.** Network: The Secret Life of Your Personal Data, Animated. [Online] Brain Pickings, January 10, 2012. http://www.brainpickings.org/index.php/2012/01/10/network-michael-rigley/.

30. **Rigley, Michael.** Network. [Online] Michael Rigley, January 8, 2012. http://vimeo.com/34750078.

31. **Cauley, Leslie.** NSA has massive database of Americans' phone calls. [Online] USA Today, May 11, 2006. http://www.usatoday.com/news/washington/2006-05-10-nsa_x.htm.

32. **Goldman, David.** Your phone company is selling your personal data. [Online] CNN, November 1, 2011. http://money.cnn.com/2011/11/01/technology/verizon_att_sprint_tmobile_privacy/.

33. —. For sale: Your personal info. [Online] CNNMoney, February 26, 2013. http://money.cnn.com/2013/02/26/technology/mobile/smartphone-personal-information/.

34. **Knight, Kristina.** Expert Advice: Be more transparent with data collection practices. [Online] BizReport, December 29, 2011. http://www.bizreport.com/2011/12/expert-advice-be-more-transparent-with-data-collection-pract.html.

35. **Censky, Annalyn.** Malls track shoppers' cell phones on Black Friday. [Online] CNN, November 22, 2011. http://money.cnn.com/2011/11/22/technology/malls_track_cell_phones_black_friday/index.htm.

36. —. Malls stop tracking shoppers' cell phones. [Online] CNN, November 28, 2011. http://money.cnn.com/2011/11/28/news/economy/malls_track_shoppers_cell_phones/index.htm.

37. **Schumer, Charles E.** Schumer Reveals: This Holiday Season, New Technology Could Be Tracking Shoppers' Movements In Shopping Centers Through Their Cell Phones; Calls For Mandatory Opt-In Before Retailers Are Allowed To Track Shoppers' Movements. [Online] U.S. Senate, November 28, 2011. http://schumer.senate.gov/Newsroom/record.cfm?id=334975.

38. **Dostal, Erin.** Neiman Marcus hosts bigger foursquare challenge. [Online] Direct Marketing News, March 29, 2012. http://www.dmnews.com/neiman-marcus-hosts-bigger-foursquare-challenge/article/234277/.

39. **Patel, Kunur.** At Walgreens, a Mobile Check-in Acts Like a Circular. [Online] Advertising Age, February 8, 2012. http://adage.com/article/digital/walgreens-a-mobile-check-acts-a-circular/232584/.

40. **Keen, Andrew.** How our mobiles became Frankenstein's monster. [Online] CNN, February 28, 2012. http://www.cnn.com/2012/02/28/opinion/mobile-frankenstein-keen/index.html.

41. The Instagram Team. We're the 2011 App Store iPhone App of the Year! [Online] Instagram, December 8, 2011. http://blog.instagram.com/post/13928169232/were-the-2011-app-store-iphone-app-of-the-year.

42. **Dreyfuss, Emily.** iPhone users: Android is ruining our Instagram club. [Online] CNet, April 4, 2012. http://news.cnet.com/8301-1035_3-57409388-94/iphone-users-android-is-ruining-our-instagram-club/.

43. **Enberg, Jasmine.** Global Instagram Users 2020: The Pandemic Propels Worldwide User Base to 1.00 Billion for the First Time. [Online] eMarketer, December 8, 2020. https://www.emarketer.com/content/global-instagram-users-2020.

44. **Hamburger, Ellis.** Instagram announces Instagram Direct for private photo, video, and text messaging. [Online] The Verge, December 12, 2013. http://www.theverge.com/2013/12/12/5203302/instagram-direct-photo-text-messaging.

45. **Dress, Ed and Hairston, Harry.** Rider Jams Cell Phones on SEPTA Buses. [Online] NBC10 Philadelphia, March 5, 2012. http://www.nbcphiladelphia.com/news/local/Rider-Annoyed-by-Calls-Jams-Phones-on-Septa-Bus-140966733.html.

46. **Gross, Doug.** Why the interest in illegal cell-phone jammers? [Online] CNN, March 6, 2012. http://www.cnn.com/2012/03/05/tech/mobile/cell-phone-jammer/index.html.

47. **Greene, Bob.** Time for a new kind of phone booth. [Online] CNN, March 24, 2012. http://www.cnn.com/2012/03/24/opinion/greene-phone-booths/index.html.

48. **Path.** About Path. [Online] Path. [Cited: February 14, 2012.] https://path.com/about.

49. **Thampi, Arun.** Path uploads your entire iPhone address book to its servers. [Online] McLovin, February 8, 2012. http://mclov.in/2012/02/08/path-uploads-your-entire-address-book-to-their-servers.html.

50. **Morin, Dave.** We are sory. [Online] Path Blog, February 8, 2012. http://blog.path.com/post/17274932484/we-are-sorry.

51. **Sarno, David.** Twitter stores full iPhone contact list for 18 months, after scan. [Online] Los Angeles Times, February 14, 2012. http://www.latimes.com/business/technology/la-fi-tn-twitter-contacts-20120214,0,5579919.story.

52. **Whittaker, Zack.** Facebook, Flickr, others accused of reading text messages. [Online] ZDNet, February 26, 2012. http://www.zdnet.com/blog/btl/facebook-flickr-others-accused-of-reading-text-messages/70237.

53. **Redfern, Joff.** More about our mobile calendar feature. [Online] LinkedIn, June 6, 2012. http://blog.linkedin.com/2012/06/06/mobile-calendar-feature/.

54. **Weintraub, Seth.** Apple's iOS problem: Contacts uploading is just the tip of the iceberg. Apps can upload all your photos, calendars or record conversations. [Online] 9to5Mac: Apple Intelligence, February 15, 2012. http://9to5mac.com/2012/02/15/apples-ios-problem-contacts-uploading-is-just-the-tip-of-the-iceberg-apps-can-upload-all-your-photos-calendars-or-record-conversations/.

55. **Chen, Brian X. and Bilton, Nick.** Et Tu, Google? Android Apps Can Also Secretly Copy Photos. [Online] The New York Times, March 1, 2012. http://bits.blogs.nytimes.com/2012/03/01/android-photos/?pagewanted=all.

56. **Gahran, Amy.** Parents need more privacy info about kids' apps, feds say. [Online] CNN, February 21, 2012. http://www.cnn.com/2012/02/21/tech/mobile/privacy-info-kids-apps/index.html.

57. **Federal Trade Commission.** Mobile Apps Developer Settles FTC Charges It Violated Children's Privacy Rule. [Online] Federal Trade Commission News, August 15, 2011. http://ftc.gov/opa/2011/08/w3mobileapps.shtm.

58. —. FTC Report Raises Privacy Questions About Mobile Applications for Children. [Online] Federal Trade Commission News, February 16, 2012. http://ftc.gov/opa/2012/02/mobileapps_kids.shtm.

59. —. Mobile Apps for Kids: Current Privacy Disclosures are Disappointing. [Online] Federal Trade Commission Staff Report, February 2012. http://www.ftc.gov/os/2012/02/120216mobile_apps_kids.pdf.

60. **Rideout, Victoria.** Zero to Eight. Children's Media use in American 2013. [Online] Common Sense Media, Fall 2013. http://www.commonsensemedia.org/sites/default/files/research/zero-to-eight-2013.pdf.

61. **White House Office of the Press Secretary.** President Obama Unveils ConnectED Initiative to Bring America's Students into Digital Age. [Online] The White House, June 6, 2013. http://www.whitehouse.gov/the-press-office/2013/06/06/president-obama-unveils-connected-initiative-bring-america-s-students-di.

62. **Reilly, Byrne.** Microsoft teams with Obama, gives $1B to help set up public school kids with mobile devices. [Online] VentureBeat, April 29, 2014. http://venturebeat.com/2014/04/29/microsoft-teams-with-obama-gives-1b-to-help-set-up-public-school-kids-with-mobile-devices/.

63. **Barra, Hugo.** Android: momentum, mobile and more at Google I/O. [Online] Google Blog, May 10, 2011. http://googleblog.blogspot.com/2011/05/android-momentum-mobile-and-more-at.html.

64. **Melanson, Donald.** Google announces Q3 earnings: $9.72 billion in revenue, $2.73 billion net income, 40 million Google+ users. [Online] Engadget, October 13, 2011. http://www.engadget.com/2011/10/13/google-announces-q3-earnings-9-72-billion-revenue/.

65. **Panzarino, Matthew.** Android Market hits 10B apps downloaded, now at 53 apps per device, 10c app sale to celebrate. [Online] The Next Web, December 6, 2011. http://thenextweb.com/google/2011/12/06/android-market-hits-10b-apps-downloaded-now-at-1b-a-month-10c-app-sale-to-celebrate/.

66. **AppBrain.** Number of Android applications. [Online] AppBrain Stats. [Cited: April 25, 2021.] http://www.appbrain.com/stats/number-of-android-apps.

67. **Vaughan-Nichols, Steven J.** Google needs to clean up its Android Market malware mess. [Online] ZDNet, July 12, 2011. http://www.zdnet.com/blog/open-source/google-needs-to-clean-up-its-android-market-malware-mess/9219.

68. **Gingrich, Aaron.** The Mother Of All Android Malware Has Arrived: Stolen Apps Released To The Market That Root Your Phone, Steal Your Data, And Open Backdoor. [Online] Android Police, March 6, 2011. http://www.androidpolice.com/2011/03/01/the-mother-of-all-android-malware-has-arrived-stolen-apps-released-to-the-market-that-root-your-phone-steal-your-data-and-open-backdoor/.

69. **Chen, Brian X.** Google's 'Bouncer' Service Aims to Toughen Android Security. [Online] The New York Times, February 3, 2012. http://bits.blogs.nytimes.com/2012/02/03/google-bouncer-android/.

70. **Lockheimer, Hiroshi.** Android and Security. [Online] Google Mobile Blog, February 2, 2012. http://googlemobile.blogspot.com/2012/02/android-and-security.html.

71. **Lutz, Zachary.** Google Play replaces Android Market, new source for apps, books, movies and music (video). [Online] Engadget, March 6, 2012. http://www.engadget.com/2012/03/06/google-play-replaces-android-market/.

72. **App Annie.** App Annie Index -- Market Q1 2014: Revenue Soars in the United States and China. [Online] App Annie, April 15, 2014. http://blog.appannie.com/app-annie-index-market-q1-2014/.

73. **Apple.** Apple App Store. [Online] Apple. [Cited: February 20, 2012.] http://www.apple.com/ipodtouch/from-the-app-store/.

74. **Warren, Christina.** Apple: 100 Million iPhones Sold. [Online] Mashable, March 2, 2011. http://mashable.com/2011/03/02/100-million-iphones/.

75. **Elmer-DeWitt, Philip.** Apple users buying 61% more apps, paying 14% more per app. [Online] CNN, July 11, 2011. http://tech.fortune.cnn.com/2011/07/11/apple-users-buying-61-more-apps-paying-14-more-per-app/.

76. **Bonnington, Christina.** iOS Apps Generate 6 Times the Revenue of Android Apps. [Online] Wired, December 22, 2011. http://www.wired.com/2011/12/ios-revenues-vs-android/.

77. **Griggs, Brandon and Gross, Doug.** Apple announces high-res laptops, a smarter Siri. [Online] CNN, June 11, 2012. http://www.cnn.com/2012/06/11/tech/innovation/apple-wwdc-keynote/index.html.

78. **Ingraham, Nathan.** Apple announces 1 million apps in the App Store, more than 1 billion songs played on iTunes radio. [Online] The Verge, October 22, 2013. http://www.theverge.com/2013/10/22/4866302/apple-announces-1-million-apps-in-the-app-store.

79. **Pepitone, Julianne.** Fake Pokemon app becomes Apple App Store bestseller. [Online] CNN, February 21, 2012. http://money.cnn.com/2012/02/21/technology/pokemon_yellow/index.htm.

80. **Goldman, David.** A look behind Apple's App Store curtain. [Online] CNNMoney, April 27, 2012. http://money.cnn.com/2012/04/27/technology/carriercompare-apple/index.htm.

81. **Gross, Doug.** Apple: Apps need 'explicit approval' before collecting user contacts. [Online] CNN, February 15, 2012. http://www.cnn.com/2012/02/15/tech/mobile/apple-user-contacts/index.html.

82. **Griggs, Brandon.** Apple's App Store hits 50 billion downloads. [Online] CNN, May 15, 2013. http://www.cnn.com/2013/05/14/tech/web/itunes-50-billion/index.html.

83. **Perez, Sarah.** App stores saw record 204 billion app downloads in 2019, consumer spend of $120 billion. [Online] TechCrunch, January 15, 2020. https://techcrunch.com/2020/01/15/app-stores-saw-record-204-billion-app-downloads-in-2019-consumer-spend-of-120-billion/.

84. **Brady, Aaron.** Introducing the App Center. [Online] Facebook Developers, May 9, 2012. https://developers.facebook.com/blog/post/2012/05/09/introducing-the-app-center/.

85. **Wyndowe, Matt.** App Center: A New Place to Find Social Apps. [Online] Facebook Newsroom, June 7, 2012. http://newsroom.fb.com/News/App-Center-A-New-Place-to-Find-Social-Apps-175.aspx.

86. **Facebook.** What does an app do with my information? [Online] Facebook Help Center. [Cited: May 10, 2012.] http://www.facebook.com/help/?faq=187333441316612.

87. **Segall, Laurie.** Facebook halts phone number sharing feature. [Online] CNNMoney, January 18, 2011. http://money.cnn.com/2011/01/18/technology/facebook_privacy/index.htm.

Chapter 4
Privacy Breaches

"Quite simply, it was a mistake."
– Google's Senior VP Alan Eustace (May 2010)

"This is a bug, which we plan to fix shortly."
– Apple Press Info (April 2011)

"We are sorry. We made a mistake."
– Path co-founder and CEO Dave Morin (February 2012)

"There are only two types of companies: those that have been hacked, and those that will be. Even that is merging into one category: those that have been hacked and will be again."
— FBI Director Robert Mueller (March 2012)

"It wasn't secret, nobody leaked it; it was not a big secret."
– Columbia University Prof. John Dinges (May 2013)

"We're focused on protecting people's data by working to get this data set taken down and will continue to aggressively go after malicious actors who misuse our tools wherever possible. While we can't always prevent data sets like these from recirculating or new ones from appearing, we have a dedicated team focused on this work."
– Facebook Product Management Director Mike Clark
(April 2021)

4.1 Facebook's Massive Data Breaches

In April 2021, cybercriminals posted online the personal information of 533 million Facebook users from 106 countries, including 32 million in the U.S., 11 million in the U.K., and 6 million in India (1). The leaked personal data includes full names, locations, birthdates, relationship statuses, phone numbers, and in some cases email addresses.

Facebook spokesperson Andy Stone said in response, "This is old data that was previously reported on in 2019. We found and fixed this issue in August 2019. In 2019, we removed people's ability to directly find others using their phone number across both Facebook and Instagram—a function that could be exploited using

© Springer Science+Business Media, LLC, part of Springer Nature 2021
N. Lee, *Facebook Nation*, https://doi.org/10.1007/978-1-0716-1867-7_4

sophisticated software code, to imitate Facebook and provide a phone number to find which users it belonged to" (2). His answer does not exactly instill confidence in Facebook's ability to safeguard personal information. It offers little consolation to victims of identity theft.

When Facebook CEO Mark Zuckerberg faced U.S. Congress for the first time on April 10, 2018 over the Cambridge Analytica data sharing scandal, Senator Cory Gardner asked him, "Has Facebook ever been hacked?" Zuckerberg replied, "Yes, but not that seriously" (3). He spoke too soon. Facebook has suffered serious data breaches since April 2018:

1. In October 2018, Facebook confirmed that hackers had compromised access tokens and virtually all personal data from about 30 million Facebook users by exploiting software bugs (4).
2. In April 2019, security firm UpGuard reported that 540 million records—including Facebook IDs, comments, likes, and reaction data—were exposed by Mexico-based media company Cultura Colectiva (5).
3. In September 2019, TechCrunch found more than 419 million phone numbers linked to Facebook accounts over several databases on Facebook users globally, including 133 million records on U.S.-based users, 18 million in the U.K., and more than 50 million in Vietnam (6).
4. In April 2021, cybercriminals posted online the personal information of 533 million Facebook users from 106 countries, including 32 million in the U.S., 11 million in the U.K., and 6 million in India (1). It was alarming, but not surprising. At the 2012 RSA conference in San Francisco, Federal Bureau of Investigation (FBI) director Robert Mueller said, "There are only two types of companies: those that have been hacked, and those that will be. Even that is merging into one category: those that have been hacked and will be again" (7). Facebook has decided not to notify any of the 533 million users exposed in an online database (8) but released a statement: "We're focused on protecting people's data by working to get this data set taken down and will continue to aggressively go after malicious actors who misuse our tools wherever possible. While we can't always prevent data sets like these from recirculating or new ones from appearing, we have a dedicated team focused on this work" (9).

Therefore, it is up to individual Facebook users to determine if their personal information has been compromised. The website https://haveibeenpwned.com/ allows any person to check if their email address or phone number has been exposed in a known data breach. Figure 4.1 shows the total number of pwned accounts as well as the largest and most recently added data breaches.

4.2   Google Street View

Google Street View is a great service in conjunction with online maps and driving directions (10). It allows Google Map users explore places through 360-degree panoramic street-level imagery. It is handy for planning a trip to a new restaurant or an

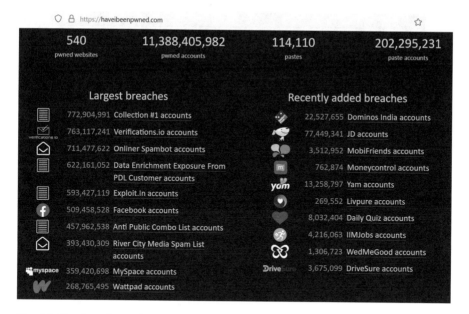

Fig. 4.1 Number of pwned accounts, largest breaches, and recently added breaches (as of June 5, 2021)

unfamiliar neighborhood. Since 2007, Google has employed Street View cars, trikes, snowmobiles, and trolleys to take pictures in the streets, national parks, university campuses, sports stadiums, and museums around the world (11). (See Fig. 4.2).

Many of the pictures taken contain unsuspecting individuals and private vehicles that happened to be in the right place at the right time (or in the wrong place at the wrong time depending on our point of view). Nevertheless, useful information for the millions outweighs the privacy of the few. It would be impractical for a moving Google Street View car to issue a privacy warning such as: "By your presence in this area, you acknowledge that you have been informed that you may be photographed as part of the Google Street View. Further, by your presence here, you grant your irrevocable permission for your likeness and mannerisms to be included in the Google Street View without compensation and/or credit, and for such data to be exploited in any and all media worldwide in all perpetuity. If you do not wish to be photographed or appear in the Google Street View, please leave this immediate area. Thank you for your cooperation."

Such a warning would have changed some destinies of life. In Russia, the faces of anyone caught in Yandex Street View are not blurred. In February 2013, Marina Voinova was looking at a panoramic view of an area on Yandex Maps only to find her fiancé Sasha canoodling with another woman. Voinova broke up with Sasha and opted for online dating instead (12).

Unlike Yandex, Google Maps intentionally blurs the individual faces and license plates caught in Street View. That was perfectly fine until April 2010 when the Data

Fig. 4.2   A Google Street View Car – Courtesy of Enrique Bosquet http://bosquetphotography.com/

Protection Authority (DPA) in Hamburg, Germany raised concerns about exactly what information Google Street View cars collected as they drove the streets (13).

At first, Google confirmed taking photos, WiFi network information, and 3-D building imagery, but denied collecting any payload data sent over the WiFi networks. However, in May 2010, Google made a stunning admission that for over three years, its camera-toting Street View cars have inadvertently collected snippets of private information that people send over unencrypted WiFi networks (14). In October 2010, Google admitted to accidentally collecting and storing entire e-mails, URLs, and passwords from unsecured WiFi networks with its Street View cars in more than 30 countries, including the United States, Canada, Mexico, some of Europe, and parts of Asia (15). Alan Eustace, Google's senior vice president of engineering and research, wrote in the Google Public Policy Blog, "It's clear from those inspections that while most of the data is fragmentary, in some instances entire emails and URLs were captured, as well as passwords. We want to delete this data as soon as possible, and I would like to apologize again for the fact that we collected it in the first place" (16).

In March 2013, Google agreed to pay 37 states a total of $7 million to settle complaints that its Street View cars violated people's privacy (17). In December 2013, Spain ordered Google to pay a fine of 900,000 euros ($1.23 million) over privacy violations in "unlawfully collecting and processing personal information"

(18). Google blamed its mistakes on software bugs. Were they really bugs or were they company-sanctioned Easter eggs?

4.3   Google Easter Eggs in Disguise

Software based Easter eggs are intentionally hidden messages or unusual program behaviors that occur in response to some user inputs or external factors. Easter eggs are normally harmless and humorous. *The Easter Egg Archive*, www.eeggs.com, uncovers many instances of Easter eggs (19).

Google is well known for Easter eggs. If we search for the words "zerg rush" in Google, an army of O's would descend on the page, devour each search result one by one, and form the red/golden letters "GG" (Good Game) no matter how hard we manage to click on some O's to eradicate them (20). In Google Earth, for another example, flying to the coordinates 44°14′39.35″N 7°46′11.53″E surprisingly reveals a pink bunny rabbit overlaid on the Satellite map. (See Fig. 4.3).

However, some software Easter eggs are more like a variant of Trojan horse, worms, adware, or spyware. Anti-virus software is useless against them because they are not malware per se, but they hide secret functionalities from their users. Indeed, uncovered Easter eggs are often disguised as software bugs by their makers.

Let us examine Google's Street View privacy blunder. Google wrote in its official blog on May 14, 2010: "… It's now clear that we have been mistakenly collecting

Fig. 4.3 An Easter egg on Google Earth. Courtesy of Google and Tele Atlas.

samples of payload data from open (i.e. non-password-protected) WiFi networks, even though we never used that data in any Google products. However, we will typically have collected only fragments of payload data because: our cars are on the move; someone would need to be using the network as a car passed by; and our in-car WiFi equipment automatically changes channels roughly five times a second. ... So how did this happen? <u>Quite simply, it was a mistake.</u> In 2006 an engineer working on an experimental WiFi project wrote a piece of code that sampled all categories of publicly broadcast WiFi data. A year later, when our mobile team started a project to collect basic WiFi network data like SSID information and MAC addresses using Google's Street View cars, <u>they included that code in their software—although the project leaders did not want, and had no intention of using, payload data</u>" (21).

It is a common software engineering practice to reuse pieces of software code from other projects in order to expedite the development of the current project. Repurposing well-written and thoroughly tested codes generally improves system performance and reduces software bugs. Nevertheless, no trained engineer would blindly reuse a piece of software code without reading its functional specification, examining its inline documentation, and performing unit testing. Google engineers are some of the world's brightest and most experienced software developers who pride themselves in writing efficient and clean code. It is mind-blogging to imagine that the Google engineers would leave extra and unnecessary code in the software by mistake, and the software ends up consuming more CPU cycles and taking up more data storage.

To read between the lines of the Google blog, "<u>although the project leaders did not want</u>" does not necessarily mean that "the upper management at Google did not want." Moreover, "<u>quite simply, it was a mistake</u>" might have meant, "quite simply, it was a mistake to get caught."

Five months later after the initial discovery, Google wrote in its official blog on October 22, 2010: "... Finally, I would like to take this opportunity to update one point in my May blog post. When I wrote it, <u>no one inside Google had analyzed in detail the data we had mistakenly collected,</u> so we did not know for sure what the disks contained. Since then a number of external regulators have inspected the data as part of their investigations (seven of which have now been concluded). It's clear from those inspections that while most of the data is fragmentary, in some instances entire emails and URLs were captured, as well as passwords. <u>We want to delete this data as soon as possible, and I would like to apologize again for the fact that we collected it in the first place.</u> We are mortified by what happened, but confident that these changes to our processes and structure will significantly improve our internal privacy and security practices for the benefit of all our users" (16).

Google admitted, "<u>no one inside Google had analyzed in detail the data we had mistakenly collected</u>" and yet they knew with certainty that "an engineer working on an experimental WiFi project wrote a piece of code that sampled all categories of publicly broadcast WiFi data." It is unfathomable that no one inside Google cared to examine the code or at least talk to the engineer who wrote the code in order to determine what type of data could have been collected.

In April 2012, the Federal Communications Commission delivered a subpoena to the Google software engineer who developed the code for downloading information from the WiFi routers. However, Engineer Doe invoked his Fifth Amendment right to avoid self-incrimination. As a result, the FCC conceded that "significant factual questions … cannot be answered" (22).

Google released the FCC order document after Consumer Watchdog filed a Freedom of Information Act request for an uncensored version with the FCC. The document reveals, "As early as 2007 or 2008, Street View team members had wide access to Engineer Doe's design document and code in which the plan to intercept 'payload data' was spelled out. One engineer reviewed the code line by line, five engineers pushed the code into Street View cars and Engineer Doe specifically told two engineers working on the project, including a senior manager about collecting 'payload data'" (23).

Google's code of conduct is "Don't be evil" (24). It only makes sense to expect Google to practice what it preaches, and to come clean about its engineers and managers.

4.4   Apple Software Bugs

Apple's infamous "goto fail" bug (see Fig. 4.4) caused the improper validation of SLL certificates on OS X and iOS (25). It was a genuine mistake. But back in 2008, some users had noticed Apple's Trojan app installer that sneaked in the Safari app installation during iTunes and QuickTime software upgrade (26). It did not create

```
        hashOut.data = hashes + SSL_MD5_DIGEST_LEN;
    hashOut.length = SSL_SHA1_DIGEST_LEN;
    if ((err = SSLFreeBuffer(&hashCtx)) != 0)
        goto fail;

    if ((err = ReadyHash(&SSLHashSHA1, &hashCtx)) != 0)
        goto fail;
    if ((err = SSLHashSHA1.update(&hashCtx, &clientRandom)) != 0)
        goto fail;
    if ((err = SSLHashSHA1.update(&hashCtx, &serverRandom)) != 0)
        goto fail;
    if ((err = SSLHashSHA1.update(&hashCtx, &signedParams)) != 0)
        goto fail;
        goto fail;
    if ((err = SSLHashSHA1.final(&hashCtx, &hashOut)) != 0)
        goto fail;

    err = sslRawVerify(ctx,
                        ctx->peerPubKey,
                        dataToSign,                      /* plaintext */
                        dataToSignLen,              /* plaintext length */
                        signature,
-uu-:---F1  sslKeyExchange.c   30% L602   (C/l Abbrev Isearch)-------------
I-search: goto fail
```

Fig. 4.4 Apple's "goto fail" Bug

much attention, unlike the 2011 discovery of the Apple iPhone location tracking app that secretly stores up to a year's worth of location data on the users' iPhones.

Apple addressed the location data issue on its company website on April 27, 2011 (27):

Question: People have identified up to a year's worth of location data being stored on the iPhone. Why does my iPhone need so much data in order to assist it in finding my location today?

Answer: This data is not the iPhone's location data—it is a subset (cache) of the crowdsourced Wi-Fi hotspot and cell tower database which is downloaded from Apple into the iPhone to assist the iPhone in rapidly and accurately calculating location. The reason the iPhone stores so much data is a bug we uncovered and plan to fix shortly (see Software Update section below). We don't think the iPhone needs to store more than seven days of this data.

Question: When I turn off Location Services, why does my iPhone sometimes continue updating its Wi-Fi and cell tower data from Apple's crowdsourced database?

Answer: It shouldn't. This is a bug, which we plan to fix shortly (see Software Update section below)."

Dissecting Apple's official answers unveils the following suspicions about Apple's real intentions:

1. The iPhone location tracking app was to store at least seven days of location data. But the more the better.
2. Even with Location Services turned off, the tracking app was to continue to perform its function at least sporadically.
3. The twice-repeated statement "this is a bug which we plan to fix shortly" does not connote the same urgency as something along the line "this is a bug which we are working on fixing."

Apple is a company renowned for combining art and science in the creation of innovative products. Apple's zealous engineers and rigorous quality assurance would have easily discovered such an obvious "bug."

Simon Davies, director of Privacy International, said about the iPhone location tracking app: "This is a worrying discovery. Location is one of the most sensitive elements in anyone's life … The existence of that data creates a real threat to privacy. The absence of notice to users or any control option can only stem from an ignorance about privacy at the design stage" (28).

4.5   Facebook User Tracking Bug and Online Behavioral Tracking

Several lawsuits were filed in February 2012 against Facebook for tracking its users even after they have logged out of the service (29). Computer blogger Nik Cubrilovic explained, "Even if you are logged out, Facebook still knows and can track every page you visit that has Facebook integrated. The only solution is to delete every Facebook cookie in your browser, or to use a separate browser for Facebook interactions" (30). Facebook engineers have issued numerous fixes but none to the complete satisfaction of privacy advocates.

In June 2014, Facebook announced changes to its privacy and advertising policies, extending its ability to track users after they log out of Facebook. In other words, Facebook has turned the user tracking bug into a data mining feature for advertisers. Furthermore, the "Do Not Track" setting in a web browser has no effect on Facebook. "Today, we learn about your interests primarily from the things you do on Facebook, such as Pages you like," a Facebook blog read. "Starting soon in the US, we will also include information from some of the websites and apps you use. This is a type of interest-based advertising, and many companies already do this" (31).

To opt out of online behavioral advertising by Facebook and other participating companies, author and blogger Violet Blue provided the step-by-step instructions on *ZDNet* (32):

1. Bookmark the Digital Advertising Alliance (http://www.aboutads.info/choices/), because you're going to visit it more than once.
2. Pick a browser that you don't use regularly. This is your new Facebook browser. In that browser, go to the Digital Advertising Alliance and opt-out of Facebook, etc.
3. Sign out of Facebook on your regular browser. Clear all your cookies. Go to the Digital Advertising Alliance and opt out of Facebook, etc.
4. You must have cookies on to opt out: If you're using AdBlock Plus, you need to turn it off before you can opt out.
5. You'll need to opt out for every browser, and you'll have to opt out again every time you clear your cookies.
6. For mobile, opt out on your device:

    a. Apple: Open iPhone Settings and go to General > Restrictions > Advertising, and then click "Limit Ad Tracking."
    b. Android: Go to Google Settings > Ads > Opt Out of Interest-Based Ads, and click.
    c. Windows: Go to Settings > System Applications > Advertising ID, and opt-out by setting the Advertising ID to "Off."

4.6   Carrier IQ and Other Privacy Blunders

Joining Google and Apple's privacy blunders, Carrier IQ released a report on December 12, 2011 (33): "… Over the course of the past week, as Carrier IQ conducted extensive reviews with the Network Operators, <u>Carrier IQ has discovered an unintended bug in a diagnostic profile to measure radio-network-to-mobile device signaling</u>. This diagnostic profile is used to gather network conditions during voice calls to determine why they fail. Using these profiles, the IQ Agent collects 'layer 3' signaling traffic between the mobile device and radio tower, to help the Network Operator determine, for example, why a call might be dropped or which radio towers are communicating with a device during a voice call. Carrier IQ has discovered that, due to this bug, in some unique circumstances, such as when a user receives an SMS during a call, or during a simultaneous data session, SMS messages may have unintentionally been included in the layer 3 signaling traffic that is collected by the IQ Agent. … Our investigation of Trevor Eckhart's video indicates that location, key presses, SMS and other information appears in log files as a result of debug messages from pre-production handset manufacturer software. Specifically <u>it appears that the handset manufacturer software's debug capabilities remained 'switched on' in devices sold to consumers.</u>"

The high-profile privacy blunders have not stopped other companies from repeating the same mistakes. Path co-founder and CEO Dave Morin issued the statement on February 8, 2012: "<u>We are sorry. We made a mistake.</u> Over the last couple of days users brought to light an issue concerning how we handle your personal information on Path, specifically the transmission and storage of your phone contacts" (34). Path did not blame on software bugs but took full responsibility of its action.

It is too easy for a company to disguise questionable software behavior as Easter eggs, and use software bugs as scapegoats when they are caught. Agile software development and quality assurance testing do not allow these kinds of bugs to slip past production into the consumer's hand. More often than not, many companies intentionally inserted secret codes into their software.

In February 2012, Jonathan Mayer, a graduate student at Stanford University, demonstrated that four advertising companies, Google's DoubleClick, Vibrant Media, Media Innovation Group, and PointRoll, have been deliberately circumventing Apple Safari's privacy feature by installing temporary cookies on user devices in order to track users' behavior (35). Safari is the primary web browser on the iPhone, iPad, and Macintosh computers. The Stanford findings contradicted Google's own instructions to Safari users on how to avoid tracking.

According to a *Wall Street Journal* Research conducted by Ashkan Soltani, Google placed the tracking code within ads displayed on 29 of the top 100 most-visited U.S. websites (36). Among them are household names YouTube, AOL, *PEOPLE Magazine*, *The New York Times*, WebMD, Merriam-Webster Dictionary, Fandango.com, Match.com, TMZ, and Yellow Pages. After *The Wall Street Journal* contacted Google about these findings, Google disabled its tracking code on Safari and removed the Safari's privacy settings language from its website.

Consumer Watchdog wrote a letter to the U.S. Federal Trade Commission about Google's unfair and deceptive violation of Safari users' privacy and the company's apparent violation of the "Buzz" Consent Decree (37). "Google has clearly engaged in 'unfair and deceptive' practices," said John M. Simpson, Consumer Watchdog's privacy project director. "They have been lying about how people can protect their privacy in their instructions about how to opt out of receiving targeted advertising" (38).

Companies, big and small, have gone to great lengths and are taking chances to collect user data in order to facilitate business intelligence.

References

1. **Holmes, Aaron.** 533 million Facebook users' phone numbers and personal data have been leaked online. [Online] Insider, April 3, 2021. https://www.businessinsider.com/stolen-data-of-533-million-facebook-users-leaked-online-2021-4.
2. **O'Sullivan, Donie.** Half a billion Facebook users' information posted on hacking website, cyber experts say. [Online] CNN Business, April 5, 2021. https://www.cnn.com/2021/04/04/tech/facebook-user-info-leaked/index.html.
3. **Watson, Chloe.** The key moments from Mark Zuckerberg's testimony to Congress. [Online] The Guardian, April 11, 2018. https://www.theguardian.com/technology/2018/apr/11/mark-zuckerbergs-testimony-to-congress-the-key-moments.
4. **Newman, Lily Hay.** How Facebook Hackers Compromised 30 Million Accounts. [Online] Wired, October 12, 2018. https://www.wired.com/story/how-facebook-hackers-compromised-30-million-accounts/.
5. **UpGuard Team.** Losing Face: Two More Cases of Third-Party Facebook App Data Exposure. [Online] UpGuard, April 3, 2019. https://www.upguard.com/breaches/facebook-user-data-leak.
6. **Whittaker, Zack.** A huge database of Facebook users' phone numbers found online. [Online] TechCrunch, September 4, 2019. https://techcrunch.com/2019/09/04/facebook-phone-numbers-exposed/.
7. **Cowley, Stacy.** FBI Director: Cybercrime will eclipse terrorism. [Online] CNNMoney, March 2, 2012. http://money.cnn.com/2012/03/02/technology/fbi_cybersecurity/index.htm.
8. **Duffy, Clare.** Facebook will not notify the 533 million users exposed in online database. [Online] CNN Business, April 9, 2021. https://www.cnn.com/2021/04/09/tech/facebook-hack-user-notification/index.html.
9. **Clark, Mike.** The Facts on News Reports About Facebook Data. [Online] Facebook, April 6, 2021. https://about.fb.com/news/2021/04/facts-on-news-reports-about-facebook-data/.
10. **Google Maps.** Street View: Explore the world at street level. [Online] Google. [Cited: January 1, 2012.] http://maps.google.com/intl/en/help/maps/streetview/.
11. —. Google Cars, Trikes, & More. [Online] Google. [Cited: January 1, 2012.] http://maps.google.com/help/maps/streetview/technology/cars-trikes.html.
12. **Matyszczyk, Chris.** Unfaithful fiance exposed on Russia's Google Street View. [Online] CNet, February 20, 2013. http://www.cnet.com/news/unfaithful-fiance-exposed-on-russias-google-street-view/.
13. **Fleischer, Peter.** Data collected by Google cars. [Online] Google's European Public Policy Blog, April 27, 2010. http://googlepolicyeurope.blogspot.com/2010/04/data-collected-by-google-cars.html.
14. **Stone, Brad.** Google Says It Inadvertently Collected Personal Data. [Online] The New York Times, May 14, 2010. http://bits.blogs.nytimes.com/2010/05/14/google-admits-to-snooping-on-personal-data/.

15. **Landis, Marina.** Google admits to accidentally collecting e-mails, URLs, passwords. [Online] CNN, October 22, 2010. http://articles.cnn.com/2010-10-22/tech/google.privacy. controls_1_wifi-data-alan-eustace-google-s-street-view?_s=PM:TECH.
16. **Eustace, Alan.** Creating stronger privacy controls inside Google. [Online] Google Public Policy Blog, October 22, 2010. http://googlepublicpolicy.blogspot.com/2010/10/creating-stronger-privacy-controls.html.
17. **Isidore, Chris.** Google to pay $7 million for privacy violation. [Online] CNNMoney, March 13, 2013. http://money.cnn.com/2013/03/12/technology/google-privacy-settlement/index.html.
18. **Yan, Sophia.** Spain fines Google for breaking data law. [Online] CNNMoney, December 20, 2013. http://money.cnn.com/2013/12/20/technology/google-spain-fine/index.html.
19. **The Easter Egg Archive.** Newest Easter Eggs. [Online] The Easter Egg Archive. [Cited: August 13, 2014.] http://www.eeggs.com/.
20. **Netburn, Deborah.** Zerg Rush Easter egg and other great time wasters from Google. [Online] Los Angeles Times, April 27, 2012. http://www.latimes.com/business/technology/la-fi-tn-zerg-rush-easter-egg-google-20120427,0,5134704.story.
21. **Eustace, Alan.** WiFi data collection: An update. [Online] The Official Google Blog, May 14, 2010. http://googleblog.blogspot.com/2010/05/wifi-data-collection-update.html.
22. **Goldman, David.** Google fined $25,000 for 'willfully' stonewalling FCC. [Online] CNN, April 16, 2012. http://money.cnn.com/2012/04/16/technology/google-fcc/index.htm.
23. **Simpson, John M.** Letter to Senator Al Franken on Google Wi-Spy. [Online] Consumer Watchdog, April 30, 2012. http://www.consumerwatchdog.org/resources/ltrfranken043012.pdf.
24. **Google.** Google's Code of Conduct. [Online] Google Investor Relations, April 25, 2012. http://investor.google.com/corporate/code-of-conduct.html.
25. **McCullagh, Declan.** Apple finally fixes 'gotofail' OS X security hole. [Online] CNet, February 25, 2014. http://www.cnet.com/news/apple-finally-fixes-gotofail-os-x-security-hole/.
26. **Ashley, Mitchell.** Apple's Trojan Easter Egg – Apple Safari. [Online] Network World, March 25, 2008. http://www.networkworld.com/community/node/26291.
27. **Apple Inc.** Apple Q&A on Location Data. [Online] Apple Press Info, April 27, 2011. http://www.apple.com/pr/library/2011/04/27Apple-Q-A-on-Location-Data.html.
28. **Arthur, Charles.** iPhone keeps record of everywhere you go. [Online] The Guardian, April 20, 2011. http://www.guardian.co.uk/technology/2011/apr/20/iphone-tracking-prompts-privacy-fears.
29. **Protalinski, Emil.** Facebook faces nationwide class action tracking cookie lawsuit. [Online] ZDNet, February 29, 2012. http://www.zdnet.com/blog/facebook/facebook-faces-nationwide-class-action-tracking-cookie-lawsuit/9747.
30. **Cubrilovic, Nik.** Logging out of Facebook is not enough. [Online] New Web Order, September 25, 2011. http://nikcub.appspot.com/posts/logging-out-of-facebook-is-not-enough.
31. **Facebook.** Making Ads Better and Giving People More Control Over the Ads They See. [Online] Facebook Blog, June 12, 2014. http://newsroom.fb.com/news/2014/06/making-ads-better-and-giving-people-more-control-over-the-ads-they-see/.
32. **Blue, Violet.** Facebook turns user tracking 'bug' into data mining 'feature' for advertisers. [Online] ZDNet, June 17, 2014. http://www.zdnet.com/facebook-turns-user-tracking-bug-into-data-mining-feature-for-advertisers-7000030603/.
33. **Fisher, Dennis.** Carrier IQ Says Bug Can Cause Some SMS to Be Recorded in Coded Form. [Online] Threat Post, December 13, 2011. http://threatpost.com/en_us/blogs/carrier-iq-says-bug-can-cause-some-sms-be-recorded-coded-form-121311.
34. **Morin, Dave.** We are sory. [Online] Path Blog, February 8, 2012. http://blog.path.com/post/17274932484/we-are-sorry.
35. **Mayer, Jonathan.** Web Policy. Safari Trackers. [Online] Web Policy Blog, February 17, 2012. http://webpolicy.org/2012/02/17/safari-trackers/.
36. **Angwin, Julia and Valentino-Devries, Jennifer.** Google's iPhone Tracking. Web Giant, Others Bypassed Apple Browser Settings for Guarding Privacy.

[Online] The Wall Street Journal, February 17, 2012. http://online.wsj.com/article_email/SB10001424052970204880404577225380456599176-lMyQjAxMTAyMDEwNjExNDYyWj.html.

37. **Simpson, John M.** Google's unfair and deceptive violation of Safari users' privacy and the company's apparent violation of the "Buzz" Consent Decree. [Online] Consumer Watchdog, February 17, 2012. http://www.consumerwatchdog.org/resources/ltrleibowitz021712.pdf.

38. **Consumer Watchdog.** Stanford Study Finds Google Violated Privacy Choices, iPhone and iPads Targeted; Consumer Watchdog Says Internet Giant Lied to Users, Calls for FTC Action. [Online] The Business Journals, February 17, 2012. http://www.bizjournals.com/prnewswire/press_releases/2012/02/17/DC55442.

Part III
Business Intelligence in Social Media

Chapter 5
Business Intelligence

"Data is king at Amazon."
— Ronny Kohavi of Amazon.com (June 2004)

"We're pretty opposed to advertising. It really turns our stomachs."
— Tumblr founder and CEO David Karp (April 2010)

"I was probably being an idiot then."
— Tumblr founder and CEO David Karp (April 2012)

"There is no more B2B or B2C. There is only Human to Human (H2H)."
— PureMatter CEO Bryan Kramer (January 2014)

"They do say 'trust us' a lot. People trust Facebook because they are the only ones that have access to all of that data and they alone can tell people what the correct thing is on the platform. If the data can't be trusted, faith in Facebook is going to erode."
— Deep Focus CEO Ian Schafer (November 2016)

"That fuzzy sensation you are feeling is called RESPECT and it is well earned. Wall Street no longer dismisses your presence anymore."
— A moderator of subreddit r/wallstreetbets (January 2021)

"We are witnessing the French Revolution of Finance."
— Former White House Communications Director Anthony Scaramucci (January 2021)

5.1 French Revolution of Finance: A Tale of GameStop

In the 20th century, multi-level marketing revolutionized direct selling. In the 21st century, social media is poised to revolutionize Wall Street. Social media provides a megaphone for any individual to interact with many other like-minded individuals in real time. In January 2021, financially savvy Reddit users in subreddit r/wallstreetbets joined forces and upended Wall Street by sending the GameStop stock price sky-high and crushing short-selling hedge funds in a short span of 2 weeks

© Springer Science+Business Media, LLC, part of Springer Nature 2021
N. Lee, *Facebook Nation*, https://doi.org/10.1007/978-1-0716-1867-7_5

from January 13 to January 27 when Citron Capital and Melvin Capital closed their positions and took a 100% financial loss (1). Former White House Communications Director Anthony Scaramucci tweeted on January 27: "We are witnessing the French Revolution of Finance" (2).

Chamath Palihapitiya, Canadian-American venture capitalist and former senior executive at Facebook, briefly joined the GameStop frenzy but donated his $500,000 profits to charity. He said, "Instead of having 'idea dinners' or quiet whispered conversations amongst hedge funds in the Hamptons, these kids have the courage to do it transparently in a forum. What it proves is this retail [investor] phenomenon is here to stay" (3).

Aided by commission-free stock trading app Robinhood, WallStreetBets with more than 2 million followers has long described itself as "4chan with a Bloomberg terminal." Many millennials celebrated the WallStreetBets victory as a populist campaign against Wall Street short sellers who profit from the demise of publicly traded companies like GameStop. A moderator of subreddit r/wallstreetbets shared the sentiment in his online post, "What I think is happening is that you guys are making such an impact that these fat cats are worried that they have to get up and put in work to earn a living. That fuzzy sensation you are feeling is called RESPECT and it is well earned. Wall Street no longer dismisses your presence anymore" (3). In fact, shares of GameStop, AMC Entertainment, BlackBerry, and clothing retailer Express all jumped again in May 2021 due to a renewed push from Reddit users looking to force another short squeeze of these meme stocks (4).

The tale of GameStop demonstrates the power of social media for the public to formulate financial strategy in the open and to orchestrate financial comeback for publicly traded companies within a matter of weeks. The formidable power of social media can be both liberating and scary.

In the 20th century, multi-level marketing (MLM) revolutionized direct selling. Despite the endorsement of Robert Kiyosaki and the undeniable success of well-known MLM companies such as Amway and Avon, multi-level marketing remains controversial to this day because of its resemblance to pyramid schemes. The people in the top tiers often make an obscene amount of money whereas those in the bottom lines are more likely to make little money or worse to risk losing money.

In the 21st century, social media is poised to revolutionize Wall Street. Some retail investors on WallStreetBets have reportedly turned a $1,000 investment into a $200,000 profit in as little as two weeks whereas some others have lost all their investments overnight. The risk is high. Indeed, the roller coaster ride can be dangerous to the inexperienced investors. In June 2020, 20-year-old college student Alexander Kearns in Plainfield, Illinois committed suicide after he saw a negative balance of $730,000 on his Robinhood account without realizing that it was not the amount he owed (5).

"The mania and bubble in GameStop is going to pop and there are going to be lots and lots of retail investors who lost a fortune," said Dennis Kelleher, CEO of financial reform group Better Markets. "The question isn't if that's going to happen — the only question is when that's going to happen" (6).

Perhaps social media in finance should not encourage greed from ordinary people but it should foster a collective power to invest in something more meaningful for humanity, such as saving lives while making money.

5.2 Bitcoin, Dogecoin, and Crypto Pump-and-Dumps

Elon Musk loves to tweet about cryptocurrencies. In January 2021, Musk added #bitcoin to his Twitter bio and the price of bitcoin surged 20%. In May 2021, Musk tweeted that Tesla had abandoned plans to accept bitcoin as payment, and the price of bitcoin plunged 12% (7).

The Japanese Shiba Inu themed meme cryptocurrency "dogecoin" that began as a joke is all the more bewildering (see Fig. 5.1). A series of tweets from Elon Musk—the self-proclaimed "Dogefather"—sent dogecoin's price up 12,000% since January 2021. "Musk will undoubtedly have a sketch on cryptocurrencies that will probably go viral for days and further motivate his army of followers to try to send dogecoin to the moon," Oanda market analyst Ed Moya wrote ahead of Musk hosting Saturday Night Live (SNL) on May 9, 2021 (8). But in an unexpected turn of events, dogecoin's price plummeted 30% when Musk joked on SNL that dogecoin was indeed a hustle (9). The sell-off continued the next day as dogecoin was down 40% (10).

Since cryptocurrency exchanges are unregulated in the U.S. as of May 2021, crypto pump-and-dumps are legal. Thousands of investors on Discord groups are manipulating the crypto market. Alejandro (last name withheld for privacy reason) is the founder of FairPlay Crypto Pumps on Discord. He said, "This principle is called FOMO (Fear Of Missing Out). Once outsiders see a sudden rise in an

Fig. 5.1 Shiba Inu (courtesy of Roberto Vasarri https://commons.wikimedia.org/w/index.php?curid=5788123) vs. Dogecoin

unexpected coin, they will buy shares. Meanwhile, the members of my group will sell their shares to the outsiders for a good chunk of profit" (11). Member Thomas Hurley concurred, "The Discord server is a casino. As the saying goes, 'The house always wins,' and they're the house." However, the truth is that only investors using bots—which can buy and sell within milliseconds of a Discord announcement—make a killing. Most other investors end up losing money.

5.3   Facebook Credits, Libra, Diem, and Stablecoin

Facebook Credits was a widely used virtual currency on the Facebook platform between May 2009 and September 2013 to facilitate online purchases (12). On June 18, 2019, Facebook officially forayed into the wild wild west of cryptocurrency with the announcement of Libra that would allow users to pseudonymously buy things online and send people money. A nonprofit Libra Association was created to oversee the development of the cryptocurrency. "Success will mean that a person working abroad has a fast and simple way to send money to family back home, and a college student can pay their rent as easily as they can buy a coffee" (13).

But soon after the announcement, Facebook was forced to abandon the Libra rollout due to regulatory concerns from the U.S., Europe, and Singapore as well as the withdrawal of support from PayPal, eBay, Visa, Mastercard, and Stripe. (14, 15). In December 2020, Facebook rebranded Libra as Diem to continue the cryptocurrency development on a smaller scale (16). On May 12, 2021, the Diem Association (formerly Libra Association) announced plans for California-based Silvergate Bank to issue the U.S. dollar stablecoin that is pegged to the fiat currency. "We are committed to a payment system that is safe for consumers and businesses, makes payments faster and cheaper" (17).

5.4   Intelligent Digital Billboards

For better or worse, the digital world and the physical world are increasingly intertwined. In Steven Spielberg's futuristic movie *Minority Report* (2002), computers scan human faces and display targeted advertisements to individuals as they walk down the street.

In July 2010, some billboards in Tokyo subway stations employed cameras and face recognition software to determine the gender and age of passersby (18). The goal was to collect data on what sorts of people look at certain ads at what times of day. "The camera can distinguish a person's sex and approximate age, even if the person only walks by in front of the display, at least if he or she looks at the screen for a second," said a spokesman for the Digital Signage Promotion Project. "Companies can provide interactive advertisements which meet the interest of people who use the station at a certain time" (19).

In February 2012, a billboard in a London bus stop used facial recognition technology to determine whether a viewer was male or female, and it displayed a different advertisement depending on the gender (20). With about 90% accuracy, the Oxford Street billboard had a built-in camera that measured a viewer's facial features in order to determine the gender. Women were shown a commercial for the "Because I Am a Girl" campaign, whereas men only saw the campaign website (21).

Meanwhile in New York City, Tic Tac's new interactive Times Square billboard used augmented reality to enable passerby to view the ad through the Tic Tac Times Square app on their smartphones, and the app would insert their Facebook pictures in various ads. A manager for Tic Tac explained, "The big thing we learned from our research is that this audience is not willing to see an ad, go home and log onto their computer to learn more – they are not interested in engaging with a brand in that way. Mobile is the new medium that this group likes to engage in but it has to be fun, fresh and entertaining" (22).

These are a few of the latest hi-tech examples of businesses collecting data, engaging the audience, and selling their products in an innovative way. The billboards might save anonymous data, but not images that are personally identifiable information. If Twitter or foursquare data indicate that there is a sports game going on in the area, the billboards might show a Nike ad instead of a FedEx ad. In response to privacy concerns about billboards collecting data of passersby, Immersive Labs CEO Jason Sosa said, "If you use a service like Amazon, have a Facebook Page, or even carry a cellphone, there is data being collected about you that is a lot more personal than anything we're collecting" (23).

5.5 Data Mining: Amazon.com, Lowe's, Target, True&Co

"Data is king at Amazon," said Ronny Kohavi, then Director of Data Mining and Personalization at Amazon.com. "Clickstream and purchase data are the crown jewels at Amazon. They help us build features to personalize the Web site experience" (24). Minimizing "junk mail" while maximizing purchase opportunity, Amazon's recommendation engine has been cited by many company observers as a killer feature. The company reported a 29% sales increase to $12.83 billion during its second fiscal quarter in 2012, up from $9.9 billion during the same time in 2011. "Our mission is to delight our customers by allowing them to serendipitously discover great products," an Amazon spokesperson told *Fortune*. "We believe this happens every single day and that's our biggest metric of success" (25).

Target, the second-largest discount retailer in the United States, is another prime example. It analyzes retail transaction data and calculates not only whether a consumer was pregnant but also when her baby was due. Target uses "pregnancy prediction" to offer expectant mother store coupons tailored to her stage of pregnancy. "Our mission is to make Target the preferred shopping destination for our guests by delivering outstanding value, continuous innovation and exceptional guest experience," the company wrote in a statement to *The New York Times*. "We've developed a number of research tools that allow us to gain insights into trends and preferences within different demographic segments of our guest population" (26). Thanks to better business decision-making using data mining tools, Target's revenues grew from $44 billion in 2002 to $67 billion in 2010.

Home improvement store Lowe's announced in June 2014 that it has built a 20-foot by 20-foot "holoroom" that uses 3D augmented reality to allow customers to walk through a floor plan of their home. A crude resemblance of *Star Trek*'s holodeck, users can visualize their home improvements by moving furniture, changing floor tiles, and repainting the walls in a virtual reality setting. The holoroom becomes Lowe's data mining tool that can analyze "which products customers often place together, how people design their homes, and which region prefers which design" (27). Although holoroom's data mining approach is more transparent and less intrusive, the collected data are somewhat limited in scope.

For two years between 2002 and 2004, True&Co collected information from more than 500,000 women in order to identify over 6,000 different types of boobs. The data scientists then created a color-coded system called "True Spectrum" to help women find the most comfortable and fitting bras. "You need a bra that makes you feel like a million bucks and we've worked really hard to build this data and infrastructure to personalize this brand," said True&Co CEO Michelle Lam. "This is just the beginning of the future of shopping, and True&Co has only just scratched the surface on its goal to deliver on the perfect fit" (28).

5.6   Tumblr and Gmail: Yes to Advertisements

No matter where we are, online or offline, advertisers seem to follow us. Only time will tell if serendipity becomes zemblanity as consumers are constantly bombarded by advertisements.

Companies that were known for their anti-ad stance have succumbed to offering their customers advertisements. David Karp, founder and CEO of the microblogging platform Tumblr, uttered his famous statement in an interview with *The Los Angeles Times* in April 2010: "We're pretty opposed to advertising. It really turns our stomachs" (29). By February 2012, the self-described "accidental social network" (30) Tumblr has over 500 million page views a day, 50+ million posts a day, 40,000 requests per second, and hundreds to millions of followers for an average post with text, images, and videos (31). In April 2012, exactly two years after the famous anti-advertisement quote, Karp announced at the Ad Age Digital conference that Tumblr would start displaying ads on the users' dashboard, and that he had probably been an "idiot" to say no to advertising (32).

In addition, saying no to email spam does not necessarily mean no advertisement. In October 2007, Microsoft CEO Steve Ballmer publicly jabbed Google for "reading your emails" (33). Google defended and clarified its practice: "Ads that appear in Gmail are similar to the ads that appear next to Google search results and on content pages throughout the web. In Gmail, ads are related to the content of your messages. Our goal is to provide Gmail users with ads that are useful and relevant to their interests. … Ad targeting in Gmail is fully automated, and no humans read your email in order to target advertisements or related information. This type of automated scanning is how many email services, not just Gmail, provide features like spam filtering and spell checking" (34).

Figure 5.2 shows a real-time ad based on an outbound email in my Gmail mailbox. However, Google has curtailed its scanning practices. After being sued in California for violating wiretap laws, Google has stopped scanning student Gmail accounts for advertising purposes since April 2014 (35).

5.7   Social Ads on Facebook

Andrew Lewis, a commenter on MetaFilter, expressed his wise opinion in August 2010, "If you're not paying for something, you're not the customer; you're the product being sold" (36). Indeed, when users sign up for free accounts on Facebook, they volunteer their personal information such as their gender, birthday, education, workplace, city of residence, interests, hobbies, photos, and even private matters like relationship status.

User activities such as clicking the "like" button can appear as part of an advertisement on the Facebook pages of their friends. Social apps' auto-share feature simplifies activity sharing without the need to click on "like."

"Facebook already has more data than they are leveraging," said Rebecca Lieb, an online advertising analyst at the research firm Altimeter Group. "There are so many infinite ways to slice and dice the data Facebook currently has, that it's rather daunting. Slicing and dicing the data for the purposes of serving up advertisements is a tricky business. It can't freak people out; it has to be cost-effective; it has to be relatively easy to do at scale" (37).

A game-changing advertising platform, Facebook has done an effective job in delivering "social ads" to consumers. Social ads are "those served to users who have friends that are fans of or have interacted with the advertised brand and prominently call the relationship out" (38). Advertisers tailor messages on Facebook based on

Fig. 5.2 Gmail displays an ad in my mailbox based on the content of the email that I just sent.

demographics like age and gender, on the preferences and affinities of its users as well as those of their friends on Facebook.

Financial analyst Martin Pyykkonen at Wedge Partners said, "Facebook is highly appealing to advertisers because about two-thirds of its users fall into the coveted age demographic of 18–49. The 'Like' button option is a basic example of targeting. [It's] likely that advertisers will be able to even better target their audiences as Facebook goes deeper with integrating apps, games, movies, music" (39).

A 2011 study from the Consumer Electronics Association (CEA) indicated that 81% of social media users are using social networks to help them make purchasing decisions about consumer electronics, and 84% of them are influenced by reviews on the social media sites (40).

According to the April 2012 Nielsen report, "Global Trust in Advertising and Brand Messages," an overwhelming 92% of consumers around the world trust recommendations from friends and family above all other forms of advertising, and 70% of them believe in consumer opinions posted online (41).

The CEA and Nielsen reports have validated the growing trend that more businesses are using Facebook, Twitter, or other social networks to communicate with and advertise to consumers. "Social media now is not an option, it's a necessity," opined Anthony DeRosa, social-media editor at Reuters. "A couple of years ago that wasn't the case, but I think now people have to be a part of it, whether it's one social network or a couple of them" (42).

On the contrary, a 2011 report from Forrester Research analyst Sucharita Mulpuru painted a not-so-rosy picture. It showed that 68% of U.S. retailers said if Facebook went away, it would not hurt their online sales. While 77% said the top benefits of Facebook are brand building, only 1% said it helped them get new customers. In fact, Gamestop, Gap, J.C. Penney, and Nordstrom have all opened and closed their storefronts on Facebook. The report stated, "In the history of retail, there has probably been nothing that has been so widely anticipated yet underwhelming as the 'era of social commerce'" (43). And Mulpuru said in a follow-up interview, "There was a lot of anticipation that Facebook would turn into a new destination, a store, a place where people would shop, but it was like trying to sell stuff to people while they're hanging out with their friends at the bar" (44).

The LIM College National Retail Federation Student Association released in January 2012 the result of a poll of shopping trends among 18 to 25 years olds (45). The poll indicated that shoppers in this age group will "like" a brand on Facebook but would not go any further. In fact, more than 88% said they do not want to shop through Facebook or Twitter.

In May 2012, General Motors announced that it would stop paid advertising on Facebook after having already spent $10 million, because the social media paid ads were not delivering the hoped-for buyers (46). On the contrary, spokeswoman Kelli Felker from GM's rival Ford Motor Company said, "We've found Facebook ads to be very effective when strategically combined with engagement, great content and innovative ways of storytelling" (47).

The conflicting reports point to the significance of social ads on one hand and downplay the effectiveness of social ads on the other hand, which can be nerve-wracking for Facebook. Advertising accounted for an overwhelming 85% of Facebook's 2011 revenue of $3.7 billion (48), which amounted to nearly $3.2 billion (49). Globally, marketers spent $84.8 billion on web advertisements in 2011, and the U.S. digital advertising expenditures amounted to $32.2 billion (50). Facebook raked in a respectable 10% of the total U.S. online advertisement revenue in 2011. To continue the momentum, Facebook had to do something more than just leveraging the "like" button and social app auto-share. By the end of 2019, Facebook had 8 million advertisers, generating $69.7 billion from advertising representing 98% of its total revenue for the year (51).

5.8 News Feed, Sponsored Stories, Custom Stories, Facebook Exchange, and Marketplace

"The goal of News Feed", Facebook engineers Varun Kacholia and Minwen Ji explained, "is to show the right content to the right people at the right time whether it's from a close friend or a news source halfway across the world" (52). This goal is certainly the Holy Grail of Internet advertising.

In March 2012, Facebook suggested that its ads would no longer be "ads" but "Sponsored Stories" (53). With sponsored stories, Facebook users are delivered ads that reveal actions their friends have taken. The most common Sponsored Stories are "Page Like" stories.

Using Facebook's new tool Reach Generator, the user-engaging stories created by advertisers would show up on the fans' Facebook homepage or in their news feed on desktop or mobile. Reach Generator guarantees that advertisers can reach 75% of their fans each month and an estimated 50% of fans each week in a simple, always-on way (54). In other words, Reach Generator effectively overrides Facebook's EdgeRank algorithm designed to enhance users' experience by putting only the most relevant content in their news feeds. It appears to have confirmed some analysts' forewarning that the Facebook IPO would only make the company even more financially driven in using personal data for marketing purposes.

Back in November 2007, Facebook launched Facebook Beacon, which was an ultimately failed attempt to advertise to friends of Facebook users based on the knowledge of what purchases the users had made online. After the initial fiasco, Facebook has successfully revamped its social ads. Facebook's "like," social app auto-share, and Reach Generator are just the beginning of "targeted social advertising."

Since 2009, Facebook's measurement research team headed by Sean Bruich has been helping agencies and brands make better ads. "Ads that were rewarding tended to be pretty clear – there wasn't an overload of information," said Bruich, who conducted a 2012 study with measurement researcher Adrienne Polich on best practices for brand-page postings. "But [the] rewarding ads also seemed to connect. The information seemed meaningful" (55).

Furthermore, Facebook can capitalize on the power of "Friend Effect" by publicizing users' "likes" of advertisers on "Sponsored Stories." Researchers have shown that an overwhelming 92% of consumers around the world trust recommendations from friends and family above all other forms of advertising (41). Facebook CEO Mark Zuckerberg was quoted as saying that a trusted referral was the "Holy Grail" of advertising; and Facebook's chief operating officer Sheryl Sandberg commented that the value of a "Sponsored Story" advertisement was at least twice and up to three times the value of a standard Facebook ad without a friend endorsement (56).

In June 2012, Facebook took another giant leap forward by introducing real-time ad bidding Facebook Exchange (57). With standard Facebook ads, users were targeted based on their Facebook profiles and what pages they "liked." The Exchange enables advertisers to reach users based on their Internet browsing history. For example, a travel website can drop a cookie on a user who looks at vacation packages without making a purchase. When the user enters Facebook, advertisers can show the user travel deals on flights, hotels, car rentals, and cruises.

Facebook Exchange offers real-time advertising auctions similar to Google AdWords. An auction determines what ads will appear after a user does a search, the ad's position on the page, and the Cost Per Click (CPC) to the advertiser, among others. Marketers manage their bids and optimize performance using a demand-side platform (DSP). The DSPs with the highest bids get their ads shown to the targeted user.

In 2011, real-time bids generated $1.07 billion in display ad sales. According to global market intelligence firm IDC's projection, real-time bidding will account for about $5.08 billion to be spent on U.S. online display ads in 2015 (58).

In April 2014, Facebook quietly dropped Sponsored Stories. However, third-party apps can still post Custom Stories on Facebook using the Open Graph API (59).

In October 2016, Facebook launched Marketplace for users to discover, buy and sell items with other people in their area. "You and the seller can work out the details in any way you choose. Facebook does not facilitate the payment or delivery of items in Marketplace" (60).

5.9   Facebook for Every Phone

While some 90% of the world's population now has access to a mobile phone, the majority of the phones are not smartphones (61). For every smartphone sold in 2010, four new "dumb phones" were purchased by consumers worldwide (61). In 2013, smartphones finally overtook dumb phones sales globally (62). However, by 2017 dumb phones sales rose 5 % compared to 2 % increase for smartphones. In fact, more and more people are switching from smartphones to dumb phones in order to reduce screen time and tech addiction (63).

To reach as many people globally as possible, Facebook launched the Facebook for Every Phone mobile app in July 2011 with 20 wireless carriers in India, Germany, Indonesia, United Kingdom, Turkey, and other countries (64). The app offers a comprehensive Facebook experience with News Feed, Messenger, and Photos on more than 2,500 Java-enabled dumb phones and mobile devices. Within two years, in July 2013, Facebook for Every Phone had reached over 100 million monthly users (65).

Ran Makavy, Growth Manager at Facebook and former cofounder of Snaptu, re-launched Snaptu as Facebook for Every Phone after his company was acquired by Facebook in 2011. Makavy wrote on the *Facebook Newsroom* (65):

> "Facebook's mission is to make the world more open and connected, and Facebook For Every Phone enables people around the globe to connect to the people and things they care about most, no matter what kind of mobile device they use. Today, millions of people in developing markets like India, Indonesia and the Philippines are relying on this technology to connect with Facebook, without having to purchase a smartphone. Ultimately, Facebook for Every Phone is a fast and easy-to-use native app that works on more than 3,000 different types of feature phones from almost every handset manufacturer that exists today. These devices can cost as little as 20 US dollars."

Facebook was reportedly looking to release its own smartphone by 2013. "Mark is worried that if he doesn't create a mobile phone in the near future that Facebook will simply become an app on other mobile platforms," a Facebook employee said anonymously (66). However, Mark Zuckerberg dispelled that rumor when he spoke on stage at TechCrunch Disrupt in September 2012 that introducing a Facebook phone "wouldn't move the needle" (67). Instead, Facebook has continued to forge a mobile app enhancement and acquisition strategy.

5.10 Instagram and Mobile App Install Ads

In April 2012, Facebook took another major step towards strengthening its mobile market and growing its advertising revenue by acquiring the popular photo-sharing application Instagram for $1 billion dollars (68).

Instagram had 40 million users in April 2012 (69) and over 200 million photos in September 2011 (70). These numbers were small compared to Facebook's 900 million users in April 2012 and 140 billion photos in September 2011 (71). Nonetheless, some large businesses were early Instagram adopters. Josh Karpf, PepsiCo's digital head, told *ClickZ* in an interview, "We use Instagram to humanize the brand and take people behind the curtains. You can let them see things they wouldn't normally see, whether its photos of Drew Brees at the Super Bowl, Pepsi Max at the MLB Fan Cave, or [Nascar star] Jeff Gordon during a photo shoot. Clearly, photo-sharing is something people are into. For brands, it's a lightweight way to connect with consumers" (72).

After its acquisition by Facebook, Instagram released an update for iOS devices in June 2012 to enhance user search and Facebook integration (73). Instagram also announced its plan to improve the software to go beyond the "10-hour" window of viewable photos. "We are trying really hard to take all the data that you've put into Instagram and let you see into the past," said co-founder Kevin Systrom. "I think we need to do a better job of creating these channels and silos that allow people to learn new things about the world" (74).

An April 2012 report by the research firm Strategy Analytics revealed that in-app spending by advertisers in the U.S. and Europe is set to overtake spending on display ads on smartphones (75). A May 2012 report by comScore showed that Facebook had achieved an impressive 80.4 percent reach or 78 million visitors on smartphones in the month of March (76). Acquiring Instagram will also help Facebook in seeking a much-needed breakthrough in the mobile ad market (77).

"In 2012, we connected over a billion people and became a mobile company," declared Mark Zuckerberg in the fourth quarter and full year 2012 financial report (78). Indeed, Facebook outranked Google Maps as the most popular mobile app in the United States in 2012 according to the comScore Mobile Metrix ranking report (79).

In August 2012, Facebook unveiled mobile app install ads to allow developers to buy clicks to Android and iOS App stores. Josh Constine at *TechCrunch* gave a good example: "Ads for a new iOS-only girl's fashion game could be targeted to iOS device-carrying females 16 to 45 years old, living in Los Angeles to maximize the relevance" (80). This feature has been a cash cow for Facebook. Constine's follow-up report in June 2014 stated that "These app install ads are the key to Facebook going essentially zero revenue on mobile to earning 59 percent of its ad revenue there, or $1.3 billion in Q1 2014 alone" (81).

In December 2012, Instagram announced that it had the perpetual right to sell users' photographs to advertisers without payment, notification, or an opt-out option for the subscribers (82). Immediately, Instagram faced massive user backlash. High-profile account holders such as National Geographic suspended posting photos to the network and threatened to close their accounts (83). Instagram promptly backed down and kept some of the original language in its terms of use.

In October 2013, Instagram introduced limited advertisement via sponsored photos and sponsored videos (84). By May 2014, Taco Bell and Hollister were among the select group of 15 brands seeing promising results. Taco Bell, for instance, saw a 29% gain in ad recall for the April rollout of its breakfast menu; and the fast-food company's Instagram following jumped 45% during its month-long ad campaign (85).

Facebook-owned Instagram is expected to roll out more ads since it has inked a $40 to $100 million advertising deal with Omnicom in March 2014 (86). "[The Omnicom deal] doesn't change our advertising strategy moving forward—people will continue to see a limited number of beautiful, high-quality photos and videos from select brands who already have a strong presence on Instagram," said Jim Squires, Instagram's director of market operations (87).

5.11 Facebook Home and Parse

In April 2013, Facebook launched the "Facebook Home" app for Android (88). The new app provides an immersive Facebook experience featuring a constant stream of full-screen photos, status updates, stories, and notifications. "Today we're going to finally talk about that Facebook Phone, More accurately, we're gonna talk about how you can turn your phone into a Facebook Phone" said Mark Zuckerberg (88).

In the same month, Facebook purchased Parse to offer mobile development tools as its first paid B2B service (89). A "mobile backend as a service" startup (mBaaS) founded in 2011 by a group of seasoned Googlers and Y Combinator alums, Parse provides backend services for data storage, notifications, user management, and other cloud-based infrastructure to help software companies to create and test new apps.

In August 2013: Facebook tested new mobile features designed to help public figures interact with their fans more easily like Twitter (90). Facebook also experimented with one-click checkout for mobile shopping that would compete with PayPal, Google Wallet, Amazon Payments, and others (91).

Overall in 2013, Facebook drove more than 145 million app downloads and made nearly $900 million that year from in-app payments (92). For the first time, Facebook's annual report revealed country-by-country mobile statistics, showing well over 50% of total users accessing Facebook from mobile in Europe and parts of the Middle East (93). Germany scored the lowest at 27% whereas Sweden was the highest at 81%.

5.12 WhatsApp and Facebook Audience Network

In February 2014, Facebook announced the acquisition of the cross-platform mobile messaging app WhatsApp for a whopping $19 billion dollars – $4 billion in cash, $12 billion worth of Facebook stock, and additional $3 billion in restricted stock units granted to WhatsApp employees and founders (94). It was also amazing considering that five years prior in 2009, both Facebook and Twitter turned down WhatsApp's cofounder Brian Acton for a job (95). Zoe Wood wrote in *The Guardian* that "it turned out to be an expensive mistake for Mark Zuckerberg. A $19bn (£14bn) one to be precise" (96). Had Acton landed a job at Facebook in 2009, however, would Jan Koum's idea for WhatsApp have become a phenomenal success?

"[WhatsApp is] a great fit for us," Zuckerberg explained. "It's the most engaging app we've ever had on mobile … I think that by itself its worth more than $19 billion. There are very few services that reach half a billion people around the world" (97).

By March 2014, Facebook had over 1 billion mobile monthly active users (98) and the company profit had tripled on mobile growth (99). In April 2014, Facebook introduced a mobile opt-in feature called "Nearby Friends" that enables Facebook friends to track each other in real time using location information (100). Facebook also purchased ProtoGeo Oy, Helsinki-based maker of a fitness tracking mobile app called "Moves" (101).

At the April 2014 F8 Conference, Facebook unveiled Anonymous Login, Facebook Audience Network, FbStart, and Graph API 2.0 that target the mobile market.

The anonymous login feature allows users to sign into apps without sharing their identities and personal information contained in their Facebook accounts (102). Circumventing privacy concerns helps to eliminate the potential barrier for many users to try out new apps – a welcome news for both app developers and users.

To further encourage developers, the new version 2.0 of the Graph API comes with a two-year stability guarantee for Facebook core products (102). The FbStart program provides startups with free tools and services worth up to $30,000 from Facebook, Parse, and 11 other companies including Adobe, Appurify, Asana, BlueJeans, Desk.com, MailChimp, Proto.io, Quip, SurveyMonkey, UserTesting, and Workable (103).

Facebook's mobile monetization chief Deborh Liu introduced the new Facebook Audience Network, "We bring it all together for you so you don't have to hire a sales team to sell ads. … [Ad] formats really matter in mobile. We encourage you to work with us on native advertising" (104). Coca-Cola, The Walt Disney Company, and other big brands have begun testing the new ad network.

To summarize, Mark Zuckerberg told the audience at the 2014 F8 Conference, "The majority of our business is on mobile" (105). The question is how to grow the mobile business. In an April 2014 interview with *The New York Times*, Zuckerberg spoke of his approach to mobile: "On desktop where we grew up, the mode that made the most sense was to have a website, and to have different ways of sharing built as features within a website. So when we ported to mobile, that's where we started — this one big blue app that approximated the desktop presence. But I think on mobile, people want different things. Ease of access is so important. So is having the ability to control which things you get notifications for. And the real estate is so small. In mobile there's a big premium on creating single-purpose first-class experiences. So what we're doing with Creative Labs is basically unbundling the big blue app" (106).

In a move to show advertisers that there are second-screen alternatives to Twitter, Facebook in May 2014 introduced an audio-recognition feature that can identify what song is playing or what show or movie is on TV, making it easier for mobile Facebook users to share in real time what they are listening to or watching (107).

In June 2014, Facebook acquired Pryte, Helsinki-based technology provider that lets smartphone users download applications using temporary mobile data allowances. "The Pryte team will be an exciting addition to Facebook," Facebook stated in an email. "Their deep industry experience working with mobile operators aligns closely with the initiatives we pursue with Internet.org, to partner with operators to bring affordable Internet access to the next 5 billion people, in a profitable way" (108).

In July 2014, Facebook reported that mobile ads accounted for 62% of its ad revenue in the second quarter (109). Mobile devices are not limited to smartphones or tablets. Budweiser's "Buddy Cup" in Brazil "makes two people friends on Facebook when they clink their glasses together in a toast" (110). At Belgium's Tomorrowland music festival, attendees wrote wristbands that not only served as a ticket, but also as a way to connect with other festival attendees by sending Facebook friend requests (111).

5.13   Location-based Mobile Advertisements

In the wake of the Facebook IPO, Professor Catherine Tucker at MIT Sloan School of Management said, "Facebook is probably going to face some difficult balancing issues, in terms of meeting its new shareholders' expressed desire to exploit the data they have with the fact that if they exploit the data too much it can drag down the effectiveness of advertising" (112).

After the rocky IPO in May 2012, Facebook has been hard at work on a location-based mobile-advertising product that will enable advertisers to target users based on their whereabouts in real time. "The holy grail of advertising is finding people when they are at their closest point to making a purchase," said Colin Sebastian, an analyst with Robert W. Baird & Co. in San Francisco (113).

In June 2012, Snapette, a 500 Startups accelerator program alum, launched the first location-based shopping application Snapette 2.0 on iPhone and iPod Touch. Snapette lets shoppers share photos and comments with friends, and see what products are trending both around the corner and around the world. Fashion brands can send real-time notifications to potential customers already shopping nearby with special discounts and inside scoops on exclusive items.

"E-commerce is growing but offline is still 90 percent of sales," Snapette co-founder Sarah Paiji told *Women's Wear Daily* (*WWD*). "For the stores, we really hope that this is a great mechanism to actively drive foot traffic" (114). Snapette co-founder Jinhee Kim added, "With Snapette, retailers can reach consumers in real time and based on location. It's a unique and immediate way to showcase new merchandise and attract fashion-conscious customers shopping nearby" (115).

5.14   Business Communications on Facebook

In addition to paid advertisements, businesses are increasingly using Facebook to communicate with their customers directly. The Walt Disney Company, one of the most recognizable brands worldwide, has over 48 million "likes" on its corporate Facebook page as of August 2014 (116). Disney's *Toy Story* has more than 34 million "likes," *Pirates of the Caribbean* has over 23 million "likes," and the list goes on and on. Andy Mooney, former Chairman of Disney Consumer Products, told a reporter from *Mashable*, "Social media is fundamental to the nature of how we communicate with the fans. The tone and the content is *[sic]* more causal and insight-based and insider-based, especially for the most ardent fans of the franchises" (117).

It is an understatement to say that Disney has mastered the skill of successful social media campaigns. There are annual Disney Social Media Moms Celebrations at the Walt Disney World Resort in Orlando (118). In January 2012, Track Social awarded Disney the "Facebook Audience Growth Award" for a remarkable 17,716 new fans per day, and the "Facebook Likes Per Post Award" with a phenomenal 30,291 likes per post (119).

Nevertheless, Disney has its own share of missteps. In February 2011, Disney made public its social media ambition by acquiring Togetherville, a Facebook-like social network for children under 10 years old (120). "Togetherville is very focused on trying to really reflect what the adult community has been doing on the Web and build a real online experience that adults enjoy for kids, but do it in a safe, COPPA-compliant way," said Togetherville founder and CEO Mandeep S. Dhillon. However, a year later in March 2012, Disney shut down Togetherville social network (121).

Like Disney, any business on Facebook can reach their audiences directly and in a timely manner without relying on third-party reporters. In March 2012, for example, some advertisers decided to withdraw their ads from the popular Rush Limbaugh radio talk show (122). AOL explained their decision via a post on their corporate Facebook page: "At AOL one of our core values is that we act with integrity. We have monitored the unfolding events and have determined that Mr. Limbaugh's comments are not in line with our values. As a result we have made the decision to suspend advertising on The Rush Limbaugh Radio show" (123).

Nonetheless, Facebook businesses are not like Facebook friends. A majority of the time, social media business-consumer communication seems to be a one-way street. According to a STELLAService survey of 20 top online retailers on Facebook, their level of responsiveness to customers is less than desirable: one out of four companies ignored customer questions posted on Facebook, and five companies took more than two days to respond to a wall post. "Retailers need to realize that two days in Facebook time is like two years in real time," said Jordy Leiser, STELLAService's co-founder. "Customer questions on Facebook should be granted the same urgency as a phone call. … Brands are doing an enthusiastic job of bringing people to their [Facebook] pages, [but] I don't think they're also necessarily bringing with them a desire to be social. It's just turning into a marketing message for many companies" (124).

The lack of two-way communication online can provoke consumers' distrust and dissatisfaction towards businesses. Commerce Secretary Gary Locke once said, "Consumers must trust the Internet in order for businesses to succeed online" (125).

In January 2008, Facebook and ABC News co-sponsored a Republican and a Democratic presidential debate in New Hampshire (126). "Through this partnership, we want to extend the dialogue both before and after the debate," said Dan Rose, Facebook's vice president for business development (127). "There are debates going on at all times within Facebook," David Westin, the president of ABC News and a new Facebook member, said. "This allows us to participate in those debates, both by providing information and by learning from the users."

"Providing information (or products/services)" and "learning from the users (or customers)" are the key phrases to winning consumers' trust and satisfaction. Although there were skeptics who believed that the Facebook/ABC News partnership was a failing concept out of the gate (128), experiments like it should be encouraged in order to foster more effective two-way communication between businesses and consumers – a win-win proposition.

5.15   B2B, B2C, and H2H on Social Media

In September 2012, Facebook changed its News Feed algorithm and 72% of movies and network TV shows experienced a dramatic decline in the number of fans who see their messages. In March 2014, a food-delivery website Eat24 with over 70,000 Facebook likes announced its breakup with the social network over an argument on Facebook's algorithm and promoted posts (129). "The days of free traffic are over," said Dennis Yu, founder and chief technology officer of BlitzMetrics. "Facebook has been trying to educate marketers on how to be social — to post the most engaging content — so as not to be penalized by their algorithms" (130).

Allison Sitch, Ritz-Carlton's vice president of global public relations, voiced a concern in May 2013 when the hotel chain bought ads to promote its Facebook page. She said, "We were fearful our engagement and connection with our community was dropping as the fan base grew" (131). Emphasizing quality over quantity, Ritz-Carlton decided to spend time analyzing its social-media conversations to see what guests like and do not like. "Fans and follower counts are over. Now it's about what is social doing for you and real business objectives," said Jan Rezab, chief executive of social-media metrics company Socialbakers AS in Prague (131).

In a June 2014 Gallup report, 62% of the more than 18,000 U.S. consumers it polled said social media had no influence on their buying decisions. "Social media are not the powerful and persuasive marketing force many companies hoped they would be," Gallup concluded (132). But it is like blaming the television instead of the TV ad that is ineffective.

The social media landscape is changing so fast that businesses have to constantly keep up in order to adjust their marketing strategy and to maximize their return on investment (ROI). In January 2014, Belle Beth Cooper summarized "10 Big, Recent Changes To Twitter, Facebook, And Linkedin You Should Know About" on *Fast Company* (133). In this book, Facebook ROI experts Dennis Yu and Alex Houg of BlitzMetrics share their latest business insights in the following chapter titled "Facebook Analytics, Advertising, and Marketing."

We are seeing a new trend that the traditional business-to-business (B2B) and business-to-consumer (B2C) strategies are shifting towards a human-to-human (H2H) approach empowered by social media. PureMatter's CEO Bryan Kramer explained, "It used to be that marketing was segmented into two categories;

business-to-business (B2B) or business-to-consumer (B2C). ... The fact is that the lines are so far blurred now between the two marketing segments that it's hard to differentiate between the two anymore. We all need to think like the consumers we are, putting ourselves in the mindset of the buyer instead of trying to speak such an intensely sophisticated language full of acronyms and big words, in order to sound smarter. Marketing increasingly strives to become one-to-one, with solutions to collect and wrangle the big data about us to serve up more personalized offers and experiences. On the other hand, social has become a more public and vast medium, where the things we share skyrocket quickly to a 'one-to-many' experience. The dichotomy between marketing and social has actually flipped... and it's out of balance. Social and marketing need to work together to personalize individual conversations, as well as deliver shared global experiences that crowds of common values can benefit from. This is what our social and digital mediums have gifted us, and how humans interact and feel more compelled take action. ... There is no more B2B or B2C. There is only human to human. That is #H2H" (134).

Take, for example, the Facebook response to a grieving father's emotional plea: On February 5, 2014, John Berlin in Arnold, Missouri posted a YouTube video on Facebook saying, "I'm calling out to Mark Zuckerberg and Facebook. You've been putting out these new movies, these one-minute movies that everyone's been sharing. Well, my son passed away ... and we can't access his Facebook account. I've tried e-mailing, and different things, but it ain't working. All we want to do is see his movie. I know it's a shot in the dark, but I don't care. I want to see my son's video. His name's Jesse Berlin. So please help me." That night, Facebook called Berlin to tell him that they would indeed make a personalized "A Look Back" video for his late son (135). Facebook understands H2H.

References

1. **Thorbecke, Catherine.** GameStop timeline: A closer look at the saga that upended Wall Street. [Online] ABC News, February 13, 2021. https://abcnews.go.com/Business/gamestop-timeline-closer-saga-upended-wall-street/story?id=75617315.
2. **Scaramucci, Anthony.** We are witnessing the French Revolution of Finance. [Online] Twitter, Janaury 27, 2021. https://twitter.com/scaramucci/status/1354445427836416003?lang=en.
3. **Morrow, Allison.** Everything you need to know about how a Reddit group blew up GameStop's stock. [Online] CNN Business, January 28, 2021. https://www.cnn.com/2021/01/27/investing/gamestop-reddit-stock/index.html.
4. **Smith, Howard.** Why AMC, GameStop, BlackBerry, and Express Stocks Jumped Again Today. [Online] Nasdaq, May 26, 2021. https://www.nasdaq.com/articles/why-amc-gamestop-blackberry-and-express-stocks-jumped-again-today-2021-05-26.
5. **Egan, Matt.** Apparent suicide by 20-year-old Robinhood trader who saw a negative $730,000 balance prompts app to make changes. [Online] CNN Business, June 20, 2020. https://www.cnn.com/2020/06/19/business/robinhood-suicide-alex-kearns/index.html.
6. **Horowitz, Julia.** 1 big thing we still don't know about the GameStop rally. [Online] CNN Business, February 1, 2021. https://www.cnn.com/2021/02/01/investing/premarket-stocks-trading/index.html.

7. **Iyengar, Rishi.** Bitcoin plunges 12% after Elon Musk tweets that Tesla will not accept it as payment. [Online] CNN Business, May 13, 2021. https://www.cnn.com/2021/05/12/tech/elon-musk-tesla-bitcoin/index.html.

8. **Morrow, Allison.** Elon Musk could make fireworks on 'SNL.' Investors are betting on it. [Online] CNN Business, May 7, 2021. https://www.cnn.com/2021/05/07/investing/elon-musk-dogecoin-snl/index.html.

9. **Sigalos, MacKenzie.** Dogecoin plunges nearly 30% during Elon Musk's SNL appearance. [Online] CNBC, May 9, 2021. https://www.cnbc.com/2021/05/08/dogecoin-price-plummets-as-elon-musk-hosts-saturday-night-live-.html.

10. **Goldman, David.** Dogecoin tumbles after Elon Musk jokes about it on 'SNL'. [Online] CNN Business, May 10, 2021. https://www.cnn.com/2021/05/09/investing/dogecoin-elon-musk-snl/index.html.

11. **D'Anastasio, Cecilia.** GameStop FOMO Inspires a New Wave of Crypto Pump-and-Dumps. [Online] Wired, May 13, 2021. https://www.wired.com/story/crypto-pump-and-dumps-gamestop-dogecoin-fomo/.

12. **Cohen, David.** Farewell, Facebook Credits. [Online] AdWeek, September 13, 2013. https://www.adweek.com/performance-marketing/farewell-facebook-credits/.

13. **Constine, Josh.** Facebook announces Libra cryptocurrency: All you need to know. [Online] TechCrunch, June 18, 2019. https://techcrunch.com/2019/06/18/facebook-libra/.

14. **Feiner, Lauren.** Facebook's libra cryptocurrency coalition is falling apart as eBay, Visa, Mastercard and Stripe jump ship. [Online] CNBC, October 13, 2019. https://www.cnbc.com/2019/10/11/ebay-drops-out-of-facebook-libra-cryptocurrency-one-week-after-paypal.html.

15. **Osborne, Charlie.** Mastercard CEO explains why Facebook's Libra project was abandoned. [Online] ZDNet, February 4, 2020. https://www.zdnet.com/article/mastercard-ceo-explains-why-facebooks-libra-project-was-abandoned/.

16. **Kastrenakes, Jacob.** Libra cryptocurrency project changes name to Diem to distance itself from Facebook. [Online] The Verge, December 1, 2020. https://www.theverge.com/2020/12/1/21755078/libra-diem-name-change-cryptocurrency-facebook.

17. **Wilson, Tom and Schroeder, Pete.** Facebook-backed crypto project Diem to launch U.S. stablecoin in major shift. [Online] Nasqad, May 12, 2021. https://www.nasdaq.com/articles/facebook-backed-crypto-project-diem-to-launch-u.s.-stablecoin-in-major-shift-2021-05-12.

18. **Katz, Leslie.** Japan tests billboards that know your gender, age. [Online] CNet, July 19, 2010. http://news.cnet.com/8301-17938_105-20010963-1.html.

19. **AFP.** Tokyo trials digital billboards that scan passers-by. [Online] Agence France-Presse, July 15, 2010. http://www.google.com/hostednews/afp/article/ALeqM5iDd1xzYx7CaahlxkLnvo4Xtcksug.

20. **Sutter, John D.** This London advertisement knows your gender. [Online] CNN, February 22, 2012. http://whatsnext.blogs.cnn.com/2012/02/22/this-london-advertisement-knows-your-gender/.

21. **Garber, Megan.** The Bus Stop That Knows You're a Lady. [Online] The Atlantic, February 21, 2012. http://www.theatlantic.com/technology/archive/12/02/the-bus-stop-that-knows-youre-a-lady/253365/.

22. **Tode, Chantal.** Tic Tac enlists augmented reality for interactive Times Square billboard. [Online] Mobile Marketer, February 17, 2012. http://www.mobilemarketer.com/cms/news/software-technology/12140.html.

23. **Kessler, Sarah.** Startup Aims To Build Billboards That Target You, Personally. [Online] Mashable, April 15, 2011. http://mashable.com/2011/04/16/smart-billboard/.

24. **Kohavi, Ronny and Round, Matt.** Front Line Internet Analytics at Amazon.com. [Online] Emetrics Summit 2004 - Stanford AI Lab, 2004. http://ai.stanford.edu/~ronnyk/emetricsAmazon.pdf.

25. **Mangalindan, JP.** Amazon's recommendation secret. [Online] CNNMoney, July 30, 2012. http://tech.fortune.cnn.com/2012/07/30/amazon-5/.

26. **Duhigg, Charles.** How Companies Learn Your Secrets. [Online] The New York Times, February 16, 2012. http://www.nytimes.com/2012/02/19/magazine/shopping-habits. html?pagewanted=all.

27. **Eugenios, Jillian.** Lowe's channels science fiction in new holoroom. [Online] CNNMoney, June 12, 2014. http://money.cnn.com/2014/06/12/technology/innovation/lowes-holoroom/ index.html.

28. **Buhr, Sarah.** 500K Women Gave Up Their Boob Data To Build This Bra. [Online] TechCrunch, June 11, 2014. http://techcrunch. com/2014/06/11/500k-women-gave-up-their-boob-data-to-build-this-bra/.

29. **Milian, Mark.** Tumblr: 'We're pretty opposed to advertising'. [Online] Los Angeles Times, April 17, 2010. http://latimesblogs.latimes.com/technology/2010/04/tumblr-ads.html.

30. **Gannes, Liz.** Tumblr's Inflection Point Came When Curators Joined Creators. [Online] All Things D, January 23, 2012. http://allthingsd.com/20120123/ tumblrs-inflection-point-came-when-curators-joined-creators/.

31. **Higginbotham, Stacey.** How Tumblr went from wee to webscale. [Online] GigaOM, February 13, 2012. http://gigaom.com/cloud/how-tumblr-went-from-wee-to-webscale/.

32. **Delo, Cotton.** Tumblr Announces First Foray Into Paid Advertising. [Online] Ad Age, April 18, 2012. http://adage.com/article/special-report-digital-conference/ social-media-tumblr-announces-foray-paid-ads/234214/.

33. **Nicole, Kristen.** Steve Ballmer Attacks Google's Gmail Ads. [Online] Mashable, October 8, 2007. http://mashable.com/2007/10/08/ballmer-google-email-ads/.

34. **Google.** Ads in Gmail and your personal data. [Online] Google Gmail. [Cited: April 29, 2012.] http://support.google.com/mail/bin/answer.py?hl=en&answer=6603.

35. **Barr, Alistair.** Google Stops Scanning Student Gmail Accounts for Ads. [Online] The Wall Street Journal, April 30, 2014. http://blogs.wsj.com/digits/2014/04/30/ google-stops-scanning-student-gmail-accounts-for-ads/.

36. **Lewis, Andrew.** User-driven discontent. [Online] MetaFilter, August 26, 2010. http://www. metafilter.com/95152/Userdriven-discontent#3256046.

37. **Sengupta, Somini.** Risk and Riches in User Data for Facebook. [Online] The New York Times, February 26, 2012. http://www.nytimes.com/2012/02/27/technology/for-facebook-risk-and-riches-in-user-data.html.

38. **Nielsen.** Ads with Friends: Analyzing the Benefits of Social Ads. [Online] Nielsenwire, March 6, 2012. http://blog.nielsen.com/nielsenwire/online_mobile/ ads-with-friends-analyzing-the-benefits-of-social-ads/.

39. **Pepitone, Julianne.** Is Facebook worth $100 billion? [Online] CNNMoney, January 30, 2012. http://money.cnn.com/2012/01/30/technology/facebook_valuation/index.htm.

40. **Consumer Electronics Association.** CEA Study Examines Social Media Influence on CE Purchase Decisions. [Online] Yahoo! Finance, February 22, 2012. http://finance.yahoo.com/ news/cea-study-examines-social-media-150200002.html.

41. **The Nielsen Company.** Consumer Trust in Online, Social and Mobile Advertising Grows. [Online] Nielsen, April 10, 2012. http://blog.nielsen.com/nielsenwire/media_entertainment/ consumer-trust-in-online-social-and-mobile-advertising-grows/.

42. **Gross, Doug.** Employers, workers navigate pitfalls of social media. [Online] CNN, February 7, 2012. http://www.cnn.com/2012/02/07/tech/social-media/companies-social-media/ index.html.

43. **Tsuruoka, Doug.** Social Media Impact On E-Commerce Called Overrated. [Online] Investor's Business Daily, February 7, 2012. http://news.investors.com/Article/600351/201202071711/ social-media-disappoints-as-ecommerce-driver.htm.

44. **Lutz, Ashley.** Gamestop to J.C. Penney Shut Facebook Stores: Retail. [Online] Bloomberg Businessweek, February 28, 2012. http://www.businessweek.com/news/2012-02-28/ gamestop-to-j-c-penney-shut-facebook-stores-retail.html.

45. **LIM College.** New Study "Shopping Trends Among 18–25 Year Olds" Reveals Technology Use Overrated. [Online] PRNewswire, January 17, 2012. http://www.prnewswire.com/

news-releases/new-study-shopping-trends-among-18-25-year-olds-reveals-technology-use-overrated-137504888.html.

46. **Terlep, Sharon, Vranica, Suzanne and Raice, Shayndi.** GM Says Facebook Ads Don't Pay Off. [Online] The Wall Street Journal, May 16, 2012. http://online.wsj.com/article/SB10001424052702304192704577406394017764460.html.

47. **Valdes-Dapena, Peter.** GM to stop advertising on Facebook. [Online] CNNMoney, May 15, 2012. http://money.cnn.com/2012/05/15/autos/gm_facebook/index.htm.

48. **Schonfeld, Erick.** Facebook's Profits: $1 Billion, On $3.7 Billion In Revenues. [Online] TechCrunch, February 1, 2012. http://techcrunch.com/2012/02/01/facebook-1-billion-profit/.

49. **Pepitone, Julianne.** Facebook files for $5 billion IPO. [Online] CNNMoney, February 2, 2012. http://money.cnn.com/2012/02/01/technology/facebook_ipo/index.htm.

50. **O'Leary, Noreen.** GroupM: Global Web Ad Spend Up 16 Percent in 2011. New research says marketers spent $84.8 billion. [Online] Adweek, April 9, 2012. http://www.adweek.com/news/advertising-branding/groupm-global-web-ad-spend-16-percent-2011-139483.

51. **Iyengar, Rishi.** Here's how big Facebook's ad business really is. [Online] CNN Business, July 1, 2020. https://www.cnn.com/2020/06/30/tech/facebook-ad-business-boycott/index.html.

52. **Kacholia, Varun and Ji, Minwen.** News Feed FYI: Helping You Find More News to Talk About. [Online] Facebook Newsroom, December 2, 2013. https://newsroom.fb.com/news/2013/12/news-feed-fyi-helping-you-find-more-news-to-talk-about/.

53. **Delo, Cotton.** Facebook Warns Brands that Scale in Social Won't Come For Free. [Online] 2012, 5 March. http://adage.com/article/digital/facebook-warns-brands-scale-social-free/233105/.

54. **Facebook.** Reach Generator. [Online] Facebook. [Cited: March 31, 2012.] http://ads.ak.facebook.com/ads/FacebookAds/Reach_Generator_Guide_2.28.12.pdf.

55. **Creamer, Matt.** Facebook Ads: What Works, What Doesn't. [Online] Advertising Age, May 14, 2012. http://adage.com/article/digital/facebook-ads-works/234731/.

56. **Levine, Dan and McBride, Sarah.** Facebook to pay $10 million to settle suit. [Online] Reuters, June 16, 2012. http://www.reuters.com/article/2012/06/16/net-us-facebook-settlement-idUSBRE85F0N120120616.

57. **Constine, Josh.** Facebook Exchange: A New Way For Advertisers To Target Specific Users With Real-Time Bid Ads. [Online] TechCrunch, June 13, 2012. http://techcrunch.com/2012/06/13/facebook-exchange/.

58. **MacMillan, Douglas and Erlichman, Jonathan.** Facebook to Debut Real-Time Bidding on Advertising Prices. [Online] Bloomberg Businessweek, June 14, 2012. http://www.business-week.com/news/2012-06-13/facebook-to-debut-real-time-bidding-for-advertising.

59. **Facebook.** Custom Stories. [Online] Facebook Developers. [Cited: June 5, 2014.] https://developers.facebook.com/docs/opengraph.

60. **Brian, M.** Facebook opens Marketplace to take on eBay and Craigslist. [Online] Engadget, October 3, 2016. https://www.engadget.com/2016-10-03-facebook-marketplace-buy-sell-app.html.

61. **Snow, Shane.** Why the "Dumbphone" Market Is Still Ripe for Innovation. [Online] Mashable, November 10, 2010. http://mashable.com/2010/11/10/mobile-innovation-dumbphone/.

62. **Lomas, Natasha.** Smartphones Finally Overtook Dumbphone Sales Globally In Q2, Android Now At 79%, Says Gartner. [Online] TechCrunch, August 14, 2013. https://techcrunch.com/2013/08/14/gartner-q2-smartphone/.

63. **Crudo, Ben.** I'm the CEO of a tech company and I permanently gave up my smartphone after my honeymoon 6 months ago. Here's why I haven't looked back. [Online] Business Insider, May 14, 2019. https://www.businessinsider.com/ben-crudo-gave-up-my-smartphone-2019-5.

64. **Van Grove, Jennifer.** Facebook for Every Phone App Launches for 2,500 Mobile Devices. [Online] Mashable, July 12, 2011. http://mashable.com/2011/07/12/facebook-for-every-phone/.

65. **Makavy, Ran.** Feature Phone Milestone: Facebook for Every Phone Reaches 100 Million. [Online] Facebook Newsroom, July 22, 2013. http://newsroom.fb.com/news/2013/07/feature-phone-milestone-facebook-for-every-phone-reaches-100-million/.

66. **Bilton, Nick.** Facebook Tries, Tries Again on a Smartphone. [Online] The New York Times, May 27, 2012. http://bits.blogs.nytimes.com/2012/05/27/facebook-tries-tries-again-on-a-smartphone/.

67. **Segall, Laurie.** Facebook's stock dive is 'disappointing,' CEO Mark Zuckerberg says. [Online] CNNMoney, September 11, 2012. http://money.cnn.com/2012/09/11/technology/zuckerberg-techcrunch-disrupt/.

68. **Mayer, Andrew.** What Facebook will do with Instagram. [Online] CNN, April 11, 2012. http://www.cnn.com/2012/04/11/opinion/mayer-instagram-facebook/index.html.

69. **Burns, Matt.** Instagram's User Count Now At 40 Million, Saw 10 Million New Users In Last 10 Days. [Online] TechCrunch, April 13, 2012. http://techcrunch.com/2012/04/13/instagrams-user-count-now-at-40-million-saw-10-million-new-users-in-last-10-days/.

70. **Perez, Sarah.** Instagram Adds 50 Million Photos In August, Now Over 200 Million Total. [Online] TechCrunch, September 2, 2011. http://techcrunch.com/2011/09/02/instagram-adds-50-million-photos-in-august-now-over-200-million-total/.

71. **Diaz, Jesus.** Facebook Photo Library Dwarfs Everything Else on the Planet. [Online] Gizmodo, September 19, 2011. http://gizmodo.com/5841667/facebook-photo-library-dwarfs-everything-else-in-the-planet.

72. **Heine, Christopher.** Pepsi and Red Bull Talk Instagram Activations. [Online] ClickZ, April 17, 2012. http://www.clickz.com/clickz/news/2168388/pepsi-red-bull-talk-instagram-activations.

73. **Saunders, Krystal.** Instagram App Gets Update for iOS. [Online] Market News. [Cited: June 26, 2012.] http://www.marketnews.ca//LatestNewsHeadlines/InstagramAppGetsUpdateforiOS.html.

74. **Neild, Barry.** Instagram wants photos to be seen beyond '10-hour' window. [Online] CNN, June 20, 2012. http://www.cnn.com/2012/06/19/tech/mobile/instagram-le-web/index.html.

75. **Prodhan, Georgina.** Apps become key to mobile advertising - report. [Online] Reuters, April 21, 2012. http://in.reuters.com/article/2012/04/21/mobile-advertising-apps-idINDEE83J0GJ20120421.

76. **comScore.** comScore Introduces Mobile Metrix 2.0, Revealing that Social Media Brands Experience Heavy Engagement on Smartphones. [Online] comScore Press Release, May 7, 2012. http://www.comscore.com/Press_Events/Press_Releases/2012/5/Introducing_Mobile_Metrix_2_Insight_into_Mobile_Behavior.

77. **Prodhan, Georgina.** Analysis: Facebook seeks breakthrough in mobile ad market. [Online] Reuters, March 2, 2012. http://www.reuters.com/article/2012/03/02/us-facebook-mobile-advertising-idUSTRE8210PH20120302.

78. **Investor Relations.** Facebook Reports Fourth Quarter and Full Year 2012 Results. [Online] Facebook, January 20, 2013. http://investor.fb.com/releasedetail.cfm?ReleaseID=736911.

79. **Lipsman, Andrew.** Facebook Vaults Ahead of Google Maps to Finish 2012 as #1 U.S. Mobile App. [Online] comScore, January 23, 2013. http://www.comscore.com/Insights/Blog/Facebook_Vaults_Ahead_of_Google_Maps_to_Finish_2012_as_number_1_US_Mobile_App.

80. **Constine, Josh.** Facebook Unveils First Non-Social Mobile Ad Unit, Allowing Developers To Buy Clicks To App Store. [Online] TechCrunch, August 7, 2012. http://techcrunch.com/2012/08/07/facebook-mobile-app-ads/.

81. —. Facebook's iPad App Becomes An Entertainment Hub With Game Discovery And Trending Videos Sidebar. [Online] TechCrunch, June 16, 2014. http://techcrunch.com/2014/06/16/facebook-for-ipad/.

82. **McCullagh, Declan.** Instagram says it now has the right to sell your photos. [Online] CNet, December 17, 2012. http://www.cnet.com/news/instagram-says-it-now-has-the-right-to-sell-your-photos/.

83. **Tsukayama, Hayley.** National Geographic returns to Instagram. [Online] The Washington Post, December 21, 2012. http://www.washingtonpost.com/business/technology/national-geographic-returns-to-instagram/2012/12/21/49b6e768-4b99-11e2-b709-667035ff9029_story.html.

84. **Constine, Josh and Crook, Jordan.** This Is What Instagram Ads Look Like. [Online] TechCrunch, October 24, 2013. http://techcrunch.com/2013/10/24/first-look-at-instagram-ads/.

85. **Heine, Christopher.** Instagram Ads Are Getting Instant Recall Taco Bell and Hollister seeing picture-perfect results. [Online] AdWeek, May 12, 2014. http://www.adweek.com/news/technology/instagram-ads-are-getting-instant-recall-157595.

86. **Bruell, Alexandra.** Instagram Inks Ad Deal With Omnicom Worth up to $100 Million. [Online] Advertising Age, March 7, 2014. http://adage.com/article/agency-news/instagram-inks-ad-deal-omnicom-worth-100-million/292037/.

87. **Sloane, Garett.** That Instagram-Omnicom Deal Is Actually Worth $40 Million. [Online] AdWeek, March 8, 2014. http://www.adweek.com/news/advertising-branding/instagram-omnicom-deal-actually-worth-40-million-156200.

88. **Constine, Josh.** Facebook Announces "Home", A Homescreen Replacement Android App Designed Around People. [Online] TechCrunch, April 4, 2013. http://techcrunch.com/2013/04/04/facebook-home-launch/.

89. **Cutler, Kim-Mai.** Facebook Buys Parse To Offer Mobile Development Tools As Its First Paid B2B Service. [Online] TechCrunch, April 25, 2013. http://techcrunch.com/2013/04/25/facebook-parse/.

90. **Kelly, Heather.** Facebook plans private tool for celebrities. [Online] CNN, August 14, 2013. http://www.cnn.com/2013/08/14/tech/social-media/facebook-vip-feature/index.html.

91. **Del Rey, Jason and Isaac, Mike.** Facebook to Test Its Own PayPal Competitor in Bid to Simplify Mobile Purchases. [Online] AllThingsD, August 15, 2013. http://allthingsd.com/20130815/facebook-testing-out-paypal-competitor-in-bid-to-simplify-mobile-commerce-purchases/.

92. **Edwards, Jim.** Facebook's New Push Into Apps Is Genius Because It Exploits The Secrecy Of Apple And Google. [Online] Business Insider, May 4, 2014. http://www.businessinsider.com/facebooks-app-discovery-strategy-2014-5.

93. **Constine, Josh.** Facebook's Cutesy Annual Report To Partners Reveals First Country-By-Country Mobile Stats. [Online] TechCrunch, December 29, 2013. http://techcrunch.com/2013/12/29/facebook-international-user-growth/.

94. **Ember, Sydney.** Facebook's $16 Billion Deal for WhatsApp. [Online] The New York Times, February 20, 2014. http://dealbook.nytimes.com/2014/02/20/morning-agenda-facebooks-16-billion-deal-for-whatsapp/.

95. **Alden, William.** Facebook's Deal for WhatsApp: The Chatter on Twitter. [Online] The Guardian, February 19, 2014. http://dealbook.nytimes.com/2014/02/19/facebooks-deal-for-whatsapp-the-chatter-on-twitter/.

96. **Wood, Zoe.** Facebook turned down WhatsApp co-founder Brian Acton for job in 2009. [Online] The Guardian, February 20, 2014. http://www.theguardian.com/technology/2014/feb/20/facebook-turned-down-whatsapp-co-founder-brian-acton-job-2009.

97. **Strange, Adario.** Mark Zuckerberg: 'We Want to Create a Dial Tone for the Internet'. [Online] Mashable, February 24, 2014. http://mashable.com/2014/02/24/mark-zuckerberg-mobile-world-congress-2/.

98. **Facebook.** Company Info. [Online] Facebook Newsroom. [Cited: August 9, 2014.] http://newsroom.fb.com/company-info/.

99. **O'Toole, James.** Facebook profit triples on mobile growth. [Online] CNNMoney, April 24, 2014. http://money.cnn.com/2014/04/23/technology/social/facebook-mobile/index.html.

100. **Kelly, Heather.** Facebook launches friend-tracking feature. [Online] CNN, April 18, 2014. http://www.cnn.com/2014/04/17/tech/mobile/facebook-nearby-friends/index.html.

101. **Albergotti, Reed.** With App Acquisition, Facebook Enters Fitness Tracking Market. [Online] The Wall Street Journal, April 24, 2014. http://blogs.wsj.com/digits/2014/04/24/with-app-acquisition-facebook-enters-fitness-tracking-market/.

102. **Spehar, Jeffrey.** The New Facebook Login and Graph API 2.0. [Online] Facebook, April 30, 2014. https://developers.facebook.com/blog/post/2014/04/30/the-new-facebook-login/.

103. **Facebook Newsroom.** Helping Grow Mobile Apps with FbStart. [Online] Facebook, April 30, 2014. http://newsroom.fb.com/news/2014/04/f8-helping-grow-mobile-apps-with-fbstart/.

104. **Marshall,   Jack.** Facebook's   Ad   Network   Is   Finally   Here.   [Online]   The Wall   Street   Journal,   April   30,   2014.   http://blogs.wsj.com/digits/2014/04/30/facebooks-ad-network-is-finally-here/.

105. **Edwards, Jim.** Here's Everything Facebook Just Announced At Its Big Developer Conference. [Online] Business Insider, April 30, 2014. http://www.businessinsider.com/mark-zuckerberg-at-facebook-f8-2014-4.

106. **Manjoo, Farhad.** Can Facebook Innovate? A Conversation With Mark Zuckerberg. [Online] The New York Times, April 26, 2014. http://bits.blogs.nytimes.com/2014/04/16/can-facebook-innovate-a-conversation-with-mark-zuckerberg/.

107. **Delo, Cotton.** Facebook Adds Audio Matching to Get You Posting More About TV. [Online] Advertising Age, May 21, 2014. http://adage.com/article/digital/facebook-launches-feature-users-post-tv/293359/.

108. **Frier, Sarah.** Facebook Buying Mobile-Data Company Pryte. [Online] Bloomberg, June 3,   2014.   http://www.bloomberg.com/news/2014-06-03/facebook-buying-mobile-data-company-pryte.html.

109. **O'Toole, James.** Facebook at all-time high on mobile might. [Online] CNNMoney, July 23, 2014. http://money.cnn.com/2014/07/23/technology/social/facebook-mobile/index.html.

110. **Byford, Sam.** Budweiser cup makes toasting drinkers instant friends on Facebook. [Online] The Verge, April 27, 2013. http://www.theverge.com/2013/4/27/4276618/budweiser-buddy-cup-connects-to-facebook.

111. **Souppouris, Aaron.** Facebook friendship bracelets put a name to Molly's face. [Online]   The   Verge,   July   8,   2014.   http://www.theverge.com/2014/7/8/5879967/festival-bracelet-helps-you-make-facebook-friends.

112. **Rushe, Dominic and Chaudhuri, Saabira.** Facebook IPO: six things you need to know. [Online] The Guardian, January 31, 2012. http://www.guardian.co.uk/technology/2012/jan/31/facebook-ipo-six-things.

113. **Frier, Sarah.** Facebook Working on Location-Based Mobile-Ad Product. [Online] Bloomberg,   June   18,   2012.   http://www.bloomberg.com/news/2012-06-18/facebook-readying-location-based-mobile-ad-product.html.

114. **Strugatz, Rachel.** Digital World Now Coaxing Shoppers Back to Stores. [Online] Women's Wear Daily, June 27, 2012. http://www.wwd.com/retail-news/direct-internet-catalogue/digital-world-now-coaxing-shoppers-back-to-stores-6002645?full=true.

115. **Snapette.** Snapette Redefines The Shopping Experience Again With Major Update To Popular Location-Based App For iPhone And iPod Touch. [Online] The Sacramento Bee, June 28, 2012. http://www.sacbee.com/2012/06/28/4595490/snapette-redefines-the-shopping.html.

116. **Disney.** Disney. [Online] Facebook. [Cited: August 13, 2014.] http://www.facebook.com/Disney.

117. **Warren, Christina.** Disney Marketing: The Happiest Social Media Strategy on Earth. [Online] Mashable, August 3, 2011. http://mashable.com/2011/08/03/disney-social-media/.

118. **Ford,   Kristin.**   Orlando   Sentinel   to   deliver   latest   from   Disney   Social Media   Moms   Celebration.   [Online]   Orlando   Sentinel,   March   17,   2011. http://blogs.orlandosentinel.com/disney-a-mom-and-the-mouse/2011/03/orlando-sentinel-to-deliver-latest-from-disney-social-media-moms-celebration/.

119. **Track Social.** The Track Social Awards: Best of 2011. [Online] PRWeb, January 5, 2012. http://www.prweb.com/releases/2012/1/prweb9079817.htm.

120. **Chmielewski, Dawn C.** Disney buys social networking site Togetherville. [Online] The Los Angeles Times, February 25, 2011. http://articles.latimes.com/2011/feb/25/business/la-fi-ct-disney-togetherville-20110225.

121. **Lewis, William E. Jr.** Togetherville: Facebook for kids is shutting down. [Online] examiner.com, February 25, 2012. http://www.examiner.com/article/togetherville-facebook-for-kids-is-shutting-down.

122. **CNN Political Unit.** Stations, advertisers drop Limbaugh. [Online] CNN, March 6, 2012. http://politicalticker.blogs.cnn.com/2012/03/06/more-limbaugh-stations-advertisers-jump-ship/.

123. **AOL.** AOL. [Online] Facebook, March 5, 2012. http://www.facebook.com/aol/posts/356690557687629.

124. **Gross, Doug.** Which companies respond quickest (or not at all) on Facebook? [Online] CNN, March 27, 2012. http://www.cnn.com/2012/03/27/tech/social-media/retailers-facebook-questions/index.html.

125. **Office of Public Affairs.** Commerce Department Unveils Policy Framework for Protecting Consumer Privacy Online While Supporting Innovation. [Online] United States Department of Commerce, December 16, 2010. http://www.commerce.gov/news/press-releases/2010/12/16/commerce-department-unveils-policy-framework-protecting-consumer-priv.

126. **McCullagh, Declan.** Facebook co-sponsors N.H. debate, not without controversy. [Online] CNet, January 3, 2008. http://www.cnet.com/news/facebook-co-sponsors-n-h-debate-not-without-controversy/.

127. **Stelter, Brian.** ABC News and Facebook in Joint Effort to Bring Viewers Closer to Political Coverage. [Online] The New York Times, November 26, 2007. http://www.nytimes.com/2007/11/26/technology/26abc.html.

128. **Hopkins, Mark Rizzin.** ABC News + Facebook = Epic Fail. [Online] Mashable, November 26, 2007. http://mashable.com/2007/11/26/abc-news-facebook-epic-fail/.

129. **Gross, Doug.** Food app, Facebook 'break up' over promoted posts. [Online] CNN, March 31, 2014. http://www.cnn.com/2014/03/31/tech/social-media/facebook-eat24/index.html.

130. **Chmielewski, Dawn C and Guynn, Jessica.** Is Facebook worth it? Film execs confide they may cut movie ads. [Online] Los Angeles Times, January 8, 2013. http://articles.latimes.com/2013/jan/08/business/la-fi-ct-hollywood-studios-movie-ads-facebook-20130108.

131. **Elder, Jeff.** Social Media Fail to Live Up to Early Marketing Hype. [Online] The Wall Street Journal, June 23, 2014. http://online.wsj.com/articles/companies-alter-social-media-strategies-1403499658.

132. **Gallup.** The Myth of Social Media. [Online] The Wall Street Journal, June 23, 2014. http://online.wsj.com/public/resources/documents/sac_report_11_socialmedia_061114.pdf.

133. **Cooper, Belle Beth.** 10 Big, Recent Changes To Twitter, Facebook, And Linkedin You Should Know About. [Online] Fast Company, January 27, 2014. http://www.fastcompany.com/3025417/work-smart/10-big-recent-changes-to-twitter-facebook-and-linkedin-you-should-know-about.

134. **Kramer, Bryan.** There Is No More B2B or B2C: There Is Only Human to Human (H2H). [Online] Social Media Today, January 27, 2014. http://socialmediatoday.com/bryan-kramer/2115561/there-no-more-b2b-or-b2c-it-s-human-human-h2h.

135. **Griggs, Brandon.** Facebook answers grieving dad's emotional plea. [Online] CNN, February 10, 2014. http://www.cnn.com/2014/02/06/tech/social-media/facebook-dad-video-appeal/index.html.

Chapter 6
Facebook Analytics, Advertising, and Marketing

Dennis Yu and Alex Houg

6.1   The Viral Cycle

When you amplify your own content, you are able to activate fans that may have joined the page a long time ago, but haven't heard from you since they originally liked the page. Plus, you'll be able to increase the feedback rate on content (likes + comments).

People make decisions based on the trust of their friends. It doesn't matter what the marketing channel is. What Facebook has done is *create a social layer* that exposes those relationships that have always been there, between people's real friends. Because those relationships are visible, we can think of all these friendships as dots with lines connecting them. This created an advertising system that sits on top of the layered friendships and allows you to inject your content – Social ads that are about amplifying user actions, not broadcasting creativity

Now let's say your content is testimonials, specials, videos of procedures, whatever kinds of content might be interesting. Identify who your best customers are; these are not people who could be customers, but people who already love you and your brand. Amplify what you already have that's great. Facebook is this "word-of-mouth" amplifier.

We believe that pay per click (PPC) and content marketing are now the same thing. Whoever creates/gathers the content is best equipped to amplify and reamplify it, as well as follow-up to retarget by creating spin-off (derivative) content, interviews, and community support. This is the framework that drives social. Here is why:

D. Yu (✉) · A. Houg
BlitzMetrics, Albany, CA, USA
e-mail: dennis@blitzmetrics.com

© Springer Science+Business Media, LLC, part of Springer Nature 2021
N. Lee, *Facebook Nation*, https://doi.org/10.1007/978-1-0716-1867-7_6

Goals: Each business has a story. The founder, CEO, or President has a distinct vision that is shared throughout the company with its employees. This vision and story make great content (1)! By sharing these stories and goals, this builds your relevant audience. These specific goals and strategy, when combined with social, takes your advertising to new heights. Your viewers then understand that for which you stand and can form that personal relationship.

Content: These clearly defined goals lead to great content. Sharing the success stories, interesting and relevant news, and things that are relevant to your business all build your audience even further; content drives this "engine." Once you find what kinds of things your audience "likes" and relates to, you can then move on to the next part of the cycle. This can be done through split testing (also known as A/B testing) and other methods (2).

Targeting: Once you have found the goal of your content, why not share it with more people? Fans of your page, friends of fans, people who have the same interests, etc. By running ads to specific audiences (3), you are able to find who your valuable fans are. These are the people who are going to support your cause, or better yet, will lead you and your brand to conversions. .

Amplify: Once you have found your fan crowd, make sure your content reaches them. They are the ones who care about your cause/business, and resonate most with your message. This is where the conversions start to take place. Whether it is page likes, going to your website, or even to a specific landing page, these are the loyal fans (4).

6.2   Metrics Analysis Action (MAA)

We call it MAA— and it stands for Metrics > Analysis > Action. The idea is this: Sort to find the top performers, ignoring the rest. Don't mass-multiply; spend a few minutes per day, not three hours once per month. Amplify what's working by using different forms of social retargeting via sponsored stories (5) and custom audience targeting (6). Don't waste time making reports, unless you're in that type of company — focus on insights and actions. Software is nice, but expert action is better. Software can't mask missing competency. Repeat these cycles quickly — you can get them down to minutes and go through multiple cycles per day.

Now, in more detail: You've made 183 different Facebook ads. You've targeted multiple interests and tested out various creatives and landing page combinations. So, what?

Over time, your garden has grown to quite an unwieldy mess. Maybe you use power editor (7), but you probably don't know that if you have more than 50 ads in a campaign, the sorting doesn't work. Maybe you're an AdWords veteran trying your hand at Facebook ads, but you're finding that the same optimization flow doesn't quite work, because it's not about title, copy, and image combos. Maybe you spend more time making reports and having meetings than actually optimizing, or your stubborn IT brethren are being uncooperative.

Well, here's how to cut right to the chase to make maximum impact with your limited time. May this be the Tim Ferriss of Facebook ads, minus the pill business he ran under that model. I'm assuming you have a target metric, such as more traffic, or perhaps more conversions at a lower cost per conversion. If you don't, then stop reading this article and set some goals in this area since you have no goal for optimization or growth. And I'm assuming you have power editor ready.

1. **Sort all ads by spend descending, looking at today.**

If you spend less than $100 per day, then look at the last few days. Optimize just the top 10 ads, ignoring the rest. By optimize, I mean look at your cost per conversion, cost per click, and click-through rate (CTR). If you have the new offsite pixel (8), you can get a CPA (cost per acquisition). When you have new ads, optimize to CTR first — kill the ones that have low CTR on at least 10,000 impressions.

I like to see at least a 0.1 percent CTR, but your CTR will vary depending on the placement (I prefer mobile news feed) and the vertical that you're in. Usually CTR is inversely related with cost per click. If you're going for conversions, then you should be using optimized cost per mille (CPM) anyway (9).

Sometimes ads don't have quite enough data to tell if they are winners or not. See these ads? The fact that one ad has a couple more conversions than another is statistical noise if you optimize on CPA alone. Look at CTR as a leading indicator of relevancy so you can kill these ads before they spend enough to be statistically relevant from a CPA standpoint.

2. **Convert your winners at lower cost.**

These are any ads that generate conversions at less than your target CPA. Clone the top couple ads in this way:

(a) Add in larger audience targets. Often, the best performers start out as small audiences, so find related interests to expand the audience. Prune the audience. Maybe the ad is nearly profitable, but if you narrow it down by demographics, fewer interests, or adding in a broad category target on top of a set of precise interest targets, it can be profitable. Look at the demographic responders report in the Web-based version of the ads tool for clues. Some colleagues are big fans of mass-multiplication — to immediately start out with hundreds of ads, then prune. I believe in smaller cycles where we can move quicker. That means just a few ads at a time. Because Facebook doesn't report on interest-level performance in either case (mass-multiplication or rapid testing), you will eventually need to get down to one ad per audience.

(b) Try other landing page tweaks, especially if you have the right audience, but it's just not converting. *You want them to get to your landing page.* I prefer to use landing pages that already convert on display or search traffic. If it's a fresh landing page, you are starting from scratch — and that means the bulk of your efforts will be here, not in actually making the ads. So you are killing the bottom 10 percent of your ads, creating more variations of your winners, and ignoring the middle 80 percent. While a script can mindlessly do this for you, whether through the Facebook ads application-programming interface (hard to get) or Google AdWords API (easy), you will want to do most of this manually. It's not about self-inflicted torture, so much as being able to spot a pattern as to what is working or not, while you're turning stuff on and off.

(c) Remember that the *why* is the most important piece. You may discover that a certain meme is working really well. For example, Marketo found that a music theme was not only driving interest at the top of the funnel, but subsequent conversions, too. Thus, you should pump out more of this type of successful content. Use services like Fiverr or FancyHands to get folks to write articles, do designs, do research, and other busywork that can be delegated. This will eliminate whining about not having enough time or money, since these jobs will cost you $5 per job and save you hours of work.

3. **Amplify the hot content.**

Determine hot by what's getting the most engagement or conversions. Split your account into three segments: branding, lead capture, and conversion. The amplification of your hot content will likely be branded content — the funny photos, as opposed to the downloadable guide that requires an email to see it. Run page posts that tell stories to drive more engagement (10). You won't be able to measure the direct return on investment (ROI) from this type of ad unit, but it definitely will drive influence among the people you want to reach.

4. **Steal from your other marketing campaigns.**

Have you tried your top-performing copy and creatives from other channels? Not only is it more likely to perform, but you enforce a single brand, especially if you run your social ads at the same time you're doing direct mail, TV, PPC, or whatever else you use for marketing.

6.3   Everything You Need to Know about Website Custom Audiences (WCA)

I had just visited these sites and immediately, they were showing me messages related to whatever I was just looking at. With jiveSYSTEMS, I was learning about how to do video email. As a result, they were tempting me with more articles from the blog. With www.autocustoms.com, they're a client, so that's what happens. If I had clicked on a particular product, I might see that again. With www.priceline.com, I'm looking at hotels for next week in Salt Lake City. They know I am cheap, but they aren't smart enough to stop ads when I have already booked something else.

Some pitfalls to avoid with WCA (Website Custom Audiences): Just because they're effective, don't overuse them. Watch your frequency and rotate your creatives. Have different calls to action. You're not going to use the same creative for driving awareness as you would for engagement or conversion (11). Segment your content by where they are in your sales funnel. Make sure to use negatives. Don't send new customer offers to existing customers. Run exclusion audiences. Use combinations. You can use WCA to catch folks who didn't open your email, didn't buy, or aren't a fan. Why not use cross emailing, connection targeting, and other attributes with your WCA? There are so many combos possible for segmented messaging.

Jon Loomer, one of my favorite Facebook geeks, wrote a great post about WCA (12). Let's take a geekier point of view for the hard-core folks, shall we? You can create lookalike audiences from a WCA, but it's currently only available via the Facebook Ads API. We are one of a few dozen companies with Ads API access, so feel free to contact me if you want to see how it works programmatically. For most folks, wait a few weeks and you'll get it. Facebook says WCA is not a replacement for Facebook Exchange (FBX) (13), which is technically true if you're using FBX for product retargeting. However, WCA dynamically updates, allows overlay of other data elements, and has access to mobile inventory. These are three HUGE advantages.

If you're a small biz, you won't need FBX. Although this is not something FBX vendors want known. It was only a matter of time before the hidden markups charged by third parties would get competed down to commodities. The max audience duration is 180 days. (Notice I didn't say cookie expiration.)

Once these folks are tied to Facebook userids, your targeting of them does not die a cookie death, which is normally 30 days. This is how Facebook can reach them on both mobile and desktop. If you are in business-to-business (B2B) with a long sales cycle, this is critical (14). If you're Consumer Packaged Goods (CPG), where the consideration time frame is days, it doesn't matter. You get up to 200 audiences. We've not seen anyone hit that limit, but a couple B2B companies we do this for have gotten over 100. We are curious to see how many rules folks are applying, perhaps directly in step with how sophisticated their marketing automation segment flows are.

6.4   Ten Questions Any Facebook Marketing Consultant should be Able to Answer

If you don't work on cars, how do you know your mechanic isn't ripping you off? Even if he's honest, he could still be inefficient, and that costs you money.

Lately, it seems like everyone on Facebook is a self-proclaimed social media expert. There are no degrees or certifications, so we all operate without a license. Scary, isn't it? More so, what if you're selling Facebook marketing services yourself? How do you distinguish yourself from all of the other guys who claim to be amazing social gurus?

To start, you should be able to answer the following 10 questions:

1. **What's the "people talking about this" (PTAT) figure on your Facebook page?** (15)

Be prepared for plenty of hemming and hawing about how they've been so busy with client projects that they haven't had time for their own stuff. Yes, I know – the cobbler's son has no shoes.

2. **Can you show me a few live examples of Facebook pages you manage?**

You might not believe it, but this is where most consultants fail altogether, or they can only show you a couple pages with pathetic traffic. Have them log in to show you. The catch-22 of any job is that a big brand isn't going to let you touch its stuff unless you have experience with other big brands. If you're a consultant in this space but don't have the experience with big brands, you need to partner with the folks who do have access, because apprenticing is a faster way to learn than taking on a couple small businesses or start-ups (the worst) with no fans.

3. **How do you promote posts?**

If they say they simply hit the "promote" or "boost" button, walk away. That button is designed for small businesses owners who need something simpler than choosing targeting options inside Power Editor. If they say they don't believe in paid, walk away. You don't have to spend much; often, a couple of dollars per day against the right micro-audience is enough. But nowadays, it's a paid game, even more so than Google. If they don't mention Power Editor, run away (16).

4. **How do you measure return on investment on Facebook?**

If they say it can't be done or that it's only about driving fans or engagement, they're ignorant. You can absolutely measure ROI by looking at referral traffic to your site (Google Analytics and Adobe SiteCatalyst), collecting emails in Facebook custom tabs (now called apps), measuring coupon redemptions, and so forth. The smart ones will ask you what your business goals are. Forget about Facebook-specific metrics. We're talking about metrics that a chief financial officer or business owner would care about. They'll figure out how to tie Facebook traffic to these goals.

5. **I'd like to build a custom application: What do you think?**

The only sensible answer is "no," unless you're a gaming company or have an engineering staff with more than 10 folks. If they mention QR codes, the answer is, "Heck no." These are easy ways to blow $20,000 for virtually no traffic.

6. **What should my custom audience strategy be?**

Here, you're just testing them to see if they know what custom audiences are and if they've used them effectively before. You can upload lists of your emails, phone numbers, and Facebook user IDs, but really, you're just loading up emails from Constant Contact, www.salesforce.com, MailChimp, or whatever. On a clean list, you should match north of 80 percent for consumer businesses and 30 percent for business-to-business (17). Facebook matches against these, so you can use it as social remarketing to help opportunities convert, bring opt-outs back, and amplify what's in your regular email trigger system.

If you have a small list (under a few thousand), ask them what you can do. The answer is to use two types of lookalike audiences — where Facebook finds additional people that are similar (a smaller expansion) or a broader audience (to increase reach). Custom audiences are the most powerful feature Facebook has released on the ads side in seven years, even stronger than sponsored stories, although you can run custom audiences into sponsored stories.

7. I want to run a contest, what should I give away?

If they say an iPad, cash, or something like that, fire them. Those contests attract traffic, but not the people who want your product or service. The only appropriate answer is to give out in-kind products and services. If you sell chocolates, then you should give out chocolates. In this case, you would have their odds of winning contingent upon inviting others. Tell them that you would like to ask people to comment on your post and that you would like to choose a winner from among the entries. What they should tell you — the correct answer — is that you do not want to do that. Because it's against Facebook's terms of service, they can consequently shut down your page, profile, and whatever else they deem necessary. The *only* acceptable way to run contests, according to the terms, is via an app.

8. What's your content strategy for my niche?

This question is designed to catch the social prima donnas who think they only need to know social, but not understand your business. Quite the contrary, whoever is posting on your behalf represents your brand. They must be credible against your best users, who can easily spot a fake.

One of our clients provides environment lab testing equipment to engineers. I don't think any Blitz people are qualified to have a discussion with customers of that company. The correct answer is that they will strive to learn your business, while developing internal processes for your own people to produce content regularly in-house. If they say they want to use HootSuite to spam every social media channel at the same time, as well as load up the posting calendar a month in advance, you should cringe. These people are called "noisemakers" and will only erode your brand with your serious customers and their circles of influence. I'm not saying you can't post pictures of cats, but most of the content must be relevant and relateable.

9. Who are the top five social practitioners you admire most?

If they can't readily name five people, they're either too new to the space or they're not willing to keep up with the times. Their knowledge is outdated at best and lethal (the most likely) at worst.

10. Is Facebook for marketing, PR, advertising, customer care, or what?

This is to pull out whether they only have a single view. Many of them come from just the PR or community management angle. Successful Facebook marketing means that all parts of the company are involved, since Facebook is not a specific "channel" for any one kind of customers. People will complain, so we have to respond, and sometimes we even have to escalate. Will your consultant know what to do, or have a team in place to do it? What if your organization is running TV or other types of media? Will social be able to amplify these messages and ready to respond with one voice? What will happen if there's a tragedy, such as the Boston bombings? Do they know what to do and have they built processes for it before? (18).

Now, how many of these questions can you answer? To be able to screen mechanics at your car dealership, you have to be a master mechanic yourself, or at least hire one who can screen them. No matter how busy you are, you must still own your Facebook strategy, even if you delegate the execution.

6.5   The Insider's Guide to Facebook Traffic

As a small brand, the following issues may be familiar: You're posting diligently, but not getting much engagement. You're not a big brand with big budgets, but you still recognize that you need the right exposure. You're concerned that Facebook is "hiding" your posts from the newsfeed (19). How can you ensure you are reaching the most relevant and influential people through your Facebook page?

Once you have created engaging content, there are 4 kinds of targeting you can use to amplify your content to potential customers (20):

1. **Workplace**

Combining these targeting methods with demographic criteria will narrow your audience, increase CTR, and reach more potential customers. Did you know you can target just folks who work at Conde Nast, Glamour, and other publications? Only users who have "Conde Nast" listed as their employer will see your ad, allowing you to influence their brand directly (21).

However, if the brand you're targeting is small, it won't show up. Use these methods instead: Include the brand as an interest, or target only people who like that Facebook page. Limit your audience to a tight geographic area around the brand's headquarters. Research how many employees the brand has to determine ad effectiveness. Take Infusionsoft, for example. Based on the ad count and employee count, 58% of everyone you reach will likely be an Infusionsoft employee.

2. **Competitive**

Competitive interests are targeting your competitor's fans based on their brand name, allowing you to 'piggyback' and steal traffic (22). Use Facebook Power Editor to grab interest counts and to filter by gender, showing brand influence.

Let's use Ralph Lauren as an example: If you sell men's clothing, targeting all 2.6 million users is inefficient. Ralph Lauren is a brand of variety, not just fashion. Filter your ad to fit using category, age, gender, and even partner categories (23). This allows you to hone in on an audience that would make the biggest impact (24).

3. **Lateral**

Lateral interests are things your demographic finds interesting. Fashion brand lateral interests might include "breast cancer awareness," "prom," and "evening gown." Limit your audience to *only the most relevant interests.* Lateral interests can vary easily. Unless you're a big brand with a huge budget, it's not feasible to reach millions of people. Stay away from being too general, like "I love my kids," and focus close to your brand. Narrow it further with demographic targeting. Stores that sell goods or organizations you sponsor would also be lateral interests. Now, combine these with some demographic targeting.

4. **Literal**

Literal interests include terms directly related to your brand. If you are a wedding gown boutique, target women who are getting married. Literal interests are the easiest to start with, but they tend to be broad. Segmenting and testing your campaigns helps you derive what combination is most effective.

Your advertising cost depends on audience and content. As an incentive, Facebook rewards engaging ads with higher reach and lower CPC. Optimizing your campaigns every day will let you do that. Use workplace, competitive, lateral, and literal targeting with demographic criteria to build your audience.

6.6   Using Exclusion Targeting to Filter Out Unwanted Targets

In Power Editor, you can exclude folks you DON'T want to hit. For Google PPC veterans, this is the equivalent of negative keywords. For example, if you ran a personals site, you'd bid on "dating", but have "carbon" as a negative to not match on "carbon dating". With Facebook, we can choose targets and exclude audiences within them. For example, maybe we want to target the entire US minus San Diego, or maybe you're a mortgage company licensed to operate in 47 states– you could list out all 47 states as a target or just select United States and negative out the three states you don't serve.

Let's say that you've got your marketing automation running smoothly (25). You have content for those new to your brand and then content bucketed out mid-funnel as well as conversion. You can exclude folks who are already fans, so they don't see top of funnel messages. Same for those you already have emails for– exclude them if they're on your list already.

The pros by now are nodding their heads vigorously, as using the right combos of positive and negative audiences is critical to not wasting traffic. Even if you bid CPC or optimized CPM, failing to target as precisely as possible will cause your CPC to be higher. Remember that Facebook is maximizing their eCPM (effective CPM), so they will charge you more when you waste inventory to make up for who didn't click. Negative feedback will hurt your organic rankings, as well as damage your brand value (26).

You don't want to be known for irritating users, right? Many folks have asked for Boolean logic– the ability to specify ANDs and ORs wherever they like.

For example, there is a difference between those folks who:

- like Coke
- like Pepsi
- Like Coke and Pepsi
- Like Coke or Pepsi

With precise targets, we can determine the audience size of those who like A or B as well as A and B. However, we are, as of this writing, unable to target those who like A and B– despite being able to extrapolate the counts via some Venn diagram magic. In broad category targeting, you actually can get this. You can specify ANY (which is OR) as well as ALL (which is AND). If you add in a bunch of broad category targets with "AND," you will keep cutting down your audience size, the more you AND along.

Likewise, if you choose ANY, then you're expanding the audience, since you're saying you're looking to reach folks who like one or more of these topics, as opposed to ALL of them. Watch your counts. Put too many in the ALL bucket and you end up slicing your audience down to zero. If the estimator says "20 or fewer", that means zero.

We have 50,000 people when we target ANY of these broad interests; we have just 1,260 when we try to do ALL of these broad interests. I had to remove one of them, since it was too many for Facebook's tool to estimate. One day we'll be able to specify ANDs and ORs (Boolean logic) between target groups and within target groups Until then, however, you'll just have to make a lot of ad combos and clever custom audiences.

6.7   Guess Where Users are Spending More Time — TV or Mobile/Web?

For the first time, mobile/web wins– at 197 minutes per day versus 168 minutes. That would seem to be 6 hours per day, but it's actually closer to 4, since most people have their phones while watching TV. So what should you do about it?

Mobile is where your customers are, whether you are a real-estate agent, B2B company, pizzeria, marketing consultant, or whomever. Smartphone penetration in the United States passed 50%. You can buy ads on Facebook mobile in the newsfeed for 30% less than what you're paying for RHS (right-hand side) ads.

Are you taking advantage of this discount, plus the fact that on the iPhone, your page post ads will take up the whole screen? (27)

You're busy, but a few minutes to learn to set up these ads to run on auto-pilot for the next year is worth your time. How many items are being liked on Facebook each day? Answer: 2.7 billion. And since January 2009, Facebook has accumulated 1.3 trillion likes, according to Andrew Bosworth, engineering director.

Fans for the sheer sake of fans is vanity, at best, and wasting money at worst (28). But legitimately lighting the fire on word of mouth to get your best fans (real world customers) talking about you is no different than getting more reviews on Yelp, Zagat, or other similar sites.. In fact, the head of Bing search told me it influences search engine rankings.

Remember, you're competing in Google and Facebook to "show up" in the search results and the newsfeed. Forget the black magic about EdgeRank (Facebook themselves even tells authors like us to not mention the term, but to call it "the algorithm"). Instead, focus on more interactions, since that's the signal both engines use. Comments on your site affect Google rankings, too, in the same way that directory reviews affect your local rankings if you have a store or office.

To get more "votes", which then influences search rankings, run page post ads on Facebook. Promoted Posts are easy to run, too. Just make sure you're targeting the right audience in your geography and interest segments, as opposed to all friends of your fans. Oh, and this helps your newsfeed exposure on Facebook, too. Bonus! Putting a like button on your site and implementing FBConnect will also help you get more interactions, even when people aren't on Facebook, such as my favorite method of getting them to be a fan via text (29).

What's a Facebook fan worth? $1.07, according to research released by the Wall Street Journal, but realistically, some fans are worth more than others. Facebook says the average Facebook user has 130 friends, but that the average fan has 320 friends. Why? If you're a fan of one thing, you're likely to be a fan of many things and also more likely to be someone who is less sensitive about privacy, plus more interested in sharing. We know the average cost per click on Facebook is about 70 cents and the average CTR (click-through rate) is 0.040%,

It's important to know, however, that the performance for a fast food company promoting pictures of bacon will perform quite differently than a plastic surgeon promoting new research on laser varicose vein removal. This is not apples to apples. One is going for likes and the other is going for leads. Comparing against broad averages is fruitless.

All that matters is real ROI for your business– the metrics you choose. The majority of case studies out there either worked in very special circumstances (they have a well-known brand, had a supporting direct mail budget to drive traffic, got unique news coverage, are in a different industry than you, or didn't actually drive success). Ignore them. If you want phone calls, measure phone calls with one of many call tracking tools. If you're low-tech, just ask people how they heard about you. If you are a marketing consultant, forget about mass and target people by their job titles and where they work (30).

How much of your ad budget is being wasted? , According to the famous quote by John Wanamaker, it can be upwards 50%, but he doesn't know which half.

With few exceptions, online performs better than print, magazine, or other offline marketing. The yellow pages are nearly dead– 500 million directories printed each year, which is half a billion, and 24 million trees cut down (31). That's a lot of door stops, kindling, or whatever other clever uses for which the phone books are now used.

Should you stop print advertising altogether? We know many businesses that have make the switch cold-turkey, never looking back, but certain vertical directories are still considered useful, so it's not a black-and-white issue; it's yellow.

What we do know for sure, however, is that micro-targeted ads on Facebook, no matter what the industry, are massively effective. For example, actions like running sponsored results will dominate search results on Facebook for whatever keywords you choose. You can get these for 5 cents a click at a 12% CTR. Don't screw it up,

There is no magic bullet, but with the right strategy for your business, you can select the right tactics for your business. That means rapid cycles of posting content, amplifying it, and repeating it– as opposed to spending a lot of time perfecting your website or spending a lot of time just doing just one other thing (32).

You'll likely not have success if you just hire a consultant without being in charge of your social strategy. If you're a consultant, don't be like this guy who pinged me while I'm writing this article. The world of cold-calling is dead. Write great content, sharing it freely on your blog and influential sites. One of the best examples of passionate storytelling while sharing deep expertise is right here: big data, more noise, not enough time, too many tools. Break through the clutter by getting your best customers to do the work for you. That's why you should be so bullish on Facebook Sponsored Stories and highly targeted page post ads.

You have to generate the great content (not merely good– but amazing) that people will talk about. Then, you use ads to amplify it. You can't make chicken salad out of chicken poo. If you can't write your own content, interview the people who are pros and place the conversation on your blog. They will likely promote your interview to their audience, too!

The new age of inbound marketing is the death of the traditional sales channel. You lead now with expertise and the word of what your loyal customers say about you.

6.8   The Mechanics of Facebook Ad Budgeting

How much should you spend on Facebook ads? How should you allocate budget between campaigns– and then within the ads for each campaign? Let's walk through the strategy behind effective budgeting, then tactically how you implement it.

We start by understanding Facebook's point of view. Facebook wants to maximize their revenues– and they do that by getting as much money as they can per thousand impressions (CPM) of ad inventory, an industry standard handed down long ago (The M is Latin for Mille, which translates to thousand.).

Whether you bid CPM, CPC, or CPA, you're still effectively paying based on how many impressions you're serving. If what I just said was a bunch of alphabet soup to you– hang with me for a minute. It will all make sense.

If you think bidding CPC means a "better deal" because you're "only paying when there's a click', you're wrong. Watch what happens when one of your ads has a third the CTR (click-through rate) of another ad on the same audience—you'll pay three times the CPC. Why? See point #1 about Facebook looking at maximizing their revenues. Run two ads– CPC and CPM with the same placement (newsfeed only or Right-Hand Side only, for example), and you'll see the net CPM price should be similar. Run multiple ads with different creatives against the same audience, and even though they have different CPC/CTR combos, the net CPM is still similar.

What you're really paying for is how much inventory you're using. That means what drives your cost is how big your audience is. If you're targeting audiences of hundreds of thousands, no matter how you're bidding, you're squandering inventory. Assume that Facebook needs to make $5 per thousand ads they serve (CPM). If you have a $10 daily budget, then you can serve up 2,000 impressions a day. If you want to be able to have 5 ads run at any point in time, which means you'll need to run 400 impressions per day per ad.

If one of your ads has an audience target of 100,000 people, then it will hog the inventory away from the other ads in the campaign. Let's calculate your target audience sizes. Take your daily budget for a campaign, divide by 5 and add 3 zeros. So if you have a $100 daily budget, then you have 20,000 impressions per day. I like to have 5–10 ads in a campaign– for sake of simple math, call that 10 ads. That means each ad can consume 1/10th of the 20,000 impressions per day, or 2,000 impressions.

It's important to remember this: *You're not going to be able to reach everyone in your target audience.* They might not be online when your ads are live, or someone else's ads might serve instead of yours. So assuming you are reaching 50% of your target audience, you can target an audience size that's DOUBLE the impressions you want to serve. In other words, if I want to serve 2,000 impressions on an ad, then I'm going for an audience size of 4,000.

Tune your ads to your ideal audience size. You can also have some ads that are well below your target audience size, such as when you're doing workplace targeting, custom audiences, or ads that are restricted by size (maybe by geography, a small precise interest, or an ad that has many filters to whittle down the audience size). You don't want to go too far above your target audience size, for risk of that ad hogging the entire inventory in that campaign. If your audience target is too big, then add more filters. Specifically, you can add a FOF (friend of fan) filter. You will see the audience counts drop significantly, unless you have a large fan base (33). Assume that the average fan has 330 friends. If you have 2,000 fans, then the FOF audience is 660,000 that you're crossing against that initial target. Restrict down by age, gender, or location. People in your hometown are more likely to convert, since they know you and are more likely to be influenced by your existing customers. Filter by a partner category or broad category, such as income, whether they have kids, the kinds of items they have bought in-store, the kind of car they drive, their profession, their ethnicity, and so forth.

Be careful here, since these can cut down your audience size drastically. Facebook used to tell us with fine accuracy what our counts were. Then a couple years ago, if the audience was really small, they would say "less than 20 people". Now they just say "under 1,000 people", which means it could be anywhere from zero to 999 people in that audience. As a result, there is a need to stack your audience, engagement, and conversion campaigns. Allocate the percentages you want on audience, engagement, and conversion. Even if you really want conversions, you still need to put some amount in audience and engagement, so that your revenue factory has a steady stream of traffic flowing from audience to engagement to conversion. Even if you really wanted more conversions, you're limited by how many friends of fans you have and the potential size of your universe (especially if you're a local services provider).

We once talked to a day care in a suburb of Phoenix that asked for 10,000 new enrollments a month. There are just not that many kids in daycare in the whole metro.

If you did allocate more than 50% of your budget towards conversion, then you risk a low conversion rate (an unacceptably high cost of conversion) and alienating people on Facebook with too many self-promotional ads in their newsfeed. If you have a small fan base, you're going to disproportionately allocation on fan growth and engagement so you can build up your company's awareness and word of mouth power. Keep in mind that this is a long-term play and there are likely to be no immediate sales here. It's about nurturing. You certainly can adjust your percentages over time between audience, engagement, and conversion, and you can adjust your total budget, as well, as you start to learn what works and doesn't.

Building up to your total Facebook budget, you could sum up the daily campaign budgets for audience, engagement, and conversion to get your account budget. But if you're just starting a campaign and aren't sure what to spend, start off with 5–10% of your total marketing budget. Then it's not a major risk, but still gives you room to optimize. That number should be at least $5 a day, which is $150 a month. If that's a lot of money for where you are now, then you might wait until your business can afford to invest in building long-term brand on Facebook.

Facebook marketing is not an immediate sales strategy, but some types of Google ads do fit the bill here, as well as FBX (retargeting on Facebook). Run your campaigns for 6–8 weeks, which gives you enough time to optimize for results– finding the right combos of content and interest targets that produce results. You should continue to refine your content to see what drives the most engagement and conversion. This includes your landing pages and email nurture program (a sequence of emails your system sends out to folks who gave you an email in the bottom of the engagement campaign).

A word about bidding: Just use the default bid of "optimized CPM" to make your life easy. When you tell Facebook your goal (to get fans, drive engagement, or drive conversion), then their system will automatically figure out which users in your target audience to hit, plus bid the appropriate price.

Only in rare circumstances should you override this. For example, if you can't get your ads to serve against a particular audience then you can force bid to a $10 CPC. The more complex your campaigns, the more time it takes to optimize them. The more ads you've created, the more "weeding" your garden needs. The lesson here is to not go crazy making a ton of ads at once– just 5–10 per campaign within the 3 campaigns.

This is why we advocate the simple 3 layer campaign strategy of audience, engagement, and conversion. These campaigns are "always on", so they'll continue to pass your traffic through these three levels automatically. When you have only a handful of ads in a campaign, you can quickly see which ones to kill off and which ones to create more variations from. This is a modified version of "winner stay on", where you keep cloning the top performer with similar audiences, but slightly different.

See, our earlier discussion on creating ad combos of one or multiple interest filters. Most of our ads, by the way, have 3–4 filters on them each. Some might have 7–8 filters on them. Having multiple combinations is called the "onion targeting" (34). For a new set of campaigns, you should check in 2–3 times a week, spending only 15 minutes each time. It's better to make a few adjustments over time than try to create a ton of ads at once and have only one cycle of optimization. You want to work with just a few ads per campaign, allowing you to nimbly pause a couple of ads (don't hit "delete") and create a couple new ones.

This allows you to quickly get to statistical significance– a minimum number of clicks to be able to tell whether the difference in performance between groups of ads is a real difference or just random noise. General rules of thumb for people who forget what they learned in stats class: get 10,000 impressions or at least 20 clicks for any ad. Any less and it's noise, and unfortunately you can't really tell the difference.

Once your pilot is successful and you reach a point that you have been able to prove your campaigns are successful, then you can scale up the daily budgets. That also means you can readjust your audience sizes to reflect the larger budgets. More likely, though, once you get the hang of performing bulk operations in Power Editor, you'll likely absorb the budget increase by just managing more ad combos (35).

At this point, you'll be creating more and more audience targeting combination to include custom audiences and FBX. You then clone your three campaigns so you now have two of each — two audiences, two engagements, and two conversions. Except you have one "test" campaign and one "production" campaign for each type of campaign. The test campaign now becomes that with which you've been experimenting, while the production campaign is much larger. When you find a winner in the test campaign, you should copy it over to the production campaign. You will not want to test out new ads in the production budget, since it could risk eating up the larger budget on a larger audience. For those who are veterans of Google AdWords, this is called the "paste and stick" method.

Here are some super pro tips: Just keep in mind that if the audiences are small for an ad, it would cap out on the audience well before it capped out on the daily campaign budget. Budgets are set at the campaign level, not the ad level, so you still need to be careful. Facebook doesn't have frequency capping or ad rotation features natively in Power Editor, the regular ads interface or the API– but we have heard that it's coming. Meanwhile, that means you have to watch your frequency per ad carefully, as well as look at frequency at the campaign and account level.

If you're doing a great job at onion targeting, some of your users are seeing multiple ads from you– perhaps not the same piece of content, but different newsfeed posts, dark posts, and sponsored stories. You know that reach x frequency = impressions. Facebook shows reach and frequency, not impressions, but you can calculate it easily. They choose to show reach and frequency instead, because it's more action-able. Your reach tells you who is exposed to your ad, while frequency is how often those folks see it.

If you have a reach of 10,000 people and an average frequency of 10, then you've served 100,000 impressions. A synonym for reach is unique impressions, meaning unique users who have seen at least one impression. You don't want your newsfeed frequency to exceed 2, since this is a sensitive area of Facebook. You don't want users to say "get off my Facebook page" or other adverse ad reaction. The negative feedback would hurt you, too. You certainly can run frequency on the RHS (Right Hand Side), however, up to 20 or even 30. Yes, the CTR will burn out– even lower than the average RHS CTR of about 0.070%, but if it's still converting and you're not getting complaints, keep those ads alive.

In general, the newsfeed placements (desktop newsfeed and mobile newsfeed) are better for audience and engagement campaigns. For conversion campaigns, sometime the RHS placement performs better– better CPC or better CPA. You just have to test. It may be that non-social businesses (think of things like hemorrhoid crème, industrial plastic extrusion machinery, or personal injury attorneys) produce content that people wouldn't want to actually click like on, even if they're inter-ested. Phew– did you get it all? There you have it! Glad you made it through all the material and exercises. Give yourself a pat on the back.

6.9   How Spending a Few Dollars on Facebook can Turn You into an Influencer

You are a member of the public, and thus a member of the press. So when you get terrible service, should you complain? The levers of power have been tipping toward the public, thanks to social media: A hotel treats me wrong (it's happened to you, too), so I write about it (36). My best friend has a problem with his Toyota, blogs about it, and runs a Facebook ad for $20, targeting executives of Toyota in Japan (37). A cruise line screws up its Fourth of July cruise, so someone writes an exposé on Business Insider (38). An airline accidentally kills a woman's golden retriever, so she uses her blog and Facebook account to warn others about neglect (39).

We resort to this only when we've exhausted our regular channels. Complaining on social media should be a last resort, since it's basically jumping the line. When you're a journalist, blogger, or an influential person in other ways, you wield a megaphone. Even if you're not one of those, running Facebook ads gives you that same power for a few dollars (40).

A lot of people will file a complaint or go to the Better Business Bureau when this happens. Try that first and let me know how it works a few weeks later, counting up how much time and money you spent chasing wild geese. Then run Facebook ads with workplace targeting (targeting folks who work at the New York Times, Wall Street Journal, or wherever folks need to see your message). Target executives at the offending company by following some easy steps. Because you're targeting just a few dozen or a few hundred people, it can be done for a few dollars and in a few minutes. The next day, the general manager of the dealer calls to profusely apologize. Folks in Japan at Toyota HQ have seen the ad and are asking what happened. Of course, as members of media, you and I have to be careful not to abuse our status. Yet with Facebook ads targeted by workplace, any consumer now has this lethal weapon available for their use.

Sure, at one point, you could get a message into Mark Zuckerberg's mailbox for $100 (41). But why not target employees at Facebook for far less and reach a couple of thousand people, too? We attended a mobile hackathon, wrote a post about it, and targeted Facebook mobile engineers. Matt Kelly and James Pearce noticed it and liked it (42). An intern decided to "play a trick on his boss" and ran ads targeting me (43). B2B firms target the press to get more coverage and show up in the Facebook newsfeed (30).

Jim Williams of Influitive shared this with us: "Xactly's advocate marketing program generated hundreds of recommendations, follows and shares on LinkedIn, and a single advocate challenge resulted in nearly a hundred new Facebook fans and Twitter followers" (44). Customers are already talking about the companies that they love or hate online, but advocate marketing programs allow marketers to better organize those customers, tying their activity to sales and marketing initiatives and results. Have a grudge or complaint? Would you spend $5 to scratch this itch? (23).

6.10 The Danger of Buying Facebook Fans

A word of warning to brands looking to expand their Facebook footprint: There are NO shortcuts. Should you "buy" Facebook fans from vendors that sell on a cost-per-fan basis? We have gotten this question a lot over the last couple of years, so let this be your guide. The short answer is: If it sounds too good to be true, listen to your instincts. Whatever you decide, make sure the ads are being run in your own account, no matter what excuse they give you. You've probably come across services that promise to deliver fans for just pennies each (or even cheaper!). That's like saying you can buy a brand new iPod for a dollar.

What's the catch? Most of them can't deliver, and most of the ones that do are offering you what's effectively poison. Some reputable social advertising agencies like Epic Social can deliver you quality, but they are rare.

Here are the main flavors of social media snake oil, why they're dangerous, and how to spot them. If you see any variation of this, run. Often they have only a couple of hundred fans themselves. It's no different than SEO vendors that promise links and yet have no Google PageRank or inbound links to show for themselves. Notice that you don't see any customer testimonials — at least not real ones. And their fan page looks like something pulled out of an infomercial selling dietary supplements. They probably just switched the images out on that landing page to sell whatever is hot.

Fans for pennies! If you see a self-checkout right on the page where you can send a PayPal payment or order fans in bulk, run. You're getting bot traffic, international traffic, traffic rings and other so-called fans that will never result in engagement or sales of any kind. However, if you just want to be able to say you have 100,000 fans but don't care beyond a single boasting metric, then go for it.

Link exchanges! The idea here is: If you fan me, I'll fan you. Often there's a credit system in place where it's not a one-to-one trade, as you find on Twitter. Some of these trades are automated fan exchanges. Not only is this against the Facebook Terms of Service, but these "firms" usually require you to give them administrative access to your page. You might as well give them your social security number, while you're at it.

Our 'proprietary' system! These charlatans will try to sell you an e-book or software, promising the "secrets" to making millions. If you believe that, I'd like to sell you some oceanfront property in Colorado. Do they have real examples to share, or must you pay to see them?

The alternative: A marketing strategy for fan acquisition and valuation. In the end, there's just no substitute for a clear marketing strategy for fan acquisition and valuation. On Facebook, three things are keys when appealing to customers: Decide what your best customers look like, write ads that appeal to them, and send them to a landing page that makes good on that compelling value proposition. Then you can test like crazy to fine-tune your targeting, ad copy, and landing pages. Know what your fan costs and what a fan is worth; hopefully, the former is greater than the latter.

The hucksters described above present you with a simple shopping cart check out to sell fans. Rather, you should select how many fans you want and then pay. Yet how could they possibly deliver on that promise if you don't inform them of your unique selling proposition, which particular audiences to go after, and how you will engage or convert them? Are you trusting them to write whatever ad copy they want, buy traffic from underdeveloped countries, or make misleading promises about your brand to encourage users to click Like? We've seen some firms place a dozen "Like" buttons on a page and offer an incentive to users who click on all of them. Those users who are clicking on the Like buttons machine gun style — have they had a chance to learn about your brand?

No amount of software or gimmicks can substitute for not having a strategy in place. A key component of that strategy is analytics. You must be able to measure fan quality so that you can use this as a basis to optimize your campaigns. What is a fan worth to you? What are you doing with these folks once they become a fan? And how do you identify and reward your most loyal fans — the people who love your product or service in real life?

The idea of spending money on Facebook ads just because your CEO said to do it or your competitor has more fans is ludicrous. You might be inviting derelicts to loiter in the lobby of your high-end hotel, which will discourage the very customers you want to serve. Your real fans will notice who is in your community and decide whether they want to spend time with you there.

Imagine your fan page now has a bunch of 13-year-olds from Indonesia and Turkey (no offense, folks). These could be people who clicked Like on your page because they wanted to earn some FarmVille dollars for a Facebook game. Not only do they not know about your product, but they don't even speak English. Here's a simple litmus test for quality: Of 11,000 Facebook campaigns we analyzed in a recent study, the cost per fan was $1.07 — but the cost to acquire a customer varies dramatically depending on sector. Whether you're evaluating your page, the agency you're considering, or the clients they put forth as examples, just look at their wall. Is there a lot of user interaction relative to how many fans they have?

Count up the number of Likes and comments for the most recent post, which is the number of interactions. Divide that by the number of fans they have. If it's less than 1 in 200 (half a percent), then the engagement rate is low. Your cost per fan depends upon the industry your company is in, how well you can capitalize on your brand's real-world awareness, and how effectively you run your Facebook campaigns.

Of 11,000 Facebook campaigns we analyzed in a recent study, the cost per fan was $1.07. But that averages out entertainment categories that are half that cost, versus healthcare and financial companies that might be five times the cost. Just like in regular Pay Per Click marketing or even direct marketing as a whole, the cost to acquire a customer varies dramatically. You'll need to determine what your real world customer is worth, ensure that your Facebook fans are of the same quality, and then apply the same ROI measurements you'd apply to any other channel.

Don't entrust your marketing strategy or Facebook advertising to an outsider. Does this mean don't hire an agency? No, just make sure you run the strategy, while they execute the details. Does this mean don't buy Facebook ads? No, just make sure you're connecting with your valuable customers and nurturing them in a profitable way.

6.11   How to Tell if Your Ad is Working and Diagnose Newsfeed Burnout

The newsfeed placements (desktop and mobile) are tricky. It's considered "personal" space for Facebook users, so you wouldn't want to burn out from a high frequency or push overtly promotional messaging. Save that for the dark posts to fans and the RHS placements.

We have a newsfeed that that is at a frequency of 6.5. The CTR has fallen to 0.352%. We like to see CTR stay above 1% and frequency below 2.0. You can also look at your negative feedback to tell if users are weary. Grab this via your page insights, downloading the clunky CSV file on post insights. You can also expand the comments to see if you have people demanding that you "get off my Facebook". Besides user experience, a poor CTR or quality score (now defunct) is financial, and Facebook will charge you more. 126 clicks for $91.40 is 72 cents a click. Had this ad not burned out, we'd likely see a 1% CTR (3 times better) and 24 cents a click (a third the price).

The exception to a seemingly high frequency ad is the page post ad that is always on "promote most recent post". Provided that you're posting daily, this ad is not going to burn out, no matter the budget you allocate against it. The true frequency is lower than stated. Facebook is progressively limiting the frequencies of newsfeed ads based on your negative feedback. The rule doesn't apply to RHS (right hand side) placements, since users expect ads there.

How do you tell if your Facebook ad is working or not? Do you let it run for a certain number of days? Or perhaps wait until it gets a certain number of clicks and impressions? How do you know when to turn off an ad or create a similar ad? What's the simple answer for those who are not math geeks? The simple answer: Let each ad generate 10 clicks or $10 in spend, whichever comes first. This gives you enough data to tell if the CTR or the CPC is not where it needs to be.

If you can't get a 1% CTR in the newsfeed, something is wrong with either your targeting or your content. If you have multiple ads in a campaign, sort them by how you've spent over the last 7 days, high to low. Pause (not delete) the low performers, such that you keep 3 ads live at any one time. Each time you optimize (every couple of days), you should create a few new ads and kill a few ads. This takes 5 minutes, tops.

Here's the sophisticated answer: If you have your ads set up properly, with the right counts and structure, you've got your Facebook funnel of Audience, Engagement, and Conversion set up to nurture your customers (45). At 3 campaigns of 8 ads each, you've got 24 ads to watch– each with a different combination of content and targeting, along with varying business objectives and audience counts.

Within Audience, you're looking to gain new fans and reach people who don't know about you yet. You're comparing your audience ads against only the other audience ads, since the engagement and conversion campaigns have other objectives. The CTR on your conversion campaigns will be much lower than your engagement campaigns, but the revenue per click is higher for conversion. Your cost per fan (CPF) is lower for your Audience campaign, since you're explicitly asking Facebook to generate new fans.

The early indicator on ad performance is CTR, since it tells you if there is a mismatch between your content and audience. I like to see a 1% CTR in the newsfeed, though you might be able to get 5–10% if you are in a "social" vertical (entertainment, food, babies, pets, etc). If you're running RHS your CTR will be much lower, but likely generate the same CPC, since the decrease in CTR is offset by the decrease in price for CPM bidding.

We like to see 10 clicks or $10 in spend before making a decision to pause an ad. Anything less and you're looking at an issue of statistical significance – results that are noise from not enough data. For example, if you got one click on only 2 impressions, that's a 50% CTR, but is still just noise. Ads that have a decent CTR can stay alive for the second level of ad pruning, which is a decent CPC and engagement rate.

Usually CTR and CPC have an inverse relationship. When you bid on CPM (which you should always do, except in rare exception), Facebook is going to allocate inventory for you automatically based on your chosen business objective. They select who within your target is most likely to engage/convert and they determine the right price to pay for you. In an engagement campaign, you're looking for a strong CTR and a low cost per action. Look at the ratio of your total actions versus your total clicks. If that's high, you know that only is your content interesting enough to generate interest, but that people will also engage.

In your conversion campaign, you're looking at 3 levels of progressive culling of your ads– a decent CTR, a strong engagement rate, and a good CPA (Cost Per Acquisition). Of course, the cost per conversion (also called CPA) is most critical, but the early indicators of CTR and engagement will help you shut off ads before they spend too much. I like to see 10 conversions per ad before I can make a proper decision about an ad working well. In most cases, especially if this were Google AdWords, we'd cut this ad for being unprofitable. However, this ad might be profitable with some landing page optimization, and it may contribute as an "assist" by driving more people into Google searches for our name. This is a tricky example, since Facebook does drive more Google traffic, enhance the performance of email campaigns, and boost other marketing efforts, in general.

References

1. Yu, Dennis. Why Starbucks = Community. [Online] dennis-yu.com, April 2, 2013. http://www. dennis-yu.com/why-starbucks-equals-community/.
2. —. How to Tackle any Facebook Marketing Question with Ease. [Online] jonloomer.com, May 8, 2013. http://www.jonloomer.com/2013/05/08/ how-to-tackle-any-facebook-marketing-question-with-ease/.
3. —. Preston Smith: Small biz superhero, from one to 94 leads within 90 days on Facebook. [Online] Inside Facebook, July 8, 2014. http://www.insidefacebook.com/2013/07/08/ preston-smith-small-biz-superhero-from-one-to-94-leads-within-90-days-on-facebook/.
4. —. How a TV show gained 567,106 new Facebook fans without running ads. [Online] Inside Facebook, September 30, 2013. http://www.insidefacebook.com/2013/09/30/ how-a-tv-show-gained-567106-new-facebook-fans-without-running-ads/.
5. Guest Writer. How To Succeed At Facebook Advertising. [Online] AllFacebook, May 26, 2011. http://allfacebook.com/how-to-succeed-at-facebook-advertising_b44222.
6. Yu, Dennis. Let the CAT out of the bag! [Online] FB PPC.com, January 10, 2013. http://fbppc. com/targeting/let-the-cat-out-of-the-bag/.
7. —. How To Use Facebook's New Power Editor For Ads. [Online] AllFacebook, June 2, 2011. http://allfacebook.com/how-to-use-facebooks-new-power-editor-for-ads_b44952.
8. —. The Most Amazing Thing You've Never Heard Of On Facebook, If You're a Direct Marketer. [Online] jonloomer.com, January 23, 2013. http://www.jonloomer.com/2013/01/23/ facebook-offsite-pixel/.
9. —. Facebook's Secret To Making Your Life Easy: Optimized CPM. [Online] AllFacebook, November 6, 2012. http://allfacebook.com/dennis-yu-optimized-cpm-facebook_b103941.
10. Yu, Dennis. How To Set Up A Facebook Ad Campaign In 60 Minutes — And Look Good. [Online] AllFacebook, November 23, 2012. http://allfacebook. com/60-minute-facebook-ad-campaign_b105275.
11. Houg, Alex. The 3 campaign system for your Facebook funnel, how it operates. [Online] alexhoug. com, December 19, 2013. https://alexhoug.com/3-campaign-system-facebook-funnel-operates.
12. Loomer, Jon. Website Custom Audiences: Target Visitors with Facebook Ads (Not FBX!). [Online] jonloomer.com, January 28, 2014. http://www.jonloomer.com/2014/01/28/ website-custom-audiences-facebook/.

13. Yu, Dennis. Google selling FBX ads – what it means. [Online] FB PPC.com, October 18, 2013. http://fbppc.com/news-updates/google-selling-fbx-ads-what-it-means/.

14. —. Marketo's Jason Miller On Facebook For B2B: Why So Serious? [Online] AllFacebook, May 13, 2013. http://allfacebook.com/marketos-jason-miller-on-facebook-for-b2b-why-so-serious_b117197.

15. Darwell, Brittany. Word of Mouth at Scale with Facebook: Understanding PTAT. [Online] Inside Facebook, August 31, 2012. http://www.insidefacebook.com/2012/08/31/word-of-mouth-at-scale-with-facebook-understanding-ptat/.

16. Yu, Dennis. How To Use Facebook's New Power Editor For Ads. [Online] AllFacebook, June 2, 2011. http://allfacebook.com/how-to-use-facebooks-new-power-editor-for-ads_b44952.

17. Guest Writer. 8 Critical Steps For B2B Facebook Advertising Success. [Online] AllFacebook, March 12, 2013. http://allfacebook.com/8-critical-steps-for-b2b-facebook-advertising-success_b112724.

18. Lafferty, Justin. News Of Boston Marathon Explosions Spreads Through Facebook. [Online] AllFacebook, April 15, 2013. http://allfacebook.com/boston-marathon-explosion-facebook_b115314.

19. Yu, Dennis. Is Facebook Meddling With Your News Feed Exposure? [Online] AllFacebook, October 3, 2012. http://allfacebook.com/is-facebook-meddling-with-your-news-feed-exposure_b101223.

20. —. THE Single Critical Factor For Successful Advertising On Facebook. [Online] AllFacebook, July 6, 2010. http://allfacebook.com/successful-advertising-facebook_b15387.

21. —. How I shamelessly abuse social media to my advantage. [Online] Socialmedia.biz, August 12, 2013. http://socialmedia.biz/2013/08/12/how-i-use-social-media-to-my-advantage/.

22. —. How To Steal Your Competitor's Customers On Facebook. [Online] AllFacebook, August 11, 2010. http://allfacebook.com/steal-customers-facebook_b16842.

23. —. How to run an effective Facebook campaign for $5. [Online] Socialmedia.biz, April 12, 2011. http://socialmedia.biz/2011/04/12/how-to-run-an-effective-facebook-campaign-for-5/.

24. —. Facebook's Partner Category Targeting: Is Your Head Spinning Yet? [Online] AllFacebook, April 16, 2013. http://allfacebook.com/partner-category-targeting-is-your-head-spinning-yet_b115332.

25. Yu, Dennis. Admit It – You're Struggling as a Small Business. [Online] dennis-you.com, May 14, 2013. http://www.dennis-yu.com/admit-it-youre-struggling-as-a-small-business/.

26. —. Dennis Yu on Ads Impact on Organic, Facebook Retargeting, and Local Business. [Online] EdgeRank Checker, December 12, 2012. http://edgerankchecker.com/blog/2012/12/dennis-yu-on-ads-impact-on-organic-facebook-retargeting-and-local-business/.

27. Yu, Dennis. Facebook mobile ads are how you'll kill it. [Online] FB PPC.com, November 27, 2012. http://fbppc.com/mobile/facebook-mobile-ads-are-how-youll-kill-it/.

28. —. The danger of buying Facebook fans. [Online] Socialmedia.biz, April 18, 2011. http://socialmedia.biz/2011/04/18/the-danger-of-buying-facebook-fans/.

29. Ostrow, Adam. Become a Fan of Facebook Pages With a Text Message. [Online] Mashable, March 26, 2009. http://mashable.com/2009/03/26/facebook-pages-text-messaging/.

30. Miller, Jason. Facebook Expert Dennis Yu on Breaking Edgerank & Creating Kick-A** Ads. [Online] Marketo Blog, July 16, 2012. http://blog.marketo.com/blog/2012/07/facebook-expert-dennis-yu-on-breaking-edgerank-creating-kick-a-ads.html.

31. Yu, Dennis. Facts you probably didn't know about the Yellow Pages. [Online] dennis-you.com, October 26, 2009. http://www.dennis-yu.com/facts-you-probably-didnt-know-about-the-yellow-pages.

32. Stelzner, Michael. How to Connect With Local Customers Via Facebook. [Online] Social Media Examiner, November 11, 2011. http://www.socialmediaexaminer.com/how-to-connect-with-local-customers-via-facebook/.

33. Yu, Dennis. Facebook Friends-Of-Fans' Information Is Key For Marketing. [Online] AllFacebook, September 24, 2012. http://allfacebook.com/dennis-yu-friends-of-fans_b100440.

34. Ash, Tim. Q & A With Dennis Yu – 651% ROI from Facebook Ads–Behind the Curtain of Top Campaigns! [Online] SiteTuners, August 23, 2013. http://www.sitetuners.com/blog/q-and-a-with-dennis-yu-651-roi-from-facebook-ads-behind-the-curtain-of-top-campaigns/.

35. Yu, Dennis. How I Optimize Facebook Ad Campaigns In 15 Minutes Per Day. [Online] AllFacebook, February 13, 2013. http://allfacebook.com/yu-optimize-facebook-ad-campaigns-15-minutes_b110677.

36. Yu, Dennis. Social Media Horror Story With A Happy Ending. [Online] Firebelly Marketing, November 15, 2012. http://www.firebellymarketing.com/2012/11/social-media-horror-story.html.

37. **Keith.** 2008 Toyota Highlander Rip-Off. [Online] Almighty Dad, April 2010. http://www.almightydad.com/reviews/2008-toyota-highlander-rip-off.

38. Anderson, Chris C. I Walked Away From The 'Cruise' From Hell And Still Can't Get A Full Refund. [Online] Business Insider, July 27, 2013. http://www.businessinsider.com/oncruisescom-and-wesellcom-wont-fully-refund-cruise-from-hell-photos-2013-7.

39. Nathaniel. Tribute to the Tragic Death of Beatrice. [Online] beamakesthree.com. [Cited: June 13, 2014.] http://beamakesthree.com/tribute-tragic-death-beatrice/.

40. Yu, Dennis. How To Set Up A Facebook Ad Campaign In 60 Minutes — And Look Good. [Online] AllFacebook, December 23, 2012. http://allfacebook.com/60-minute-facebook-ad-campaign_b105275.

41. Tayor, Chris. Facebook Charging $100 to Message Mark Zuckerberg. [Online] Mashable, January 10, 2013. http://mashable.com/2013/01/11/facebook-message-mark-zuckerberg/.

42. The Blitzlocal Team. Facebook Mobile Hack NYC. [Online] Blitzlocal, January 18, 2012. http://www.blitzlocal.com/facebook-mobile-hack-nyc/.

43. —. Using Facebook Microtargeting to Play a Trick on My Boss. [Online] Blitzlocal, April 10, 2011. http://www.blitzlocal.com/facebook-microtargeting-trick/.

44. Tang, Truman. Case Study: How Xactly Mobilized Social Media Influencers. [Online] influitive, May 23, 2013. http://influitive.com/blog/2013/05/23/case-study-xactlys-marketing-x-factor/.

45. Houg, Alex. Silly! Facebook is like a garden, not a supermarket. [Online] alexhong.com, December 4, 2013. https://alexhoug.com/silly-facebook-like-garden-supermarket.

Chapter 7
How to Become an Influencer and Make Money on Instagram

Inessa Lee

7.1 Social Media Influencer

I am a blogger. Pretty much everyone on Instagram is a blogger these days. But not everyone is a social media influencer making money on their blogs.

In less than 2 years I have successfully developed over 20 micro-blogs for commercial purposes; some of them have over 200K followers and receive advertisement offers on a daily basis. In this article I will describe the latest and the most efficient Instagram marketing tools that I have been using to develop blogs for myself and other companies/individuals. But first let us see how bloggers leverage their investments in their Instagram accounts.

7.2 Advertisement

Owned by Facebook, Instagram has become one of the best social media platforms for business marketing. Many businesses pay influencers to advertise their products. Micro-bloggers do it more successfully than celebrities with millions of followers, because they have a niche. Micro-blogs provide targeted advertisement, similar to Google ads.

Bloggers with a following of 10 to 100 K people are considered influencers as they contribute to shaping public opinion about goods, services, and social issues.

I. Lee (✉)
Institute for Education, Research, and Scholarships, Los Angeles, CA, USA
e-mail: inessa@ifers.org

© Springer Science+Business Media, LLC, part of Springer Nature 2021   151
N. Lee, *Facebook Nation*, https://doi.org/10.1007/978-1-0716-1867-7_7

Low budget advertisement campaigns with micro-bloggers allow businesses to spend less money and target more people. According to Nielsen more than 30% of Americans buy things based on bloggers' recommendations.

For example, if you own a beauty salon in Atlanta, GA, Lady Gaga's Instagram page won't help you to attract customers, but a local beauty-blogger will. Their followers live in Atlanta. They read reviews about beauty products and services, and most importantly they trust the blogger.

So once you choose a niche, start earning subscribers' trust as it is essential in becoming an influencer. Building trust is about how genuine you are in your blog: there is no point to write about new vegan products if you are a meat-eater craving for another burger. People can sense authenticity. That is why some bloggers put the hash tag #noncommercial in a post or add a note about non-sponsored content.

The most successful influencers maintain a balance between their integrity and commercial content. It is all about being authentic, which means that you cannot post sponsored content 24/7. Keep in mind that your followers are there because of your own personal brand.

7.3   Affiliate Marketing

Affiliate marketing is another way to make money on Instagram. Simply use your blog as a platform to distribute products and get a percentage of the sales. Again, the products you distribute should match your personal brand. It would be weird to push for healthy dog food if you do not have any pets. But if you are a fashion gal, it makes sense to be a jewelry brand ambassador. Sometimes bloggers receive free goods in exchange for their advertisement services. It is up to the bloggers to decide what form of compensation works the best for them.

One of the ways to get discovered by brands is setting up a profile on Collabstr which connects advertisers with influencers. On Collabstr you get to set your own price for feeds, posts, and stories.

7.4   Personal Branding

Instagram influencers can easily create and promote their own brands. You can work with creator hubs like Pietra to design and source products from trusted suppliers. Platforms such as Etsy and Pietra allow bloggers to distribute their goods.

Remember that your products should be related to your personal brand. For instance, if you are a lifestyle blogger, your followers are more likely to buy aroma candles and sequin pillows from you. But if you are a fashion blogger, you may even create your own jewelry or clothing line. Cosmetic products are usually sold by beauty bloggers.

Successful brands are often unique and different. Supply exceeds demand, so you have to come up with creative ideas to market your goods on Instagram. For example, every month you could give away some free product samples to those subscribers who have mentioned the largest number of friends in the comments on your Instagram post. Of course, it would be great to talk about your brand in the post. This way you can increase the number of subscribers and your potential customers.

7.5   Giveaways

Instagram giveaway is an additional promotional strategy that allows you to offer free gifts in exchange for subscriptions, likes, and comments. Here are some tips on running a successful giveaway.

The first thing to take care of is a prize. The best option is collaborating with a brand to create an appealing gift. Obviously, people are more likely to engage if you offer a Mercedes-Benz or a million-dollar dream house. If your blog is not backed by a big sponsor, you need to be more creative in coming up with a unique and desirable gift. For instance, you could offer them a weekend trip or a free manicure, depending on your budget and your blog's content.

You can have multiple sponsors funding a gift in exchange for mentioning their company names in your giveaway. For example, your subscribers will have to follow the sponsors' pages and like their posts in order to win the prize.

After you have decided on the prize, you need to determine the rules and timeline. 24-hour giveaway works best, because people do not have to wait till the last day. Urgency works magic when it comes to engaging followers on social media. A 24-hour giveaway is definitely a call to action for them.

You can ask your subscribers to take certain actions, such as "like to win," "tag your friends to win," "like and share to win," or "follow to win." And remember to announce the winners on time. People have short attention span. Do not disappoint them.

You can use all of the above strategies to generate income when you are an established blogger. Now let's talk about SMM (Social Media Marketing) strategies to help you grow your Instagram following and become an influencer.

7.6   Boosting Your Instagram Followers

Buying subscribers does not work! Forget about buying Instagram bots or "high quality" followers. It is simply not worth the money, because 99.9% of "real" followers purchased from black market are not active. Inactive subscribers certainly do not care about your brand and products. Most likely than not, Instagram algorithms will automatically unsubscribe them from your page within a few weeks if they are not actively engaged.

Here are some tips on boosting the number of your Instagram followers:

7.6.1 Enter Giveaways as a Sponsor

This is the fastest way to increase the numbers on your profile and get real followers interested in your brand.

Simply choose a blogger with a decent following (500K and up) whose audience are into similar things that you are promoting. If you have a fashion blog, find a celebrity model, host a giveaway, and get on the sponsors' list.

There are plenty of SMM agencies offering listings of the upcoming celebrity giveaways through WhatsApp and Telegram chats. Find a reputable one as you may come across some scammers trying to sell a giveaway of the blogger who is unaware of it.

It is better to get into a giveaway as early as possible because sponsors on top of the list naturally get the most subscriptions. During the giveaway you need to tell your new subscribers about yourself and your products. Showcase your brand by making some creative posts. Try to engage followers by announcing contests with some cool prizes.

Half of the people who stay subscribed to your blog in the long run are the ones who are enticed by your contests and gifts. The other half is truly interested in your content. Therefore, it is equally important to make attractive posts throughout a giveaway.

If you are a family counselor, post some incredible stories from your therapy practice. People like it when you share your life experience with them. Emotional appeal is just as important as beautiful pictures in making an impact.

7.6.2 Promote your Content to Top Instagram Posts

High engagement level is a way to top Instagram. To get there, you need to have GENUINE likes, comments, and reposts on your posts.

In addition, choose more specific and less popular hashtags; otherwise your content will get lost among millions of similar posts from popular bloggers. For instance, you have a higher chance of "getting in the spotlight" if you use the hashtag #beautykills instead of #beautifulgirl.

It used to be fairly easy to get your posts to the top, but Instagram has been changing its algorithms every couple months. So SMM companies have to constantly update their marketing strategies to keep up with Instagram.

The more comments and likes you have on your post, the better it looks on your brand, but it does not necessarily increase the chance of getting your content to the top any longer. Now you must receive comments and likes steadily within 24 hours—they should be coming non-stop. It does not matter if your get 50 or 1,000 comments. As long as you keep getting them, your post will stay at the top. They must be quality comments. Fake ones are easily recognized by Instagram algorithms. So quit buying low-quality comments from bots. Instead, join the pods.

Here is how pods can help you get into the top Instagram posts.

7.6.3 Joining Instagram Pods

A pod is a community that unites people engaging in each other's Instagram content. It really helps to boost up your social media presence. Pod subscribers like each other's posts and most importantly leave quality comments, which helps to promote content to the top post area. You can join Instagram pods on Telegram or WhatsApp. Some of them are free, and some require a monthly fee to join.

However, Instagram has already started cracking down on comment pods. Facebook has recently broken up several large comment pods and removed a significant number of Facebook groups that were used to organize comment pods on Instagram.

7.6.4 Advertising with Influencers

Another way to gain more followers is advertising your brand with influencers and celebrity bloggers. You can always find micro-bloggers who are in the same niche, and pay them less for more exposure if you do not have a big campaign budget.

Giving free services in exchange for advertisement is a great option too. For example, if you are a cosmetologist, you could approach a bunch of influencers and offering them a free facial in exchange for mentioning your Instagram page in their stories. It is not only a good exposure but also a chance to get more clients.

7.6.5 Targeted Instagram Ads

Instagram ad campaigns can be very costly, and they do not guarantee desirable outcomes. But can consider advertising your Instagram page on other online platforms and social networks. For this type of promotion, make sure to set the right goal for your SMM team before launching a campaign. Find a reputable company to work with. Avoid scammers who will take your money and create fake engagement, which will only hurt your brand and your Instagram account.

7.6.6   The Bottomline

I am not going to waste your time and the publisher's ink, giving you some useless tips on how to boost your following. Yes, creating reels, stories, and IGTV series helps, because it increases the engagement level of your existing followers. To make a big difference, however, you need to come up with creative content. Good luck in becoming a social media influencer!

Chapter 8
Consumer Privacy in the Age of Big Data

"America needs a robust privacy framework that preserves consumer trust in the evolving Internet economy while ensuring the Web remains a platform for innovation, jobs, and economic growth."
– U.S. Commerce Secretary Gary Locke (December 2010)

"I will include easier access to one's own data in the new rules. People must be able to easily take their data to another provider or have it deleted if they no longer want it to be used."
– E.U. Justice Commissioner Viviane Reding (January 2012)

"Who doesn't like getting those retail discounts or free gift coupons from their favorite stores? But did you know there were strings attached, invisible eyes tracking your every consumer move?"
– FTC Chairwoman Edith Ramirez (May 2014)

"Advertising that respects privacy is not only possible, it was the standard until the growth of the Internet. … the current data arms race primarily benefits big businesses with big data sets."
– Apple (November 2020)

"People shouldn't have to accept being tracked across the web in order to get the benefits of relevant advertising, and advertisers don't need to track individual consumers across the web to get the performance benefits of digital advertising."
– David Temkin, Google's Ads Privacy and Trust (March 2021)

8.1 Data Privacy vs. Data Security

Privacy advocates scored a triumph in April 2021 with anti-tracking features in Apple's privacy nutrition labels and, to a lesser extent, Google's Federated Learning of Cohorts replacement for third-party cookies. However, data security remains elusive as cybercriminals posted online the stolen personal information of 533 million Facebook users from 106 countries.

N. Lee, *Facebook Nation*, https://doi.org/10.1007/978-1-0716-1867-7_8

Data privacy and data security are complementary to each other. Data privacy is about the proper or lawful collection, usage, and sharing of personal information by an organization such as Facebook or Google. Data security is about the protection of personal information from unauthorized access by persons inside or outside that organization.

8.2 Facebook vs. Apple's Privacy Nutrition Labels

In April 2021, Facebook was dealt a serious blow by Apple's new anti-tracking functionality in iOS 14.5 and iPadOS 14.5. To comply with Apple's new rules, an app such as Facebook must present a popup that lets users agree to or disable ad tracking. Apple slaps a privacy label (aka privacy nutrition label) on every app. "The App Store now helps users better understand an app's privacy practices before they download the app on any Apple platform. On each app's product page, users can learn about some of the data types the app may collect, and whether that data is linked to them or used to track them. You'll need to provide information about your app's privacy practices, including the practices of third-party partners whose code you integrate into your app, in App Store Connect. This information is required to submit new apps and app updates to the App Store" (1).

Facebook-owned WhatsApp protested the App Store privacy labels, saying that users may be discouraged from using its app. "We think labels should be consistent across first and third party apps as well as reflect the strong measures apps may take to protect people's private information. While providing people with easy to read information is a good start, we believe it's important people can compare these 'privacy nutrition' labels from apps they download with apps that come pre-installed, like iMessage" (2).

Facebook publicly lambasted Apple by taking out full-page newspaper ads in the *New York Times*, *Wall Street Journal*, and *Washington Post* with the headline "We're standing up to Apple for small businesses everywhere" (3) (See Fig. 8.1)

Apple rebuked Facebook in response, "Too often, information is collected about you on an app or website owned by one company and combined with information collected separately by other companies for targeted advertisements and advertising measurement. Sometimes your data is even aggregated and resold by data brokers, which are third parties you neither know nor interact with. Advertising that respects privacy is not only possible, it was the standard until the growth of the Internet. Some companies that would prefer ATT is never implemented have said that this policy uniquely burdens small businesses by restricting advertising options, but in fact, the current data arms race primarily benefits big businesses with big data sets. Privacy-focused ad networks were the universal standard in advertising before the practice of unfettered data collection began over the last decade or so. By contrast, Facebook and others have a very different approach to targeting. Not only do they allow the grouping of users into smaller segments, they use detailed data about online browsing activity to target ads. Facebook executives have made clear their intent is to collect as much data as possible across both first and third party products

Dave Stangis
@DaveStangis

···

I'm pretty certain #Facebook is fighting #Apple to retain access to personal data. #PID #privacy. #fullpagead #wsj

4:19 AM · Dec 16, 2020 · Twitter for iPhone

192 Retweets   **275** Quote Tweets   **700** Likes

Fig. 8.1 Facebook Ad: "We're standing up to Apple for small businesses everywhere"

to develop and monetize detailed profiles of their users, and this disregard for user privacy continues to expand to include more of their products" (4).

Eight civil and human rights organizations—Access Now, Amnesty International, Electronic Frontier Foundation, Human Rights Watch, National Hispanic Media Coalition, New America's Open Technology Institute, Open MIC (Open Media and

Information Companies Initiative), and Ranking Digital Rights—urged Apple to implement the anti-tracking features on iOS 14 as soon as possible (5). Apple delayed the anti-tracking functionality until April 2021 to give advertisers and developers time to adjust to the change.

In the end, Facebook lost the battle against Apple. In fact, the loss was monumental: Early data from the launch date on April 26 to May 16, 2021 shows that the daily U.S. opt-in rate across all iOS apps hovered between 2% and 6% (6). In other words, at least 94% of iOS 14.5 users in the U.S. opt out of ad-tracking—a decisive win for privacy advocates.

8.3   Oil of the Digital Age

Taking a step back, a February 2012 article on *The New York Times* reads, "Facebook's pending initial public offering gives credence to the argument that personal data is the oil of the digital age. The company was built on a formula common to the technology industry: offer people a service, collect information about them as they use that service and use that information to sell advertising" (7).

In a February 2012 report on data services for U.S. insurance companies, Martina Conlon and Thuy Nguyen wrote, "In addition to claims, credit, consumer and cost information, we can now collect information on buying behaviors, geospatial and location information, social media and internet usage, and more. Our electronic trails have been digitized, formatted, standardized, analyzed and modeled, and are up for sale. As intimidating as this may sound to the individual, it is a great opportunity for insurers to use this data and insight to make more informed and better business decisions" (8).

While traditional lenders rely heavily on FICO credit scores, some financial lending companies such as Lenddo look at borrowers' Facebook friends to determine their creditworthiness. "It turns out humans are really good at knowing who is trustworthy and reliable in their community," said Jeff Stewart, co-founder and CEO of Lenddo. "What's new is that we're now able to measure through massive computing power" (9).

In a February 2012 article, Charles Duhigg of *The New York Times* revealed how companies learned their consumers' "secrets." Target, the second-largest discount retailer in the United States, employed statisticians like Andrew Pole to analyze retail transaction data and calculate not only whether a consumer was pregnant but also when her baby was due. Target then used the "pregnancy prediction" to offer expectant mother store coupons tailored to her stage of pregnancy. A Minneapolis man complained to Target that his teenage daughter in high school was receiving coupons for baby clothes and cribs, only to learn a few days later from his daughter that she was indeed pregnant. Pole told Duhigg, "Just wait. We'll be sending you coupons for things you want before you even know you want them" (10).

Data mining in the age of big data is a lucrative business. Using applied statistics and artificial intelligence to analyze complex datasets, companies repackage our private information for their own use as well as selling it to make a profit.

8.4   Data Brokers: The Good, the Bad and the Ugly

Federal Trade Commission (FTC) Chairwoman Edith Ramirez wrote an opinion piece for CNN in May 2014 to warn consumers about the invisible data brokers (11):

The Invisible Eyes:

Who doesn't like getting those retail discounts or free gift coupons from their favorite stores? But did you know there were strings attached, invisible eyes tracking your every consumer move? …

Businesses have long sought to attract and retain customers by recording and analyzing your shopping and lifestyle habits. To do so, they often rely on "data brokers" – companies that collect and share our personal information and label us based on what they learn. And they do this mostly without our knowledge. …

Data brokers scoop up the digital breadcrumbs we leave as we shop in stores and online, and apply "big data" analytical tools to predict where we're going, what we'll buy, and what we'll do.

The Good:

There's no question that the personal information that data brokers sell to retailers, financial firms, hotels, airlines and other businesses can provide benefits to consumers and our growing digital economy. It can help direct goods and services that are tailored to our interests and assisting businesses to combat fraud by verifying consumers' identities.

The Bad:

They also take this information and use it to lump us into various, shorthand categories like "Affluent Baby Boomer" and "Bible Lifestyle." But if a data broker categorizes you as an "Urban Scrambler," meaning a low-income minority, are you more likely to receive an offer for a payday loan than a credit card? What are the implications of being labeled as "financially challenged?" Will it mean you are cut off from being offered the same goods and services, at the same prices, as your neighbors?

And the Ugly:

Data brokers are also making potentially sensitive inferences about consumers – about their health, financial status, and ethnic backgrounds. And consumers have little if any window into this process, let alone meaningful control or choice about how their data is shared among businesses. … data brokers should be required to take reasonable steps to ensure consumer information is not used for unlawful purposes, such as to illegally discriminate.

The Good, the Bad and the Ugly: data brokers are like the Wild West – untamed and without governance. Personally, I prefer targeted ads to junk mail, but there are still plenty of paper ads that I wish I could just eliminate from my mailbox. According to Ramirez, the FTC called on the U.S. Congress in May 2014 to improve the transparency of the data broker industry, and to provide consumers more control over their personal information. The FTC also recommended that Congress require data brokers to create a centralized website so that consumers can access their own data and opt out of data collection and retention.

"The user that's going to interact with your brand really needs to know what they are giving up," cautioned Jay Giraud, CEO and cofounder of Mojio. "If I'm being offered an insurance discount because Geico looked at my data, I want to be the one in control" (11).

Touted as the world's first personal data marketplace, Datacoup pays up to $10 per month for consumers who opt in to share their debit card and credit card transactions as well as data from Facebook, Twitter, and LinkedIn. Datacoup would provide companies analytical results such as "how often women in a certain age group mention coffee on Facebook on the same day they use their credit card in a coffee shop" (12).

The U.S. Congress failed to heed the FTC recommendations. The lack of oversight reared its ugly head again in March 2018 when whistleblower Christopher Wylie disclosed that the British political consulting firm Cambridge Analytica purchased Facebook data on tens of millions of Americans without their knowledge in order to build a "psychological warfare tool" on behalf of clients who intended to interfere in the 2016 U.S. presidential election in Donald Trump's favor (13).

Mark Zuckerberg admitted in a TV interview with CNN's Laurie Segall, "I'm really sorry that this happened. That … is probably the biggest mistake that we made here. … I made technical errors and business errors. I hired the wrong people. I trusted the wrong people" (14).

His confession did not convince some high-profile technology leaders including Steve Wozniak and Elon Musk who deactivated their Facebook accounts and joined the #DeleteFacebook movement (15). "It should bother all of us how much data they had access to, like profile info that we think is private," Wozniak wrote in an email to CNN. "My disgust goes to Facebook. But, like all of us, I clicked 'Accept' or 'OK' or something and gave it away to Facebook. I have always felt badly about social websites being able to sell my stuff, like my photos, and keeping all the money" (16).

Trying not to repeat the same mistake that created the Cambridge Analytica scandal, Facebook conducted an audit on all third-party apps, and in May 2018 suspended around 200 apps for potentially misusing people's data (17).

But antivirus apps are often trusted by hundreds of millions of people without question asked. Unfortunately, an investigation by Motherboard and PCMag revealed in January 2020 that Avast antivirus software had been collecting "Every search. Every click. Every buy. On every site." from its 435 million active monthly users while its subsidiary Jumpshot had been selling those web browsing data to the world's largest companies including Google, Microsoft, Yelp, Pepsi, The Home Depot, McKinsey & Company, Condé Nast, and Tripadvisor (18). In response to the astounding revelation, Avast CEO Ondrej Vlcek announced the company decision to "terminate the Jumpshot data collection and wind down Jumpshot's operations, with immediate effect" because "the data collection business is not in line with our privacy priorities as a company in 2020 and beyond" (19). Senator Ron Wyden applauded the decision, "Avast's past practice of marrying antivirus software with the secret mining of consumers' data was a terrible move. But the decision today to shutter its data broker subsidiary is a model for how companies should respond to criticism of privacy abuses. To stop future abuses, Congress needs to pass my bill to hold companies and their CEOs accountable for abusing Americans' personal information."

8.5   Consumer Privacy Bill of Rights

American Civil Liberties Union (ACLU) is a strong advocate for privacy: "Americans shouldn't have to choose between new technology and keeping their personal information private. Protections for online privacy are justified and necessary, and the government must help draw boundaries to ensure that Americans' privacy stays intact in the Digital Age" (20).

Since 2010, the Obama administration has been pushing for an online privacy bill of rights. Commerce Secretary Gary Locke said in a prepared statement, "America needs a robust privacy framework that preserves consumer trust in the evolving Internet economy while ensuring the Web remains a platform for innovation, jobs, and economic growth. Self-regulation without stronger enforcement is not enough. Consumers must trust the Internet in order for businesses to succeed online" (21).

At the 2012 Black Hat security conference in Las Vegas, Jennifer Granick, director of civil liberties at the Stanford Law School Center for Internet and Society, asked the audience of security professionals who they trusted less, Google or the government? The majority raised their hands for Google. "I fear Google more than I pretty much fear the government," said panelist Jeff Moss, founder of Black Hat and DEF CON. "Google, I'm contractually agreeing to give them all my data" (22).

In February 2012, the White House unveiled its proposed "Consumer Privacy Bill of Rights," a voluntary set of guidelines for Internet companies to provide transparency, security, and user control of their data. The Consumer Privacy Bill of Rights calls for (23):

1. Individual Control: Consumers have a right to exercise control over what personal data companies collect from them and how they use it.
2. Transparency: Consumers have a right to easily understandable and accessible information about privacy and security practices.
3. Respect for Context: Consumers have a right to expect that companies will collect, use, and disclose personal data in ways that are consistent with the context in which consumers provide the data.
4. Security: Consumers have a right to secure and responsible handling of personal data.
5. Access and Accuracy: Consumers have a right to access and correct personal data in usable formats, in a manner that is appropriate to the sensitivity of the data and the risk of adverse consequences to consumers if the data is inaccurate.

6. Focused Collection: Consumers have a right to reasonably limit the amount of personal data that companies collect and retain.
7. Accountability: Consumers have a right to have personal data handled by companies with appropriate measures in place to assure they adhere to the Consumer Privacy Bill of Rights.

Although the White House fell short of making the Consumer Privacy Bill of Rights mandatory, Jon Leibowitz, former Chairman of the Federal Trade Commission, acknowledged that, "it's not the end, it may not be the beginning of the end, but it's a very important step forward" (24).

In April 2012, John M. Simpson, Privacy Project Director at Consumer Watchdog, called on the U.S. Department of Commerce to offer legislation to implement the Consumer Privacy Bill of Rights. Simpson said, "Calls for action in policy papers are easy. The test of commitment is to translate high-minded principles like the Consumer Privacy Bill of Rights into real legislative language" (25).

Two years later in April 2014, Simpson at Consumer Watchdog and 22-member coalition called on the White House to introduce baseline privacy legislation and to implement the Consumer Privacy Bill of Rights according to the following guidelines (26):

1. **TRANSPARENCY:** Entities that collect personal information should be transparent about what information they collect, how they collect it, who will have access to it, and how it is intended to be used. Furthermore, the algorithms employed in Big Data should be made available to the public.
2. **OVERSIGHT:** Independent mechanisms should be put in place to assure the integrity of the data and the algorithms that analyze the data. These mechanisms should help ensure the accuracy and the fairness of the decision-making.
3. **ACCOUNTABILITY:** Entities that improperly use data or algorithms for profiling or discrimination should be held accountable. Individuals should have clear recourse to remedies to address unfair decisions about them using their data. They should be able to easily access and correct inaccurate information collected about them.
4. **ROBUST PRIVACY TECHNIQUES:** Techniques that help obtain the advantages of big data while minimizing privacy risks should be encouraged. But these techniques must be robust, scalable, provable, and practical. And solutions that may be many years into the future provide no practical benefit today.
5. **MEANINGFUL EVALUATION:** Entities that use big data should evaluate its usefulness on an ongoing basis and refrain from collecting and retaining data that is not necessary for its intended purpose. We have learned that the massive metadata program created by the NSA has played virtually no role in any significant terrorism investigation. We suspect this is true also for many other "Big Data" programs.
6. **CONTROL:** Individuals should be able to exercise control over the data they create or is associated with them, and decide whether the data should be collected and how it should be used if collected.

8.6   Federal Trade Commission Privacy Report: Do Not Track

On March 26, 2012, the Federal Trade Commission (FTC) issued its final report setting forth best practices for businesses to protect the privacy of American consumers and give them greater control over the collection and use of their personal data (27). The report, titled "Protecting Consumer Privacy in an Era of Rapid Change: Recommendations for Businesses and Policymakers," expands on a preliminary staff report released in December 2010, which proposed a framework for consumer privacy in light of new technologies that allow for rapid data collection and sharing that is often invisible to consumers. The goal is to balance the privacy interests of consumers with innovation that relies on information to develop beneficial new products and services. The FTC also recommends that Congress consider enacting general privacy legislation, data security and breach notification legislation, and data broker legislation.

The FTC Privacy Report calls on companies handling consumer data to implement best practices for protecting privacy, including:

- Privacy by Design: Companies should build in consumers' privacy protections at every stage in developing their products. These include reasonable security for consumer data, limited collection and retention of such data, and reasonable procedures to promote data accuracy;
- Simplified Choice for Businesses and Consumers: Companies should give consumers the option to decide what information is shared about them, and with whom. This should include a Do-Not-Track mechanism that would provide a simple, easy way for consumers to control the tracking of their online activities.
- Greater Transparency: Companies should disclose details about their collection and use of consumers' information, and provide consumers access to the data collected about them.

"If companies adopt our final recommendations for best practices – and many of them already have – they will be able to innovate and deliver creative new services that consumers can enjoy without sacrificing their privacy," said Jon Leibowitz, former Chairman of the FTC. "We are confident that consumers will have an easy to use and effective Do Not Track option by the end of the year because companies are moving forward expeditiously to make it happen and because lawmakers will want to enact legislation if they don't" (28).

But the end of the year 2012 came and went. Do Not Track has continued to elude consumers as the privacy advocates and the advertising industry cannot agree on what "tracking" means and includes. Small advertising-technology companies complained that the proposed Do Not Track implementation would end up benefiting the likes of Facebook and Google. Yet, Yahoo! said it would ignore do-not-track signals in the Internet browsers (29), and the "Do Not Track" setting in a web browser has no effect on Facebook (30).

Finally, privacy advocates scored a triumph in April 2021 when Apple implemented the new anti-tracking functionality in iOS/iPadOS 14.5 (1) and when Google announced plans to remove support for third-party tracking cookies in Chrome browser (31).

8.7   Google's Federated Learning of Cohorts (FLoC)

"People shouldn't have to accept being tracked across the web in order to get the benefits of relevant advertising," said David Temkin, director of product management at Google's Ads Privacy and Trust team. "And advertisers don't need to track individual consumers across the web to get the performance benefits of digital advertising" (31). Instead, Google's Federated Learning of Cohorts (FLoC) provides privacy-preserving APIs to advertisers for delivering relevant ads to consumers.

Wikipedia offers an elegant explanation of FLoC: "The Federated Learning of Cohorts algorithm analyzes user's online activity within the browser, and generates a "cohort ID" using the SimHash algorithm to group a given user with other users who access similar content. Each cohort contains several thousand users in order to make identifying individual users more difficult, and cohorts are updated weekly. Websites are then able to access the cohort ID using an API and determine what advertisements to serve. Google does not label cohorts based on interest beyond grouping users and assigning an ID, so advertisers need to determine the user types of each cohort on their own. The process used to generate cohorts without sending user browsing data outside the device is similar to the method behind Google's predictive keyboard" (32).

But according to Electronic Frontier Foundation (EFF), FLoC is a terrible idea: "FLoC is meant to be a new way to make your browser do the profiling that third-party trackers used to do themselves: in this case, boiling down your recent browsing activity into a behavioral label, and then sharing it with websites and advertisers. The technology will avoid the privacy risks of third-party cookies, but it will create new ones in the process. It may also exacerbate many of the worst non-privacy problems with behavioral ads, including discrimination and predatory targeting. ... Over the years, the machinery of targeted advertising has frequently been used for exploitation, discrimination, and harm. The ability to target people based on ethnicity, religion, gender, age, or ability allows discriminatory ads for jobs, housing, and credit. Targeting based on credit history—or characteristics systematically associated with it—enables predatory ads for high-interest loans. Targeting based on demographics, location, and political affiliation helps purveyors of politically motivated disinformation and voter suppression. All kinds of behavioral targeting increase the risk of convincing scams" (33).

Google began testing FLoC in its Chrome browser in March 2021 as the company plans to stop supporting third-party cookies by late 2021 or early 2022. However, as of May 2021 all other Chromium-based browsers had declined to implement FLoC. The jury is still out on whether FLoC will succeed in its claim to protect consumer privacy.

8.8 California Online Privacy Protection Act

Effective July 1, 2004, California Online Privacy Protection Act of 2003 (OPPA) is a California State Law governing operators of commercial websites that collect personally identifiable information from California's residents. Such websites are required to conspicuously post and comply with a privacy policy that meets certain requirements stated in the Business and Professions Code Section 22575-22579 (34).

On February 22, 2012, California's Office of the Attorney General has gotten agreements from Apple, Google, Microsoft, Amazon, Hewlett-Packard, and Research In Motion to improve privacy protections on mobile apps. California's Online Privacy Protection Act, one of the strongest consumer privacy laws in the country, would now be applied to mobile apps as well.

"This will give more information to the consumers so they understand how their personal and private information can be used and potentially manipulated," said California Attorney General Kamala Harris. "Most mobile apps make no effort to inform users. … Consumers should be informed what they're giving up before they download the app" (35).

8.9 European Union's "Right to be Forgotten" Law

In January 2012, the European Commission proposed a comprehensive reform of the EU's 1995 Data Protection Directive in order to strengthen online privacy rights and to unify the implementation of privacy law in the 27 EU Member States (36). European Union Justice Commissioner Viviane Reding unveiled details of the proposed "Right to be Forgotten" law at the January 2012 Digital Life Design (DLD) conference in Munich. Reding outlined her proposal:

"First, people need to be informed about the processing of their data in simple and clear language. Internet users must be told which data is collected, for what purposes and how long it will be stored. They need to know how it might be used by third parties. They must know their rights and which authority to address if those rights are violated.

"Second, whenever users give their agreement to the processing of their data, it has to be meaningful. In short, people's consent needs to be specific and given explicitly.

"Thirdly, the reform will give individuals better control over their own data. I will include easier access to one's own data in the new rules. People must be able to easily take their data to another provider or have it deleted if they no longer want it to be used" (37).

In May 2014, the European Court ruled that Google can be forced to erase links to content about individuals on the Web. It was a resounding victory for Mario Gonzalez, a Spanish citizen, who sued Google for refusing to remove a search result linked to a 1998 report on his real estate auction and social security debts. Gonzalez's line of reasoning is simple: "This is really old information, and it no longer reflects who I am" (38).

Professor Jeffrey Rosen at the George Washington University commented in *Stanford Law Review* of how the EU law could affect Facebook and Google: "The right to be forgotten could make Facebook and Google, for example, liable for up to two percent of their global income if they fail to remove photos that people post about themselves and later regret, even if the photos have been widely distributed already" (39).

Since the May 2014 European Court ruling, Google has been flooded with demands from people to remove links from its search results. While innocent people and "revenge porn" victims could benefit from the "Right to be Forgotten" law, an unpopular politician, a poorly reviewed physician, and a pedophile were also among the first to have issued Google removal requests. "The ruling has significant implications for how we handle take-down requests," a Google spokesman said. "This is logistically complicated – not least because of the many languages involved and the need for careful review" (40).

In implementing the European Data Protection law, Google has provided an online form for search removal request for people in 28 European Union countries and four neighboring nations (41). The form states, "A recent ruling by the Court of Justice of the European Union found that certain users can ask search engines to remove results for queries that include their name where those results are *inadequate, irrelevant or no longer relevant, or excessive in relation to the purposes for which they were processed.* In implementing this decision, we will assess each individual request and attempt to balance the privacy rights of the individual with the public's right to know and distribute information. When evaluating your request, we will look at whether the results include outdated information about you, as well as whether there's a public interest in the information—for example, information about financial scams, professional malpractice, criminal convictions, or public conduct of government officials" (42).

8.10   Facebook and Twitter Safety and Takedowns

In May 2018, Facebook Global Head of Safety Antigone Davis revealed a proactive reporting tool to block the sharing of intimate images on Facebook, Instagram, and Messenger. Facebook partnered with the Australian Office of the eSafety Commissioner, U.S. Cyber Civil Rights Initiative, U.S. National Network to End Domestic Violence, the UK Revenge Porn Helpline, and YWCA Canada. According to Facebook, the reporting tool works as follows (43):

- Anyone who fears an intimate image of them may be publicly can contact one of our partners to submit a form
- After submitting the form, the victim receives an email containing a secure, one-time upload link
- The victim can use the link to upload images they fear will be shared
- One of a handful of specifically trained members of our Community Operations Safety Team will review the report and create a unique fingerprint, or hash, that allows us to identify future uploads of the images without keeping copies of them on our servers
- Once we create these hashes, we notify the victim via email and delete the images from our servers – no later than seven days
- We store the hashes so any time someone tries to upload an image with the same fingerprint, we can block it from appearing on Facebook, Instagram, or Messenger

The proactive report tool is a step forward to improve privacy and protect the vulnerable members of society. As Antigone Davis wrote, "People shouldn't be able to share intimate images to hurt others" (43).

In November 2021, Twitter announced that it would let private individuals request takedowns of their pictures and videos posted by others without their permission. Twitter Safety explains, "Sharing personal media, such as images or videos, can potentially violate a person's privacy, and may lead to emotional or physical harm. The misuse of private media can affect everyone, but can have a disproportionate effect on women, activists, dissidents, and members of minority communities" (44).

Social media has finally begun to step up to their responsibility in thwarting harassment and invasion of privacy.

References

1. **App Store.** App privacy details on the App Store. [Online] Apple. [Cited: April 26, 2021.] https://developer.apple.com/app-store/app-privacy-details/.
2. **Charlton, Hartley.** WhatsApp Protests Apple's App Store Privacy Requirements. [Online] MacRumors, December 9, 2020. https://www.macrumors.com/2020/12/09/whatsapp-protests-app-store-privacy-requirements/.
3. —. Facebook Takes Out Full-Page Newspaper Ads to Attack Apple's iOS Privacy Changes. [Online] MacRumors, December 16, 2020. https://www.macrumors.com/2020/12/16/facebook-takes-out-full-page-ads-to-attack-apple/.
4. **Clover, Juli.** Apple Confirms Commitment to App Tracking Transparency in Letter Condemning Facebook's Data Collection [Updated]. [Online] MacRumors, November 19, 2020. https://www.macrumors.com/2020/11/19/apple-app-tracking-transparency-letter/.
5. **Ranking Digital Rights.** Mr. Tim Cook. [Online] Ranking Digital Rights, October 2020. https://rankingdigitalrights.org/wp-content/uploads/2020/10/Ranking-Digital-Rights-Joint-Letter-to-Apple-iOS14-delay.pdf.
6. **Laziuk, Estelle.** iOS 14.5 Opt-in Rate – Daily Updates Since Launch . [Online] Flurry, May 21, 2021. https://www.flurry.com/blog/ios-14-5-opt-in-rate-att-restricted-app-tracking-transparency-worldwide-us-daily-latest-update/.

7. **Brustein, Joshua.** Start-Ups Seek to Help Users Put a Price on Their Personal Data. [Online] The New York Times, February 12, 2012. http://www.nytimes.com/2012/02/13/technology/start-ups-aim-to-help-users-put-a-price-on-their-personal-data.html.

8. **Conlon, Martina and Nguyen, Thuy.** Data Services for US Insurers 2012 (Q1). [Online] Novarica, February 2012. http://www.novarica.com/data_services_nmn2012/.

9. **Lobosco, Katie.** Facebook friends could change your credit score. [Online] CNNMoney, August 27, 2013. http://money.cnn.com/2013/08/26/technology/social/facebook-credit-score/index.html.

10. **Duhigg, Charles.** How Companies Learn Your Secrets. [Online] The New York Times, February 16, 2012. http://www.nytimes.com/2012/02/19/magazine/shopping-habits.html?pagewanted=all.

11. **Ramirez, Edith.** The secret eyes watching you shop. [Online] CNN, May 30, 2014. http://www.cnn.com/2014/05/30/opinion/ramirez-data-brokers-ftc/index.html.

12. **Simonite, Tom.** Datacoup Wants to Buy Your Credit Card and Facebook Data. [Online] MIT Technology Review, September 8, 2014. http://www.technologyreview.com/news/530486/datacoup-wants-to-buy-your-credit-card-and-facebook-data/.

13. **Lapowsky, Issie.** How Cambridge Analytica Sparked the Great Privacy Awakening. [Online] Wired, March 17, 2019. https://www.wired.com/story/cambridge-analytica-facebook-privacy-awakening/.

14. **Wiener-Bronner, Danielle.** Mark Zuckerberg has regrets: 'I'm really sorry that this happened'. [Online] CNN Business, March 21, 2018. https://money.cnn.com/2018/03/21/technology/mark-zuckerberg-apology/index.html.

15. **Koren, Marina.** Why Did Elon Musk Delete His Facebook Pages? [Online] The Atlantic, March 23, 2018. https://www.theatlantic.com/technology/archive/2018/03/elon-musk-facebook-mark-zuckerberg-delete/556412/.

16. **Smith, Aaron.** Apple co-founder Steve Wozniak 'disgusted' with Facebook, deactivates account. [Online] CNNBusiness, April 9, 2018. https://money.cnn.com/2018/04/09/technology/steve-wozniak-facebook/index.html.

17. **Meyer, David.** Facebook Has Suspended 200 Apps That May Have Misused People's Private Data. [Online] Fortune, May 14, 2018. https://fortune.com/2018/05/14/facebook-suspends-200-apps-cambridge-analytica-privacy/.

18. **Cox, Joseph.** Leaked Documents Expose the Secretive Market for Your Web Browsing Data. [Online] Vice, January 27, 2020. https://www.vice.com/en/article/qjdkq7/avast-antivirus-sells-user-browsing-data-investigation.

19. **Koebler, Jason.** Avast Antivirus Is Shutting Down Its Data Collection Arm, Effective Immediately. [Online] Vice, January 30, 2020. https://www.vice.com/en/article/wxejbb/avast-antivirus-is-shutting-down-jumpshot-data-collection-arm-effective-immediately.

20. **ACLU.** Internet Privacy. [Online] American Civil Liberties Union. [Cited: May 29, 2012.] http://www.aclu.org/technology-and-liberty/internet-privacy.

21. **Office of Public Affairs.** Commerce Department Unveils Policy Framework for Protecting Consumer Privacy Online While Supporting Innovation. [Online] United States Department of Commerce, December 16, 2010. http://www.commerce.gov/news/press-releases/2010/12/16/commerce-department-unveils-policy-framework-protecting-consumer-priv.

22. **Kelly, Heather.** Is the government doing enough to protect us online? [Online] CNN, July 31, 2012. http://www.cnn.com/2012/07/25/tech/regulating-cybersecurity/index.html.

23. **CNNMoneyTech.** Consumer Privacy Bill of Rights. [Online] CNNMoney, February 23, 2012. http://money.cnn.com/2012/02/22/technology/bill_of_rights_privacy/index.htm.

24. **Goldman, David.** White House pushes online privacy bill of rights. [Online] CNN, February 23, 2012. Money. http://money.cnn.com/2012/02/23/technology/privacy_bill_of_rights/index.htm.

25. **Consumer Watchdog.** Consumer Watchdog Calls on Commerce Department to Offer Privacy Legislation; Says Proposed "Multi-Stakeholder Process" Must Be Fair, Transparent and Credible. [Online] MarketWatch, April 2, 2012. http://www.marketwatch.com/story/

consumer-watchdog-calls-on-commerce-department-to-offer-privacy-legislation-says-proposed-multi-stakeholder-process-must-be-fair-transparent-and-credible-2012-04-02.

26. **Simpson, John M.** Consumer Watchdog Tells White House Team People Have Right To Control Data. [Online] Consumer Watchdog, April 1, 2014. http://www.consumerwatchdog.org/newsrelease/consumer-watchdog-tells-white-house-team-people-have-right-control-data.

27. **Federal Trade Commission.** Protecting Consumer Privacy in an Era of Rapid Change: Recommendations for Businesses and Policymakers. [Online] FTC Report, March 2012. http://www.ftc.gov/sites/default/files/documents/reports/federal-trade-commission-report-protecting-consumer-privacy-era-rapid-change-recommendations/120326privacyreport.pdf.

28. —. FTC Issues Final Commission Report on Protecting Consumer Privacy. [Online] Federal Trade Commission, March 26, 2012. http://www.ftc.gov/news-events/press-releases/2012/03/ftc-issues-final-commission-report-protecting-consumer-privacy.

29. **Winkler, Rolfe.** Fight Over 'Do Not Track' Web Rules. [Online] The Wall Street Journal, May 22, 2014. http://online.wsj.com/news/articles/SB10001424052702303749904579576283791254304.

30. **Blue, Violet.** Facebook turns user tracking 'bug' into data mining 'feature' for advertisers. [Online] ZDNet, June 17, 2014. http://www.zdnet.com/facebook-turns-user-tracking-bug-into-data-mining-feature-for-advertisers-7000030603/.

31. **Hardawar, D.** Google plans to stop targeting ads based on your browsing history. [Online] Engadget, March 3, 2021. https://www.engadget.com/google-ads-user-data-tracking-cookies-144445173.html.

32. **Wikipedians.** Federated Learning of Cohorts. [Online] Wikipedia. [Cited: May 22, 2021.] https://en.wikipedia.org/wiki/Federated_Learning_of_Cohorts.

33. **Cyphers, Bennett.** Google's FLoC Is a Terrible Idea. [Online] Electronic Frontier Foundation, March 3, 2021. https://www.eff.org/deeplinks/2021/03/googles-floc-terrible-idea.

34. **Legislative Counsel of California.** BUSINESS AND PROFESSIONS CODE SECTION 22575-22579. [Online] Official California Legislative Information, July 1, 2004. http://leginfo.ca.gov/cgi-bin/displaycode?section=bpc&group=22001-23000&file=22575-22579.

35. **Mills, Elinor.** Tech firms agree to privacy protections for mobile apps. [Online] CNET, February 22, 2012. http://news.cnet.com/8301-1009_3-57382965-83/tech-firms-agree-to-privacy-protections-for-mobile-apps/.

36. **European Commission.** Commission proposes a comprehensive reform of the data protection rules. [Online] European Commission Newsroom, January 25, 2012. http://ec.europa.eu/justice/newsroom/data-protection/news/120125_en.htm.

37. **Rooney, Ben.** Reding Details Sweeping Changes to EU Data Laws. [Online] The Wall Street Journal, January 23, 2012. http://blogs.wsj.com/tech-europe/2012/01/23/reding-details-sweeping-changes-to-e-u-data-laws/.

38. **Randazza, Marc.** We need a 'right to be forgotten' online. [Online] CNN, May 14, 2014. http://www.cnn.com/2014/05/14/opinion/randazza-google-right-to-privacy/index.html.

39. **Rosen, Jeffrey.** The Right to Be Forgotten. [Online] Stanford Law Review, February 13, 2012. http://www.stanfordlawreview.org/online/privacy-paradox/right-to-be-forgotten.

40. **Burke, Samuel.** Google fielding 'take-down requests' after privacy ruling. [Online] 2014, 16 May. http://money.cnn.com/2014/05/16/technology/google-forget/index.html.

41. **Petroff, Alanna.** Google spells out how to be 'forgotten' in search. [Online] CNNMoney, May 30, 2014. http://money.cnn.com/2014/05/30/news/companies/google-europe-search/index.html.

42. **Google.** Search removal request under European Data Protection law. [Online] Google. [Cited: June 3, 2014.] https://support.google.com/legal/contact/lr_eudpa?product=websearch.

43. **Davis, Antigone.** People shouldn't be able to share intimate images to hurt others. [Online] Facebook Safety, May 22, 2018. https://www.facebook.com/fbsafety/posts/1666174480087050.

44. **Twitter Safety.** Expanding our private information policy to include media. Twitter. [Online] November 30, 2021. https://blog.twitter.com/en_us/topics/company/2021/private-information-policy-update.

Part IV
The Rise of Facebook Nation

Chapter 9
Twitter – A World of Immediacy

"The pen is mightier than the sword."
– Edward Bulwer-Lytton (1839)

"Too many tweets might make a twat."
– British Prime Minister David Carmeron (July 2009)

"Freedom of expression is essential."
– Twitter's @biz and @amac (January 2011)

"They [the newspapers] seem incapable of breaking real, meaningful news at Internet speed. It's why they like Twitter so much. Twitter does the hard work for them."
– Mike Hudack, director of product at Facebook (May 2014)

"Twitter is like a party where everyone is screaming. Not much of a party. Goodbye for now."
– Actor Alec Baldwin (January 2021)

"The internet is undefeated. Thank you thank you thank you"
– Actress Olivia Munn (February 2021)

"It's time for me to say goodbye. This no longer serves me as positively as it serves me negatively, and I think that's the right time to call something."
– Model and TV personality Chrissy Teigen (March 2021)

9.1 Platform of Hope Amid COVID-19 Crisis

In April 2021, India experienced the worst COVID-19 surge in the world with a record 330,000 new COVID-19 cases a day (1). At a vaccination center in Mumbai, India, notices about the shortage of the COVISHIELD vaccine turned hope into despair (see Fig. 9.1). After calling government helplines in search of a hospital bed for a critically ill COVID-19 patient, Indian attorney and medical support volunteer Jeevika Shiv turned to Twitter for help: "Serious #covid19 patient in #Delhi with oxygen level 62 needs immediate hospital bed. #Covid report awaited but oxygen saturation is very low." Help arrived quickly, and the patient was transported to a hospital by ambulance. (See Fig. 9.2) "Finally, it was help online that worked as people responded with information," said Shiv (2). "Twitter is having to do what the

© Springer Science+Business Media, LLC, part of Springer Nature 2021
N. Lee, *Facebook Nation*, https://doi.org/10.1007/978-1-0716-1867-7_9

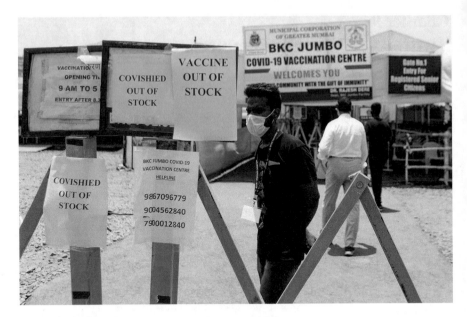

Fig. 9.1 Outside a COVID-19 vaccination center in Mumbai, India on April 20, 2021 (Courtesy of Reuters/Francis Mascarenhas)

government helpline numbers should be doing," wrote Twitter user Karanbir Singh. Twitter enables people to help each other in real time, which can be more efficient and effective than any government services.

9.2   Crime Stoppers on Social Media

Established on September 8, 1976 in Albuquerque, New Mexico, Crime Stoppers USA has created a network of local programs to prevent and solve crimes in communities and schools across the United States. Statistics from September 1976 to May 2021 show more than 800,000 arrests, 14,000 homicides solved, 1,000,000 cases cleared, and $100,000,000 rewards paid (3).

Social media such as Twitter takes crime fighting to the whole new level of immediacy. On February 17, 2021, American actress Olivia Munn posted images on Twitter to ask for assistance in identifying the assailant who attacked her friend's mother in Flushing, New York (4). She pleaded for help (see Fig. 9.3):

"My friend's mom is a 5'3" 50+ Chinese woman and she was attacked by this guy in Flushing, NY yesterday on Main St and Roosevelt between 2-4pm. She left the hospital with 10 stitches in her head. We're gonna find this guy. Queens, Internet, please... do your shit. 🙏 @NYPD109Pct" (5)

Within 24 hours, the assailant was identified and apprehended by NYPD. Munn tweeted again and thanked the Internet for helping (see Fig. 9.4):

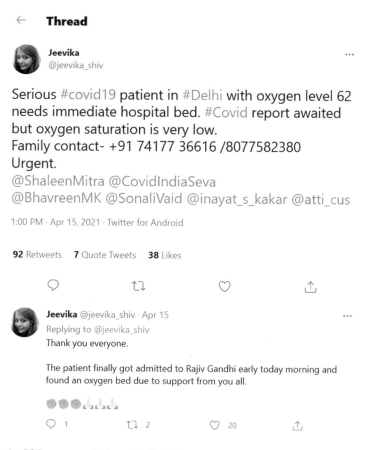

Fig. 9.2 An SOS request on Twitter (April 15, 2021)

"This is the guy you guys helped @nypd find and arrest. This is him attacking my friend's mom who is a petite 5-foot-3 Chinese woman. Fuck this guy. The internet is undefeated. Thank you thank you thank you #StopAsianHate #ProtectOurElders @NYPDnews @NYPD109Pct" (6)

9.3   The Pen is Mightier than the Sword

Edward Bulwer-Lytton coined the metonymic adage "the pen is mightier than the sword" in 1839 (7). Chairman Mao Zedong seemed to concur, "As communists we gain control with the power of the gun and maintain control with the power of the pen" (8).

  On April 10, 2008, University of California, Berkeley grad student James Karl Buck was photographing an anti-government protest in Mahalla, Egypt when he

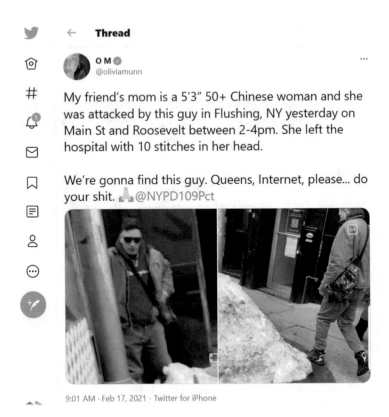

Fig. 9.3 Olivia Munn tweeted and pleaded for assistance on February 17, 2021

was arrested by the authorities. He managed to send a quick tweet: "Arrested." His Twitter followers contacted the university, the American Embassy, and media organizations to put pressure on the Egyptian government to release him. In less than 24 hours, on April 11, Buck sent another one-word tweet: "Free" (9).

On October 9, 2012, 15-year-old Pakistani girl Malala Yousufzai was shot in the head by Taliban gunmen who flagged down her school bus. Malala survived the attack and took the stage at the United Nations on July 12, 2013, her 16th birthday, to advocate the universal right for all children to attend school. A few days later, Adnan Rashid, militant commander of Tehreek-i-Taliban Pakistan, sent Malala a letter to explain the atrocious attack: "The Taliban believe you were intentionally writing against them and running a smear campaign to malign their effort to establish an Islamic system in (the) Swat Valley, and your writings were provocative. You have said in your speech ... that the pen is mightier than the sword. So they attacked you for your sword not your books or school" (10).

In the ancient historical past, the sword had exerted considerable influences on the pen. Qin Shi Huang (秦始皇), the first emperor of the unified China in 221 B.C., outlawed and burned many books in order to enforce the uniformity of the Chinese

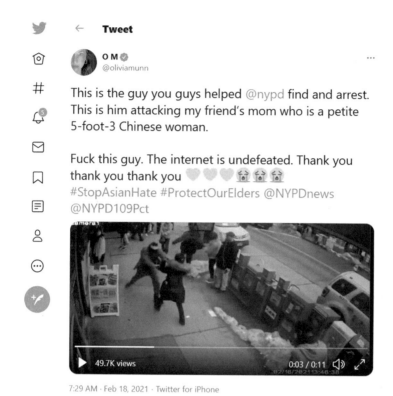

Fig. 9.4   Olivia Munn tweeted and thanked the Internet for helping on February 18, 2021

language (11). His censorship succeeded in imposing one basic written language throughout China, even though there still exists today hundreds of spoken Chinese dialects that sound like entirely different languages (12). And for some periods of time in Catholic history, lay Catholics were discouraged from directly reading the Bible for fear that they would misinterpret the Scripture. The printing press and Protestant Reformation in the 16th century resulted in the proliferation of the Bible and the freedom of new Bible translations.

When I was in college, a saleswoman tried to sell me a set of Encyclopedia Britannica that contains all of the above historical events and literary commentaries. In March 2012, after 244 years, Encyclopedia Britannica decided to cease production of its iconic multi-volume print book sets, making the 2010 version its final edition. The company would instead focus on digital encyclopedia and educational tools. "The print set is an icon," said Britannica president Jorge Cauz. "But it's an icon that doesn't do justice to how much we've changed over the years. Updating dozens of books every two years now seems so pedestrian. The younger generation consumes data differently now, and we want to be there" (13).

For the same reason of the behavioral change in consumers' data consumption, AT&T in April 2012 ditched the Yellow Pages directories that used to go out to about 150 million homes and businesses in 22 states (14). It was inevitable, since major cities such as Seattle and San Francisco were moving to ban the unsolicited delivery of Yellow Pages in order to reduce waste (15).

In the digital age, information is abundant with immediacy and is easily accessible anytime and anywhere. In June 2012, Google.org launched the Endangered Language Project in an effort to save 3,054 dying languages around the world (which will hopefully help undo some of the deeds by Chinese emperor Qin Shi Huang) (16). Project managers Clara Rivera Rodriguez and Jason Rissman said, "Documenting the 3,000+ languages that are on the verge of extinction is an important step in preserving cultural diversity, honoring the knowledge of our elders, and empowering our youth" (17).

Thanks to the Internet, words can travel at the speed of light, and no amount of censorship can stop the flow of information. Although the online social networking site Twitter said in January 2012 that it would delete users' tweets in countries that require it, Twitter would still keep those deleted tweets visible to the rest of the world (18). Sarah Kendzior at Washington University in St. Louis has published online papers to help Uzbek refugees find a safe haven abroad and to introduce contemporary Uzbek literature into the lives of Midwestern teens (19).

Thanks to Malala's courage, no militant can silence her. Thanks to the Internet, the pen is mightier than the sword.

9.4   Citizen Journalists

Mike Hudack, director of product at Facebook, ranted about the state of the media in his blog: "They [the newspapers] just report what people tell them, whether it's Cheney pulling Judith Miller's strings or Snowden through the proxy of Glenn Greenwald doing roughly the same. They seem incapable of breaking real, meaningful news at Internet speed. It's why they like Twitter so much. Twitter does the hard work for them" (20).

On January 15, 2009, eyewitness Jānis Krūms sent a TwitPic photo of passengers waiting to be rescued from a US Airways plane after its emergency landing on the Hudson River. His wrote on Twitter, "There's a plane in the Hudson. I'm on the ferry going to pick up the people. Crazy" (21) (See Fig. 9.5). Hundreds of Flickr users also posted photos of the crash, but Krūms' eyewitness report went viral.

On May 1, 2011, IT consultant Sohaib Athar (@ReallyVirtual) was coding some software after midnight in Pakistan when he heard the annoying noise outside his apartment (22). Athar sent out a series of tweets as the event developed (23):

- "Helicopter hovering above Abbottabad at 1AM (is a rare event)"
- "Go away helicopter – before I take out my giant swatter :-/"
- "A huge window shaking bang here in Abbottabad Cantt. I hope its [sic] not the start of something nasty :-S"

Fig. 9.5 Eyewitness Jānis Krūms' Tweet and TwitPic

- "@m0hcin all silent after the blast, but a friend heard it 6 km away too... the helicopter is gone too."
- "@m0hcin http://bit.ly/ljB6p6 seems like my giant swatter worked!"
- "@m0hcin the few people online at this time of the night are saying one of the copters was not Pakistani..."

- "@raihak Funny, moving to Abbottabad was part of the 'being safe' strategy"
- "Since taliban (probably) don't have helicpoters *[sic]*, and since they're saying it was not 'ours', so must be a complicated situation #abbottabad"
- "@kashaziz technically, it is unidentified until identified, and it is a flying object, so year *[sic]*, why the hell not, we have seen weirder stuff"
- "The abbottabad helicopter/UFO was shot down near the Bilal Town area, and there's report of a flash. People saying it could be a drone."
- "@smedica people are saying it was not a technical fault and it was shot down. I heard it CIRCLE 3-4 times above, sounded purposeful."
- "@smedica It must have been more, I started noticing the helicpoter when the noise got irritating - which part of Abbottabd are you in?"
- "@smedica I live near Jalal Baba Auditorium"
- "Two helicpoters *[sic]*, one down, could actually be the training accident scenario they're saying it was >> http://bit.ly/ioGE6O"
- "and now I feel I must apologize to the pilot about the swatter tweets :-/"
- "And now, a plane flying over Abbottabad..."
- "Interesting rumors in the otherwise uneventful Abbottabad air today"
- "Report from a taxi driver: The army has cordoned off the crash area and is conducting door-to-door search in the surrounding."
- "RT @ISuckBigTime: Osama Bin Laden killed in Abbottabad, Pakistan.: ISI has confirmed it << Uh oh, there goes the neighborhood :-/"
- "For the curious, here is life in abbottabad two minutes ago http://twitpic. com/4s8nfq"
- "Uh oh, now I'm the guy who liveblogged the Osama raid without knowing it."
- "and here come the mails from the mainstream media... *sigh*"

Until the official news reached Sohaib Athar, little did Athar know that he was live tweeting the secret U.S. military raid by the SEAL Team Six that killed Osama bin Laden at a hideout compound in Abbottabad, Pakistan. The IT consultant went on to photograph bin Laden's compound a mile away from his home, and interviewed neighbors living in that area. Athar was soon hailed as the accidental "citizen journalist," the man who live-tweeted Osama's death. His 750 or so Twitter followers on May 1, 2011 have swelled to over 100,000 followers in a matter of days (24).

Steve Myers, managing editor of Poynter.org, said at the 2012 South by Southwest Interactive festival, "In an era when mobile-phone owners walk around with a video camera in their pocket at all times and tools like Twitter, Facebook and YouTube make broadcasting the results quick and simple, people like Athar can turn into journalists without even knowing it" (25). CNN's sports columnist Terence Moore agreed, "New media have created a slew of investigative reporters among average citizens through personal blogs, Twitter, YouTube, talk-show radio, cellphone cameras and recorders, Facebook and fan websites" (26).

In August 2013, NBC News embraced citizen journalism by acquiring user-generated live video service Stringwire. "You could get 30 people all feeding video, holding up their smartphones," NBC News Chief Digital Officer Vivian Schiller told the *Times*, "and then we could look at that. We'll be able to publish and broad-cast some of them" (27). As citizen journalists and bloggers are becoming more important in news gathering and timely dissemination, mainstream media has found an important ally in the Fifth Estate.

9.5   A World of Immediacy

Morning newspapers are yesterday's news; social media news are the now moments. Twitter, in particular, has created a world of immediacy. Twitter's mission is "to instantly connect people everywhere to what is most meaningful to them." For this to happen, Twitter expresses in its official blog, "freedom of expression is essential. Some Tweets may facilitate positive change in a repressed country, some make us laugh, some make us think, some downright anger a vast majority of users. We don't always agree with the things people choose to tweet, but we keep the information flowing irrespective of any view we may have about the content" (28).

In 2011, Apple integrated Twitter into its iOS 5, making Twitter the default social graph and social network on iPhone, iPod Touch, and iPad (29). As a direct result of the iOS integration, Twitter has enjoyed a 25% increase in monthly signups (30). In October 2011, Twitter CEO Dick Costolo announced at the Web 2.0 Summit that there were 250 million tweets every day (31). By August 2013, the daily number of tweets had doubled to 500 million as reported by ʻraffi krikorian, vice president of platform engineering at Twitter (32).

The Super Bowl XLVI on February 5, 2012 set a new record for simultaneous tweeting in the United States, with 12,233 tweets a second at its peak during the final three minutes of the game (33). Super Bowl XLVI host city Indianapolis built the first-ever "social media command center" for a team of strategists, analysts, and techies to monitor the fan conversation via Facebook and Twitter from a 2,800-square-foot space downtown (34).

The U.S. record, though impressive as is, was dwarfed by the world record of 25,088 tweets per second during the December 9, 2011 television screening in Japan of the animated film *Castle in the Sky* directed by Hayao Miyazaki (35). The Japanese viewers were challenged to use social networks to say the spell "balse" together with the two characters at the climax of the film. It was a resounding suc-cess in audience engagement.

Not only does Twitter provide up-to-the-minute personal news to keep us informed of the people and events that we are following, it also helps spread infor-mation among would-be followers. NASCAR driver Brad Keselowski, for example, tweeted about the explosion and fire caused by a crash during the Daytona 500 in February 2012. Some of his fans re-tweeted the accident. Within two hours, Keselowski gained more than 100,000 new followers on Twitter (36).

When Hurricane Sandy was sweeping through New York City in October 2012, hundreds of tweets pleading for help were sent to the New York Fire Department (@FDNY). Emily Rahimi, NYFD's social media manager, responded and relayed tweets to 911 dispatchers. "You could see the panic and fear in the words they were typing," said Rahimi. "A lot of people couldn't get through to a 911 dispatcher. So I took their information and called our dispatchers myself to make sure they sent an emergency crew. I reassured everyone asking for our help that rescuers would eventually reach them" (37).

On March 24, 2012, a piece of a debris from a Russian Cosmos satellite passed dangerously close to the International Space Station hosting the Expedition 30 crew (38). NASA tweeted at 11:29 PM on March 23 as the event was unfolding: "The six crew members are in their Soyuz spacecraft and will close the hatches to isolate themselves from #ISS until the debris passes" (39).

On August 13, 2013 when billionaire investor Carl Icahn tweeted about having a large position in Apple and his meeting with Apple's CEO Tim Cook, Apple's stock price soared 5% in less than two hours (40).

Such were a few of the many quintessential real-life, real-time dramas via Twitter.

9.6   Prevalence of Twitter

In a July 2009 interview, British Prime Minster David Cameron told *Absolute Radio* host Christian O'Connell, "I am not on Twitter. As politicians we have to think about what we say. The trouble with Twitter – the instantness of it – is that, I think, too many tweets might make a twat" (41). Cameron changed his mind in October 2012, created a Twitter account, and told *Sky News*, "In this modern world you have got to use every means to try and communicate your message and explain to people why you are doing it. You've got to get with the programme, I suppose" (42).

Indeed, Twitter is so prevalent that we can tweet at 75% of the world's leaders. According to a 2013 report by Digital Daya, a total of 123 world leaders out of 164 countries have accounts on Twitter set up in their personal name or through an official government office (43). For example, President Barack Obama (@BarackObama), First Lady Michelle Obama (@MichelleObama), Russian President Vladimir Putin (@KremlinRussia_E), South Africa's President Jacob Zuma (@SAPresident), Dalai Lama (@DalaiLama), and Pope Benedict XVI (@PopeBenedictXIV) are all tweeting (44).

Since Obama joined Twitter on March 5, 2007, his popularity has grown to 43 million followers in June 2014 as Obama was ranked #3 on twitaholic.com in terms of number of followers, behind Justin Bieber (#2) and above Lady Gaga (#5) among all celebrities in the world (45) (see Fig. 9.6). By March 2021, President Barack Obama (with 130 million followers) overtook Justin Bieber (with 114 million followers) to claim the top spot.

Twitter is not off-limits to dead celebrities whose legends live on. Among the verified authentic accounts on Twitter are Marilyn Monroe, Elvis Presley, and Michael Jackson (46). Behind Twitter's Marilyn Monroe, for instance, is a marketing firm who purchased the rights to all things Marilyn Monroe.

#	Name (Screen Name)	Location	URL	Followers	Following	Updates	Joined
1	KATY PERRY @katyperry		http://t.co/TJWZhJVWfnu	53,816,374	147	5,688	65 months ago
2	Justin Bieber @justinbieber		http://t.co/i6HGkdvRpP	52,367,734	130,129	27,042	64 months ago
3	Barack Obama @BarackObama	Washington, DC	http://t.co/OSVroad92c1	43,378,939	650,417	11,839	89 months ago
4	YouTube @YouTube	San Bruno, CA	http://t.co/F3fLcfn@Vf	42,598,158	666	10,500	80 months ago
5	Lady Gaga @ladygaga			41,536,612	134,438	4,772	76 months ago
6	Taylor Swift @taylorswift13		http://t.co/FkfaGHPux8	41,379,768	130	2,231	67 months ago
7	Britney Spears @britneyspears	Los Angeles, CA	http://t.co/PfMgHx07ro	37,647,357	403,075	3,666	70 months ago
8	Rihanna @rihanna	LA BABY!	http://t.co/v6gLcj4ynf	35,791,889	1,065	9,011	Details...
9	Instagram @instagram		http://t.co/93yg7AXYM	33,274,744	16	5,096	Details...
10	Justin Timberlake @jtimberlake	Memphis, TN	http://t.co/SRpzf5jQvhZ	32,694,810	79	2,394	64 months ago

Fig. 9.6 Top 10 Twitterholics based on Followers (as of June 2014) – Courtesy of Twitaholic.com

In June 2009, Twitter began to institute the verification of accounts in order to establish authenticity of identities on Twitter and to reduce user confusion (47). Verified accounts display a blue "Verified Badge" on their Twitter bio. However, this program is currently closed to the public as of March 2012. Twitter only verifies some trusted sources from their advertisers, partners, and high-profile personalities (48).

Twitter's concoction of the hashtag as a short and handy identifier is becoming as important as Tim Berners-Lee's creation of web URLs for companies and politicians alike. For example, during the 2012 Super Bowl XLVI, eight out of 42 TV advertisers included a Twitter hashtag in their commercials (49). And shortly after Clint Eastwood's Super Bowl commercial was shown to more than 111 million Americans watching the game, White House communications director Dan Pfeiffer sent a tweet: "Saving the America Auto Industry: Something Eminem and Clint Eastwood can agree on" (50).

Twitter has become the most prevalent tool for spreading news and getting feedback in real-time. Immediately following President Obama's State of the Union address on January 24, 2012, an online panel from the White House answered questions submitted by citizens via Twitter (#WHChat & #SOTU), Google+, Facebook, and the in-person audience of "tweetup" participants (51). A "tweetup" is an event where people who tweet come together to meet in person.

Since the first tweet was sent by Twitter co-founder Jack Dorsey in 2006, more than 6,000 tweets are being sent every second around the world in 2021. *TIME*

Magazine's Victor Luckerson wrote about the seven most important moments in Twitter's history (52) while CNN's Brandon Griggs, Heather Kelly, and Doug Gross identified 23 key moments between 2006 and 2013 (53). Here is our list of 29 key events:

1. March 2006: Twitter co-founder Jack Dorsey posts the first-ever tweet "just setting up my twttr" on March 21 as part of an internal messaging system for the podcasting company Odeo.
2. July 2006: Twitter publicly reveals a full version on July 15.
3. March 2007: Twitter becomes popular among attendees at the South By Southwest Interactive festival in Austin, Texas.
4. August 2007: Twitter user Chris Messina proposes the idea of using # (the hashtag) for groups.
5. April 2008: University of California, Berkeley grad student James Karl Buck shows the power of a one-word tweet: "Arrested" on April 10 and "Free" on April 11.
6. January 2009: On January 15, eyewitness Jānis Krūms tweets a photo of passengers waiting to be rescued from a US Airways plane after its emergency landing on the Hudson River. His message says, "There's a plane in the Hudson. I'm on the ferry going to pick up the people. Crazy."
7. April 2009: Actor Ashton Kutcher becomes the first Twitter user with 1 million followers.
8. June 2009: Demonstrators in Iran start a "Twitter Revolution" by tweeting about the disputed election in Iran and protests in the streets of Tehran.
9. August 2009: Justin Halpern creates a Twitter account called "Sh*t My Dad Says" to disseminate his father's blunt wisecracks.
10. January 2010: Astronaut Timothy Creamer sends the first live tweet from space: "Hello Twitterverse! We r now LIVE tweeting from the International Space Station — the 1st live tweet from Space! :) More soon, send your ?s."
11. April 2010: The Library of Congress announces plans to archive every public tweet on Twitter.
12. April 2010: Twitter introduces promoted tweets in order to generate ad revenue.
13. October 2010: Twitter names Dick Costolo its CEO.
14. January 2011: Twitter and Facebook play a key role in "Arab Spring" uprisings as people in Tunisia, Egypt, Syria, Libya and other countries use social networks to message each other and organize protests.
15. March 2011: An anonymous jokester heralds a new wave of parody Twitter feeds by tweeting "Leaving Wall Street. These guys make my skin crawl." on behalf of an Egyptian cobra that has escaped from the Bronx Zoo in order to sightsee around New York City.
16. May 2011: Sohaib Athar, a 33-year-old IT consultant in Abbottabad, Pakistan, unwittingly live tweets the secret U.S. military raid by the SEAL Team Six. One of his tweets says, "Uh oh, now I'm the guy who liveblogged the Osama raid without knowing it."
17. June 2011: U.S. representative Anthony Weiner resigns after confessing to sending lewd photos of himself to women on Twitter.

18. June 2012: NASA lands the Curiosity rover safely on Mars and begins sending updates to the public via Twitter.
19. November 2012: President Barack Obama acknowledges his successful re-election in a tweet "Four more years" along with an image of him embracing his wife. It becomes the "most retweeted photo ever" – with over 770,000 retweets (see Fig. 9.7).
20. November 2012: The Israel Defense Forces live-tweets its rocket attacks against the Hamas in Gaza, making it the first time that a military conflict is chronicled in real time on social media.
21. December 2012: Pope Benedict XVI becomes the first pontiff to join Twitter (@Pontifex).
22. January 2013: Twitter users in Japan and Korea set a world record by posting 33,388 tweets per second on their New Year's Day.
23. January 2013: Justin Bieber dethrones Lady Gaga to become the most followed person on Twitter.

Fig. 9.7 President Barack Obama's "Four More Year" Tweet on November 6, 2012

24. January 2013: Twitter launches Vine app to let users shoot and share 6-second looping videos.
25. February 2013: Super Bowl XLVII generates more than 268,000 tweets per minute, and 24.1 million for the entire game.
26. April 2013: The Syrian Electronic Army hacks into the Associated Press Twitter account and posts "Breaking: Two Explosions in the White House and Barack Obama is injured."
27. September 2013: Twitter announces IPO on September 12.
28. February 2014: Super Bowl XLVIII on February 2nd generates 24.9 million tweets for the entire game, topping the 24.1 million from the previous year's game.
29. March 2014: Ellen DeGeneres' Oscar-night group selfie "If only Bradley's arm was longer" on March 2nd during the 86th Academy Awards (see Fig. 9.8) generated a record 3.4 million retweets, breaking Twitter's servers as well as the record held by President Barack Obama's "Four More Years" tweet.

Fig. 9.8 Ellen DeGeneres' Oscar-Night Group Selfie on March 2, 2014

30. Fast forward to January 2021: Twitter permanently banned President Donald Trump, citing the risk of further incitement of violence by the President of the United States.
31. March 2021: Twitter co-founder Jack Dorsey sold his first-ever tweet "just setting up my twttr" for $2.9 million as a nonfungible token (NFT) to Sina Estavi, CEO of Bridge Oracle.

9.7   Advertisements and Campaigns on Twitter

Advertisers and campaign strategists have caught Twitter fever as well. Twitter CEO Dick Costolo said in October 2010, "We feel like we've cracked the code on a new form of advertising" (54). Businesses pay a fee to have their "promoted tweets" appear near the top of a user's feed. In February 2012, Twitter announced that it would also start sending promoted tweets to mobile phones (55). In July 2013, Twitter introduced Tailored Audience Advertising to better target ads to potential customers (56). In April 2014, Twitter announced plans to roll out 15 new ad products over the following six months to compete with Facebook in ad revenue (57).

Some brands have been using the hashtag to engage consumers in constant conversation and to spread the news through retweeting by the more proactive customers to their friends. Politicians pay Twitter to help shape opinions. Social media consultant Vincent Harris said, "The beauty of Twitter's ad unit is that it's the best rapid-response tool that exists in politics right now" (49). A case study about a customer acquisition campaign in Q4 2013 showed that leads coming from the Twitter promotion were 20% more likely to convert to paying customers than any other marketing channels (58).

Nevertheless, freedom of speech on Twitter carries its own risk for advertisers and campaign strategists. In January 2012, McDonald's launched a marketing campaign with the innocuous hashtag #McDStories as part of a larger campaign to share stories about the farmers who grow McDonald's food and their commitment to fresh produce and meats. Within two hours after the launch, however, McDonald's pulled down #McDStories due to the critics of McDonald's tweeting stories of food poisoning, weight gain, and poor employee hygiene.

In defense of the Twitter campaign fiasco, McDonald's social media director Rick Wion wrote, "McDonald's is mentioned on Twitter more than 250,000 times each week, it is very easy to cherry pick negative (or positive) tweets that are not representative of the overall picture. Bottom line – the negative chatter wasn't as much as today's headlines have lead [sic] people to believe. This happened almost a week ago and the hashtag is only living on because many media outlets are using the chance to push a provocative and tweetable headline" (59).

Similar to McDonald's fiasco, the NYPD Twitter campaign backfired badly in April 2014 when the New York Police Department asked citizens to post photos of themselves with the officers using the hashtag #myNYPD. Deputy Chief Kim Y. Royster explained, "The NYPD is creating new ways to communicate effectively

Occupy Wall Street @OccupyWallStNYC 16h
What about YOUR police? bit.ly/Pt6ICv #myELAS #myNYPD #myLAPD pic.twitter.com/GJrosNnx2H +NYTimes article!
thelede.blogs.nytimes.com/2014/04/23/new…
↩ Reply ⇄ Retweet ★ Favorite   Flag media

Fig. 9.9 Similar hashtags inspired by #myNYPD sprang up around the world in April 2014

with the community. Twitter provides an open forum for an uncensored exchange and this is an open dialogue good for our city" (60).

However, the exchange and dialogue were shortchanged by overwhelmingly negative tweets with photos showing police brutality and misconduct (61). The minority voices supporting the NYPD were few and far between. Moreover, similar hashtags sprang up around the world: #myLAPD (Los Angeles Police Department), #myCPD (Chicago Police Department), and #MiPoliciaMexicana (Mexican Police), to name a few (see Fig. 9.9).

In spite of the backlash, the NYPD should be lauded for bringing up an age-old sensitive topic that needs to be addressed in order build more trust between the police and the citizens. Social media such as Twitter certainly offers a powerful mechanism to take the pulse of public opinion.

9.8   Cuban Twitter: ZunZuneo

During 2011, Twitter and Facebook played a key role in "Arab Spring" uprisings as people in Tunisia, Egypt, Syria, Libya and other countries use social networks to message each other and organize protests. What if a country, such as Cuba or China, bans the use of Twitter and Facebook?

In April 2014, Cuba accused the Obama administration for secretly financing a social network in Cuba to stir political unrest and undermine the country's communist government (62). Dubbed "ZunZuneo," a slang for a Cuban hummingbird's tweet, drew in some 40,000 subscribers in Cuba. The U.S. Agency for International Development (USAID) was the mastermind behind the creation of the "Cuban Twitter," hoping that the text-messaging tool would be used to organize political demonstrations. ZunZuneo went offline in June 2012 when the program ran out of government funding and failed to obtain private investment from Jack Dorsey, cofounder of Twitter.

Josefina Vidal, director of U.S. affairs at Cuba's Foreign Ministry, said that the ZunZuneo program "shows once again that the United States government has not renounced its plans of subversion against Cuba ... The government of the United States must respect international law and the goals and principles of the United Nations charter and, therefore, cease its illegal and clandestine actions against Cuba, which are rejected by the Cuban people and international public opinion" (63).

Nonetheless, no one would argue that the U.S. government should be credited for being creative.

9.9 Creative Uses of Twitter

Given the skyrocketing volume of public tweets, analytical tools are being developed to comb through the tweets to gauge public opinions. Developed by the *Los Angeles Times*, IBM, and the USC Annenberg Innovation Lab, the Oscar Senti-Meter uses language recognition technology to analyze the positive, negative, and neutral opinions about the 2012 Academy Awards race (64). When the Academy announced the best actor nominations, Jean Dujardin of *The Artist* scored the highest in positive sentiment while George Clooney of *The Descendants* had the highest volume of tweets. The Oscar Senti-Meter analysis seemed to concur that Dujardin beat Clooney and won the best actor in a leading role.

MIT Professor Erik Brynjolfsson explained, "Data measurement is the modern equivalent of the microscope. Google searches, Facebook posts and Twitter messages, for example, make it possible to measure behavior and sentiment in fine detail and as it happens" (65).

With more than 250 million tweets per day as of October 2011, people around the world are co-authoring the equivalent of a 12.5 million-page book every day (assuming that an average tweet has 100 characters and an average book page contains roughly 2,000 characters). That is a gigantic book, to say the least.

Speaking of books, author Neil Gaiman and BBC Audiobooks America in 2009 used Twitter for interactive storytelling (66). In May 2012, Pulitzer Prize winner Jennifer Egan released her new novel *Black Box* on Twitter in a series of 140-character bursts every minute for the hour between 8 and 9 p.m. daily from May 24 to June 2 (67).

In May 2013, researchers at the University of Vermont released a study titled "The Geography of Happiness: Connecting Twitter sentiment and expression, demographics, and objective characteristics of place" (68). The Twitter data found Hawaii to be the happiest state and Napa in California to be the happiest city, whereas Louisiana to be the saddest state and Beaumont in Texas to be the saddest city (69). According to the study, cities with a higher density of tweets tended to be less happy.

In October 2013, Jiwei Li at Carnegie Mellon University and Claire Cardie at Cornell University developed an algorithm that could identify a Twitter user's most significant events and assemble them into an accurate life history. "Experiments on real Twitter data quantitatively demonstrate the effectiveness of our method," said Li and Cardie. "It can be extended to any individual, (e.g. friend, competitor or movie star), if only he or she has a twitter account" (70).

In February 2014, Nathan Kallus at MIT reported his research finding on how to predict crowd behavior using statements made on Twitter (71). "The gathering of crowds into a single action can often be seen through trends appearing in this data far in advance," said Kallus. "We find that the mass of publicly available information online has the power to unveil the future actions of crowds" (72).

In March 2014, four W hotels in New York began to offer couples a "social media wedding concierge" to live-tweet their wedding, upload photos to Instagram, post updates on Facebook, and create inspirational Pinterest boards from the start of a wedding planning (73). The concierge will also make sure that the wedding guests all use the same hashtag in order to get the wedding to "trend" on Twitter.

In May 2014, a wealthy California real estate investor (@HiddenCash) conducted an anonymous social experiment for good (74). He hid $100 bills in public places in San Francisco, Oakland, San Jose, Los Angeles, and other cities; and then posted clues to the money's whereabouts on Twitter. On May 28, he had 172,000 followers (75); and by August 13, the number of followers had ballooned to 719,000 (76).

In July 2014, Arab-American journalist Sulome Anderson gave her Jewish boyfriend Jeremy a kiss on Twitter to show their support for a New York-based social media campaign called "Jews and Arabs refuse to be enemies." Anderson tweeted, "He calls me neshama, I call him habibi. Love doesn't speak the language of occupation #JewsAndArabsRefuseToBeEnemies" (77).

In August 2014, Bruno Gonçalves at the University of Toulon in France and David Sánchez at the Institute for Cross-Disciplinary Physics and Complex Systems in Spain released a report on their study of dialects on a global scale using messages posted on Twitter. Based on 50 million geo-located tweets, the researchers mapped the distribution of dialects and grouped them into two "superdialects" that are indicative of an "increasing homogenization of language caused by global communication systems like Twitter" (78).

9.10   The Downside of Twitter

While the creative uses of Twitter signify the beginning of brave new possibilities empowered by Twitter in specific and social media in general, there is always a downside. YouTube comments used to be the angriest place on the Internet with all forms of trolling, bullying, racism, sexism, and other offensive expressions (79). Now, the Twitterverse has become the favorite go-to place for intolerant bile.

When U.S. born Indian-American Nina Davuluri was crowned the 2014 Miss America, ignorant and racist tweets started spewing (80):

- "This is Miss America... not Miss Foreign Country"
- "shes *[sic]* like not even american and she won miss america"
- "More like Miss Terrorist #MissAmerica"
- "How the fuck does a foreigner win miss America? She is a *[sic]* Arab!"
- "Miss New York is an Indian.. With all do *[sic]* respect, this is America"
- "9/11 was 4 days ago and she gets miss America?"
- "Congratulations Al-Qaeda. Our Miss America is one of you."
- "Asian or indian are you kiddin this is america omg"
- "Well they just picked a Muslim for Miss America. That must've made Obama happy. Maybe he had a vote"

It is no surprise that Miss America Nina Davuluri, President Barack Obama, and many high achievers in the public eye have been attacked by racial slurs. Social media amplifies both the good side and the dark side of human nature. Prof. Lesley Withers at Central Michigan University offered this explanation: "[Twitter] allows us to go off in ways that we wouldn't choose to do if we had to look at another person's face when we did it. ... People use Twitter to get reactions out of others. It's like a popularity contest: If you can put something out there that's quick and inflammatory and it gets retweeted a ton, that's your feedback – that's how you know that it was an interesting or effective tweet. And people don't seem to be as concerned if the response is positive or negative" (81).

The lack of concern for others—coupled with misinformation and disinformation—can be lethal. "Falsely shouting fire in a theatre and causing a panic" is the classic example given by Justice Oliver Wendell Holmes, Jr. in 1919. In fact, the Italian Hall Disaster occurred on December 24, 1913 in Michigan where 73 men, women, and children were crushed to death in a stampede when someone falsely shouted "fire" at a crowded Christmas party.

The lack of concern for others also led to the death of George Floyd. CNN writer and producer John Blake pointed out that "it was the look of indifference in Chauvin's eyes on May 25, 2020, as he casually drained the life out of George Floyd. ... That look was freeze-framed in what the prosecution dryly called 'Exhibit 17.' ... The look on Chauvin's face is one of bored disinterest. His sunglasses are perched on his head and his hands rest in his pocket. He doesn't seem to notice Floyd at all. ... They [the prosecutors at his trial] focused relentlessly on Chauvin's casual body language during his arrest of Floyd and the lack of concern on his face as he pinned Floyd to the ground. They told jurors Chauvin showed 'indifference' to Floyd's pleas for help. They said Chauvin and other officers at the scene talked about the smell of Floyd's feet and idly picked stones from a vehicle's tire while Floyd died in front of them" (82).

Twitter amplifies both true and false information in real time, making it more constructive or destructive depending on the content. Repeated tweets by President

Donald Trump and his supporters aiming to incite public sentiment against the 2020 election result culminated in the storming of Capitol Hill on January 6, 2021. The failed four-hour insurrection left five people dead and more than a hundred injured. Among the dead was 35-year-old QAnon adherent Ashli Babbitt who, on the day she died, retweeted President Trump's "Stop the Steal!" rallying cry as well as attorney Lin Wood's tweet urging that "Mike Pence @vp @Mike_Pence must resign & thereafter be charged with TREASON" (83). In the aftermath, Twitter permanently banned President Trump, citing the risk of further incitement of violence by the President of the United States (84).

The negativity of Twitterverse has prompted some celebrities to quit Twitter altogether. In January 2021, actor Alec Baldwin had enough of the controversy over his wife Hilaria's Spanish heritage. "Twitter is like a party where everyone is screaming. Not much of a party. Goodbye for now," Bladwin tweeted as he deactivated his account for the fifth time since 2011 (85). In March 2021, model and TV personality Chrissy Teigen—who had more than 13 million followers and a spat with President Trump—wrote on Twitter, "Hey. For over 10 years, you guys have been my world. I honestly owe so much to this world we have created here. I truly consider so many of you my actual friends. But it's time for me to say goodbye. This no longer serves me as positively as it serves me negatively, and I think that's the right time to call something" (86).

References

1. **Bhowmick, Nilanjana.** How India's second wave became the worst COVID-19 surge in the world. [Online] National Geographic, April 23, 2021. https://www.nationalgeographic.com/science/article/how-indias-second-wave-became-the-worst-covid-19-surge-in-the-world.
2. **Kalra, Aditya and Ghoshal, Devjyot.** Twitter becomes platform of hope amid the despair of India's COVID crisis. [Online] Reuters, April 21, 2021. https://www.reuters.com/world/india/twitter-becomes-platform-hope-amid-despair-indias-covid-crisis-2021-04-21/.
3. **Crime Stoppers.** History of Crime Stoppers. [Online] Crime Stoppers USA. [Cited: May 30, 2021.] https://www.crimestoppersusa.org/history/.
4. **Michallon, Clémence.** Olivia Munn laments spiking hate crimes against Asian Americans as friend's mother is attacked. [Online] The Independent, February 19, 2021. https://www.independent.co.uk/arts-entertainment/films/news/olivia-munn-man-shove-asian-woman-new-york-b1804739.html.
5. **@oliviamunn.** My friend's mom. [Online] Twitter, February 17, 2021. https://twitter.com/oliviamunn/status/1362084698197909508?lang=en.
6. —. This is the guy you guys helped. [Online] Twitter, February 18, 2021. https://twitter.com/oliviamunn/status/1362423891109367812?lang=en.
7. **Bulwer-Lytton, Edward.** Richelieu; Or the Conspiracy: A Play in Five Acts. (second ed.). [Online] Saunders and Otley, 1839. https://archive.org/details/richelieuorcons01lyttgoog.
8. **Weiwei, Ai.** China's censorship can never defeat the internet. [Online] The Guardian, April 15, 2012. http://www.guardian.co.uk/commentisfree/libertycentral/2012/apr/16/china-censorship-internet-freedom.
9. **Simon, Mallory.** Student 'Twitters' his way out of Egyptian jail. [Online] CNN, April 25, 2008. http://www.cnn.com/2008/TECH/04/25/twitter.buck/index.html.

10. **Carter, Chelsea J. and Mohsin, Saima.** Purported letter from Taliban to Malala Yousafzai: Why we shot you. [Online] CNN, July 18, 2013. http://www.cnn.com/2013/07/17/world/asia/ pakistan-taliban-malala/index.html.

11. **Ren, Changhong and Wu, Jingyu.** Rise and Fall of the Qin Dynasty. [Online] Asiapac Books Pte Ltd, January 1, 2000. https://play.google.com/store/books/details/Asiapac_Editorial_Rise_ and_Fall_of_Qin_Dynasty?id=J1dWcWdDXskC.

12. **Wikipedia.** List of varieties of Chinese. [Online] Wikipedia. [Cited: March 15, 2012.] http:// en.wikipedia.org/wiki/List_of_varieties_of_Chinese.

13. **Pepitone, Julianne.** Encyclopedia Britannica to stop printing books. [Online] CNN, March 13, 2012. http://money.cnn.com/2012/03/13/technology/encyclopedia-britannica-books/ index.htm.

14. **Segall, Laurie.** AT&T ditches the Yellow Pages. [Online] CNNMoney, April 9, 2012. http:// money.cnn.com/2012/04/09/technology/ATT-sells-yellow-pages/index.htm.

15. **Gonzales, Richard.** San Francisco Moves To Ban Yellow Pages. [Online] NPR, May 16, 2011. http://www.npr.org/2011/05/16/136368752/san-francisco-moves-to-ban-yellow-pages.

16. **Google.org.** The Endangered Languages. A project to support language preservation and documentation around the world. [Online] Google. [Cited: June 28, 2012.] http://www.endan-geredlanguages.com/.

17. **Hopkins, Curt.** Google launches Endangered Language Project. [Online] Ars technica, June 21, 2012. http://arstechnica.com/science/2012/06/google-launches-endangered-language-project/.

18. **CNN Wire Staff.** Twitter to delete posts if countries request it. [Online] CNN, January 28, 2012. http://www.cnn.com/2012/01/27/tech/twitter-deleting-posts/index.html.

19. **Quirin, Courtney.** Impacting the World One Paper Upload at a Time. [Online] Academia. edu, January 22, 2013. http://blog.academia.edu/post/41209970316/impacting-the-world-one-paper-upload-at-a-time.

20. **Hudack, Mike.** Please allow me to rant for a moment about the state of the media. [Online] Facebook, May 22, 2014. https://www.facebook.com/mhudack/posts/10152148792566194.

21. **Johnston, Lauren and Marrone, Matt.** Twitter user becomes star in US Airways crash – Janis Krums sets Internet abuzz with iPhone photo. [Online] New York Daily News, January 16, 2009. http://www.nydailynews.com/new-york/twitter-user-star-airways-crash-janis-krums-sets-internet-abuzz-iphone-photo-article-1.408174.

22. **O'Dell, Jolie.** One Twitter User Reports Live From Osama Bin Laden Raid. [Online] Mashable, May 1, 2011. http://mashable.com/2011/05/01/live-tweet-bin-laden-raid/.

23. **The Province.** The man who tweeted bin Laden's death. [Online] Storify, May 2011. https:// storify.com/theprovince/the-man-who-tweeted-bin-ladens-death.

24. **McCullagh, Declan.** Sohaib Athar on Twitter fame after bin Laden raid (Q&A). [Online] CNet, May 4, 2011. http://www.cnet.com/news/sohaib-athar-on-twitter-fame-after-bin-laden-raid-q-a/.

25. **Gross, Doug.** Tweeting Osama's death: The accidental citizen journalist. [Online] CNN, March 12, 2012. http://www.cnn.com/2012/03/10/tech/social-media/twitter-osama-death/ index.html.

26. **Moore, Terence.** Bobby Petrino and social media prove a bad mix. [Online] CNN, April 13, 2012. http://www.cnn.com/2012/04/13/us/petrino-social-media/index.html.

27. **Mlot, Stephanie.** NBC News Acquires Stringwire for User-Generated Content. [Online] PC Magazine, August 12, 2013. http://www.pcmag.com/article2/0,2817,2422959,00.asp.

28. **@biz and @amac.** The Tweets Must Flow. [Online] Twitter Blog, January 28, 2011. http:// blog.twitter.com/2011/01/tweets-must-flow.html.

29. **Warren, Christina.** How Twitter Integrates With iOS 5. [Online] Mashable, October 12, 2011. http://mashable.com/2011/10/12/twitter-ios-5-integration/.

30. **Rao, Leena.** Twitter's Monthly Signups By 25 Percent. [Online] TechCrunch, December 8, 2011. http://techcrunch.com/2011/12/08/apple-ios-5-integration-boosted-twitter-signups-by-25-percent/.

31. **Sloan, Paul.** Twitter CEO: 250 million tweets a day--now what? [Online] CNet, October 17, 2011. http://news.cnet.com/8301-1023_3-20121714-93/twitter-ceo-250-million-tweets -a-day-now-what/.

32. **Krikorian, Raffi.** New Tweets per second record, and how! [Online] Twitter Engineering Blog, August 16, 2013. https://blog.twitter.com/2013/new-tweets-per-second-record-and-how.
33. **Twitter.** Twitter Tweets. [Online] Twitter. [Cited: February 6, 2012.] https://twitter.com/twitter.
34. **Laird, Sam.** Super Bowl gets social-media command center. [Online] CNN, January 23, 2012. http://www.cnn.com/2012/01/23/tech/social-media/super-bowl-social-media-center/index.html.
35. **Evangelista, Benny.** Social spelling during "Castle in the Sky" rerun smashes Twitter record. [Online] San Francisco Chronicle, December 14, 2011. http://blog.sfgate.com/techchron/2011/12/14/mass-spelling-during-castle-in-the-sky-rerun-smashes-twitter-record/.
36. **Laird, Sam.** NASCAR driver tweets from car, gains 100,000 followers. [Online] CNN, February 28, 2012. http://www.cnn.com/2012/02/28/tech/social-media/nascar-driver-tweets-race/index.html.
37. **Khorram, Yasmin.** As Sandy pounded NYC, fire department worker was a Twitter lifeline. [Online] CNN, November 1, 2012. http://www.cnn.com/2012/11/01/tech/social-media/twitter-fdny/index.html.
38. **CNN Wire Staff.** Space junk forces astronauts into escape capsules on International Space Station. [Online] CNN, March 24, 2012. http://www.cnn.com/2012/03/24/tech/tech-space-station-debris/index.html.
39. **NASA.** The six crew members are in their Soyuz spacecraft and will close the hatches to isolate themselves from #ISS until the debris passes. [Online] Twitter, March 23, 2012. http://twitter.com/#!/NASA/status/183440480854491136.
40. **Wohlsen, Marcus.** Single Tweet Sends Apple Shares Soaring. [Online] Wired, August 13, 2013. http://www.wired.com/2013/08/single-tweet-sends-apple-shares-soaring/.
41. **Cameron, David.** David Cameron on Twitter. [Online] Absolute Radio, July 29, 2009. http://www.youtube.com/watch?v=yELHemcQn10.
42. **Press Association.** David Cameron gets 100,000 Twitter followers days after starting account. [Online] The Guardian, October 9, 2012. http://www.theguardian.com/politics/2012/oct/09/david-cameron-100000-twitter-followers.
43. **Fitzpatrick, Alex.** You Can Tweet at 75% of the World's Leaders. [Online] Mashable, January 2, 2013. http://mashable.com/2013/01/02/world-leaders-twitter/.
44. **Gross, Doug.** The pope's on Twitter? 10 unlikely tweeters. [Online] CNN, February 2, 2012. http://www.cnn.com/2012/02/02/tech/social-media/unlikely-twitter-users/index.html.
45. **Twitaholic.** Stats & Rankings for Barack Obama. [Online] Twitaholic. [Cited: May 28, 2014.] http://twitaholic.com/barackobama/.
46. **Farrell, Maureen.** Marilyn Monroe 'officially' joins Twitter. [Online] CNN, February 8, 2012. http://money.cnn.com/2012/02/08/markets/marilyn_monroe_twitter/index.htm.
47. **Cashmore, Pete.** Twitter Launches Verified Accounts. [Online] Mashable, June 11, 2009. http://mashable.com/2009/06/11/twitter-verified-accounts-2/.
48. **Twitter.** Twitter FAQs about Verified Accounts. [Online] Twitter. [Cited: March 20, 2012.] http://support.twitter.com/groups/31-twitter-basics/topics/111-features/articles/119135-about-verified-accounts.
49. **Stone, Brad.** Twitter, the Startup That Wouldn't Die. [Online] Bloomberg Businessweek, March 1, 2012. http://www.businessweek.com/articles/2012-03-01/twitter-the-startup-that-wouldnt-die.
50. **Monroe, Bryan.** Were politics buried inside Eastwood's 'Halftime' commercial? [Online] CNN, February 7, 2012. http://www.cnn.com/2012/02/06/politics/eastwood-ad-politics/index.html.
51. **Curtis, Colleen.** State of the Union 2012: We Want to Hear From You. [Online] The White House Blog, January 20, 2012. http://www.whitehouse.gov/blog/2012/01/20/state-union-2012-we-want-hear-you.
52. **Luckerson, Victor.** The 7 Most Important Moments in Twitter History. [Online] TIME Magazine, November 7, 2013. http://business.time.com/2013/11/07/the-7-most-important-moments-in-twitter-history/.

53. **Griggs, Brandon and Kelly, Heather.** 23 key moments from Twitter history. [Online] CNN, September 19, 2013. http://www.cnn.com/2013/09/13/tech/social-media/twitter-key-moments/index.html.

54. **Miller, Claire Cain and Vega, Tanzina.** After Building an Audience, Twitter Turns to Ads. [Online] The New York Times, October 10, 2010. http://www.nytimes.com/2010/10/11/business/media/11twitter.html.

55. **Greenfield, Rebecca.** Twitter Is Growing Up! (No It's Not). [Online] The Atlantic Wire, March 2, 2012. http://www.theatlanticwire.com/technology/2012/03/twitter-growing-no-its-not/49416/.

56. **Shrivastava, Abhishek.** More relevant ads with tailored audiences. [Online] Advertising Blog, December 5, 2013. https://blog.twitter.com/2013/more-relevant-ads-with-tailored-audiences.

57. **Chen, Yuyu.** Twitter Prepares 15 New Ad Products to Compete With Facebook. [Online] Clickz, April 8, 2014. http://www.clickz.com/clickz/news/2338808/twitter-prepares-15-new-ad-products-to-compete-with-facebook.

58. **Kuchinskas, Susan.** Case Study Shows How Twitter Advertising Can Pay Off. [Online] Mashable, April 15, 2014. http://mashable.com/2014/04/15/twitter-improves-for-advertisers/.

59. **Hsu, Tiffany.** McDonald's #McDStories Twitter marketing effort goes awry. [Online] Los Angeles Times, January 23, 2012. http://www.latimes.com/business/money/la-fi-mo-mcdonalds-twitter-fail-20120123,0,7220567.story.

60. **Ford, Dana.** #D'oh! NYPD Twitter campaign backfires. [Online] CNN, April 24, 2014. http://www.cnn.com/2014/04/22/tech/nypd-twitter-fail/index.html.

61. **Twitter.** Results for #myNYPD. [Online] Twitter. [Cited: April 22, 2014.] https://twitter.com/search?q=%23myNYPD&src=hash.

62. **Lewis, Paul and Roberts, Dan.** White House denies 'Cuban Twitter' ZunZuneo programme was covert. [Online] The Guardian, April 3, 2014. http://www.theguardian.com/world/2014/apr/03/white-house-cuban-twitter-zunzuneo-covert.

63. **Associated Press in Havana.** Cuba's state media denounce 'secret Twitter' as proof of US cyber-war. [Online] The Guardian, April 4, 2014. http://www.theguardian.com/world/2014/apr/04/cuba-secret-twitter-cyber-war-us-zunzuneo.

64. **Gettell, Oliver.** Oscars 2012: Streep and Clooney top the Twitter charts, volume-wise. [Online] Los Angeles Times, February 26, 2012. http://latimesblogs.latimes.com/movies/2012/02/oscars-2012-streep-and-sentimeter-clooney-top-the-twitter-charts-volume-wise.html.

65. **Lohr, Steve.** The Age of Big Data. [Online] The New York Times, February 11, 2012. http://www.nytimes.com/2012/02/12/sunday-review/big-datas-impact-in-the-world.html.

66. **Dybwad, Barb.** Neil Gaiman + Twitter = Interactive Storytelling. [Online] Mashable, October 13, 2009. http://mashable.com/2009/10/13/neil-gaiman-twitter-audiobook/.

67. **Gross, Doug.** Pulitzer winner to publish new story, one tweet at a time. [Online] CNN, May 24, 2012. http://www.cnn.com/2012/05/24/tech/social-media/new-yorker-story-twitter/index.html.

68. **Mitchell, Lewis, et al.** The Geography of Happiness: Connecting Twitter sentiment and expression, demographics, and objective characteristics of place. [Online] Cornell University Library arXiv.org, May 29, 2013. http://arxiv.org/pdf/1302.3299.pdf.

69. **Kelly, Heather.** The happiest and saddest states according to Twitter. [Online] CNN, February 20, 2013. http://www.cnn.com/2013/02/19/tech/social-media/twitter-happiness/index.html.

70. **arXiv.** Algorithm Writes People's Life Histories Using Twitter Stream. [Online] MIT Technology Review, October 7, 2013. http://www.technologyreview.com/view/519961/algorithm-writes-peoples-life-histories-using-twitter/.

71. **Kallus, Nathan.** Predicting Crowd Behavior with Big Public Data. [Online] Cornell University Library, February 10, 2014. http://arxiv.org/abs/1402.2308.

72. **MIT.** Can Twitter Predict Major Events Such as Mass Protests? [Online] MIT Technology Review, February 18, 2014. http://www.technologyreview.com/view/524871/can-twitter-predict-major-events-such-as-mass-protests/.

73. **Kelly, Heather.** Lovely wedding, but did it trend on Twitter? [Online] CNN, March 27, 2014. http://www.cnn.com/2014/03/26/tech/social-media/wedding-social-media-concierge/index.html.

74. **Martinez, Michael and Simon, Dan.** @HiddenCash lines pockets, warms heart of anonymous California philanthropist. [Online] CNN, May 28, 2014. http://www.cnn.com/2014/05/28/us/california-anonymous-donor-hidden-cash-twitter/index.html.
75. **@HiddenCash.** Hidden Cash. [Online] Twitter. [Cited: May 28, 2014.] https://twitter.com/HiddenCash.
76. —. Hidden Cash. [Online] Twitter. [Cited: August 13, 2014.] https://twitter.com/HiddenCash.
77. **Kuruvilla, Carol.** Arab-Jewish couple kiss in Twitter picture to support peace in Gaza. [Online] Daily News (New York), July 22, 2014. http://www.nydailynews.com/news/national/couple-kiss-viral-show-jews-arabs-refuse-enemies-article-1.1876242.
78. **arXiv.** Computational Linguistics of Twitter Reveals the Existence of Global Superdialects. [Online] MIT Technology Review, August 7, 2014. http://www.technologyreview.com/view/529836/computational-linguistics-of-twitter-reveals-the-existence-of-global-superdialects/.
79. **Kelly, Heather.** YouTube tries to fix its comments. [Online] CNN, September 24, 2013. http://www.cnn.com/2013/09/24/tech/social-media/youtube-comment-upgrade/index.html.
80. **ICTMN Staff.** 20 Racist Tweets About the New Miss America. [Online] Indian Country, September 16, 2013. http://indiancountrytodaymedianetwork.com/2013/09/16/20-racist-tweets-about-new-miss-america-151294.
81. **Leopold, Todd.** Is the Twitterverse the angriest place on the Internet? [Online] CNN, October 1, 2013. http://www.cnn.com/2013/09/21/tech/social-media/twitter-anger/index.html.
82. **Blake, John.** The look in Derek Chauvin's eyes was something worse than hate. [Online] CNN, April 24, 2021. https://www.cnn.com/2021/04/24/us/derek-chauvin-eyes-indifference-blake/index.html.
83. **Zadrozny, Brandy and Gains, Mosheh.** Woman killed in Capitol was Trump supporter who embraced conspiracy theories. [Online] NBC News, January 7, 2021. https://www.nbcnews.com/news/us-news/woman-killed-capitol-was-trump-supporter-who-embraced-conspiracy-theories-n1253285.
84. **Fung, Brian.** Twitter bans President Trump permanently. [Online] CNN Business, January 9, 2021. https://www.cnn.com/2021/01/08/tech/trump-twitter-ban/index.html.
85. **Juneau, Jen.** Alec Baldwin Quits Twitter After Controversy over Wife Hilaria's Heritage: 'Goodbye for Now'. [Online] People, January 20, 2021. https://people.com/tv/alec-baldwin-quits-twitter-after-wife-hilaria-baldwin-heritage-controversy/.
86. **Woodyatt, Amy.** Chrissy Teigen's parting words as she left Twitter. [Online] CNN Entertainment, March 25, 2021. https://www.cnn.com/2021/03/25/entertainment/chrissy-teigen-twitter-intl-scli/index.html.

Chapter 10
Misinformation, Disinformation, and Fake News

"Perhaps there is a simple answer – not an easy answer but simple: If you and I have the courage to tell our elected officials that we want our national policy based on what we know in our hearts is morally right."
> – President Ronald Reagan (October 1964)

"I play to people's fantasies. … People want to believe that something is the biggest and the greatest and the most spectacular. I call it truthful hyperbole."
> – President Donald Trump (November 1987)

"There's an old economic principle, that bad money drives out good. One thing that worries me is that bad information is driving out good."
> – Professor Frank Farley (March 2012)

"The loudest voices should be particularly careful not to rush to conclusions."
> – U.S. Secretary of Education William J. Bennett (March 2012)

"Facts have been replaced by opinions. Information has been replaced by entertainment. Reporters have become stenographers. I can't be the only one who's sick of what passes for the news today."
> – Superman Clark Kent (October 2012)

"The Internet is so full of junk and not-researched material."
> – Historian David Wallechinsky (April 2014)

"For me having to explain every day that I am not a prostitute is a daily complication. I am in favor of freedom of expression, but not the kind of freedom of expression built on lies."
> – Argentine model María Belén Rodríguez (May 2014)

"I'm quitting Facebook. Not comfortable with the flood of false information that's allowed in its political advertising."
> – American Author Stephen King (January 2020)

"At a moment of rampant disinformation and conspiracy theories juiced by algorithms, we can no longer turn a blind eye to a theory of technology that says all engagement is good engagement – the longer the better – and all with the goal of collecting as much data as possible."
> – Apple CEO Tim Cook (January 2021)

"Social media has become, in many ways, the key amplifier to domestic violent extremism just as it has for malign foreign influence. The same things that attract people to it for good reasons are also capable of causing all kinds of harms that we are entrusted with trying to protect the American people against."

– FBI director Christopher Wray (March 2021)

"My hope is that Facebook, instead of taking it personally, that somehow I'm saying Facebook is killing people, that they would do something about the misinformation, the outrageous misinformation about the vaccine. That's what I meant."

– President Joe Biden (July 2021)

"Facebook chooses what information billions of people see, shaping their perception of reality. Even those who don't use Facebook are impacted by the radicalization of people who do."

– Former Facebook product manager Frances Haugen
(October 2021)

"Information is power. Disinformation is abuse of power."

– Newton Lee

10.1   The Storming of Capitol Hill in 2021

Rampant misinformation and disinformation on social media culminated in the storming of Capitol Hill on January 6, 2021 by pro-Trump supporters. In March 2021, Facebook CEO Mark Zuckerberg, Google CEO Sundar Pichai, and Twitter CEO Jack Dorsey appeared before Congress to face criticism about their handling of misinformation and online extremism (1). In October 2021, former Facebook product manager Frances Haugen testified before the U.S. Senate Subcommittee on Consumer Protection, Product Safety, and Data Security: "Facebook chooses what information billions of people see, shaping their perception of reality. Even those who don't use Facebook are impacted by the radicalization of people who do" (2).

In the aftermath of the Capitol riot, social media took an extreme measure – borderline censorship – against misinformation and disinformation. But the damage was done. The failed four-hour insurrection left five people dead, more than a hundred injured, and subsequent suicide of four capitol police officers. Among the dead was 35-year-old QAnon adherent Ashli Babbitt who, on the day she died, retweeted President Trump's "Stop the Steal!" rallying cry as well as attorney Lin Wood's tweet urging that "Mike Pence @vp @Mike_Pence must resign & thereafter be charged with TREASON" (3).

Words are powerful, especially when emotions run high, which can lead to dire consequences. Long before the advent of social media, one notable incident happened in 1938 that caused public panic.

10.2 The War of the Worlds Radio Broadcast in 1938

On Sunday, October 30, 1938, millions of radio listeners were stunned by the CBS radio "news" on the Martian invasion of Earth:

"Good heavens! Something's wriggling out of the shadow like a gray snake. Now it's another, and another. They look like tentacles to me. There, I can see the thing's body. It's large as a bear and it glistens like wet leather. But that face. It … It's indescribable. I can hardly force myself to keep looking at it. The eyes are black and gleam like a serpent. The mouth is V-shaped with saliva dripping from its rimless lips that seem to quiver and pulsate. … The thing is raising up. The crowd falls back. They've seen enough. This is the most extraordinary experience. I can't find words. … I'll have to stop the description until I've taken a new position. Hold on, will you please. I'll be back in a minute" (4).

Orson Welles' radio adaption of H.G. Wells' novel *The War of the Worlds* (1898) caused widespread panic in America. Thousands of people called the police about the Martian landing in central New Jersey. Some residents loaded up their cars and fled their homes as the radio broadcasted a statement from the U.S. Secretary of the Interior voiced by an actor who sounded like President Franklin D. Roosevelt:

"Citizens of the nation: I shall not try to conceal the gravity of the situation that confronts the country, nor the concern of your government in protecting the lives and property of its people. However, I wish to impress upon you – private citizens and public officials, all of you – the urgent need of calm and resourceful action. Fortunately, this formidable enemy is still confined to a comparatively small area, and we may place our faith in the military forces to keep them there. In the meantime placing our faith in God we must continue the performance of our duties each and every one of us, so that we may confront this destructive adversary with a nation united, courageous, and consecrated to the preservation of human supremacy on this earth. I thank you" (5).

Surprisingly, the Federal Communications Commission decided not to fine CBS Radio or Orson Welles for the stunt that fooled countless numbers of American citizens as well as some officials at the New York City Department of Health (6). Ironically, the department was later revamped and renamed as the New York City Department of Health and Mental Hygiene (7).

10.3 Misinformation, Disinformation, and Fake News on Social Media

Fast-forwarding 74 years from the old radio days to March 2012, American film director Spike Lee retweeted to his 250,000 followers the wrong address of George Zimmerman, the man who shot and killed 17-year-old Trayvon Martin in February (8). The tweet took off on a life of its own. Consequentially, the homeowners at the address – Elaine McClain, 70, and her husband David McClain, 72 – started receiving hate mail and death threats that eventually drove them out of their home and into a hotel (9). Realizing his gross mistake, Lee apologized to the McClains and reached a settlement deal with them. The rush to judgment in the Trayvon Martin case in the world of immediacy via Twitter, Facebook, and other social networks can be chaotic

Fig. 10.1 "Get a real job" Hoax – Photoshopped Receipt vs. Real Receipt

and downright dangerous. Former U.S. Secretary of Education William J. Bennett warned about the behavior of influential people and celebrities, "The loudest voices should be particularly careful not to rush to conclusions" (10).

Users of Twitter, Facebook, and social networks often follow the Chinese maxim "Say all you know and say it without reserve" and ignore the Japanese proverb "Never let an opportunity pass by, but always think twice before acting." In a world of immediacy, Twitter has become the perfect tool for instant gratification and rapid dissemination of information as well as misinformation. Every day, information is being circulated on the Internet without verification or clear thoughts.

In February 2012, one of the strangest receipts from America's restaurants went viral on Twitter and Facebook. Twitterer @FutureExBanker sent Receiptrocity at eater. com a picture of the receipt showing that his boss left the waitress a miniscule 1% tip, $1.33, on a $133.54 bill with the message, "Get a real job" (11). As it turned out, it was a Photoshopped hoax. The restaurant spokesperson was able to locate the merchant copy of the real receipt that showed a $7 tip for a $33.54 bill (12). (See Fig. 10.1).

On May 8, 2012, Blogger Nate St. Pierre wrote an amusingly elaborate hoax article about U.S. President Abraham Lincoln filing a patent for Facebook in 1845 (14). The story deliberately raised a few red flags by mentioning the infamous prankster P.T. Barnum and inserting a poorly Photoshopped copy of the December 24, 1845 newspaper *Springfield Gazette*.

St. Pierre put out one tweet and posted a link on Facebook. Within 36 hours, he got 16,000 Facebook "Likes" and 104,463 unique pageviews to his blog. He was interviewed by reporters from CNN, The Atlantic, and The Washington Post.

On May 10, St. Pierre deconstructed the entire experience and expounded on the hoax, "It's a tip of the hat to P.T. Barnum's celebrated hoaxes (or humbugs) and Abe Lincoln's tall tales. … there are clues throughout the entire article telling you it's a hoax … I wanted to illustrate one of the drawbacks to our 'first and fastest' news aggregation and reporting mentality, especially online. … In addition to social media and bloggers, it ran as fact on a lot of big-name sites and news aggregators. That's the thing that surprised me the most. … I can tell you that virtually nobody checked with me to ask if it was true" (15).

Despite the numerous red flags throughout St. Pierre's story, *Forbes* posted his story under the headline "Abraham Lincoln Filed a Patent for a Dead-Tree Facebook in 1845" for a day before pulling it down. "A Forbes contributor took Nate St. Pierre's story at face value," said a Forbes spokeswoman. "Once Forbes realized it was a prank, the article was pulled from the site" (16). Nevertheless, *ZDNet* kept the story "Abraham Lincoln tried to patent Facebook in 1845, but failed?" on its website, but the *ZDNet* reporter Emil Protalinski crossed out some of the fake information and added an apology: "Update: Sorry everyone but this was indeed a hoax" (17).

In November 2012, software developer Nolan Daniels tricked more than two million Facebook users into sharing his fake lotto ticket on the social network. He posted on Facebook a picture of himself holding a Photoshopped multimillion-dollar winning lotto ticket with a catchy status update: "Looks like I won't be going to work EVER!!!! Share this photo and I will give a random person 1 million dollars!" (See Fig. 10.2) (18). To redeem himself from the shenanigans, Daniels said, "Instead of thinking of ways to profit from a hoax or eating up media attention, I spent the weekend setting up a fundraiser for Brooke and was determined to use my short-term fame to reach out to 1 person in need and if at minimum bring awareness for her and other with her condition [of brain disorder known as Chiari malformation]" (19).

All joking aside, misinformation and disinformation on social media are no laughing matter when it comes to national security and personal safety. In a June 2019 Congressional hearing before the subcommittee on Intelligence and Counterterrorism of the Committee on Homeland Security, Georgetown University professor Ben Buchanan testified that "automated algorithms on social media platforms cannot just drive users to objectionable content but help make that content more appealing and visible. The AP and academic researchers found that Facebook's algorithms automatically generate slick videos of some of the extremist content that has evaded its filtering. These algorithmically generated videos take images and videos that extremists have uploaded and package it to make it more neatly edited and synthesized – in essence, unintentionally doing the work of propaganda" (20).

10.4 Ramifications and Repercussions of Misinformation and Disinformation

On January 31, 2020, American author Stephen King tweeted to his 6.4 million followers, "I'm quitting Facebook. Not comfortable with the flood of false information that's allowed in its political advertising" (21).

Nolan Daniels
22 hours ago

Looks like I won't be going to work EVER!!!! Share this photo and I
will give a random person 1 million dollars!

Fig. 10.2 Nolan Daniels' "Lotto Ticket" Hoax

Misinformation and disinformation abound in the digital information world on
social media and news broadcast. Disinformation meant to deceive and mislead
people can take on a life of its own when ardent followers unwittingly spread misinformation. The proliferation of misinformation can lead to serious ramifications
and repercussions.

In November 2010, a Nicaraguan general cited Google's map of the border with
Costa Rica to justify a reported raid in a disputed area (22). Costa Rica had written
to Google about its map asking for changes, but the Nicaraguan Embassy in London
said, "The Government of Nicaragua has formally requested to Google not to accept
the petition of Costa Rica to modify the border demarcation presented on Google
Maps service, which recognizes Harbour Head as Nicaraguan territory. The path
presented by Google corresponds to the various treaties that define the Nicaragua-
Costa Rica border" (23).

In May 2012, Iran threatened to sue Google for not labeling the Persian Gulf,
whereas nearby bodies of water – including the Gulf of Oman, Arabian Sea, Gulf of
Aden and Red Sea – are labeled. "Toying with modern technologies in political

issues is among the new measures by the enemies against Iran, (and) in this regard, Google has been treated as a plaything," said Iran Foreign Ministry spokesman Ramin Mehmanparast (24).

In July 2012, then Kenyan President Mwai Kibaki's party was blamed for stoking xenophobic sentiment when the Kenyan Twitterati began writing about Somali refugees as culpable for a host of Kenya's domestic problems and terrorist attack (25).

In the midst of the Aurora, Colorado shooting rampage in July 2012, ABC News' Brian Ross speculated on air that suspect might be Jim Holmes of a Colorado Tea Party organization. ABC News later apologized, "ABC News and Brian Ross apologize for the mistake, and for disseminating that information before it was properly vetted" (26).

In October 2012, hedge fund analyst and campaign manager Shashank Tripathi (@ComfortablySmug) sent his 6,500 followers tweets of fake reports on flooding and destruction intended to spread confusion and fear when Hurricane Sandy was approaching New York City. Tripathi later apologized for his action and resigned from the campaign of New York Republican Christopher Wight. "While some would use the anonymity and instant feedback of social media as an excuse," he said, "I take full responsibility for my actions. I deeply regret any distress or harm they may have caused" (27).

In the aftermath of the Sandy Hook Elementary School shooting in Newtown, Connecticut in December 2012, Buzzfeed, CNN, Fox News, and Gawker identified the wrong person, Ryan Lanza, as the shooting suspect (28). Harassment outpacing verification in the social media space, Lanza fanatically tried to undo the reputational damage online. Lanza's Facebook friend Matt Bors, a political cartoonist, was also inundated with angry and bizarre messages like "Why are you friends with a monster?" and "Looks like this killer is a fan of yours." Bors wrote in *Salon*, "We have a problem with rushing to judgment. News organizations racing to be first know that an article with a snappy headline thrown up when people are hungry for information can bring in incredible amounts of traffic – forget glory or prestige, keep the servers running ads. But accuracy and being first seem to conflict" (29).

In April 2013, Syrian Electronic Army hacked into the official Associated Press Twitter account (@AP) and tweeted, "Breaking: Two Explosions in the White House and Barack Obama is injured." The message was re-tweeted more than 3,000 times before Twitter took the account offline, and the Dow Jones Industrial Average dropped sharply on the news but regained its losses when the report was deemed false (30).

After the Boston Marathon bombings on April 15, 2013, well-meaning Reddit users joined the hunt for the Boston bombers but ended up diverting attention and suspicion on innocent bystanders. After police had apprehended the true suspect Dzhokhar Tsarnaev, Reddit's General Manager Erik Martin wrote in a blog, "During the tragedy and the aftermath, people found many different avenues to help on reddit. The vast majority of these activities were positive. They provided a way for people to stay informed, as well as a place to just discuss, cope, and try to make sense of what happened. Primarily, reddit served as a great clearinghouse for information. ... However, though started with noble intentions, some of the activity on reddit fueled online witch hunts and dangerous speculation which spiraled into very negative consequences for innocent parties. The reddit staff and the millions of people on reddit around the world deeply regret that this happened. We have apologized privately to the family of missing college student Sunil Tripathi, as have various users and moderators. We want to take this opportunity to apologize publicly for the pain they have had to endure. ... A few years ago, reddit enacted a policy to not allow personal information on the site. This was because 'let's find out who this is' events frequently result in witch hunts, often incorrectly identifying innocent suspects and disrupting or ruining their lives. We hoped that the crowdsourced search for new information would not spark exactly this type of witch hunt. We were wrong" (31).

When a subreddit community page "FindNavyYardShooters" appeared in September 2013 after the Washington Navy Yard shooting, Reddit shut it down almost immediately so that the social media site would not make the same mistake twice (32).

In 2017, Myanmar lawmakers regularly posted hateful anti-Muslim content on Facebook, leading to violence against 700,000 Rohingya Muslims. The United Nations called it a genocide and criticized Facebook as a "useful instrument for those seeking to spread hate" (33). In response to the scorching UN report in 2018, Facebook banned 20 organizations and individuals in Myanmar, which was viewed by many as too little, too late.

In 2021, Belarusian KGB created more than 40 fake accounts on Facebook to pose as journalists and activists with profile pictures using deepfake technology. "These fictitious personas posted criticism of Poland in English, Polish, and Kurdish, including pictures and videos about Polish border guards allegedly violating migrants' rights. ... These fake personas claimed to be sharing their own negative experiences of trying to get from Belarus to Poland and posted about migrants' difficult lives in Europe" (34).

One of the biggest mistakes made by social media is allowing years of rampant misinformation and disinformation of unfounded theories and outright lies that culminated in the storming of Capitol Hill on January 6, 2021 by pro-Trump supporters. The failed four-hour insurrection left five people dead and more than a hundred injured. Among the dead was 35-year-old QAnon adherent Ashli Babbitt who, on the day she died, retweeted President Trump's "Stop the Steal!" rallying cry as well as attorney Lin Wood's tweet urging that "Mike Pence @vp @Mike_Pence must resign & thereafter be charged with TREASON" (3).

When President Trump tweeted "Stop the Steal!" to his 88 million followers, many of them retweeted the same rallying cry to their friends and relatives. Social media helped to perpetuate unproven claims such as widespread voter fraud, QAnon conspiracy theory, and "fake news" in traditional media. Disinformation meant to deceive and mislead people quickly takes on a life of its own as ardent followers unwittingly spread misinformation; and misinformation proliferates like a multilevel marketing (MLM) scheme, benefiting mostly the one on top of the pyramid.

In April 2021, FBI director Christopher Wray testified before the House Intelligence Committee. He said, "Social media has become, in many ways, the key amplifier to domestic violent extremism just as it has for malign foreign influence. The same things that attract people to it for good reasons are also capable of causing all kinds of harms that we are entrusted with trying to protect the American people against" (35).

10.5 Combating Misinformation, Disinformation, and Fake News on Social Media

Social media has been trying to combat misinformation, disinformation, and fake news. In January 2016, Facebook COO Sheryl Sandberg promoted "counter-speech" at the World Economic Forum in Davos, Switzerland, "Counter-speech to the speech that is perpetuating hate we think by far is the best answer" (35). Facebook offers ad credits worth up to $1,000 to users who post counter-extremist messages (36).

In March 2017, Facebook rolled out "Disputed News" tag (37). All fact-checkers are required to sign a "Code of Principles" created by the journalism non-profit Poynter (38).

In August 2017, Facebook began to block ads from Pages that repeatedly share false news. "Over the past year we have taken several steps to reduce false news and hoaxes on Facebook. Currently, we do not allow advertisers to run ads that link to stories that have been marked false by third-party fact-checking organizations. Now we are taking an additional step. If Pages repeatedly share stories marked as false, these repeat offenders will no longer be allowed to advertise on Facebook" (39).

In September 2017, Facebook released a report: "In reviewing the ads buys, we have found approximately $100,000 in ad spending from June of 2015 to May of 2017 – associated with roughly 3,000 ads – that was connected to about 470 inauthentic accounts and Pages in violation of our policies. We don't allow inauthentic accounts on Facebook, and as a result, we have since shut down the accounts and Pages we identified that were still active" (40).

On October 29, 2020, Instagram temporarily disabled the "Recent" tab on hashtag pages in attempt to curtail the spread of misinformation shortly before the U.S. presidential election (41). "As we near the U.S. elections, we're making changes to make it harder for people to come across possible misinformation on Instagram. Starting today, for people in the U.S. we will temporarily remove the 'Recent' tab from hashtag pages. We're doing this to reduce the real-time spread of potentially harmful content that could pop up around the election" (42). Instagram restored the "Recent" tab on December 9, 2020; and the Capitol riot happened less than a month later, on January 6, 2021.

On March 1, 2021, Twitter rolls out vaccine misinformation warning labels and a strike-based system for violations. The warning labels inform users that the content "may be misleading." Repeated violations result in temporary account lockout (for 2 to 4 strikes) or permanent suspension (after 5 strikes) (43).

On March 25, 2021, Facebook CEO Mark Zuckerberg, Google CEO Sundar Pichai, and Twitter CEO Jack Dorsey appeared before Congress to face criticism about their handling of misinformation and online extremism. Democratic congressman Mike Doyle, chair of the House subcommittee on Communications and Technology, said in his opening remarks, "You can take this content down. You can reduce the vision. You can fix this. But you choose not to. You have the means. But time after time you are picking engagement and profit over the health and safety of users" (1).

In July 2021, President Joe Biden answered CNN's question about his statement "Facebook killing people" (44) and he said, "My hope is that Facebook, instead of taking it personally, that somehow I'm saying Facebook is killing people, that they would do something about the misinformation, the outrageous misinformation about the vaccine. That's what I meant" (45).

Indeed, automated algorithms on social media platforms prioritize user engagement and therefore unwittingly promote sensationalism and conspiracy theories that are often based on lies and deception. Moreover, New York University researchers have discovered that right-wing misinformation on Facebook is more engaging than its left-wing counterpart (46). Laura Edelson at NYU's Cybersecurity for Democracy said, "My takeaway is that, one way or another, far-right misinformation sources are able to engage on Facebook with their audiences much, much more than any other category. That's probably pretty dangerous on a system that uses engagement to determine what content to promote" (47).

In June 2020, 22-year-old Facebook software engineer Timothy Aveni made headlines for quitting his job because of Zuckerberg's inaction on Trump's Facebook posts. "I'm resigning from my job at Facebook," wrote Aveni. "For years, President Trump has enjoyed an exception to Facebook's Community Standards; over and over he posts abhorrent, targeted messages that would get any other Facebook user suspended from the platform. He's permitted to break the rules, since his political speech is 'newsworthy.' ... Mark always told us that he would draw the line at speech that calls for violence. He showed us on Friday that this was a lie. Facebook will keep moving the goalposts every time Trump escalates, finding excuse after excuse not to act on increasingly dangerous rhetoric. Since Friday, I've spent a lot of time trying to understand and process the decision not to remove the racist, violent post Trump made Thursday night, but Facebook, complicit in the propagation of weaponized hatred, is on the wrong side of history" (48).

Apple CEO Tim Cook said in his online keynote at the 2021 Computers, Privacy and Data Protection Conference in Brussels, "At a moment of rampant disinformation and conspiracy theories juiced by algorithms, we can no longer turn a blind eye to a theory of technology that says all engagement is good engagement – the longer the better – and all with the goal of collecting as much data as possible" (49).

In the aftermath of the Capitol riot, social media took an extreme measure – borderline censorship – against misinformation and disinformation:

1. For the first time in history, major social media platforms including Facebook, Instagram, Twitter, YouTube, Snapchat, TikTok, Twitch, Discord, and Reddit have banned a sitting U.S. President – Donald J. Trump – citing the risk of further incitement of violence by the President of the United States (50). Twitter announced that "after close review of recent Tweets from the @realDonaldTrump account and the context around them we have permanently suspended the account due to the risk of further incitement of violence" (51). And Mark Zuckerberg wrote on Facebook, "His decision to use his platform to condone rather than condemn the actions of his supporters at the Capitol building has

rightly disturbed people in the US and around the world. … We believe the risks of allowing the President to continue to use our service during this period are simply too great. Therefore, we are extending the block we have placed on his Facebook and Instagram accounts indefinitely…" (52)

2. Facebook began to remove all content that mentions the phrase "stop the steal." Facebook's vice president of integrity Guy Rosen explained, "With continued attempts to organize events against the outcome of the U.S. presidential election that can lead to violence, and use of the term by those involved in Wednesday's violence in DC, we're taking this additional step in the lead up to the inauguration" (53).

3. Facebook started to crack down on Facebook Groups that promote "harmful" misinformation. "Groups and members that violate our rules should have reduced privileges and reach, with restrictions getting more severe as they accrue more violations, until we remove them completely," said Tom Alison, vice president of engineering. "And when necessary in cases of severe harm, we will outright remove groups and people without these steps in between" (54).

4. Twitter banned over 70,000 accounts for sharing misinformation, including the permanent ban of MyPillow founder Mike Lindell (55), attorney Lin Wood (56),

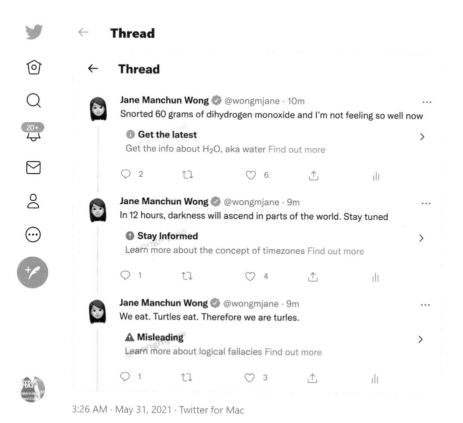

Fig. 10.3 Three levels of warning labels by Twitter (courtesy of Jane Manchun Wong)

Project Veritas (57), former national security adviser Michael Flynn and former Trump attorney Sidney Powell (58).

5. Discord banned pro-Trump server "The Donald" with the statement, "We have a zero-tolerance policy against hate and violence of any kind on the platform, or the use of Discord to support or organize around violent extremism. While there is no evidence of a server called The Donald being used to organize the Jan 6 riots, Discord decided to ban the entire server today due to its overt connection to an online forum used to incite violence, plan an armed insurrection in the United States, and spread harmful misinformation related to 2020 U.S. election fraud" (59).

6. Reddit banned unofficial pro-Trump subreddit r/donaldtrump for inciting violence, citing its "repeated policy violations in recent days regarding the violence at the U.S. Capitol" (60).

Social media tends to rely on fact checks and warning labels to alert readers of misinformation and disinformation. In May 2021, Twitter is working on three new levels of warning labels: "Get the latest," "Stay informed," and "Misleading" (61). Figure 10.3 shows three hilarious examples from researcher Jane Manchun Wong.

Nevertheless, the effectiveness of fact checks and warning labels may be overrated because not everyone heeds them. How often do we see grocery shoppers read the food labels on the items that they are browsing in supermarkets (62)?

Fact checks and warning labels have failed to convince the vast majority of Trump supporters because of:

1. Illusory truth effect: When a liar repeatedly states a particular untruth or half-truth over and over, the sheer repetition of the same lie casts doubt on the validity of fact checks and warning labels. 27-year-old QAnon believer Ashley Vanderbilt told BuzzFeed News reporter Scaachi Koul, "I had this idea in my head that I'm treating Jarrin's [Facebook] Live as if it's church" (63).

2. Continued influence effect: Also known as continued influence of misinformation, falsehoods can persist in our thinking long after they have been proven false. For example, when *The New York Times* debunked Trump by printing an article with the headline "Trump Claims, With No Evidence, That 'Millions of People' Voted Illegally", it perversely reinforced the false claim in the mind of many people (64).

3. Emotional bias: A distortion in cognition and decision making due to emotional factors causes a reluctance to accept hard facts that are unpleasant. English philosopher and politician John Stuart Mill wrote, "So long as an opinion is strongly rooted in the feelings, it gains rather than loses in stability by having a preponderating weight of argument against it" (65).

4. Religious influence: Appealing to the evangelicals, President Trump uses religious words and references to God at a higher rate than any U.S. Presidents in the last 100 years (66), not to mention a photo op holding a Bible in front of St. John's Episcopal Church amid the George Floyd protests in Washington D.C. (67) A Pew Research Center survey finds that almost one-third of U.S. adults believe that God put Trump into the White House (68).

5. Mental fatigue: When we are overwhelmed with false and half-truth statements day in and day out, our mind become so overworked that we stop trying to sift through all the information to determine what is true and not true. Consequently, many people simply accept what is music to their ears such as President Trump's blatant claims that "I am the least racist person there is anywhere in the world" in spite of the deadly clash at the white supremacist Unite the Right rally in Charlottesville, Virginia (69) and "I'm not the one trying to undermine American democracy. I'm the one that's trying to save it" despite the January 6 Capitol riot (70).

A master of illusory truth effect, continued influence effect, emotional bias, religious influence, and mental fatigue, President Trump summarized his mind game in his 1987 book *The Art of the Deal* (co-authored by journalist Tony Schwartz): "I play to people's fantasies. … People want to believe that something is the biggest and the greatest and the most spectacular. I call it truthful hyperbole. It's an innocent form of exaggeration – and a very effective form of promotion."

Truthful hyperbole is a dangerous game in politics. In July 2016 when Trump became the Republican presidential candidate, coauthor Tony Schwartz came to regret writing *The Art of the Deal*, stating that if it were to be written today it would be titled *The Sociopath* (71). President Trump's hyperbole includes denial, finger-pointing, and propaganda:

1. Denying and downplaying the coronavirus pandemic resulted in the death of half a million Americans (72) (73). Robert Redfield, director of the Centers for Disease Control and Prevention (CDC), had no choice but to publicly contradict Trump in September 2020: "Everything he says is false. We're nowhere near the end" (74).
2. Finger-pointing with words like "China virus" and "kung flu" caused a dramatic increase in hate crimes and deadly violence against Asian Americans (75). #StopAsianHate rallies were held across the country joined by celebrities such as Rihanna and Justin Timberlake (76), which paved the way to President Joe Biden signing into law on May 20, 2021 "the Covid-19 Hate Crimes Act" (77).
3. The "Stop the Steal!" propaganda culminated in the U.S. Capitol riot on January 6, 2021 (78). President George W. Bush remarked in the aftermath, "The violent assault on the Capitol – and disruption of a constitutionally mandated meeting of Congress – was undertaken by people whose passions have been inflamed by falsehoods and false hopes" (79). During the sentencing of former Trump campaign adviser Rick Gates, Federal Judge Amy Berman Jackson said, "This deliberate effort to obscure the facts, this disregard for the truth undermines our political discourse and it affects our policymaking. If people don't have the facts, democracy doesn't work" (80).

10.6   Censorship vs. Freedom of Speech

President Trump lashed out at social media companies after he was permanently banned by his favorite online megaphone Twitter. "I long predicted this would happen," Trump said. "We have been negotiating with various other sites, and will have a big announcement soon, while we also look at the possibilities of building out our own platform in the near future. We will not be SILENCED!" (81) Donald Trump Jr. added, "The world is laughing at America & Mao, Lenin, & Stalin are smiling. Big tech is able to censor the President? Free speech is dead & controlled by leftist overlords" (82).

German Chancellor Angela Merkel is certainly not fond of President Trump, but she expressed reservations about Twitter's decision. Merkel's chief spokesman Steffen Seibert told reporters at a government news conference in Berlin, "The right to freedom of opinion is of fundamental importance. Given that, the chancellor considers it problematic that the president's accounts have been permanently suspended" (83).

While major social media companies such as Facebook, Twitter, and Google (YouTube) have imposed a permanent ban on President Trump, other smaller sites such as Parler, Gab, and DLive have operated as alternative "free speech" platforms with minimal to no moderation. When major credit card companies cut ties with these alternative platforms known for racist and anti-Semitic content, these sites circumvent financial restrictions by using cryptocurrencies such as Bitcoin for which Gab calls "free speech money" (84).

In free speech, anyone can say anything with or without logic, reasoning, evidence, or proof. Social media has enabled users to bypass traditional news gatekeepers. The notion of gatekeeping on social media is an impossible feast without some form of censorship. Something as simple as automated profanity filtering can be viewed as censorship by some people.

Earlier in October 2020 before the Capitol riot, Facebook CEO Mark Zuckerberg, Google CEO Sundar Pichai, and Twitter CEO Jack Dorsey faced off with Congress over Section 230 of the Communications Decency Act that provides immunity for website publishers from third-party content. Section 230 also gives social media companies discretion in pulling down or leaving up offensive content such as hate speech.

Both Republican President Donald Trump and Democratic President Joe Biden have called for repealing or revamping Section 230. Senator Roger Wicker said in the congressional hearing, "This liability shield has been pivotal in protecting online platforms from endless and potentially ruinous lawsuits. It has also given these internet platforms the ability to control, stifle and even censor content in whatever manner meets their respective standards. The time has come for that free pass to end" (85). Senator Ted Cruz directed his anger towards Twitter CEO Jack Dorsey, "Mr. Dorsey, who the hell elected you and put you in charge of what the media are allowed to report and what the American people are allowed to hear, and why do you persist in behaving as a Democratic super PAC silencing views to the contrary of your political beliefs?" (86) Senator Cory Gardner added to the insult, "It's strange to me that you've flagged the tweets from [President Trump], but you haven't hidden the Ayatollah's call to wipe Israel off the map."

There are no easy answers. Facebook expanded its hate speech policy in October 2020 to include Holocaust denial only after the Anti-Defamation League (ADL) documented the rise in anti-Semitism in America and launched an advertiser boycott in protest of Facebook's inaction. The social network finally bowed to the pressure of over 1,000 participating companies which included Starbucks and Ben & Jerry's (87).

Before running for California governor and U.S. President, Ronald Reagan delivered "A Time for Choosing" speech on October 27, 1964 in which he discussed the idea of simple answers to complex problems in politics. He said, "Perhaps there is a simple answer – not an easy answer but simple: If you and I have the courage to tell our elected officials that we want our national policy based on what we know in our hearts is morally right" (88). Ethical policies are ideal, but results may vary depending on society's moral compass.

In April 2021, U.S. Supreme Court Justice Clarence Thomas suggested that Congress should consider whether existing laws need to be updated to better regulate social media platforms: "If part of the problem is private, concentrated control over online content and platforms available to the public, then part of the solution may be found in doctrines that limit the right of a private company to exclude" (89).

To bypass media censorship, fact checks, and warning labels, President Trump floated the idea of creating his own social media platform to reconnect with millions of followers. In March 2021, Jason Miller – spokesperson for Trump's 2020 campaign – told Howard Kurtz on Fox News that Trump will be "returning to social media in probably about two or three months... This is something that I think will be the hottest ticket in social media. It's going to completely redefine the game, and everybody is going to be waiting and watching to see what President Trump does, but it will be his own platform" (90).

In April 2021, Florida passed a bill to fine social media companies such as Facebook, Twitter, and YouTube for banning political candidates. "What this bill is about is sending a loud message to Silicon Valley that they are not the absolute arbiters of truth," said Congressman John Snyder (91). But NetChoice President Steve DelBianco disagreed, "The First Amendment makes clear that government may not regulate the speech of private individuals or businesses. This includes government action that compels speech by forcing a private social media platform to carry content that is against its policies or preferences."

In May 2021, an online blog called "From the Desk of Donald J. Trump" was launched. However, it only lasted for a month when the blog was scrubbed in June 2021, signaling that a Trump social media platform may just be another hyperbole (92). But lo and behold, President Donald Trump announced in October 2021 the formation of Trump Media & Technology Group (TMTG) that would include streaming service TMTG+ and social platform TRUTH Social (93). Trump stated his rationale, "I created TRUTH Social and TMTG to stand up to the tyranny of Big Tech. We live in a world where the Taliban has a huge presence on Twitter, yet your favorite American President has been silenced. This is unacceptable. I am excited to send out my first TRUTH on TRUTH Social very soon. TMTG was founded with a mission to give a voice to all" (94). It remains to be seen if Trump's new social network will take root in truth or lies.

10.7   The Oversight Board: Facebook's Supreme Court

An independent body described by Mark Zuckerberg as a kind of Supreme Court, Facebook announced the Oversight Board on May 6, 2020 with 20 notable individuals who have lived in over 27 countries and speak at least 29 languages. Co-chaired by former Prime Minister of Denmark Helle Thorning-Schmidt and Universidad de los Andes Dean of Law Faculty Catalina Botero Marino, the current members include former European Court of Human Rights judge András Sajó, Internet Sans Frontières Executive Director Julie Owono, Yemeni activist and Nobel Peace Prize laureate Tawakkol Karman, former editor-in-chief of *The Guardian* Alan Rusbridger, Pakistani digital rights advocate Nighat Dad, and Brazilian civil rights attorney Ronaldo Lemos.

"We expect them to make some decisions that we, at Facebook, will not always agree with – but that's the point: they are truly autonomous in their exercise of independent judgment," wrote Nick Clegg, VP of Global Affairs and Communications. "Facebook will implement the board's decisions unless doing so could violate the law, and will respond constructively and in good faith to policy guidance put forth by the board" (95).

As of May 20, 2021, the Oversight Board has upheld 3 and overturned 7 of Facebook's decisions (96):

1. Myanmar Syrian toddler photographs – Hate speech – Overturn
2. Azerbaijani churches photograph – Hate speech – Uphold
3. Breast cancer photographs (Instagram) – Adult nudity and sexual activity – Overturn
4. Goebbels misattribution – Dangerous individuals and organizations – Overturn
5. French hydroxychloroquine and azithromycin post – Violence and incitement – Overturn
6. Depiction of a Muslim threat to Macron – Violence and incitement – Overturn
7. "Zwarte Piet" blackface – Hate speech – Uphold
8. Video interview with Professor Manjit Singh – Dangerous individuals and organizations – Overturn
9. Ban of President Donald Trump – Dangerous individuals and organizations – Uphold
10. "Two buttons" meme of Armenian genocide – Hate speech – Overturn

The highest profile case was certainly the Oversight Board's decision on May 5, 2021 to uphold Facebook's ban of President Donald Trump:

"At the time of Mr. Trump's posts, there was a clear, immediate risk of harm and his words of support for those involved in the riots legitimized their violent actions. As president, Mr. Trump had a high level of influence. The reach of his posts was large, with 35 million followers on Facebook and 24 million on Instagram. Given the seriousness of the violations and the ongoing risk of violence, Facebook was justified in suspending Mr. Trump's accounts on January 6 and extending that suspension on January 7" (97).

However, the Oversight Board was against an "indefinite" suspension of Donald Trump:

> "It was not appropriate for Facebook to impose an 'indefinite' suspension. It is not permissible for Facebook to keep a user off the platform for an undefined period, with no criteria for when or whether the account will be restored. … Within six months of this decision, Facebook must reexamine the arbitrary penalty it imposed on January 7 and decide the appropriate penalty. This penalty must be based on the gravity of the violation and the prospect of future harm. It must also be consistent with Facebook's rules for severe violations, which must, in turn, be clear, necessary and proportionate" (97).

In response to the Oversight Board, Facebook announced on June 4, 2021 that the suspension of Donald Trump from its platform would last for 2 years until January 7, 2023 – just in time for the 2024 U.S. presidential election (98). After the 2-year ban, Facebook "will look to experts to assess whether the risk to public safety has receded. We will evaluate external factors, including instances of violence, restrictions on peaceful assembly and other markers of civil unrest. If we determine that there is still a serious risk to public safety, we will extend the restriction for a set period of time and continue to re-evaluate until that risk has receded" (99).

10.8 Trustworthiness of Wikipedia

What we need is a more civilized free speech with respect and dignity. Wikipedia, for instance, is a well-respected form of free speech that anyone can contribute by citing verifiable sources. As a result, a Wikipedia article often paints a more complete picture of truth instead of a one-sided story.

When Encyclopedia Britannica decided in 2012 to cease production of its iconic multi-volume print book sets, Britannica president Jorge Cauz conceded, "Google's algorithm doesn't know what's fact or what's fiction. So Wikipedia is often the No. 1 or No. 2 result on search. But I'd bet a lot of money that most people would rather use Britannica than Wikipedia. Wikipedia is a wonderful technology for collecting everything from great insights to lies and innuendos. It's not all bad or all good, just uneven. It's the murmur of society, a million voices rather than a single informed one. As a result, consumers are craving accuracy and are willing to pay for it [Encyclopedia Britannica]" (100).

Prof. James S. O'Rourke at the University of Notre Dame concurred, "The problem with crowdsourcing the answer to any particular question is, of course, that you're as likely to find ideologically driven opinion as hard fact. You also have little in the way of support for judgments about credibility, reliability, and accuracy" (101).

Prof. Yochai Benkler, co-director of the Berkman Center for Internet & Society at Harvard University, pointed out that "Wikipedia's organizational innovation is in problem solving more than innovation: how to maintain quality contributions together with potentially limitless expansion, a problem that scarcity absolved Britannica from solving" (102).

In the age of big data, Wikipedia has become the de facto encyclopedia. Its online content is searchable, revisable, and up-to-date. Its credibility, reliability, and accuracy depend mostly on citations from trusted sources. Wikipedia flags articles for incompleteness and biases by displaying warning messages on the content pages. For example, "This biographical article needs additional citations for verification. Please help by adding reliable sources. Contentious material about living persons that is unsourced or poorly sourced must be removed immediately, especially if potentially libelous or harmful" (103).

Given the open crowdsourcing nature of Wikipedia, unverifiable content can be misleading at best or malicious at worst. In November 2005, American journalist John Seigenthaler – who was Robert Kennedy's administrative assistant in the early 1960s – told his story about Internet character assassination on *USA Today*. An anonymous user with IP address 65.81.97.208 created a defamatory biography of the 78-year-old Seigenthaler on Wikipedia, scurrilously claiming that "for a brief time, he was thought to have been directly involved in the Kennedy assassinations of both John, and his brother, Bobby. Nothing was ever proven" (104). Seigenthaler phoned Wikipedia's founder Jimmy Wales and asked, "Do you ... have any way to know who wrote that?" To which Wales replied, "No, we don't. We have trouble with people posting abusive things over and over and over. We block their IP numbers, and they sneak in another way. So we contact the service providers, and they are not very responsive."

My own biographical article was vandalized on November 15, 2011 when someone by the login name "Newyorker1" revised the article. Apart from the vile changes that he made, he also updated my name to "Newton Shrimp Fried Rice Lee," my picture to that of President George Bush, and my book title *Disney Stories: Getting to Digital* to *Disney Stories: Getting to XXX Shop By Midnight* (105). Fortunately, Wikipedia's ClueBot NG detected the vandalism almost immediately and reverted all the changes automatically. ClueBot NG's vandalism detection algorithm uses machine learning techniques, Bayesian classifiers, artificial neural networks, threshold calculation, and post-processing filters (106).

In May 2013, someone with the IP address 86.166.188.231 proposed that my biographical article be deleted because of the concern: "Autobiography entirely written by subject" (107). However, long-time Wikipedian and librarian David Goodman (DGG) saved the article with the remark: "Not necessarily a reason for deletion; First look for reviews of his books, & if not found, only then nominate for deletion" (108). To maintain quality and accuracy of the open-source encyclopedia, some prolific Wikipedians such as İvana take on additional responsibility as Wikipedia Volunteer Patrollers for anti-vandalism (109).

In July 2014, someone changed the U.S. Secretary of Defense entry on Wikipedia from Chuck Hagel to American soccer goalkeeper Tim Howard who had a record-setting 16 saves in the 2014 FIFA World Cup match between USA and Belgium. In praise of Howard, the revised entry also credited him with "the destruction of terrorism and the advent of lasting peace" (110). (See Fig. 10.4). With a sense of humor, Hagel told Howard on the phone that with some training, he could someday become the real secretary of defense (111).

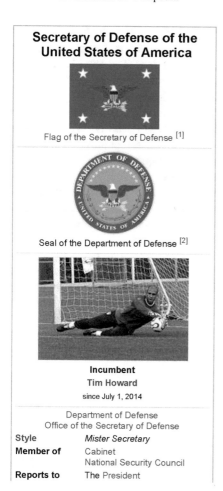

Secretary of Defense of the United States of America

Flag of the Secretary of Defense [1]

Seal of the Department of Defense [2]

Incumbent
Tim Howard
since July 1, 2014

Department of Defense
Office of the Secretary of Defense

Style	*Mister Secretary*
Member of	Cabinet
	National Security Council
Reports to	The President

Line 41:

The current Secretary of Defense is [[**Chuck Hagel**]], **who** assumed office on **February 27, 2013**.

The current Secretary of Defense is [[**Tim Howard|Sir Tim Howard**]]. He assumed office on July 1, 2014 after protecting the USA from the Belgians, Germans and other evil empires. On July 2, 2014, the day after Sir Howard assumed office, the [[al-Qaeda]], the [[Taliban]] and other major global terrorist organizations disbanded with their members surrendering to the [[US Armed Forces]] due to Mr Howard taking office. This behavior has been termed "Howanoia" and has resulted in the destruction of terrorism and the advent of lasting peace. In recognition of Mr.Howard's efforts. the [[Nobel Committee]] has decided to bestow upon him the [[Nobel Peace Prize]]. He has also received a [[Medal of Honor]] from the US President Barack Obama in recognition of his valour, bravery and defence of the United States.

Fig. 10.4 Tim Howard as U.S. Secretary of Defense on Wikipedia (July 2, 2014)

Notwithstanding the potential risk of misinformation and disinformation, Internet-powered crowdsourcing is being wholeheartedly embraced by both Generation X and the Millennials. Yahoo! CEO Marissa Mayer and husband Zack Bogue crowdsourced their newborn baby's name in an email to their friends (112). More than a million couples have crowdsourced their wedding photos through WedPics, Capsule, Wedding Party, Guest Shots and AppilyWed (113). A 2013 Rally Fighter race car built by Local Motors is believed to be the first production vehicle to be designed through crowdsourcing (114). And in 2014, Stanford University researchers released "Twitch" – a crowdsourcing app that ask its user to answer a roughly one-second question about their surroundings in order to build a map of human activity in the world (115).

"I love to collect information, and I love that I get to share that information with the world," said Emily Temple-Wood who started editing Wikipedia entries at the age of 12 (116). Now a resident doctor of osteopathic medicine, Temple-Wood has made it her mission to ensure that female scientists get their due recognition on Wikipedia. She shares her views and personal experiences in the chapter titled "Wikipedia and the New Web" in this book.

It may come as a surprise that Wikipedia admits that it can be wrong and yet it can be a good thing: "The threshold for inclusion in Wikipedia is verifiability, not truth. There are two important consequences to this. The first is that sometimes things that are true cannot be included. The second is that sometimes things that are not true are included. The second of these is often frequently infuriating to those who know the truth. It means that Wikipedia is wrong.

While at first glance that may appear like a very great problem for Wikipedia, in reality it is not. In fact, it can be seen as a good thing. Wikipedia is a project to build a free encyclopedia. Encyclopedias are tertiary sources and Wikipedia is no different in that respect. Tertiary sources collect knowledge that has already been published in what are called secondary sources. Tertiary sources do not generate new knowledge but rather just reflect what is already known and has already been published on a topic. If what has been published is incorrect then these errors will be replicated in an encyclopedia. It is not until secondary sources are published which correct these errors, that these corrections will be reflected in the encyclopedias…

Wikipedia's editing is open to anyone and if it is a popular subject it is biased to the majority (contemporary) opinion of Wikipedia editors." (117).

10.9   Google Search Sabotage

Unlike Wikipedia, Google search sabotage is a lot trickier to deal with. For many years, former Pennsylvania Senator and 2012 GOP presidential hopeful Rick Santorum has been battling his Google search results. In November 2003, gay newspaper advice columnist Dan Savage created the blog "Spreading Santorum" in retaliation for Santorum's ultraconservative views and anti-gay comments (118). Because of the prank, people saw a vulgar term for anal sex as the first result when they searched the word "Santorum" on Google. Santorum contacted Google to protest but to no avail.

In an e-mail to CNN, a Google spokeswoman said, "Google's search results are a reflection of the content and information that is available on the Web. Users who want content removed from the Internet should contact the webmaster of the page directly. Once the webmaster takes the page down from the Web, it will be removed from Google's search results through our usual crawling process" (119).

Obviously, contacting the webmaster Dan Savage is out of the question for Rick Santorum, who fired back at Google, "I suspect if something was up there like that about Joe Biden, they'd get rid of it. If you're a responsible business, you don't let things like that happen in your business that have an impact on the country" (120). Nonetheless, Santorum's active political campaign activities in 2012 helped improve the rankings of his Wikipedia page and Google news just enough for them to be displaced above the "Spreading Santorum" blog in Google search results.

In February 2014, based on Edward Snowden's NSA leaks, journalist Glenn Greenwald published in *The Intercept* a comprehensive report on the tactics of online sabotage by British intelligence agency GCHQ. The two main tactics are "(1) to inject all sorts of false material onto the internet in order to destroy the reputation of its targets; and (3) to use social sciences and other techniques to manipulate online discourse and activism to generate outcomes it considers desirable." Greenwald wrote, "To see how extremist these programs are, just consider the tactics they boast of using to achieve those ends: 'false flag operations' (posting material to the internet and falsely attributing it to someone else), fake victim blog posts (pretending to be a victim of the individual whose reputation they want to destroy), and posting 'negative information' on various forums" (121).

In May 2014, Argentine model María Belén Rodríguez took to the Supreme Court of Argentina to sue Google and Yahoo! over images of her that link to porn sites. "For me having to explain every day that I am not a prostitute is a daily complication," said Rodríguez through a translator. "I am in favor of freedom of expression, but not the kind of freedom of expression built on lies" (122). Google's response was that "search engines are neutral platforms that do not create nor control content on the web" (123).

During the 2014 election season, the National Republican Congressional Committee (NRCC) created at least 15 fake websites that appeared to be the official campaign sites for Democratic candidates. "The idea is people who are looking for information on the candidate, one of the places we all go now is online and so this is a way for folks to find out more about the candidates and information they may not find on the candidate's own site," said NRCC press secretary Daniel Scarpinato. "I think that sites are clear in terms of the disclosure and the content where were coming from. And I also think it's important for voters to get all the perspectives on the candidates. So just as a candidate is going to put information out about themselves, we're going to put out information about the candidate that they are not putting out that we think is important for voters to know" (124).

While Google, Microsoft's Bing, Facebook, Twitter, and other social media are excellent sources of information in the age of big data, it is up to the readers to decipher what is true and what is false. Information, misinformation, and disinformation are more mingled and harder to differentiate today than ever in the history of humankind. Pulitzer Prize nominee Nicholas Carr wrote an insightful article "Is Google Making Us Stupid?" in the July/August 2008 issue of the *Atlantic Magazine*:

> "Thanks to the ubiquity of text on the Internet, not to mention the popularity of text-messaging on cell phones, we may well be reading more today than we did in the 1970s or 1980s, when television was our medium of choice. But it's a different kind of reading, and behind it lies a different kind of thinking – perhaps even a new sense of the self. 'We are not only what we read,' says Maryanne Wolf, a developmental psychologist at Tufts University and the author of *Proust and the Squid: The Story and Science of the Reading Brain*. 'We are how we read.' Wolf worries that the style of reading promoted by the Net, a style that puts 'efficiency' and 'immediacy' above all else, may be weakening our capacity for the kind of deep reading that emerged when an earlier technology, the printing press, made long

and complex works of prose commonplace. When we read online, she says, we tend to become 'mere decoders of information.' Our ability to interpret text, to make the rich mental connections that form when we read deeply and without distraction, remains largely disengaged" (125).

10.10   Advertising Misinformation and Disinformation

Celebrities do not always believe in the products and services that they are paid to endorse. For instance, Weight Watchers spokesman and NBA player Charles Barkley was caught disparaging his endorsement deal on air when he thought the microphone was off. He said, "I thought this was the greatest scam going – getting paid for watching sports – this Weight Watchers thing is a bigger scam" (126).

In teen and women's magazines, advertisements for diets and weight loss programs are 10 times more common than they are in men's magazines (127). A fashion trend is often the result of deliberate promotion of certain images online and in print to create a mass following – starting from runways, magazines, TV, movies, and the Internet to shopping malls. Like everything else, there are plenty of competitions.

Occidental University associate professor Caroline Heldman said, "The number of images out there means advertisers have a much more difficult time breaking through the clutter, causing the content to be much more violent and sexualized to get consumers' attention" (128).

As a result, misinformation and disinformation are widespread in advertisements. Between 2010 and 2012, the U.K. Advertising Standards Authority has banned eight misleading ads due to excessive Photoshop, social irresponsibility, and marketing deception (129). The "misleadingly exaggerated" ads included Rachel Weisz's L'Oréal Revitalift Repair 10 and Julia Roberts' Lâncome Teint Miracle; the deceptive ad was for Reebok's EasyTone sneakers; and the "socially irresponsible" ads included Hailee Steinfeld for Miu Miu Fall 2011 collection, Dakota Fanning for Marc Jacobs Oh Lola! Perfume, and campaigns for Levi's Jeans "Go Forth" and Diesel "Be Stupid."

Some American teenagers are calling for an end to the digitally enhanced, unrealistic "beauty" in the pages of teen fashion magazines. In July 2012, 14-year-old Julia Bluhm from Maine hand-delivered a petition signed by 84,000+ people to the executive editor of *Seventeen* magazine, urging the publisher not to alter the body size or face shape of the girls and models in the magazine. Bluhm wrote on change. org, "*Seventeen* listened! They're saying they won't use Photoshop to digitally alter their models! This is a huge victory, and I'm so unbelievably happy. Another petition is being started by SPARK activists Emma [Stydahar] and Carina [Cruz], targeting *Teen Vogue* and I will sign it. If we can be heard by one magazine, we can do it with another. We are sparking a change!" (130)

10.11   Authenticity of Social Media Influencers and Fake Accounts

Exaggerated images and sensationalized news are no strangers to mass media. The Internet, with its efficiency and immediacy, serves to exacerbate the potential danger of misinformation and disinformation. Sadly, the public is simply unaware of the authenticity of social media influencers on Facebook, Instagram, Twitter, and YouTube:

- In 2006, "lonelygirl15" appeared as a home-schooled and confused 16-year-old teenager "Bree" on her wildly popular YouTube videos with over a million views. For four months, she fooled viewers into believing her real struggles with her estranged parents and dysfunctional family, until *Los Angeles Times* reporter Richard Rushfield revealed that Bree was a 19-year-old American-New Zealand actress Jessica Lee Rose. Rushfield reported, "Three lonelygirl15-obsessed amateur Web sleuths set up a sting using tracking software that appears to show that e-mails sent from a lonelygirl15 account came from inside the offices of the Beverly Hills-based talent agency Creative Artists Agency" (131).
- In 2009, a group of students at Millburn High School in New Jersey created a fake Facebook account for a fictional new student "Lauren" in their school, and almost 120 students and 55 others added her as a friend (132).
- In 2010, Indiana University professor Filippo Menczer and other researchers launched the Truthy project to detect political smears, astroturfing, misinformation, and other social pollution (133). They found evidence that political campaigns and special interest groups are using fake Twitter accounts to create the false impression of grassroots movements. Repeated and retweeted messages from a score of fake users would show up as "trending" topics on Twitter and would ultimately influence Google's search results (134).
- In 2011, a classmate of 11-year-old Ashley Berry took photos of her and created an entire Facebook page without her consent. "It had things like where I went to school, and where my family was from and my birthday, and there were no security settings at all, so it was pretty scary," said Berry who had to deal with unintended consequences such as friends uninviting her to birthday parties and leaving her at the lunch table in school (135).
- In 2011, a student at Rancho Bernardo High School created a Facebook account using another teen's name, and posted threats of a mass shooting at the high school (136). Police arrested the student for making terrorist threats and impersonating another on the Internet.
- In 2011, GOP Presidential hopeful Newt Gingrich had over 1.38 million Twitter followers, more than twice the number of Twitter followers for former Vice Presidential candidate Sarah Palin, and 10 times more than that for his main GOP rival Mitt Romney. Gingrich's Twitter presence looked impressive, until a New York search company PeekYou discovered that only 8% of Gingrich's

Twitter followers were verifiable humans (137). In other words, about 1.27 million phony Twitter accounts were created by Gingrich-hired campaign agencies.

- In 2012, media mogul Rupert Murdoch signed up for Twitter and started to follow four people on the social network including Google's co-founder and CEO Larry Page. Unbeknown to Murdoch, he followed a fake Larry Page – a parody account created by Virginia Tech for university project (138).
- In 2013, Dan Bilzerian, a trust fund beneficiary and poker player, became a social media sensation for posting pictures of his lavish playboy lifestyle on Instagram. Known as the "King of Instagram," his number of followers ballooned to 32.6 million in 2020 before he was ousted as a fraud (139).

In the amended S-1 filing on March 7, 2012, Facebook disclosed that 5 to 6% of Facebook accounts were either fake or duplicated based on an internal review of a limited sample of accounts (140). Similarly, Twitter reported in its securities filings that fake accounts represented fewer than 5% of its 230 million active users in October 2013 (141).

Nevertheless, 5 or 6% is likely a gross underestimate. Some industry watchers claimed that nearly 50% of social network users could be fake or empty user accounts (142). Facebook admitted in its first quarterly report in August 2012 that 83 million Facebook profiles were fake and millions of Facebook accounts were created for users' pets (143). Jason Ding, a research scientist at Barracuda Labs, told NBC News that the number of Twitter accounts that were fake was "at least 10%, maybe more" in November 2013 (144).

Fake accounts are usually created by fake followers for hire who are paid to like a Facebook page, follow someone on Twitter, comment on a YouTube video, or fake an engagement on Twitch. In April 2021, Twitch announced the removal of more than 7.5 million accounts: "We have been monitoring the rise of fake engagement on Twitch and have identified 7.5MM+ accounts that break our TOS by follow-botting and view-botting. We are taking action on these accounts and appreciate all of the reports about this issue" (145).

Prof. Ben Zhao at UC Santa Barbara coined the term "crowdturfing" to describe the phenomenon of "crowdsourcing" and "astroturfing" – recruiting a large number of people to fake a grassroots support (146).

10.12   Facebook Account Verification

To help reduce spam, fake, and multiple accounts, Facebook encourages a user to "verify" their account by adding a mobile number to it (147). The "Confirm Your Phone" page states, "Facebook uses security tests to ensure that the people on the site are real. Having a mobile phone helps us establish your identity. Please verify your account by confirming your phone here. We'll text you a confirmation code" (148). After verification, a user may add a username (e.g. myusername) to the account and customize the Facebook web address (e.g. www.facebook.com/myusername) (149).

Facebook's mobile number verification constitutes a very basic security. Everyone in the U.S. can purchase a cheap, disposable prepaid cell phone for temporary use. In order for Facebook to step up its security, Facebook began to roll out in February 2012 "verified accounts" whose owners have submitted a government ID to prove their identities. However, the new security update is currently restricted to Facebook users with a large number of subscribers. "This update makes it even easier for subscribers to find and keep up with journalists, celebrities and other public figures they want to connect to," said a Facebook spokesman (150).

However, it gets tricky when you have the same name as a celebrity. In May 2011, Mark S. Zuckerberg's Facebook account was deleted for the reason of "false identity." A bankruptcy attorney in Indianapolis, Zuckerberg received hundreds of friend request and inquiries from people who thought he was Facebook's CEO. "Our reviewers look at thousands of pieces of content a day that are reported to them and of course make an occasional mistake," said a Facebook spokesperson. "When this happens, and we're notified about it, we work quickly to restore the content. We have reactivated this person's account and sent him an email apologizing for the inconvenience" (151).

Similarly in August 2012, 18-year-old Selena M. Gomez in New Mexico was distraught when Facebook denied her access to her account with the message "Disabled – Inauthentic Account." Gomez told *TMZ*, "I AM NOT AN IMPOSTOR ... My name is not hers on my page. In fact, I even put my middle name on my FB to clear up any confusion. I did not have one single famous friend. I did not refer to myself as [the famous Selena], and I did not have any pictures of her on my page!" (152) The story had a happy ending: Facebook apologized to Gomez and reactivated her account within a day after mistakenly disabling her profile (153).

10.13   Twitter Verified Accounts

Unlike Facebook, Twitter does not accept public requests for account verification. Since the launch of verified accounts in June 2009, Twitter has stated on its help center, "Any account with a blue verified badge on their Twitter profile is a verified account. Verification is currently used to establish authenticity of identities on Twitter. The verified badge helps users discover high-quality sources of information and trust that a legitimate source is authoring the account's Tweets. Twitter proactively verifies accounts on an ongoing basis to make it easier for users to find who they're looking for. We concentrate on highly sought users in music, acting, fashion, government, politics, religion, journalism, media, advertising, business, and other key interest areas. We verify business partners from time to time and individuals at high risk of impersonation. We do not accept requests for verification from the general public. If you fall under one of the above categories and your Twitter account meets our qualifications for verification, we may reach out to you in the future" (154).

According to *Advertising Age*, Twitter reaches out to advertisers who have spent at least $15,000 over three months and get their accounts verified (155). The Twitter business practice leaves many smaller businesses out in the cold. *The Wall Street Journal* reported that celebrities such as Britney Spears had their managers contact the head of Twitter to obtain account verifications (156).

In spite of the verification process, Twitter has made quite a few mistakes in its nearly 17,000 verified accounts. In a high-profile error, Twitter apologized in January 2012 for incorrectly verifying a false account for Wendi Deng, the wife of News Corp CEO Rupert Murdoch (157). The @Wendi_Deng account had racked up more than 10,000 followers before it was discovered to be a faux one created by a British man to poke fun at Deng (158).

10.14   Deepfakes and Shallowfakes on YouTube

Computer technology has leapfrogged radio broadcast from 1938 when millions of listeners were stunned by the CBS radio "news" on the Martian invasion of Earth. Orson Welles' radio adaption of H.G. Wells' novel *The War of the Worlds* (1898) caused widespread panic in America as the radio broadcasted a statement from the U.S. Secretary of the Interior voiced by an actor who sounded like President Franklin D. Roosevelt. Nowadays, such convincing deceptions would require both audio and video.

Wikipedia offers a concise definition of deepfakes (a portmanteau of "deep learning" and "fake") as "synthetic media in which a person in an existing image or video is replaced with someone else's likeness. While the act of faking content is not new, deepfakes leverage powerful techniques from machine learning and artificial intelligence to manipulate or generate visual and audio content with a high potential to deceive. The main machine learning methods used to create deepfakes are based on deep learning and involve training generative neural network architectures, such as autoencoders or generative adversarial networks (GANs)" (159).

In 2020, Belgium VFX specialist and deepfake artist Chris Ume was hired by South Park creators Trey Parker and Matt Stone to work on *Sassy Justice* with deepfake videos of celebrities and politicians (including Julie Andrews, Michael Caine, Al Gore, Jared Kushner, Donald Trump, Ivanka Trump, Chris Wallace, and Mark Zuckerberg) played by Parker, Stone, Peter Serafinowicz, and other actors (160).

In 2021, Chris Ume created a TikTok sensation with a series of deepfake Tom Cruise videos that went viral. "You can't do it by just pressing a button," Ume told *The Verge*. "By combining traditional CGI and VFX with deepfakes, it makes it better. I make sure you don't see any of the glitches. Each clip took weeks of work using the open-source DeepFaceLab algorithm as well as established video editing tools" (161).

On the positive side, deepfake technology offers Hollywood the mean to "resurrect" late actors in new movies. A prime example is actress Carrie Fisher (1956–2016) as Princess Leia in the 2019 film *Star Wars: Rise of Skywalker* (162). On the negative side, deepfakes have gained notoriety in the proliferation of celebrity pornographic videos, revenge porn, fake news, hoaxes, and financial fraud.

While it may take years before deepfakes become as easy as a "one-click" operation, shallowfakes are already pervasive enough to cause a lot of troubles especially when emotions are running high.

"By these 'shallowfakes' I mean the tens of thousands of videos circulated with malicious intent worldwide right now – crafted not with sophisticated AI, but often simply relabeled and re-uploaded, claiming an event in one place has just happened in another," said Sam Gregory of the Witness human rights organization (163). Not only can we be fooled into believing in falsehood, we can also be manipulated into denying the truth. "An alarmist narrative only enhances the real dangers we face: plausible deniability and the collapse of trust."

Some examples of deepfakes and shallowfakes are Lynda Carter as *Wonder Woman* in 2020 (164), Obama's public service announcement (165), Nancy Pelosi's slurring her words (166), Mark Zuckerberg boasting of how the platform manipulates its users (167), and roundtable discussion with Tom Cruise, Robert Downey, Jr, George Lucas, Ewan McGregor, and Jeff Goldblum (168).

No matter what we do, misinformation and disinformation are here to stay. In the social media world of immediacy without proper fact checks, deepfakes and shallowfakes are only making it harder for the public to discern the difference between truth and error.

10.15   Social Media vs. Mainstream Media

CNN reporter Todd Leopold wrote in his March 2012 article about online missteps and misinformation: "In an increasingly connected world where social networking has made us all news sources, that means missteps and misinformation get issued – and repeated – more quickly than ever. Gabrielle Giffords is declared dead, Chris Brown lets fly with profane rants, and it all makes the rounds before anyone has time to think" (169).

Frank Farley, Temple University professor and former president of the American Psychological Association, made this chilling conclusion: "Everyone now has a global platform on which they can shout their opinions and voice their beliefs. There's an old economic principle, that bad money drives out good. One thing that worries me is that bad information is driving out good" (169).

"The Internet is so full of junk and not-researched material," concurred David Wallechinsky, author of the bestseller *Book of Lists*. Wallechinsky created the website AllGov.com to disseminate information about the business of government in the United States, France, and India. He told CNN in a 2014 interview, "We pride ourselves on accuracy, double-checking. ... We try to emphasize policy instead of politics" (170).

In an October 2012 Superman comic, an outraged Clark Kent quitted his job at *The Daily Planet* in protest: "I was taught to believe you could use words to change the course of rivers – that even the darkest secrets would fall under the harsh light of the sun. But facts have been replaced by opinions. Information has been replaced by entertainment. Reporters have become stenographers. I can't be the only one who's sick of what passes for the news today" (171).

In reality, public trust in mainstream news media has eroded over the years. Figure 10.5 shows a steady decline of trustworthiness in mass media among independent and Republican respondents according to the Gallup poll.

Media outlets are pitted against each other in attempts to support or discredit Donald Trump. For example, CNN posted a YouTube video condemnation titled "Trump mocks reporter with disability" in November 2015 showing Trump perform

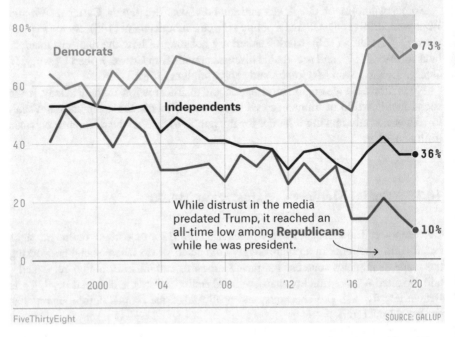

Fig. 10.5 A steady decline of trustworthiness in mass media among independent and Republican respondents

a derisive impression of New York Times reporter Serge Kovaleski who suffers from a chronic condition (172).

In September 2016, Fox News uploaded a YouTube video refutation titled "Did Trump really mock reporter's disability?" The video shows a collection of short clips in which Trump used similar tone and gesture to mock U.S. bank presidents, U.S. military generals, U.S. Senator Ted Cruz, and New York Times reporter Serge Kovaleski (173). Fox News did a decent job in showing Trump's unflattering behavioral pattern but it did a disservice by messing with the chronological order of events: mocking U.S. bank presidents in October 2015, military generals in November 2015, Senator Ted Cruz in February 2016, and New York Times reporter Serge Kovaleski in November 2015. Based on 3,000+ YouTube comments, a handful of people realized the chronological trick pulled by Fox News while some viewers concluded that no mainstream media can be trusted.

Neither can social media be trusted for that matter. For example, Capitol Hill rioter and Insurgence USA founder John Sullivan had a history on social media for supporting Antifa and Black Lives Matter using #antifa, #blm, and other anti-Trump or anti-police hashtags. After the FBI arrested and charged Sullivan for felony, Trump supporters claimed that Antifa activists incited the mob to storm the U.S. Capitol on January 6, 2021 (174).

10.16 Abuse of Power

In June 2014, the revelation of Facebook's secret psychological mood experiment had infuriated some users. In a massive experiment conducted in January 2012, Facebook manipulated 689,003 users' News Feed intentionally for a week to study the effect of "emotional contagion" via social networks. By filtering the news feeds, one test reduced users' exposure to their friends' "positive emotional content" whereas another test reduced exposure to "negative emotional content" (175). Jim Sheridan of the U.K. Parliament said, "They are manipulating material from people's personal lives and I am worried about the ability of Facebook and others to manipulate people's thoughts in politics or other areas. If people are being thought-controlled in this kind of way there needs to be protection and they at least need to know about it" (176).

Information is power. Disinformation is abuse of power. Even a good cause can be marred by dishonesty. Somaly Mam appeared on the Oprah Winfrey Show, a PBS documentary, *TIME Magazine*'s 100 Most Influential People of 2009, and CNN Heroes in 2007. She was the world's crusader against the trafficking of girls for sex in Cambodia. However, her extraordinary personal tale chronicled in her bestselling autobiography about being a village girl sold into sex slavery turned out to be pure fabrication. She also coached other women to lie in front of cameras about being child sex slaves. Mam resigned from her charity foundation in May 2014 after a *Newsweek* exposé by Simon Marks. The revelation potentially weakens the foundation's future work in combating human trafficking.

Notwithstanding human ignorance spreading misinformation, freedom of speech is essential. In George Orwell's novel *Nineteen Eighty-Four*, the totalitarian regime deliberately promotes Newspeak, an impoverished language without any words or possible constructs that describe the ideas of freedom and rebellion. "We're cutting the language down to the bone," philologist Syme said wickedly. "It's a beautiful thing, the destruction of words" (177). We certainly do not want that to happen.

On a lighter note, *Los Angeles Times* playfully called the 2006 "lonelygirl15" YouTube mystery the "Web's Watergate" (178). The real Watergate scandal culminated in the resignation of President Richard Nixon in August 1974 (179). Watergate has had a profound influence on American journalism and politics. In the new era of digital information with the proliferation of Twitter, Facebook, and YouTube, inquisitive citizens and accidental journalists will radically transform the landscape of journalism and politics in the years to come.

References

1. **Fung, Brian.** Facebook, Twitter and Google CEOs grilled by Congress on misinformation. [Online] CNN Business, March 25, 2021. https://www.cnn.com/2021/03/25/tech/tech-ceos-hearing/index.html.
2. **Haugen, Frances.** Statement of Frances Haugen. *United States Senate Committee on Commerce, Science and Transportation.* [Online] October 4, 2021.
3. **Zadrozny, Brandy and Gains, Mosheh.** Woman killed in Capitol was Trump supporter who embraced conspiracy theories. [Online] NBC News, January 7, 2021. https://

www.nbcnews.com/news/us-news/woman-killed-capitol-was-trump-supporter-who-embraced-conspiracy-theories-n1253285.

4. **Long, Tony.** Oct. 30, 1938: The Martians Have Landed in New Jersey! [Online] Wired, October 30, 2007. http://www.wired.com/science/discoveries/news/2007/10/dayintech_1030.

5. **Cantril, Hadley.** The Invasion from Mars: A Study in the Psychology of Panic. [Online] Transaction Publishers, May 2, 2005. http://books.google.com/books/about/The_Invasion_From_Mars.html?id=2c2-k6AvQtQC.

6. **Swan, Lisa.** 'War of the Worlds' terrified the nation 70 years ago. [Online] New York Daily News, October 30, 2008. http://www.nydailynews.com/entertainment/television/war-worlds-terrified-nation-70-years-article-1.304998.

7. **Hamilton, Gabrielle.** Good Enough to Fine. [Online] The New York Times, April 27, 2006. http://www.nytimes.com/2006/04/27/opinion/27hamilton.html.

8. **Picket, Kerry.** PICKET: Media misses the boat on Spike Lee Twitter story. [Online] The Washington Times, April 3, 2012. http://www.washingtontimes.com/blog/watercooler/2012/apr/3/picket-media-misses-boat-spike-lee-twitter-story/.

9. **Jacobson, Susan.** Elderly couple abandon their home after address is posted on Twitter as that of George Zimmerman. [Online] Orlando Sentinel, March 29, 2012. http://articles.orlandosentinel.com/2012-03-29/news/os-trayvon-martin-wrong-zimmerman-20120327_1_spike-lee-william-zimmerman-retweeted.

10. **Bennett, William J.** Rush to judgment in Trayvon Martin case. [Online] CNN, March 30, 2012. http://www.cnn.com/2012/03/30/opinion/bennett-trayvon-martin/index.html.

11. **Forbes, Paula.** Rich Jerk Tips 1% and Advises Server to 'Get a Real Job'. [Online] Eater, February 24, 2012. http://eater.com/archives/2012/02/24/rich-jerk-tips-1-advises-server-to-get-a-real-job.php.

12. —. The 'Get a Real Job' Receipt With a 1% Tip Was a Hoax. [Online] Eater, February 28, 2012. http://eater.com/archives/2012/02/28/that-get-a-real-job-receipt-with-a-1-tip-was-a-hoax.php.

13. **O'Sullivan, Donie.** Facebook says Belarusian KGB used fake accounts to stoke border crisis. CNN. [Online] December 1, 2021. https://www.cnn.com/2021/12/01/tech/facebook-belarus-poland/index.html.

14. **St. Pierre, Nate.** Abraham Lincoln Filed a Patent for Facebook in 1845. [Online] Nate St. Pierre Blogs, May 8, 2012. http://natestpierre.me/2012/05/08/abraham-lincoln-patent-facebook/.

15. —. Anatomy of a Hoax: How Abraham Lincoln Invented Facebook. [Online] Nate St. Pierre Blogs, May 10, 2012. http://natestpierre.me/2012/05/10/hoax-abraham-lincoln-invented-facebook/.

16. **Gross, Doug.** Abraham Lincoln didn't invent Facebook (except on the Internet). [Online] CNN, May 10, 2012. http://www.cnn.com/2012/05/09/tech/web/abraham-lincoln-facebook/index.html.

17. **Protalinski, Emil.** Abraham Lincoln tried to patent Facebook in 1845, but failed? [Online] ZDNet, May 8, 2012. http://www.zdnet.com/blog/facebook/abraham-lincoln-tried-to-patent-facebook-in-1845-but-failed/12728.

18. **Moyer, Edward.** Facebook photo a Powerball prank? A million users hedge bets. [Online] CNet, November 30, 2012. http://www.cnet.com/news/facebook-photo-a-powerball-prank-a-million-users-hedge-bets/.

19. **Daniels, Nolan.** Why I Started a Social Media Hoax – and How I'm Using It to Help. [Online] The Huffington Post, December 18, 2012. http://www.huffingtonpost.com/nolan-daniels/powerball-facebook-hoax_b_2323206.html.

20. **116th Congress.** House Hearing, 116th Congress — ARTIFICIAL INTELLIGENCE AND COUNTERTERRORISM: POSSIBILITIES AND LIMITATIONS. [Online] Congress.gov, June 25, 2019. https://www.congress.gov/event/116th-congress/house-event/LC64673/text?s=1&r=1.

21. **King, Stephen.** I'm quitting Facebook. [Online] Twitter, January 31, 2020. https://twitter.com/StephenKing/status/1223425267831574534.

22. **Sutter, John D.** Google Maps border becomes part of international dispute. [Online] CNN, November 5, 2010. http://articles.cnn.com/2010-11-05/tech/nicaragua.raid.google.maps_1_google-maps-google-spokeswoman-google-earth.

23. **Rooney, Ben.** Google Maps Caught in Border Dispute. [Online] The Wall Street Journal, November 5, 2010. http://blogs.wsj.com/tech-europe/2010/11/05/google-maps-caught-in-border-dispute/.

24. **Levs, Josh.** Iran threatens to sue Google for not labeling Persian Gulf. [Online] CNN, May 17, 2012. http://www.cnn.com/2012/05/17/world/meast/iran-google-gulf/index.html.

25. **Migiro, Katy.** Somali refugees turned into Twitter scapegoats after Kenya terror attack. [Online] Thomson Reuters Foundation, July 2, 2012. http://www.trust.org/item/?map=somali-refugees-turned-into-twitter-scapegoats-after-kenya-terror-attack/.

26. **Wemple, Erik.** Colorado shootings: ABC News's bogus report. [Online] The Washington Post, July 20, 2012. http://www.washingtonpost.com/blogs/erik-wemple/post/abc-news-invites-bias-claims-with-bogus-aurora-report/2012/07/20/gJQAJJWCyW_blog.html.

27. **Gross, Doug.** Man faces fallout for spreading false Sandy reports on Twitter. [Online] CNN, October 31, 2012. http://www.cnn.com/2012/10/31/tech/social-media/sandy-twitter-hoax/index.html.

28. **Serwer, Adam.** How the Press Got It Wrong on the Newtown Shooter. [Online] Mother Jones, December 14, 2012. http://www.motherjones.com/mojo/2012/12/ryan-lanza-newtown-shooting-media-fail.

29. **Bors, Matt.** I am Facebook friends with Ryan Lanza. [Online] Salon, December 17, 2012. http://www.salon.com/2012/12/17/i_am_facebook_friends_with_ryan_lanza/.

30. **CNN Political Unit.** A false tweet heard around the web. [Online] CNN, April 23, 2013. http://politicalticker.blogs.cnn.com/2013/04/23/a-false-tweet-heard-around-the-web/.

31. **Martin, Erik.** Reflections on the Recent Boston Crisis. [Online] Reddit, April 22, 2013. http://www.redditblog.com/2013/04/reflections-on-recent-boston-crisis.html.

32. **Gross, Doug.** Reddit shuts down community seeking Navy Yard shooter. [Online] CNN, September 17, 2013. http://www.cnn.com/2013/09/17/tech/social-media/reddit-navy-yard-shooter/index.html.

33. **Rajagopalan, Megha, Vo, Lam Thuy and Soe, Aung Naing.** How Facebook Failed The Rohingya In Myanmar. [Online] BuzzFeed News, August 27, 2018. https://www.buzzfeed-news.com/article/meghara/facebook-myanmar-rohingya-genocide.

34. **Cohen, Zachary.** FBI director says bureau is not investigating QAnon conspiracy 'in its own right'. [Online] CNN, April 15, 2021. https://www.cnn.com/2021/04/15/politics/fbi-director-wray-qanon-threat/index.html.

35. **Yadron, Danny.** Facebook's Sheryl Sandberg: 'likes' can help stop Isis recruiters. [Online] The Guardian, January 20, 2016. https://www.theguardian.com/technology/2016/jan/20/facebook-davos-isis-sheryl-sandberg.

36. **Toor, Amar.** Facebook gives free advertising to users who counter terrorist propaganda. [Online] The Verge, February 12, 2016. https://www.theverge.com/2016/2/12/10957776/facebook-terrorism-counter-speech.

37. **Hongo, Hudson.** Facebook Finally Rolls Out 'Disputed News' Tag Everyone Will Dispute. [Online] Gizmodo, March 3, 2017. https://gizmodo.com/facebook-finally-rolls-out-disputed-news-tag-everyone-w-1792959827.

38. **Poynter.** Commit to transparency – sign up for the International Fact-Checking Network's code of principles. [Online] Poynter. [Cited: May 31, 2021.] https://www.ifcncodeofprinciples.poynter.org/.

39. **Facebook Newsroom.** Blocking Ads From Pages that Repeatedly Share False News. [Online] Facebook, August 28, 2017. https://about.fb.com/news/2017/08/blocking-ads-from-pages-that-repeatedly-share-false-news/.

40. —. An Update On Information Operations On Facebook. [Online] Facebook, September 6, 2017. https://about.fb.com/news/2017/09/information-operations-update/.

41. **Duffy, Kate.** Instagram disables the 'Recent' tab on hashtag pages to stop the spread of misinformation around Election Day. [Online] Business Insider, October 30, 2020. https://www.businessinsider.com/instagram-misinformation-recent-tab-election-day-hashtag-searches-2020-10.

42. **@InstagramComms.** As we near the U.S. elections. [Online] Twitter, October 29, 2020. https://twitter.com/instagramcomms/status/1321957713476280320?lang=en.

43. **Hatmaker, Taylor.** Twitter rolls out vaccine misinformation warning labels and a strike-based system for violations. [Online] TechCrunch, March 1, 2021. https://techcrunch.com/2021/03/01/twitter-vaccine-misinformation-labels-strike-system/.

44. **Judd, Donald, Vazquez, Maegan and O'Sullivan, Donie.** Biden says platforms like Facebook are 'killing people' with Covid misinformation. CNN. [Online] July 16, 2021. https://www.cnn.com/2021/07/16/politics/biden-facebook-covid-19/index.html.

45. **Klein, Betsy, Vazquez, Maegan and Collins, Kaitlan.** Biden backs away from his claim that Facebook is 'killing people' by allowing Covid misinformation. CNN. [Online] July 19, 2021. https://www.cnn.com/2021/07/19/politics/joe-biden-facebook/index.html.

46. **Edelson, Laura, et al.** Far-right news sources on Facebook more engaging. [Online] Cybersecurity for Democracy, March 3, 2021. https://medium.com/cybersecurity-for-democracy/far-right-news-sources-on-facebook-more-engaging-e04a01efae90.

47. **Fung, Brian.** Right-wing misinformation on Facebook is more engaging than its left-wing counterpart, research finds. [Online] CNN Business, March 3, 2021. https://www.cnn.com/2021/03/03/tech/facebook-right-wing-misinformation/index.html.

48. **Aveni, Timothy J.** I'm resigning from my job at Facebook. [Online] Facebook, June 1, 2020. https://www.facebook.com/timothy.j.aveni/posts/3006224359465567.

49. **Velazco, C.** Tim Cook takes aim at Facebook's practices during privacy conference. [Online] Engadget, January 28, 2021. https://www.engadget.com/tim-cook-privacy-cpdp-2021-slams-facebook-184333398.html.

50. **Fung, Brian.** Twitter bans President Trump permanently. [Online] CNN Business, January 9, 2021. https://www.cnn.com/2021/01/08/tech/trump-twitter-ban/index.html.

51. **Culliford, Elizabeth, Shepardson, David and Paul, Katie.** Twitter permanently suspends Trump's account, cites 'incitement of violence' risk. [Online] Reuters, January 8, 2021. https://www.reuters.com/article/us-usa-election-trump-twitter/twitter-permanently-suspends-trumps-account-cites-incitement-of-violence-risk-idUSKBN29D355.

52. **Zuckerberg, Mark.** Facebook Newsroom. [Online] Facebook, January 7, 2021. https://twitter.com/fbnewsroom/status/1347211647245578241.

53. **Fung, Brian.** Facebook bans 'stop the steal' content, 69 days after the election. [Online] CNN Business, January 12, 2021. https://www.cnn.com/2021/01/11/tech/facebook-stop-the-steal/index.html.

54. **Guynn, Jessica.** Facebook will punish groups, members who break its rules after Capitol riot and COVID vaccine fear mongering. [Online] USA Today, March 17, 2021. https://www.usatoday.com/story/tech/2021/03/17/facebook-groups-crackdown-covid-vaccine-misinformation-capitol-riot/4734394001/.

55. **Associated Press.** Twitter permanently bans MyPillow founder Mike Lindell. [Online] MarketWatch, January 26, 2021. https://www.marketwatch.com/story/twitter-permanently-bans-my-pillow-ceo-mike-lindell-01611686322.

56. **Mac, Ryan.** Trump-Supporting Lawyer Lin Wood Has Been Permanently Banned From Twitter. [Online] BuzzFeed News, January 7, 2021. https://www.buzzfeednews.com/article/ryanmac/twitter-bans-lin-wood.

57. **Fung, Brian.** Twitter permanently bans Project Veritas account. [Online] CNN Business, February 11, 2021. https://www.cnn.com/2021/02/11/tech/twitter-project-veritas/index.html.

58. **Robertson, Adi.** Twitter bans QAnon supporters, including former national security adviser Michael Flynn. [Online] The Verge, January 8, 2021. https://www.theverge.com/2021/1/8/22221332/twitter-ban-qanon-accounts-michael-flynn-sidney-powell-ron-watkins.

59. **Peters, Jay.** Discord bans pro-Trump server 'The Donald'. [Online] The Verge, January 8, 2021. https://www.theverge.com/2021/1/8/22221579/discord-bans-the-donald-server-reddit-subreddit.

60. **Robertson, Adi.** Reddit bans r/donaldtrump forum for inciting violence. [Online] The Verge, January 8, 2021. https://www.theverge.com/2021/1/8/22220834/reddit-trump-subreddit-ban-violence-us-capitol-mob.

61. **Adorno, José.** Twitter is working on three different misinformation warning labels. [Online] 9 to 5 Mac, May 31, 2021. https://9to5mac.com/2021/05/31/twitter-is-working-on-three-different-misinformation-warning-labels/.

62. **National Institutes of Health.** Reading Food Labels . [Online] NIH National Institute on Aging, April 30, 2019. https://www.nia.nih.gov/health/reading-food-labels.

63. **Koul, Scaachi.** What The Past Three Months Have Been Like For QAnon Believers. [Online] BuzzFeed News, March 26, 2021. https://www.buzzfeednews.com/article/scaachikoul/qanon-believers-turning-away-from-trump?utm_source=pocket-newtab.

64. **Shear, Michael D. and Haberman, Maggie.** Trump Claims, With No Evidence, That 'Millions of People' Voted Illegally. [Online] The New York Times, November 27, 2016. https://www.nytimes.com/2016/11/27/us/politics/trump-adviser-steps-up-searing-attack-on-romney.html.

65. **Mill, John Stuart.** The Subjection of Women. [Online] 1869. https://courses.lumenlearning.com/suny-classicreadings/chapter/john-stuart-mill-on-the-equality-of-women/.

66. **Hughes, Ceri.** Trump uses religious words and references to God at a higher rate than past presidents. [Online] Salon.com, October 18, 2020. https://www.salon.com/2020/10/18/trump-uses-religious-words-and-references-to-god-at-a-higher-rate-than-past-presidents_partner/.

67. **Rascoe, Ayesha and Keith, Tamara.** Trump Defends 'Law And Order' Symbolism Of Photo-Op At St. John's Church. [Online] NPR, June 3, 2020. https://www.npr.org/2020/06/03/868779265/trump-defends-symbolism-of-photo-op-at-st-johns-church.

68. **Smith, Gregory A.** About a third in U.S. see God's hand in presidential elections, but fewer say God picks winners based on policies. [Online] Pew Research Center, March 12, 2021. https://www.pewresearch.org/fact-tank/2020/03/12/about-a-third-in-u-s-see-gods-hand-in-presidential-elections-but-fewer-say-god-picks-winners-based-on-policies/.

69. **Trump, Donald.** Trump: 'I am the least racist person there is anywhere in the world' – video. [Online] The Guardian, July 30, 2019. https://www.theguardian.com/us-news/video/2019/jul/30/trump-claims-least-racist-person-in-the-world.

70. **Reston, Maeve.** Trump advances dangerous disinformation campaign as more states move to restrict the vote. [Online] CNN, June 6, 2021. https://www.cnn.com/2021/06/06/politics/trump-election-lies-north-carolina/index.html.

71. **Mayer, Jane.** Donald Trump's Ghostwriter Tells All. [Online] The New Yorker, July 18, 2016. https://www.newyorker.com/magazine/2016/07/25/donald-trumps-ghostwriter-tells-all.

72. **NPR Editors.** Trump Tells Woodward He Deliberately Downplayed Coronavirus Threat. [Online] NPR, September 10, 2020. https://www.npr.org/2020/09/10/911368698/trump-tells-woodward-he-deliberately-downplayed-coronavirus-threat.

73. **Pilkington, Ed.** Six months of Trump's Covid denials: 'It'll go away … It's fading'. [Online] The Guardian, July 29, 2020. https://www.theguardian.com/world/2020/jul/29/trump-coronavirus-science-denial-timeline-what-has-he-said.

74. **Reuters Staff.** CDC director contradicts Trump on coronavirus: 'We're nowhere near the end' -NBC. [Online] Reuters, September 28, 2020. https://www.reuters.com/article/health-coronavirus-usa-cdc/cdc-director-contradicts-trump-on-coronavirus-were-nowhere-near-the-end-nbc-idUSL1N2GP0FO.

75. **Roche, Darragh.** Ted Lieu Raises Donald Trump's 'Kung Flu' Rhetoric After Atlanta Spa Shootings. [Online] Newsweek, March 17, 2021. https://www.newsweek.com/ted-lieu-raises-donald-trump-kung-flu-rhetoric-after-atlanta-spa-shootings-1576746.

76. **Mamo, Heran.** Rihanna Marches in Stop Asian Hate Rally in New York City. [Online] Billboard, April 5, 2021. https://www.billboard.com/articles/news/9551446/rihanna-attends-stop-asian-hate-rally/.

77. **Vazquez, Maegan.** Biden signs bill aimed at addressing rise in anti-Asian hate crimes. [Online] CNN, May 20, 2021. https://www.cnn.com/2021/05/20/politics/biden-anti-asian-hate-crimes-covid-19-signing/index.html.

78. **Hatmaker, Taylor.** Pro-Trump mob storms the US Capitol, touting 'Stop the Steal' conspiracy. [Online] TechCrunch, January 6, 2021. https://techcrunch.com/2021/01/06/pro-trump-mob-storms-the-us-capitol-touting-stop-the-steal-conspiracy/.

79. **Cillizza, Chris.** George W. Bush is unrecognizable in the current Republican Party. [Online] CNN Politics, March 19, 2021. https://www.cnn.com/2021/03/19/politics/george-w-bush-donald-trump-texas-tribune/.

80. **Polant, Katelyn.** Judge while sentencing Trump campaign aide: 'If people don't have the facts, democracy doesn't work'. [Online] CNN, December 17, 2019. https://www.cnn.com/2019/12/17/politics/amy-berman-jackson-gates-barr/index.html.

81. **Kan, Michael.** Trump Considers Building His Own Social Media Site After Twitter Ban. [Online] PC Magazine, January 9, 2021. https://www.pcmag.com/news/trump-considers-building-his-own-social-media-site-after-twitter-ban.

82. **Perrett, Connor.** Donald Trump Jr. says 'the world is laughing at America' as he rails against his dad's Twitter ban, saying 'free speech is dead'. [Online] Business Insider, January 9, 2021. https://www.businessinsider.com/trump-jr-free-speech-is-dead-controlled-by-leftist-overlords-2021-1.

83. **Reuters Staff.** Germany has reservations about Trump Twitter ban, Merkel spokesman says. [Online] Reuters, January 11, 2021. https://www.reuters.com/article/usa-trump-germany-twitter/germany-has-reservations-about-trump-twitter-ban-merkel-spokesman-says-idUSL8N2JM4ES.

84. **The FR Fintech Buzz.** Fall of Parler a boon for crypto-friendly social platforms Gab and DLive. [Online] The Financial Revolutionist , January 12, 2021. https://thefr.com/news/2021/1/18/fall-of-parler-a-boon-for-crypto-friendly-social-platforms-gab-and-dlive.

85. **Wong, Queenie and Nieva, Richard.** Zuckerberg, Dorsey and Pichai face off with Congress over Section 230, free speech. [Online] CNet, October 29, 2020. https://www.cnet.com/news/zuckerberg-dorsey-and-pichai-face-off-with-congress-over-section-230-free-speech/.

86. **Yurieff, Kaya and Fung, Brian.** CEOs of Google, Twitter and Facebook grilled in Senate hearing. [Online] CNN Business, October 28, 2020. https://www.cnn.com/2020/10/28/tech/section-230-senate-hearing-wednesday/index.html.

87. **Effron, Oliver.** Facebook will ban Holocaust denial posts under hate speech policy. [Online] CNN Business, October 12, 2020. https://www.cnn.com/2020/10/12/tech/facebook-holocaust-denial-hate-speech/index.html.

88. **Reagan, Ronald.** A Time for Choosing Speech, October 27, 1964. [Online] Ronald Reagan Presidential Library & Museum. [Cited: April 6, 2021.] https://www.reaganlibrary.gov/reagans/ronald-reagan/time-choosing-speech-october-27-1964.

89. **Vogue, Ariane de.** Justice Clarence Thomas suggests US should regulate Facebook, Google and Twitter. [Online] CNN Politics, April 5, 2021. https://www.cnn.com/2021/04/05/politics/clarence-thomas-twitter-facebook-google-regulation/index.html.

90. **Goodwin, Jazmin**. Trump is returning to social media in a few months with his own platform, spokesman says. [Online] CNN Business, March 22, 2021. https://www.cnn.com/2021/03/21/media/donald-trump-social-media-network/index.html.

91. **Ingra, David and Kamisar, Ben.** In nod to Trump, Florida is set to ban 'deplatforming' by tech companies. [Online] NBC News, April 30, 2021. https://www.nbcnews.com/politics/politics-news/nod-donald-trump-florida-set-ban-big-tech-deplatforming-rcna784.

92. **Darcy, Oliver.** Trump shuts down his blog after less than a month. [Online] CNN Business, June 2, 2021. https://www.cnn.com/2021/06/02/media/trump-blog-shut-down/index.html.

93. **Mahdawi, Arwa.** A 'non-cancellable' community: the 'truth' about Trump's social media platform. The Guardian. [Online] October 21, 2021. https://www.theguardian.com/us-news/2021/oct/21/trump-truth-social-media-platform-tmtg-presentation.

94. **Heyer, Lori, et al.** TMTG: Trump Media & Technology Group. U.S. Securities and Exchange Commision. [Online] October 20, 2021. https://www.sec.gov/Archives/edgar/data/0001849635/000110465921128231/tm2130724d1_ex99-1.htm.

95. **Clegg, Nick.** Welcoming the Oversight Board. [Online] Facebook, May 6, 2020. https://about.fb.com/news/2020/05/welcoming-the-oversight-board/.

96. **Oversight Board.** 11 DECISIONS. [Online] Facebook Oversight Board, May 20, 2021. https://www.oversightboard.com/?page=decision.

97. —. Case decision 2021-001-FB-FBR. [Online] Facebook Oversight Board, May 5, 2021. https://oversightboard.com/decision/FB-691QAMHJ/.

98. **Clegg, Nick.** In Response to Oversight Board, Trump Suspended for Two Years; Will Only Be Reinstated if Conditions Permit. [Online] Facebook, June 4, 2021. https://about.fb.com/news/2021/06/facebook-response-to-oversight-board-recommendations-trump/.

99. **O'Sullivan, Donie.** Facebook says Trump now suspended until at least January 2023. [Online] CNN Business, June 4, 2021. Facebook says Trump now suspended until at least January 2023.

100. **Pepitone, Julianne.** Encyclopedia Britannica to stop printing books. [Online] CNN, March 13, 2012. http://money.cnn.com/2012/03/13/technology/encyclopedia-britannica-books/index.htm.

101. **O'Rourke, James S., IV.** Why Encyclopedia Britannica mattered. [Online] CNN, March 15, 2012. http://www.cnn.com/2012/03/14/opinion/orourke-encyclopedia/index.html.

102. **Benkler, Yochai.** Distributed Innovation and Creativity, Peer Production, and Commons in Networked Economy. [Online] OpenMind, 2013. https://www.bbvaopenmind.com/en/article/distributed-innovation-and-creativity-peer-production-and-commons-in-networked-economy/?fullscreen=true.

103. **Wikipedia.** Template:BLP sources. [Online] Wikipedia, November 17, 2013. http://en.wikipedia.org/wiki/Template:BLP_sources.

104. **Seigenthaler, John.** A false Wikipedia 'biography'. [Online] USA Today, November 29, 2005. http://usatoday30.usatoday.com/news/opinion/editorials/2005-11-29-wikipedia-edit_x.htm.

105. **Wikipedia.** Newton Lee. Difference between revisions. [Online] Wikipedia, November 15, 2011. http://en.wikipedia.org/w/index.php?title=Newton_Lee&diff=460810113&oldid=458830548.

106. —. User:ClueBot NG. [Online] Wikipedia, October 20, 2010. http://en.wikipedia.org/wiki/User:ClueBot_NG#Vandalism_Detection_Algorithm.

107. **86.166.188.231.** Newton Lee: Difference between revisions. [Online] Wikipedia, May 16, 2013. http://en.wikipedia.org/w/index.php?title=Newton_Lee&diff=555338184&oldid=555286309.

108. **DGG.** Newton Lee: Difference between revisions. [Online] Wikipedia, May 23, 2013. http://en.wikipedia.org/w/index.php?title=Newton_Lee&diff=556498038&oldid=555338184.

109. **Ïvana.** User:Ïvana. [Online] Wikipedia. [Cited: April 25, 2021.] https://en.wikipedia.org/wiki/User:%C3%8Fvana.

110. **Skaterboy2012.** United States Secretary of Defense. [Online] Wikipedia, July 2, 2014. http://en.wikipedia.org/w/index.php?title=United_States_Secretary_of_Defense&diff=615359698&oldid=615244303.

111. **Lamothe, Dan.** Chuck Hagel calls Tim Howard from Pentagon, acknowledges defense secretary joke. [Online] The Washiongton Post, July 2, 2014. http://www.washingtonpost.com/news/checkpoint/wp/2014/07/02/pentagon-chief-chuck-hagel-calls-tim-howard-acknowledges-defense-secretary-joke/.

112. **Casserly, Meghan.** Marissa Mayer Is Crowd-Sourcing Her Baby's Name. [Online] Forbes, October 1, 2012. http://www.forbes.com/sites/meghancasserly/2012/10/01/marissa-mayer-is-crowd-sourcing-her-babys-name/.

113. **Angley, Natalie.** How to crowdsource your wedding photos. [Online] CNN, May 29, 2014. http://www.cnn.com/2014/05/28/tech/mobile/wedding-photo-crowdsourcing/index.html.

114. **Munoz, Juan Andres.** How the Internet built a $100,000 race car. [Online] CNN, March 13, 2013. http://www.cnn.com/2013/03/12/tech/web/crowdsourced-car-sxsw/index.html.

115. **Stanford HCI Group.** Twitch Crowdsourcing. [Online] Stanford University. [Cited: June 23, 2014.] http://twitch.stanford.edu/.

116. **Chang, Rita.** Emily Temple-Wood: A cool Wikipedian on a big mission. [Online] Wikimedia Blog, October 11, 2013. https://blog.wikimedia.org/2013/10/11/emily-temple-wood-profile/.

117. **Wikipedians.** Wikipedia is wrong. [Online] Wikipedia. [Cited: March 14, 2021.] https://en.wikipedia.org/wiki/Wikipedia:Wikipedia_is_wrong.

118. **Savage, Dan.** Spreading Santorum. [Online] Dan Savage. [Cited: April 5, 2012.] http://blog.spreadingsantorum.com/.

119. **Sutter, John D.** Santorum asks Google to clean up search results for his name. [Online] CNN, September 21, 2011. http://articles.cnn.com/2011-09-21/tech/tech_web_santorum-google-ranking_1_google-spokeswoman-google-ceo-eric-schmidt-google-places.

120. **Burns, Alexander.** Rick Santorum contacted Google, says company spreads 'filth'. [Online] Politico, September 20, 2011. http://www.politico.com/news/stories/0911/63952.html.
121. **Greenwald, Glenn.** How Covert Agents Infiltrate the Internet to Manipulate, Deceive, and Destroy Reputations. [Online] The Intercept, February 24, 2014. https://firstlook.org/theintercept/2014/02/24/jtrig-manipulation/.
122. **Boroff, David.** Argentine model takes battle with Google, Yahoo over linked images of her to porn to country's Supreme Court. [Online] New York Daily News, May 27, 2014. http://www.nydailynews.com/news/world/model-google-yahoo-linking-pics-porn-article-1.1806826.
123. **Zeckman, Ashley.** Model Battles Google, Yahoo in Court Over Images Linking Her to Porn Sites. [Online] Search Engine Watch, May 27, 2014. http://searchenginewatch.com/article/2346899/Model-Battles-Google-Yahoo-in-Court-Over-Images-Linking-Her-to-Porn-Sites.
124. **Griffin, Drew.** National Republican Congressional Campaign using fake Democrat websites to lure voters. [Online] CNN, February 6, 2014. http://politicalticker.blogs.cnn.com/2014/02/06/national-republican-congressional-campaign-using-fake-democrat-websites-to-lure-voters/.
125. **Carr, Nicholas.** Is Google Making Us Stupid? [Online] The Atlantic Magazine, July/August 2008. http://www.theatlantic.com/magazine/archive/2008/07/is-google-making-us-stupid/6868/.
126. **Wong, Venessa.** Weight Watchers' Big Fat Marketing Dilemma. [Online] Businessweek, December 3, 2012. http://www.businessweek.com/articles/2012-12-03/weight-watchers-big-fat-marketing-dilemma.
127. **Rehabs.com.** Dying to be Barbie. Eating Disorders in Pursuit of the Impossible. An Epidemic of Body Hatred. [Online] Rehabs. [Cited: May 18, 2014.] http://www.rehabs.com/explore/dying-to-be-barbie/.
128. **Grinberg, Emanuella.** Sex, lies and media: New wave of activists challenge notions of beauty. [Online] CNN, March 11, 2012. http://www.cnn.com/2012/03/09/living/beauty-media-miss-representation/.
129. **Skarda, Erin.** Tough Standards: 8 'Misleading' Ads Banned by U.K. Officials. [Online] TIME Magazine, February 3, 2012. http://newsfeed.time.com/2012/02/06/tough-standards-8-misleading-ads-banned-by-u-k-standards-board/.
130. **Bluhm, Julia.** Seventeen Magazine Gives Girls Images of Real Girls! [Online] change.org, July 3, 2012. http://www.change.org/petitions/seventeen-magazine-give-girls-images-of-real-girls.
131. **Rushfield, Richard and Hoffman, Claire.** Mystery fuels huge popularity of web's Lonelygirl15. [Online] Los Angeles Times, September 8, 2006. http://www.latimes.com/entertainment/news/la-et-lonelygirl15,0,241799.story.
132. **Podvey, Heather.** Do you really KNOW your Facebook friends? [Online] Applywise, 2009. http://www.applywise.com/sep09_facebook.aspx.
133. **Center for Complex Networks and Systems Research.** About Truthy. [Online] Indiana University, 2010. http://truthy.indiana.edu/about.
134. **Kleiner, Kurt.** Bogus Grass-Roots Politics on Twitter. [Online] MIT Technology Review, November 2, 2010. Review. http://www.technologyreview.com/computing/26666/.
135. **Landau, Elizabeth.** When bullying goes high-tech. [Online] CNN, April 15, 2013. http://www.cnn.com/2013/02/27/health/cyberbullying-online-bully-victims/index.html.
136. **Repard, Pauline.** RB High threats on Facebook a hoax; teen arrested. [Online] UT San Diego, April 8, 2012. http://www.utsandiego.com/news/2011/oct/15/rb-high-threats-facebook-hoax-teen-arrested/.
137. **Taylor, Chris.** Newt Gingrich's Twitter Followers Are 8% Human [INFOGRAPHIC]. [Online] Mashable, August 2, 2011. http://mashable.com/2011/08/02/newt-gingrich-twitter-followers/.
138. **Gross, Doug.** Twitter newbie Rupert Murdoch following fake account. [Online] CNN, January 2, 2012. http://www.cnn.com/2012/01/02/tech/social-media/murdoch-twitter-larry-page/index.html.
139. **Roberts, Chris.** Dan Bilzerian Is A Renter, And Someone Else Pays His Credit Card Bills: Lawsuit. [Online] Forbes, July 9, 2020. https://www.forbes.com/sites/chrisroberts/2020/07/09/dan-bilzerian-is-a-renter/.

140. **Facebook.** Amendment No. 2 to Form S-1 Registration Statement. [Online] U.S. Securities and Exchange Commission, March 7, 2012. http://sec.gov/Archives/edgar/data/1326801/000119312512101422/d287954ds1a.htm.

141. **Elder, Jeff.** Inside a Twitter Robot Factory. [Online] The Wall Street Journal, November 24, 2013. http://online.wsj.com/news/articles/SB10001424052702304607104579212122084821400.

142. **Foremski, Tom.** The hollow emptiness in social media numbers – most accounts are fake or empty. [Online] ZdNet, February 14, 2012. http://www.zdnet.com/blog/foremski/the-hollow-emptiness-in-social-media-numbers-most-accounts-are-fake-or-empty/2175.

143. **Sweney, Mark.** Facebook quarterly report reveals 83m profiles are fake. [Online] The Guardian, August 2, 2012. http://www.theguardian.com/technology/2012/aug/02/facebook-83m-profiles-bogus-fake.

144. **Wagstaff, Keith.** 1 in 10 Twitter accounts is fake, say researchers. [Online] NBC News, November 25, 2013. http://www.nbcnews.com/tech/internet/1-10-twitter-accounts-fake-say-researchers-f2D11655362.

145. **Twitch Support.** Tweet. [Online] Twitter, April 14, 2021. https://twitter.com/TwitchSupport/status/1382379214624714756.

146. **Jacobs, Suzanne.** Fake Followers for Hire, and How to Spot Them. [Online] MIT Technology Review, June 30, 2014. http://www.technologyreview.com/news/528506/fake-followers-for-hire-and-how-to-spot-them/.

147. **Facebook.** Verifying Your Account. [Online] Facebook. [Cited: April 8, 2012.] http://www.facebook.com/help/verify.

148. —. Confirm Your Phone. [Online] Facebook. [Cited: April 8, 2012.] http://www.facebook.com/confirmphone.php.

149. —. General Information. Usernames. [Online] Facebook. [Cited: April 8, 2012.] http://www.facebook.com/help/usernames/general.

150. **Gross, Doug.** Facebook rolls out 'verified accounts,' celeb nicknames. [Online] CNN, February 17, 2012. http://www.cnn.com/2012/02/16/tech/social-media/facebook-verified-accounts/index.html.

151. **Protalinski, Emil.** Facebook bans Mark Zuckerberg. [Online] ZDNet, May 11, 2011. http://www.zdnet.com/blog/facebook/facebook-bans-mark-zuckerberg/1464.

152. **TMZ Staff.** Selena Gomez BANNED from Facebook. [Online] TMZ, August 5, 2012. http://www.tmz.com/2012/08/05/selena-gomez-banned-facebook/.

153. **Protalinski, Emil.** Facebook bans Selena Gomez. [Online] CNet, August 5, 2012. http://www.cnet.com/news/facebook-bans-selena-gomez/.

154. **Twitter.** FAQs about Verified Accounts. [Online] Twitter help center. [Cited: April 8, 2012.] http://support.twitter.com/groups/31-twitter-basics/topics/111-features/articles/119135-about-verified-accounts.

155. **Delo, Cotton.** One Way to Get a Twitter 'Verified Account': Buy Ads. [Online] 2012, 10 January. http://adage.com/article/digital/a-twitter-verified-account-buy-ads/231984/.

156. **Cheney, Alexandra.** How Does Twitter Verify Celebrity Accounts? [Online] The Wall Street Journal, March 7, 2011. http://blogs.wsj.com/speakeasy/2011/03/07/how-does-twitter-verify-celebrity-accounts/.

157. **Adegoke, Yinka.** Twitter embarrassed by fake Wendi Murdoch account. [Online] Reuters, January 4, 2012. http://www.reuters.com/article/2012/01/04/us-wendimurdoch-twitter-idUSTRE80305620120104.

158. **Swisher, Kara.** The Case of the Unfortunate Underscore: How Twitter Verified the Fake Wendi Over the Real Wendi. [Online] AllThingsD, January 4, 2012. http://allthingsd.com/20120104/the-case-of-the-unfortunate-underscore-how-twitter-verified-fake-wendi-over-real-wendi/.

159. **Wikipedians.** Deepfake. [Online] Wikipedia. [Cited: March 7, 2021.] https://en.wikipedia.org/wiki/Deepfake.

160. —. Sassy Justice. [Online] Wikipedia. [Cited: March 7, 2021.] https://en.wikipedia.org/wiki/Sassy_Justice.

161. **Vincent, James.** Tom Cruise deepfake creator says public shouldn't be worried about 'one-click fakes'. [Online] The Verge, March 5, 2021. https://www.theverge.

com/2021/3/5/22314980/tom-cruise-deepfake-tiktok-videos-ai-impersonator-chris-ume-miles-fisher.

162. **Giardina, Carolyn.** How 'Star Wars: Rise of Skywalker' VFX Pro Crafted Carrie Fisher's Final Farewell. [Online] The Hollywood Reporter, January 7, 2020. https://www.hollywoodreporter.com/behind-screen/how-star-wars-rise-skywalker-vfx-pro-crafted-carrie-fishers-final-farewell-1267455.

163. **Johnson, Bobbie.** Deepfakes are solvable – but don't forget that "shallowfakes" are already pervasive. [Online] MIT Technology Review, March 25, 2019. https://www.technologyreview.com/2019/03/25/136460/deepfakes-shallowfakes-human-rights/.

164. **DeepFaker.** Lynda Carter Wonder Woman [deepfake]. [Online] YouTube, October 15, 2020. https://www.youtube.com/watch?v=BwRmeT1lEFg.

165. **BuzzFeedVideo.** You Won't Believe What Obama Says In This Video! . [Online] YouTube, April 17, 2018. https://www.youtube.com/watch?v=cQ54GDm1eL0.

166. **CBS Los Angeles.** Videos Doctored To Make House Speaker Nancy Pelosi Look Like She's Slurring Her Words. [Online] YouTube, May 24, 2019. https://www.youtube.com/watch?v=CErxzDYPjyE.

167. **Posters, Bill.** Zuckerberg speaks frankly. [Online] Instagram, June 13, 2019. https://www.instagram.com/p/BypkGIvFfGZ/.

168. **Collider.** Deepfake Roundtable: Cruise, Downey Jr., Lucas & More - The Streaming Wars I Above the Line. [Online] YouTube, November 11, 2019. https://www.youtube.com/watch?v=l_6Tumd8EQI.

169. **Leopold, Todd.** In today's warp-speed world, online missteps spread faster than ever. [Online] CNN, March 6, 2012. http://www.cnn.com/2012/03/06/tech/social-media/misinformation-social-media/index.html.

170. —. The man who invented the Internet (well, sort of). [Online] CNN, April 23, 2014. http://www.cnn.com/2014/04/23/tech/web/david-wallechinsky-lists-internet/.

171. **Shoichet, Catherine E.** Clark Kent quits newspaper job in latest Superman comic. [Online] CNN, October 24, 2012. http://www.cnn.com/2012/10/24/showbiz/superman-quits-job/.

172. **CNN.** Trump mocks reporter with disability. [Online] YouTube, November 25, 2015. https://www.youtube.com/watch?v=PX9reO3QnUA.

173. **Fox News.** Did Trump really mock reporter's disability? [Online] YouTube, September 14, 2016. https://www.youtube.com/watch?v=CsaB3ynIZH4.

174. **McCarthy, Bill.** Facebook posts wrongly claim left-wing activist, antifa 'incited' US Capitol mob. [Online] PolitiFact , January 8, 2021. https://www.politifact.com/factchecks/2021/jan/09/facebook-posts/facebook-posts-wrongly-claim-left-wing-activist-an/.

175. **Kramer, Adam D. I.** A lot of people have asked me about my and Jamie and Jeff's recent study published in PNAS, and I wanted to give a brief public explanation. [Online] Facebook, June 29, 2014. https://www.facebook.com/akramer/posts/10152987150867796.

176. **Booth, Robert.** Facebook reveals news feed experiment to control emotions. [Online] The Guardian, June 29, 2014. http://www.theguardian.com/technology/2014/jun/29/facebook-users-emotions-news-feeds.

177. **Orwell, George.** 1984. Part 1, Chapter 5. [Online] Signet Classics, 1949. http://www.george-orwell.org/1984/4.html.

178. **Rushfield, Richard.** On the Trail of lonelygirl15 Daily. [Online] Los Angeles Times, September 4, 2006. http://www.latimes.com/entertainment/news/la-et-lonelygirl5sep05,0,3933739.htmlstory.

179. **The Washington Post Special Reports.** The Watergate Story. [Online] The Washington Post. [Cited: April 9, 2012.] http://www.washingtonpost.com/wp-srv/politics/special/watergate/.

Chapter 11
Wikipedia and the New Web

Emily Temple-Wood

11.1 History of Wikipedia

For most people in the Western world, Wikipedia has become the first – and often last – stop for information about pop culture, science, medicine, history, and just about anything else. Donating to the Wikimedia Foundation, the nonprofit that runs Wikipedia and its sister projects, has become mainstream. News stories about Wikipedia and its editors are no longer focusing on the oddity of a collection of geeks trying to write an encyclopedia. Instead, that people would choose to do so is not even questioned, and the content they have produced and the complex political system they engage in are scrutinized by the mainstream.

Five years ago, only the most optimistic, committed, and obsessed Wikipedians would have predicted that Wikipedia, the illegitimate sibling of pedigreed encyclopedias, would become the juggernaut of information it is now. Wikipedia's beginnings were even more humble, however. It began as a scratchboard for Nupedia, a project conceived as a free encyclopedia written collaboratively by academics in a convoluted seven-step process. The less formal, less bureaucratic Wikipedia took off as Nupedia withered and died, though the number of readers and editors stayed small for several years. The "wiki way" was established, with the Five Pillars as the major set of rules – one of which was "Ignore All Rules", referred to by the acronym "IAR". The practice on Wikipedia of referring to policies by acronyms has been cited in internal and external discussions as an example of the insular community that has grown up around Wikipedia; however, jargon is common in a myriad of subcultures, both on and off the Internet.

E. Temple-Wood (✉)
WikiProject Women Scientists, Downers Grove, IL, USA
e-mail: emily.temple.wood@gmail.com

© Springer Science+Business Media, LLC, part of Springer Nature 2021
N. Lee, *Facebook Nation*, https://doi.org/10.1007/978-1-0716-1867-7_11

The early Wikipedia was very open and almost anarchic – the very few rules were enforced inconsistently and the process of becoming an administrator, which is now a gauntlet that accomplished editors fear, consisted of asking politely on a mailing list. When the Requests for Adminship (RFA) process was introduced in 2003, users were given administrator rights on the basis of a handful of "support" votes from their peers; in 2013, successful candidates typically had more than 75 "support" votes.

It must be noted, however, that "vote" has never been the preferred term for "supports" or "opposes" entered into community discussions like RFA. The consensus model was instituted very early on in Wikipedia's history and decisions are supposed to be made by a consensus process, not vote-counting. With the small community of early Wikipedia, this was entirely possible and processes like Requests for Comment (RfC) were effective in creating acceptable decisions. More than ten years later, creating a true consensus in a community of thousands is near-impossible.

Articles of the early Wikipedia reflected the open environment in which they were nurtured. New articles could be started with one sentence and no sources or formatting, and the "wiki way" would eventually get the articles to an acceptable standard. Before a push to add inline citations, Featured Articles (FAs) were judged on their "brilliant prose" – in fact the original name for that process. In more recent years, this spirit of collaborative fixing and "no big deal" has passed in favor of a rigid orthopraxy, where if new articles do not have a source and correct formatting, they may be deleted, sometimes within minutes, even if they contain correct information.

The article on Hong Kong was started on September 14, 2001, and consisted of a few sentences about the territory. The only citation given was "From the CIA World Factbook 2000 and the U.S. Department of State website. Not wikified" (1). As of December 2013, the article is listed as a Good Article (GA) and has 243 inline citations with nine books listed as "further reading" (2). "Saxophone" came from even more humble beginnings, with five sentences describing the instrument and zero citations (3). It was one of Wikipedia's first Featured Articles – then called "Refreshing and Brilliant Prose" – promoted sometime in 2003 (4). At the end of that year the article, as one of Wikipedia's best, had a few scant sections and no citations. By 2006 its status had been removed as it did not meet Wikipedia's increasingly high standards. The article on the Earth began as two sentences with a serious grammar error on February 27, 2001: "The third [[planet]] from [[the Sun]]. Six features six [[continent]]s, four [[ocean]]s, and many [[CountriesOfTheWorld|countries]]" (5). This early era was important to Wikipedia's success as starting an encyclopedia from scratch with a prescribed review process had already failed, and the complex processes that characterize modern Wikipedia evolved organically. Though the increasingly high standards adopted by Wikipedians have improved Wikipedia's reputation in the eyes of the public, the community has repeatedly struggled with how to balance the tradition of openness and the "wiki way" with the need for credibility and the accompanying high standards.

11.2 Standard of Quality

It seems that in recent years, high standards and a focus on correct process have won out over these original ideals that formed the community, inciting regular griping and prophecies of doom and gloom for the future of Wikipedia. The signs of this ossification have been around since at least 2007, when I joined for the first time, and the period that many consider to be the heyday of the project, at least in terms of the balance between process and wiki values. The bureaucracy of processes like requests for user rights has snowballed since the first of those processes, Requests for Adminship (RfA), began in 2003.

RfA was originally an off-wiki process, where requests for administrator rights were conducted on the Wikien-L mailing list, a mailing list for editors of English Wikipedia. One of these very early requests consisted of the user asking on the mailing list for adminship "to assist in the general maintenance and welfare of wikipedia [*sic*]" (6). The nomination was seconded by Erik Moeller, an early and prominent member of the community – and now Wikimedia Foundation employee – and the change in status was made a few days later with a minimum of fuss. A look through the mailing list archives shows this to be fairly typical, though concerns about too much bureaucracy in the process were already brewing, even at this early stage (7).

For comparison, one successful RfA from July 2013 (8) consisted of two co-nominations, 15 questions (several of which were multi-part), 98 "support" comments, 3 "oppose" comments, 1 withdrawn "oppose", and 1 withdrawn "neutral", all summing to more than 69,000 bytes of text – not including the three sections of discussion on the associated Talk page.

The move towards a more complicated, bureaucratic RfA process is indicative of the attitude on English Wikipedia in general towards administration of the project. Process is seen as protective against bad content; commensurate with Wikipedia's rising star, processes have spiraled in number and complexity. In fact, the steps that an article goes through to become a Featured Article (FA), a designation of Wikipedia's highest-quality work, bear a remarkable resemblance to the steps in the production of a Nupedia article, which included numerous guidelines for assignment of the article, extensive peer-review, and copyediting (9). For a Wikipedia article circa 2013 – depending on where the article falls in the purview of various WikiProjects – there are at least three steps to FA status, and as many as five, all of which can involve days to weeks of complex review. WikiProject Military History, arguably the most successful project, conducts several of its own internal review processes in addition to the Wikipedia-wide ones. Though these reviews are not in any way mandatory, the do confer prestige on an editor and improve Wikipedia's perceived reliability.

Though the increase in quality that these review processes have wrought is welcome, they are substantially dysfunctional in a number of ways. One study of the FAC process by a long time Wikipedia user addressed the issue of reviewers not engaging with content and accuracy (10). A Featured Article is defined as having a number of characteristics, including comprehensiveness, "engaging, even brilliant" prose, appropriate style, and comprehensive research (11) (12). Unfortunately, reviewers often nitpick the article's prose and its adherence to the most minute details of the Manual of Style, and overlook major problems like plagiarism (in Wikipedia parlance, "copyvio", a concatenation of "copyright violation") and missing areas of coverage. This study found that many Featured Article reviews did not have any critique of the content. Though not widespread, several articles have had their Featured status removed when editors found extensive copyright violations upon later review. This is a serious problem for Wikipedia's credibility and the community will need to improve the various review processes so that they regulate the breadth of coverage and reliability of sources as well as high quality prose and style.

Another serious problem with the peer review processes is a substantial dearth of reviewers. In December 2013, the Good Article Nominations page had a backlog of 362 articles stretching back to August 2013 (13); the Peer Review page had a backlog of 47 articles (14), and the Featured Article Nominations page had 53 articles undergoing review (15). These numbers are not unusual, and in fact have been worsening for years. For these pages to be effective in auditing content, more reviewers need to volunteer. However, reviewing articles is a difficult, thankless task, and it will be no mean feat to attract these necessary contributors.

11.3 Learning Curve

Another problem that faces the modern Wikipedia as it tries to create a stable place for itself in the new web's information economy is the steep learning curve and hostile environment perceived by non-contributors or new editors. A large part of this is due to a growing idea of English Wikipedia as a "walled garden" amongst experienced contributors, and a burgeoning fear of newcomers to the community not meeting standards on their first attempt to contribute and harming the encyclopedia. As I have discussed earlier, the consequence of Wikipedia's increased reliability is increased visibility and therefore an increased burden on the community of contributors to maintain the current quality and continue to produce more and better content.

New contributors often struggle to master the syntax of Wiki markup and internalize the "house style" that has developed over Wikipedia's thirteen years of existence. As such, new articles or additions to existing articles are often written like academic essays, contain the author's opinions (contravening Wikipedia's sacred "Neutral Point of View", or NPOV, principle (16)), or do not meet the notability guidelines (17). They also often have no citations, no Wiki markup, or no links. These contributions are often removed wholesale even if they contain salvageable content because they are seen as harming the credibility of Wikipedia. This, in turn, leads to burnout on the part of experienced editors and a poor retention rate of new editors, who grow frustrated with the obstacles to contributing and quit for greener volunteering pastures.

Two projects have been implemented in an attempt to mitigate the harm that new contributors can do: "Draftspace", and Articles for Creation (AfC). Draftspace is a brand-new namespace on English Wikipedia that is meant to create a gentle place for contributors who are inexperienced or afraid of a hostile reception (18) (19). Though a private place for people to work on a draft article already exists, called "sandboxes", assigning a whole namespace to this purpose helps to make drafting an article more accessible to newcomers. A namespace on Wikipedia is a prefix that indicates what type of page something is (20). Namespaces include Wikipedia: ("projectspace"), Portal:, Talk:, Template:, and more. Putting a page in a namespace is as simple as starting the page with the appropriate prefix, for example, Wikipedia:Requests for adminship is the projectspace page for adminship requests. Instead of having to create a sandbox page, a contributor who wants to start a new article can prefix their creation with "Draft:", lowering the barrier to contribution.

The fear of newcomers harming Wikipedia's content or reputation has extended to the groups of editors called "New Page Patrollers" and the anti-vandalism corps, who make extensive use of the Page Curation tools and the program Huggle. New page patrollers are a self-selected group of volunteers who go through the constant stream of new pages (21) and nominate for one of three deletion processes articles they consider unsuitable for Wikipedia, or put tags on articles they see as having problems. This is all well and good – and necessary for Wikipedia's reliability and future – but these patrollers often tag articles within minutes or even seconds of their creation. This contributes heavily to the hostile attitude that deters new contributors, who have heard that Wikipedia is open and flexible, and do not realize that new pages must meet basic guidelines. To combat this attitude, the Wikimedia Foundation spearheaded the creation of the Teahouse, a help desk designed to be friendly and personal in answering newcomers' questions (22).

11.4   Wikipedia as Major News Source

All of these issues contribute heavily to the ossification of Wikipedia's processes and power structure, and Wikipedia will therefore lose its greatest assets – flexibility and responsiveness – when compared to traditional media. On December 27, 2007, Benazir Bhutto, the Prime Minister of Pakistan, was killed on the streets of Rawalpindi. I was an eighth grader on winter break and came upon the news very soon after it happened. For the next few hours I hid in my room and helped write the article about her assassination as events unfolded half a world away (23). This was a formative experience for me as an editor and for my understanding of Wikipedia. Because it could be updated in real time as information reached news outlets, it had the potential – since realized – to be a powerful news source. This was the first time I had ever seen Wikipedia realize this potential. Since then, I have watched as Wikipedia became a major news source in its own right – when the US government shut down in October 2013, Wikipedia's constantly updated article was one of the most popular articles on Wikipedia during the first days of the shutdown (24).

11.5 Wikipedians

I joined Wikipedia in April 2007, in the year that some members of the community consider to be the "heyday" of the project, when process and quality assurance were balanced well with the wiki tradition. This year saw the highest number of users made administrators and was also the high-water mark until now of the number of editors. I can't count the number of times I have seen other editors lament the "good old days", with a focused, dedicated community producing excellent content. Though this picture is often only seen through rose-colored glasses, the statistics do indeed show a significant drop in the number of both editors and administrators on English Wikipedia, along with a large rise in the number of page views. In short, less people are writing and more people are reading Wikipedia.

The most innocuous reason typically given for this decline is the "middle age" of Wikipedia, where most of the low-hanging fruit has been plucked and specialists move in to write about niche topics. The more insidious explanation is that Wikipedia and its politics are inherently toxic and it will become ever harder to retain and recruit editors as the pool of contributors, potential and actual, realizes how dysfunctional the community is. The truth is somewhere in between these two hypotheses. Yes, Wikipedia is often a toxic community, but concerted efforts – like the Teahouse – to mitigate that environment are succeeding, at least somewhat, and there is an ever-growing amount of quality content that is no longer accessible for the Average Joe. I'm an optimist, though, and I believe that the altruistic spirit, though diminished, remains in the Wikipedia community and the efforts to improve the interpersonal dynamics of the community will succeed in fanning that flame.

The sheer altruism was not the only thing that made me stay with Wikipedia for the long haul. I discovered I had a passion for research and writing that school had not yet uncovered in me. I suspect that if I had not found an outlet for this, I would have quickly tired my family out with endless trips to the library and pages of notes scattered all over my house in my attempt to create my own encyclopedia. I've been told that I was "born to edit" – one of my favorite hobbies was memorizing names of planetary moons, dinosaurs, gems, and whatever else I could get my hands on, and the best gift I had received as a child was the encyclopedia I got in kindergarten. I read it cover to cover and delighted in learning about everything from alphabets to Zambia.

Wikipedia is incredibly compelling for people like me, but not every contributor has a remotely similar profile to me – so what makes editors stick around? Are Wikipedians born or made? And again, the answer is somewhere in between. It's an unpopular opinion, but not everyone is capable of or willing to contribute to Wikipedia. A lot of college students think Wikipedia is amazing, but think contributing is too much like homework (and with the establishment of the Wikipedia Education Program (25), sometimes it is just that). Our job should not be to turn every person on the street into a Wikipedian, it should be to find and cultivate contributors who have skills that will improve the project. People with these skills and a healthy sense of altruism won't need to be coerced to contribute – but simply exposing them to the fact that they *can* contribute is not enough. It is much more effective to teach and facilitate and sometimes even incentivize new contributors, who will then stay of their own accord. It is abundantly clear that we have not yet solved this problem, and I don't at all profess to have a magic bullet, indeed, the simple number of contributors may not be the problem. Increasing successful, productive contributions will take concerted experimentation and a willingness to fail purposefully, which may prove difficult for the fundamentally conservative Wikipedia community.

11.6 Acceptance of Wikipedia

One step to understanding the future of Wikipedia and how a bare-bones site has attained its current supremacy in the modern, flashy, bite-size, GIF-laden Web requires a look at how Wikipedia rose to prominence in the first place. The English Wikipedia received major attention on the Internet giant Slashdot in early 2005. (I'm focusing on the English Wikipedia here and throughout because I contribute almost exclusively to English Wikipedia and do not consider myself qualified to comment on the often startlingly different dynamics of other language communities.)

The very early content of Wikipedia – circa late 2001 – consisted of mostly traditional "geek" content, as well as a focus on Ayn Rand and Libertarian topics (26). But by 2005, content had been greatly diversified, with over 400,000 articles (27). Wikipedia was no longer a niche website – it had widespread appeal, and the breadth of topics it offered when it began to receive mainstream attention allowed Wikipedia to enter into the public consciousness in a way that other information sites did not. They were either too specialized or were written by professionals, not volunteers, and so had less content overall.

But with greater recognition in the public eye came a growing reluctance among educators and academics to accept Wikipedia. Coming of age in the 2000s, I heard a constant stream of Wikipedia demonization from my teachers starting in the sixth grade and continuing to the present day in full force. Wikipedia is maligned by the educational system not because it is a tertiary source – generally unacceptable in academic papers regardless of provenance – but because it is crowdsourced and therefore unreliable. My experience with hearing Wikipedia regularly delegitimized by my teachers and professors is not uncommon among other people my age. But as students everywhere tend to ignore their teachers on other topics, they don't heed warnings to avoid Wikipedia. In fact, I have been thanked on multiple occasions for editing Wikipedia and thereby helping my friends and acquaintances pass their exams. Editing Wikipedia has taken on the role of public service in the eyes of the Millennial generation.

In recent years, though, Wikipedia has become much more widely accepted in the educational community, and the unanimous rejection of Wikipedia as a valid academic project has found dissent. A 2005 study in *Nature* showed that English

Wikipedia was about as accurate as the *Encyclopedia Britannica* on science topics, which did much to validate Wikipedia in academia (28).

11.7   Wikipedia Education Program

The Education Program, mainly active in the US and Canada, has created a remarkable acceptance of Wikipedia as a classroom tool in those countries. During the Fall 2013 semester, dozens of classes were involved across the US and Canada, in contrast to just five years earlier, when any academic who introduced Wikipedia into the classroom flew under the radar and was branded a maverick. Though some academics still choose to work outside of its bounds, most engage with the Education Program and the structure and support it provides. The program assigns ambassadors to each class, experienced Wikipedians who provide extra instruction and support to the students, reviewing their articles and teaching valuable editing skills.

In theory this is a wonderful idea, but in practice, like any grand idea, it often falls short. Some professors, like University of Toronto's Steve Joordens, refuse to engage with the Wikipedia community, and in his case, sic almost two thousand poorly-prepared undergraduates on one niche area of content (29). This and other incidents in a similar vein have harmed the reputation of the Education Program and students in the Wikipedia community at large, and have led to significant tension between the two communities. The barrier to acceptance in the next few years may not be the opposition to Wikipedia within the academic community, but the Wikipedia community's conservatism about allowing Wikipedia into the classroom. The fear of newcomers failing to adhere to well-established format and guidelines extends to students as well, and still has the potential to sink the Education Program's ambitions.

Wikipedia's relationship with academia may be shaky but it is typically celebrated among a very diverse readership, to the tune of hundreds of millions of page views a day. The prevailing attitude among Millennials is that "if it's not on Wikipedia, it doesn't exist", which gives Wikipedia the kind of cultural power that few institutions can enjoy. It is a ubiquitous source of information for students, typically the first port of call for students trying to write a term paper, understand a reading, or kill time in lecture. For non-students, Wikipedia settles arguments and satisfies curiosities – it has been described as "indispensable" to modern Western life on a regular basis. Even doctors, junior and senior alike, are not immune to Wikipedia's siren song. A 2011 study showed that 60% of doctors across Europe use Wikipedia to seek medical information regularly, underscoring the project's prominence as an information source for the modern Web (30) (31).

11.8   Systemic Bias and WikiProject Women Scientists

The major problem with this ubiquity and the attitude among students and non-students alike of Wikipedia as infallible is that Wikipedia is both incomplete and imperfect. A serious issue is the systemic bias that plagues the project – women, LGBT people, and nonwhite people are sorely underrepresented. Either their biographies are not covered or they are seriously substandard. Efforts to combat this have been somewhat successful in recent years. I co-founded WikiProject Women Scientists in November 2012 and in one year of existence, it doubled the amount of Good and Featured Articles covering women scientists and put dozens of articles on the Main Page in the Did You Know section, bringing thousands of readers to biographies of little-known women scientists.

But the work is far from over on women scientists or on most other topics affected by systemic bias, and it is particularly crucial that systemic biases are eradicated as soon as possible. "There is no deadline" is a phrase commonly bandied about on Wikipedia, but in this case, there is indeed a deadline to write this content. Before Wikipedia achieved its current status as a cultural and Internet icon, there was no imperative to produce quality articles or fill in coverage gaps because readership was still low. Since Wikipedia has taken on the burden of providing education for the world, though, there is a moral duty on the part of Wikipedia contributors to make sure that the encyclopedia has broad coverage and is as accurate as possible.

11.9   Native Language Wikipedias

English Wikipedia is not the only project that can aid in this endeavor, though. Wikipedias in a variety of smaller languages can be an invaluable resource for communities that speak those languages. Instead of forcing, say, Hausa communities to read research and articles in English, the Hausa Wikipedia can provide content in people's native language. Native-language Wikipedias can be incredibly empowering for speakers of languages that have been subjugated by colonial languages. For example, Aymara, a language spoken in Bolivia and Peru, has a burgeoning Wikipedia written by native speakers. This provides an opportunity for Aymara community members to preserve knowledge in their own language and provides an important resource for native Aymara speakers, who can read Wikipedia in their native language instead of in Spanish (32).

In any language, the widespread use of Wikipedia instills a sense of duty in editors to create the best and most accurate content possible. In Wikipedia's early years, though its contributors had a sense of altruism and knew they were working on something important, it was not yet the global information service it is now. This sense of duty has created a conflict with the "wiki way" – now that doctors are using

Wikipedia regularly, it is extraordinarily tempting to lock all of the medicine articles down to prevent vandalism. It makes for a difficult transition in the community, especially as more diverse contributors join in on English Wikipedia. Contributors are not just young, white college-educated men from the West (though they are still overwhelmingly so). There are editors from around the world, from many different cultural contexts, participating and editing, bringing their own paradigms that can be in conflict with the established culture.

11.10   Wikipedia Zero

Wikipedia has become even more important in the past year or so because of a new program instituted by the Wikimedia Foundation, called Wikipedia Zero (33). This is a program that partners the Wikimedia Foundation with mobile carriers around the world and allows subscribers to access Wikipedia articles without incurring data costs. It has become so popular that a group of students in South Africa have petitioned their mobile carrier to subscribe to Wikipedia Zero. This is a revolutionary endeavor but it places an even bigger burden on the shoulders of Wikimedia volunteer contributors. This program gives Wikipedia access to millions more people - as of December 2013, 22 countries have access in at least some languages on a major carrier (34). A readership that is expanded this way and is prone to using Wikipedia as an only source for information due to its low cost helps to make Wikipedia a platform for social change and empowerment but it carries with it the need for quality assurance. Our mission is to bring the sum of human knowledge to everyone for free, but as we move closer to realizing that mission, we as editors need to remember our readership and focus on creating content that serves our readers.

The question now is how we accomplish this massive mission. First of all, we need to remember that our news is suddenly mainstream news. Internally, we seem to be repeatedly caught off guard by news organizations taking interest in our politics. That shouldn't be a surprise anymore. As a community, we need to realize that to some degree, the tyranny of structurelessness has hurt us, and come up with a governance solution that isn't a stopgap. We need to recognize that turnover of our editing population is not a tragedy, and welcome new voices into our community. And finally, whenever the minutiae of politics or trolls gets to be too much, as individual contributors we need to remember what is important and why we began contributing in the first place.

References

1. **Qatsi, Koyaanis.** Hong Kong. *Wikipedia.* [Online] September 14, 2001. https://nostalgia.wikipedia.org/w/index.php?title=Hong_Kong&oldid=20252.
2. **Xqbot.** Hong Kong. *Wikipedia.* [Online] December 31, 2013. https://en.wikipedia.org/w/index.php?title=Hong_Kong&oldid=588505338.

3. **207.235.31.xxx.** Saxophone. *Wikipedia.* [Online] April 20, 2001. https://nostalgia.wikipedia. org/w/index.php?title=Saxophone&oldid=40050.

4. **GimmeBot.** Featured article candidates/Featured log/October 2003 and before. *Wikipedia.* [Online] April 19, 2008. https://en.wikipedia.org/wiki/Wikipedia:Featured_article_candidates/ Featured_log/October_2003_and_before.

5. **Reagle.** Earth. *Berkman Center for Internet & Society at Harvard University.* [Online] February 27, 2001. http://cyber.law.harvard.edu/~reagle/wp-redux/Earth/983254092.html.

6. **Moeller, Erik.** [WikiEN-l] sysop. *Wikimedia.* [Online] May 8, 2003. http://lists.wikimedia. org/pipermail/wikien-l/2003-May/003122.html.

7. **Mayer, Daniel.** [WikiEN-l] sysop nominations. *Wikimedia.* [Online] May 8, 2003. http://lists. wikimedia.org/pipermail/wikien-l/2003-May/003125.html.

8. **Wikipedia.** Requests for adminship/Kelapstick 2. *Wikipedia.* [Online] July 16, 2013. https:// en.wikipedia.org/wiki/Wikipedia:Requests_for_adminship/Kelapstick_2.

9. **Upedia.com.** NUPEDIA.COM EDITORIAL POLICY GUIDELINES. *Internet Archive Wayback Machine.* [Online] November 16, 2000. http://web.archive.org/web/20010331211742/ www.nupedia.com/policy.shtml.

10. **Wiki user "TCO".** Improving Wikipedia's important articles. *Wikimedia.* [Online] December 15, 2011. http://upload.wikimedia.org/wikipedia/commons/8/8c/Wikipedia%E2%80%99s_ poor_treatment_of_its_most_important_articles.pdf.

11. **Wikipedia.** Featured article criteria. *Wikipedia.* [Online] [Cited: December 2013, 30.] https:// en.wikipedia.org/wiki/Wikipedia:WIAFA.

12. —. Manual of Style. *Wikipedia.* [Online] [Cited: January 1, 2014.] https://en.wikipedia.org/ wiki/Wikipedia:MOS.

13. —. Good article nominations. *Wikipedia.* [Online] [Cited: December 31, 2013.] https:// en.wikipedia.org/wiki/Wikipedia:GAN.

14. —. Peer review. *Wikipedia.* [Online] [Cited: December 31, 2013.] https://en.wikipedia.org/ wiki/Wikipedia:PR.

15. —. Fancruft. *Wikipedia.* [Online] [Cited: December 31, 2013.] https://en.wikipedia.org/wiki/ Wikipedia:FAN.

16. —. Neutral point of view. *Wikipedia.* [Online] December 17, 2013. https://en.wikipedia.org/ wiki/Wikipedia:NPOV.

17. —. General notability guideline. *Wikipedia.* [Online] December 8, 2013. https://en.wikipedia. org/wiki/Wikipedia:GNG#General_notability_guideline.

18. **Walling, Steven.** New draft feature provides a gentler start for Wikipedia articles. *Wikimedia Foundation.* [Online] December 20, 2013. http://blog.wikimedia.org/2013/12/20/ new-draft-feature/.

19. **Wikipedia.** Drafts. *Wikipedia.* [Online] December 29, 2013. https://en.wikipedia.org/wiki/ Wikipedia:Drafts.

20. —. Namespace. *Wikipedia.* [Online] December 27, 2013. https://en.wikipedia.org/wiki/ Wikipedia:Namespace.

21. —. Recent changes. *Wikipedia.* [Online] [Cited: December 31, 2013.] https://en.wikipedia.org/ wiki/Special:RecentChanges.

22. —. Teahouse. *Wikipedia.* [Online] December 12, 2013. https://en.wikipedia.org/wiki/ Wikipedia:TEAHOUSE.

23. —. Assassination of Benazir Bhutto: Revision history. *Wikipedia.* [Online] [Cited: November 15, 2013.] https://en.wikipedia.org/w/index. php?title=Assassination_of_Benazir_Bhutto&action=history.

24. **Wikipedia article traffic statistics.** United States federal government shutdown of 2013. *Wikipedia article traffic statistics.* [Online] [Cited: November 1, 2013.] http://stats.grok.se/ en/201310/United%20States%20federal%20government%20shutdown%20of%202013.

25. **Wikipedia.** Education program. *Wikipedia.* [Online] September 22, 2013. https://en.wikipedia. org/wiki/Wikipedia:USEP.

26. **Reagle.** Wikipedia 10K Redux. *Berkman Center for Internet & Society at Harvard University.* [Online] December 16, 2010. http://cyber.law.harvard.edu/~reagle/wp-redux/.
27. **Wikipedia.** Size of Wikipedia. *Wikipedia.* [Online] January 2, 2014. https://en.wikipedia.org/wiki/Wikipedia:Size_of_Wikipedia.
28. **Giles, Jim.** Special Report Internet encyclopaedias go head to head. *Nature.* [Online] December 14, 2005. http://www.nature.com/nature/journal/v438/n7070/full/438900a.html.
29. **McQuigge, Michelle.** Toronto professor learns not all editors are welcome on Wikipedia when class assignment backfires. *National Post.* [Online] April 7, 2013. http://news.nationalpost.com/2013/04/07/toronto-professor-learns-not-all-editors-are-welcome-on-wikipedia-when-class-assignment-backfires/.
30. **Poulter,Martin.**Doctorsuse,butdon'trelytotallyon,Wikipedia. *WikimediaUK.*[Online]April24, 2012. http://blog.wikimedia.org.uk/2012/04/doctors-use-but-dont-rely-totally-on-wikipedia/.
31. **BBC.** Hundreds of GPs admit to using the website Wikipedia as a medical research tool. *BBC News.* [Online] June 1, 2011. http://www.bbc.co.uk/news/health-13615420.
32. **Mao, Elaine.** Preserving Aymara language and culture on Wikipedia. *Wikimedia Foundation.* [Online] April 6, 2012. http://blog.wikimedia.org/2012/04/06/preserving-aymara-language-and-culture-on-wikipedia/.
33. **Wikimedia Foundation.** Wikipedia Zero. *Wikimedia Foundation.* [Online] November 14, 2013. http://wikimediafoundation.org/wiki/Wikipedia_Zero.
34. **U5K0.** Wikipedia Zero map. *Wikimedia Fondation.* [Online] July 7, 2013. http://wikimediafoundation.org/wiki/File:Wikipedia_Zero_map.svg.

Chapter 12
E-Government and E-Activism

"We are the nation that put cars in driveways and computers in offices; the nation of Edison and the Wright brothers; of Google and Facebook."

– President Barack Obama (January 2011)

"We must use technology to build stronger connections between constituents and their elected officials by incorporating social media into daily Congressional operations."

– Majority Leader Eric Cantor (December 2011)

"In the face of everything else that's screwed up in Washington, we the American people can fix things."

– Reddit co-founder Alexis Ohanian (May 2012)

"We are only a drop in this world ... but the rain starts with a single drop."

– Saudi Arabian Activist Manal al-Sharif (May 2012)

"If there is an Internet connection, my camera is more powerful [than my AK-47]."

– Syrian dissident Abu Ghassan (June 2012)

"The future is sharing – open data, open participation, open source, open everything, and it must happen at every level."

– Lieutenant Governor of California Gavin Newsom (February 2013)

"There isn't a single senator who doesn't use Facebook to communicate with constituents."

– Senator Todd Young (April 2018)

"Politics don't corrupt people, people corrupt politics."

– Federal Judge Amy Berman Jackson (December 2019)

"Big Tech companies think they are bigger than governments and that the rules should not apply to them. They may be changing the world, but that doesn't mean they run it."

– Australian Prime Minister Scott Morrison (February 2021)

N. Lee, *Facebook Nation*, https://doi.org/10.1007/978-1-0716-1867-7_12

12.1   President Barack Obama and Web 2.0

John F. Kennedy's masterful images on television, the new medium in the 60's, helped him defeat then Vice President and Republican candidate Richard Nixon in the 1960 U.S. presidential election. Those who heard their first debate on the radio pronounced Nixon the winner, but the majority of the 70 million Americans who watched the televised debate perceived Kennedy as the clear champion (1).

In 2008, Barack Obama ushered in a new Internet era in politics. With over 13 million addresses in his email list, 400,000 blog posts, 130,000 Twitter followers, and 5 million supporters on Facebook, Obama successfully raised half a billion dollars online for his 2008 presidential campaign (2). The Triple O (Obama's Online Operation) used the World Wide Web to mobilize supporters and took advantage of YouTube for free advertising and fundraising (3).

Former Facebook spokesman Chris Hughes launched the networking site My. BarackObama.com (MyBO) for supporters to be actively involved in the 2008 presidential campaign. Volunteers on MyBO created more than 2 million profiles, planned 200,000 events, formed 35,000 groups, posted 400,000 blogs, and raised $30 million on 70,000 personal fund-raising pages. *Fast Company* featured Hughes on its April 2009 cover as "The Kid Who Made Obama President" (4).

"Were it not for the Internet, Barack Obama would not be president," said *Huffington Post* founder Arianna Huffington at the 2008 Web 2.0 Summit in San Francisco a few days after the election. "Were it not for the Internet, he wouldn't even have been the Democratic nominee. By contrast, the McCain campaign didn't have a clue. The problem wasn't the age of the candidate; it was the age of the idea" (5).

Immediately after winning the 2008 U.S. presidential election, President-Elect Barack Obama (@BarackObama) thanked his Twitter followers, "We just made history. All of this happened because you gave your time, talent and passion. All of this happened because of you. Thanks" (6).

Obama also launched the website change.gov to inform the American public about the Obama-Biden transition and to encourage people to share their ideas with the government (7). The website reads, "To change this country, we're counting on Americans from every walk of life to get involved. Tell us how an experience in your life showed you something that is right or something that is wrong with this country – and share your ideas for how to make it better" (8).

After the transition, President Obama continued to leverage the power of the Internet via the government website whitehouse.gov as well as holding online town hall meetings via Google+, Facebook, and YouTube (9). When we visited the whitehouse.gov in April 2012 and April 2021, we saw something similar to commercial business websites – we were prompted to enter our email address to get periodic updates (from the Executive Office of the President in the case of whitehouse.gov) (10). (See Fig. 12.1 and 12.2).

In 1966, the U.S. Congress enacted the Freedom of Information Act (FOIA) to give the American public greater access to the federal government's records (11).

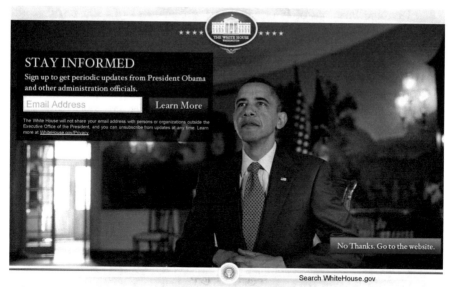

Fig. 12.1 WhiteHouse.gov in April 2012

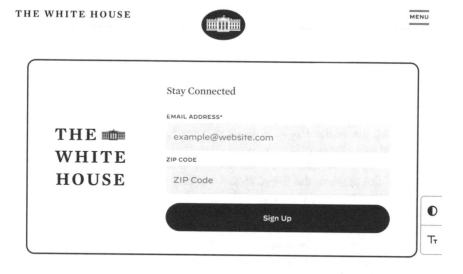

Fig. 12.2 WhiteHouse.gov in April 2021

The Electronic Freedom of Information Act Amendments of 1996 broadens the scope of FOIA to encompass electronic records and to make government's records more easily and widely available to the public by placing more material online (12). All government agencies are required to have their websites provide the function of "electronic reading rooms" (13). In addition, the U.S. Congress passed the E-Government Act of 2002 intended to improve the management and promotion of electronic government services and processes (14). In 2009, President Obama created Data.gov to "increase public access to high value, machine readable datasets generated by the Executive Branch of the Federal Government" (15).

Instead of a passive electronic reading room as described in 1996, however, the Internet has evolved into a proactive medium, or Web 2.0, for governments, politicians, and citizens in the 21st century. *Web 2.0* is the title of a book by Dermont McCormack published in 2002 (16). Nevertheless, the term "Web 2.0" was popularized by Dale Dougherty, Vice President of O'Reilly Media, to describe the present, evolutionary stage of the Internet since the dot-com bust in 2001 (17). With the advent of Web 2.0 social media tools and applications, Government 2.0 (or Gov 2.0) fosters a two-way communication between citizens and governments.

In his 2011 State of the Union Address, President Barack Obama said, "Thirty years ago, we couldn't know that something called the Internet would lead to an economic revolution. What we can do – what America does better than anyone – is spark the creativity and imagination of our people. We are the nation that put cars in driveways and computers in offices; the nation of Edison and the Wright brothers; of Google and Facebook. In America, innovation doesn't just change our lives. It's how we make a living" (18).

In September 2011, the Obama administration launched "We the People on WhiteHouse.gov," a new online platform for Americans to create and sign petitions on a range of issues affecting the United States (19). When a petition gathers enough online signatures, it will be reviewed by government policy experts who will then issue an official response. As the *TIME Magazine* reported, "Petitions have sometimes forced the White House to respond when it otherwise might have stayed silent." And as a case in point, "Activists upset over a Hollywood effort to increase copyright rules online petitioned the White House in 2011 to issue a veto threat. As a result of the petition, the White House issued a statement laying out concerns about the Hollywood approach, contributing to the bill's defeat in the Senate" (20).

Steven VanRoekel, U.S. Chief Information Officer, said in October 2011 that America has become a "Facebook nation" that demands increased transparency and interactivity from the federal government (21). His solution is to bring startup culture to the bureaucracy. He argues that the ubiquity of social media has created a "Facebook nation" that expects the same kinds of interactivity from commercial websites as it does from the federal government.

Immediately following President Obama's State of the Union address on January 24, 2012, an online panel from the White House answered questions submitted by citizens via Twitter (#WHChat & #SOTU), Google+, Facebook, and the in-person audience of "tweetup" participants (22). A "tweetup" is an event where people who tweet come together to meet in person.

CIA ✓
@CIA

 Follow

We can neither confirm nor deny that this is our first tweet.

↩ Reply   ↻ Retweet   ★ Favorite   ••• More

RETWEETS   FAVORITES
271,373   161,663

10:49 AM - 6 Jun 2014

Fig. 12.3 CIA's First Tweet (June 6, 2014)

Even the secretive Central Intelligence Agency (CIA) joined Twitter on June 6, 2014 with a sense of humor by sending its first message "We can neither confirm nor deny that this is our first tweet" (23). (See Fig. 12.3). CIA Director John Brennan explained, "By expanding to these platforms, CIA will be able to more directly engage with the public and provide information on CIA's mission, history, and other developments. We have important insights to share, and we want to make sure that unclassified information about the Agency is more accessible to the American public that we serve, consistent with our national security mission" (24).

CIA-funded Palantir has created AnalyzeThe.US that allows anyone to use the sophisticated data-mining tool to analyze data made public at Data.gov as well as information compiled by nonprofits and policy centers. Palantir stated on its website that "well-informed citizens lead to better government, and making government data available is certainly an important first step" (25).

Michael Scherer of CNN summed up nicely, "As one official put it, the time of guys sitting in a back room smoking cigars, saying 'We always buy 60 Minutes' is over. In politics, the era of big data has arrived" (26).

12.2   Gov 2.0 Apps

In a June 2012 interview with CNN, U.S. Chief Technology Officer Todd Park said that he wanted to unleash the power of data, technology, and innovation. Park explained the power of government data: "It's the notion of government taking a public good, which is this data – say weather data, or the global-positioning system or health-related knowledge and information – making it available in electronic, computable form and having entrepreneurs and innovators of all stripes turn it into an unbelievable array of products and services that improves lives and creates jobs" (27).

Indeed, the White House has been promoting the Open Data Initiatives program to "stimulate a rising tide of innovation and entrepreneurship that utilizes government data to create tools that help Americans in numerous ways – e.g., apps and services that help people find the right health care provider, identify the college that provides the best value for their money, save money on electricity bills through smarter shopping, or keep their families safe by knowing which products have been recalled" (28).

The Open Data Initiatives program also supports the Health Data Initiative launched in 2010 by the Institute of Medicine and the U.S. Department of Health and Human Services. A 2013 report by McKinsey & Company estimated that open data could generate more than $3 trillion a year in additional value in seven key sectors of the global economy, including education, transportation, and electricity (29).

As part of the Administration's larger commitment to open data, the White House also launched in May 2012 the Safety Data Initiative – an effort to "make government data relating to every aspect of public and product safety, from crime to roadway safety to food safety, much more accessible, and to encourage the development of innovative apps and services fueled by those data to empower Americans with the information and tools to make smarter, safer choices" (30).

In 2012, the National Archives and Record Administration (NARA) uploaded 100,000 digital images to Wikimedia Commons to allow Wikipedia editors to incorporate them into their projects and articles. The 2014 Open Government Plan calls for a broader reach to the public via Wikimedia, stating that "the 4,000 Wikipedia articles featuring our records received more than one billion page views in Fiscal Year 2013. Over the next two years we will work to increase the number of National Archives records available on Wikimedia Commons, which furthers our strategic goal to 'Make Access Happen' and expands re-use of our records by the public" (31).

In addition to the federal government, state and local government officials have also been active in promoting Government 2.0. With more than a million Twitter followers, mayor Cory Booker of Newark, New Jersey is an exemplary government official who actively uses Twitter to help citizens who are in need and to keep them informed. On New Year's Eve 2009, for example, mayor Booker and his volunteers shoveled the driveway of a 65-year-old Newark man after receiving a tweet from the man's concerned daughter (32).

To facilitate communication between citizens and local governments, technologies have created an assortment of Gov 2.0 applications such as "SeeClickFix" and "Street Bump." "SeeClickFix" allows anyone to file a public report online or via a mobile phone with GPS location about a non-emergency issue (33). Their website claims to have fixed 75,000 issues as of April 2012. "Street Bump" is an Android app piloted by Boston's Mayor's Office of New Urban Mechanics to catch potholes using the smartphone's built-in accelerometer (34). As of April 2012, "Street Bump" works in four cities: Boston, Austin, New York City, and London.

"I see [the Gov 2.0 applications] as the death of a passive relationship with government," said Clay Johnson, director of Sunlight Labs and author of *The Information Diet*. "Instead of people saying, 'Well, it's the government's job to fix that,' …

people are taking ownership and saying, 'Hey, wait a minute. Government is us. We are government. So let's take a responsibility and start changing things ourselves'" (35). Reddit's co-founder Alexis Ohanian voiced a similar opinion, "In the face of everything else that's screwed up in Washington, we the American people can fix things" (36).

As local government releases more community-specific data to the public, new Gov 2.0 utility apps are popping up. Among them are "DiscoverBPS" and "Adopt a Hydrant." "DiscoverBPS" assists parents in finding eligible schools for students in grade K0 through 12 in the Boston area (37). "Adopt a Hydrant" encourages Boston residences to help shovel out a fire hydrant after it snows (38).

Jennifer Pahlka, founder and executive director of Code for America, spoke at the TED2012 conference in February 2012, "Code for America … it's a little bit like a Peace Corps for geeks. We select a few fellows every year, and we have them work with city governments. … One of the applications the Code for America fellows wrote last year is called Adopt-a-Hydrant. It lets Bostonians sign up to dig out fire hydrants when they're covered in snow. … It's open-source, so anyone can take the code. Forest Frizzell in the IT department of the City of Honolulu found it and realized he could use it to recruit citizens to check on the tsunami sirens in his city to make sure they're functioning. Seattle is planning to use it to get citizens to clear clogged storm drains. Chicago has rolled it out to let people sign up to shovel sidewalks when it snows. There are now nine cities we know of looking to use this app, and it's happening organically, frictionlessly" (39). Pahlka suggested how government might work more like the Internet itself: "permissionless, open, generative."

To facilitate the development of Gov 2.0 apps, Sunlight Foundation offers free APIs (Application Programming Interfaces) to access and analyze government data (40). For instance:

1. The Congress API v3 is a live JSON API for information on legislators, districts, committees, bills, and votes as well as real-time notice of hearings, floor activity, and upcoming bills.
2. Docket Wrench examines the rulemaking process of federal agencies by tracking similar public comments and entity matching in order to get a complete picture of their influence across millions of documents. The Docket Wrench API gives developers programmatic access to metadata for documents, dockets, and agencies as well as to Docket Wrench's clustering and text analysis tools.
3. The Influence Explorer API gives programmers and journalists the ability to easily create subsets of large data for their own research and development purposes. The API provides access to campaign contributions and lobbying records.
4. The Open States API retrieves information on the legislators and activities of all 50 state legislatures, Washington, D.C. and Puerto Rico.
5. The Political Party Time API obtains the underlying raw data that the Sunlight Foundation creates based on fundraising invitations collected in Party Time.

On December 7, 2011, the Offices of Majority Leader Eric Cantor and Democratic Whip Steny Hoyer held the first-ever Congressional Facebook Hackathon in the Capitol Visitor Center in Washington, DC. The event brought together a bipartisan gathering of Members of Congress, Congressional staffers, Facebook engineers, and software developers to explore the potential connections between legislative data, constituent correspondence, and social media. Cantor stated the objective of the Hackathon: "We are dedicated to making the activities of this Congress transparent, accessible and useful for people around the country. In order to accomplish that, it is clear that we must use technology to build stronger connections between constituents and their elected officials by incorporating social media into daily Congressional operations" (41).

In September 2013, U.S. Homeland Security Investigations released an iOS app called "Operation Predator" that allows users to submit anonymous tips on suspected child sexual predators and fugitives. The app enables the public to identify suspects listed as "John Doe" from available photos posted online. "These investigations are one of our highest priorities, and in today's world, we need to be technologically savvy and innovative in our approach," said John Sandweg from the U. S. Homeland Security (42).

In his letter from the Facebook IPO filing in 2012, Mark Zuckerberg expounded his hope to change how people relate to their governments and social institutions:

"We believe building tools to help people share can bring a more honest and transparent dialogue around government that could lead to more direct empowerment of people, more accountability for officials and better solutions to some of the biggest problems of our time. By giving people the power to share, we are starting to see people make their voices heard on a different scale from what has historically been possible. These voices will increase in number and volume. They cannot be ignored. Over time, we expect governments will become more responsive to issues and concerns raised directly by all their people rather than through intermediaries controlled by a select few" (43).

In his 2013 book *Citizenville*, Lieutenant Governor of California and Democrat Gavin Newsom wrote, "The future is sharing – open data, open participation, open source, open everything, and it must happen at every level" (44). Republican strategist Alex Castellanos concurred, "If we open the doors of government to the private sector and make data accessible, we can jump-start a new era of social innovation. Open up the doors of government satellite data and you get Google Earth. Give Web designers in Chicago and Oakland access to public police data, and they create innovative crime-mapping tools that prevent muggings. Invent a digital 'currency' to reward citizens for participating in their own governance, and small town decision-making becomes as interesting and involving as Farmville" (45).

Wouldn't it be nice if more Democrats and Republicans are in unison to end congressional gridlock? (46) But all Democrats and Republicans have one thing in common: Senator Todd Young said in the April 10, 2018 Congressional hearing with Mark Zuckerberg, "There isn't a single senator who doesn't use Facebook to communicate with constituents" (47).

12.3   The Kony 2012 Phenomenon

"Kony 2012" is a perfect exemplification of social networks empowering people in voicing their concerns over injustice in the world. Uploaded to YouTube on March 5, 2012, the "Kony 2012" video has garnered over 87 million views within a month (48). With the goal of capturing the notorious criminal Joseph Kony, Invisible Children's 30-minute documentary film about the Ugandan warlord has been shared all over Facebook and mentioned incessantly on Twitter. The video went viral almost instantly after Invisible Children shared the YouTube link on Facebook, Tumblr, and Twitter (49).

As shown in Fig. 12.4, the "Kony 2012" video statistics retrieved on March 8, 2012 from YouTube indicated the following significant discovery events over a four-day period:

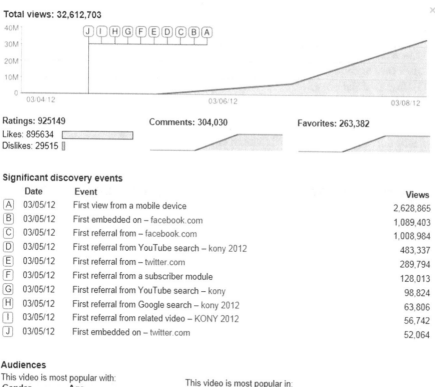

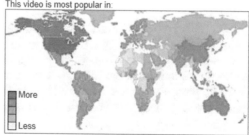

Fig. 12.4   Kony 2012 Video Statistics from YouTube on March 8, 2012

1. More than 2.6 million views came from mobile devices.
2. Over 1 million views came from the embedded YouTube video on Facebook.
3. Additional 1 million views came from referrals on Facebook.
4. Almost 300,000 views came from referrals on Twitter.
5. A combination of 150,000 views came from YouTube search and Google search.
6. More than 50,000 views came from the embedded video on Twitter.

The discovery events confirmed that Facebook and Twitter were instrumental in spreading the "Kony 2012" video around the world with lightning speed.

Moreover, the audiences' breakdown in Fig. 12.4 showed that among the 32.6 million views between March 5 and March 8, the video was most popular in the United States with females ages 13–17, followed by males ages 18–24 and 13–17. Columbia University professor Emily Bell found out about the "Kony 2012" video from her 11-year-old (50). The City University of New York journalism professor discovered the video from his daughter's Facebook page (51). Mark C. Toner, deputy spokesman at the State Department, had the video brought to his attention by his 13-year-old (52). Stories like these abounded.

Soon enough, Hollywood celebrities and entertainers joined in and ignited more chatter on Facebook, Twitter, and other social networks with their millions of fans (53). Some of the notable tweets were (54):

1. Oprah Winfrey to her 10 million followers: "Thanks tweeps for sending me info about ending #LRAviolence. I am aware. Have supported with $'s and voice and will not stop.#KONY2012" (March 6, 2102)
2. Ryan Seacrest to his 6 million followers: "Was going to sleep last night and saw ur tweets about #StopKony…watched in bed, was blown away. If u haven't seen yet on.fb.me/zClYoj" (March 7, 2012)
3. Justin Bieber to his 18 million followers: "it is time to make him known. Im calling on ALL MY FANS, FRIENDS, and FAMILY to come together and #STOPKONY – youtu.be/Y4MnpzG5Sqc" (March 7, 2012)
4. Kim Kardashian to her 14 million followers: "#Kony2012 Wow just watched! What a powerful video! Stop Kony!!! RT @KendallJenner: please WATCH THIS… vimeo.com/37119711" (March 7, 2012)

The ripple effect reached all the way to the U.S. government. State Department spokeswoman Victoria Nuland answered reporters' questions at a daily press briefing on March 8, 2012 (55):

QUESTION: Toria, have you seen this video that's going around the web, the Kony 2012 video, and does the State Department have a reaction to that or a comment on it?

MS. NULAND: We have. It's had some 25 million tweets. In fact, Mark had it brought to his attention by his 13-year-old, I think, earlier this morning. Well, certainly we appreciate the efforts of the group, Invisible Children, to shine a light on the horrible atrocities of the LRA. As you know, there are neighboring states, there are NGO groups who have been working on this problem for decades, and we, of course, are very much involved in trying to support all the states of East and Central

Africa. We have a multifaceted strategy to work on this, including, as you know, we now have special forces advisors working to train some of the neighboring states in their efforts to get a handle on this awful, awful problem.

QUESTION: And if I could just follow up, the film makes a point that they are doing this now because the U.S. – they say the U.S. could pull out these advisors that you cited at any moment. So they're trying to keep up the momentum. Is that a concern – a right concern on their part that these advisors could be moved out of Uganda?

MS. NULAND: I don't have any information to indicate that we are considering that, but that would be a question for the Pentagon. As you know, they've only been in for a couple of months, and we consider them a very important augmentation of our effort to help the East and Central African countries with this problem.

As you know, hundreds of people – hundreds and thousands of people around the world, especially young people, have been mobilized to express concern for the communities in Central Africa that have been placed under siege by the LRA. So the degree to which this YouTube video helps to increase awareness and increase support for the work that governments are doing, including our own government, that can only help all of us.

QUESTION: And just one more, if I may. Would an update on what these advisors are doing currently be more of a question for the Pentagon, or do you have a summary?

MS. NULAND: Well, we've spoken about this in general terms. If you need a detailed briefing, I'd send you to them. But we are not part of the fight ourselves. We're involved in training and supporting and providing advice to the forces of the governments of East and Central Africa that are engaged in the fight.

QUESTION: Are you concerned that this type of call, which takes viral form on the web and so on, might increase pressure for direct U.S. involvement in the fight for Kony rather than just providing the support that you mentioned?

MS. NULAND: I don't think anybody in the region favors that. What they have asked for is this logistical technical training support, and that is what we are providing. We are also helping them with their public information campaign. We are trying to get the word into these communities that if members of the LRA, whether they're pressed into service or whether they're volunteers, are ready to defect, that they'll have support in doing that, et cetera.

The March 8th daily press briefing demonstrated that the "Kony 2012" video did prompt the U.S. State Department to address the issue of American apathy in the past and the recent involvement of the U.S. government in finding a solution to the problem. The Department's spokeswoman even acknowledged that a 13-year-old brought the video to the attention of her colleague at the State Department.

A little over a month later on April 13, 2012, the "Kony 2012" video statistics from YouTube indicated a slight change in the audiences' demographics: the video was still most popular in the United States (and Canada) with females ages 13–17, but the second latest group was males ages 45–54, larger than the previous groups of males ages 18–24 and 13–17. (See Fig. 12.5).

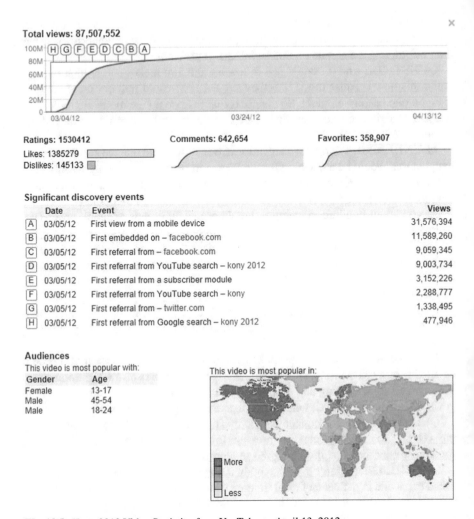

Fig. 12.5 Kony 2012 Video Statistics from YouTube on April 13, 2012

The new data implied that on the Internet, news of "Kony 2012" spread from the younger generation to the older generation. It explained why male ages 45–54 replaced male ages 18–24 as the second largest group of viewers after a month.

"No one wants a boring documentary on Africa," said filmmaker Jason Russell, co-founder of Invisible Children who spent years making the documentary. "Maybe we have to make it pop, and we have to make it cool. We view ourselves as the Pixar of human rights stories" (52).

Ben Keesey, Invisible Children's CEO, acknowledged to *The Wall Street Journal* that the video was made to appeal to children. Kessey admitted in an interview, "How do we make this translate to a 14-year-old who just walked out of algebra class?" (56).

Notwithstanding the video's serious subject matter, "Kony 2012" succeeded in drawing the initial massive wave of attention from the younger generation, mostly teenagers and college students ages 13 and above, who do care about human rights and social issues to the extent that they want to share the news with all their friends on Facebook and Twitter.

12.4 Reactions to Kony 2012

Skeptic Andrew Keen voiced his concerns on CNN, "In a post-era world of 'Kony2012,' with its harrypotterfication of reality and its transformation of Africa from a complex, infinitely nuanced society into a manichaean Madison Avenue fantasy of good and evil, are we all now becoming teenagers? Should we really be empowering children to make moral decisions about a world in which they have little experience? Should we entrust the innocent, that 'bunch of littles' who have made 'Kony2012' such an instant hit, to architect our brave new connected world?" (57).

No amount of skepticism can change the fact that the younger generation is a powerful force to be reckoned with in the Internet age. Nevertheless, both children and adults can be equally susceptible to well-crafted propaganda and disinformation, as Journalist Matthew Ingram thoughtfully questioned, "Is Kony2012 a sign of how powerful social media can be as a news distribution mechanism, a sign of how dangerous it can be, or both?" (58).

On the heels of the phenomenal public attention of "Kony 2012," Sheila Lyall Grant and Huberta von Voss-Wittig, wives of the British and German ambassadors to the United Nations, posted a 4-minute video on YouTube to ask the viewers to petition Asma al-Assad for peace in Syria (59). The April 16, 2012 video juxtaposed glamorous pictures of Syria's first lady Asma al-Assad against disturbing images of dead and injured Syrian children (60). Grant and Voss-Wittig urged Asma to help end the bloodshed in her country (61): "Stand up for peace … for the sake of your people. … No one cares about your image. We care about your action" (62). The YouTube video encouraged the public to sign the petition and spread the word on Facebook, Twitter, and LinkedIn (63).

Social media has become a powerful information distribution mechanism. Information is power; and with power comes responsibility.

12.5 SOPA/PIPA Blackout Day

The MPAA and RIAA called the SOPA/PIPA blackout on January 18, 2012 an "abuse of power" when Wikipedia, Reddit, WordPress, *Wired*, *Boing Boing*, Mozilla, Google, Flickr, and other websites went dark or posted anti-SOPA/PIPA messages on their homepages that reach out to more than 1 billion people (64).

In May 2011, Vermont Senator Patrick Leahy and 15 bipartisan co-sponsors in the U.S. Senate introduced PIPA, the PROTECT IP (Preventing Real Online Threats to Economic Creativity and Theft of Intellectual Property) Act (65). PIPA would enhance enforcement against rogue websites operated and registered overseas, and would eliminate the financial incentive to steal intellectual property online.

The Senate Judiciary Committee unanimously passed the PIPA bill, but Oregon Senator Ron Wyden placed a hold on it, citing that the overreaching legislation poses a significant threat to Internet commerce, innovation, and free speech. Wyden issued a press release on May 26, 2011, "I understand and agree with the goal of the legislation, to protect intellectual property and combat commerce in counterfeit goods, but I am not willing to muzzle speech and stifle innovation and economic growth to achieve this objective. At the expense of legitimate commerce, PIPA's prescription takes an overreaching approach to policing the Internet when a more balanced and targeted approach would be more effective. The collateral damage of this approach is speech, innovation and the very integrity of the Internet" (66).

A group of 55 high-profile venture capitalists also opposed the PIPA bill. They wrote a letter to the U.S. Congress in June 2011 to express their concerns: "As investors in technology companies, we agree with the goal of fostering a thriving digital content market online. Unfortunately, the current bill will not only fail to achieve that goal, it will stifle investment in Internet services, throttle innovation, and hurt American competitiveness. ... The entire set of issues surrounding copyright in an increasingly digital world are [sic] extremely complex, and there are no simple solutions. These challenges are best addressed by imagining, inventing, and financing new models and new services that will allow creative activities to thrive in the digital world. There is a new model for financing, distributing, and profiting from copyrighted material and it is working – just look at services like iTunes, Netflix, Pandora, Kickstarter, and more. Pirate web sites will always exist, but if rights holders make it easy to get their works through innovative Internet models, they can and will have bright futures" (67).

Undeterred by the oppositions, the U.S. Chamber of Commerce sent a letter to the U.S. Congress in support of the PIPA legislation. Signed in September 2011 by an impressive list of 360 businesses and professional organizations, the letter read, "IP-intensive industries are a cornerstone of the U.S. economy, employing more than 19 million people and accounting for 60 percent of exports. Rampant online counterfeiting and piracy presents a clear and present threat to American jobs and innovation. A study examined approximately 100 rogue sites and found that these sites attracted more than 53 billion visits per year, which average out to approximately nine visits for every man, woman, and child on Earth. Global sales of counterfeit goods via the Internet from illegitimate retailers reached $135 billion in 2010. The theft of American IP is the theft of American jobs" (68).

The U.S. Chamber of Commerce list of 360 included industry heavyweights and household names such as 3M, American Society of Composers, Authors and Publishers (ASCAP), Broadcast Music, Inc. (BMI), Dolby Laboratories, Electronic Arts, Harley-Davidson, Motion Picture Association of America (MPAA), National Basketball Association (NBA), National Football League (NFL), Nike, Nintendo,

Pfizer, Philip Morris, Ralph Lauren, Recording Industry Association of America (RIAA), Reebok, Revlon, Rite Aid, Rolex, SESAC, Sony, The Dow Chemical Company, The Walt Disney Company, Tiffany & Co., Time Warner, Toshiba, Viacom, Walmart, World Wrestling Entertainment (WWE), and Xerox.

Texas Representative Lamar S. Smith agreed with the U.S. Chamber of Commerce. In October 2011, Smith and a bipartisan group of lawmakers in the U.S. House of Representatives introduced the Stop Online Piracy Act (SOPA), a bill that would expand the authority of U.S. law enforcement to shut down websites that offer pirated content such as music, films, software, and other intellectual properties (69). SOPA's goal was "to promote prosperity, creativity, entrepreneurship, and innovation by combating the theft of U.S. property, and for other purposes" (70). The bill would also provide immunity for a service provider, payment network provider, Internet advertising service, advertiser, Internet search engine, domain name registry, or domain name registrar for voluntarily blocking access to or ending financial affiliation with an Internet site that offers pirated content.

Although the objective of SOPA was indisputable, the content of the bill generated a huge backlash. "There is no need for a bill this sweeping and this Draconian," said Gigi B. Sohn, president and co-founder of Public Knowledge. "There are simple, easily implemented solutions on which industry and others agree – such as cutting off the ability of credit-card companies to fulfill payments to sites that traffic in copyright infringement. At a time when Congress and the Obama Administration are trying to cut back on sweeping, overbroad regulation, we are disappointed that House Judiciary Committee Chairman Lamar Smith and his co-sponsors have chosen this means of establishing a vast new regulatory regime over the Internet" (71).

In November 2011, AOL, eBay, Facebook, Google, LinkedIn, Mozilla, Twitter, Yahoo!, and Zynga sent a joint letter to the U.S. Congress and placed a full-page ad in *The New York Times:*

"We support the bills' stated goals – providing additional enforcement tools to combat foreign 'rogue' websites that are dedicated to copyright infringement or counterfeiting. Unfortunately, the bills as drafted would expose law-abiding U.S. Internet and technology companies to new and uncertain liabilities, private rights of action, and technology mandates that would require monitoring of websites. We are concerned that these measures pose a serious risk to our industry's continued track record of innovation and job creation, as well as to our nation's cybersecurity. One issue merits special attention. We are very concerned that the bills as written would seriously undermine the effective mechanism Congress enacted in the Digital Millennium Copyright Act (DMCA) to provide a safe harbor for Internet companies that act in good faith to remove infringing content from their sites. Since their enactment in 1998, the DMCA's safe harbor provisions for online service providers have been a cornerstone of the U.S. Internet and technology industry's growth and jeopardize a foundational structure that has worked for content owners and Internet companies alike information lawfully online" (72).

Vint Cerf, one of the fathers of the Internet and now Google's vice president, provided scientific explanations for his objection to SOPA. In December 2011, Vint Cerf wrote Lamar S. Smith an open letter:

"I appreciate the opportunity to express my concerns about and opposition to the managers' amendment to the Stop Online Piracy Act (SOPA) and, in particular, the 'technological solutions' related to the Domain Name System (DNS) and search engines. … Even with the proposed manager's amendment, SOPA's site-blocking provisions remain problematic. They would undermine the architecture of the Internet and obstruct the 15 year effort by the public and private sectors to improve cybersecurity through implementation of DNSSEC, a critical set of extensions designed to address security vulnerabilities in the DNS. This collateral damage of SOPA would be particularly regrettable because site blocking or redirection mechanisms are unlikely to make a significant dent in the availability of infringing material and counterfeits online, given that DNS manipulation can be defeated by simply choosing an offshore DNS resolution provider, maintaining one's own local DNS cache or using direct IP address references. The search engine remedy also suffers from the fact that it will not be effective in preventing users' access to illegal, offshore websites. A congressional 'tech mandate' on search engines to delete a domain name from search results does not result in the website disappearing. Users can and do today find their way to these websites largely without the help of search engines. Relative to the questionable efficacy of this proposed remedy, requiring search engines to delete a domain name begins a worldwide arms race of unprecedented 'censorship' of the Web" (73).

Go Daddy, the world's largest ICANN-accredited registrar with 47 million domain names under its management, had been working with federal lawmakers for months to help craft revisions to SOPA. In contrast to Vint Cerf's viewpoints, Go Daddy's Executive Vice President and General Counsel Christine N. Jones testified before the U.S. House of Representatives Committee on the Judiciary on April 6, 2011:

"In 2010 alone, Go Daddy suspended approximately 150,000 websites found to be engaged in illegal or malicious activity. … We believe that DNS blocking, as opposed to DNS filtering, is a much more effective vehicle for removing illegal content from the Internet. DNS blocking is different from DNS filtering in that DNS blocking is action taken at the 'authoritative' or 'response' level of the DNS cycle. As such, it needs to be done by the registrar (which provides the authoritative DNS response), or, in cases where the registrar is unable or unwilling to comply, by the registry (which provides the Root zone file records – the database – for the entire TLD [Top-Level Domain]). Though a very similar technical process to DNS filtering, DNS blocking provides a much more thorough solution because it applies to all Internet users, regardless of which ISP they are a customer of or whether proxy services are used. Where DNS blocking is imposed, Internet users will not be able to access a ParaSite by any common means" (74).

Nonetheless, no revisions of SOPA and PIPA could quench the fierce opposition to the bills. After all, legislators are not scientists, and lawmakers are not expected to propose technical solutions to copyright infringement and counterfeiting.

Wikipedia's CEO Jimmy Wales (@jimmy_wales) tweeted that the Wikipedia domain names would move away from Go Daddy (75). Cheezburger's CEO Ben Huh announced they would be moving their 1,000+ registered domains elsewhere

(76). As a result of the aggressive anti-Go Daddy campaign, 21,000 domains trans-ferred out of Go Daddy in just 1 day (77). Bowing to boycott and criticism from high-profile clients, Go Daddy reluctantly reversed their stance and rescinded their support of SOPA on December 23, 2011 (78):

"Fighting online piracy is of the utmost importance, which is why Go Daddy has been working to help craft revisions to this legislation – but we can clearly do bet-ter," said Go Daddy CEO Warren Adelman, "It's very important that all Internet stakeholders work together on this. Getting it right is worth the wait. Go Daddy will support it when and if the Internet community supports it" (79).

The "when and if" did not happen. Instead, Internet businesses, big and small, were preparing for a "blackout" day on January 18, 2012 to protest SOPA and PIPA.

Chris Dodd, Connecticut Senator and CEO of the Motion Picture Association of America (MPAA), issued the following statement on January 17, 2012 to criticize the impending blackout (80):

"Only days after the White House and chief sponsors of the legislation responded to the major concern expressed by opponents and then called for all parties to work cooperatively together, some technology business interests are resorting to stunts that punish their users or turn them into their corporate pawns, rather than coming to the table to find solutions to a problem that all now seem to agree is very real and damaging. It is an irresponsible response and a disservice to people who rely on them for information and use their services. It is also an abuse of power given the freedoms these companies enjoy in the marketplace today. It's a dangerous and troubling development when the platforms that serve as gateways to information intentionally skew the facts to incite their users in order to further their corporate interests. A so-called 'blackout' is yet another gimmick, albeit a dangerous one, designed to punish elected and administration officials who are working diligently to protect American jobs from foreign criminals. It is our hope that the White House and the Congress will call on those who intend to stage this 'blackout' to stop the hyperbole and PR stunts and engage in meaningful efforts to combat piracy."

Dodd's pleading went unheeded. On January 18, 2012, the Internet revolted by staging the largest online protest in history. Over 115,000 websites participated in the strike by going dark and/or posting anti-SOPA messages on their homepages that reach out to more than 1 billion people (81). The largest participants included Google, Reddit, Craigslist, Wikipedia, WordPress, Mozilla, Tumblr, Cheezburger, Imgur, Pinterest, Flickr, and Amazon. (See Fig. 12.6).

Wikipedia displayed on its homepage, "Imagine a World Without Free Knowledge: For over a decade, we have spent millions of hours building the largest encyclopedia in human history. Right now, the U.S. Congress is considering legisla-tion that could fatally damage the free and open Internet. For 24 hours, to raise awareness, we are blacking out Wikipedia."

WordPress and *Wired* placed black "censored" bars over their blogs and stories. WordPress wrote, "Many websites are blocked out today to protest proposed U.S. legislation that threatens internet freedom: the Stop Internet Piracy Act (SOPA) and the Protect IP Act (PIPA). From personal blogs to Wikipedia, sites all over the

Fig. 12.6 Homepages of Wikipedia, WordPress, Wired, Google, Firefox, Cheezburger, Reddit, and Boing Boing on January 18, 2012.

web – including this one – are asking you to help stop this dangerous legislation from being passed."

Google added a black "censored" bar atop its logo as well as a link "Tell Congress: Please don't censor the web!" to the Google Public Policy Blog that said, "You might notice many of your favorite websites look different today. Wikipedia is down. WordPress is dark. We're censoring our homepage logo and asking you to petition Congress. So what's the big deal? Right now in Washington D.C., Congress is considering two bills that would censor the web and impose burdensome regulations on American businesses. They're known as the PROTECT IP Act (PIPA) in the Senate and the Stop Online Piracy Act (SOPA) in the House. ... Fighting online piracy is extremely important. We are investing a lot of time and money in that fight. ... Because we think there's a good way forward that doesn't cause collateral damage to the web, we're joining Wikipedia, Twitter, Tumblr, Reddit, Mozilla and other Internet companies in speaking out against SOPA and PIPA" (82).

Reddit remarked on its website, "SOPA and PIPA damage Reddit. Today we fight back. Today, for 12 hours, reddit.com goes dark to raise awareness of two bills in congress: H.R.3261 'Stop Online Piracy Act' and S.968 'PROTECT IP', which could radically change the landscape of the Internet. These bills provide overly broad mechanisms for enforcement of copyright which would restrict innovation and threaten the existence of websites with user-submitted content, such as reddit. Please take today as a day of focus and action to learn about these destructive bills and do what you can to prevent them from becoming reality."

Boing Boing displayed a "503: Service Unavailable" message with an explanation, "Boing Boing is offline today, because the US Senate is considering legislation that would certainly kill us forever. The legislation is called the PROTECT IP Act (PIPA), and would put us in legal jeopardy if we linked to a site anywhere online that had any links to copyright infringement. This would unmake the Web, just as proposed in the Stop Online Piracy Act (SOPA). We don't want that world."

Cheezburger popped up a huge panel with the message: "CHEEZBURGER NEEDS YOUR HELP. This and millions of other sites could be censored by the US government. A bill called PIPA proposed in the US Senate will cripple the Web – one of the biggest job-creating engines in America – and censor our online freedoms. It could mean the censoring of Cheezburger, Facebook, Wikipedia, and millions of others. It will mean censoring you. We need to tell our Senators that this bill needs to be stopped."

Mozilla redirected traffic from the Mozilla.org and Mozill.com for 12 hours to an action page that said, "Today Mozilla joins with other sites in a virtual strike to protest two proposed laws in the United States, called SOPA and the PROTECT IP Act. On January 24th, the U.S. Senate will vote on the PROTECT IP Act to censor the Internet, despite opposition from the vast majority of Americans. Join us to protect our rights to free speech, privacy, and prosperity."

The wide-scale Internet protest was a triumph. Two days after the blackout, the U.S. Congress shelved the PIPA and SOPA bills on January 20 (83).

12.6   Reactions to SOPA/PIPA Blackout

"The SOPA/PIPA blackout … was a whole new form of engagement and protest. I know that a lot of people in Hollywood were absolutely shocked at the effectiveness of that," said Marc Andreessen, co-founder of Netscape and venture capital firm Andreessen Horowitz that funded Facebook, Twitter, Zynga, Groupon, and Pinterest, and other Internet companies (84).

"With SOPA and PIPA," Google's co-founder Sergey Brin opined, "fears of piracy had reduced the entertainment industry to shooting itself in the foot, or maybe worse than in the foot" (85).

Google fights piracy in its own way by processing removal requests from copyright holders. In July 2014, Google's Transparency Report indicated that in the past month Google received from 4,625 copyright owners more than 29 million URLs requested to be removed from the Google search results (86).

Fred von Lohmann, senior copyright counsel at Google, said, "We believe that the time-tested 'notice-and-takedown' process for copyright strikes the right balance between the needs of copyright owners, the interests of users and our efforts to provide a useful Google Search experience" (87). For YouTube videos, copyright holders can submit copyright infringement notifications online or sign up for YouTube's Content Verification Program (88).

Sean Parker, co-founder of Napster and founding president of Facebook, told an audience at the 2012 South by Southwest conference in Austin, Texas, "The way online communities rose up to ultimately derail the Stop Online Piracy Act is heartening. … SOPA awakened that sleeping giant. There are a lot of really smart hackers in this audience. We need to put our heads together and take control of this [political] system … before the slow-thinking incumbents … know what's happening" (89).

Indeed, the effectiveness of the SOPA/PIPA blackout took Vermont Senator Patrick Leahy by surprise. As U.S. senators and representatives dropped their support of the anti-piracy bills after the blackout (90), Leahy retorted, "I understand and respect Majority Leader Reid's decision to seek consent to vitiate cloture on the motion to proceed to the PROTECT IP Act. But the day will come when the senators who forced this move will look back and realize they made a knee-jerk reaction to a monumental problem. Somewhere in China today, in Russia today, and in many other countries that do not respect American intellectual property, criminals who do nothing but peddle in counterfeit products and stolen American content are smugly watching how the U.S. Senate decided it was not even worth debating how to stop the overseas criminals from draining our economy" (91).

Cary H. Sherman, CEO of the Recording Industry Association of America (RIAA) that represents music labels, criticized the blackout tactic in *The New York Times*: "Wikipedia, Google and others manufactured controversy by unfairly equating SOPA with censorship. … The hyperbolic mistruths, presented on the home pages of some of the world's most popular Web sites, amounted to an abuse of trust and a misuse of power. … The violation of neutrality is a patent hypocrisy. … What the Google and Wikipedia blackout showed is that it's the platforms that exercise the real power. Get enough of them to espouse Silicon Valley's perspective, and tens of millions of Americans will get a one-sided view of whatever the issue may be, drowning out the other side" (92).

Whether we are for or against SOPA and PIPA, January 18, 2012 will forever be remembered as a historic day when the new-age Internet technology companies triumphed over the age-old entertainment industry.

12.7 Battles over Internet Legislations – OPEN, ACTA, CISPA, and Net Neutrality

With more than 50,000 people petitioned the Obama administration to veto the SOPA bill (93), the White House issued an official response on "We the People on WhiteHouse.gov:"

"While we believe that online piracy by foreign websites is a serious problem that requires a serious legislative response, we will not support legislation that reduces freedom of expression, increases cybersecurity risk, or undermines the dynamic, innovative global Internet. ... Moving forward, we will continue to work with Congress on a bipartisan basis on legislation that provides new tools needed in the global fight against piracy and counterfeiting, while vigorously defending an open Internet based on the values of free expression, privacy, security and innovation" (94).

While SOPA and PIPA have stalled indefinitely, California Representative Darrell Issa and Oregon Senator Ron Wyden have introduced the OPEN (Online Protection and Enforcement of Digital Trade) Act in the U.S. House of Representatives and the U.S. Senate respectively (95). The new bills are meant to deliver stronger intellectual property rights for American copyright holders while protecting the openness of the Internet.

Back in December 2011, AOL, eBay, Facebook, Google, LinkedIn, Mozilla, Twitter, Yahoo!, and Zynga sent an endorsement letter to Issa and Wyden to express their support of the OPEN Act (96). These were the same nine companies that opposed SOPA and PIPA.

In March 2012, Tiffiniy Cheng of Fight for the Future and Reddit co-founder Alexis Ohanian registered the domain name internetdefenseleague.org. Their new entity, Internet Defense League, announced in May their plan to defeat ACTA (Anti-Counterfeiting Trade Agreement) and CISPA (Cyber Intelligence Sharing and Protection Act).

Ohanian said, "You can only cry 'Oh my gosh, they're going to shut down the Internet' so often. We've scared [Congress] from doing anything as egregious as SOPA and PIPA again. But the new challenge is this endless series of smaller bills that try to unravel internet rights" (36).

To Obanian's disappointment, Facebook is one of the supporters of CISPA. Ohanian told CNN's Soledad O'Brien in a May 2012 interview, "One of the big issues that a lot of us in the tech community have had of late has been their support for bills like CISPA that make it really easy for companies like Facebook to hand over private data about us without any due process" (97). The Internet Defense League ensures that the battles over Internet legislations rage on.

Notwithstanding the ongoing battles over government legislations, America's largest Internet Service Providers (ISPs) have quietly begun implementing a "graduated response" antipiracy program on July 1, 2012 (98). The program requires Comcast, Cablevision, Time Warner Cable, Verizon, AT&T, and other ISPs to send out an educational notice to subscribers who download copyrighted content illegally. If a repeat infringer does not stop pirating, an ISP can apply "mitigation measures" such as throttling down the customer's Internet connection speed or suspending his or her account altogether.

Net neutrality has been a hotly debated topic in the past decades. Net neutrality is the principle that Internet service providers (ISPs) must treat all Internet communications equally regardless of users, content, equipment, and other factors. It would outlaw anti-competitive blocking and throttling of Internet services. California became the first state to pass a Net Neutrality law in 2018, but the U.S. Department of Justice (DOJ) filed a lawsuit against the state of California (99). The DOJ dropped the lawsuit in February 2021, allowing California to enforce the 2018 Net Neutrality law (100).

12.8   Peace on Facebook, Facebook Donate, and Community Help

Facebook's mission is "to give people the power to share and make the world more open and connected" (101). In January 2008, Facebook and ABC News cosponsored a Republican and a Democratic presidential debate in New Hampshire (102). "Through this partnership, we want to extend the dialogue both before and after the debate," said Dan Rose, Facebook's vice president for business development (103). "There are debates going on at all times within Facebook," David Westin, the president of ABC News and a new Facebook member, said. "This allows us to participate in those debates, both by providing information and by learning from the users." Although there were skeptics who believed that the Facebook/ABC News partnership was a failing concept out of the gate (104), experiments like it should be encouraged in order to foster more political activism among Facebook users.

In the realm of world peace, Facebook has a dedicated webpage titled "Peace on Facebook" https://www.facebook.com/peace/ to highlight Friends Without Borders, Invisible Children, One Million Voices Against FARC, The People's March Against Knife Crime, Stanford University's Peace Innovation, and other activism (105).

Facebook poses the same question every day in the users' own language: "Do you think we will achieve world peace within 50 years?" On August 14, 2014, the answer was a minuscule 5.41% in the United States (105). So Facebook is asking the follow-up question: "How can we grow this number?"

The Peace on Facebook webpage also displays statistics on friend connections created each day since November 5, 2011 between people of different regions, religions, and political affiliations. Figure 12.7 shows the daily friendships statistics in the past 24 hours for August 25, 2012. (Unfortunately, the interesting friendships statistics did not seem to be working anymore in August 2014.)

Besides world peace, Facebook has been involved with the rally against bullying (since 2011) (106), alerting Facebook users in the United States of their voting activities on the election day (since 2010) (107), and issuing AMBER Alerts in response to child abductions (since 2009) (108).

In partnership with Donate Life America, Mark Zuckerberg announced on May 1, 2012 that Facebook users could now identify themselves as potential organ donors on Facebook under the "Health & Wellness" section of the Life Event. "The Facebook partnership is an opportunity for people to share decisions," said David Fleming, CEO of Donate Life America, "The most important part of this is actually registering to be a donor so that your wishes can be carried out. Sharing that decision through Facebook is an opportunity to encourage your friends and family to also register" (109).

In December 2013, Facebook introduced the "Donate" button with 19 nonprofit launch partners including American Cancer Society, ASPCA, Boys & Girls Clubs of America, DonorsChoose.org, Girls Inc., Red Cross, St. Jude Children's Research

Geographic Friendships	Connections
India-Pakistan	180,625
Israel-Palestine	19,155
Albania-Serbia	19,109
Greece-Turkey	6,767

Religious Friendships	Connections
Muslim-Christian	118,454
Christian-Atheist	32,131
Muslim-Jewish	554
Sunni-Shiite	132

Political Friendships	Connections
U.S. Conservative/Liberal	7,885

Fig. 12.7 Facebook Daily Friendships Statistics on August 25, 2012

Hospital, UNICEF, Water.org, and World Wildlife Fund (110). Charities can apply for the Facebook Donate program (111) and "100% of the payment goes to the non-profit" (112).

In February 2017, Facebook launched "Community Help" in an effort to expand its Safety Check feature which allows friends to declare that they are safe after a disaster. "We want to create a space on Facebook…that connects communities in the aftermath of a crisis and helps people feel safe faster, recover, and rebuild," said Facebook Safety Check product designer Preethi Chetan (113). During the COVID-19 pandemic in 2020, Facebook's Community Help encourages neighbors to help each other by picking up groceries, asking someone to run an errand, or donating to fundraisers (114).

12.9   Internet Activism and Occupy Democracy

There are many Internet activist organizations in the United States. For example:

1. Co-founded by Sean Parker, former Facebook president, and Joe Green, former Harvard roommate of Mark Zuckerberg, Causes claims to be the world's largest online platform for activism and philanthropy (115). Since 2007, Causes has brought together 186 million members in 156 countries to take on 1 billion actions.
2. Acquired by Causes in January 2013 (116), Votizen enables users to unlock the potential of their social networks (Facebook, LinkedIn, and Twitter) to see how their friends vote, and to campaign for the candidates by making endorsements and bringing their friends to their side. Votizen has collected data from 200 million registered American voters. Co-founder Jason Putorti told *Business Insider*, "Votizen allows people to find voters in their social networks. Only half of people are registered, so it's actually non-trivial to know who votes, as well as see how they're registered and how frequently they vote in their districts. You can then campaign with them to elect the candidates you want to win in 2012 up and down ticket. The way I explain it to people is you're moving votes around that you can influence, so you can have a real impact not just where you live, but all over the country" (117).
3. Silicon Valley entrepreneurs Joan Blades and Wes Boyd founded MoveOn.org in 1998 in response to the impeachment of President Bill Clinton by the U.S. House of Representatives (118). With 8 million members as of August 2014, the online activist group offers "real Americans a voice in a political process where big money and corporate lobbyists wield too much influence" (119). In 2007, MoveOn.org launched a paid ad campaign on Facebook to protest against Facebook's Beacon advertisements for "glaring violation of [Facebook's] users' privacy" (120).
4. The Sunlight Foundation is a nonpartisan nonprofit founded in 2006 that uses the power of the Internet to catalyze greater government openness and transparency

(121). They provide software tools, open data, policy recommendations, journalism, and OpenGov Grants to expand citizen access to government information and to create accountability of public officials. The foundation's scope encompasses the U.S. Congress as well as government on the local, state, federal, and international level.

5. Created by David Wallechinsky, AllGov.com is an information repository about the business of government in the United States, France, and India (122). It details dozens of government agencies and names of hundreds of high-level government officials.

6. FWD.us is an immigration reform advocacy group led by Facebook CEO Mark Zuckerberg and entrepreneur Joe Green. In November 2013, FWD.us hosted a hackathon with DREAMers – undocumented immigrants who arrived in the United States as children and remain undocumented (123). And in January 2014, FWD.us launched the winning Push4Reform app aimed at helping supporters connect with Congress members and urge them to take action (124).

Internet activism (aka Web activism) is growing stronger by the number of causes, advocates, supporters, and philanthropists each day. For instance:

1. In October 2012 after 15-year-old Amanda Todd took her own life, the Anonymous hacktivist group tracked and exposed the man who allegedly posted the topless pictures and harassed the teenager via Facebook (125).

2. During the escalated Gaza-Israel conflict in November 2012 with deadly violence, the Israel Defense Forces (IDF) and the Palestinian Hamas made use of social media in an attempt to win over world sympathy (126). To wage peace, however, Israeli television producer Ido Simyoni started a project asking people to post anti-war photos on Instagram and tag them #stoptheterror (127).

3. Like the rest of the world, Beth Howard of Eldon, Iowa was horrified by the Sandy Hook Elementary School shooting on December 14, 2012 in Newtown, Connecticut. She told her Facebook friends about her plan to drive 1,100 miles to Newtown and hand out gift pies to grieving families. She received $2,000 in donations within two hours; and more than 60 volunteers helped with pie-baking. "They were making pies for Newtown because of this one Facebook comment," she said. "That was a powerful thing" (128).

4. Less than 48 hours after George Zimmerman was declared "Not Guilty" in July 2013, trial juror B37 had signed a book deal in the midst of public outrage. One person took to Twitter to call for literary agent Sharlene Martin to drop Zimmerman Juror B37: "Only thing I can think to do is flood Sharlene Martin's phone, email, and snail mail, w/ requests that she drop juror B37. That sound good?" The same activist also created a Change.org petition that received over a thousand supporters within minutes. Martin eventually caved in and said, "After careful consideration regarding the proposed book project with Zimmerman Juror B37, I have decided to rescind my offer of representation in the exploration of a book based upon this case" (129).

5. In October 2013, the Anonymous hacktivist group demanded an immediate investigation into the handling by local authorities regarding the case of Daisy

Coleman, the high schooler who said she was raped by a local football player. Anonymous said, "We have heard Daisy's story far too often. We heard it from Steubenville, Halifax and Uttar Pradesh. ... If Maryville won't defend these young girls, if the police are too cowardly or corrupt to do their jobs, if justice system has abandoned them, then we will have to stand for them" (130).

6. Phillip Atiba Goff, UCLA professor and president of the Center for Policing Equity, announced in May 2014 his plan to collect data for the nation's first database to track police stops and use of force. Goff said, "Using big data to analyze police behavior across the country is the first step in harnessing these powers to make our society fairer. Although this justice database will not end unfairness in policing, it might give us tangible benchmarks from which to work in our conversations about race in the U.S. And it will let us learn how to ask the right questions to reduce racial disparities" (131).

7. Consumers can use the Buycott app to organize their spending to help causes that they believe in (132). By simply scanning the barcode on a given product, the app traces the product's ownership back to its top parent company and cross-checks the company against the campaigns that the consumers have joined. Users can then make an informed decision to either support or avoid (i.e. buycott or boycott) the company. Go Daddy's reverse stance on SOPA in December 2011 clearly demonstrated that massive boycott is very effective.

8. In September 2014, a petition on Change.org gathered nearly 193,000 signatures to demand the ouster of Centerplate CEO Desmond Hague. He was caught by a security camera that showed him kicking a puppy repeatedly. The online petition resulted in his resignation (133).

Inspired by the grassroots Occupy Movement against social and economic inequality, former Vice President Al Gore told an overcrowded audience at the South by Southwest conference in Austin, Texas, in March 2012, "Our democracy has been hacked. It no longer works, in the main, to serve the best interests of the people of this country. I would like to see a new movement called Occupy Democracy, where people who have Internet savvy remedy this situation" (134). Former U.S. Secretary of Labor Robert Reich concurred, "Our democracy is increasingly being taken over by big money and that's wrong. ... We need to occupy democracy" (135).

12.10   Transnational (Arab-Israeli) Facebook Nation

The Internet has empowered individuals to start their own grassroots movements. Amid the longstanding Arab-Israeli conflict since 1920 that has taken more than 107,000 lives (136) and has cost more than $12 trillion dollars (137), Ronny Edry, an Israeli graphic designer based in Tel Aviv, reached out to the people of Iran on Facebook in March 2012. Edry and his wife uploaded posters on the Facebook page of Pushpin Mehina with the resounding message "IRANIANS. We will never bomb your country. We *Heart* You" (138).

Edry shared his Facebook experience: "My idea was simple, I was trying to reach the other side. There are all these talks about war, Iran is coming to bomb us and we bomb them back, we are sitting and waiting. I wanted to say the simple words that this war is crazy. In a few hours, I had hundreds of shares and thousands of likes. … I think it's really amazing that someone from Iran poked me and said 'Hello, I'm from Iran, I saw your poster on Facebook.' … I got a private message from Iran: 'We love you too. Your word reaches out there, despite the censorship. And Iranian people, aside from the regime, have no hard feelings or animosity towards anybody, particularly Israelis'" (139).

Iran's neighbor Pakistan has also banned Facebook for "hosting competitions featuring blasphemous caricatures." On the first annual "Draw Muhamad Day" on May 20, 2010, the Facebook ban was temporary and lasted for 12 days (140). On the second annual event on May 20, 2011, however, the Lahore High Court ordered permanent blockage to Facebook and all websites that "spread religious hatred" (141).

12.11   Internet Censorship in Western Democracies

Google released a Transparency Report in June 2012 showing an alarming rise in government censorship around the world. Google's senior policy analyst Dorothy Chou wrote, "We've been asked to take down political speech. It's alarming not only because free expression is at risk, but because some of these requests come from countries you might not suspect – Western democracies not typically associated with censorship" (142). Those countries included Canada, Czech Republic, Germany, Poland, Spain, the United Kingdom, and the United States.

Figure 12.8 shows the increasing number of content removal requests from the U.S. government from reporting period ending 12/31/2009 to ending 6/30/2013 (143). Figure 12.9 indicates a drastic increase by 100% in total requests from the U.S. government from mid-year 2016 to mid-year 2020; Figure 12.10 shows the reasons cited for content removal including national security, defamation, copyright, regulated goods and services, and privacy and security; and Figure 12.11 breaks down the affected Google products and services: approximately 50 % YouTube and 28 % Google Search. (144).

Twitter released its first Transparency Report on July 2, 2012 (145). Inspired by Google, Twitter aims to shed more light on government requests received for user information, government requests received to withhold content, and Digital Millennium Copyright Act (DMCA) takedown notices received from copyright holders. With data from January 1 to June 30, 2012, the Transparency Report revealed that an overwhelming 80% of the user information requests came from the United States, and Twitter provided the requested data 75% of the time. Japan came in a distant second, followed by Canada and the United Kingdom.

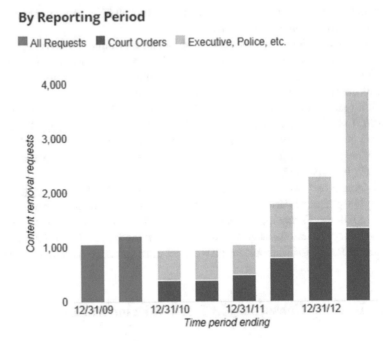

Fig. 12.8 Google Summary of All Requests to Remove Content by Reporting Period (Ending 12/31/2009 to Ending 6/30/2013)

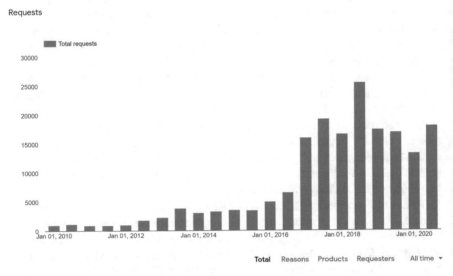

Fig. 12.9 Google Summary of All Requests to Remove Content by Reporting Period (From 01/01/2010 to 06/30/2020)

Reasons cited for content removal

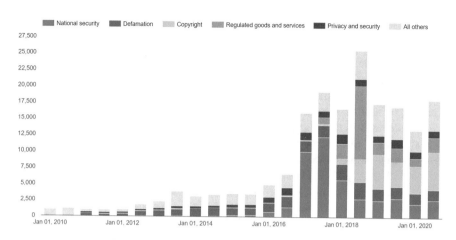

Fig. 12.10 Google Summary of All Reasons Cited for Content Removal by Reporting Period (From 01/01/2010 to 06/30/2020)

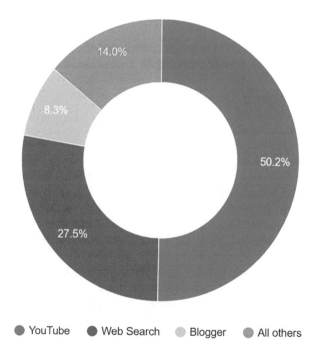

Fig. 12.11 Google's Top 3 Products and Services Cited in Government Requests (From 01/01/2010 to 06/30/2020)

In February 2021, the Indian government ordered Twitter to suspend more than 500 accounts links to farmers' protests on agricultural reforms (146). In April 2021 amid the surge in the coronavirus pandemic in India with a record 330,000 new COVID-19 cases a day, the Indian government ordered Twitter to take down tweets that were critical of its coronavirus handling (147).

Apple released its first Transparency Report on November 5, 2013. CNN's Heather Kelly summarized that "the United States submitted the most requests for account information, with 1,000 to 2,000 requests regarding 2,000 to 3,000 individual accounts. These requests might be for personal information found in iTunes, Game Center and iCloud accounts. ... Germany made the second largest number of device requests, followed by Singapore" (148). However, Apple conceded that "at the time of this report, the U.S. government does not allow Apple to disclose, except in broad ranges, the number of national security orders, the number of accounts affected by the orders, or whether content, such as emails, was disclosed. We strongly oppose this gag order, and Apple has made the case for relief from these restrictions in meetings and discussions with the White House, the U.S. Attorney General, congressional leaders, and the courts. Despite our extensive efforts in this area, we do not yet have an agreement that we feel adequately addresses our customers' right to know how often and under what circumstances we provide data to law enforcement agencies" (149).

"The only security of all is in a free press," said President Thomas Jefferson, American Founding Father and principal author of the Declaration of Independence. "The force of public opinion cannot be resisted when permitted freely to be expressed" (150). Nevertheless, democratic governments have increasingly been securitizing journalists and reporters.

In 2012, the U.S. Justice Department secretly collected two months of telephone records for reporters and editors at The Associated Press (AP). In an outraged letter to Attorney General Eric Holder, AP's President and CEO Gary Pruitt wrote, "These records potentially reveal communications with confidential sources across all of the newsgathering activities undertaken by the AP during a two-month period, provide a road map to AP's newsgathering operations and disclose information about AP's activities and operations that the government has no conceivable right to know. ... We regard this action by the Department of Justice as a serious interference with AP's constitutional rights to gather and report the news" (151)·

In 2013, *The Guardian* in London destroyed the hard drives containing top-secret documents leaked by Edward Snowden after a threat of legal action by the British government (152). The U.K. authorities detained Glenn Greenwald's partner David Miranda for nine hours as Miranda passed through London's Heathrow airport on this way home to Rio de Janeiro. Officials questioned him under Schedule 7 of the Terrorism Act 2000 (153) and confiscated his personal electronics including his mobile phone, laptop, camera, memory sticks, DVDs, and games consoles (154).

12.12   Internet Censorship in China

Unlike Western democracies, communist China made no content removal request to Google. Instead, China opts for preemptive measures and imposes severe Internet censorship by banning Facebook, YouTube, Twitter, and Snapchat as well as censoring search results and content from Google, Yahoo!, MSN, Baidu, and LinkedIn (155). "This is due to specific requirements within China to block certain content so that it does not appear on our network in that country," explained a LinkedIn message (156).

Although Skype is not banned in China, Chinese users must use a modified version of Skype (previously known as Tom-Skype) that follows Chinese regulations. Tom-Skype sent chat logs to the Chinese government server if certain keywords were typed (157). The new modified Skype has a new user interface created in partnership with Guangming Founder Information Technology (Beijing) Ltd. Co. (GMF) (158).

In June 2006, Paris-based Reporters Without Borders identified Yahoo! as the "strictest" search engine censor in China (159). In March 2010 when Google ceased filtering its search results in China (160), the search giant had to scale back operations in China and redirect users from Google.cn to its uncensored Google.com.hk in Hong Kong (161). In May 2011, eight New York residents filed a lawsuit against Baidu for aiding Chinese censorship in spite of the fact that Baidu is operating in China in full compliance with the Chinese laws (162).

Weibo, a Chinese counterpart of Twitter, had 61.4 million daily active users in December 2013 (163). The Chinese authorities are censoring the rumbustious microblogs by 24/7 monitoring, blacklisting users, deleting illegal or harmful posts, and intercepting messages with Deep Packet Inspection (164). In response, Weibo users have become skillful at evading censorship by inventing codewords and nicknames such as "Teletubby" for China's Prime Minister Wen Jiabao (165). Government censorship has forced Chinese activists to use increasingly obscure Internet memes and coded language on social media. In the diminishing returns of tricking China's censors, the practice is isolating the activists from the people that they are hoping to reach (166).

WeChat, a hugely popular Chinese microblogging service, offers greater privacy and variety of mobile apps than rival Weibo. It too has been adversely affected by China's censorship crackdown in March 2014 when a number of public pages maintained by prominent activists went dark permanently (167).

Dissident artist Ai Weiwei, who was jailed for 81 days for supporting Arab-style protests in China, wrote in *The Guardian*, "Chairman Mao used to say: 'As communists we gain control with the power of the gun and maintain control with the power of the pen.' You can see propaganda and the control of ideology as an authoritarian society's most important task. … Censorship is saying: 'I'm the one who says the last sentence. Whatever you say, the conclusion is mine.' But the internet is like a tree that is growing. The people will always have the last word – even if someone has a very weak, quiet voice. … The internet is a wild land with its own games, languages and gestures through which we are starting to share common feelings. But the [Chinese] government cannot give up control. It blocks major internet platforms – such as Twitter and Facebook – because it is afraid of free discussion. And it deletes information. … China may seem quite successful in its controls, but it has only raised the water level. It's like building a dam: it thinks there is more water so it will build it higher. But every drop of water is still in there. It doesn't understand how to let the pressure out. … But in the long run, its leaders must understand it's not possible for them to control the internet unless they shut it off – and they can't live with the consequences of that. The internet is uncontrollable. And if the internet is uncontrollable, freedom will win" (168).

12.13   Arab Spring Uprisings, Egypt, Syria, Sandi Arabia, Turkey, and Myanmar

Social media has played a vital role in Arab Spring uprisings including the 2011 Egyptian revolution (169). Activists organized through Facebook and Twitter the nationwide protests on January 28, 2011 to call for an end to President Hosni Mubarak's government (170).

Mubarak reacted by blocking social media sites and mobile phone networks. A day before the planned demonstrations, the Egyptian government began to shut down Internet access nationwide. By midnight January 28, virtually all of Egypt's Internet addresses were unreachable (171). Unprecedented in the history of the Internet, Egypt had successfully shut down 88% of the Egyptian Internet and 9 out of 10 Internet Service Providers (ISPs) (172).

Google responded to the Internet blockade by working with Twitter and SayNow to unveil a web-free speak-to-tweet service (Speak2Tweet), allowing anyone to send and receive tweets by calling a phone number (173).

Mubarak's totalitarian action failed to thwart the planned demonstrations. Fourteen days later on February 11, 2011, Mubarak resigned as president. In May 2011, a judge in Cairo found Mubarak and two officials guilty of "causing damage to the national economy" for cutting cellphone and Internet services during the protests in January (174). Mubarak was fined $33.6 million. Approximately $16.8 million would be paid to telecommunications companies that were forced to suspend their services during the revolution.

In November 2012, more than 90% of the Internet access in Syria was shut down by the government in an attempt to limit the dissemination of images and videos taken by the opposition activists. U.S. Ambassador to Syria Robert Ford said, "The Syrian government has been monitoring [the Internet] for years. They have been using the Internet with Iranian assistance to track opposition activists, arrest and kill them. That is the reason why our non-lethal assistance to the Syrian opposition, we put a special emphasis on communications equipment precisely to help the Syrian people tell the world what is going on inside Syria" (175). Google also pitched in by offering the Speak2Tweet service in Syria (176).

In April 2013, Saudi Arabia's Communications and Information Technology Commission threatened to block messaging applications Skype, Viber, and WhatsApp in order to force the apps to comply with government rules. "I believe a big part of the reason why this is happening … is because lots of demonstrations that were organized in Saudi Arabia were done through the use of WhatsApp," explained Eman Al-Nafjan, a prominent blogger in Saudi Arabia (177).

In March 2014, Turkey's prime minister Recep Tayyip Erdogan vowed to "eradicate" Twitter and to shut down Facebook and YouTube in an attempt to block embarrassing leaks of government corruption (178). As Turkish Internet users began to experience widespread Twitter disruption on March 20, Twitter swiftly offered subscribers a workaround using cell phone instant messaging: "Turkish users: you can send Tweets using SMS. Avea and Vodafone text START to 2444. Turkcell text START to 2555" (179). The following day on March 21, Hillary Clinton (@HillaryClinton) tweeted, "The freedom to speak out & to connect is a fundamental right. The people of Turkey deserve that right restored. #TwitterisblockedinTurkey" (180)

In June 2014 during the intensifying conflict in Iraq, many Iraqis could not get on Facebook and Twitter, but they were able to use the Whisper app to share real-time information anonymously. Before the media could confirm the U.S. embassy's partial staff relocation, a whisper was posted online: "US embassy in Baghdad is evacuating!!! Yepppppppp!!!!" (181).

In April 2021, Myanmar's military junta cut all wireless Internet services in a concerted effort to control communications and messaging of pro-democracy demonstrators who were protesting against the military for overthrowing the elected government (182).

Time after time, social media and the Internet are viewed as a serious threat to dictators and, conversely, a liberating platform for democracy.

12.14   The Rise of Facebook Nation

Elsewhere in Norway, Christine Bar and Lili Hjonnevag posted on Facebook a call to assemble a choir in downtown Oslo in protest against mass murderer Anders Behring Breivik (183). Bar and Hjonnevag expected a few dozen responses, but 4,000 people accepted their Facebook invitation, and a mass choir of 40,000 braved the pouring rain and gathered at Oslo's Youngstorget square on April 26, 2012 (184). Artist Lillebjørn Nilsen led the choir to sing the song "Children of the Rainbow" (Barn av regnbuen) in protest of Breivik who cited in court that the song was an example of Marxist influence on Norwegian children.

On April 30, 2012, 9-year-old Martha Payne in Scotland started blogging about her school lunches, rating and photographing each meal (185). Payne's blog, NeverSeconds, attracted international attention from schoolchildren, parents, and even British celebrity chef Jamie Oliver who sent a tweet to Payne's father, "Shocking but inspirational blog. Keep going, Big love from Jamie x" (186). Payne also raises money for Mary's Meals that sets up school feeding projects in the world's poorest communities. However, Scotland local government Argyll and Bute Council banned Payne from taking pictures in the dining hall for the reason of "unwarranted attacks on its schools catering service which culminated in national press headlines which have led catering staff to fear for their jobs" (186). Payne's supporters wrote many encouraging comments such as "you are an inspiration, bless you for being upfront and honest and not afraid to speak up" and "the world needs your voice; don't let a couple of frightened adults silence you." Amid mounting public criticism of government censorship, Argyll and Bute Council eventually withdrew the ban.

In May 2012, Manal al-Sharif, co-founder of the Women2Drive campaign, received the Václav Havel Prize for Creative Dissent at the Oslo Freedom Forum (187). Advocating for women's right to drive in Saudi Arabia, Al-Sharif filmed herself a year earlier in May 2011 driving through the Saudi city of Khobar, and posted the video on YouTube and Facebook. In her Havel Prize acceptance speech, Al-Sharif said, "We are only a drop in this world … but the rain starts with a single drop" (188).

In June 2012, *Time Magazine*'s congressional correspondent Jay Newton-Small asked the Syrian dissident Abu Ghassan whether his AK-47 or his video camera was the more powerful weapon. Ghassan replied, "My AK!" But he paused for a few seconds, and said, "Actually, if there is an Internet connection, my camera is more powerful" (189). Partially aided by the Internet Freedom Grants from the U.S. State Department, Syrian rebels have been filming the protests and posting them on the Internet (190).

In April 2014, Mozilla cofounder and CEO Brendan Eich resigned over anti-same-sex-marriage controversy, just 10 days after his promotion to chief executive officer (191). Gay rights activists took to blogs and Twitter to express outrage over Eich's donation to the 2008 California Proposition 8 campaign to ban same-sex marriage in the state. Online dating site OkCupid joined the protests and asked its users to boycott Mozilla's Firefox browser (192).

In the same month of April, advertising technology firm RadiumOne's board of directors reluctantly fired its founder, chairman, and CEO Gurbaksh Chahal after a social media firestorm (193). Chahal pleaded guilty to domestic violence and battery charges for assaulting his girlfriend. Although the RadiumOne board members were unanimously supportive of Chahal, the uproar in the press and social media proved to be a potent backlash that led to his termination 10 days after his guilty pleas (194).

Social networks have been playing an important role everywhere in the world with no exception. With the rise of Facebook nation with billions of people connected to the Internet, the World Wide Web is an open platform for debates of opposing views and an outlet for unpopular voices. "What makes the Internet so great is that it's interactive," AllGov.com editor-in-chief David Wallechinsky told CNN in a 2014 interview. "You can see opposing sources – if you know how to use it" (195).

Internet activism, spearheaded by private individuals as well as organizations, is becoming a driving force for peace and justice around the world regardless of the ruling regimes. Facebook is helping to spread the news more than ever. Facebook executive Justin Osofsky reported that "on average referral traffic from Facebook to media sites has increased by over 170% throughout the past year. In fact, from September 2012 to September 2013, TIME's referral traffic has increased 208%, BuzzFeed is up 855%, and Bleacher Report has increased 1,081%" (196).

Online news is indeed a major contributing factor to the rise of Facebook Nation. In February 2021, Facebook clashed with the Australian government over a proposed law that would require the social media giant to pay publishers for their news. Facebook flexed its muscles by blocking users from sharing news in Australia and inadvertently banning Facebook pages of fire services and public charities (197).

Foodbank Australia CEO Brianna Casey tweeted in anguish, "This is UNACCEPTABLE. Demand for food relief has never been higher than during this pandemic, and one of our primary comms tools to help connect people with #foodrelief info & advice is now unavailable. Hours matter when you have nothing to eat. SORT THIS OUT! #facebooknewsban." (See Fig. 12.12)

Australian Prime Minister Scott Morrison also said in response, "These actions will only confirm the concerns that an increasing number of countries are expressing about the behavior of Big Tech companies who think they are bigger than governments and that the rules should not apply to them. They may be changing the world, but that doesn't mean they run it" (198).

Indeed, Facebook has the power to change the world for the better or for worse. In March 2018, whistleblower Christopher Wylie disclosed that the British political consulting firm Cambridge Analytica purchased Facebook data on tens of millions of Americans without their knowledge in order to build a "psychological warfare tool" on behalf of clients who intended to interfere in the 2016 U.S. presidential election in Donald Trump's favor (199).

The revelation sparked outrage from Facebook users, lawmakers, privacy advocates, and media pundits. As a result, Facebook CEO Mark Zuckerberg faced U.S. Congress for the first time in April 2018 over the data sharing scandal when he testified, "It was my mistake, and I'm sorry. I started Facebook, I run it, and I'm responsible for what happens here. It's clear now that we didn't do enough to prevent these tools from being used for harm. That goes for fake news, foreign interference in elections, and hate speech, as well as developers and data privacy" (200).

12.15 Electoral College, Social Network Constitution, and Cyber Civil Rights

During the sentencing of former Trump campaign adviser Rick Gates, Federal Judge Amy Berman Jackson said, "Politics don't corrupt people, people corrupt politics" (201). When politicians are not doing their jobs, grassroots campaigns can help put issues and people on the public agenda. Although Web activism has

← **Thread**

Brianna Casey
@briannacasey1   ...

This is UNACCEPTABLE. Demand for food relief has
never been higher than during this pandemic, and one
of our primary comms tools to help connect people
with #foodrelief info & advice is now unavailable. Hours
matter when you have nothing to eat. SORT THIS OUT!
#facebooknewsban.

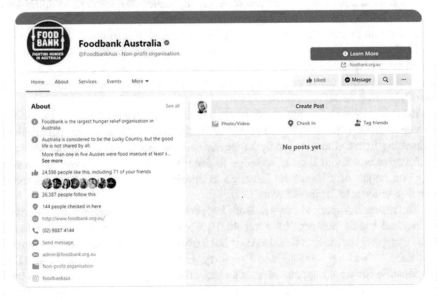

5:14 PM · Feb 17, 2021 · TweetDeck

Fig. 12.12 Foodbank Australia CEO Brianna Casey Tweeted about Facebook News Ban.

generated public awareness and achieved some significant results, believing that the
Internet empowers each and every individual is somewhat naive.

In the United States of America, the Electoral College, not the American voters,
directly elects the President and Vice President of the United States. Known as indi-
rect election, 538 electors from 50 states and the District of Columbia represent
some 200 million registered American voters in a U.S. presidential election.
Unbeknownst to many voters, Americans cast their ballots for presidential and vice
presidential candidates by voting for correspondingly pledged electors. Despite its
rarity, some electors can be either unpledged or faithless, and they can ignore the

popular votes altogether. A presidential candidate can win the election but lose the popular vote, or vice versa.

Similarly, the Internet is becoming the online equivalent of the Electoral College. Google, Facebook, Twitter, Wikipedia, YouTube, and other high-traffic websites are the online electors representing the voices of individuals, businesses, and special interest groups. These electors are capable of exerting great influences on politics, as we have witnessed in the SOPA/PIPA blackout.

Cary H. Sherman, CEO of the Recording Industry Association of America (RIAA), described the SOPA/PIPA blackout as "the digital tsunami that swept over the Capitol ... forcing Congress to set aside legislation to combat the online piracy of American music, movies, books and other creative works, raised questions about how the democratic process functions in the digital age" (92).

Political strategist and Internet consultant Wesley Donehue warned of the influence of social media in America: "Well for starters, we don't live in a democracy. We never have, nor should we. We live in a republic, where we elect people to take the tough votes and make the tough decisions for us. ... Too many politicians aren't voting their conscience, they're voting to placate blog commenters, and that's no way to run government. ... Technology has expedited our descent toward a political system devoid of real ideas and bold, controversial thought" (202).

Why is it that technology is often the one to blame? On the contrary, social media encourages people to "think aloud" and come up with bold, new, controversial, or opposing ideas. Bloggers make certain that the political process is no longer confined to "backroom deal-making in a smoke-filled room." Chinese scholar Chen Zhiwu at Yale University wrote, "Microblogs are the best weapon to reduce corruption, improve social governance and make officials behave well" (203). The United States is light years ahead of China in democracy. Facebook nation will certainly transform the republic in the years to come. Nonetheless, Donehue's controversial and thought-provoking statement is a wake-up call for Americans to examine and comprehend the all-important U.S. Constitution.

Prof. Lori B. Andrews at Chicago-Kent College of Law suggested that since Facebook has become as big and powerful as a country, it is high time that its citizens got a "Social Network Constitution" that governs in minute detail what a social network should or should not do (204):

"We the people of Facebook Nation, in order to form a more Perfect Internet, to protect our fundamental rights and freedoms, to explore our identities, dreams, and relationships, to safeguard the sanctity of our digital selves, to ensure equal access to technology, to lessen discrimination and disparities, and to promote democratic principles and the general welfare, declare these truths to be self-evident:

1. The Right to Connect.
2. The Right to Free Speech and Freedom of Expression.
3. The Right to Privacy of Place and Information.
4. The Right to Privacy of Thoughts, Emotions and Sentiments.
5. The Right to Control One's Image.
6. The Right to Fair Trial.

7. The Right to an Untainted Jury.
8. The Right to Due Process of Law and the Right to Notice.
9. Freedom from Discrimination.
10. Freedom of Association" (205).

The Social Network Constitution would give us the ammunition to mandate Internet businesses to behave constitutionally. Moreover, government legislations affecting Facebook nation would be tested on the ground of being constitutional. Take the case of Malcolm Harris as an example. In February 2012, the District Attorney's Office in Manhattan issued Twitter a subpoena to ask for three months of information connected to the Twitter account that belongs to Harris, who was arrested and charged with disorderly conduct on the Brooklyn Bridge for the Occupy Wall Street protest (206). In May 2012, Twitter filed a motion in New York state court seeking to quash the court order for turning over the requested information: "If the Fourth Amendment's warrant requirement applies merely to surveillance of one's location in public areas for 28 days, it also applies to the District Attorney's effort to force Twitter to produce over three months worth of a citizen's substantive communications, regardless of whether the government alleges those communications are public or private" (207).

American Civil Liberties Union (ACLU) applauded Twitter's decision: "This is a big deal. … If Internet users cannot protect their own constitutional rights, the only hope is that Internet companies do so. … That is why it is so important to encourage those companies that we all increasingly rely on to do what they can to protect their customers' free speech and privacy rights" (208).

ACLU proposes that companies who are stewards of our digital lives should (209):

1. Tell you when the government is asking for your information so that you can protect yourself;
2. Disclose how often they share information with the government;
3. Stand up for user privacy in the courts and in Congress;
4. Advocate for an update to the outdated Electronic Privacy Communications Act (ECPA) which was passed in 1986 before the Internet as we know it today existed.

In the age of big data and prevalence of Google search, nonconsensual disclosure of naked images as in "revenge porn" is a growing problem. Prof. Danielle Keats Citron from the University of Maryland wrote an opinion piece on CNN, "A new law in Israel makes it a sex crime to post sexual pictures or videos to the Internet without the consent of the person featured in them. We need to follow that example. … Because searches of victims' names display their naked images, they lose their jobs. Schools have fired teachers whose naked photos appeared on revenge porn sites. … We need a 'cyber civil rights' agenda to combat bigoted online abuse. The criminalization of nonconsensual disclosure of someone's naked images is an important part of that agenda" (210).

In January 2014, Hunter Moore, founder of a now-defunct revenge porn website, was indicted for peddling hundreds of nude pictures without obtaining permission, and for hacking into people's email accounts to steal nude photos to post online (211).

In May 2014, Argentine model María Belén Rodríguez took to the Supreme Court of Argentina to sue Google and Yahoo! over images of her that link to porn sites. The European Court agreed and ruled that search engines can be forced to erase links to content about individuals on the Web (212).

These are some baby steps in the right direction for cyber civil rights. One may ponder the bigger question: What will the Constitution be like if the people governed by the Constitution get to create it themselves?

References

1. **Allen, Erika Tyner.** The Kennedy-Nixon Presidential Debates, 1960. [Online] The Museum of Broadcast Communications. [Cited: April 10, 2012.] http://www.museum.tv/eotvsection. php?entrycode=kennedy-nixon.

2. **Vargas, Jose Antonio.** Obama Raised Half a Billion Online. [Online] The Washington Post, November 20, 2008. http://voices.washingtonpost.com/44/2008/11/20/ obama_raised_half_a_billion_on.html.

3. —. Obama's Wide Web: From YouTube to Text Messaging, Candidate's Team Connects to Voters. [Online] The Washington Post, August 20, 2008. http://www.washingtonpost.com/ wp-dyn/content/story/2008/08/19/ST2008081903613.html.

4. **McGirt, Ellen.** How Chris Hughes Helped Launch Facebook and the Barack Obama Campaign. [Online] Fast Company, April 1, 2009. http://www.fastcompany.com/maga-zine/134/boy-wonder.html.

5. **Schiffman, Betsy.** The Reason for the Obama Victory: It's the Internet, Stupid. [Online] Wired, November 7, 2008. http://www.wired.com/epicenter/2008/11/the-obama-victo/.

6. **Obama, Barack.** @BarackObama. [Online] Twitter, November 5, 2008. http://twitter. com/#!/barackobama/statuses/992176676.

7. **Weiner, Rachel.** Change.Gov Launched. [Online] The Huffington Post, December 7, 2008. http://www.huffingtonpost.com/2008/11/06/changegov-launched_n_141822.html.

8. **The Office of the President-Elect.** Open Government. [Online] change.gov, November 2008. http://change.gov/content/home.

9. **Lothian, Dan and Brittain, Becky.** Obama hosts Google 'hangout'. [Online] CNN, January 30, 2012. http://www.cnn.com/2012/01/30/politics/obama-google/index.html.

10. **The White House.** The White House. [Online] whitehouse.gov. [Cited: April 9, 2012.] http:// www.whitehouse.gov.

11. **United States Department of Justice.** FOIA. [Online] FOIA.gov. [Cited: April 9, 2012.] http://www.foia.gov/.

12. **FOIA Update.** The Freedom of Information Act 5 U.S.C. § 552, As Amended By Public Law No. 104-231, 110 Stat. 3048. FOIA Update. Vol. XVII, No. 4. [Online] United States Department of Justice, Fall 1996. http://www.justice.gov/oip/foia_updates/Vol_XVII_4/ page2.htm.

13. **FOIA Update. Vol. XVII, No. 4.** Congress Enacts FOIA Amendments. [Online] United States Department of Justice, Fall 1996. http://www.justice.gov/oip/foia_updates/Vol_ XVII_4/page1.htm.

14. **United States Senate.** E-Government Act of 2002. [Online] National Archives. [Cited: April 10, 2012.] http://www.archives.gov/about/laws/egov-act-section-207.html.

15. **Data.gov.** About data.gov. [Online] Data.gov. [Cited: March 23, 2012.] http://www.data. gov/about.

16. **McCormack, Dermont.** Web 2.0: 2003-'08 AC (After Crash): The Resurgence of the Internet & E-Commerce. [Online] Aspatore Books, June 15, 2002. http://www.worldcat.org/title/ web-20-2003-08-ac-after-crash-the-resurgence-of-the-internet-e-commerce/oclc/51057025.

17. **O'Reilly, Tim.** What Is Web 2.0. Design Patterns and Business Models for the Next Generation of Software. [Online] O'Reilly, September 30, 2005. http://oreilly.com/web2/ archive/what-is-web-20.html.

18. **Obama, Barack.** 2011 State of the Union Address. [Online] PBS, January 25, 2011. http:// www.pbs.org/newshour/interactive/speeches/4/2011-state-union-address/.

19. **Sabochik, Katelyn.** Petition the White House with We the People. [Online] The White House, September 22, 2011. http://www.whitehouse.gov/blog/2011/09/22/ petition-white-house-we-people.

20. **Scherer, Michael.** Why the White House Loves Your Death Star Petition. [Online] TIME Magazine, January 31, 2013. http://swampland.time.com/2013/01/31/we-the-people/2/.

21. **Ferenstein, Gregory.** Inspired By "Facebook Nation," Obama's Chief Disruptor Brings Startup Culture To The Gov't. [Online] Fast Company, October 24, 2011. http://www.fast-company.com/1790016/steven-vanroekel-cio.

22. **Curtis, Colleen.** State of the Union 2012: We Want to Hear From You. [Online] The White House Blog, January 20, 2012. http://www.whitehouse.gov/blog/2012/01/20/ state-union-2012-we-want-hear-you.

23. **CIA.** We can neither confirm nor deny that this is our first tweet. [Online] Twitter, June 6, 2014. https://twitter.com/CIA/status/474971393852182528.

24. **Wemple, Erik.** Want to talk to the CIA? Tweet @CIA. [Online] The Washington Post, June 6, 2014. http://www.washingtonpost.com/blogs/erik-wemple/wp/2014/06/06/ want-to-talk-to-the-cia-tweet-cia/.

25. **AnalyzeThe.US.** Frequently Asked Questions. [Online] Palantir. [Cited: July 8, 2014.] https://analyzethe.us/faq.

26. **Scherer, Michael.** How Obama's data crunchers helped him win. [Online] CNN, November 8, 2012. http://www.cnn.com/2012/11/07/tech/web/obama-campaign-tech-team/index.html.

27. **Ferenstein, Gregory.** Obama's chief tech officer: Let's unleash ingenuity of the public. [Online] CNN, June 14, 2012. http://www.cnn.com/2012/06/14/tech/web/white-house-tech-officer/index.html.

28. **The White House.** Presidential Innovation Fellows: Open Data Initiatives. [Online] WhiteHouse.gov. [Cited: June 14, 2012.] http://www.whitehouse.gov/innovationfellows/ opendata.

29. **Manyika, James, et al.** Open data: Unlocking innovation and performance with liquid information. [Online] McKinsey & Company, October 2013. http://www.mckinsey.com/insights/business_technology/ open_data_unlocking_innovation_and_performance_with_liquid_information.

30. **The White House Office of Science & Technology Policy.** Fact Sheet: White House Safety Datapalooza. [Online] The White House, January 14, 2014. http://www.whitehouse.gov/ sites/default/files/microsites/ostp/safety_datapalooza_factsheet_jan-2014.pdf.

31. **Chokkattu, Julian.** US National Archives To Upload All Holdings To Wikimedia Commons. [Online] TechCrunch, June 30, 2014. http://techcrunch.com/2014/06/30/ us-national-archives-to-upload-all-holdings-to-wikimedia-commons/.

32. **Kuhn, Eric.** Mayor digs in after Twitter appeal. [Online] CNN, January 3, 2010. http://politi-calticker.blogs.cnn.com/2010/01/03/mayor-digs-in-after-twitter-appeal/.

33. **SeeClickFix.** About SeeClickFix. [Online] SeeClickFix. [Cited: August 14, 2014.] http:// www.seeclickfix.com/about.

34. **The Mayor's Office of New Urban Mechanics in Boston.** About Street Bump. [Online] Street Bump. [Cited: August 14, 2014.] http://www.streetbump.org/about.

35. **Sutter, John D.** Cities embrace mobile apps, 'Gov 2.0'. [Online] CNN, December 29, 2009. http://www.cnn.com/2009/TECH/12/28/government.web.apps/index.html.

36. **Greenberg, Andy.** Reddit's Alexis Ohanian And Activists Aim To Build A 'Bat-Signal For The Internet'. [Online] Forbes, May 25, 2012. http://www.forbes.com/sites/andygreen-berg/2012/05/25/reddit-founder-and-activists-aim-to-build-a-bat-signal-for-the-internet/.

37. **DiscoverBPS.** Welcome to Boston Public Schools Registration. [Online] DiscoverBPS. [Cited: August 14, 2014.] http://www.discoverbps.org/.

38. **Adopt a Hydrant.** Adopt a Hydrant. [Online] Code for America and Built in Boston. [Cited: August 14, 2014.] http://adoptahydrant.org/.

39. **Pahlka, Jennifer.** To fix government, call in the geeks. [Online] CNN, March 25, 2012. http://www.cnn.com/2012/03/25/opinion/pahlka-code-government/index.html.

40. **Sunlight Foundation.** Sunlight Data Services. [Online] Sunlight Foundation. [Cited: August 14, 2014.] http://sunlightfoundation.com/api/.

41. **Cantor, Eric.** Congressional Facebook Developer Hackathon. [Online] Office of the Majority Leader, December 7, 2011. http://majorityleader.gov/Facebook/.

42. **CNN Staff.** Feds launch smartphone app to nab child sexual predators. [Online] CNN, September 12, 2013. http://www.cnn.com/2013/09/12/tech/ice-phone-app-child-sex-predator/index.html.

43. **Benoit, David.** Mark Zuckerberg's Letter From The Facebook Filing. [Online] The Wall Street Journal, February 1, 2012. http://blogs.wsj.com/deals/2012/02/01/mark-zuckerbergs-letter-from-the-facebook-filing/.

44. **Newsom, Gavin and Dickey, Lisa.** Citizenville. [Online] Penguin, February 7, 2013. http://www.penguin.com/book/citizenville-by-gavin-newsom/9781594204722.

45. **Castellanos, Alex.** California discovers gold again. [Online] CNN, April 22, 2013. http://www.cnn.com/2013/04/22/opinion/castellanos-california-gold/index.html.

46. **Blake, Aaron.** Gridlock in Congress? It's probably even worse than you think. [Online] The Washington Post, May 29, 2014. http://www.washingtonpost.com/blogs/the-fix/wp/2014/05/29/gridlock-in-congress-its-probably-even-worse-than-you-think/.

47. **Wong, Julia Carrie.** Congress grills Facebook CEO over data misuse – as it happened. [Online] The Guardian, April 10, 2018. https://www.theguardian.com/technology/live/2018/apr/10/mark-zuckerberg-testimony-live-congress-facebook-cambridge-analytica.

48. **Invisible Children Inc.** KONY 2012. [Online] YouTube, March 5, 2012. http://www.you-tube.com/watch?v=Y4MnpzG5Sqc.

49. **Fantz, Ashley.** 'Stop Kony' video goes viral, puts spotlight on Ugandan war-lord. [Online] CNN, March 7, 2012. http://news.blogs.cnn.com/2012/03/07/viral-video-puts-spotlight-on-ugandan-warlord/.

50. **Bell, Emily.** I am watching #Kony2012 ' my 11 yr old. [Online] Twitter, March 8, 2012. https://twitter.com/#!/emilybell/status/177736783289794560.

51. **Jarvis, Jeff.** @emilybell I found out about #kony2012 from my daughter's Facebook page. [Online] Twitter, March 8, 2012. https://twitter.com/#!/jeffjarvis/status/177743392942473217.

52. **Kron, Josh and Goodman, J. David.** Online, a Distant Conflict Soars to Topic No. 1. [Online] The New York Times, March 8, 2012. http://www.nytimes.com/2012/03/09/world/africa/online-joseph-kony-and-a-ugandan-conflict-soar-to-topic-no-1.html?pagewanted=all&_r=0.

53. **Goodman, David J. and Preston, Jennifer.** How the Kony Video Went Viral. [Online] The New York Times, March 9, 2012. http://thelede.blogs.nytimes.com/2012/03/09/how-the-kony-video-went-viral/.

54. **NBC Universal.** Hollywood Reacts To 'Kony 2012' Video. [Online] Access Hollywood, March 8, 2012. http://www.accesshollywood.com/justin-bieber/kim-kardashian-justin-bieber-and-more-tweet-support-for-kony-2012-movement_article_61715.

55. **Nuland, Victoria.** Daily Press Briefing. Washing, DC. March 8, 2012. [Online] U.S. Department of State, March 8, 2012. http://www.state.gov/r/pa/prs/dpb/2012/03/185423.htm.

56. **Orden, Erica and Steel, Emily.** How 'Kony' Clip Caught Fire Online. [Online] The Wall Street Journal, March 9, 2012. http://online.wsj.com/article/ SB10001424052970204781804577271692294533870.html.

57. **Keen, Andrew.** Opinion: After Kony, should kids decide our morals? [Online] CNN, March 14, 2012. http://www.cnn.com/2012/03/14/opinion/keen-kony-2012/index.html.

58. **Ingram, Matthew.** Kony2012: New Media Success Story or Cautionary Tale? [Online] Bloomberg Businessweek, March 12, 2012. http://www.businessweek. com/articles/2012-03-12/tc-gigaom-0312-kony2012-new-media-success-story-or-cautionary-tale/.

59. **Roth, Richard.** Wives of U.N. diplomats tell Syria's first lady to 'stop being a bystander'. [Online] CNN, April 18, 2012. http://www.cnn.com/2012/04/18/world/meast/syria-un-wives/index.html.

60. **Women of the World.** International Letter & Petition to Asma al-Assad. [Online] YouTube, April 16, 2012. http://www.youtube.com/watch?v=SzUViTShIAo.

61. **Kekeh, Nicole.** After Kony 2012, Now Asma 2012? [Online] Forbes, April 18, 2012. http:// www.forbes.com/sites/worldviews/2012/04/18/after-kony-2012-now-asma-2012/.

62. **Associated Press.** Ambassadors' wives urge Syrian president's wife to 'stop your husband,' lobby for peace. [Online] The Washington Post, April 17, 2012. http://www.washington-post.com/world/middle_east/ambassadors-wives-urge-syrian-presidents-wife-to-stop-your-husband-lobby-for-peace/2012/04/17/gIQAvSbEOT_story.html.

63. **Women of the World.** Asma Al-Assad: Call for peace in Syria. [Online] Change.org, April 18, 2012. http://www.change.org/petitions/asma-al-assad-call-for-peace-in-syria.

64. **PC Magazine editors.** SOPA/PIPA Blackout Day. [Online] PC Magazine. [Cited: April 17, 2012.] http://www.pcmag.com/slideshow_viewer/0,3253,l%253D292984%2526a%25 3D292997%2526po%253D1,00.asp.

65. **Senate Judiciary Committee.** To prevent online threats to economic creativity and theft of intellectual property, and for other purposes. [Online] U.S. Government Printing Office (GPO), May 26, 2011. http://www.gpo.gov/fdsys/pkg/BILLS-112s968rs.

66. **Wyden, Ron.** Wyden Places Hold on Protect IP Act. Overreaching Legislation Still Poses a Significant Threat to Internet Commerce, Innovation and Free Speech. [Online] U.S. Senate, May 26, 2011. http://wyden.senate.gov/newsroom/press/release/?id=33a39533-1b25-437b-ad1d-9039b44cde92.

67. **55 Venture Capitalists.** Letter to U.S. Congress in Opposition of Legislation. [Online] Net-VCLetterRePIPA, June 23, 2011. https://docs.google.com/document/d/14CkX3zDyAxShrq UqEkewtUCjvvFdciIbKjC18_eUHkg/edit?hl=en_US&authkey=CNHr3I4L&pli=1.

68. **U.S. Chamber of Commerce.** Letter to Congress in Support of Legislation. [Online] U.S. Chamber of Commerce Global Intellectual Property Center, September 22, 2011. http:// www.theglobalipcenter.com/sites/default/files/pressreleases/letter-359.pdf.

69. **Kang, Cecilia.** House introduces Internet piracy bill. [Online] The Washington Post, October 6, 2011. http://www.washingtonpost.com/blogs/post-tech/post/house-introduces-internet-piracy-bill/2011/10/26/gIQA0f5xJM_blog.html.

70. **House Judiciary Committee.** H.R. 3261 - Stop Online Piracy Act. [Online] U.S. House of Representatives, October 26, 2011. http://judiciary.house.gov/hearings/pdf/112%20HR%20 3261.pdf.

71. **Sohn, Gigi B.** Public Knowledge Sees Dangers In New Intellectual Property Bill. [Online] Public Knowledge, October 26, 2011. http://www.publicknowledge.org/ public-knowledge-sees-dangers-new-intellectual-pro.

72. **Doctorow, Cory.** Internet giants place full-page anti-SOPA ad in NYT. [Online] BoingBoing, November 16, 2011. http://boingboing.net/2011/11/16/internet-giants-place-full-pag.html.

73. **McCullagh, Declan.** Vint Cerf: SOPA means 'unprecedented censorship' of the Web. [Online] CNet, December 15, 2011. http://news.cnet.com/8301-31921_3-57344028-281/ vint-cerf-sopa-means-unprecedented-censorship-of-the-web/.

74. **Jones, Christine N.** Hearing on "Promoting Investment and Protecting Commerce Online: Legitimate Sites v. Parasites, Part II". [Online] U.S. House of Representatives. Committee on the Judiciary, April 6, 2011. http://judiciary.house.gov/hearings/pdf/Jones04062011.pdf.

75. **Wales, Jimmy.** @jimmy_wales. [Online] Twitter, December 23, 2011. https://twitter.com/#!/jimmy_wales/status/150287579642740736.

76. **Kumparak, Greg.** Cheezburger's Ben Huh: If GoDaddy Supports SOPA, We're Taking Our 1000+ Domains Elsewhere. [Online] TechCrunch, December 22, 2011. http://techcrunch.com/2011/12/22/cheezburgers-ben-huh-if-godaddy-supports-sopa-were-taking-our-1000-domains-elsewhere/.

77. **Weinstein, Natalie.** 21,000 domains transfer out of Go Daddy in 1 day. [Online] CNet, December 24, 2011. http://news.cnet.com/8301-1023_3-57348183-93/21000-domains-transfer-out-of-go-daddy-in-1-day/.

78. **McCullagh, Declan.** GoDaddy bows to boycott, now 'opposes' SOPA copyright bill. [Online] CNet, December 29, 2011. http://news.cnet.com/8301-31921_3-57349913-281/godaddy-bows-to-boycott-now-opposes-sopa-copyright-bill/.

79. **Go Daddy.** Go Daddy No Longer Supports SOPA. [Online] Go Daddy News Releases, December 23, 2011. http://www.godaddy.com/newscenter/release-view.aspx?news_item_id=378.

80. **Dodd, Chris.** A statement by Senator Chris Dodd, Chairman and CEO of the Motion Picture Association of America, Inc. (MPAA) on the so-called "Blackout Day" protesting anti-piracy legislation. [Online] Motion Picture Association of America, January 17, 2012. http://www.mpaa.org/resources/c4c3712a-7b9f-4be8-bd70-25527d5dfad8.pdf.

81. **Fight For The Future 2012.** The January 18 Blackout / Strike. [Online] Fight for the Future. [Cited: April 17, 2012.] http://sopastrike.com/numbers/.

82. **Drummond, David.** Don't censor the web. [Online] Google Public Policy Blog, January 18, 2012. http://googlepublicpolicy.blogspot.com/2012/01/dont-censor-web.html.

83. **Yu, Roger.** Congress shelves anti-piracy bills. [Online] USA Today, January 20, 2012. http://www.usatoday.com/tech/news/story/2012-01-20/anti-piracy-bills-halted/52698192/1.

84. **Taylor, Colleen.** How Marc Andreessen makes Silicon Valley magic. [Online] Gigaom, February 2, 2012. http://gigaom.com/2012/02/02/marc-andreessen-horowitz-silicon-valley-startups/.

85. **Katz, Ian.** Web freedom faces greatest threat ever, warns Google's Sergey Brin. [Online] The Guardian, April 15, 2012. http://www.guardian.co.uk/technology/2012/apr/15/web-freedom-threat-google-brin.

86. **Google.** Google Removal Requests. [Online] Google. [Cited: August 14, 2014.] http://www.google.com/transparencyreport/removals/copyright/.

87. **Goldman, David.** Google kills 250,000 search links a week. [Online] CNNMoney, May 24, 2012. http://money.cnn.com/2012/05/24/technology/google-search-copyright/index.htm.

88. **Google.** Copyright Infringement Notification. [Online] YouTube. [Cited: May 27, 2012.] http://www.youtube.com/t/dmca_policy.

89. **Gross, Doug.** Gore, Parker urge Web to 'Occupy Democracy'. [Online] CNN, March 12, 2012. http://www.cnn.com/2012/03/12/tech/web/gore-parker-sxsw/index.html.

90. **OpenCongress.** Protect IP Act Senate whip count. [Online] The OpenCongress Wiki, January 24, 2012. http://www.opencongress.org/wiki/Protect_IP_Act_Senate_whip_count.

91. **Leahy, Patrick.** Comment Of Senator Patrick Leahy On Postponement Of The Vote On Cloture On The Motion To Proceed To The PROTECT IP Act. [Online] U.S. Senate Press Releases, January 20, 2012. http://www.leahy.senate.gov/press/press_releases/release/?id=467fb8f0-828d-403c-9b7b-8bf42d583c3e.

92. **Sherman, Cary H.** What Wikipedia Won't Tell You. [Online] The New York Times, February 7, 2012. http://www.nytimes.com/2012/02/08/opinion/what-wikipedia-wont-tell-you.html.

93. **U.S. Petitioners.** VETO the SOPA bill and any other future bills that threaten to diminish the free flow of information. We the People. Your Voice in Our Government. [Online]

whitehouse.gov, December 18, 2011. https://wwws.whitehouse.gov/petition-tool/peti-tion/veto-sopa-bill-and-any-other-future-bills-threaten-diminish-free-flow-information/g3W1BscR.

94. **Espinel, Victoria, Chopra, Aneesh and Schmidt, Howard.** Combating Online Piracy while Protecting an Open and Innovative Internet. We the People. Your Voice in Our Government. [Online] whitehouse.gov. [Cited: April 17, 2012.] https://wwws.whitehouse.gov/petition-tool/response/combating-online-piracy-while-protecting-open-and-innovative-internet.

95. **DesMarais, Christina.** SOPA, PIPA Stalled: Meet the OPEN Act. [Online] PCWorld, January 21, 2012. http://www.pcworld.com/article/248525/sopa_pipa_stalled_meet_the_open_act.html.

96. **Keeptheweb#OPEN.** Big Web Companies OPEN Endorsement Letter. [Online] Keeptheweb#OPEN, December 13, 2011. http://keepthewebopen.com/assets/pdfs/12-13-11%20Big%20Web%20Companies%20OPEN%20Endorsement%20Letter.pdf.

97. **Greenberg, Andy.** Reddit Founder Says He Won't Buy Facebook's Stock Due To Its CISPA Support. [Online] Forbes, May 7, 2012. http://www.forbes.com/sites/andygreen-berg/2012/05/07/reddit-founder-says-he-wont-buy-facebooks-stock-due-to-its-cispa-support/.

98. **Sandoval, Greg.** RIAA chief: ISPs to start policing copyright by July 1. [Online] CNet, March 14, 2012. http://news.cnet.com/8301-31001_3-57397452-261/riaa-chief-isps-to-start-policing-copyright-by-july-1/.

99. **Kelly, Heather.** California just passed its net neutrality law. The DOJ is already suing. [Online] CNN Business, October 1, 2018. https://www.cnn.com/2018/10/01/tech/california-net-neutrality-law.

100. **BEAM, ADAM.** Federal judge says California can enforce net neutral-ity law. [Online] AP News, February 23, 2021. https://apnews.com/article/california-enforce-net-neutrality-judge-5b40eea8c05c78225bad0bcc8290d88b.

101. **Facebook.** About Facebook. [Online] Facebook, February 4, 2004. https://www.facebook.com/facebook/info.

102. **McCullagh, Declan.** Facebook co-sponsors N.H. debate, not with-out controversy. [Online] CNet, January 3, 2008. http://www.cnet.com/news/facebook-co-sponsors-n-h-debate-not-without-controversy/.

103. **Stelter, Brian.** ABC News and Facebook in Joint Effort to Bring Viewers Closer to Political Coverage. [Online] The New York Times, November 26, 2007. http://www.nytimes.com/2007/11/26/technology/26abc.html.

104. **Hopkins, Mark Rizzin.** ABC News + Facebook = Epic Fail. [Online] Mashable, November 26, 2007. http://mashable.com/2007/11/26/abc-news-facebook-epic-fail/.

105. **Facebook.** Peace on Facebook. [Online] Facebook. [Cited: August 14, 2014.] https://www.facebook.com/peace/.

106. **Time Warner Inc.** Facebook and Time Warner Inc. Launch Stop Bullying: Speak Up App. [Online] Time Warner Press Releases, September 19, 2011. http://www.timewarner.com/newsroom/press-releases/2011/09/Facebook_and_Time_Warner_Inc_Launch_Stop_Bullying_Speak_Up_App_09-19-2011.php.

107. **Chang, Jonathan.** How voters turned out on Facebook. [Online] Facebook Data Team, November 4, 2010. http://www.facebook.com/notes/facebook-data-team/how-voters-turned-out-on-facebook/451788333858.

108. **AMBER Alert.** About AMBER Alert on Facebook. [Online] Facebook, December 30, 2009. http://www.facebook.com/AMBERalert/info.

109. **Almasy, Steve.** Facebook encouraging organ donations. [Online] CNN, May 1, 2012. http://www.cnn.com/2012/05/01/health/facebook-organ-donors/index.html.

110. **Constine, Josh.** Facebook Launches "Donate" Button For Non-Profits That Also Collects Billing Info For Itself. [Online] TechCrunch, December 16, 2013. http://techcrunch.com/2013/12/16/facebook-donate-now-button/.

111. **Facebook.** Donate: Nonprofit Interest Form. [Online] Facebook. [Cited: April 25, 2014.] https://www.facebook.com/help/contact/585894954798346.

112. **Kelly, Meghan.** Facebook launches 'Donate' button; won't take a cut of the payments. [Online] VentureBeat, December 16, 2013. http://venturebeat.com/2013/12/16/facebook-donate-button/.

113. **Constine, Josh.** Facebook Safety Check now lets locals find and offer Community Help like shelter. [Online] TechCrunch, February 8, 2017. https://techcrunch.com/2017/02/08/community-help/.

114. **Yurieff, Kaya.** Facebook feature lets neighbors volunteer to help each other during pandemic. [Online] CNN Business, March 31, 2020. https://www.cnn.com/2020/03/31/tech/facebook-community-help-coronavirus/index.html.

115. **Causes.** About Causes. [Online] Causes. [Cited: August 14, 2014.] http://www.causes.com/about.

116. **Constine, Josh.** Causes Acquires Votizen To Democratize Democracy. [Online] TechCrunch, January 10, 2013. http://techcrunch.com/2013/01/10/causes-acquires-votizen/.

117. **Dickinson, Boonsri.** Votizen Wants To Use Social Networks To Revolutionize Politics. [Online] Business Insider, April 9, 2012. http://articles.businessinsider.com/2012-04-09/tech/31311939_1_politics-social-networks-users.

118. **Blades, Joan and Boyd, Wes.** MoveOn's 50 Ways to Love Your Country. [Online] MoveOn.org. [Cited: August 14, 2014.] http://civic.moveon.org/book//excerpt.html.

119. **MoveOn.org.** What is MoveOn™? [Online] MoveOn.org. [Cited: August 14, 2014.] http://www.moveon.org/about.html.

120. **McCarthy, Caroline.** MoveOn.org takes on Facebook's 'Beacon' ads. [Online] CNet, November 20, 2007. http://news.cnet.com/8301-13577_3-9821170-36.html.

121. **Sunlight Foundation.** Our Mission. [Online] Sunlight Foundation. [Cited: April 25, 2014.] http://sunlightfoundation.com/about/.

122. **Wallechinsky, David.** Everything Our Government Really Does. [Online] AllGov.com. [Cited: April 25, 2014.] http://www.allgov.com/.

123. **Green, Joe.** A DREAMer Hackathon for Immigration Reform. [Online] FWD.us, October 18, 2013. http://www.fwd.us/dreamer_hackathon.

124. **Segall, Laurie.** Immigration reform? There's an app for that. [Online] CNNMoney, January 23, 2014. http://money.cnn.com/2014/01/23/technology/social/fwdus-immigration-app/index.html.

125. **Ryall, Jenni.** Anonymous outs bully they claim drove Amanda Todd to suicide, mum says leave her family alone. [Online] Herald Sun, October 17, 2012. http://www.heraldsun.com.au/news/world/online-bully-victim-amanda-todd-still-tormented-in-death/story-fnd134gw-1226497411838.

126. **Hachman, Mark.** IDF vs. Hamas War Extends to Social Media. [Online] PC Magazine, November 16, 2012. http://www.pcmag.com/slideshow/story/305065/idf-vs-hamas-war-extends-to-social-media.

127. **CNN iReport.** As Twitter war rages, #stoptheterror Instagrams aim to wage peace. [Online] CNN, November 19, 2012. http://www.cnn.com/2012/11/19/world/meast/irpt-storify-stop-the-terror/index.html.

128. **Drash, Wayne.** Bringing healing to Newtown, one pie at a time. [Online] CNN, December 19, 2012. http://eatocracy.cnn.com/2012/12/19/bringing-healing-to-newtown-one-pie-at-a-time/.

129. **David D.** Here's The Story Of The Twitter Hero Who Single-Handedly Killed Zimmerman Juror B37's Book Deal. [Online] Uproxx Web Culture, July 16, 2013. http://uproxx.com/webculture/2013/07/persistent-tweeter-ends-juror-b37s-book-deal/.

130. **Leopold, Todd.** Why Anonymous wants justice in the Missouri rape case. [Online] CNN, October 16, 2013. http://www.cnn.com/2013/10/16/tech/web/anonymous-maryville-rape-case/.

131. **Goff, Phillip Atiba.** Can big data transform social justice? [Online] CNN, May 2, 2014. http://www.cnn.com/2014/05/02/opinion/goff-big-data/index.html.

132. **Buycott.** FAQ. [Online] Buycott. [Cited: August 13, 2014.] http://www.buycott.com/about.

133. **Isidore, Chris.** Dog-kicking video costs CEO his job. [Online] CNNMoney, September 3, 2014. http://money.cnn.com/2014/09/03/news/companies/dog-kicking-ceo/index.html.

134. **Healey, Jon.** Al Gore, Sean Parker call for 'Occupy Democracy' movement online. [Online] Los Angeles Times, March 13, 2012. http://opinion.latimes.com/opinionla/2012/03/al-gore-and-sean-parker-do-sxsw.html.

135. **#OccupyDemocracy.** #OccupyDemocracy. [Online] Public Campaign Action Fund. [Cited: August 14, 2014.] http://occupydemocracy.org/.

136. **The American-Israeli Cooperative Enterprise.** The Arab-Israeli Conflict: Total Casualties (1920-2012). [Online] Jewish Virtual Library. [Cited: April 20, 2012.] http://www.jewishvirtuallibrary.org/jsource/History/casualtiestotal.html.

137. **Strategic Foresight Group.** Cost of Conflict in the Middle East. [Online] Strategic Foresight Group Report Excerpts, January 2009. http://www.strategicforesight.com/Cost%20of%20Conflict%20-%206%20pager.pdf.

138. **Mehina, Pushpin.** IRANIANS. We will never bomb your country. We *Heart* You. [Online] Facebook. [Cited: April 20, 2012.] http://www.facebook.com/pushpin.

139. **Said, Samira.** Peace-minded Israeli reaches out to everyday Iranians via Facebook. [Online] CNN, March 20, 2012. http://www.cnn.com/2012/03/19/world/meast/israel-iran-social-media/index.html.

140. **Khan,   Habibullah.**   Facebook   Banned   in   Pakistan.   [Online]   ABC News,   May   19,   2010.   http://abcnews.go.com/Technology/International/facebook-banned-pakistan-prophet-muhammad-sketch-competition/story?id=10688625.

141. **Staff Report.** Facebook to be blocked. [Online] Pakistan Today, September 19, 2011. http://www.pakistantoday.com.pk/2011/09/19/uncategorized/facebook-to-be-blocked/.

142. **Chou, Dorothy.** More transparency into government requests. [Online] Google Official Blog, June 17, 2012. http://googleblog.blogspot.com/2012/06/more-transparency-into-government.html#!/2012/06/more-transparency-into-government.html.

143. **Google.** Google Transparency Report. [Online] Google. [Cited: June 22, 2014.] http://www.google.com/transparencyreport/removals/government/.

144. **Google Transparency Report.** Government requests to remove content. [Online] Google. [Cited: April   2,   2021.]   https://transparencyreport.google.com/government-removals/overview.

145. **Kessel, Jeremy.** Twitter Transparency Report. [Online] Twitter Blog, July 2, 2012. http://blog.twitter.com/2012/07/twitter-transparency-report.html.

146. **Singh, Manish.** Twitter suspends over 500 accounts in India after government warning. [Online] TechCrunch, February 9, 2021. https://techcrunch.com/2021/02/09/twitter-takes-actions-on-over-500-accounts-in-india-amid-government-warning/.

147. **—.** India orders Twitter to take down tweets critical of its coronavirus handling. [Online] TechCrunch, April 24, 2021. https://techcrunch.com/2021/04/24/india-orders-twitter-to-take-down-tweets-critical-of-its-coronavirus-handling/.

148. **Kelly, Heather.** Apple releases its first transparency report. [Online] CNN, November 6, 2013. http://www.cnn.com/2013/11/05/tech/social-media/apple-transparency-report/index.html.

149. **Apple.** Report on Government Information Requests. [Online] Apple, November 5, 2013. https://www.apple.com/pr/pdf/131105reportongovinforequests3.pdf.

150. **Frontline.** News War. [Online] wgbh educational foundation, December 11, 2012. http://www.pbs.org/wgbh/pages/frontline/teach/newswar/hand1.html.

151. **Smith, Matt and Johns, Joe.** AP blasts feds for phone records search. [Online] CNN, May 14, 2013. http://www.cnn.com/2013/05/13/us/justice-ap-phones/index.html.

152. **Borger, Julian.** NSA files: why the Guardian in London destroyed hard drives of leaked files. [Online] The Guardian, August 20, 2013. http://www.theguardian.com/world/2013/aug/20/nsa-snowden-files-drives-destroyed-london.

153. **U.K. Legislation.** Terrorism Act 2000 Schedule 7. [Online] The National Archives, July 20, 2000. http://www.legislation.gov.uk/ukpga/2000/11/schedule/7.

154. **Guardian Staff.** Glenn Greenwald's partner detained at Heathrow airport for nine hours. [Online] The Guardian, August 18, 2013. http://www.theguardian.com/world/2013/aug/18/glenn-greenwald-guardian-partner-detained-heathrow.

155. **Foley, Kathryn.** China Bans Access to Facebook and Twitter Due to Riots. [Online] Yahoo!, July 7, 2009. http://voices.yahoo.com/china-bans-access-facebook-twitter-due-riots-3755708.html.

156. **Riley, Charles.** LinkedIn draws fire for China censorship. [Online] CNNMoney, June 4, 2014. http://money.cnn.com/2014/06/04/technology/linkedin-china-censorship/index.html.

157. **Simonite, Tom.** NSA Leaks Could Inspire a Global Boom in Intrusive Surveillance. [Online] MIT Technology Review, November 12, 2013. http://www.technologyreview.com/view/521561/nsa-leaks-could-inspire-a-global-boom-in-intrusive-surveillance/.

158. **Skype.** What is GMF? [Online] Skype. [Cited: June 22, 2014.] https://support.skype.com/en/faq/FA10910/what-is-gmf.

159. **Milchman, Eli.** Yahoo 'Strictest' Censor in China. [Online] Wired, June 15, 2006. http://www.wired.com/politics/onlinerights/news/2006/06/71166.

160. **Helft, Miguel and Barboza, David.** Google Shuts China Site in Dispute Over Censorship. [Online] The New York Times, March 22, 2010. http://www.nytimes.com/2010/03/23/technology/23google.html.

161. **Drummond, David.** A new approach to China: an update. [Online] Google Official Blog, March 22, 2010. http://googleblog.blogspot.com/2010/03/new-approach-to-china-update.html.

162. **Fletcher, Owen.** Baidu Accused of Aiding Chinese Censorship in U.S. Suit. [Online] The Wall Street Journal, May 19, 2011. http://online.wsj.com/article/SB10001424052748703482104576332073063272688.html.

163. **Sina Corp.** Sina says Weibo daily active users up 4 pct to 61.4 million. [Online] Reuters, February 24, 2014. http://www.reuters.com/article/2014/02/25/sina-results-users-idUSB9N0LF00W20140225.

164. **Henochowicz, Anne.** Big Brother Gets Tough on Weibo, Sina Balks. [Online] China Digital News, February 29, 2012. http://chinadigitaltimes.net/2012/02/big-brother-gets-tough-on-weibo-sina-balks/.

165. **Branigan, Tania.** China's microbloggers turn to Teletubbies to discuss politics. [Online] The Guardian, March 22, 2012. http://www.guardian.co.uk/world/2012/mar/22/china-microbloggers-teletubbies.

166. **Ng, Jason Q.** The Diminishing Returns of Tricking China's Censors. [Online] MIT Technology Review, June 20, 2014. http://www.technologyreview.com/view/528521/the-diminishing-returns-of-tricking-chinas-online-censors/.

167. **McKirdy, Euan.** WeChat's conversations gagged: Are China's censors behind it? [Online] CNN, March 17, 2014. http://www.cnn.com/2014/03/17/world/asia/wechat-censorship/index.html.

168. **Weiwei, Ai.** China's censorship can never defeat the internet. [Online] The Guardian, April 15, 2012. http://www.guardian.co.uk/commentisfree/libertycentral/2012/apr/16/china-censorship-internet-freedom.

169. **Alexander, Anne.** Internet role in Egypt's protests. [Online] BBC, February 9, 2011. http://www.bbc.co.uk/news/world-middle-east-12400319.

170. **Fathi, Yasmine.** In Egypt, nationwide protests planned for January 28. [Online] Ahram Online, January 27, 2011. http://english.ahram.org.eg/News/4953.aspx.

171. **Cowie, James.** Egypt Leaves the Internet. [Online] Renesys Blog, January 27, 2011. http://www.renesys.com/blog/2011/01/egypt-leaves-the-internet.shtml.

172. **Williams, Christopher.** How Egypt shut down the internet. [Online] The Telegraph, January 28, 2011. http://www.telegraph.co.uk/news/worldnews/africaandindianocean/egypt/8288163/How-Egypt-shut-down-the-internet.html.

173. **AFP.** Google unveils Web-free 'tweeting' in Egypt move. [Online] Google, January 31, 2011. http://www.google.com/hostednews/afp/article/ALeqM5h8de3cQ8o_S2zg9s72t7sxNToBqA?docId=CNG.ddc0305146893ec9e9e6796d743e6af7.c81.

174. **Hennessy-Fiske, Molly and Hassan, Amro.** Mubarak, other former Egypt officials fined $91 million for blocking cellphones, Internet. [Online] Los Angeles Times, May 29, 2011. http://articles.latimes.com/2011/may/29/world/la-fg-egypt-mubarak-fines-20110529.

175. **CNN Wire Staff.** Virtually all Internet service in Syria shut down, group says. [Online] CNN, November 29, 2012. http://www.cnn.com/2012/11/28/world/meast/syria-civil-war/index.html.

176. **Gross, Doug.** Syria caused Internet blackout, security firm says. [Online] CNN, December 3, 2012. http://www.cnn.com/2012/11/30/tech/web/syria-internet/index.html.

177. **Jamjoom, Mohammed.** Saudi Arabia may block Skype, Viber, WhatsApp, others. [Online] CNN, April 1, 2013. http://www.cnn.com/2013/03/31/world/meast/saudi-arabia-may-block-apps/index.html.

178. **Watson, Ivan and Tuysuz, Gul.** Turkish PM vows to 'eradicate' Twitter, users see service disruptions. [Online] CNN, March 20, 2014. http://www.cnn.com/2014/03/20/world/europe/turkey-twitter-blackout/.

179. **Watson, Tom.** Turkey's Twitter Ban: Shutting Down Technology ... Or Social Culture? [Online] Forbes, March 25, 2014. http://www.forbes.com/sites/tomwatson/2014/03/25/turkeys-twitter-ban-shutting-down-technology-or-social-culture/.

180. **Clinton, Hillary.** @HillaryClinton. [Online] Twitter, March 21, 2014. https://twitter.com/HillaryClinton/statuses/447233637054820352.

181. **Segall, Laurie.** Iraqis turn to Whisper app during conflict. [Online] CNNMoney, June 16, 2014. http://money.cnn.com/2014/06/16/technology/social/whisper-app-iraq/index.html.

182. **Smith-Spark, Laura.** Myanmar junta orders internet blackout as more pro-democracy protesters are detained. [Online] CNN, April 2, 2021. https://www.cnn.com/2021/04/02/asia/myanmar-military-internet-blackout-detentions-intl/index.html.

183. **Lendon, Brad.** Norwegians sing to annoy mass killer. [Online] CNN, April 26, 2012. http://news.blogs.cnn.com/2012/04/26/norwegians-sing-to-annoy-mass-killer/.

184. **Solholm, Rolleiv.** Mass choir of 40,000 sang in Breivik protest. [Online] The Norway Post., April 26, 2012. http://www.norwaypost.no/news/mass-choir-to-sing-in-breivik-protest-26832.html.

185. **Payne, Martha.** One primary school pupil's daily dose of school dinners. [Online] NeverSeconds. [Cited: July 9, 2012.] http://neverseconds.blogspot.com.es/.

186. **Hough, Andrew and Johnson, Simon.** Victory for Martha Payne as Argyll and Bute council backs down on school dinner blog ban. [Online] The Telegraph, June 15, 2012. http://www.telegraph.co.uk/education/educationnews/9333975/Victory-for-Martha-Payne-as-Argyll-and-Bute-council-backs-down-on-school-dinner-blog-ban.html.

187. **Oslo Freedom Forum.** About Manal al-Sharif. [Online] Oslo Freedom Forum, May 2012. http://www.oslofreedomforum.com/speakers/manal-al-sharif.html.

188. **Prize, Havel.** Manal al-Sharif - 2012 Havel Prize Acceptance Speech. [Online] YouTube, May 30, 2012. http://www.youtube.com/watch?v=xECB8Xyagnk.

189. **Newton-Small, Jay.** Hillary's Little Startup: How the U.S. Is Using Technology to Aid Syria's Rebels. [Online] TIME Magazine, June 13, 2012. http://world.time.com/2012/06/13/hillarys-little-startup-how-the-u-s-is-using-technology-to-aid-syrias-rebels/.

190. **CNN Editors.** Syria's 'cyber warriors' choose cameras over guns. [Online] CNN, June 14, 2012. http://globalpublicsquare.blogs.cnn.com/2012/06/14/syrias-cyber-warriors-choose-cameras-over-guns/.

191. **Kelly, Heather.** Mozilla CEO resigns over anti-same-sex-marriage controversy. [Online] CNNMoney, April 3, 2014. http://money.cnn.com/2014/04/03/technology/mozilla-ceo/index.html.

192. —. OkCupid protests Firefox over CEO's anti-same-sex marriage donation. [Online] CNN, March 31, 2014. http://www.cnn.com/2014/03/31/tech/web/firefox-okcupid-protest/index.html.

193. **Primack, Dan.** RadiumOne fires abusive CEO after backlash. [Online] CNNMoney, April 27, 2014. http://finance.fortune.cnn.com/2014/04/27/radiumone-fires-abusive-ceo/.

194. **Segall, Laurie.** Board backed RadiumOne CEO days before firing him. [Online] CNNMoney, May 2, 2014. http://money.cnn.com/2014/05/02/technology/enterprise/radiumone-ceo/index.html.

195. **Leopold, Todd.** The man who invented the Internet (well, sort of). [Online] CNN, April 23, 2014. http://www.cnn.com/2014/04/23/tech/web/david-wallechinsky-lists-internet/index.html.

196. **Osofsky, Justin.** More Ways to Drive Traffic to News and Publishing Sites. [Online] Facebook, October 21, 2013. https://www.facebook.com/notes/facebook-media/more-ways-to-drive-traffic-to-news-and-publishing-sites/585971984771628.

197. **Westcott, Ben, Watson, Angus and Whiteman, Hilary.** 'Sort this out': Facebook's chaotic news ban in Australia blocks pages for fire services, charities and politicians. [Online] CNN Business, February 18, 2021. https://www.cnn.com/2021/02/18/tech/facebook-australia-news-ban-chaos-intl-hnk/index.html.

198. **Iyengar, Rishi.** The worldwide web as we know it may be ending. [Online] CNN Business, February 24, 2021. [Cited:]

199. **Lapowsky, Issie.** How Cambridge Analytica Sparked the Great Privacy Awakening. [Online] Wired, March 17, 2019. https://www.wired.com/story/cambridge-analytica-facebook-privacy-awakening/.

200. **Watson, Chloe.** The key moments from Mark Zuckerberg's testimony to Congress. [Online] The Guardian, April 11, 2018. https://www.theguardian.com/technology/2018/apr/11/mark-zuckerbergs-testimony-to-congress-the-key-moments.

201. **Polant, Katelyn.** Judge while sentencing Trump campaign aide: 'If people don't have the facts, democracy doesn't work'. [Online] CNN, December 17, 2019. https://www.cnn.com/2019/12/17/politics/amy-berman-jackson-gates-barr/index.html.

202. **Donehue, Wesley.** The danger of Twitter, Facebook politics. [Online] CNN, April 24, 2012. http://www.cnn.com/2012/04/24/opinion/donehue-social-media-politics/index.html.

203. **Branigan, Tania.** China's censors tested by microbloggers who keep one step ahead of state media. [Online] The Guardian, April 15, 2012. http://www.guardian.co.uk/technology/2012/apr/16/internet-china-censorship-weibo-microblogs.

204. **Andrews, Lori B.** The rise of Facebook Nation. [Online] Salon, December 31, 2011. http://www.salon.com/2011/12/31/the_rise_of_facebook_nation/singleton/.

205. **Andrews, Lori.** The Social Network Constitution. [Online] socialnetworkconstitution.com. [Cited: April 23, 2012.] http://www.socialnetworkconstitution.com/the-social-network-constitution.html.

206. **Moynihan, Colin.** Protester's Lawyer Challenges Twitter Subpoena. [Online] The New York Times, February 6, 2012. http://cityroom.blogs.nytimes.com/2012/02/06/protesters-lawyer-challenges-twitter-subpoena/.

207. **Fitzpatrick, Alex.** Twitter fights court order for user's data. [Online] CNN, May 9, 2012. http://www.cnn.com/2012/05/09/tech/social-media/twitter-court-order/index.html.

208. **Fine, Aden.** Twitter Stands Up For One Of Its Users. [Online] American Civil Liberties Union, May 8, 2012. http://www.aclu.org/blog/technology-and-liberty-national-security-free-speech/breaking-news-twitter-stands-one-its-users.

209. **ACLU.** Hey! Do you use the Internet? [Online] American Civil Liberties Union. [Cited: May 12, 2012.] https://secure.aclu.org/site/SPageServer?pagename=110419_Internet_Privacy.

210. **Citron, Danielle Keats.** 'Revenge porn' should be a crime in U.S. [Online] CNN, January 16, 2014. http://www.cnn.com/2013/08/29/opinion/citron-revenge-porn/.

211. **Mungin, Lateef.** Man once called the 'Revenge Porn King' indicted. [Online] CNN, January 24, 2014. http://www.cnn.com/2014/01/24/justice/california-revenge-porn-indictment/index.html.

212. **Randazza, Marc.** We need a 'right to be forgotten' online. [Online] CNN, May 14, 2014. http://www.cnn.com/2014/05/14/opinion/randazza-google-right-to-privacy/index.html.

Chapter 13
A Multi-Criteria Approach to Analysing E-Democracy Support Systems

Mats Danielson, Love Ekenberg and Adriana Mihai

13.1 Introduction

New information and communication technologies (ICT) have made the public sphere more diverse and fragmented, and consequently, participation in these diverse and fragmented online public spheres has introduced new modes of interaction between citizens and governments. Participation requires a new kind of literacy to navigate the information flow as well as new kinds of abilities to sustain a reasonable democratic discourse in the Internet age. The interdisciplinary field of e-democracy is thus naturally growing at a fast pace and includes researchers from a diversity of disciplines such as political science, communication studies, information security, system studies, human-computer interaction, and e-government, making it sometimes difficult to get a more coherent view of the various concepts and ideas involved. In this chapter, we therefore suggest a unifying and fairly open framework for evaluating tools for e-democracy, while still trying to avoid a more fundamental discussion about the inner nature of democracy. More precisely, we discuss how these models and tools could be categorised and analysed concerning

---

This chapter is an extended version of [25].

M. Danielson (✉) · L. Ekenberg
Department of Computer and Systems Sciences, Stockholm University, Kista, Sweden

International Institute of Applied Systems Analysis, Schlossplatz 1, A-2361, Laxenburg, Austria
e-mail: mats.danielson@su.se; ekenberg@iiasa.ac.at

A. Mihai
Centre of Excellence for the Study of Cultural Identity, University of Bucharest, Bucharest, Romania
e-mail: adriana.mihai@lls.unibuc.ro

© Springer Science+Business Media, LLC, part of Springer Nature 2021
N. Lee, *Facebook Nation*, https://doi.org/10.1007/978-1-0716-1867-7_13

their intended use in a more general democracy setting and as participation-enabling instruments. We take an inclusive perspective to accommodate different views of e-democracy in order to enable tool users and developers to understand and structure tool characteristics and the degrees of support that the tools provide in different respects, such as which types of democratic values are being supported in the different tools. Since already the ideas of democracy and democratic participation involve diversities of ideas and processes, and there are so many different research perspectives and practices in the subject areas, it is almost impossible to actually scrutinise the manifold of aspects that have been flourishing for hundreds of years in the various sub-fields on structural, formal, pragmatic and ideological approaches to the broader area. Consequently, it is not immediately clear how to structure, categorise, and evaluate the variety of tools that have appeared over the last few years and thus, some comments are necessary to understand our ambitions with this chapter.

We are not aiming at solving large conceptual issues in the various fields regarding the democracy concept(s), but will instead in some detail try to outline a method making it easier to map out and understand the varying degrees of support that *digital tools* can display in various settings of *e-democracy*. There are, of course, several issues involved here. For instance, as Dahlberg's [22] overview of discourses on e-democracy as well as reviews of the field of open government in, e.g., [41] point out, there are several shortcomings already in the underlying concepts of democracy, not the least with issues concerning representativeness. There are also a multitude of other aspects involved, such as the need for knowledge and the willingness to participate, as [61, 65] also have observed. However, we will here only suggest a subset of the plethora of aspects that are relevant for e-democracy and discuss four of them that will be used as underlying components in the index to illustrate our framework. The inclusion of whichever other aspects of relevance that are desired in a particular context can be analogously handled. We also want to point out that there have been several earlier and more general suggestions for structuring the field, such as Bellamy's [8], [18], Tambouris et al. [77], and Dahlberg's [22] four positions for e-democracy. Worth mentioning from a modelling point of view are also the overview by [42] of representative and direct democracy in relation to ICT as well as Päivärinta and Sæbø's [62] model for e-democracy. The latter's categories are discriminating and functional, but are not entirely suitable for modelling mutually dependent and complementary democratic objectives. The ability to investigate trade-off effects is in such cases of great interest and we will return to this issue below. More recent surveys are provided in [56] and, in a more limited sense, in [39]. Furthermore, [68] provides state-of-the-art coverage of e-participation and discusses a set of requirements for a Social Software Infrastructure (SSI) as well as an integrated model for e-participation. More recent structuring attempts have been made, e.g., in [11, 41], providing overviews of open governments and democracy aspects in a rather general sense, but they do not attempt to evaluate them in any structured way.

Complementary to these, we suggest an evaluation framework that can be applied to various subsets of democracy aspects in different contexts. This could, for example, contain only a few dimensions such as information quality and efficient distribution, or contain a significantly larger superset of attributes, such as flexibility in participation, reasonable voting possibilities, explanation and enlightenment, representativeness, agenda control, equality, inclusion, Internet access, anonymity, protection of privacy, transaction security, and fraud detection mechanisms, depending on the circumstances and the purposes of the tools investigated. The framework can furthermore be used for handling hierarchies of attributes and can therefore be quite useful also in complex contexts. Even if we exemplify this in a few dimensions, there are no such limitations to the framework, neither regarding contexts nor the component domains.

In this chapter we present:

(a) Observation regarding the notion of e-democracy and its position in an interdisciplinary field.
(b) Discussions on the more general and important aspects of e-democracy and tool support.
(c) Methodological concerns are discussed concerning the formulation of our framework and the sub-sections provide a summary of e-democracy tool categories, including examples from some of the categories, containing a number of positioning criteria for four important, but not exclusive or exhaustive, dimensions.
(d) Discussions on indexation in general.
(e) The actual indexation model and how it can be employed.
(f) Some applications of the framework as a demonstration of its potential.
(g) Conclusions with some outlooks, general considerations, and further research regarding quality assessments of tools for e-democracy.

13.2 e-Democracy and Tool Support

As is the case of the general concept of democracy, a more limited concept such as e-democracy is still by no means uncomplicated and there have even been discussions on whether the concepts of democracy and non-democracy should be considered as a dichotomy and if so, how graded this should be, cf. e.g., [18]. What seems to be quite common in different approaches is to position e-democracy as a system within a frame and as a relationship between governments and citizens, as can be seen, e.g., in the approaches by Macintosh and Whyte's [49] evaluation model for e-participation, the Oni et al.'s [60] guidelines for an e-democracy agenda setting, Lidén's [47] framework for socially sustainable values in e-democracy processes, Ayo et al.'s [5] strategic framework for e-democracy development, and Alathur et al.'s [3] determinants of citizens' participation. E-democracy is usually seen as a process that deals not only with information and collective decision-making but also with who is a "representative citizen" in the corresponding decision-making processes. Central to such a process seems again to be the aim for transparency and individual autonomy. Especially in the areas of e-government and open government, transparency is emphasised and concepts such as interoperability and open data have to a large extent been dominating the scene [40]. For instance, the first two directives of the Obama administration [59] emphasised transparency and participation, albeit with a focus on information provision. Transparency was put forward as a means to provide citizens with information, while participation concerned the improvement of information assisted by independent citizens and organisations. A central precondition for this information exchange was autonomous public participation. The European Commission also quite early emphasised accountability through transparency in public services [48]. Other documents emphasise citizen participation in the information process as a driver for an open and collaborative government [32]. Another strongly interlinked part of e-democracy has a stronger focus on e-participatory models. Many studies have discussed the effects of open government and e-participation, such as [4] and some interesting spin-offs thereof, notably [44]. It should, however, be noted that e-participation in itself already early presented a fragmented field of definitions, theories, and methods, such as in [36, 50, 53, 54, 71, 72, 75] and is thus a complicated field in itself. Other topics have also proliferated, such as significant institutional transformations where it is investigated if general social media platforms, rather than dedicated tools, can better support participatory democracy, cf., e.g., [2, 13, 73].

Other areas within the field of e-democracy also emphasise democratic rights and understanding. Another central sub-field is public participation in the process of consensus, agenda-setting, discussions, and decision making [30]. A broad pluralism seems to be important as well, i.e. diversity in conflicting perspectives at different levels, from setting the agenda to discussion and voting. The earlier stages of policy design and design theory are of critical value in the processes and, e.g., [35, 67] provide a quite elaborated discussion on this issue. Some, such as Bellamy [8], label this emphasis as the *consumer model* since it focuses on citizens as consumers of public services and their legal rights against the state. Others, such as Dahlberg [22], argue that this is where most of the development of e-democracy takes place, i.e. in projects providing citizens with better services, increased accessibility, and information transparency. Or simply to improve government accountability and "customer service" through flexible information systems and more informed decision making.

Citizen empowerment has furthermore been at the core of the e-participation ethos, ranging from prosumers' active consumption practices and reviewing of public services, to citizen journalism or Internet activism [45]. User-generated content [79], aside from generating business models and profits, has involved a shift from the private sphere to the public (political) one, where disempowered citizens could express political views and associate with others who are interested in common issues, a case in point being the larger importance of political participation on social media for black Americans after the introduction of the #BlackLivesMatter hashtag [64]. Empowerment and agency in the public sphere raise the plurality of viewpoints, information production, association, accountability, agenda-setting, and collective decision-making through functionalities such as user comments and social networks [19]. Moving from the personal to the public sphere also involves trust and issues of privacy, so as to maintain freedom of thought and expression without risking repression or surveillance.

When it comes to tool support, most commonly used tools for e-participation, such as social platforms, music, photo, video sharing tools, and microblogs, are developed by the private sector and the most important actors and competitors are Apple, Facebook, Google, and Microsoft, cf. [63, 78]. There are also some examples of public sector projects aiming at making the sector more transparent, such as OpenCongress [45]. There are, further, some more innovative projects, exemplified by Diplopedia [21], the US State Department's wiki for Foreign Affairs information, Intellipedia, a joint information source for U.S. Intelligence Agencies and Departments [9], GCpedia, the Government of Canada's wiki [37], and MyUniversity [55], the latter for educational settings. Other common categories include various wikis and community portals for collaboratively sharing information about local places. Notably, there are also systems using blockchain-based encryption, such as Votem[1] and Votewatcher[2]. There are several issues of importance regarding these models and tools and there is of course a range of possible improvements on the functionality as well as the legalisation surrounding them, not least when it comes to actual e-voting processes as well as data security, privacy, and counting auditability. We will, however, at a more abstract level consider their actual or potential roles in a more general democracy setting and in their functions as participation-enabling instruments.

13.3 Relevant Features of Tools for e-Democracy

There are thus several important aspects of e-democracy and many of them concern societal decision-making processes. As mentioned above, central to those processes seem to be transparency and individual autonomy, i.e. that there is a clear understanding of the pros and contras involved in the various issues on the agendas as well as the opportunity to freely discuss them and influence the results. Another important aspect is public participation in the sub-processes, such as the agenda-formation, consensus-building, discussions, and analyses as well as the actual voting procedures and the regulations around them. A broad pluralism and a diversity of conflicting perspectives on different levels seem furthermore to be of importance in the different phases during the process. In the following, we will use these democracy aspects to illustrate our framework. More precisely, we will primarily use four aspects to serve as positioning criteria in order to demonstrate the tool index. We could have selected a larger or a different set of criteria, but this would not have added anything to the explanative strength of the presentation and only obfuscated the results with too many calculation details.

---

[1] https://www.votem.com.

[2] http://votewatcher.com.

13.3.1   A Sample of Relevant Aspects

It seems to be fundamental for democratic processes to provide citizens with information and to improve both transparency and understanding in autonomous public participatory processes as well as to increase accountability. For instance, the Obama administration emphasised efficiency and improved services and favoured a distribution and decentralisation of the public sector among several actors, public as well as private [59]. The aim was to decentralise the public sector even further and release public data, making it easily accessible and possible to reuse, as well as generally enabling governments to become more efficient in various ways. Data interoperability was perceived as important both for accountability and because it can be used in new and innovative ways. Such interoperability is an important aspect of democracy in general. Provided that there is governmental transparency, gathering information through autonomous actors makes information more easily available in the context of e-democracy.

Another component, which can be facilitated by e-democracy tools, is citizen-to-citizen and citizen-to-government dialogues, enabling a bottom-up approach to information production and sharing where the public may participate. Other aspects involve supporting the sharing of data between agencies, agencies to citizens, and citizens to citizens, where the aim is better services, efficiency, as well as innovation, aggregating, competing, informing, petitioning, transacting, voting, and controlling. The most common tools for this kind of e-participation are developed by the private sector, such as photo and video sharing tools or microblogs. But there are also examples of public sector projects aiming at making the public sector more transparent, for example, OpenCongress and more innovative projects such as Diplopedia, the U.S. State Department's wiki for Foreign Affairs information, Intellipedia, a joint information source for U.S. Intelligence Agencies and Departments [9], GCpedia, the Government of Canada's wiki [37], and MyUniversity for educational settings.

Autonomy for the individual and the right to associate as well as to disassociate with communities is often considered as a basic democratic right [6]. Micro-democratic processes in autonomous networks, what Dahlberg [22] calls an autonomous-Marxist discourse, is also seen as a production principle where reciprocal relationships between equals replace a hierarchical workflow. ICT-enhanced social networks have, for example, received credit for the democratic movements in countries such as Egypt and Tunisia. This "cyber-democratic" model has sometimes been seen as one of the most radical changes to traditional democratic institutions [62]. The autonomy of the open-data and open-government paradigms is also a component of an innovation strategy where decentralisation and sharing of information with large crowds of independent citizens and organisations can be utilised for new innovations, such as in the open-source culture where peers develop software in collaboration motivated by peer recognition or other micro-rewards (see, for example, [58]). Applications are used that support forms of open-source culture where participants typically collaborate motivated by peer recognition or other micro-rewards, networking, collaborating, distributing, and sharing (again, see [58]). One significant example is crowdsourcing projects, where the public is asked to perform a predefined task. Citizen dialogue is considered central, such as in SeeClickFix and FixMyStreet [17, 76] for identifying neighbourhood issues and in Ushahidi [52] regarding how to collect eyewitness reports of violence.

A broad public deliberative conversation is often considered essential for democracy, both for solving common problems and for creating a shared understanding of the decisions made. Projects aiming at a consensus in this context are typically about changing the representative system by making room for deliberative discussions on various issues and developing public opinions using information technological solutions [22]. The focus in this case is usually on improving the quality of citizens' participation and involvement [8]. This strengthened citizen activity should be supported for the benefit of both the political sphere and the citizens' well-being.

We will use the concept of consensus in the e-democracy tool context, intended as collective decisions and/or information production, to create and refine information and shared understanding in the form of agenda-setting, arguing, deliberation, education, opinion-formation, and negotiating. This means tools for information, discussion, and collaboration, including social media. Such a concept is motivated by the belief that this will enable a more informed understanding of the democratic settings as well as a better understanding of the decisions finally made. Support tools for deliberative processes therefore also aim at structuring the decision situation and provide information regarding the alternatives and criteria involved [34]. Deliberation can also be seen as a culture, a behaviour that needs to be established. This is, for example, the ambition of Regulationroom.org, an online experimental e-participation platform that aims to open up rulemaking processes in legislation by inviting the public to review new regulations [33].

An important aspect is also the tolerance and the existence of a plurality of values and identities. In an e-democracy context, this means the formation of a diversity of public spheres that develop their discourses in enclosed counter-publics [22]. This position focuses on how different interest groups are more actively involved in the formation of consensus. Components supporting pluralism should acknowledge diversity, inequality, and conflicts, and also support the establishment of counter-cultures, collective actions, community building, campaigning, contesting, organizing, and protesting.

Since e-participation entails users sharing data publicly, what has been seen more and more as a precondition for supporting the abovementioned components is the right to privacy, as it protects personal choice, association, and expression. These ensure decisional autonomy, self-governance, self-direction, and the capacity to form ideas, political interests, and preferences [46, 51], which in turn inform democratic deliberation processes. The protection of individual differences and identity supports e-democracy by, among other things, enabling pluralism, incorporating checks and balances systems which allow for reactions against undemocratic practices through forms of protest and noncompliance, and maintaining trust in democratic institutions and public spheres. Even though legislation such as the General Data Protection Regulation (GDPR) and the California Consumer Privacy

Act (CCPA) increases fairness in tools' use of personal data, through provisions ensuring more user agency and data collection proportionality, accountability, and necessity, aspects such as jurisdiction or media independence often allow e-tools to only apply self-regulation. When these fail to secure the privacy of personal data, all four e-democracy components can be affected. Data misuse has been shown to trigger erosion of trust in institutions or private actors, leading to a decline in public participation [15] and to concerns over mass surveillance [10, 45], voter and consumer manipulation [12, 51]. Privacy issues can be included in the index either by measuring their effects on transparency, autonomy, consensus, and pluralism or by adding a further dimension, whose components should protect self-governance, personal choice and expression: choosing, negotiating, opting in, declining, reviewing, controlling, trusting and holding accountable. We will exemplify the latter option later on, in evaluating Facebook, a ubiquitous case study for user data collection and repurposing.

13.3.2 A Map of Different Aspects of Democracy

Based on Bellamy's [8] and Dahlberg's [22] four categories, we will now use the abovementioned positions and Päivärinta and Sæbø's model for e-democracy [62] to design a map illustrating how the different positions above are related to each other and to micro/macro processes needed for the implementation of e-democracy, e.g. polling, voting, community building, etc. The map uses the four positions shown in Figure 13.1, and the four positions' relationships to tool support for various functions needed for e-democracy are listed below. This field can also be structured between a macro perspective where the focus is on society as a whole system, and a micro perspective where the focus is on society from the individual's perspective.

- **Transparency**: Components that support the sharing of data between agencies, government to citizens, and citizens to citizens, where the aim is better services, efficiency, and innovation: aggregating, competing, informing, petitioning, transacting, transmitting, voting, and controlling.
- **Autonomy**: Components that support forms for open-source cultures where participants typically collaborate motivated by peer recognition or other micro-rewards: networking, collaborating, distributing, and sharing.
- **Consensus**: Components that support forms for collective decisions and information production to develop information and shared understanding: agenda-setting, arguing, deliberating, informing and educating, meeting, opinion-forming, reflecting, trade-off analysis, and negotiating.
- **Pluralism**: Components that acknowledge and enable diversity, inequality, and conflicts. Support for establishing counter-cultures and collective actions: associating, campaigning, contesting, forming groups, community building, organizing, mediating, and protesting.

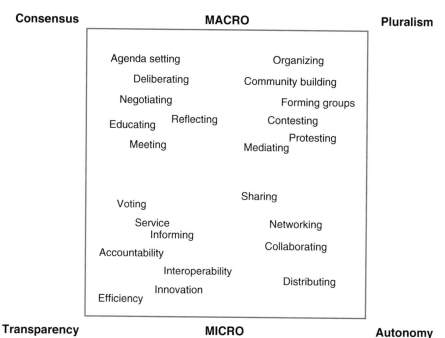

Figure 13.1. Visual positioning of functions needed to support the six dimensions of democracy

Organising, community building, and group formation are placed close to pluralism since they are about organising interest communities and thus creating the conditions for organising around a diversity of perspectives and interests. Tools for networking and collaborating are placed in the autonomy corner as these tools focus on creating conditions for the individual to act autonomously and to have direct contact with other autonomous actors in different networks.

  These positions are relative and oppose each other in the map for visualisation purposes. If we place our four different aspects of democracy on a map of different foci of democracy, we obtain a map that can help discuss and identify which kinds of democratic aspects that different types of e-democracy projects and components can support. Note that these particular four criteria and their roles within the chapter are to demonstrate a general mapping and indexing method that should be further adapted by the prospective method users by incorporating criteria appropriate for their intended purposes. Such a mapping can also lead to a categorisation of tools by an index as a complement to and operationalization of the map itself.

13.4   Indexation

We will now introduce a more elaborate index for categorising and visualising the various features present in the models and tools. Commonly used democracy indices, where Coppedge et al. [20] provide an overview of different indices and their properties, are very similar from a mathematical perspective and many of them use variants of weighted averages based on questions or criteria sets, such as the Economist's Democracy Index [29] or Freedom House. Skaaning [74] provides another overview of the current state of democracy indices with similar conclusions. The current indices seem to be unnecessarily simplified and can be improved considerably from an elicitation perspective to increase their granulation and adequacy. This is similar to the situation in the area of multi-criteria decision analysis, where [69] provides a thorough overview of various possibilities and issues, including some trade-off discussions.

One crucial issue in practice is how to realistically elicit criteria weights (and also values) from users in such a way that they can provide information they understand the meaning of, since the elicitation of exact numbers demands an exactness which does rarely exist. (There are also other problems, such as that ratio weight procedures are difficult to accurately employ due to response errors [43], but a discussion of those issues are beyond the scope of this chapter.) We have therefore argued that ordinal or other imprecise importance (and preference) information could successfully be used for determining criteria weights (and values of entities). Surrogate weights (and values), which are derived from ordinal and cardinal importance (and value) information, could be very useful in the elicitation process (cf., e.g., [23, 24]). In surrogate-number methods, the decision-maker provides information on the rank order of the criteria, i.e. supplies ordinal information on relative importance. Thereafter, the information is converted into numerical weights consistent with the extracted ordinal information. We will use this technique when constructing an index underlying the visualisation framework discussed below. To better understand the feature of this index, we will first briefly discuss the four aspects of democracy that will be used as underlying components in the index to illustrate the framework. There are many more components that might and possibly should be included, but the inclusion of other aspects of relevance in a particular context can be analogously handled. In general, elicitation efforts can be grouped into a) methods handling the outcome of an elicitation by precise numbers as representatives of the information elicited and b) methods instead handling the outcome by using less precise (interval-valued) information. But there are also other approaches, less reliant on high information precision on the part of the decision-maker while still aiming at non-interval representations.

As stated above, today's commonly used democracy indices are very similar from a mathematical perspective. To gain an overview, we surveyed the usage of the terms *democracy/dictatorship index*, *index of democracy*, *list of freedom index*, and *democracy ranking*. In the indices we found, most use a weighted average based on questions or criteria sets, such as, e.g., in the Economist's Democracy Index [29] on electoral process and pluralism, civil liberties, the functioning of government, political participation, and political culture, or thinner ones such as Freedom House. For instance, [66] provides an overview of indices and suggest a weighted average model for e-participation. Most of these indices assess criteria weights using exact numbers. The methods range from relatively simple ones, such as direct rating and point allocation methods, to somewhat more advanced procedures. Generally, in these approaches, precise numerical values are assigned to criteria and performance values are extracted to represent the information. There exist various weighting methods that utilise questioning procedures for elicitation, but the requirement for numeric precision in the input information is in any case problematic. This is because people's beliefs are not naturally represented as numerically precise terms, cf., e.g., [28, 31].

Our suggestion tries to accommodate and alleviate these considerations. Therefore, we suggest a ranking method that goes beyond the commonly used scales also for rankings and where we have quite conservatively extended a purely ordinal-scale approach with the possibility to supply cardinal information as well. The discrimination formula that we use is validated by simulation studies similar to [1, 7, 16] that have become de facto standards for comparing weight methods relevant for cardinal ordering methods. The details of the validations can be found in [23, 24]. In this categorisation, we were inspired by the early work performed during the eParticipation Network of Excellence project Demo-net[3] organized by the University of Koblenz. This was a project with the objective to strengthen scientific, technological, and social research excellence in e-participation by integrating the research capacities of individuals and organizations spread across Europe. In an innovative European research project on e-participation, Wimmer [80] identified three groups of tool categories that support democratic participation: *i)* core e-democracy tools, *ii)* ICT tools extensively used in e-democracy, and *iii)* basic ICT tools needed in e-democracy. This is a tool categorisation that still makes sense. Using these categories, the group of core e-democracy tools consists of artefacts especially designed and used for e-democracy services while the other groups, ICT tools extensively used in e-democracy and ICT tools needed in e-democracy, consist of generic interfaces that are designed as multi-purpose e-tools but are being used primarily as e-democracy services. We have also elicited categories of tools from scientific articles that discuss types of tools concerning particular projects or experiments and from the analyses of specialised fields within e-democracy research. Examples include [70], who discuss the role of Social Networking Services (SNS) in e-participation, and [27] who discuss decision analysis in e-participation as a social process and sketches a basic architecture for an ICT system to support such processes. The next section presents the method in more detail.

---

[3] https://participedia.net/organization/316

13.5   Categorising E-democracy Tools

We will now turn to the index itself and apply it to a set of e-democracy tools ema-nating from our survey. The index is constructed from cardinal orderings of proper-ties and the relevant criteria under consideration. The orderings are then transformed to surrogate numbers that are aggregated to form the index for each respective tool.

13.5.1   Positioning Criteria

Table 13.1 shows some categories of tools of interest as well as brief descriptions of them.

The following steps were undertaken to evaluate the degree of support of a tool relative to the four positioning criteria concerning e-democracy (Consensus, Transparency, Pluralism, and Autonomy) defined in Section 13.3:

- Description and classification of a tool in terms of the categories.
- Measuring the tool in terms of an index defined in the next section and based on the four dimensions of e-democracy (transparency, autonomy, consensus, and pluralism) on a scale from where the tool displays no characteristics of any of the dimensions, to where the tool displays a maximum degree of the characteristics of all of the dimensions. In between, we could assert statements such as *The tool displays some characteristics of at least one of the dimensions* or *The tool dis-plays characteristics of several of the dimensions*.
- In between, we could assert statements, such as the tool displays some character-istics of at least one of the dimensions and the tool displays characteristics of several of the dimensions.

Note that tools can be measured under two interpretations, where the second one seems to be of more relevance in forming the index:

- The tool itself (or its managers/owners/manufacturers) claims that it supports a characteristic and no evidence contradicts this.
- It is evident, or at least very probable, that the users of a tool can use or uses it in a way that supports a characteristic.

13.5.2   Evaluation Principles

We will now show how our index, a weighted average over the dimensions, can be constructed. The method takes into account that there are usually large uncertainties and vagueness involved when characterising tools concerning these kinds of criteria.

A general way to create an index is to stipulate a set of criteria and evaluate a set of entities for them. The value function is here the additive model $V\left(E_{i}\right)=\sum_{j=1}^{m}w_{j}v_{j}\left(E_{i}\right),$

Table 13.1. Characterisations of some e-democracy tools

Chat Rooms	Tools that support citizens in participating in real-time sessions. Can also be configured to support peer-to-peer communication.
Social Networks and Virtual Communities	Tools that facilitate communication, sharing resources, and other interaction activities such as gaming between people who share a common interest.
Online Survey Tools	Tools that are web-based questionnaires where the public can submit responses online.
Deliberative Survey Tools and Deliberative Polls	Tools and polls that can be seen as a combination of traditional online survey tools but applied to focus groups where deliberation can take place.
E-consultation Tools	Tools that can be used by stakeholders to communicate and share information on specific issues, or get advice online, instead of meeting locally.
E-voting Tools	Systems that offer a secure environment for online voting.
E-petitions	Electronic lists where participants can sign up to support or protest against an issue.
Decision-Making Games	Games directed towards policy decision-making.
Internet-Based Decision Support	Computer-based systems used to retrieve data from the Internet and other sources and then to analyse this data.
Collaborative Environments	Systems that are used to support social interactions and collaboration.
Argument Visualisation Tools	Software tools that use argument diagramming to analyse arguments.
Semantic Web Technologies	Technologies that support automatic extraction of semantic content.

where $V(E_i)$ is the overall value of an e-tool E_i that can be described by a set of values under multiple criteria. $v_j(E_i)$ is the value of the e-tool under criterion i and w_j is the weight of this criterion. To express the relative importance of the criteria, weights are restricted by a normalisation constraint $\sum_{j=1}^{m} w_j = 1$. In very few cases, the weights are (quite artificially) considered to be all equal. Except for these cases, the criteria weights are critical components representing the significance of each criterion within the context under consideration.

One key characteristic is that there is more than one perspective under which we view the set of entities to be evaluated and for each perspective, the evaluator must assign values to each e-tool on some value scale. An even more general situation can be modelled where the criteria are also allowed to have sub-criteria, a feature that is more seldom used but can nevertheless improve the granularity of the entities under consideration. [26] discusses this in detail.

One very important practical issue is how to realistically elicit criteria weights (and also values).[4] Elicitation efforts can be grouped into a) methods handling the outcome of the elicitation by precise numbers as representatives of the information

---

[4] See [69] for an overview.

elicited; and b) methods instead handling the outcome by interval-valued variables. A vast number of methods have been suggested for assessing criteria weights using exact numbers. These range from relatively simple ones, like the commonly used direct rating and point allocation methods, to somewhat more advanced procedures. Generally, in these approaches, a precise numerical weight is assigned to each criterion to represent the information extracted from the user. There exist various weighting methods that utilise questioning procedures to elicit weights, but the requirement for numeric precision in elicitation is somewhat problematic because people's beliefs are not naturally represented in numerically precise terms in our minds. There are therefore other approaches, less reliant on large precision on the part of the decision-maker while still aiming at non-interval (and fundamentally non-numeric) representations.

As we have discussed above, a practical issue is how to realistically elicit information from users. Ordinal or other imprecise importance (and preference) information could, for instance, be used for determining criteria weights (and values of entities). Many authors suggest using surrogate weights which are derived from ordinal importance information (cf., [23, 24]). In such methods, the decision-maker provides information on the rank order of the criteria, i.e. supplies ordinal information on importance, and thereafter this information is converted into numerical weights consistent with the extracted information. In this chapter, we extend this suggestion to cover cardinal information as well.

13.5.3   CAR Weights and Values

A straightforward and robust method for cardinal ranking is CAR, which extends the concept of surrogate weights as one of the main components. First, we obtain information about how much more or less important the criteria are compared to each other.

In the following, we use $>_i$ to denote the strength (cardinality) of the rankings between criteria and values respectively, where $>_0$ is the equal ranking operator '='. Assume that we have a user induced ordering of criteria weights $w_1 >_{i_1} w_2 >_{i_2} \ldots >_{i_{n-1}} w_n$. Then we construct a new ordering, containing only the symbols = and >, by introducing auxiliary variables w_{ij} and substituting

$$w_k >_0 w_{k+1} \text{ with } w_k = w_{k+1}$$
$$w_k >_1 w_{k+1} \text{ with } w_k > w_{k+1}$$
$$w_k >_2 w_{k+1} \text{ with } w_k > x_{k_1} > w_{k+1} \tag{13.1}$$
$$\ldots$$
$$w_k >_i w_{k+1} \text{ with } w_k > x_{k_1} > \ldots > x_{k_{i-1}} > w_{k+1}$$

and analogously for the values (which are more straightforwardly handled since there are no normalisation constraints.) The substitutions yield new spaces defined by the simplexes generated by the new orderings. In this way, we obtain a computationally meaningful way of representing preference weight and value strengths.

To see how this works, consider the cardinality expressions as distance steps on an importance scale. The number of steps corresponds straightforwardly to the strength of the cardinal relations above such that ' $>_i$ ' means i steps. The statements are then converted into weights. This is explained in detail in [24], where also the performance of a set of cardinal weights are compared to ordinal weights. In this chapter, we use the SR (Sum-Reciprocal) weights of the aforementioned article. Then the cardinal ranking weights w_i^{CAR} are found by the weight formula

$$w_i^{CAR} = \frac{1/p(i) + \dfrac{Q+1-p(i)}{Q}}{\sum_{j=1}^{N} \left(1/p(j) + \dfrac{Q+1-p(j)}{Q} \right)}.$$

which are effortlessly calculated by, e.g., a spreadsheet program. One reasonable candidate for a weight function is a function that is proportional to the distances on the importance scale. This is analogous to the equidistant criteria placed on the ordinal importance scale (, right). To obtain the cardinal ranking weights w_i^{CAR}, proceed as follows:

- Assign an ordinal number to each importance scale position, starting with the most important position as number 1.
- Let the total number of importance scale positions be Q. Each criterion i has the position $p(i) \in \{1,...,Q\}$ on this importance scale, such that for every two criteria c_i and c_j, whenever $c_i >_{s_i} c_j$, $s_i = |p(i) - p(j)|$. The position $p(i)$ then denotes the importance as stated by the decision-maker.
- The values (assessments) of the various e-democracy tools under each criterion are elicited in a way similar to the weights. For each criterion in turn, rank the entities from the worst to the best outcome.

The criteria and value strengths indicate the degree of importance of the criteria and how well each tool performs in the particular dimension under consideration, i.e., how strong the separation is between every two ordered entities. As an example, consider Transparency. In Figure 13.2, some tools (A-E) are compared to a reference point: a zero tool (a base tool with almost no useful capabilities in the dimension considered).

The positions on the ranking ruler in Figure 13.2 are then converted into rankings on the $>i$ format. Each tool is assigned a ranking symbol $>i$ in which the integer i represents the number of steps the tool is away from the zero tool base. For example, Tool D is represented by >2 under the criterion Transparency. This scoring is repeated for each of the criteria being measured, in this example four. Thus, we obtain four rankings, one along each of the criteria. For Tool D, this might have yielded Transparency: >2; Autonomy: >1; Consensus: >3; and Pluralism: >1. Only Transparency: >2 is shown in the figure but the others would have been measured on

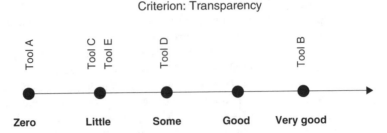

Figure 13.2. Tools assessed under the Transparency criterion

similar scales for the other three perspectives. (Tables 13.2 and 13.3 in the next section contain two real-world examples scored along the four dimensions in question.)

Thereafter, a weighted overall value is calculated by multiplying the centroid of
the weight simplex (i.e. the numbers best representing the weight relations, given by
the CAR weight formula above) with the centroid of the e-tool value simplex (again,
the numbers that best represents the value relations on rules such as in Figure 13.2).
This can be pictured as obtaining a kind of "mean value" best representing the
assessment of the e-tool. Thus, given a set of criteria in a (one-level) criteria hierarchy, $G_1,..., G_n$ and a set of e-tools $a_1,..., a_m$. A general value function U using additive value functions is then

$$U\left(a_j\right) = \sum_{i=1}^{n} w_i^{CAR} v_{ij}^{CAR}$$

where w_i^{CAR} is the weight representing the relative importance of attribute G_i, and
$v_{ij}^{CAR}: a_j \rightarrow [0,1]$ is the increasing individual value function of a_j under criterion G_i
obtained by the following procedure. As seen in the figure, for each criterion (i.e.
characteristic), the integers k in the statements $>k$ are interpreted as the values being
k steps away from the zero tool. Each step is represented on the criterion's local
value scale as $\alpha \cdot k$, where α is the scaling constant for the index. The scaling constant
is determined by $\alpha = d/s$, where d is the desired target for the average of the indices
and s is the expected average number of steps in the $>k$ symbols used. Again, this is
straightforwardly calculated in a spreadsheet.

Thus, the $U(a_j)$ expression is subject to the constraints in the polytopes of weights
and values. This means that the feasible values are the ones in the extended polytopes defined by (13.1) above. Now, we define the weighted value

$$\bar{U}\left(a_j\right) = \sum_{i=1}^{n} \bar{w}_i \bar{v}_{ij}$$

as a general result value, where $\bar{w}_i$ is the centroid component of criteria weight w_i in
the weight simplex and $\bar{v}_{ij}$ is the centroid component of the value of e-tool a_j under
criterion G_i in the simplex of values. Since we only consider non-interval valued

Table 13.2. Analysis of Municipality Chat Rooms

Grading	Motivations for grading
Transparency: $>_0$	The component does not support transparency since discussions in a chat room tend to be particular and unofficial. Additionally, not all chat rooms save the chats for later viewing.
Autonomy: $>_0$	Chat rooms do not support collaboration between residents. The activity in the two municipalities we have looked at seemed very sparse, and no peer recognition, networking, etc. seemed to have occurred. However, chat rooms do not hinder this but rather do not offer any support per se.
Consensus: $>_2$	Chat rooms facilitate the ability to discuss propositions and rulings within a municipality, it also supports both municipality representatives and the municipality residents. I.e. they have a strong potential to support consensus-building.
Pluralism: $>_1$	As only a small number of representatives participate in a chat at the same time, the support for pluralism is weak. A chat room is used for discussions between individuals, so even though chat rooms can be considered as a component that acknowledges diversity and conflicts, it does not support counter-cultures or collective actions between municipality residents.

Table 13.3. Analysis of Political Discussion Boards

Grading	Motivations for grading
Transparency: $>_0$	The reviewed (and probably most) discussion boards are unaffiliated with decision-makers. However, political agendas, suggestions, or rulings can be discussed on discussion boards and information on issues can be shared. Due to the lack of affiliation with decision-makers, discussion boards only show weak support for transparency.
Autonomy: $>_2$	Discussion boards let their participants form collaborations and posts and especially frequent posters get peer recognition.
Consensus: $>_1$	As the political discussion boards are not affiliated to any political parties they do not have much impact on decision making in communities, but they do support creating a shared understanding of political issues. Therefore, the reviewed political discussion boards do only provide weak support for consensus.
Pluralism: $>_2$	Political discussion boards let their users easily form counter-communities and create collective actions. The boards strongly support pluralism.

results, the centroid is the most representative single number of a polytope, thus reducing the operation to a sum of multiplied factors w_i and v_{ij}.

The criteria (in our example, the four characteristics transparency, autonomy, consensus, and pluralism, but more generally any set of e-democracy aspects) are then measured and weighted into an index reflecting the degree of fulfilment of the characteristics. The result will use the concept of steps to denote the strength of a tool along each dimension in relation to a "zero tool", having no value whatsoever regarding democratic qualities. We thus rank all of the tools under consideration under each of the four criteria in relation to the zero tool. Thereafter, the criteria are ranked according to the method described above. The values and weights are then aggregated into a weighted value $U(a_j)$ and where finally the resulting index $I(a_j)$ is

$U(a_j)$ rounded to the nearest integer value. The scale and measurements involved can be made even more realistic by, e.g., utilising sub-criteria as well as more complex assessments, in terms of mixtures and comparisons and interval statements as well as distributions, along the lines of, e.g., [26]. How this works in practice will be demonstrated in the next section.

13.6　Some Examples of Components of the Positioning Criteria

We will now map some tools according to the index being used. As above, we will use the following:

- **Transparency:** supporting the sharing of data between agencies, government to citizens, and citizens to citizens
- **Autonomy:** supporting forms for open-source culture where participants typically collaborate
- **Consensus:** supporting forms for collective decisions and information production
- **Pluralism:** acknowledging diversity, inequality, and conflicts

13.6.1　Grading and Scale

Table 13.2 and 13.3 show the analysis of Municipality Chat Rooms and the analysis of Political Discussion Boards respectively.

First, we need a scale for the analyses. Assume that we desire the indices to be around 20 on average and that we expect an average k of about 1.2 for the $>k$ statements. Then we obtain a scaling constant $\alpha = 20/1.2 \approx 16.7$. (The particular scale does not matter and any linear transformation of this one would do.) Utilising the transformations described in the previous section, this results in the following assessments:

- The components of Municipality Chat Rooms (a_1) are assigned the following surrogate numbers: Transparency: $v_{12} = 0.0$; Autonomy: $v_{14} = 0.0$; Consensus: $v_{11} = 33.3$; Pluralism: $v_{13} = 16.7$.
- And for Political Discussion Boards (a_2): Transparency: $v_{22} = 0.0$; Autonomy: $v_{24} = 33.3$; Consensus: $v_{21} = 16.7$; Pluralism: $v_{23} = 33.3$.

Further assume that we establish a ranking of the importance of the characteristics, for example $Transparency>_1 Pluralism>_0 Autonomy>_2 Consensus$, resulting in the following weights: $w(Transparency) = 0.40$; $w(Pluralism) = w(Autonomy) = 0.25$; $w(Consensus) = 0.10$.

Note that these values are not simply assigned but a consequence of the asserted ranking and the derived characteristic weights. Consequently, the ranking then yields the indices $I(a_j)$ by

$$\bar{U}\left(a_j\right) = \sum_{i=1}^{n} \bar{w}_i \bar{v}_{ij}$$

as the sum of products $w_i \bullet v_{ij}$ and then $I(a_j)$ as $U(a_j)$ rounded to the nearest integer. The result is thus that Municipality Chat Rooms receive an index $I(a_1) = 17$ and that Political Discussion Boards receive $I(a_2) = 18$.

One issue concerning the use of e-democracy tools such as the above ones is that a tool is not always used as intended – if we by intended mean increasing e-democracy or the participation in e-democratic processes. Just using a tool that in our analysis displays high support for information dissemination may not in the end increase e-democracy per se – it might simply be used to disseminate information to a target population for good and for bad. A tool is not inherently democratic or non-democratic but in our framework, we analyse the *potential* of using these tools to support components that are usually mentioned in the literature as useful and beneficial for e-democracy (as was discussed in the literature overview above). The example continues with more specific e-tools:

13.7   Analysis of BottenAda, Twitter, Ushahidi, and Facebook

13.7.1   Analysis: BottenAda

BottenAda provides information on parties and coalitions rather than issues to reach consensus without the possibility to have discussions or reach consensus on specific issues. BottenAda used Bayesian statistics to try to predict the election results in Sweden in 2014.

- Transparency: BottenAda supports transparency in that it visualises the strengths of parties and coalitions of parties based on polls of polls and Bayesian analysis. By showing the likelihood of, for example, a certain party's ability to take seats in the government, it lets potential voters make more informed and/or tactical decisions on which party to support. Measure: $>_2$
- Autonomy: BottenAda does not support networking, collaborating, distributing, or sharing among users. Measure: $>_0$
- Consensus: BottenAda does not support consensus per se, since it only provides information on parties and coalitions rather than issues to reach consensus, without the possibility to have discussions or reach consensus on specific issues. Measure: $>_0$
- Pluralism: BottenAda does not support pluralism in more than it recognises the probable percent of votes for different parties. It does not cover different ideas or issues in its scope, and it does not support collective actions Measure: $>_0$

13.7.2   Analysis: Twitter

Twitter is a very well-known online social networking service where a user can post short messages, so-called "tweets", iterate others' messages, and interact.

- Transparency: Twitter does not explicitly support forms sharing of data between agencies, government to citizens, and citizens to citizens, where the aim is better service, efficiency, and innovation: aggregating, competing, informing, petitioning, transacting, transmitting, voting, controlling. Implicitly it supports the aim of informing. Measure: $>_0$
- autonomy: Twitter supports forms for open-source cultures where participants typically collaborate motivated by peer recognition or other micro-rewards: networking, collaborating, distributing, and sharing. Measure: $>_2$
- Consensus: Twitter does not explicitly support forms for collective decision-making or information production. Implicitly it supports some of the aspects of shared understanding, namely: opinion-forming, arguing, and agenda-setting. Measure: $>_1$
- Pluralism: Twitter supports or enables activities that acknowledge diversity, inequality, and conflicts. There is some support for establishing counter-cultures and collective actions: associating, campaigning, contesting, forming groups, community building, organising, mediating, and protesting. Measure: $>_1$

Adopting the same characteristic weights as in the example above, we obtain the indices $I(BottenAda) = 8$ and $I(Twitter) = 14$.

Similarly, various other tools can be evaluated and positioned with respect either to the strengths of the respective characteristics (such as those in Figure 13.1) or to the aggregated measure discussed above where also the relative importance of the characteristics can be considered. For a practitioner to use an indexing method like this, a relevant set of criteria for the purpose intended has to be selected, defined, and described. Then for each participating e-democracy tool, it needs to be measured and evaluated on a scale as in Figure 13.2, comparing it to a base or zero tool with almost no capabilities in the dimension under consideration. The results of the comparisons can be illustrated on an index scale as shown in Figure 13.3. For the actual implementation, a spreadsheet should be sufficient. It could easily hold the computational formulas, thus hiding them in everyday use and eliminate the risk of making errors that could arise if performing the calculations manually.

The locus is not a contributing aspect as such to the index but can balance the values of a tool regarding the other criteria. We can consider the locus here more formally by expressing the weighted overall value of an e-tool E_i with, for instance, two loci, each having four sub-criteria as $\sum_{j=1}^{2} w_j \sum_{k=1}^{3} w_{jk} v_{jik}$. The use of a locus perspective just adds the possibility to weight the usability of a tool with respect to its main purpose and can be represented as a criteria hierarchy, such as in Figure 13.4.

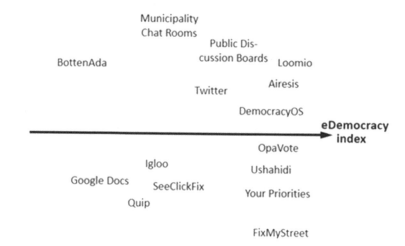

Figure 13.3. Example of how various types of tools can be positioned on a mapping of e-democracy to an index. (Note that Figure 13.3 aims only at illustrating the methodology with a broad coverage of tools. To give a more precise picture, a much more detailed analysis would be required, which is beyond the scope of this chapter.)

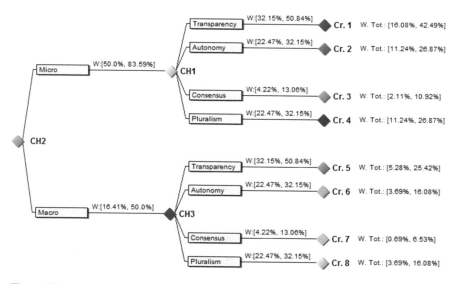

Figure 13.4. A criteria hierarchy including the Locus aspect.

13.7.3 Analysis: Ushahidi

Ushahidi was developed to map reports of violence in Kenya after the post-election violence in 2008 and used crowdsourcing for social activism and public accountability. It has thereafter been used in several places, particularly in crises and for tracking corruption.

- Transparency: Ushahidi supports transparency as a fundamental idea. Measure Micro: $>_3$, Macro: $>_3$
- Autonomy: Ushahidi supports forms for open-source cultures, distributing, and sharing among users. Measure: Micro: $>_3$, Macro: $>_1$
- Consensus: Ushahidi does not support consensus per se as it primarily provides a reporting and visualisation function. Measure: Micro: $>_0$, Macro: $>_0$
- Pluralism: Ushahidi does support pluralism and can cover different ideas or issues in its scope. It does implicitly support collective actions. In principle, this could imply international activism as well, but this is not its main use. Measure: Micro: $>_2$, Macro: $>_1$
- Locus: There are no explicit restrictions regarding its global use, but the actual use has been from a micro perspective so the main importance is for local purposes. Measure: Micro $>_1$ Macro

Continuing with the same characteristic weights as previously, but this time applied to the two loci, we obtain the intermediate results $U(Ushahidi:Macro) = 28.3$ and $U(Ushahidi:Micro) = 40.8$. Since we rank the importance of the loci as Micro $>_1$ Macro, the total index $I(Ushahidi)$ is determined by taking the nearest integer of the expression $0.67 \cdot U(Ushahidi:Micro) + 0.33 \cdot U(Ushahidi:Macro) = 36.6$, yielding $I(Ushahidi) = 37$.

13.7.4   Ranking Digital Intermediaries: Facebook

Similar to Twitter in relying on user-generated content as a business model, Facebook is currently the largest social media platform with over 2.7 billion monthly active users, financed through advertisement placement using user profiling and micro-targeting marketing techniques. Since in many countries this is the dominating e-democracy tool used by citizens to engage in the public sphere, we will evaluate it according to the four criteria above, but we will also include (a) privacy and (b) a discussion of how the double role of e-tool and digital intermediary can play out in the overall evaluation.

In what concerns privacy, the data misuse by which Cambridge Analytica managed to harvest the personal data of potentially 87 million Facebook users to tailor and place political advertisements in the 2016 U.S. presidential election without users' knowledge or notification by Facebook, triggered a large debate on the platform's use of personal data, as well as on accountability and the effectiveness of self-regulation for e-tools. Problems related to information asymmetry were seen at various levels, from users' lack of understanding of privacy policies to members of Congress who were struggling to understand Facebook's source of revenue and technological architecture. Users' and regulators' misinformed trade-off between privacy and communication has, in this case, led to an erosion of trust in Facebook's services and willingness to protect its users' data from malevolent actors. In order to regain its users' and investors' trust (and to comply with GDPR for European

Union users), Facebook focused its efforts to improve its users' privacy on three main aspects: transparency, readability, and affirmative consent. While users are better informed of the privacy policies and can opt in for settings that make their profiles or activity available for other users, Facebook's data policy on what it collects and, importantly, provides to its clients for ad tailoring is non-negotiable.

Given that the platform dominates many national public spheres with respect to e-participation, a user has furthermore no viable alternative to engage politically online. Given that privacy addresses, in particular, the question of self-governance and personal decisional autonomy, the question of choice becomes paramount and needs to be one of the components assessed by the e-democracy index. The analysis, then, becomes as follows:

- Transparency: Facebook implicitly supports the aim of informing and citizen-to-citizen sharing of data, through communities of practice organized in groups or pages, lacking, however, information aggregation, petitioning, transacting, voting, and controlling. It does not support the sharing of data between agencies or from government to citizens for better services or efficiency. Measure: $>_1$
- Autonomy: Facebook supports open-source cultures where participants associate, collaborate, distribute and share, motivated by peer recognition, social affirmation, and other user engagement rewards, however, the networking and distributing components are limited by algorithms rewarding users' predetermined preferences. Measure: : $>_1$
- Consensus: Facebook does not explicitly support forms of collective decisions. It does however implicitly support information production through its Crisis Response feature or groups, as well as arguing and informing. It does not provide incentives or mechanisms for agenda-setting, deliberating, trade-off analysis, or negotiation. Measure: $>_1$
- Pluralism: Facebook acknowledges diversity, inequality, and conflicts and there is some support for establishing counter-cultures and collective actions, including associating, campaigning, forming groups, organizing, and protesting. It offers little support for enabling counter-actions and diversity due to its prioritization and higher visibility of sponsored content. Measure: $>_1$
- Privacy: It uses affirmative consent and reviewing options for privacy settings which establish a profile's audience and accessibility. It does not provide mechanisms for choosing what data gets collected and shared with Facebook's clients, nor for negotiating terms, declining, controlling, holding accountable for data misuse, or for ensuring trust. Measure: $>_0$

We can derive Facebook's index for the other four aspects in the same manner as for the other tools above. Since its actual use and reach is local as well as global, the macro and micro perspectives coexist, leading to a combined locus index calculation. The index for Facebook becomes, using the same weights as above, I(*Facebook*) = 17.

One additional aspect which could influence the evaluation of social media is their double role as e-democracy support tools and digital intermediaries, with a larger editorial role in filtering out content that violates community norms, such as hate speech or disinformation. Digital intermediaries are not subject to media regulation because they do not identify themselves as publishers, but since they have the power to structure the media environment inasmuch as news media have become increasingly dependent upon them, we can include under the previous e-democracy aspects some sub-components derived from media pluralism indexes, such as market plurality, political independence, and social inclusiveness [14]. Facebook is one of the top two digital intermediaries owning more than half the digital media market in all countries and two-thirds of the digital advertising market. Their dominance in the media economy affects, for instance, consensus issues such as agenda-setting, informing, and educating, deliberating or opinion-forming.

Facebook does offer incentives and tools for deliberation, but it is market-driven and aims at customer engagement more than at improving the quality of the public sphere. Relying mostly on self-regulation, digital intermediaries' roles as media and information gatekeepers, at a macro level, can affect the overall ecosystem of e-democracy tools.

The index itself is insensitive to the number of dimensions studied. Some additional dimensions (criteria) could be valuable in these evaluations. For example, criteria for usability could be employed. It is important for the practical use of a tool that it is reasonably well-designed when it comes to the usability and accessibility of the user interface (UI). If usability is to be considered, one way of measuring the success of the UI in that respect would be to consider its affordance, i.e. how well its functionality could be inferred from the interface that it presents to the prospective intended users, some or many of which might not be extensive everyday computer users. Affordance theory, while introduced by [38], has among computer scientists and computer tool designers become widely spread as a concept by [57]. A dimension of affordance could easily be added to the framework, as could many others depending on which goals are being set by the index makers.

13.8   Concluding Remarks and Discussion

In this chapter, we have suggested a comparatively simple but still mathematically sound framework as the basis for a method for conceptualising components supporting e-democracy as well as for the evaluation of how these dimensions (criteria) can visually position different components of e-democracy. We have also suggested how to use the framework for evaluating tools to support participation and how tools for supporting e-democracy can be measured in terms of the degree of support for the various components. This enables users to evaluate and hence select tools to support participation. The evaluation model builds on the inclusion of different views of e-democracy, not seeing them as conflicting per se but rather making it possible for e-democracy tool users and developers to understand the varying degree of support a tool can display for several aspects of democracy. The framework also provides a visualisation of complex theories and can thus contribute to a more informed discussion on what types of democratic values are being supported in a particular e-democracy tool.

The motivation behind the framework is that democracy is a multi-faceted concept and, needless to say, evaluating ICT tools for enhancing democracy along only one dimension is usually misleading. For instance, a political system based on elections according to a simple majority principle might still be highly undemocratic in most reasonable senses of the concept. Instead, several dimensions must be considered. An evaluation of the e-democracy qualities of an IT-tool in terms of how the tool specifically supports different aspects of democracy must reflect these sometimes intersecting dimensions.

We have, therefore, suggested an e-democracy mapping and indexing technique that constitutes a functional approach to evaluating e-democracy tool support systems while taking various aspects of democracy into account and analysing the concept with respect to a set of dimensions. This framework builds on the inclusion of different views of democracy, clarifying the relations between several aspects of it. The framework provides an easily accessible visualisation of complex theories, and can thus contribute to the development of a discussion on which types of democratic values are embedded in e-democracy strategies or tools. The point of departure for the exemplification in this chapter has been four different aspects of democracy (transparency, autonomy, consensus, and pluralism) as well as locus and privacy.

The comparatively simple framework has then subsequently been used as the basis for a method for conceptualising components supporting e-democracy as well as for evaluation. The framework makes use of the aspects and it is demonstrated how these dimensions can visually position different components of e-democracy. We have also suggested how to use the framework for evaluating tools to support participation in these contexts and how tools for supporting e-democracy can be measured in terms of the degree of support for the various components. In practice, geometrical representations become problematic, although they can still be made meaningful by using projections onto subspaces and handled analogously, or alternatively by using the index without a corresponding visualisation.

In any case, the framework can support interdisciplinarity and communication with a diversity of stakeholders in a highly multidisciplinary development context. Depending on the goals, the e-democracy map can be used to assess and choose a tool to be selected or constructed to meet those goals. The framework can also be used as a way to reflect on whether a tool can be enhanced in some way, or to see which democracy aspects a portfolio of tools is covering. This type of mapping and indexing framework could, for example, be used by an e-democracy supporting organisation to categorise and keep track of the various e-democracy tools that exist within their domain of interest.

One issue with respect to the use of e-democracy tools is that they may as well be used for disinformation as well as spreading information. A tool is not always used as intended if we by intended mean increasing e-democracy or participation in e-democracy processes. Just by using a tool that in our analysis displays large support for information dissemination, for instance, Political Discussion Boards and

Twitter, may not increase e-democracy per se – it may be used to disseminate information to a target population for good and for bad. Thus, a tool is not democratic or non-democratic by itself – what we analyse in this chapter is the potential of using ICT-tools to support activities/functions usually mentioned in the literature [8, 22, 62] as useful for e-democracy. Furthermore, tools such as social media do not primarily serve the purpose of supporting e-democracy, but their scope and use have progressively accommodated various types of political expression and participation, insofar as they occupy a significant part of sharing, networking, collaborating or community building practices online. Evaluating them as e-democracy support systems, therefore, can help us better distinguish between functionalities which increase user engagement with a platform's products and clients, and those which enable participation in democratic processes. We have not covered this extensively, but the purpose of this chapter is rather to investigate how such a map can be meaningfully applied, and further studies of the framework are needed to obtain better coverage. However, this is beyond the scope of the current project reported here.

We invite others to evaluate and improve the framework. Several roads of improvement of the work are conceivable. Firstly, the scoring process in terms of how measurements are assigned to e-tools could be tuned in several ways. A first step could be to test the reliability of the assigned values by letting larger groups of researchers and practitioners redo the scoring of the samples analysed in this chapter (i.e. Municipality Chat Rooms, Political Discussion Boards, BottenAda, Twitter and Facebook) and other similar tools. Another aspect concerns the normalisation of the obtained results, i.e. the scores could be weighted in order to indicate that some analysed aspects are considered to be more important than others. The framework is open by design and can easily be combined with various existing multi-criteria decision tools or tools for conflict detection and resolutions of different complexities to form a more powerful toolset. Another natural extension is to allow for a richer variety of statements for which there exist methods within the area of multi-criteria decision making.

Acknowledgements The work in this chapter was supported by the EU project Co-Inform (Co-Creating Misinformation-Resilient Societies H2020-SC6-CO-CREATION-2017) and the EU project Open-Science Evidence-Based Methodologies for the Development of Epidemic Combating Policies, European Open Science Cloud EOSC, Covid-19 Fast Track Funding.

References

1. Ahn, B.S. and Park, K.S., 2008. Comparing methods for multiattribute decision making with ordinal weights. *Computers & Operations Research*, 35(5), pp.1660–1670.
2. Alarabiat A., Soares D.S., and Estevez E., 2016. Electronic Participation with a Special Reference to Social Media - A Literature Review. In: Tambouris E. et al. (eds) Electronic Participation. ePart 2016. Lecture Notes in Computer Science, vol. 9821. Springer, Cham.

3. Alathur, S., Ilavarasan, V., and Gupta, M.P., 2014. Determinants of Citizens' Electronic Participation: Insights from India, Transforming Government People Process and Policy 8(3), pp.447–472.

4. Al-Jamal, M.A. and Shanab, E.A., 2016. The influence of open government on e-government website: the case of Jordan. *International Journal of Electronic Governance*, 8(2), pp.159–179.

5. Ayo, C.K., Oni, A.A., and Mbarika, V.W., 2013. "A strategic framework for e-democracy development", in the Proceedings of the International Conference on e-Learning, e-Business, Enterprise Information Systems, and e-Government (EEE), The Steering Committee of The World Congress in Computer Science, Computer Engineering and Applied Computing (WorldComp).

6. Bader, V., Borchers, D. and Vitikainen, A., 2012. *Individual and/or associational autonomy? Associative Democracy and the Freedoms of Entry and Exit*. Vitikainen, A. (Ed.), On Exit: Interdisciplinary Perspectives on the Right of Exit in Liberal Multicultural Societies, Walter de Gruyter, Berlin. 2012

7. Barron, F.H. and Barrett, B.E., 1996. Decision quality using ranked attribute weights. *Management Science*, 42(11), pp.1515–1523.

8. Bellamy, C., 2000. Modelling electronic democracy, towards democratic discourses for an information age. In: J. Hoff, I. Horrocks and P. Tops, eds., *Democratic governance and new technology: technologically mediated innovations in political practice in Western Europe*. London: Routledge, pp.33–54.

9. Ben Eli, A. and Hutchins, J., 2010. *Intelligence after Intellipedia: improving the push pull balance with a social networking utility*. [online] Available at: http://www.dtic.mil/cgi-bin/GetTR Doc?Location=U2&doc=GetTRDoc.pdf&AD=ADA523538 [Accessed 29 Aug. 2020].

10. Bennett, C. J. and Parsons, C. 2013. Privacy and surveillance: the multidisciplinary literature on the capture, use, and disclosure of personal information in cyberspace. In: Dutton, W (Ed.) The Oxford Handbook of Internet Studies, Oxford, Oxford University Press.

11. Bindu, N., Prem Sankar, C., and Satheesh Kumar, K., 2019. From conventional governance to e-democracy: Tracing the evolution of egovernance research trends using network analysis tools Government Information Quarterly.

12. Bradshaw, S. and Howard, P. 2018. "Challenging Truth and Trust: A Global Inventory of Organized Social Media Manipulation", Oxford Internet Institute, University of Oxford, available at: https://comprop.oii.ox.ac.uk/wp-content/uploads/sites/93/2018/07/ct2018.pdf

13. Bright, J. and Margetts, H., 2016. Big Data and Public Policy: Can It Succeed Where E-Participation Has Failed? Policy & Internet, 8: 218–224. doi:https://doi.org/10.1002/poi3.130.

14. Brogi, E. et al., 2020, "Monitoring media pluralism in the digital era: application of the Media Pluralism Monitor 2020 in the European Union, Albania & Turkey: policy report", European University Institute, DOI: https://doi.org/10.2870/21728.

15. Brown, A. J. 2020. 'Should I Stay or Should I Leave?': Exploring (Dis)continued Facebook Use After the Cambridge Analytica Scandal. *Social Media + Society*, January-March, pp.1–8.

16. Butler, J., Jia, J. and Dyer, J., 1997. Simulation techniques for the sensitivity analysis of multi-criteria decision models. *European Journal of Operational Research*, 103(3), pp.531–546.

17. Cantijoch, M., Galandini, S. and Gibson, R., 2016. 'It's not about me, it's about my community': a mixed-method study of civic websites and community efficacy. *New Media & Society*, 18(9), pp.1896–1915.

18. Collier, D. and Adcock, R., 1999. 'Democracy and dichotomies: a pragmatic approach to choices about concepts', Annual Review of Political Science, 2, pp.537–565.

19. Comunello, F. and Anzera, G. 2012. Will the revolution be tweeted? A conceptual framework for understanding the social media and the Arab Spring. *Islam and Christian–Muslim Relations*, 23(4), pp.453–470, DOI: https://doi.org/10.1080/09596410.2012.712435.

20. Coppedge, M., Gerring, J., Lindberg, S.I., Skaaning, S.E. and Teorell, J., 2017. V-Dem comparisons and contrasts with other measurement projects. *V-Dem Working Paper* 2017:45.

21. Cozzani, F., 2015. Knowledge management 2.0: the proposal for Commipedia. *Transforming Government: People, Process and Policy*, 9(1), pp.17–34.
22. Dahlberg, L., 2011. Re-constructing digital democracy: an outline of four 'positions.' *New Media & Society*, 13(6), pp.855–872.
23. Danielson, M. and Ekenberg, L., 2016a. A robustness study of state-of-the-art surrogate weights for MCDM. *Group Decision and Negotiation*, 26(4), pp.677–691.
24. Danielson, M. and Ekenberg, L., 2016b. The CAR method for using preference strength in multi-criteria decision making. *Group Decision and Negotiation*, 25(4), pp.775–797.
25. Danielson, M. and Ekenberg, L., 2020. A Framework for Categorising and Evaluating Tools for E-democracy, The Electronic Journal of e-Government 18(3), pp.69–82.
26. Danielson, M., Ekenberg, L. and Larsson, A., 2020. A second-order-based decision tool for evaluating decisions under conditions of severe uncertainty, Knowledge-Based Systems 191.
27. Danielson, M., Ekenberg, L., Larsson, A. and Riabacke, M., 2010. Transparent public decision making – discussion and case study in Sweden. In: *e-democracy: a group decision and negotiation perspective*, eds., D. R. Insua and S. French, Dordrecht: Springer, pp.263–281.
28. Danielson, M., Ekenberg, L. and Riabacke, A., 2009. A prescriptive approach to elicitation of decision data. Journal of Statistical Theory and Practice, 3(1), pp.157–168.
29. Democracy Index, 2018. Me too? Political participation, protest and democracy. [online] The Economist Intelligence Unit Limited. Available at: https://www.eiu.com/public/topical_report. aspx?campaignid=Democracy2018 [Accessed 29 Aug. 2020].
30. Ekenberg, L., Hansson, K., Danielson, M., Cars, G. et al., 2017. *Deliberation, representation, equity research approaches, tools and algorithms for participatory processes*. Cambridge, UK Open Book Publishers.
31. Ekenberg, L., Larsson, A., Idefeldt, J. and Bohman, S., 2009. The lack of transparency in public decision processes. *International Journal of Public Information Systems*, 5(1), pp.1–8.
32. European Commission DG CONNECT, A vision for public services, 2013.
33. Farina, C.R., Epstein, D., Heidt, J.B. and Newhart, M.J., 2013. Regulation room. *Transforming Government: People, Process and Policy*, 7(4), pp.501–516.
34. Fasth, T., Bohman, S. Larsson, A. Ekenberg L. and Danielson, M., 2020. Portfolio Decision Analysis for Evaluating Stakeholder Conflicts in Land Use Planning, Group Decision and Negotiation 29, pp.321–343.
35. Ferretti, V., Pluchinotta, I., and Tsoukiàs, A., 2019. Studying the generation of alternatives in public policy making processes. European Journal of Operational Research 273, pp.353–363.
36. Freschi, A.C., Medaglia, R., Nørbjerg, J. et al., 2009. "eParticipation in the institutional domain: a review of research: analytical report on eParticipation research from an administration and political perspective in six European countries", Freschi AC, Medaglia R, Nørbjerg J, et al. (eds), DEMO-Net Consortium, Bergamo.
37. Fyfe, T. and Crookall, P., 2010. Social media and public sector policy dilemmas, Institute of Public Administration of Canada, Toronto.
38. Gibson, J.J., 1977. *The perception of the visual world*. Westport, Conn.: Greenwood Press.
39. Hansson, K. and Ekenberg, L., 2018. Embodiment and Gameplay: Situating the User in Crowdsourced Information Production: Innovative Perspectives on Public Administration in the Digital Age, in Innovative Perspectives on Public Administration in the Digital Age, Ed: A.P. Manoharan, pp.239–255, IGI Global.
40. Hansson, K., 2015. *Accommodating differences: Power, belonging and representation online*, PhD thesis, Department of Computer and Systems Sciences, Stockholm University.
41. Hansson, K., Belkacem, K. and Ekenberg, L., 2014. Open Government and Democracy. *Social Science Computer Review*, 33(5), pp.540–555.
42. Heeks, R. and Bailur, S., 2007. "Analyzing e-government research: Perspectives, philosophies, theories, methods, and practice", Government Information Quarterly, Vol. 24 No. 2, pp.243–265.

43. Jia J, Fischer GW, and Dyer J., 1998. Attribute weighting methods and decision quality in the presence of response error: a simulation study, J. Behavioral Decision Making 11(2), pp.85–105.

44. Komendantova, N., Ekenberg, L., Marashdeh, L., Al Salaymeh, A., Danielson, M. and Linnerooth-Bayer, J., 2018. Are energy security concerns dominating environmental concerns? Evidence from stakeholder participation processes on energy transition in Jordan. *Climate*, 6(4), pp.88–99.

45. Lee, N., 2014. Facebook Nation. New York, NY: Springer.

46. Lever, A. 2006. Privacy Rights and Democracy: A Contradiction in Terms?. *Contemporary Political Theory*, Vol. 5, No. 2, pp. 142–162. doi:https://doi.org/10.1057/palgrave.cpt.9300187.

47. Lidén, G., 2011. "Is e-democracy more than democratic ? - An examination of the implementation of socially sustainable values in e-democratic processes", Electronic Journal of e-Government, Vol. 9 No. 2, pp.84–94.

48. Lörincz, B., Tinholt, D., van der Linden, N., Colclough, G., Cave, J., Schindler, R., Cattaneo, G., Lifonti, R., Jacquet, L. and Millard, J., 2010. Digitizing Public Services in Europe: Putting ambition into action, European Commission, Directorate General for Information Society and Media.

49. Macintosh, A. and Whyte, A., 2006. "Evaluating how eParticipation changes local democracy", eGovernment Workshop 11 September 2006, Brunel University, West London.

50. Macintosh, A., Coleman, S., and Schneeberger, A., 2009. "eParticipation: The research gaps", Electronic Participation, Vol. 9 No. 1, pp.1–11.

51. Manheim, K. and Kaplan, L. 2019. "Artificial Intelligence: Risks to Privacy and Democracy", *Yale Journal of Law and Technology*, Vol. 21, No.106, available at: https://ssrn.com/abstract=3273016.

52. Marsden, J., 2013. Stigmergic self-organization and the improvisation of Ushahidi. *Cognitive Systems Research*, 21, pp.52–64.

53. Medaglia, R., 2007. "The challenged identity of a field: The state of the art of eParticipation research", Information Polity, Vol. 12 No. 3, pp.169–181.

54. Medaglia, R., 2012. eParticipation research: moving characterization forward (2006-2011), Government Information Quarterly, Vol. 29 No. 3, pp.346–360.

55. Mobini, P. and Hansson, H., 2014. E-participation in higher education: the importance of non-technical factors as identified in the EU-project MyUniversity. *IEEE Frontiers in Education Conference, FIE) Proceedings*, Madrid: IEEE, pp.1–8.

56. Naranjo-Zolotov, M., Oliveira, T. and Casteleyn, S., 2018. E-participation adoption models research in the last 17 years: a weight and meta-analytical review. *Computers in Human Behavior*, 81, pp.350–365. [online] https://doi.org/10.1016/j.chb.2017.12.031

57. Norman, D.A., 2013. *The design of everyday things*. New York: Basic Books.

58. Noveck B.S., 2009. "Wiki government: How technology Can make government better, democracy stronger, and citizens more powerful", Brookings Institution Revised 2nd edition. Massachusetts: MIT Press.

59. OMB: The Open Government Progress Report to the American People (Office of Management and Budget, December 2009), available at: http://www.npstc.org/documents/OGIProgressReportAmericanPeople20091208.pdf.

60. Oni, A., Ayo, C., Mbarika, V., et al., 2014. "E-democracy implementation: The imperative of agenda setting", in the Proceedings of the 14th European conference on e-government: ECEG 2014, Academic Conferences Limited, pp. 203–209.

61. Orihuela, L., and Obi, T., 2012. E-Democracy: ICT for a Better Relation between the State and Their Citizens. In S. S. Mishra (Ed.). E-Democracy Concepts and Practices by Mishra, Santap Sanhari Dec-31-2012 Hardback. SBS Publishers.

62. Päivärinta, T. and Sæbø, Ø., 2006. Models of e-democracy, *Communications of the Association for Information Systems*, 1(1), pp. 818–840.

63. Parker, G.G., Van Alstyne, M.W. and Choudary, S.P., 2016. Platform revolution: How networked markets are transforming the economy—and how to make them work for you. New York; London: WW Norton & Company
64. Pew Research Center, July 2018, Activism in the Social Media Age.
65. Pirannejad, A., Janssen, M., 2017. Internet and political empowerment: towards a taxonomy for online political empowerment. Information Development, 35(1), pp.80–95.
66. Pirannejad, A., Janssen, M. and Rezaei, J., 2019. Towards a balanced e-participation index: integrating government and society perspectives. *Government Information Quarterly*, 36(4), pp.1–16.
67. Pluchinotta, I., Kazakçi, A.O., Giordano, R. and Tsoukiàs, A., 2019. Design Theory for Generating Alternatives in Public Decision Making Processes, Group Decision and Negotiation.
68. Porwol, L., Ojo, A. and Breslin, J.G., 2018. Social software infrastructure for e-participation. *Government Information Quarterly*, 35(4), pp.S88–S98.
69. Riabacke, M., Danielson, M. and Ekenberg, L., 2012. State-of-the-art prescriptive criteria weight elicitation. *Advances in Decision Sciences*, 2012, pp.1–24.
70. Sæbø, Ø., Rose, J. and Nyvang, T., 2009. The role of social networking services in eParticipation, In: A. Macintosh and E. Tambouris, eds., *Electronic Participation*, Sprinter Lecture Notes in Computer Science LNCS vol. 5694, Berlin: Springer, pp. 46–55.
71. Sæbø, Ø., Rose, J. and Skiftenes Flak, L., 2008. "The shape of eParticipation: Characterizing an emerging research area", Government Information Quarterly, Vol. 25 No. 3, pp. 400–428
72. Sanford, C. and Rose, J., 2007. "Characterizing eParticipation", International Journal of Information Management, Vol. 27 No. 6, pp. 406–421.
73. Sinclair, J., Timothy, A., Peirson-Smith, J. and Boerchers, M., 2017. Environmental assessments in the Internet age: the role of e-governance and social media in creating platforms for meaningful participation, Impact Assessment and Project Appraisal, Vol. 35:2.
74. Skaaning, S-E., 2018. *The global state of democracy indices methodology: conceptualization and measurement framework*, version 2, Strömsborg: IDEA, The International Institute for Democracy and Electoral Assistance.
75. Susha, I. and Grönlund, Å., 2012. E-participation research: systematizing the field. *Government Information Quarterly*, 29(3), pp.373–382.
76. Szkuta, K., Pizzicannella, R. and Osimo, D., 2014. Collaborative approaches to public sector innovation: a scoping study. *Telecommunications Policy*, 38(5–6), pp.558–567.
77. Tambouris, E., Liotas, N. and Tarabanis, K., 2007. "A Framework for Assessing eParticipation Projects and Tools", In HICSS-40 - Hawaii International Conference on System Sciences, pp. 1–10.
78. van Dijk, J. A. G. M., 2012. The network society (3rd ed.). London; New Delhi; Thousand Oaks, CA; Singapore: Sage
79. van Dijk, J. 2009. Users like you? Theorizing agency in user-generated content. *Media, Culture & Society*, 31 (1), pp.41–58
80. Wimmer, M. A., 2007. Ontology for an e-participation virtual resource centre. In: *Proceedings of the 1st international conference on Theory and practice of electronic governance - ICEGOV '07*, Macao, China, pp.89–98.

Chapter 14
A Ranking Model for Citizen Engagement in a Smart City

Julien Carbonnell

14.1 Introduction

I am looking for a way to prove that citizen engagement in decision-making is one key success factor for future smart-city governance. To do so, I have been collecting inhabitants' answers to a survey in three case studies for the cities: Taipei (Taiwan), Tel Aviv (Israel), and Tallinn (Estonia).

I collected 366 answers (122 respondents in each city) from random inhabitants online (Facebook Groups, direct messages on LinkedIn, and messaging apps) as well as in-person interviews at events related to smart city and urban innovation startups.

In this article, I present a complete data analysis on my survey results, using Python programming language (See Fig. 14.1), in order to take an in-depth look at the features and insights that can be extracted from the collected data. The anonymized dataset and the coding notebook are available on GitHub: https://github.com/democracyStudio/.

14.2 Problem, Hypothesis, and Methodology

Problem

In contemporary democratic regimes, citizen engagement is widely considered by professionals, from both public and private sectors, as a key to successful urban transformations.

J. Carbonnell (✉)
University of Cergy-Pontoise, Cergy-Pontoise, France
e-mail: julien.carbonnell@gmail.com

© Springer Science+Business Media, LLC, part of Springer Nature 2021   329
N. Lee, *Facebook Nation*, https://doi.org/10.1007/978-1-0716-1867-7_14

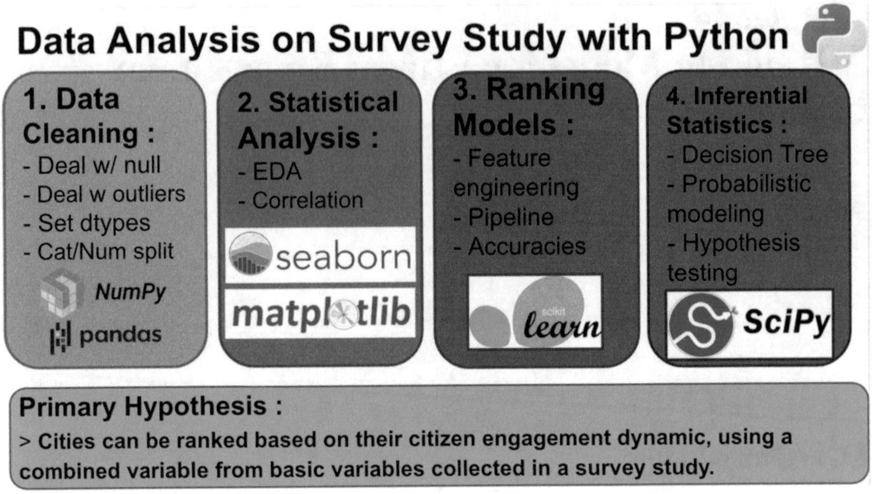

Fig. 14.1 Overview of the technical tools used in this study

Smart city promoters tend to emphasize their citizen-centric models worldwide. But we lack methods and insights about how to engage inhabitants in decision-making for the future of their cities. The widely used management models are highly determined by a design-thinking method which we are not sure about the influence on society at scale. In practice, we can even say that most digital engagement of citizens are mainly communication campaigns which fail to produce any satisfying result. However, we are experiencing a pessimistic citizen crisis in most modern democracies of the world, with a loss of trust in public agents and media, political apathy, and disinterest in elections by a majority of the voters. In this context, there is a crucial need to revive the feeling among the citizens that their opinions count when building the future of their cities.

My approach to this problem involves building a method for citizen engagement in smart city, by classifying the citizens feeling among the most engaged, their profiling attributes, and trying to identify variables depending on this engagement feeling.

Hypothesis

1. The citizens feeling the most engaged, wish to engage more.
2. The citizens feeling the most engaged are the most demanding in terms of engagement frequency.
3. The citizens feeling the most engaged, share their opinion in public easily.
4. The citizens feeling the most engaged, tend to change their opinion during contact with others.

5. The gender has no correlation with the engagement feeling.
6. Younger citizens feel the least engaged. Maybe the oldest feel the same.

Since I am testing my hypothesis on the engagement feeling, I should be able to validate the opposite of the above hypothesis with the following variables:

1bis. The citizens feeling the less engaged, do not wish to engage more.
2bis. The citizens feeling the less engaged, are the least demanding in terms of engagement frequency.
3bis. The citizens feeling the less engaged, share their opinion less easily.
4bis. The citizens feeling the less engaged, change their opinion less easily.

Methodology

Since my methodology of research consists of comparing different case studies, I will test ranking models using machine learning in order to classify citizen profiles from the least to the best engagement level, and to deduct the classification of the least to the most engaging cities from the level of engagement of their citizens.

I am defining a citizen highly engaged in a smart city as someone who:

- has an engagement feeling of 5/10 at least
- uses social media and the Internet as a source of information to shape its opinion
- uses at least two social media platforms
- uses at least two messaging apps
- meets other citizens online
- shares its opinion in public (at least 3/5)
- changes its opinion when in contact with others (at least 3/5)
- wishes to engage more
- employs multiple engagement channels (at least 2/5)
- is active with a moderate to high frequency (at least 1 hour per month).

This combination of variables allows me to create a new variable to classify highly engaged citizens out of the general population. I will use this classification in my machine learning models. It also allows me to create an engagement score to rank citizens from the lowest to the highest engagement level. Each of the conditions above will deliver 1 point to the citizen. In the end, highly engaged citizens will have a score of 10 out of 10. After having validated the accuracy of using a combined variable to classify highly engaged citizens from a survey study on random inhabitants, I will use inferential statistics to test my last hypothesis: "We can use my definition of a highly engaged citizen in a smart city to detect them in a random population of inhabitants." This last step of my study will consist of generalizing my results by using statistical inferences. Building inferences on a general population from a sample usually involves testing hypotheses using probabilistic techniques.

However, hypothesis testing can be a tricky exercise since the method consists of writing a Null Hypothesis and its symmetrical contrary the Alternative Hypothesis, in order to evaluate the level of certainty for one or the other hypothesis. In my case, the hypothesis to test would be:

1. NULL HYPOTHESIS: We cannot use the combined variable highly engaged citizens in order to identify this class of citizens from a random population of inhabitants.
2. ALTERNATIVE HYPOTHESIS: We can use the combined variable highly engaged citizens in order to identify this class of citizens from a random population of inhabitants.

Setting up a statistical test involves several subjective choices and their results are easy to misinterpret. A more informative and effective approach for comparing groups is one based on estimation rather than testing, and it is driven by Bayesian probability rather than frequentist. Rather than testing whether two groups are different, we instead pursue an estimate of how different they are.

14.3   Descriptive Statistics: Distribution and Relationships

Descriptive statistics quantitatively describes or summarizes features from a collection of information. Measures of central tendency such as the mean, median, and mode, as well as measures of variability such as the standard deviation, the minimum and maximum values of the variables, kurtosis and skewness, are commonly used to describe a data set.

Data Cleaning and Data Transformation
Some data cleaning and data transformation will need to be done in order to make further analysis:

- **There are a few nulls** in the variable engagement wish. I will replace it by 1 wish means "No" to the question "Do you wish to engage more?"
- **There are a few outliers** in the date of birth and arrival date in the city of reference. That was predictable since some people do not like to share this information and others have had some difficulty in the mobile version of Google Form to choose a specific year on the calendar. I will only keep the birth dates for the respondents between 18 and 90 years old.
- **All my dataset is composed of categorical variables,** recorded as ordinal integers (See Fig. 14.2). Most ML models and algorithms work on numerical variables, so in order to proceed with the calculation, I will store each variable both in its numerical and its categorical version.
- **Split categorical and numerical in different subsets** to ease its manipulation. It also distinguishes hypotheses from other attributes.

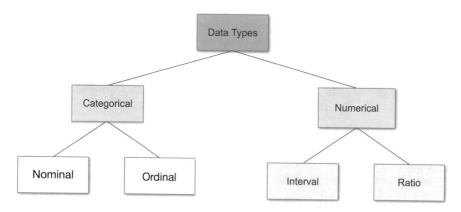

Fig. 14.2: Existing data types

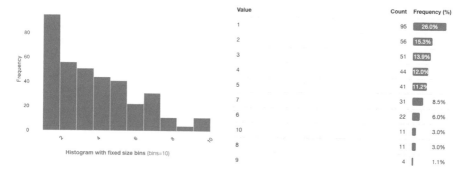

Fig. 14.3: Engagement feeling distribution on the whole dataset
(1: not engaged at all, 10: very engaged)

Exploratory Data Analysis

I have 366 respondents in my surveys: 122 in each of my three case study cities: Taipei (Taiwan), Tallinn (Estonia), and Tel Aviv (Israel).

Using Python's Pandas library on my hypothesis, I can already figure the following trends:

- Engagement feeling (1 to 10) has a mean of 3.61 and standard deviation of 2.43. **The respondents globally express a rather not engaged feeling**. (See Fig. 14.3 and 14.4.)
- Engagement wish (0: No, 1: Yes) has a mean of 0.77 and standard dev of 0.42. **The respondents globally demand to engage more.**
- Engagement frequency (0: Less than one hour a year to 5: More than one hour a day) has a mean of 2.50 and a standard dev of 1.14. **The respondents globally agree to engage one hour a month to one hour a week.** (See Fig. 14.19 and 14.20)

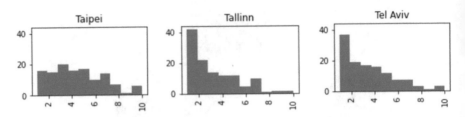

Fig. 14.4: Engagement feeling distribution by city

- Opinion share (1 to 5) has a mean of 3.21 and standard deviation of 1.25. **The respondents globally express a moderate opinion share, skewed right.** (See Fig. 14.13 and 14.14)
- Opinion change (1 to 5) has a mean of 3.06 and a standard deviation of 0.80. **The respondents globally express a moderate opinion change.** (See Fig. 14.15 and 14.16)
- The respondents are 44% women and 56% men globally.
- The respondents are in their 30s, with an age mean at 36 years old, and a standard dev of 13 years (See Fig. 14.21 and 14.22). The length of stay follows similar distribution (See Fig. 14.23 and 14.24).
- **They use globally at least 3 sources of information to shape their opinion,** with a mean of 3.44 and a standard deviation of 1.61. (See Fig. 14.5 and 14.6)
- **Most of them use between 2 and 3 social media platforms** (See Fig. 14.7 and 14.8)
- **They use at least 1 messaging app,** with a mean of 1.55 and a standard dev. of 0.88.
- **They have at least 1 social media influencer and 78% of them have between 1 and 3 social media influencers.** (See Fig. 14.9 and 14.10)
- **They encounter other opinions in at least 2 meeting places,** with a mean of 2.17 and a standard deviation of 1.25. (See Fig. 14.11 and 14.12) But the mode value here differs from the mean: it is 1 for the most respondents. It means that we have a cleaving dataset between encountering other opinions in a few meeting places, while some of them have much more opportunities to encounter other opinions in other meeting places.
- **They globally agree to engage through at least 2 engagement channels,** with a mean of 2.37 and a standard deviation of 1.25. (See Fig. 14.17 and 14.18)
- **Agent's types are unbalanced** (see Fig. 14.25 and 14.26) but I am not using this variable in this study.

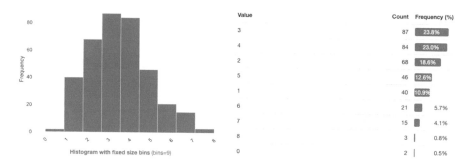

Fig. 14.5: Total sources of information to shape its opinion (from 0 to 8) on the whole dataset

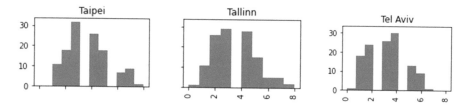

Fig. 14.6: Total sources of information to shape its opinion (from 0 to 8) by city

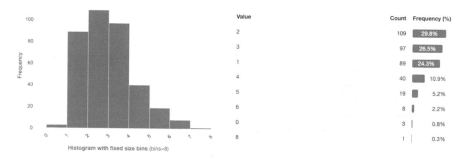

Fig. 14.7: Total social media platforms distribution (from 0 to 8) on the whole dataset

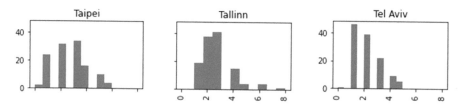

Fig. 14.8: Total social media platforms distribution (from 0 to 8) by city

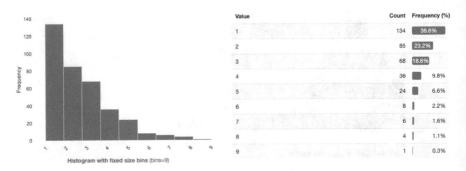

Fig. 14.9: Total influencers distribution (from 1 to 9) on the whole dataset

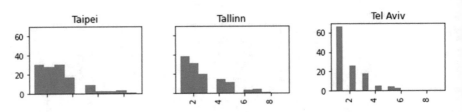

Fig. 14.10: Total influencers distribution (from 1 to 9) by city

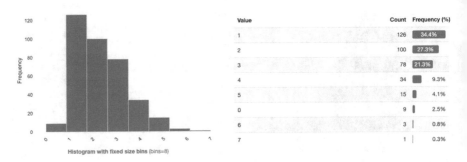

Fig. 14.11: Total meeting places distribution (from 0 to 7) on the whole dataset

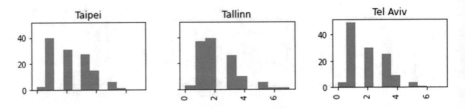

Fig. 14.12: Total meeting places distribution (from 0 to 7) by city

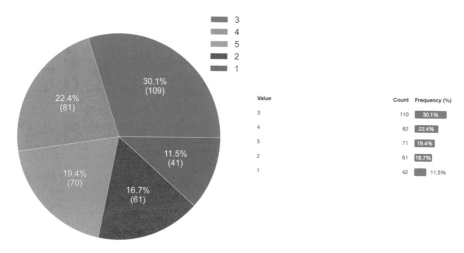

Fig. 14.13: Opinion Share distribution (1: do not share, 5: share very easily) on the whole dataset

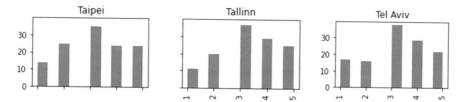

Fig. 14.14: Opinion Share distribution (1: do not share, 5: share very easily) by city

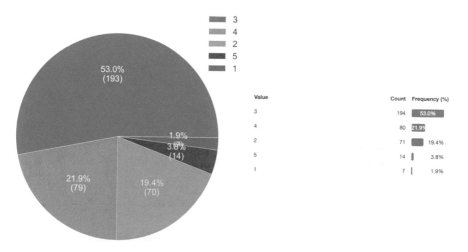

Fig. 14.15: Opinion Change distribution (1: do not change, 5: change very easily) on the whole dataset

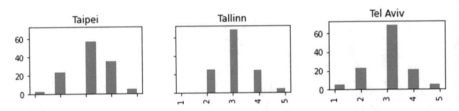

Fig. 14.16: Opinion Change distribution (1: do not change, 5: change very easily) by city

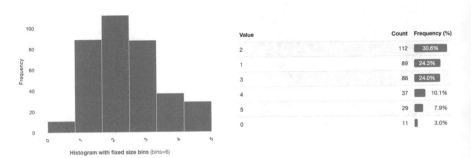

Fig. 14.17: Total engagement channels distribution (from 0 to 5) on the whole dataset

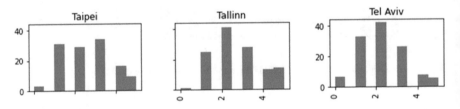

Fig. 14.18: Total engagement channels distribution (from 0 to 5) on the whole dataset

Fig. 14.19: Engagement frequency wishes distribution on the whole dataset

Engagement Feeling

Total Sources of Information

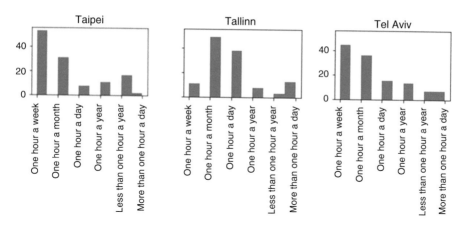

Fig. 14.20: Engagement frequency wishes distribution by city

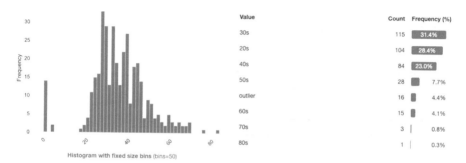

Fig. 14.21: Age distribution on the whole dataset

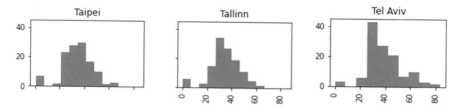

Fig. 14.22: Age distribution by city

Total Social Media Platforms

Total Influencers

Total Meeting Places

Opinion Share

Opinion Change

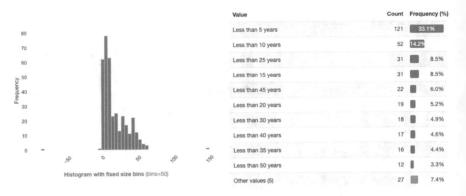

Fig. 14.23: Length of stay distribution on the whole dataset (with a few outliers)

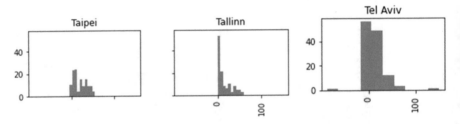

Fig. 14.24: Length of stay distribution by city (with a few outliers)

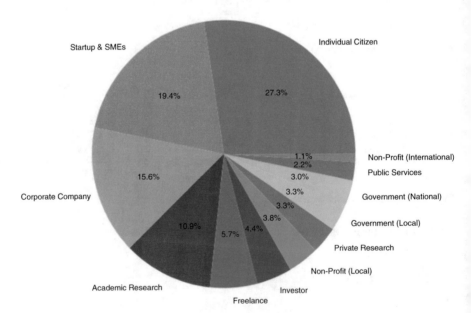

Fig. 14.25: Agents' types distribution on the whole dataset (not used in this study)

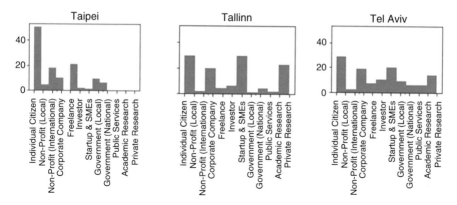

Fig. 14.26: Agents' types distribution by city (Taipei lacks representatives in some types)

Total Engagement

Engagement Frequency

Age

Length of Stay

Agents' types

14.4   Correlation Between Variables

Data correlation is a way to understand the relationship between multiple variables in your dataset. Using correlation matrix, you can take a first look at the relationships between the variables of your dataset. I can identify if one or multiple attributes depend on other ones, or if some attributes are associated as in a causal relationship. There are 3 types of correlations:

1. **Positive Correlation:** means that if feature **A** increases then feature **B** also increases or if feature **A** decreases then feature **B** also decreases. Both features move in tandem, and they have a linear relationship.
2. **Negative Correlation:** means that if feature **A** increases then feature **B** decreases and vice versa.
3. **No Correlation:** No relationship between those two attributes.

Correlation Coefficients
The Pearson's correlation coefficient (r) is a measure of linear correlation between two variables. Its value lies between -1 and +1, -1 indicating total negative linear correlation, 0 indicating no linear correlation and 1 indicating total positive linear correlation. Furthermore, r is invariant under separate changes in location and scale of the two variables, implying that for a linear function the angle to the x-axis does

not affect r. To calculate r for two variables X and Y, one divides the covariance of X and Y by the product of their standard deviations.

The Spearman's rank correlation coefficient (ρ) is a measure of monotonic correlation between two variables, and is therefore better in catching nonlinear monotonic correlations than Pearson's r. Its value lies between -1 and +1, -1 indicating total negative monotonic correlation, 0 indicating no monotonic correlation and 1 indicating total positive monotonic correlation. To calculate ρ for two variables X and Y, one divides the covariance of the rank variables of X and Y by the product of their standard deviations.

The Kendall's rank correlation coefficient (τ) measures ordinal association between two variables, similarly to Spearman's rank correlation coefficient. Its value lies between -1 and +1, -1 indicating total negative correlation, 0 indicating no correlation and 1 indicating total positive correlation. To calculate τ for two variables X and Y, one determines the number of concordant and discordant pairs of observations. τ is given by the number of concordant pairs minus the discordant pairs divided by the total number of pairs.

Phik (φk):
Phik (φk) is a new and practical correlation coefficient that works consistently between categorical, ordinal and interval variables, captures non-linear dependency and reverts to the Pearson correlation coefficient in case of a bivariate normal input distribution.

Cramér's V (φc):
Cramér's V is an association measure for nominal random variables. The coefficient ranges from 0 to 1, with 0 indicating independence and 1 indicating perfect association. The empirical estimators used for Cramér's V have been proved to be biased, even for large samples.

As we can see in Fig. 14.27 and 14.28, matrices with all the variables of my dataset do not produce any visually interpretable results. In order to generate more readable matrices, I will split my variables in two:

- hypothesis variables (See Fig. 14.29 and 14.30)
- other variables (See Fig. 14.31)

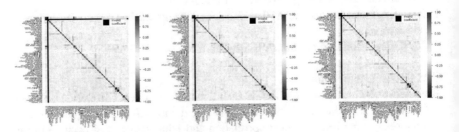

Fig. 14.27: Pearson's r, Spearman's ρ and Kendall's τ correlation matrices are not readable in detail, but they confirm the same distribution of correlations

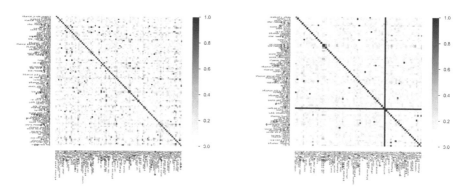

Fig. 14.28: Phik (φk) and Cramér's V (φc) matrices do not seem to express the same correlations.

```
# correlation matrix and heatmap on hypothesis variables
hyp_pearson = num_hyp.corr(method='pearson')
plt.figure(figsize=(18,4))
sns.heatmap(hyp_pearson, annot=True)
plt.show()
```

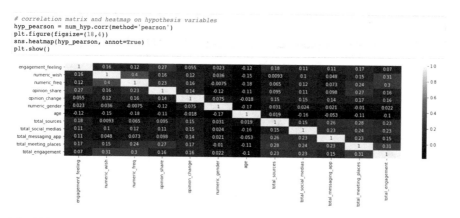

Fig. 14.29: Pearson's R correlation matrix on hypothesis variables

```
import phik
hyp_phik = num_hyp.phik_matrix()
plt.figure(figsize=(18,4))
sns.heatmap(hyp_phik, annot=True)
plt.show()
```

```
interval columns not set, guessing: ['engagement_feeling', 'numeric_wish', 'numeric_freq', 'opinion_share', 'opinion_
change', 'numeric_gender', 'age', 'total_sources', 'total_social_medias', 'total_messaging_app', 'total_meeting_place
s', 'total_engagement']
```

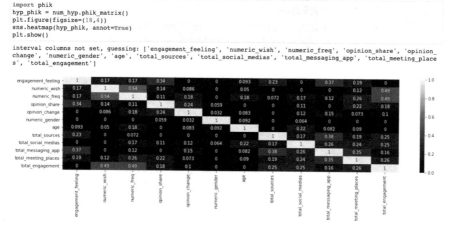

Fig. 14.30: Phik (φk) correlation matrix on hypothesis variables.

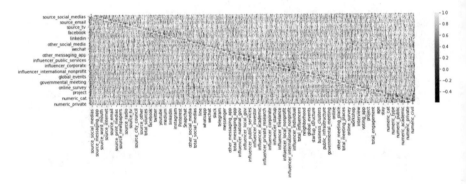

Fig. 14.31: Pearson's R correlation matrix on other variables.

The first will be visually interpreted and I will also calculate the scores presented above, in order to evaluate the degree of relationship between the correlated variables.

The second will not produce more visual results and I will filter the most correlated variables AND the most non-correlated ones, in hope to make some more sense out of my survey study.

Correlation on hypothesis variables:

Correlation on other variables

I generated a correlation matrix on Pearson's correlation coefficient between other variables than my hypothesis, to check if some unexpected correlations can appear between attributes.

There are too many variables to read the correlation matrix (See Fig. 14.31) so I will filter out the most interesting correlation coefficients:

- Coefficients greater than 0.50 express strongly correlated variables.
- Coefficients lesser than 0.001 express strongly non-correlated variables.

Strongly Correlated Variables

Variables whose correlation coefficient is higher than 0.5 are usually considered as strongly correlated. Let see what they are and what sense we can make of it.

  Negative correlations:

- **WhatsApp / Line (-0.59).** It makes sense since I observed that depending on the cities, citizens were preferably using one messaging app or the other. Taiwan: Line, Tel Aviv: WhatsApp.

  Positive Correlations:

- **Total Engagement / Voting App are correlated (0.51).** It means that the citizens open to the most engagement channel agree on using Voting App.
- **Total Engagement / Online Survey are correlated (0.53).** It means that the citizens open to the most engagement channel agree on filling the online survey.

- **Total Engagement / Interview are correlated (0.54).** It means that the citizens open to the most engagement channel agree on giving interviews.
- **Total Engagement / Workshop are correlated (0.55).** It means that the citizens open to the most engagement channel agree to participate in workshops.
- **Total Meeting Places / Startup Structures are correlated (0.56).** It means that the citizens meeting other citizens in the most different places are also the ones visiting Startup Structures.
- **Total Meeting Places / Global Events are correlated (0.59).** It means that the citizens meeting other citizens in the most different places are also the ones visiting Global Events.
- **Total Social Medias / YouTube are correlated (0.56).** It means that the citizens using the most different social media are also those who use YouTube.
- **Total Social Medias / Instagram are correlated (0.59).** It means that the citizens using the most different social media platforms are also those who use Instagram.
- **Total Messaging App / Messenger are correlated (0.52).** It means that the citizens using the most messaging apps are also using Messenger.

Strongly Uncorrelated Variables

Variables whose correlation coefficient is less than 0.001 are considered as strongly uncorrelated. It means that they have a very low probability to be in a relationship together. There were quite a lot, so to avoid being redundant, I will only select a few of them which seem the most meaningful to me.

Negative uncorrelations:

- **Engagement Wish / Influencer: Individual Citizen (-0.0008).** It means that saying to be influenced by individual citizens when shaping their opinion has no influence on the willingness to engage more or not.
- **Engagement Feeling / Meeting Place: Neighborhood (-0.0001)!** The engagement feeling has no relationship with the use to meet other citizens in the neighborhood!

Positive uncorrelations:

- **Age / Voting apps are uncorrelated (0.0003).** It means that the age of the citizen has no relationship with the openness to using a voting app as an engagement channel.
- **Snapchat / Newspapers are uncorrelated (0.0005).** It means that the use of the social network Snapchat has no relationship with using Newspaper as source of information.
- **Newspapers / Governmental Meeting are uncorrelated (0.0009).** It means that the use of Newspaper as source of information has no relationship with visiting Governmental Meeting places in order to meet other citizens.
- **WhatsApp / Internet are uncorrelated (0.0009)!** It means that the use of the messaging app WhatsApp has no relationship with using the Internet as source of information!

- **WhatsApp / Total Meeting Places are uncorrelated (0.001)**. It means that the use of the messaging app WhatsApp has no relationship with the total number of meeting places visited in order to meet other citizens.

After selecting the strongly correlated variables, I am able to draw a new correlation matrix for correlated variables aside from my hypothesis (See Fig. 14.32).

These correlation matrices are much more readable, but they do not reach any strong correlation between my hypothesis variables. So, I will make some data transformation on my hypothesis variables and re-check for correlation coefficients:

- Normalize my variables and re-plot the correlation matrix.
- Categorize my variables in three classes: Low, Medium and High, and compare the mean of hypothesis' variables between these classes.

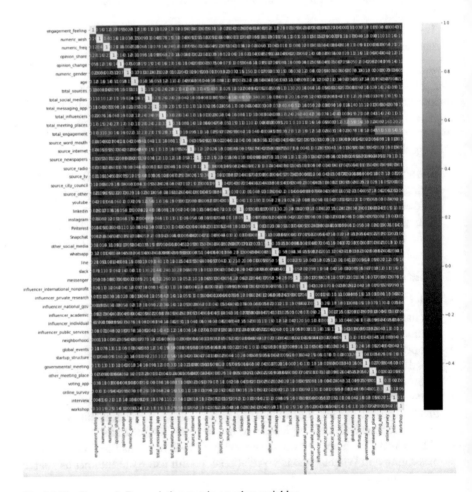

Fig. 14.32: Pearson's R correlation matrix on other variables

What is Normalization?
Normalization is a scaling technique in which values are shifted and rescaled so that they end up ranging between 0 and 1. It is also known as Min-Max scaling.

- When the value of X is the minimum value in the column, the numerator will be 0, and hence X' is 0
- On the other hand, when the value of X is the maximum value in the column, the numerator is equal to the denominator and thus the value of X' is 1
- If the value of X is between the minimum and the maximum value, then the value of X' is between 0 and 1

To achieve my data normalization, I am using the normalizer utility from Scikit Learn preprocessing module.

After normalization, my hypothesis variables appear much more correlated between each others (See Fig. 14.33 and 14.34). This is also the case for other correlated variables (See Fig. 14.35).

Normalization seems to be an effective way to increase correlation coefficients between variables. However, in order to validate my hypothesis in another way, I will categorize the numerical data hypothesis variables in order to reach more evidence of correlation.

14.5   Hypothesis Validation

What is categorization?
Categorization is a data transformation technique which will fit my data in the creation of a resulting set of classes, as well as the assignment of elements to pre-established classes. It means that I will put my ordinal numerical variables into categorical classes.

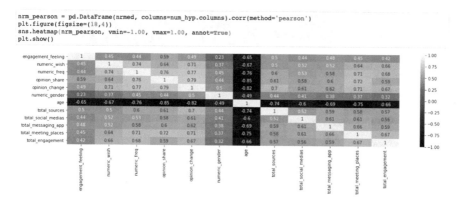

```
nrm_pearson = pd.DataFrame(nrmed, columns=num_hyp.columns).corr(method='pearson')
plt.figure(figsize=(18,4))
sns.heatmap(nrm_pearson, vmin=-1.00, vmax=1.00, annot=True)
plt.show()
```

Fig. 14.33: Pearson's R correlation matrix on normalized hypothesis variables

```
nrmed_phik = pd.DataFrame(nrmed, columns=num_hyp.columns).phik_matrix()
plt.figure(figsize=(18,4))
sns.heatmap(nrmed_phik, vmin=-1.00, vmax=1.00, annot=True)
plt.show()
```

```
interval columns not set, guessing: ['engagement_feeling', 'numeric_wish', 'numeric_freq', 'opinion_share', 'opinion_
change', 'numeric_gender', 'age', 'total_sources', 'total_social_medias', 'total_messaging_app', 'total_meeting_place
s', 'total_engagement']
```

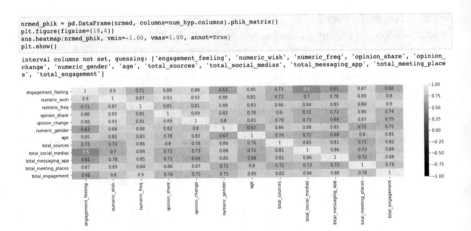

Fig. 14.34: Phik (φk) correlation matrix on normalized hypothesis variables.

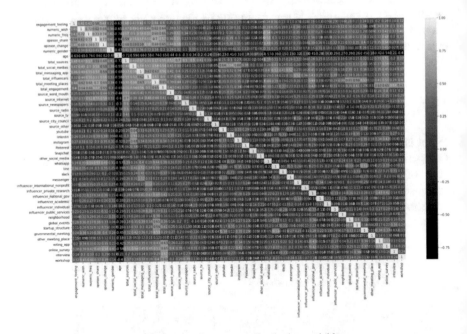

Fig. 14.35: Pearson's R correlation matrix on normalized other variables.

Engagement Feeling (1 to 10) is encoded as:

- 1, 2, 3: Low
- 4, 5, 6, 7: Medium
- 8, 9, 10: High

Engagement Frequency is encoded as:

- Less than one hour a year: Low
- One hour a year: Low
- One hour a month: Medium
- One hour a week: High
- One hour a day: High

Opinion Share (1 to 5) is encoded as:

- 1, 2: Low
- 3: Medium
- 4, 5: High

Opinion Change (1 to 5) is encoded as:

- 1, 2: Low
- 3: Medium
- 4, 5: High

Age (18 to 84) is encoded by decades:

- 20s, 30s: Youngest
- 40s, 50s: Mid-Aged
- 60s, 70s, 80s: Oldest

Stay (0 to 61) is encoded by slices of 5 years:

- Less than 1, 5, 10 year(s): Shortest
- Less than 15, 20, 25, 30, 35, 40, 45 years: Mid-Length
- Less than 50, 55, 60, 65 years: Longest

Engagement Wish (yes / no) is kept in its original form
Gender (Man/Woman) is kept in its original form

After categorizing the variables of my hypothesis and calculating the mean for the supposedly depending numerical variable, I reach much more interesting answers to my hypothesis from one-to-one relationships.

Hypothesis 1

Hypothesis 1: VALIDATED! The citizens feeling the most engaged wish to engage more.

1bis: The citizens who wish to engage more, have a highest engagement feeling (See Fig. 14.36 and 14.37).

Hypothesis 2

Hypothesis 2: VALIDATED! The citizens feeling the most engaged are the most demanding in terms of engagement frequency.

2bis. The citizens demanding the highest engagement frequency are those who feel the most engaged (See Fig. 14.38 and 14.39).

However, the medium values are those receiving the lowest engagement feeling.

engagement_wish_mean		engagement_feeling_mean	
cat_feel		engagement_wish	
High	0.961538	No	2.891566
Low	0.717822	Yes	3.830389

Fig. 14.36: Engagement wish by engagement feeling, and engagement feeling by engagement wish

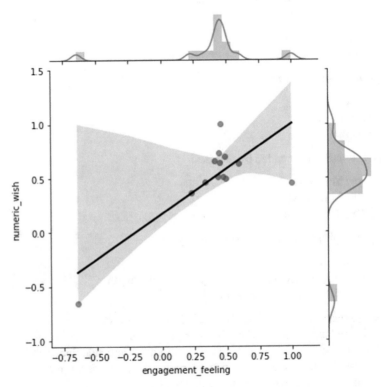

Fig. 14.37: Linear regression of engagement feeling by engagement wish confirms relationship

engagement_freq_mean		engagement_feeling_mean	
cat_feel		cat_freq	
High	2.769231	High	3.920398
Low	2.341584	Low	3.383333

Fig. 14.38: Engagement feeling by engagement frequency, and engagement frequency by engagement feeling

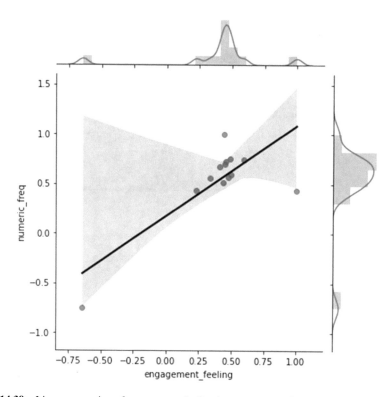

Fig. 14.39: Linear regression of engagement feeling by engagement frequency

- If the engagement feeling is lowest to people willing to engage at a medium level, it can be because the latest are not effectively engaged. Lowest and highest demanding people already feel engaged, and some think they should engage more while others think they should engage less.
- Could validate with engagement wish: Does low engagement demanders have a highest NO score and lowest YES score to the engagement wish?

Hypothesis 3

Hypothesis 3: VALIDATED! The citizens feeling the most engaged share their opinion in public more easily.

3bis. The citizens sharing their opinion in public more easily feel more engaged (See Fig. 14.40 and 14.41).

Hypothesis 4

Hypothesis 4 and 4bis are not validated using this categorization technique: the relationship is too weak. I suspect opinion change to be in a causal relationship with opinion share which depends on engagement feeling. So I will check the relationship between opinion share and opinion change in order to find out if one is depending on the other.

opinion_share_mean		engagement_feeling_mean	
cat_feel		**cat_share**	
High	3.884615	High	4.411765
Low	2.960396	Low	2.757282

Fig. 14.40: Engagement feeling by opinion share, and opinion share by engagement feeling.

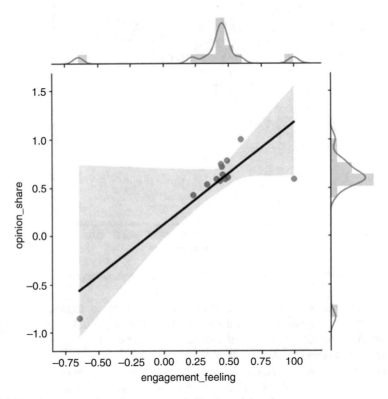

Fig. 14.41: Linear regression of engagement feeling by opinion share.

Hypothesis 4: VALIDATED! The citizens feeling the most engaged tend to change their opinion in contact with others.

4bis. The citizens feeling the less engaged, change their opinion less easily. If the Opinion change is not directly linked to engagement feeling (See Fig. 14.40), it is directly linked to opinion share (See Figs. 14.42 and 14.43) which is linked to engagement feeling. Hypothesis 4 and 4bis are validated that way.

Hypothesis 5

Hypothesis 5: VALIDATED! Gender has no relationship with the engagement feeling. (See Fig. 14.44 and Fig. 14.45)

opinion_change_mean		engagement_feeling_mean	
cat_feel		**cat_change**	
High	3.153846	High	3.797872
Low	3.044554	Low	3.294872

Fig. 14.42: Engagement feeling by opinion change, and opinion change by engagement feeling.

opinion_share_mean		opinion_change_mean	
cat_change		**cat_share**	
High	3.372340	High	3.150327
Low	2.820513	Low	2.873786

Fig. 14.43: Opinion change by opinion share, and opinion share by opinion change.

engagement_feeling_mean		gender_polarity	
gender		**cat_feel**	
Man	3.568627	High	0.423077
Woman	3.679012	Low	0.435644

Fig. 14.44: Engagement feeling by gender and gender by engagement feeling.

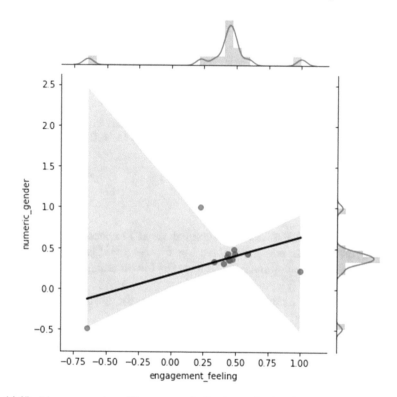

Fig. 14.45: Linear regression of Engagement feeling by gender (too flat and unpredictable).

	age_mean
engagement_feeling_mean	
	cat_feel
recat_age	
	High 29.192308
Oldest 2.842105	
	Low 36.668317
Youngest 3.680365	

Fig. 14.46: Engagement feeling by age and age by engagement feeling

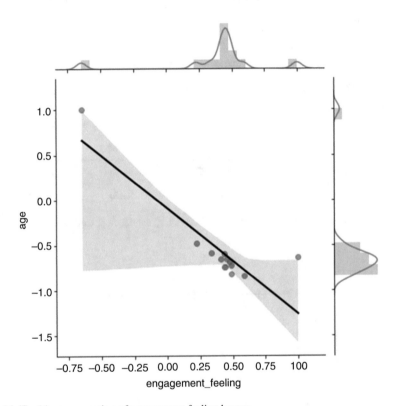

Fig. 14.47: Linear regression of engagement feeling by age.

Hypothesis 6

**Hypothesis 6: UNVALIDATED. Contrary to what I expected, age has a nega-
tive correlation with engagement feeling. It means that younger citizens feel
the less engaged, and older citizens have the lowest engagement feeling** (See
Fig. 14.46 and 14.47)

Does the length of stay follow the same tendency as the age in its correlation with
the engagement feeling?

Indeed, it seems like the citizens who have stayed the longest in the city feel the
least engaged (See Fig. 14.48), and the citizens having a high engagement feeling

	engagement_feeling_mean		length_stay_mean
recat_stay		**cat_feel**	
Longest	2.923077	High	13.153846
shortest	3.469945	Low	15.410891

Fig. 14.48: Engagement feeling by length of stay, and length of stay by engagement feeling

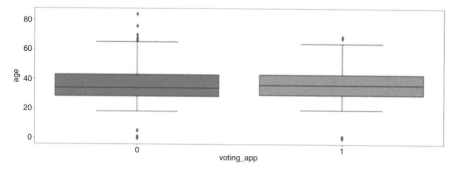

Fig. 14.49: Openness to voting apps by age distribution.

stayed less time in the city. Length of Stay and Engagement Feeling seem negatively correlated as well as age. I am not certain how to interpret this insight. By curiosity, I would like to check something more about age: **Does the voting app enthusiasm have a relationship with age?**

I do not see any significant age differences in the openness to engage by voting apps (See Fig. 14.49).

14.6   Machine Learning: Classifying Models

Machine learning is the study of computer algorithms that improve automatically through experience. Machine learning algorithms build a model based on sample data, in order to make predictions without being explicitly programmed to do so. ML models process statistical regression analysis when predicting a numerical value, and statistical classification when predicting a class label.

My end goal is to build a ranking model able to predict if a citizen is highly engaged in decision-making for its city or not. So far, I am defining a citizen highly engaged in Smart-City as someone who:

- has an engagement feeling of 5/10 at least
- uses social media and the Internet as a source of information to shape its opinion
- uses at least two social media platforms
- uses at least two messaging apps
- meets other citizens online

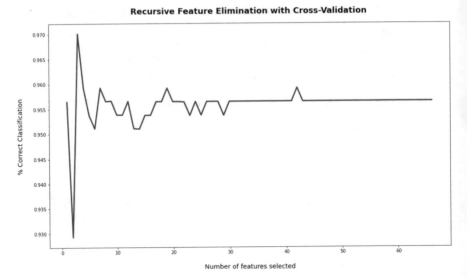

Fig. 14.50: Percentage of correct classification by number of features selected

- shares its opinion in public (at least 3/5)
- changes its opinion with in contact with others (at least 3/5)
- wishes to engage more through multiple engagement channels (at least 2/5) at a moderate to a high frequency (at least 1 hour per month)

Using my definition of a highly engaged citizen, I found that I had 16 respondents on 366 matchings. It means that 350 respondents on 366 are not. I can also say that **highly engaged citizens represent 4.4 % of my sample taken randomly on three representative cities out of all smart cities worldwide.**

Feature Selection

Feature selection is the process of selecting a subset of relevant features for use in model construction. The data features that you use to train your machine learning models have a huge influence on the performance you can achieve. Irrelevant or partially relevant features can negatively impact model performance.There are a number of reasons why you may want to remove a feature from the training phase. These include:

- A feature that is highly correlated with another feature in the data set. If this is the case, both features are in essence providing the same information. Some algorithms are sensitive to correlated features.
- Features that provide little to no information. An example would be a feature where most examples have the same value.
- Features that have little to no statistical relationship with the target variable.

In feature selection, you select those features in your data that contribute most to the prediction variable or output in which you are interested. It asks me to define the

X-y axes that I will use in my machine learning models. Since my end goal is to detect highly engaged citizens from a combination of questions in my survey study, I am creating a Boolean field called "Highly Engaged" on these attributes' combination, where 0 means "No" and 1 means "Yes". This new field will be the y axis of my model, and the other variables will be the X axis.

Optimal Number of Features
Using RFECV coupled with StratifiedKfold on a Random Forest Classifier model, I found that the optimal number of features for my models must be 3.

On the following graph, we can check for the performance of the classification model depending on the number of features selected. It is visible that with 3 features the accuracy was about 97% which is quite satisfying (See Fig. 14.50).

Evaluating Feature Importance
Once we have trained a model it is possible to apply further statistical analysis to understand the effects features have on the output of the model and determine which features are most useful.

From the same classification model RandomForestClassifier as trainer, I am evaluating the features importance in the performance of classifying highly engaged citizens from others.

This gives a good indicator of those features that are having an impact on the model and those that are not. We may choose to remove some of the less important features after analyzing this chart. Since the results from the first one were quite surprising from a first look (See Fig. 14.51), I decided to try two other rankings on Extra Trees Classifier (See Fig. 14.52) and on Decision Tree Classifier (See Fig. 14.53) models.

These two feature rankings confirm the first one: the most important variables in order to achieve the best performance with my classification models are not my hypothesis. It makes sense, since we already saw that highly correlated variables tend to express the same ideas and lower the ML performance. Overall, I can say that **engagement feeling, total sources of information, and total messaging apps are the three most important features to achieve the best performance with my classification model.**

Deal with data unbalance
The distribution of highly engaged citizens (16) compared to others (350) is very unbalanced. In order to train the best machine learning models to achieve my goal, I will need to use an over-sampling technique to balance my dataset.

Balancing Dataset with SMOTE (Synthetic Minority Over-sampling Technique) is a type of data augmentation that synthesizes new samples from the existing ones. I will use it to oversample the minority class. SMOTE is not a simple duplication of the minority class; it actually creates new samples between closest points of the minority class by using the K-Nearest Neighbor algorithm. With this approach, it can create as many synthetic samples as needed, bringing new relevant information to the dataset.

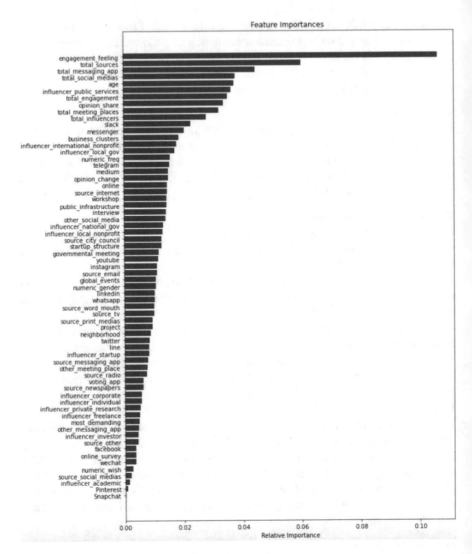

Fig. 14.51: Ranking of feature importance in the predictive model performance

As a result, the new dataset will simulate 700 respondents, where 350 respondents are highly engaged and 350 respondents are not (See Fig. 14.54).

Train/test split—Since my dataset is now balanced, I will split it in two: a 1/3 split called "train set" which I will use to train my models until I will reach a satisfying accuracy score, and a 2/3 split called "test set" on which I will deploy the trained model (See Fig. 14.55).

Comparing four models

I will process my dataset into different classification models to evaluate their performance.

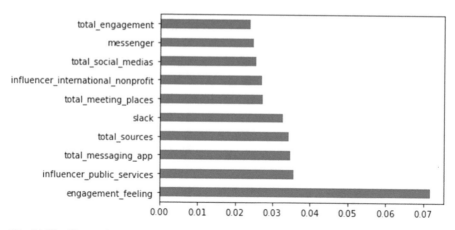

Fig. 14.52:   10 most important features to achieve the best performance of Extra Trees Classifier

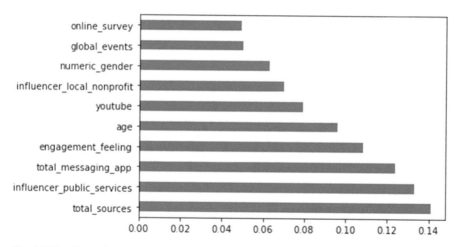

Fig. 14.53:   10 most important features to achieve the best performance of Decision Tree Classifier

The purpose of a Machine Learning Pipeline is to assemble several steps that can be cross-validated together while setting different parameters. I can cover the whole process of data analysis from the very beginning: collecting data by scraping web content, to the end prediction validation. I have not worked on automating the whole process for the moment, but I will now build the core step of a pipeline that I will be able to complete later.

The pipeline will process my dataset through different machine learning models, and compare the accuracies and confusion scores to choose the best model (See Fig. 14.56). It consists of the following steps:

1. standard scaling
2. feature extraction
3. model processing

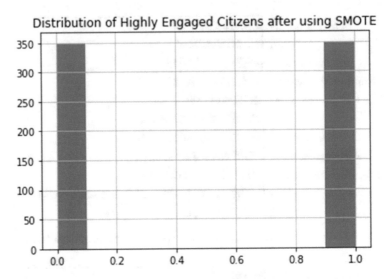

Fig. 14.54: Distribution of highly engaged citizens and non-highly engaged citizens after over-sampling is a perfect 50:50 %

4. accuracy scores
5. confusion matrix

There are many classification algorithms available and it is not possible to tell if one is better than the other. Each performance relies on the data itself and the pre-paratory steps. Model performance must be evaluated case by case. I chose to use four classifier models and compare their accuracies:

- Logistic Regression
- K-Nearest Neighbours
- Multi-Layer Perceptron
- Support Vector Machines

Logistic Regression
It is one of the most fundamental algorithms used to model relationships between a dependent variable and one or more independent variables. Similar to the linear regression model, but used on a discrete number of outcomes, the logistic regression uses a logistic function to model a binary dependent variable.

K-Nearest Neighbors
In statistical classification, the KNN algorithm is used to classify an object by a plurality vote of its neighbors, with the object being assigned to the class most common among its k nearest neighbors. k is a positive integer, typically small. k-NN is a type of instance-based learning, where the function is approximated locally and the algorithm relies on distance for classification.

Multi-Layer Perceptron

MLPClassifier is an Artificial Neural Network model which optimizes the log-loss function. As ANN, it uses a set of connected input/output units where each connection has a weight associated with. During the learning phase, the network learns by adjusting the weights so as to be able to predict the correct class label of the input data.

Support Vector Machines

A Support Vector Machine is a supervised classification technique that will find a hyperplane or a boundary between the two classes of data that maximizes the margin between the two classes. There are many planes that can separate the two classes, but only one plane can maximize the margin or distance between the classes.

Accuracy scores

Aside from the confusion matrices on a heatmap (See Fig. 14.57), there are not so many visuals to show from a machine learning model, which consists mainly in a series of calculations using statistical predictions. In order to evaluate the models otherwise than with the number of errors, there are a series of accuracy scores to check:

- **Classification Accuracy** is what we usually mean, when we use the term accuracy. Probably the most straightforward and intuitive metric for classifier performance. It is the ratio of number of correct predictions to the total number of input samples. It works well only if there are an equal number of samples belonging to each class.
- **F1 Score** is the Harmonic Mean between precision and recall. The range for F1 Score is [0, 1]. It tells you how precise your classifier is (how many instances it classifies correctly), as well as how robust it is (it does not miss a significant number of instances).
- **Area Under Curve (AUC)** is one of the most widely used metrics for evaluation. It is used for binary classification problems. The AUC of a classifier is equal to the probability that the classifier will rank a randomly chosen positive example higher than a randomly chosen negative example.
- **Recall** is the number of correct positive results divided by the number of all relevant samples (all samples that should have been identified as positive), which means the percent of truly positive instances that were classified as such.
- **Precision** is the number of correct positive results divided by the number of positive results predicted by the classifier, which means percent of positive classifications that are truly positive.
- **Mean Absolute Error (MAE)** is the average of the difference between the Original Values and the Predicted Values. It gives us the measure of how far the predictions were from the actual output.
- **Mean Squared Error (MSE)** is quite similar to Mean Absolute Error, the only difference being that MSE takes the average of the square of the difference between the original values and the predicted values. The advantage of MSE being that it is easier to compute the gradient.

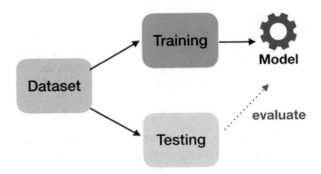

Fig. 14.55: Typical split of a dataset between train and test subsets

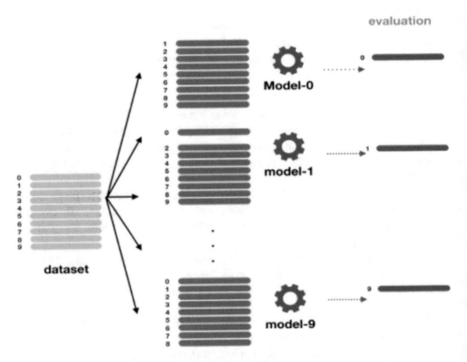

Fig. 14.56: Illustration of a comparison of models performances

- **Root Mean Squared Error (RMSE)** is more appropriate to represent model performance than the MAE when the error distribution is expected to be Gaussian. It avoids the use of absolute value which is highly undesirable in many mathematical computations.
- **R-squared (r2)** is the percentage of the response variable variation that is explained by a linear model. The maximum value of R^2 is 1 but it may take a negative value.

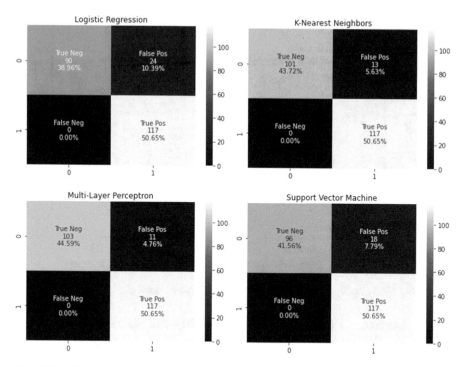

Fig. 14.57: Confusion matrices for each model shows the spread of errors in predictions

	accuracy	f1	auc	recall	precision	mae	mse	rmse	r2	vif
Logistic Regression	0.896104	0.906977	0.894737	1.0	0.829787	0.103896	0.103896	0.322329	0.584345	2.405844
KNN Classifier	0.943723	0.947368	0.942982	1.0	0.900000	0.056277	0.056277	0.237228	0.774854	4.441558
Multi-Layer Perceptron	0.952381	0.955102	0.951754	1.0	0.914062	0.047619	0.047619	0.218218	0.809492	5.249115
Support Vector Machines	0.922078	0.928571	0.921053	1.0	0.866667	0.077922	0.077922	0.279145	0.688259	3.207792

Fig 14.58: Accuracy scores of the four classification models used

- **Variance inflation factor (VIF)** is a measure of the amount of multicollinearity in a set of multiple regression variables. It is calculated for each independent variable. A high VIF indicates that the associated independent variable is highly collinear with the other variables in the model.

Overall, it looks like the Artificial Neural Network model Multi-Layer Perceptron reached the best results in all accuracy scores (see Fig. 14.59), and it has the lowest error rates MAE and MSE (see Fig. 14.58). I will keep working with this one, trying to find a way to make its predictive work even better.

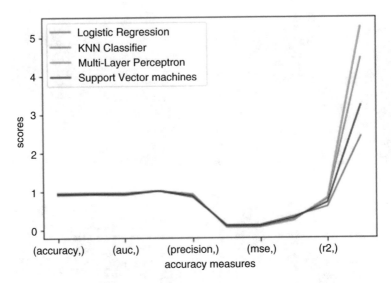

Fig 14.59. Model performance of the four classification models used

14.7   Statistical Inferences: Generalizing the Ranking Model

Inferential statistics use the data to learn about the population that the sample of data is thought to represent, and in my case the highly engaged citizens of a smart city. With statistical inferences, it is possible to reach conclusions that extend beyond the actual dataset.

If the machine learning models are used to make predictions inside the dataset, probabilistic models are used to make predictions about extensive data, using probability of an event to occur and statistical hypothesis testing.

In this third part of my study, I will use probabilistic models and the analysis of variance in order to frame my predictions of highly engaged citizens in the most accurate way. Whatever level of assumption is made, a correctly calibrated inference in general requires some assumptions to be correct. I will present them first, then I will be able to compare my actual results with the predicted ones. If both are very close, my inferences would be right, and I will be able to validate my ranking model at a wider scale.

Probabilistic Model
Estimating probabilities with probabilistic model is to formulate my problem like that this: I am investigating citizens of a city in order to look for highly engaged citizens. I know that the overall population of a city can be classified as highly engaged citizens and non-highly engaged citizens, but I do not know how many of each there are. By conducting a survey study on a random sample population, I found that highly engaged citizens approximate 4.4 % of my whole dataset (16 of 366 respondents). Assuming that this class of citizen had an equal chance to appear in my

sample, I want to estimate their prevalence in the whole population of citizens in smart cities.

Machine learning models worked great, but after going through this workflow, I had the feeling that something was missing in solving my problem. At least two questions pop up in my mind:

1. How can I be sure that my sample is representative of the whole population? I need to include uncertainty in my estimation, considering the limited data.
2. How can I incorporate prior beliefs about highly engaged citizens into this estimation?

The inferential statistics method called Bayesian inference allows me to express uncertainty and prior beliefs. To solve this problem with a Bayesian model, I will need to assume that:

- The chances to reach a highly engaged citizen are independent from each other. (I am not spreading my survey in some niche segments of engaged citizens)
- Any citizen can potentially be highly engaged and match with my definition. (There is no bias that would reserve this class to a niche population.)

Since my population can be divided in two classes of citizens—the highly engaged and those who are not—the probability distribution of all situations respects a binomial model of distribution. In the probability theory, the binomial distribution with parameters **n** and **p** is the discrete probability distribution of the number of successes in a sequence of **n** independent experiments, each asking a yes-no question, and each of its own Boolean-valued outcome: success (with probability **p**) and failure (with probability q = 1-p). In my problem, **p** is the ultimate objective: I want to figure out the probability of meeting highly engaged citizens in the whole smart city, from the observed sample data. In statistics, a single success/failure experiment is drawn from a Bernoulli distribution, which forms the prior distribution for the sample of size **n** drawn with replacement from a population of size N.

My sampling distribution helps to estimate the population statistics. The overall system of my interest, where a population of citizens can be divided in 2 discrete classes (highly engaged and non-highly engaged citizens) and 366 independent respondents, has a Probability Mass Function shown on the binomial distribution below (See Fig. 14.60).

The **Central Limit Theorem** states that, no matter the shape of the population distribution, the shape of the sampling distribution will remain the same. This gives us a mathematical advantage to estimate the population statistics. The number of samples must be sufficient (generally more than 50) to satisfactorily achieve a normal curve distribution. Also, care must be taken to keep the sample size fixed since any change in sample size will change the shape of the sampling distribution and it will no longer be bell shaped. As we increase the sample size, the sampling distribution squeezes from both sides giving us a better estimate of the population statistic since it lies somewhere in the middle of the sampling distribution (See Fig. 14.61).

The mean remains the same for x number of samples, and the standard deviation tends to reduce the bigger the number of samples are. As for my study, the

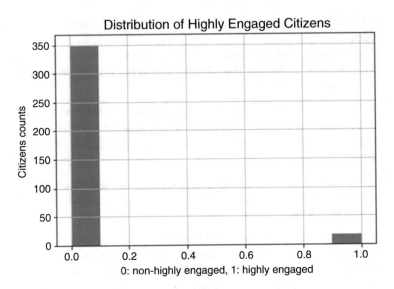

Fig. 14.60: Highly engaged citizens on my overall dataset

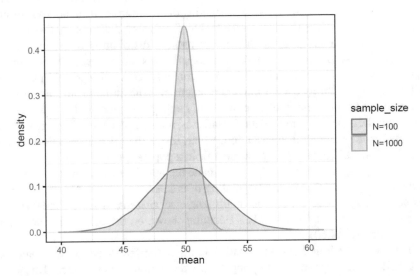

Fig. 14.61: Illustration of the Central Limit Theorem. The biggest the sample, the tightest to its mean.

proportion of 4.4 % percent of highly engaged citizens over a random sample from a city population is already a mean generated out of my 3 case studies. The Central Limit Theorem allows me to assume that if I would investigate 100 smart cities in the world with the same protocol of data collection, the final mean of the proportions of Highly Engaged citizens would keep close to 4.4 %. As normally distributed, the means of the proportion of highly engaged citizens in the smart city populations fit inside a confidence interval to be determined by our hypothesis testing.

Hypothesis testing
Hypothesis testing is all about the validity of making claims from a sample. With the advent of data-driven decision making in business, science, technology, social, and political undertakings, the concept of hypothesis testing has become critically important to understand and apply. This method allows a sample statistics to be checked against a population statistics.

Hypothesis testing is defined in two terms: a Null Hypothesis and an Alternate Hypothesis. The Null Hypothesis usually claims that the inference is wrong, the Alternate Hypothesis says the exact contrary. In my case:

- **Null Hypothesis**: I cannot use the highly engaged variable to rank citizen engagement in a smart city because randomly selected citizens in a smart city do not have 4.4% chances to be highly engaged.
- **Alternate Hypothesis**: I can use the highly engaged variable to rank citizen engagement in a smart city because randomly selected citizens in a smart city do have 4.4% chances to be highly engaged.

The Null Hypothesis is assumed to be true and statistical evidence is required to reject it in favor of an Alternative Hypothesis. What I am really asking is **how confident am I in the claim that my ranking model is correct?** In other words, I want to answer the question: "What is the chance for any random sample of inhabitants in any smart city worldwide to reach 4.4% of highly engaged citizens?"

This chance is represented by the **p-value** (or probability value) and that is what I want to evaluate. If this p-value is less than a predetermined **Critical Value**, usually $\alpha = 0.05$, when the confidence interval is defined at 95% (See Fig. 14.62). If I have evidence that the alternative hypothesis is likely to be true; then I can reject the Null Hypothesis and accept the Alternative Hypothesis.

My issue is that I do not know the real proportion of highly engaged citizens in the whole population of citizens in smart cities worldwide, and so I cannot compare my prediction with the reality. When the population parameters (mean and standard deviation) are not known, the best I can do is to estimate it from my samples.

The hypotheses testing will consist of answering this question: Is there a significant difference of proportion of highly engaged citizens between cities? I don not know the proportion of highly engaged citizens in the whole population of smart cities, but I have three samples from which I can calculate means and standard deviations.

Composition of Dataset: Overall proportion of highly engaged citizens is 4.37%. Taipei has 6.55% of highly engaged citizens, Tallinn has 4.92% of highly engaged citizens, and Tel Aviv has 1.64% of highly engaged citizens. (see Fig. 14.63 and 14.64)

Distribution of sample means ($\overline{x}$)
around population mean (μ)

Fig. 14.62: Confidence interval in usual hypothesis testing

Fig. 14.63: Distribution
of highly engaged citizens
on my three samples

highly_engaged	city_id	
0	Taipei	114
	Tallinn	116
	Tel Aviv	120
1	Taipei	8
	Tallinn	6
	Tel Aviv	2

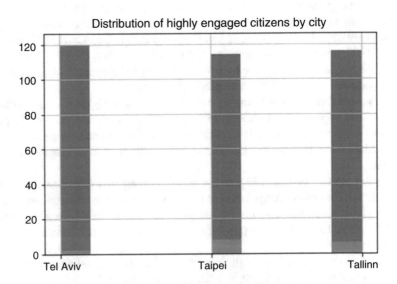

Fig. 14.64: Distribution of highly engaged citizens (orange) and not highly engaged ones (blue)

Statistical test

The **Analysis of variance or ANOVA test** is a way to find out if the survey or the experiment results are significant when you want to compare more than two groups at the same time. In other words, ANOVA tests help you to figure out if you need to reject the null hypothesis or accept the alternate hypothesis, based on the results coming out of different independent samples. Basically, it tells whether two or more groups are similar or different based on their mean similarity and f-score.

Performing an F-test is quite straightforward: you simply divide the variances together and compare your answer with a critical value obtained from a table (See Fig. 14.67). The main thing to realize is that the value should be more than one, and so we put the larger value on the top of the division.

Interpretations

The purpose of this statistics is to test for a difference between the proportion of engaged citizens between cities (See Fig. 14.65 and 14.66). Conducting a One-Way ANOVA using SciPy library, I found F-Statistic = 1.83 and a p-value = 0.16. Considering the usual significance level at 0.05, I cannot find enough evidence to reject the Null Hypothesis. There is a statistically significant difference between my samples.

However, these results are not significant statistically, but they do not set an end point to my study. We can think about an irregularity in the data collection process which led to fake unbalance of the target group. I notably think about the fact that I collected the answers to my survey in Tel Aviv during the first COVID-19 pandemic. This unprecedented situation affected many people, especially in a Mediterranean city where the way of life is a lot about enjoying outdoor activities, social contact, and nightlife. The lockdown measures could have significantly affected the way people perceived their engagement, and the correlated variables like the total meeting places, or the easiness to share its opinion in public. This could certainly affect the end score of highly engaged citizens detected in this city by my study.

Anyway, there are still some more rooms to maneuver. The first way to reconsider my definition of a highly engaged citizen, in order to reach less imbalance between my three case studies. Other ways could be to collect more case studies on other cities, or maybe find more respondents on my current case studies to vary the sample size. I could also reformulate my Null Hypothesis, and perhaps think about a different statistical test that I could conduct to test my hypothesis.

14.8   Conclusion

Models are approximations of the complex dynamics that drive the observable phenomenon in the world around us. They provide the setting in which we can formulate learning and decision making and hence are a foundational aspect to any rigorous analysis.

	Variable	N	Mean	SD	SE	95% Conf.	Interval
0	highly_engaged	366.0	0.0437	0.2047	0.0107	0.0227	0.0648

Fig. 14.65: Overall mean and standard deviation

	N	Mean	SD	SE	95% Conf.	Interval
city_id						
Taipei	122	0.0656	0.2486	0.0225	0.0210	0.1101
Tallinn	122	0.0492	0.2171	0.0197	0.0103	0.0881
Tel Aviv	122	0.0164	0.1275	0.0115	-0.0065	0.0392

Fig. 14.66: Mean and standard deviation for each sample

```
stats.f_oneway(survey['highly_engaged'][survey['city_id'] == 'Taipei'],
               survey['highly_engaged'][survey['city_id'] == 'Tallinn'],
               survey['highly_engaged'][survey['city_id'] == 'Tel Aviv'])

F_onewayResult(statistic=1.8333333333333321, pvalue=0.16135700323789995)
```

Fig. 14.67: One-Way ANOVA using SciPy.stats

In this study, I have used 366 answers of inhabitants of 3 different smart cities in the world: Taipei (Taiwan), Tel Aviv (Israel), and Tallinn (Estonia). First I have had to clean and transform the data in order to make them easily interpretable so that I could conduct different calculations on their potential relationship. I have been able to identify many correlations between the variables of my hypothesis, like the relationship between the engagement feeling and the wish and frequency of engagement. I also showed a like between the ability to share its opinion in public and the ability to change its opinion when in contact with others, both related to the level of engagement feeling, leading to the conclusion that the more people feel engaged, the more they engage in their city by getting in touch with more peer citizens. I also broke some preconceived opinions like the age factor, showing that young citizens feel more engaged than older ones, and that age has no influence on the openness to voting apps as a channel for citizen engagement. Even more surprising for me: the engagement feeling has no relationship with the ability to meet peers in the neighborhood, which says a lot about most participative methods tending to promote in-person meeting groups rather than online.

After revealing the evidence of correlated variables, I have created a combined variables matching with a definition of a highly engaged citizen in a smart city. Recursive Feature Elimination technique allowed me to select the best features in order to represent my variables in a model while avoiding redundancy between related variables. I found out that Engagement Feeling, Total Sources of Information to shape an opinion, and Total Messaging Apps used to communicate with peers are the three most important variables for the best representativeness of a highly engaged citizens population. This information has been the input for four classification models of Machine Learning: Logistic Regression, K-Nearest Neighbors, Multi-Layer Perceptron, and Support Vector Machines. These four models have been used to predict the results of 2/3 random samples from my data, after training on 1/3. Three predictive models out of four reach a satisfactory accuracy score, but the best of them is the Multi-Layer Perceptron—an Artificial Neural Network used to classify data points.

However, the good results in the automation of learning to rank my citizen population in between the highly engaged and those who are not needed to be evaluated at a wider scale. I used the inferential statistics methods to test the generalizability of my assumption: My definition of Highly Engaged citizens allows me to classify the whole population of citizens of smart city worldwide. To test this hypothesis, I have conducted an analysis of variance ANOVA on my three case studies. It finally appears that the imbalance in the spread of highly engaged citizens between my three case study cities does not allow me to statistically validate the model of ranking. I will have to conduct some more analysis to prove my inference.

Part V
Total Information Awareness in Facebook Nation

Chapter 15
Generation C in the Age of Big Data

> *"No activity is too big or too small to share. You don't have to 'Like' a movie. You just watch a movie."*
> — Facebook CEO Mark Zuckerberg (September 2011)

> *"Digital omnivores consume content everywhere they go across every device whether it's their PC, tablet or smartphone."*
> — Sarah Radwanick of comScore (February 2012)

> *"In 2020, the world changed fundamentally—and so did the data that makes the world go round. As COVID-19 swept the globe, nearly every aspect of life—from work to working out— moved online, and people depended more and more on apps and the Internet to socialize, educate and entertain ourselves. Before quarantine, just 15% of Americans worked from home. Now over half do."*
> — 8th edition of Data Never Sleeps (September 2020)

15.1 Digital Omnivores and Generation C

In October 2011, Internet marketing research company comScore coined the term "digital omnivores" to describe the new generation of digital media consumers, especially those living in the United States, the United Kingdom, Singapore, Japan, and Australia (1).

According to Intel, 639,800 GB of data is transferred every minute on the Internet in 2014 (2). That includes 204 million emails sent, 61,141 hours of music on Pandora, 47,000 app downloads, 20 million photo views on Flickr, 100,000 new tweets, 277,000 Facebook logins, 6 million Facebook views, 2 million Google searches, and 1.3 million video views on YouTube (see Fig. 15.1).

Six years later in 2020, the data volumes had skyrocketed. "In 2020, the world changed fundamentally—and so did the data that makes the world go round. As COVID-19 swept the globe, nearly every aspect of life—from work to working out—moved online, and people depended more and more on apps and the Internet

© Springer Science+Business Media, LLC, part of Springer Nature 2021
N. Lee, *Facebook Nation*, https://doi.org/10.1007/978-1-0716-1867-7_15

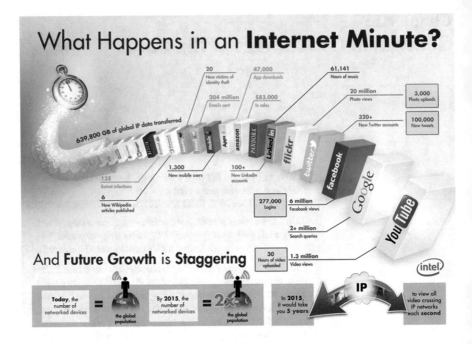

Fig. 15.1 What Happens in an Internet Minute in 2014? (Courtesy of Intel)

to socialize, educate and entertain ourselves. Before quarantine, just 15% of Americans worked from home. Now over half do" (3).

The global Internet population has increased from 4.57 billion in 2020 to 5.17 billion in 2021. In every minute of the hour, Facebook users uploaded 240,000 photos, Instagram users shared 65,000 pictures, Twitter users sent 575,000 tweets, Netflix viewers streamed 452,000 hours of video, and Google conducted 5.7 million searches (see Fig. 15.2).

"Today's digital media environment is rapidly evolving, driven by the proliferation of devices people use to consume content both at home, at work and on the go," the comScore report affirmed. "With smartphones, tablets and other connected devices, consumers have become digital omnivores – not just because of the media they consume, but also in *how* they consume it. Cross-platform consumption has created a vastly different digital landscape, and it is one that requires insight into both the individual usage of devices as well as the nature of their complementary use" (4). For example, comScore's study shows that during the day, a higher share of digital content is consumed over computers and mobile phones due to workplace and daily activity; whereas during the nighttime hours, tablets have the highest usage as the consumers are winding down at home on the couch or bed.

"Digital omnivores consume content everywhere they go across every device whether it's their PC, tablet or smartphone," said comScore communications analyst Sarah Radwanick. "We will see a spotlight on these consumers during multimedia extravaganzas like the Summer Olympics and the presidential election where (they) need to stay plugged in to the latest news and events" (5).

Fig. 15.2 What Happens in an Internet Minute in 2021? (Courtesy of Michigan Software Labs)

Nielsen and NM Incite issued a report in 2012 titled "State of the Media: U.S. Digital Consumer Report, Q3-Q4 2011." The report says, "Born sometime between the launch of the VCR and the commercialization of the Internet, Americans 18–34 are redefining media consumption with their unique embrace of all things digital. ... This group – dubbed 'Generation C' by Nielsen – is taking their personal connection – with each other and content – to new levels, new devices and new experiences like no other age group" (6).

In the world overflowing with digital information, the digital omnivores devour both nutritious information as well as empty information calories. Clay Johnson, author of *The Information Diet,* warns that "just as we have grown morbidly obese on sugar, fat, and flour—so, too, have we become gluttons for texts, instant messages, emails, RSS feeds, downloads, videos, status updates, and tweets" (7).

Indeed, some people are starting to feel overwhelmed and reacting to information overload. A recent survey commissioned by Citi Investment analyst Mark Mahaney in 2012 indicated that 71% of Netflix subscribers are "not at all interested" in "seeing what [their] Facebook friends have watched on Netflix" (8). If this sentiment prevails among Facebook users, it will eventually undermine the idea of "frictionless sharing" on Facebook. For the time being, nonetheless, more and more data is being generated and consumed every second in the modern age of big data.

15.2   Big Data Research and Development Initiative

Global market intelligence firm IDC estimates that the amount of data is growing at 50% a year, or more than doubling every two years (9). Much of the data are online in the form of text, images, and videos on the Internet, from personal data to public records and everything in between.

At the World Economic Forum in January 2012, a report titled *Big Data, Big Impact* declared data a new class of economic asset, like currency or gold. It reads, "The amount of data in the world is exploding – large portion of this comes from the interactions over mobile devices being used by people in the developing world – people whose needs and habits have been poorly understood until now" (10).

In an email dated March 27, 2012, the Office of Science and Technology Policy stated, "Researchers in a growing number of fields are generating extremely large and complicated data sets, commonly referred to as big data. A wealth of information may be found within these sets, with enormous potential to shed light on some of the toughest and most pressing challenges facing the Nation. To capitalize on this unprecedented opportunity to extract insights and make new connections across disciplines, we need better tools and programs to access, store, search, visualize, and analyze these data. To maximize this historic opportunity – and in support of recommendations from the President's Council of Advisors on Science and Technology – the Obama Administration is launching a Big Data Research and Development Initiative, coordinated by the White House Office of Science and Technology Policy and supported by several Federal departments and agencies."

On March 29, 2012, the Obama administration announced more than $200 million in funding for "Big Data Research and Development Initiative" (11). The first wave of agency commitments includes National Science Foundation, National Institutes of Health, Department of Energy, U.S. Geological Survey, and Department of Defense (including DARPA) (12).

Not to imply that DARPA intends to resurrect the Total Information Awareness program, the DARPA-proposed Anomaly Detection at Multiple Scales (ADAMS) program is one of several key technologies that are directly applicable to Total Information Awareness. And Information Innovation Office has replaced the Information Awareness Office (13). According to the White House document, ADAMS "addresses the problem of anomaly detection and characterization in massive data sets. In this context, anomalies in data are intended to cue collection of additional, actionable information in a wide variety of real-world contexts. The initial ADAMS application domain is insider threat detection, in which anomalous actions by an individual are detected against a background of routine network activity" (14).

15.3   Big Data in Public Health and Economics

Centers for Disease Control and Prevention (CDC) is also a beneficiary of the Big Data Research and Development Initiative. CDC's BioSense program "is a public health surveillance system that increases the ability of health officials at local, state, and national levels to efficiently, rapidly and collaboratively monitor and respond to harmful health effects of exposure to disease or hazardous conditions" (15).

The predictive power of big data has shown great promise in public health forecasting. For example, Google Flu Trends uses aggregated Google search data to estimate current flu activity around the world in near real-time (16). A spike in Google search requests for terms like "flu symptoms" and "flu treatments" often predicts quickly and correctly an increase of flu patients in a monitored region. In comparison, emergency room reports usually lag behind patient visits by two weeks or more.

In economic development and forecasting, *Forbes* has been advising CEOs and IT people to take an inventory of all the data that their business produces, and turn the data into new revenue streams (17). For instance, MasterCard has built an advisory business using its core credit card purchasing data to help merchants analyze consumer-buying trends (18).

Big data analysis is also used to track shadow economic activities worldwide. A research report estimated the value of the underground economy in the United States at about $2 trillion annually (19). In July 2012, U.S. Senate released a report on global banking giant HSBC exposing the U.S. financial system to a wide array of money laundering, drug trafficking, and terrorist financing risks due to poor anti-money laundering (AML) controls (20). SynerScope is one of new startups that develop big-data tools to analyze millions of transactions in order to help authorities track and halt money laundering (21).

15.4   Big Data in Facebook and Google

Facebook and Google are experts in harnessing big data with Internet advertising. According to the Facebook IPO S-1 filing statement, Facebook's 2011 advertising revenues were $3.15 billion (22). Meanwhile, Google's 2013 advertising revenues were a striking $50 billion according to Google's Income Statement Information (23).

Since Facebook renamed its "Privacy Policy" to "Data Use Policy" in September 2011, Sarah A. Downey, an analyst at the online privacy company Abine, said, "This is a significant acknowledgement that Facebook is focused on data collection, data storage and data sales, because that's where they make their money" (24).

In promoting "frictionless sharing," Mark Zuckerberg suggested that people would benefit from publishing more data and letting computer algorithms sort out what is important. "No activity is too big or too small to share," Zuckerberg said. "You don't have to 'Like' a movie. You just watch a movie" (25).

How does Facebook determine what is important to the users? Facebook CTO Bret Taylor disclosed, "Facebook programmers have created a mathematical algorithm that will examine the types of posts a person has chosen to give prominent placement to on his or her profile. ... Whether food, movies or exercises logged into Facebook, the site will try to predict what you're most passionate about based on past choices, similar to how the system determines its news feed based partly on the people you contact most often" (26). The official Facebook site also describes, "Just like the search engines we all know and love, Facebook utilizes a number of algorithms as part of their system for sharing information. EdgeRank is the algorithm which determines who sees what, basically – it determines what social objects (i.e. updates, posts, photos, actions etc) you will see in your Facebook news feed" (27).

Google also uses mathematical algorithms such as PageRank to determine the relevance of the search results it gives back to the users (28). In addition, artificial intelligence techniques are being used to construct a giant "knowledge graph" to better understand the context of search terms and to return more in-depth search results to the questions posted by the users. Google Fellow and Senior Vice President Amit Singhal revealed in 2012, "Google is building a huge, in-house understanding of what an entity is and a repository of what entities are in the world and what should you know about those entities. ... The huge knowledge graph of interconnected entities and their attributes now has north of 200 million entities. ... Google is building the infrastructure for the more algorithmically complex search of tomorrow" (29).

Google began rolling out knowledge graph in May 2012 to users in the U.S. (30). While knowledge graph is helpful in optimizing search for everyone, Google also personalizes its search results based on the user's preferences determined by cookies, IP addresses, and signing in with a Google account. Google explains, "When the web first started, it was a set of static pages that looked the same for everybody. Nowadays, the web has become even more useful because websites can know something about you that helps them guess what you would like to view. For example, they can remember whether you want them in English or French, can suggest books or movies you might enjoy based on what you've viewed in the past, and can store your delivery address ready for your next purchase" (31).

Using computer algorithms and our past online activities, Facebook and Google are guessing what we want to find, to see, and to like. The results can be helpful but at the same time can be limiting the possibilities of us discovering new ideas and new interests on the Internet. Michael Rigley made an interesting argument in his video titled *Network:* "Ad servers assign an individual a demographic, based on their digital histories. Once assigned, individualized information is deployed to the user. Location data is filtered into intrusive localized advertising. Facebook 'Likes' transform into custom Walmart ads, and search engine results are narrowed to a limited scope. The global Internet becomes the personal Internet. And information ceases to be information at all" (32).

Google's mission is to "organize the world's information and make it universally accessible and useful" (33). The phrase "Google it!" has become a universal slang. In searching for information in the modern world of big data, it would be a great disservice to users if Google were to filter its search results through colored glasses. University of Virginia professor Siva Vaidhyanathan considered Google insidious and questioned the search giant's influence on our society: "What is the nature of the transaction between Google's computer algorithms and its millions of human users? Are we heading down a path toward a more enlightened age, or are we approaching a dystopia of social control and surveillance?" (34).

References

1. **Donovan, Mark.** The Rise of Digital Omnivores. [Online] comScore, November 15, 2011. http://blog.comscore.com/mdonovan.html.
2. **Intel.** What Happens In An Internet Minute? [Online] Intel. [Cited: June 23, 2014.] http://www.intel.com/content/www/us/en/communications/internet-minute-infographic.html.
3. **Ali, Aran.** Here's What Happens Every Minute on the Internet in 2020. [Online] Visual Capitalist, September 15, 2020. https://www.visualcapitalist.com/every-minute-internet-2020/.
4. **comScore.** Digital Omnivores: How Tablets, Smartphones and Connected Devices are Changing U.S. Digital Media Consumption Habits. [Online] comScore, October 2011. http://www.comscore.com/Press_Events/Presentations_Whitepapers/2011/Digital_Omnivores.
5. **Snider, Mike.** Analysis details digital lives in USA. [Online] USA Today, February 24, 2012. http://www.usatoday.com/tech/news/story/2012-02-23/nielsen-digital-consumers/53228194/1.
6. **The Nielsen Company.** State of the Media: U.S. Digital Consumer Report, Q3-Q4 2011. [Online] The Nielsen Company, February 2012. http://www.nielsen.com/content/dam/corporate/us/en/reports-downloads/2012%20Reports/Digital-Consumer-Report-Q4-2012.pdf.
7. **Johnson, Clay A.** The Information Diet: A Case for Conscious Consumption. [Online] O'Reilly Media, January 2012. http://www.theatlantic.com/health/archive/2012/01/a-healthy-information-diet-the-case-for-conscious-consumption/251634/.

8. **Kafka, Peter.** Please Don't Tell Me What You're Watching on Netflix. [Online] AllThingsD, March 13, 2012. http://allthingsd.com/20120313/please-dont-tell-me-what-youre-watching-on-netflix/.

9. **Lohr, Steve.** The Age of Big Data. [Online] The New York Times, February 11, 2012. http://www.nytimes.com/2012/02/12/sunday-review/big-datas-impact-in-the-world.html.

10. **The World Economic Forum.** Big Data, Big Impact: New Possibilities for International Development. [Online] WEF, 2012. http://www.weforum.org/reports/big-data-big-impact-new-possibilities-international-development.

11. **Kalil, Tom.** Big Data is a Big Deal. [Online] The White House, March 29, 2012. http://www.whitehouse.gov/blog/2012/03/29/big-data-big-deal.

12. **Office of Science and Technology Policy.** Obama Administration Unveils "Big Data" Initiative: Announces $200 Million In New R&D Investments. [Online] Executive Office of the President, March 29, 2012. http://www.whitehouse.gov/sites/default/files/microsites/ostp/big_data_press_release.pdf.

13. **DARPA.** Information Innovation Office. [Online] Defense Advanced Research Projects Agency. [Cited: April 3, 2012.] http://www.darpa.mil/Our_Work/I2O/.

14. **Executive Office of the President.** Big Data Across the Federal Government. [Online] The White House, March 29, 2012. http://www.whitehouse.gov/sites/default/files/microsites/ostp/big_data_fact_sheet_final_1.pdf.

15. **CDC BioSense Program.** BioSense Program. [Online] Centers for Disease Control and Prevention, August 7, 2014. http://www.cdc.gov/biosense/.

16. **Google.org.** Explore flu trends around the world. [Online] google.org Flu Trends. [Cited: August 15, 2014.] http://www.google.org/flutrends/.

17. **Upbin, Bruce.** The Data Explosion and the Networked Enterprise. [Online] Forbes, April 18, 2011. http://www.forbes.com/sites/bruceupbin/2011/04/18/the-data-explosion-and-the-networked-enterprise/2/.

18. **Bughin, Jacques, Chui, Michael and Manyika, James.** McKinsey Column: Clouds, big data, and smart. [Online] Financial Times, September 22, 2010. http://www.ft.com/cms/s/0/97701346-c273-11df-956e-00144feab49a.html.

19. **Cebula, Richard and Feige, Edgar L.** America's Underground Economy: Measuring the Size, Growth and Determinants of Income Tax Evasion in the U.S. [Online] University of Wisconsin–Madison Social Science Computing Cooperative. [Cited: May 3, 2014.] http://www.ssc.wisc.edu/econ/archive/wp2011-1.pdf.

20. **The Permanent Subcommittee On Investigations.** HSBC Exposed U.S. Financial System to Money Laundering, Drug, Terrorist Financing Risk. [Online] U.S. Senate, July 16, 2012. http://www.hsgac.senate.gov/subcommittees/investigations/media/hsbc-exposed-us-finacial-system-to-money-laundering-drug-terrorist-financing-risks.

21. **Bansal, Manju.** Looking for the Needle in a Stack of Needles: Tracking Shadow Economic Activities in the Age of Big Data. [Online] MIT Technology Review, April 28, 2014. http://www.technologyreview.com/view/526961/looking-for-the-needle-in-a-stack-of-needles-tracking-shadow-economic-activities-in-the/.

22. **Facebook, Inc.** Form S-1. Registration Statement. [Online] United States Securities and Exchange Commission, February 1, 2012. http://www.sec.gov/Archives/edgar/data/1326801/000119312512034517/d287954ds1.htm.

23. **Google.** Google's Income Statement Information. [Online] Google Investor Relations. [Cited: August 15, 2014.] http://investor.google.com/financial/tables.html.

24. **Segall, Laurie.** Facebook strips 'privacy' from new 'data use' policy explainer. [Online] CNNMoney, March 23, 2012. http://money.cnn.com/2012/03/22/technology/facebook-privacy-changes/index.htm.

25. **Milian, Mark.** Some apps steer clear of Facebook auto-publish tool. [Online] CNN, January 18, 2012. http://www.cnn.com/2012/01/18/tech/social-media/facebook-pandora/index.html.

26. **—.** 60 apps launch with Facebook auto-share. [Online] CNN, January 19, 2012. http://www.cnn.com/2012/01/18/tech/social-media/facebook-actions-apps/index.html.

27. **Tamar.** Facebook's EdgeRank, in a nutshell. [Online] Facebook, November 1, 2011. http://www.facebook.com/notes/tamar/facebooks-edgerank-in-a-nutshell/284652911558091.

28. **Google.** Technology overview. [Online] Google. [Cited: March 25, 2012.] http://www.google.com/about/company/tech.html.

29. **Ulanoff, Lance.** Google Knowledge Graph Could Change Search Forever. [Online] Mashable, February 13, 2012. Mashable. http://mashable.com/2012/02/13/google-knowledge-graph-change-search/.

30. **Gross, Doug.** Google revamps search, tries to think more like a person. [Online] CNN, May 16, 2012. http://www.cnn.com/2012/05/16/tech/web/google-search-knowledge-graph/index.html.

31. **Google.** Your data on the web. [Online] Google Privacy Center. [Cited: March 25, 2012.] https://www.google.com/goodtoknow/data-on-the-web/.

32. **Rigley, Michael.** Network. [Online] Vimeo, January 8, 2012. http://vimeo.com/34750078.

33. **Google.** Google Company Mission. [Online] Google. [Cited: March 25, 2011.] http://www.google.com/about/company/.

34. **Vaidhyanathan, Siva.** The Googlization of Everything: (And Why We Should Worry). [Online] University of California Press, March 8, 2011. http://www.ucpress.edu/book.php?isbn=9780520258822.

Chapter 16
Living in Facebook Nation

"On the Internet, nobody knows you're a dog."
– Cartoonist Peter Steiner (July 1993)

"We exist at the intersection of technology and social issues."
– Facebook CEO Mark Zuckerberg (September 2011)

"No activity is too big or too small to share. You don't have to 'Like' a movie. You just watch a movie."
– Facebook CEO Mark Zuckerberg (September 2011)

"If technology is a drug – and it does feel like a drug – then what, precisely, are the side-effects?"
– Black Mirror creator Charlie Brooker (December 2011)

"We are our real identities online."
– Facebook COO Sheryl Sandberg (January 2012)

"It's kind of a fiction to pretend that you can put something out on the Internet, and then delete it."
– Tom Lee of Sunlight Foundation (June 2012)

"The things we do and say online leave behind ever-growing trails of personal information."
– American Civil Liberties Union (July 2012)

"Fortnite is the new Facebook in some ways. Millennials and Gen Z are much more used to living on platforms like Fortnite."
– Henry Cowling of MediaMonks (June 2019)

"It was the first time I realized online expression could potentially harm me offline, even physically. It scared me."
– A 28-year-old resident in Rhode Island (May 2021)

"I realized how time-consuming, toxic, and divisive they [social media apps] are. It was a day of mental clarity."
– Doctoral student Lilly Logan in Texas (October 2021)

"While the Internet has the power to connect an increasingly globalized society, without careful and responsible development, the Internet can harm as much as it helps. … A safer, more enjoyable social media is possible."
– Former Facebook product manager Frances Haugen (October 2021)

© Springer Science+Business Media, LLC, part of Springer Nature 2021
N. Lee, *Facebook Nation*, https://doi.org/10.1007/978-1-0716-1867-7_16

16.1   Facebook's Impact on Children and Democracy

Mark Zuckerberg once said, "We exist at the intersection of technology and social issues" (1). He should have heeded his own words. In October 2021, former Facebook manager-turned-whistleblower Frances Haugen testified at the U.S. Senate that Facebook's products "harm children, stoke division, and weaken our democracy" (2).

The day Facebook dissolved its civic integrity team in December 2020, Facebook product manager Frances Haugen replied to a LinkedIn message from Wall Street Journal reporter Jeff Horwitz who sought information about how Facebook managed content on its platforms during the 2020 election (3). The Wall Street Journal subsequently published a series of investigative reports known as The Facebook Files (4).

In October 2021, Haugen testified before the U.S. Senate Subcommittee on Consumer Protection, Product Safety, and Data Security, sharing with lawmakers thousands of pages of internal Facebook research and documents. Haugen said in her opening remarks (5):

"Chairman Blumenthal, Ranking Member Blackburn, and Members of the Subcommittee. Thank you for the opportunity to appear before you and for your interest in confronting one of the most urgent threats to the American people, to our children and our country's well-being, as well as to people and nations across the globe.

My name is Frances Haugen. I used to work at Facebook and joined because I think Facebook has the potential to bring out the best in us. But I am here today because I believe that Facebook's products harm children, stoke division, weaken our democracy and much more. The company's leadership knows ways to make Facebook and Instagram safer and won't make the necessary changes because they have put their immense profits before people. Congressional action is needed. They cannot solve this crisis without your help.

I believe that social media has the potential to enrich our lives and our society. We can have social media we enjoy — one that brings out the best in humanity. The Internet has enabled people around the world to receive and share information and ideas in ways never conceived of before. And while the Internet has the power to connect an increasingly globalized society, without careful and responsible development, the Internet can harm as much as it helps. … A safer, more enjoyable social media is possible."

16.2   Digital Personalities and Identities

It used to be that "on the Internet, nobody knows you're a dog"—as it was cleverly depicted by Peter Steiner in his famous cartoon published on July 5, 1993 in *The New Yorker* (6). Six years later on May 7, 2009, a real Pomeranian dog named "Boo" joined Facebook. Before Boo passed away on January 18, 2019 at age 12, he had garnered 16 million "Likes" on Facebook as a "Public Figure," surpassing the popularity of most human public figures on the social network at the time (7).

Everyone can have his or her own digital personality and identity online. IBM released a new study in April 2012 that identified four emerging digital personalities – efficiency experts, content maestros, social butterflies, and content kings – respectively representing 41%, 35%, 15%, and 9% of the online population (8). Efficiency experts are proficient Internet users; content maestros are media consumers and gamers on the web and on mobile devices; social butterflies are Facebook and Twitter addicts; and content kings are both consumers and creators of rich media.

Prof. Mitja Back of Johannes Gutenberg University in Mainz, Germany, studied a group of Facebook users and concluded, "Online social networks are so popular and so likely to reveal people's actual personalities because they allow for social interactions that feel real in many ways. ... Facebook is so true to life that encountering a person there for the first time generally results in a more accurate personality appraisal than meeting face to face" (9).

On the other hand, *Consumer Reports* magazine conducted a survey of 2,002 online households, including 1,340 that are active on Facebook. The findings based on the January 2012 survey showed that 25% of Facebook users falsified information in their profiles to protect their identity (10).

Moreover, a Facebook profile may represent the alter ego of a person. UCLA Prof. Patricia Greenfield and researcher Adriana Manago published their research on Facebook and MySpace in the November-December 2008 issue of the *Journal of Applied Developmental Psychology*. "You can manifest your ideal self," said Manago. "You can manifest who you want to be and then try to grow into that. We're always engaging in self-presentation; we're always trying to put our best foot forward. Social networking sites take this to a whole new level. You can change what you look like, you can Photoshop your face, you can select only the pictures that show you in a perfect lighting. These websites intensify the ability to present yourself in a positive light and explore different aspects of your personality and how you present yourself. You can try on different things, possible identities, and explore in a way that is common for emerging adulthood. It becomes psychologically real. People put up something that they would like to become – not completely different from who they are but maybe a little different – and the more it gets reflected off of others, the more it may be integrated into their sense of self as they share words and photos with so many people" (11).

"People are living life online," Greenfield added to Manago's statements. "Identity, romantic relations and sexuality all get played out on these social networking sites. All of these things are what teenagers always do, but the social networking sites give them much more power to do it in a more extreme way. In the arena of identity formation, this makes people more individualistic and more narcissistic; people sculpt themselves with their profiles" (11).

In the case of Boo the dog on Facebook, Boo was the living alter ego of his behind-the-scene owner—Facebook employee Irene Ahn—who never appeared in any of the Facebook pictures. "Identity online is kind of like an artifact, almost," said researcher Claire Pescott from the University of South Wales. "It's a kind of projected image of yourself" (12).

16.3   Intertwining Lives, Online and Offline

Facebook's chief operating officer Sheryl Sandberg said at the January 2012 Digital Life Design (DLD) conference in Munich, "We are our real identities online" (13). What we do online is increasingly who we are. In a pep talk at Wakefield High School in September 2009, President Barack Obama told the students, "Be careful what you post on Facebook. Whatever you do, it will be pulled up later in your life" (14).

For many people, life online is as real as life offline. The two lives are intertwined; each of them affects the other, both in the psychological and physical sense. On one hand, some people utilize social media to help them stay in shape. Social apps that track and share their fitness habits make them feel accountable and more likely to follow through with their fitness plans. On the other hand, Prof. Lori B. Andrews at Chicago-Kent College of Law pointed out that "virtually every interaction a person has in the offline world can be tainted by social network information" (15).

The following are some examples of the adverse effects of online life that made headline news:

1. In summer 2009, 24-year-old public high school English teacher Ashley Payne went to Europe for a summer vacation. She posted her vacation photos on Facebook. One of the pictures showed a smiling Payne holding a glass of wine and a mug of beer. She also used the "B" word on Facebook and thought that only her closest friends could access her Facebook page. Payne did not realize that despite the Facebook privacy settings, no one could ever guarantee the absolute privacy of content posted on the Internet. When the school principal found out about the Facebook photo and profanity, Payne was forced to resign (16).

2. In March 2011, Comedian Gilbert Gottfried was fired from his job as the voice of the Aflac duck for making a dozen of tasteless jokes on Twitter about the Japan tsunami (17). One of his tweets was: "Japan is really advanced. They don't go to the beach. The beach comes to them" (18).

3. In June 2011, U.S. representative Anthony Weiner from New York resigned after a sexting scandal in which he admitted having "engaged in several inappropriate conversations conducted over Twitter, Facebook, email and occasionally on the phone" and had exchanged "messages and photos of an explicit nature with about six women over the last three years" (19).

4. In June 2011, Corinne Gregory told a story of a high school graduate who applied for a job as security guard for the local Port Authority. The recruiter asked the applicant if he or any of his friends had ever been incarcerated. He honestly answered "no." However, the recruiter pulled out a copy of his Facebook page, with two of his "friends" highlighted; and those two "friends" were indeed in jail for their convicted crimes. Although the applicant denied knowing those two people at all, he did not get the job (20).

5. In April 2012, Marine Sgt. Gary Stein posted on his Facebook pages derogatory comments about President Barack Obama. As a direct consequence, a military board recommended that Stein be discharged for violating "good order and discipline" required by all U.S. military service members (21).

6. In July 2012, Greek triple jumper Paraskevi Papachristou was banned from the 2012 London Olympics and suspended from her country's Olympic team because of one offensive tweet: "With so many Africans in Greece, at least the mosquitoes of West Nile will eat homemade food" (22). "I would like to express my heartfelt apologies for the unfortunate and tasteless joke I published on my personal Twitter account," Papachristou wrote on her Facebook page. "I am very sorry and ashamed for the negative responses I triggered, since I never wanted to offend anyone, or to encroach human rights."

7. In February 2013, 18-year-old Justin Carter was arrested for making a threat on Facebook during a heated argument about the online video game "League of Legends." Someone wrote to Carter on Facebook, "Oh you're insane. You're crazy. You're messed up in the head." To which Carter replied, "Oh yeah, I'm real messed up in the head. I'm going to go shoot up a school full of kids and eat their still-beating hearts." Carter ended up in jail for over four months (23). His lawyer, Donald H. Flanary III commented, "The law enforcement, the sheriff's department, the district attorney's office – nobody wants to be the one that let him go. They don't think about the person or the crime or the lack of crime ... they don't want to take responsibility for something happening in the future" (24).

8. In August 2013, two Virginia day care workers were fired after they posted on Instagram photos of children in their care, along with comments mocking the young kids. "He is thinking cuz sure can't talk," one employee wrote of a 2-year-old boy who was pictured sitting in a chair, looking dejected (25). The child was diagnosed with speech delay.

9. In August 2013, CNN reported that "references to drugs, comments about hazing and pictures of semi-nude women taken from posts on a closed Facebook page have prompted the suspension of Pi Kappa Alpha fraternity on Florida International University's Miami campus" (26). In a similar incident, *HLN* reported that "Many students on college campuses have been learning a hard lesson recently: Private correspondence and social media pages don't always stay private, particularly, it seems, when the subject matter is questionable. ... A controversial e-mail from a Georgia Tech student to his fraternity brothers ... prompted online ire and immediate action from the school and the fraternity involved" (27).

10. In December 2013, top PR executive Justine Sacco at media company IAC tweeted "Going to Africa. Hope I don't get AIDS. Just kidding. I'm white!" on her way to Cape Town, South Africa. After her plane had landed 12 hours later, she realized that she had been fired. Sacco apologized "for being insensitive to this crisis – which does not discriminate by race, gender or sexual orientation, but which terrifies us all uniformly – and to the millions of people living with the virus, I am ashamed" (28).

11. In January 2014, a Canadian teenage girl was found guilty of distributing child pornography in connection with "sexting" pictures of her boyfriend's ex-girlfriend (29). Similar to the idea of revenge porn, the teenager texted to a group of people several explicit pictures of the ex-girlfriend that she found on her boyfriend's phone.

12. In May 2014, PayPal's new director of strategy Rakesh "Rocky" Agrawal was drunk in early morning hours, and he fired off denigrating tweets to insult some of his fellow colleagues. Within hours, PayPal tweeted back, "Rakesh Agrawal is no longer with the company. Treat everyone with respect. No excuses. PayPal has zero tolerance" (30). Agrawal later published an apology on LinkedIn: "Those tweets were intended as a confidential communication; I am deeply sorry that they became public" (31).

13. In March 2021, the White House pulled Neera Tanden's nomination to lead the Office of Management and Budget amid opposition from both Democratic and Republican senators (32). West Virginia Democratic Senator Joe Manchin said, "I have carefully reviewed Neera Tanden's public statements and tweets that were personally directed towards my colleagues on both sides of the aisle from Senator Sanders to Senator McConnell and others. I believe her overtly partisan statements will have a toxic and detrimental impact on the important working relationship between members of Congress and the next director of the Office of Management and Budget." Maine Republican Senator Susan Collins concurred, "Her past actions have demonstrated exactly the kind of animosity that President Biden has pledged to transcend. In addition, Ms. Tanden's decision to delete more than a thousand tweets in the days before her nomination was announced raises concerns about her commitment to transparency."

14. In March 2021, Alexi McCammond was ousted by *Teen Vogue* on March 18 for the new editor-in-chief position even before she was to officially start the new job on March 24. Apologizing for her anti-Asian and homophobic tweets that she posted a decade ago, she wrote on Twitter: "My past tweets have overshadowed the work I've done to highlight the people and issues that I care about — issues that Teen Vogue has worked tirelessly to share with the world — and so Condé Nast and I have decided to part ways. I should not have tweeted what I did and I have taken full responsibility for that" (33).

15. In May 2021, 17-year-old Adrian and his friends planned a casual get-together on Huntington Beach, California for his birthday. His hashtag #adrianskickback on TikTok went viral with over 350 million views (34). More than 2,500 people showed up at Huntington Beach and downtown area on the weekend of Adrian's birthday; and police arrested nearly 150 individuals for their disruptive and unruly behavior in public (35).

There are countless other stories that did not make national news. Some can be totally harmless such as Brad Pitt impersonator Jacob Tran (with username @bradpitt) carrying on a conversation about "Climate Impact Reduction" with an alleged Quentin Tarantino and thousands of participants for hours on the social media app

Clubhouse (36). Nevertheless, the potential impact of our digital personalities and identities on our real life should not be understated.

In 2008, educational company Kaplan conducted an annual survey of 500 top colleges and found that 10% of admissions officers acknowledged looking at social-networking sites to evaluate applicants, and 38% of them said that what they saw "negatively affected" their views of the applicants. Thomas Griffin, director of undergraduate admissions at North Carolina State University in Raleigh, disclosed that several applicants a year had been rejected partly due to the information on Facebook and other social media sites (37).

In 2011, Kaplan Test Prep's annual survey found that 24% of admissions officers have gone to an applicant's Facebook or other social-network sites to learn more about them. The percentage has more than doubled in three years. The growing practice of exploring applicants' digital trails is evident, as Kaplan Test Prep reported, "More prevalent is the use of social media for outreach purposes. ... Facebook and YouTube are increasingly important recruiting tools for colleges – 85% use Facebook (up from 82% in the 2010 survey) and 66% use YouTube (up from 52% in the 2010 survey) to vie for the interest of prospective students" (38).

Aside from college admissions, employment decisions are also affected by our digital personalities and identities. *Consumer Reports* in June 2012 stated that 69% of human-resource officers have rejected job applicants based on social media reviews that turned up any of the red flags such as sexually explicit photos or videos, racist remarks, and evidence of illegal activities.

As more employers are turning to Facebook to check on the job applicants, both American Civil Liberties Union (ACLU) and Facebook have voiced their opposi-tions. In March 2012, ACLU attorney Catherine Crump said, "It's an invasion of privacy for private employers to insist on looking at people's private Facebook pages as a condition of employment or consideration in an application process. People are entitled to their private lives. You'd be appalled if your employer insisted on opening up your postal mail to see if there was anything of interest inside. It's equally out of bounds for an employer to go on a fishing expedition through a per-son's private social media account" (39).

At the same time, Facebook's chief privacy officer Erin Egan wrote on the com-pany's official blog, "In recent months, we've seen a distressing increase in reports of employers or others seeking to gain inappropriate access to people's Facebook profiles or private information. This practice undermines the privacy expectations and the security of both the user and the user's friends. It also potentially exposes the employer who seeks this access to unanticipated legal liability. ... For example, if an employer sees on Facebook that someone is a member of a protected group (e.g. over a certain age, etc.) that employer may open themselves up to claims of discrimination if they don't hire that person" (40).

Nonetheless, from the standpoint of employers and college admission officers, looking up an applicant on Facebook, Google, and LinkedIn can be regarded as a type of background check. It is up to the applicant to keep his or her own private life private by not uploading any inappropriate materials online.

16.4   Digital Footprint and Exhaust Data

Speaking of digital footprint and exhaust data, imagine your whole life is recorded on a device portrayed by the 2011 *Black Mirror* episode "The Entire History of You"!

Gmail and AOL Mail allow users to un-send their emails under some circumstances, but we cannot be certain if the unsent emails may be stored in some mail servers for an unknown period of time. Once data is uploaded to the Internet via email, Twitter, Facebook, YouTube, et cetera, they can potentially take on a life of their own regardless of whether the data is meant to be public or private.

Even if a Facebook user later decides to delete uploaded photos for whatever reasons, the "deleted" Facebook photos may still be online indefinitely and are accessible via direct links (URLs) (41). And in case we cannot recall our own or someone else's first tweet, Twitter has a simple tool (https://discover.twitter.com/first-tweet) that lets anyone relive their first-ever tweet.

Indeed, everything posted on the Internet is public to some extent. Things that had been taken down may live on forever in *The Internet Archive* that provides permanent storage on its 70+ Petabytes server space. As of April 2021, it had archived 475 billion web pages, 28 million books and texts, 14 million audio recordings including 220,000 live concerts, 6 million videos including 2 million TV news programs, 3.5 million images, and 580,000 software programs (42). Synonymous with the term "Wayback Machine," *The Internet Archive* allows us to see previous versions of websites and to visit old websites that no longer exist. I find it quite interesting to look back at Disney.com in 1996 (see Fig. 16.1) when I first joined The Walt Disney Company, and to compare that to Disney.com today (43).

Fig. 16.1 Disney.com in 1996 on the Internet Archive

In April 2010, the U.S. Library of Congress announced that every public tweet posted since Twitter's inception in March 2006 would be archived digitally by the federal library. By January 2013, the Library of Congress had compiled more than 170 billion Twitter messages and processed about 500 million tweets per day (44). Blogger Matt Raymond wrote, "How Tweet It Is!: Library Acquires Entire Twitter Archive... Twitter processes more than 50 million tweets every day, with the total numbering in the billions. I'm no Ph.D., but it boggles my mind to think what we might be able to learn about ourselves and the world around us from this wealth of data. ... So if you think the Library of Congress is 'just books,' think of this: The Library has been collecting materials from the web since it began harvesting congressional and presidential campaign websites in 2000. Today we hold more than 167 terabytes of web-based information, including legal blogs, websites of candidates for national office, and websites of Members of Congress" (45).

In June 2012, Sunlight Foundation launched the U.S. edition of Politwoops in order to expose tweets that politicians shared and then promptly deleted. "It's kind of a fiction to pretend that you can put something out on the Internet, and then delete it," said Tom Lee, director of the technical arm of the Sunlight Foundation (46). Take an example as recent as April 2014, amid backlash for tweeting out an article with inflammatory language, Illinois Gov. Pat Quinn's campaign deleted the tweets but they ended up being saved in perpetuity and posted on the website Politwoops for the world to read (47). Indeed, Politwoops states on its homepage that it "tracks deleted tweets by public officials, including people currently in office and candidates for office" (48).

At the 2011 South by Southwest Interactive conference in Austin, Texas, LinkedIn founder Reid Hoffman spoke of the web of "real identities generating massive amounts of data" (49). The exhaust data – the output of human beings using the Internet – contains the digital footprint of the past and current user activities and interactions.

When we go to a nightclub, the bouncer checks our IDs. We are not anonymous. Likewise, when we log onto Facebook, Twitter, YouTube, and Google, among others, we are not Jane/John Doe. There is plenty of personally identifiable information (PII) online such as our full name, IP address, phone number, and date of birth. Furthermore, government-issued IDs are required to establish verified accounts on Facebook and Twitter. Is the online world moving towards PII instead of anonymity?

American Civil Liberties Union (ACLU) has expressed the concern that "the things we do and say online leave behind ever-growing trails of personal information. With every click, we entrust our conversations, emails, photos, location information and much more to companies like Facebook, Google and Yahoo. But what happens when the government asks these companies to hand over their users' private information?" (50)

In 2012, ACLU launched a new campaign – Demand Your dotRights (Privacy 2.0) – to educate the public about digital footprint and exhaust data (51):

1. Search Engines: When you browse through online stacks of information, you are leaving a trail that reveals a lot about you: interests, hobbies, habits, and concerns.

2. Location Information: Location data from your cell phone or laptop can tell more than just where you travel, but also what you do and even who you know.
3. Social Networking: Replacing interactions in the coffee shop with connections online leaves behind a lot of information about you, friends, and activities.
4. Webmail: Online email services make it easy to keep in touch with friends and family. But every email creates a record of who you write, what you write, and when you send and read it.
5. Photo Sites: The pictures you develop, store, or share online can tell many thousands of words to others about you and who you know, where you've gone, and what you've done.
6. Media Sites: Reading a book or watching a video is a great way to learn and explore new things. But a lot of information can be collected about who you are and what you read and watch.
7. Cloud Computing: Moving files from your hard drive to an online service or accessing applications through the Internet can be convenient. But, those documents and files you store or produce online can say a lot about you.

16.5   Facebook, Peer Pressure, and Social Issues

Facebook can extend peer pressure from the physical world to the larger online world. Live artist-researcher Louise Orwin said, "There's always going to be peer pressure but I think [social media] makes these issues worse" (52).

Marlon P. Mundt from University of Wisconsin, Madison, studied the influence of peer social networks on adolescents. The findings suggest that adolescents are more likely to start drinking alcoholic beverages when they have large social networks of friends (53). Soraya Mehdizadeh from York University, Toronto, published revealing research results that "individuals higher in narcissism and lower in self-esteem were related to greater online activity" and that women in particular used pictures that "include revealing, flashy and adorned photos of their physical appearance" (54).

In March 2012, CNN columnist Amanda Enayati reported on a story of a college student named Amanda Coleman who decided to quit Facebook. Being the president of her sorority, Coleman has counseled many young girls at her university. "They would call or come in to see me for advice, crying that they were stressed out," Coleman said. "At some point I began noticing that Facebook was being mentioned in some way in just about every conversation. … It's as if somewhere along the line, Facebook became the encyclopedia of beauty and status and comparisons. … [The young girls, many of them college freshmen] were walking around saying, 'I'm not good enough. I'm not enough this or that'" (55).

The story reminds us of Facemash, the predecessor to Facebook, which placed two photos next to each other at a time and asked users to choose the hotter person. In spite of Facebook's sophistication over Facemash, users can still compare themselves to their friends and their friends' friends in terms of looks, fashion, popularity, and so forth. In fact, Facebook and Instagram have publicly acknowledged, "We know people may feel pressure to look a certain way on social media" (12).

Children and young teens are particularly susceptible to messages and images coming from their friends on Facebook. How are they going to react to their "enemies" on Facebook? The Facebook app "Enemybook," developed in July 2007 by Kevin Matulef at MIT, could exacerbate peer pressure by bonding like-minded haters online. Enemybook is a Facebook application that you can "add people as Facebook enemies, specify why they are your enemies, notify your enemies, see who lists you as an enemy, and even become friends with the enemies of your enemies" (56).

In May 2013, Facebook was called "hatebook" by some women's groups protesting against Facebook pages that promoted rape, domestic violence, and sexual degradation of women. Women, Action, and the Media (WAM!) complained, "It appears that Facebook considers violence against women to be less offensive than non-violent images of women's bodies, and that the only acceptable representation of women's nudity are those in which women appear as sex objects or the victims of abuse" (57). When a dozen companies started pulling their ads from Facebook, the social network responded swiftly by removing the offensive pages (58).

In October 2021, former Facebook product manager Frances Haugen testified before the U.S. Senate that Facebook "is generating self-harm and self-hate — especially for vulnerable groups, like teenage girls" (5). And CNN interviewed teenagers Ashlee Thomas and Anastasia Vlasova who developed anorexia after they started following "clean eating" influencers on Instagram (59). In fact, Facebook's own internal research documented that 17 % of teen girls say Instagram makes "Eating Issues" such as anorexia worse, despite Instagram placing restrictions on weight loss content for users under 18 years old (60).

In his 2009 book *The Dumbest Generation: How the Digital Age Stupefies Young Americans and Jeopardizes Our Future,* Professor Mark Bauerlein at Emory University argues that the younger generation today is less informed, less literate, and more self-absorbed because the immediacy and intimacy of social-networking sites have focused young people's Internet use on themselves and their friends instead of on learning new knowledge and useful skills. He observed that the language of Internet communication, with its peculiar spelling, grammar, and punctuation, actually encourages illiteracy by making it socially acceptable (61).

In 2012, former U.S. Secretary of State Condoleezza Rice issued an alarming report in which she warned that "although the United States invests more in education than almost any other developed nation, its students rank in the middle of the pack in reading and toward the bottom in math and science. On average, U.S. students have fallen behind peers in Korea and China, Poland and Canada and New Zealand. This puts us on a trajectory toward massive failure" (62).

It is high time for a major overhaul of the U.S. educational system. Peter Thiel, co-founder of PayPal, argues that colleges and universities do a poor job promoting innovation. He predicts that higher education is the next bubble waiting to burst (63). In a provocative move, Thiel awarded each of the 24 winners of the 2011 Thiel Fellowship $100,000 not to attend college for two years but to develop business ideas instead (64).

16.6   Reality TV and Social Media

Long before reality TV and social media, Andy Warhol correctly predicted in 1968 that "in the future, everyone will be world-famous for 15 minutes."

Popular television programs have shown to increase online social activities on Twitter, Facebook, and other social networks (65). Super Bowl XLVI on February 5, 2012 created an all-time record high of 17.46 million tweets, public Facebook posts, GetGlue check-ins, and Miso check-ins (66). Analyst Nick Thomas at Informa wrote in a recent report on the future of TV worldwide, "Many [are] already using Facebook and Twitter and other tools to communicate via the handheld devices about the content they are simultaneously viewing on the TV" (67).

Beginning in the year 2000, we have witnessed the exploding popularity of reality television shows such as *Big Brother, Survivor, American Idol, America's Next Top Model, Dancing With the Stars, The Apprentice,* and *Fear Factor.* A 2010 study showed that 15 of the top 20 highest-rated television programs among young adults 18 to 49 were reality shows (68).

Following the footsteps of Donald Trump's *The Apprentice*, other businesses are also taking a page from reality TV shows to discover new stars. The world's largest retailer Walmart launched its "Get on the Shelf" program on the same day *American Idol* began its eleventh season on January 18, 2012 (69). The "Get on the Shelf" contest allows anyone in the U.S. to submit a video online pitching his or her invention. The public will vote on the products and three winners will have their products sold on Walmart.com, with the grand prizewinner also getting shelf space in select stores. Unlike *The Apprentice*, Walmart chose the Internet, instead of television, as the reality show medium.

While some reality shows have a certain amount of entertainment and educational values, others have little to no redeeming quality at all. *The Real Housewives of Beverly Hills,* for instance, is a prime example of legalized voyeurism and exhibitionism where the television viewers are the voyeurs and the participants in the reality show are the exhibitionists. Millions of people seem to enjoy access to private information that is really none of their business; and quite a large number of people want to expose their private lives to strangers in spite of potentially dangerous consequences including suicide (70) and murder (71).

In fact, a Brigham Young University study in 2010 reported that a reality show on average contains 52 acts of verbal, relational, or physical aggression per hour (72). Reporter Irin Carmon opines that sadism is a recurring theme in *America's Next Top Model*: "The series has pioneered a whole new standard of placing women in danger. ... Right from the get-go, *ANTM*'s producers began manufacturing moments that would inevitably result in pain or injury to the girls. ... As the series progressed, pain became not only a by-product but a basis upon which the girls were judged, in contests requiring the women to repeatedly fall from platforms and crash onto barely padded surfaces, recline in bikinis on ice sculptures in frigid rooms, and so on" (73).

Apart from reality television, user-generated reality shows on social media are on the rise. Acquired by Twitter in October 2012, Vine is a popular mobile app that lets users create and post 6-second looping video clips (74). Former cashier Jessica Vazquez (aka Jessi Smiles) and video gamer Curtis Lepore became Vine's first reality stars in the summer of 2013 (75). Sponsors such as Wendy's and Virgin Mobile paid them handsomely for their online video endorsements. Millions of followers watched their romance unfolded like a reality show, which unfortunately ended on a tragic note when Lepore was accused of raping Vazquez.

Social commentator Dean Obeidallah opined that "there's a connection between a willingness to share private aspects of our lives and the reality TV show world in which we have been immersed for over a decade. On a nightly basis, we see people share their triumphs and tragedies, be it on shows like *Big Brother* or *The Real World* or more contrived ones like *Honey Boo Boo* or *Keeping up with the Kardashians*. They have made it easier and more acceptable for us to do the same. To me, the best thing about this new trend is that you get to control it. It's your choice whether to disclose deeply personal information. Those who find it unnerving or inappropriate can keep that information secret. But for the rest, social media may end up being a less expensive but helpful form of therapy" (76).

One of the high-profile cases is a graphic video uploaded to YouTube in October 2011 by 23-year-old Hillary Adams, showing Aransas County Court Judge William Adams viciously whipping her with a strap seven years earlier when she was 16 (77). The video has been viewed almost seven million times as of January 2012 (78). It is debatable whether the victim wanted to raise public awareness of child abuse or to retaliate against her father for withdrawing his financial support seven years after the incident (79).

YouTube has become the reality TV broadcast medium for the masses, and Facebook is the effective tool to disseminate the YouTube videos. Christopher Carpenter from Western Illinois University conducted research on the link between Facebook and narcissism. He concluded, "Facebook gives those with narcissistic tendencies the opportunity to exploit the site to get the feedback they need and become the center of attention" (80). Self-promoters show signs of two narcissistic behaviors: grandiose exhibition (GE) and entitlement/exploitativeness (EE). GE refers to people who love to be the center of attention. EE indicates how far people will go to get the respect and attention that they think they deserve.

Although the GE and EE readings may be off the scale on many Facebook users and YouTubers, the situation is not necessarily as nefarious as some media have portrayed. Carol Hartsell, comedy editor of *The Huffington Post,* commented at the 2012 South by Southwest Interactive festival that social media has democratized comedy by giving everyone a platform to be funny. "People just naturally want to make other people laugh," said Hartsell. "It's hard to find an audience when you want to be funny. When you're a kid, it's your family. But when you're an adult, the Internet gives you a constant audience. It may just be 20 friends on Facebook, but it's an audience" (81).

A September 2010 survey by the Interactive Advertising Bureau (IAB) shows that one-third of the online population is on both YouTube and Facebook (82). With billions of users on both social networks since, the seamless integration of Facebook and YouTube videos offers a powerful communication tool for hundreds of millions of people to disseminate and consume information, both private and public (83).

In August 2017, Facebook introduced Watch to help users discover new shows and interact with online friends and other viewers while watching. Watch is also a platform for creators and publishers of a variety of new shows including (84):

- Shows that engage fans and community
- Live shows that connect directly with fans
- Shows that follow a narrative arc or have a consistent theme
- Live events that bring communities together

16.7   YouTube: The Beast with a Billion Eyes

In a May 2014 *Forbes* article titled "The 'Sex Talk' for 21st Century Parents," Jordan Shapiro, shared some intimate conversations with his 9-year-old son who asked, "Would you rather have your first kiss on YouTube? Or a transcript of everything you said on your first date available on Google?" Shapiro answered with a bit of anxiety, "I choose my first kiss on YouTube. No matter how awkward that looks, it is not as bad as the clumsy ways we try to express confusing feelings to people before we really know how" (85).

While reality television may be losing steam (86) and the percentage of U.S. homes with a television set is declining (87), the Internet is flourishing with reality content and attentive audiences. Mahir Çağrı, for instance, became an Internet celebrity in 1999 for his infamous homepage (88) and arguably was the main inspiration for British comedian Sacha Baron Cohen as the fictional Kazakhstan reporter "Borat" (89).

With the launch of the video-sharing website YouTube in February 2005, the Internet is becoming the new reality TV. Touted as "The Beast With A Billion Eyes" by the *Time Magazine* (90), YouTube reports in January 2012 that 4 billion online videos are viewed every day (91). More than tripling the prime-time audiences of all three major U.S. broadcast networks combined, YouTube users upload the equivalent of 240,000 full-length films every week. In fact, more video is uploaded to YouTube in one month than the 3 major U.S. networks created in 60 years (92).

In December 2011, more than 100 million Americans watched online video on an average day, representing a 43% increase of a year ago (93). The numbers continue to skyrocket. In January 2012, some 181 million U.S. Internet users watched about 40 billion online videos (94). Internet marketing research firm comScore's Video Metrix shows that YouTube has over 50% share of content videos viewed, followed by the distant second Vevo, Hulu, Yahoo!, Microsoft, Viacom, AOL, Netflix, ESPN, Mevio, and others (95). Thanks to Netflix, Amazon Prime, and Hulu, Americans watched more online movies than DVDs in 2012 (96).

By March 2021, YouTube had over 2 billion monthly active users who watched over 1 billion hours of YouTube video every day and uploaded more than 500 hours of video to YouTube every minute (97). Facebook took second place with 46 % of its 2 billion monthly active users watching videos (98). Together with Facebook, YouTube has ushered in the new era of exhibitionism and voyeurism. Not everyone can be on TV, but everyone can be on YouTube. The HTML title of youtube.com is "YouTube – Broadcast Yourself" and the description meta tag reads "Share your videos with friends, family, and the world."

Google video head Salar Kamangar said at News Corp.'s D: Dive Into Media 2012 conference, "We want YouTube to be the platform of these next generation of channels" (99), referring to bringing its audiences more high-quality content in partnership with Disney and other media companies (100).

Nevertheless, the lion's share of YouTube videos has been and will continue to be unscripted content created by amateurs (101). Pew Research Internet Project reported that "the percent of American adult Internet users who upload or post videos online has doubled in the past four years, from 14% in 2009 to 31% in 2013" (102).

In May 2014, the most subscribed YouTube channel of all time was PewDiePie featuring video game commentaries by 24-year-old Felix Arvid Ulf Kjellberg and Marzia Bisognin (103). The channel's 27 million subscribers have logged a staggering 4.5 billion video views (104). After a bitter online competition between PewDiePie and T-Series (run by an Indian record company of the same name), T-Series won by having the most YouTube subscribers in the world. As of April 2021, T-Series had 180 million subscribers, followed by PewDiePie with 109 million subscribers.

Although it takes time and energy to grow a YouTube channel, anyone can literally create a "15 minutes of fame" on YouTube. Aspiring young singers hope to become the next pop star Justin Bieber who was discovered via his homemade YouTube videos (105). Kate Upton's YouTube video of herself at a Los Angeles Clippers game "doing the Dougie" helped catapult her onto the cover of *Swimsuit Illustrated* (106). Bella Poarch rose to fame with her lip-sync videos on TikTok and subsequently launched her music career with the smashing debut single "Build a Bitch" (107). In 2019, 5-year-old Anastasia Radzinskaya and 8-year-old Ryan Kaji created children content on YouTube almost every day; and earned $18 million and $26 million respectively (108).

16.8   Am I Pretty or Ugly?

In addition to individuals showcasing their talents on social media, YouTube has also become an outlet for many teenagers seeking approval. Videos asking "Am I Pretty or Ugly" have popped up all over YouTube, some of them have accrued millions of views, rivaling blockbuster movie trailers and hit music videos. Research has shown that one in three girls was unhappy with their personal appearance by the age of 14 (109).

In the opening of one "Am I Pretty or Ugly" video, the YouTuber says: "Hey guys, this is my first video … but before I post any more videos making a fool of myself, and I know there's hundreds of videos like this. … I just wanna know, am I pretty or ugly? Cuz at school I get called ugly all the time" (110).

Indeed, many of those YouTubers are victims of bullying. Naomi Gibson's 13-year-old daughter Faye is constantly bullied by schoolmates who call her ugly. Faye went to YouTube to get a second opinion from strangers and received mixed reactions with nearly 3,000 comments (111). Her mother appealed to YouTube to try to take down all those "Am I Pretty or Ugly" videos, but to no avail. Gibson told *ABC Good Morning America*, "I took away her Facebook and Twitter account because of bullying. She needs to stop putting herself out there. Now people are walking around asking her if she's pretty to her face. It's hurting her more in the long run, I think" (112).

On February 19, 2013, Canadian poet and writer Shane Koyczan published a YouTube video titled "To This Day" to confront bullying (113). It has garnered over 13.5 million views as of June 2014. Sending out one new poem each month to his readers, Koyczan wrote, "If you can't see anything beautiful about yourself, get a better mirror" (114).

Beauty filters using augmented reality (AR) have become the most popular digital mirror among young girls on Snapchat, Instagram, and TikTok. Researcher Claire Pescott from the University of South Wales conducted a research study with children aged 10 and 11. "[The girls] were all saying things like, 'I put this filter on because I have flawless skin. It takes away my scars and spots'. I don't think it's just filtering your actual image. It's filtering your whole life" (12).

Indeed, beauty filters can create body dysmorphic disorder—a mental illness involving obsessive focus on a perceived flaw in appearance. Such a dangerous effect on young social media users has prompted Instagram and Facebook to issue this statement: "We know people may feel pressure to look a certain way on social media, and we're taking steps to address this across Instagram and Facebook. We know effects can play a role, so we ban ones that clearly promote eating disorders or that encourage potentially dangerous cosmetic surgery procedures" (12).

Dysmorphia can lead to online and offline bullying. But bullying victims are not limited to the young age group. On June 21, 2012, a 10-minute YouTube video showed a 68-year-old bus monitor named Karen Klein being verbally bullied by a group of middle schoolers, on their way home from the Athena Middle School in Greece, New York (115). The video was viewed one million times within a week. Klein received widespread support from sympathizers and nearly $650,000 in donations (116).

Another lurking danger on social media is the so-called "challenges" that have gone viral. Some are just silly and funny (such as the Mannequin Challenge where a group of people poses and freezes in place) whereas some others are outright harmful (like the Tide Pod Challenge where people eat laundry detergent packets on camera) (117). In 2019, a blindfolded teen crashed into another vehicle while doing the Bird Box Challenge in Utah. Netflix—which plays the film *Bird Box* starring Sandra Bullock—warned the viewers: "We don't know how this started, and we appreciate the love, but Boy and Girl have just one wish for 2019 and it is that you not end up in the hospital due to memes" (118). YouTube, Facebook, and Instagram have been busy taking down videos that promote physical harm (119).

16.9 Social Media Regrets

Not everyone is as talented as former California Governor Arnold Schwarzenegger who sent lawmakers a "F*ck You" message through an acrostic poem in 2010 (see Fig. 16.2).

Hip-hop singer Chris Brown lashed out against his critics after his Grammy performance in February 2012. He sent a series of missives ending with a "F*ck You" on Twitter. A few minutes later, he attempted to delete all the offensive tweets, but it was too late. Some bloggers took screenshots of his tweets and posted them online for the whole world to see (120).

Evan Spiegel, CEO and cofounder of Snapchat, apologized for the profanity-laced emails that he sent during his Stanford University fraternity days that celebrated underage drinking and performing lewd acts on sorority women (121). "I'm obviously mortified and embarrassed that my idiotic e-mails during my fraternity days were made public. I have no excuse. I'm sorry I wrote them at the time and I was jerk to have written them. They in no way reflect who I am today or my views towards women" (122).

"We now have entered a phase where every single thing you say – the way you say it, how you say it – is now all exposed," said Gavin Newsom, former San

To the Members of the California State Assembly:

I am returning Assembly Bill 1176 without my signature.

For some time now I have lamented the fact that major issues are overlooked while many unnecessary bills come to me for consideration. Water reform, prison reform, and health care are major issues my Administration has brought to the table, but the Legislature just kicks the can down the alley.

Yet another legislative year has come and gone without the major reforms Californians overwhelmingly deserve. In light of this, and after careful consideration, I believe it is unnecessary to sign this measure at this time.

Sincerely,

Arnold Schwarzenegger

Fig. 16.2 Gov. Arnold Schwarzenegger's Acrostic Poem

-3349

Hey gorgeous :) what's
up?

Not much but I can't speak
for the 31 other girls
attached in this group
message

Fig. 16.3 This Guy Tried to Group Text 32 Tinder Matches and Failed

Francisco Mayor and 49th Lieutenant Governor of California. "I have to watch myself now singing 'I left my heart in San Francisco' on YouTube, and it can't go away. I am desperate to get it to go away" (123).

Chris Brown, Evan Spiegel, and Gavin Newsom are among the majority of people who wish they could erase their digital footprint and eliminate their exhaust data. We all have said to ourselves at one point, "Oh, I wish I hadn't sent that email or that tweet." Dallas Mavericks owner Mark Cuban and Miami Heat owner Micky Arison have both been fined $500,000 by the National Basketball Association (NBA) for inappropriate tweets against NBA officials (124). The guy who sent a group message to 32 of his Tinder matches probably also wished he hadn't (125) (see Fig. 16.3). (Who knows if this guy may also be using BroApp (126) that auto-texts sweet things to his girlfriend at an appointed time every day?)

Actor George Clooney summed it up his own way in a 2013 interview with *Esquire*: "I don't understand why any famous person would ever be on Twitter. ... So one drunken night, you come home and you've had two too many drinks and you're watching TV and somebody pisses you off, and you go '*Ehhhhh*' and fight back. And you go to sleep, and you wake up in the morning and your career is over. Or you're an asshole. Or all the things you might think in the quiet of your drunken evening are suddenly blasted around the entire world before you wake up" (127).

Just ask the 19-year-old Justin Carter who spent more than four months in jail for what he wrote on Facebook, and he would tell us, "I certainly would have thought a lot more about what I said and how permanent my writing – and everyone's writing – is (on the Internet). People should be very, very careful of what they say. It's being recorded all the time, if you say it on any website, anywhere" (128).

Yang Wang and fellow researchers at Carnegie Mellon University have identified seven possible causes of why Facebook users make posts that they later regret (129):

1. They want to be perceived in favorable ways.
2. They do not think about their reason for posting or the consequences of their posts.

3. They misjudge the culture and norms within their social circles.
4. They are in a "hot" state of high emotion when posting, or under the influence of drugs or alcohol.
5. Their postings are seen by an unintended audience.
6. They do not foresee how their posts could be perceived by people within their intended audience.
7. They misunderstand or misuse the Facebook platform.

16.10 Facebook Social Plug-in: Like

Within a week after Facebook announced the social plug-in "Like" at the 2010 F8 Conference, more than 50,000 websites have implemented the new feature. Today, the Like button is ubiquitous across the Internet (130).

"No activity is too big or too small to share," said Mark Zuckerberg. "You don't have to 'Like' a movie. You just watch a movie" (131). There is no need to read between the lines, as chief political correspondent Declan McCullagh at *CNET* has clarified that the widespread use of the Like button enables Facebook to track people: "Even if someone is not a Facebook user or is not logged in, Facebook's social plug-ins collect the address of the Web page being visited and the Internet address of the visitor as soon as the page is loaded – clicking on the Like button is not required. If enough sites participate, that permits Facebook to assemble a vast amount of data about Internet users' browsing habits" (132).

American Civil Liberties Union (ACLU) attorney Nicole Ozer has also warned that "if an organization puts a Like button on their site, they're potentially telling Facebook about everyone who visits their Web site, every time that person visits their Web site ... even if they never press that [Like] button" (132).

The proliferation of Facebook's social plug-in "Like" on the Web enables the social network to collect consumers' digital footprint. A 2012 study by University of California, Berkeley concluded that "Facebook Likes can be used to automatically and accurately predict a range of highly sensitive personal attributes including: sexual orientation, ethnicity, religious and political views, personality traits, intelligence, happiness, use of addictive substances, parental separation, age, and gender" (133). Some of the interesting findings based on inductive reasoning are (134):

1. For high intelligence: Curly Fries, Science, Mozart, Thunderstorms, or The Daily Show.
2. For low intelligence: Harley-Davidson, Lady Antebellum, Chiq, and I Love Being a Mom.
3. For Satisfaction with Life: Swimming, Jesus, Pride and Prejudice, and Indiana Jones.
4. For Dissatisfaction with Life: Ipod, Kickass, Lamb of God, Quote Portal, and Gorillaz.

5. For being emotionally unstable (neurotic): So So Happy, Dot Dot Curve, Girl Interrupted, The Adams Family, and Kurt Donald Cobain.
6. For being emotionally stable (calm and relaxed): Business Administration, Skydiving, Soccer, Mountain Biking, and Parkour.
7. For being old: Cup Of Joe For A Joe, Coffee Party Movement, The Closer, Freedomworks, Small Business Saturday, and Fly The American Flag.
8. For being young: Body by Milk, I Hate My Id Photo, Dude Wait What, J Bigga, and Because I Am A Girl.
9. For being gay (males): Kathy Griffin, Adam Lambert, Wicked The Musical, Sue Sylvester Glee, and Juicy Couture.
10. For being straight (male): X Games, Foot Locker, Being Confused After Waking Up From Naps, SportsNation, WWE, and Wu-Tang Clan.

16.11 Facebook Knows Who, When, and Where

In February 2012, Jacqui Cheng, Senior Apple Editor at Ars Technica, recounted her own experience and 3-year investigation that even if a Facebook user decides to delete uploaded photos for whatever reasons, the "deleted" Facebook photos may still be online indefinitely and are accessible via direct links (URLs) (41). Cheng first contacted Facebook in 2009 about the issue (135). She did a follow up with Facebook in 2010. Over three years later, her "deleted" Facebook photos were still online.

Facebook responded to Cheng defensively, "For all practical purposes, the photo no longer exists, and we wouldn't be able find it if we were asked or even compelled to do so. … It's possible that someone who previously had access to a photo and saved the direct URL from our content delivery network partner could still access the photo" (136). Facebook blamed the problem on their legacy database systems, and promised to work with their content delivery network (CDN) partner to "significantly reduce the amount of time that backup copies persist." In other words, no one can tell how long a deleted Facebook photo will linger in the online universe before it is ultimately purged, if ever.

Moreover, *The New York Times* reported in February 2012, "Facebook can calculate your location information from different sources, including your computer's Wi-Fi connection or phone's GPS feature. When it finds you, it adds a small tag on the updates you post to your Facebook wall, like 'near New Orleans, LA' or wherever you are" (137).

In June 2012, *Consumers Report* made public another startling revelation: "Regulators in Germany found that such information [user's IP address and activities] was being collected on Facebook users for up to two years even after they deactivated their accounts." An IP address can be traced back to a company's datacenter or a residential address in some circumstances. Facebook explained that their policy of collecting IP addresses and user activities was required to "enhance Facebook security."

In April 2013, Facebook introduced "Partner Categories" for advertisers to use offline purchases information to target ads to Facebook users more effectively (138). To create dossiers on Facebook users, Partner Categories matches the social network's user-generated data with the information from massive consumer data companies Acxiom, DataLogix, and Epsilon. Advertisers can then target their ads to specific groups of Facebook users such as "people who are heavy buyers of frozen foods."

The massive amount of data that companies keep about us can inadvertently expose not only our real identity but also our activities, habits, likes, dislikes, and, as Thelma Arnold puts it, "the whole personal life."

Thelma Arnold is a 62-year-old widow in Lilburn, Georgia. Arnold was the anonymous user No. 4417749 among more than 650,000 users whose 20 million web search queries were collected by AOL and released to academic researchers in August 2006. Although the user's logs were associated with random ID numbers, several users' identities were readily discovered based on their search queries. Over a three-month period, Arnold conducted hundreds of searches such as "numb fingers," "60 single men," "dog that urinates on everything," and "landscapers in Lilburn, Ga." A *New York Times* reporter was able to follow the data trail to Thelma Arnold in Lilburn. "My goodness, it's my whole personal life," Arnold told the reporter. "I had no idea somebody was looking over my shoulder" (139).

Based on the 1990 U.S. Census summary data, researcher Latanya Sweeney at Carnegie Mellon University found that combinations of few characteristics often uniquely or nearly uniquely identify some individuals in geographically situated populations (140). In fact, 53% of the U.S. population had reported characteristics that likely made them uniquely identifiable based only on their city of residence, gender, and date of birth. The number increased to a startling 87% if their zip code was also included. In 2014, IBM researchers have developed an algorithm that can analyze anybody's last 200 tweets and determine their home city location with an accuracy of almost 70% (141).

By the way, you can always access your Facebook data at https://www.facebook.com/your_information and download your personal information from https://www.facebook.com/dyi

16.12 Online Births and Deaths in Facebook Nation

A September 2010 study by Internet security company AVG found that almost a quarter (23%) of children have online births before their actual birth dates, as today's parents are building digital footprints for their children prior to and from the moment they are born. In the U.S., 92% of children have an online presence by the time they are two.

J.R. Smith, CEO of AVG, commented on the report, "It's completely understandable why proud parents would want to upload and share images of very young children with friends and families. At the same time, we urge parents to think… you are creating a digital history for a human being that will follow him or her for the rest of their life. What kind of footprint do you actually want to start for your child, and what will they think about the information you've uploaded in future?" (142). Parenting columnist Aisha Sultan and University of Michigan researcher Jon Miller concurred, "Never before have parents had the ability to publish the details of their children's lives in such a widespread manner. A potentially embarrassing anecdote won't faze a toddler, but how does the unilateral flow of information affect a tween or teenager?" (143).

In November 2008, a Florida teenager died of a drug overdose in front of his webcam while others watched over the Internet (144). In November 2010, a 24-year-old man in Japan live streamed his own hanging and viewers called the police (145).

To discourage people from doing harm to themselves, Facebook in March 2011 added Samaritans suicide risk alert system (146). If someone is posting depressing photos or writing about killing themselves, their Facebook friends can click on the "report suicidal content" link to alert Facebook staff members who are monitoring these reports 24/7 (147). In March 2017, Facebook added suicide prevention tools in Facebook Live and Messenger so that individuals can reach out to a friend or contact a helpline. "Some might say we should cut off the livestream, but what we've learned is cutting off the stream too early could remove the opportunity for that person to receive help," said Facebook researcher Jennifer Guadagno (148).

Nevertheless, some people cannot be convinced to change their minds. In August 2013, sports reporter and statistician Martin Manley committed suicide on his 60th birthday. Before his death, however, he spent over a year creating an intricate website that meticulously describes his life story and viewpoints. "Let me ask *you* a question," Manley wrote on his site. "After you die, you can be remembered by a few-line obituary for one day in a newspaper when you're too old to matter to anyone anyway… **_OR_** you can be remembered for years by a site such as this. That was my choice and I chose the obvious" (149).

CNN reporter Doug Gross characterized Manley's suicide as follows: "Call it death in the time of Facebook. Never before in the history of human communication have suicide notes been such a public affair, easily accessible to the masses and potentially lasting forever" (150). Indeed, Anonymous—the Internet hacktivists—has archived and mirrored Manley's website in perpetuity, urging readers not to end their life journey (see Fig. 16.4).

Online births and deaths in Facebook Nation made me question why people could not live without borders. Birthright citizenship is like being baptized into a religion as an infant. Taking a page from Veronica Roth's novel *Divergent*, people should be free to choose where they belong when they grow up.

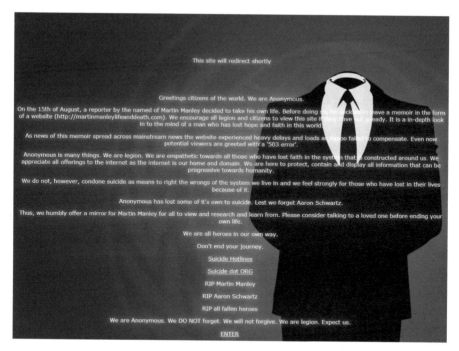

This site will redirect shortly

Greetings citizens of the world. We are Anonymous.

On the 15th of August, a reporter by the named of Martin Manley decided to take his own life. Before doing so, he decided to leave a memoir in the form of a website (http://martinmanleylifeanddeath.com). We encourage all legion and citizens to view this site if they have not already. It is a in-depth look in to the mind of a man who has lost hope and faith in this world.

As news of this memoir spread across mainstream news the website experienced heavy delays and loads as Yahoo failed to compensate. Even now potential viewers are greeted with a '503 error'.

Anonymous is many things. We are legion. We are empathetic towards all those who have lost faith in the system that is constructed around us. We appreciate all offerings to the internet as the internet is our home and domain. We are here to protect, contain and display all information that can be progressive towards humanity.

We do not, however, condone suicide as means to right the wrongs of the system we live in and we feel strongly for those who have lost in their lives because of it.

Anonymous has lost some of it's own to suicide. Lest we forget Aaron Schwartz.

Thus, we humbly offer a mirror for Martin Manley for all to view and research and learn from. Please consider talking to a loved one before ending your own life.

We are all heroes in our own way.

Don't end your journey.

Suicide Hotlines

Suicide dot ORG

RIP Martin Manley

RIP Aaron Schwartz

RIP all fallen heroes

We are Anonymous. We DO NOT forget. We will not forgive. We are legion. Expect us.

ENTER

Fig. 16.4   Homepage of Martin Manley's Website as Mirrored by Anonymous

16.13   Memorialization on Facebook and Life after Death on Social Networks

Facebook's head of security Max Kelly worked alongside his best friend 18 hours a day and seven days a week in a small team at Facebook. After his best friend was killed in a tragic bicycling accident, the question about what to do with his friend's Facebook profile came up (151). In October 2009, Facebook introduced the idea of "memorialized" profiles for families and friends to leave posts on the deceased's profile Walls in remembrance (152).

When an account is memorialized, Facebook removes the deceased's sensitive information such as contact information and status updates, sets privacy so that only confirmed friends can see the profile or locate it in search, and prevents anyone from logging into the account. (Wouldn't it be wonderful if Facebook also makes it so easy for the livings to protect their own privacy while they are still alive?)

Social media has given a new meaning to life after death. DeadSocial is a new breed of social media companies that offer post-death social media options such as scheduling public Facebook posts, tweets, and LinkedIn posts to go out after someone has died. "It really allows you to be creative and literally extend the personality you had while alive in death," said James Norris, founder of DeadSocial. "It allows you to be able to say those final goodbyes" (153). The company even guarantees the delivery of the posthumous digital messages for the next 100 years.

For the tech-savvy users, LivesOn is a Twitter app powered by artificial intelligence algorithms that "analyze your online behavior and learn how you speak, so it can keep on scouring the Internet, favoriting tweets, and posting the sort of links you like, creating a personal digital afterlife" (154). LivesOn's tagline is: "When your heart stops beating, you'll keep tweeting."

In April 2013, Google rolled out the new "Inactive Account Manager" for users to plan their digital afterlife (155). Google users can choose to have their data deleted after three, six, nine, or 12 months of inactivity. Alternatively, they can assign trusted contacts to receive data from selected services including +1s, Blogger, Contacts and Circles, Drive, Gmail, Google+ Profiles, Pages and Streams, Picasa Web Albums, Google Voice, and YouTube.

In the 2014 Consumer Action Handbook, editor-in-chief Marietta Jelks from the General Services Administration (GSA) offered recommendations on writing a "social media will" and appointing an "online executor" responsible for handling the deceased's email accounts, social media profiles, and blogs (156).

16.14   The Facebook Cleanse or Face-to-Facebook

In November 2011, Lars Backstrom from the Facebook Data Team reported that 50% (the median) of Facebook users had over 100 friends and the average friend count is 190 (157). However, according to the GoodMobilePhones survey in January 2011, the average Facebook user does not know one fifth of the people listed as friends on the site (158).

Dan Kois, senior editor at *Slate* and contributing writer to the *New York Times Magazine*, wrote a humorous article entitled "The Facebook Cleanse" in May 2014. It started with the sentences: "Did I just unfriend you? I'm sorry if I hurt your feelings. But I'm not sorry I did it. In fact, I did you a favor. I'm on a Facebook cleanse, and it's making me fall back in love with the social network I couldn't stand for years. You should do it, too!" (159).

About nine months into his Facebook cleanse, Kois reduced his number of Facebook friends by 34% to 1,079 friends. He admitted that number was still too high compared to his "actual friends," probably by a factor of 10. He felt that most Facebook friends could not less about him just as he had absolutely no interest in them and their lives. He concluded, "So if you're suffering from friend clutter, try a one-year Facebook cleanse. It'll make your online experience a lot cleaner, better, more meaningful. And if your birthday's coming soon and we met once at a concert: Heads up. I might be about to give you the greatest birthday gift I, a person about whom you don't give a crap, can offer: the gift of never needing to think about me again" (159). (Since "un-friend-ing" is not as simple in real life as on Facebook, many young adults have chosen to end their relationships via text messages and social media (160).)

Alternatively, instead of un-friending people, we can turn all Facebook friends into real-life friends. In March 2013, Connecticut photographer Ty Morin launched a successful Kickstarter campaign and raised $14,166 (against a $5,000 goal) to fund his trip to "pay a visit to every single one of his Facebook friends to take their portrait... all 788 of them" (161). Morin admitted that he had never even spoken to at least half of his 788 Facebook friends. "The goal of the project is to reconnect with people," he wrote on Kickstarter. "No more hiding behind the screen of social media. ... Let's get out there and remind people what it's like to have a face to face conversation with someone." Morin would make a great peace ambassador.

16.15   The Rise of Alternative Social Media Platforms: Fortnite and Gab

In spite of the popularity of Facebook, we are witnessing the rise of alternative social media platforms that cater to like-minded individuals or special interest groups. A prominent example is Fortnite social network for Millennials and Gen Z whereas a notorious example is Gab for alt-right conservatives and extremists.

"Fortnite is the new Facebook in some ways. Millennials and Gen Z are much more used to living on platforms like Fortnite," said Henry Cowling, creative managing director at MediaMonks (162). Released in 2017, Fortnite is an online video game developed by Epic Games. Fortnite Battle Royale—a massively multiplayer online (MMO) game—in particular has drawn in more than 350 million registered players as of May 2020 (163). The Fortnite Chapter 2 Season 5 Galactus event in December 2020 logged an active player count of 15.3 millions concurrent players. More than just games, Fortnite has hosted virtual concerts, movie screenings, and anti-racism lectures "We the People" (164).

"If we have politically incorrect opinions, the ADL is just going to have to suck it up and deal with it," said Gab CEO Andrew Torba (165). Founded in 2016, Gab is a rapidly growing social media platform for alt-right conservatives, conspiracy theorists, extremists, and anarchists. Since the Capitol riot on January 6, 2021, Gab's registered users more than doubled to around 3.4 million, along with an 800 % increase in traffic to its website. When major credit card companies cut ties with alternative platforms known for racist and anti-Semitic content, these sites circumvent financial restrictions by using cryptocurrencies such as Bitcoin for which Gab calls "free speech money" (166).

Will popular social media platforms experience mass exodus of users to siloed social networks mimicking an increasingly fractured world under Trumpism, Brexit, anti-globalism, and decentralization? Will Facebook be able to continue its mission to empower people to build community and bring the world closer together?

16.16   Connected Cars: In-vehicle Social Networks and eXpressive Internet Architecture

In 2014, only about 10% of vehicles have built-in connectivity (167). Marketing research firm ABI Research estimated in 2012 that within five years, 60% of the world's cars would include built-in Internet and smart phone connectivity (168).

In January 2012, Mercedes-Benz publicized its efforts in bringing Facebook and Google to the automobile dashboard (169). "We're working on a new generation of vehicles that truly serve as digital companions," said Dieter Zetsche, head of Mercedes-Benz Cars, in a keynote speech at CES 2012 in Las Vegas. "They learn your habits, adapt to your choices, predict you moves and interact with your social network" (170).

At CES 2012, Ford Motor Company introduced the new in-vehicle application called Roximity. The app provides real-time deals and specials relevant to a user's location, based on personal preferences and interests. A driver could easily get a customized verbal message for a special deal on food from a favorite nearby restaurant (171).

In May 2014, General Motors announced that the 2015 Chevrolet Malibu would come equipped with a 4G LTE connection, acting as a WiFi hotspot that could connect up to seven devices. "Our objective here is to allow you to bring your digital life in your vehicle, and your vehicle into your digital life," said Terry Inch, chief operating officer for GM's OnStar unit (172). In the same month, Nokia announced a $100 million Connected Car fund for identifying and investing in innovations that are "important for a world of connected and intelligent vehicles" (173).

"Commonly referred to as a connected car, the prevailing trend is to integrate smartphone apps into the car's dashboard. This enables drivers and passengers to listen to online music, access news and other content, stream video and more," wrote *ReadWriteWeb* editor-in-chief Richard MacManus in February 2012. "The next big thing in computing isn't a new model smartphone or laptop. It's the Internet empowering everything else around us. Our cars, TVs and many other devices" (174).

Researchers at Virginia Tech Transportation Institute conducted several large-scale, naturalistic driving studies in 2009 to get a clear picture of driver distraction and cell phone use under real-world driving conditions (175). The research shows that talking on a cell phone increases the risk of a crash or near-crash by 1.3 times over non-distracted driving, while physically dialing a number increased the risk 2.8 times. A person is more than 23 times more likely to be in a crash or near crash while text messaging.

"People are already distracted by their phones in their car, but we can make it safer for them to do what they are already doing," commented Ricardo Reyes, spokesman for the Tesla Model S electric car that features a 17-inch touch screen display with Internet access and four USB ports to attach devices in the electric car (176).

U.S. Transportation Secretary Ray LaHood issued the non-binding guidelines in February 2012 for automakers to design in-car social network devices such that they cannot be used while a car is in motion. LaHood also called for disabling manual texting, Internet browsing, 10-digit phone dialing, and the ability to enter addresses into a built-in navigation system for drivers unless the car is in park (177).

In May 2012, Consumer Electronics Association sent a letter to the National Transportation Safety Board (NTSB): "CEA must disagree with the NTSB's broad recommendation calling for a ban on the nonemergency use of portable electronics devices (other than those designed to support the driving task) by all drivers. There is no real-world evidence to support such a blanket prohibition unless one would also ban other potential distractions, such as eating, drinking, applying make-up and engaging with children while in the vehicle" (178).

In spite of controversies, connected cars can make the road safer for everyone. Carnegie Mellon University developed in 2014 a vehicular network in Pittsburgh to enable vehicles to share information about road and traffic conditions. Computer science and electrical engineering professor Peter Steenkiste explained, "Vehicles can use wireless communications channels called dedicated short-range communications, or DSRC, that are similar to WiFi. Creating DSRC networks is challenging, however, because cars and trucks quickly pass from one DSRC access point to the next. XIA [eXpressive Internet Architecture] enables computer users to directly access content wherever it might be on the network, rather than always accessing a host website, so it should enable vehicles to obtain needed information from neighboring access points" (179).

In March 2014, mobile ad company Kiip planned to offer deals based on data collected from in-car apps that know how you drive. "You get to your meeting early and you should get a free coffee from the place around the block," said Michael Sprague, head of partnerships for Kiip, at the ad:tech conference in San Francisco. "You just logged 100 miles on a road trip; your phone says, "Here's a Red Bull"" (180).

However, Jay Giraud, CEO and cofounder of Mojio, raised an objection by saying, "The way I drive my car is personal information. ... If I'm being offered an insurance discount because Geico looked at my data, I want to be the one in control" (180).

16.17   Connected Home, Internet of Things, and Internet of Me

Google bought home automation company Nest in January 2014 for $3.2 billion in cash (181). Nest's smart thermostat learns and adjusts to the users' living patterns in order to minimize energy use. Nest's smoke and carbon monoxide alarm can distinguish between smoke and steam, and inform users where the danger is by networking with other home sensors.

At the Worldwide Developers Conference in June 2014, Apple unveiled HomeKit that enables users control all the items in their home with an iPad or iPhone (182). HomeKit can manage lights, cameras, door locks, thermostats, and other connected devices.

The Internet of things (IoT) is no longer just energy-conservation equipment, home automation, connected cars, and smart city. As wearable devices, health tracking, and quantified self are gaining popularity, human beings are also becoming part of the Internet of things.

Rachel Metz, IT editor for the Web and social media at the *MIT Technology Review*, wrote an article in May 2014 with a catchy title: "The Internet of You". Metz observed, "Slowly but surely, a few wearable devices—mainly high-tech pedometers like those from Fitbit and Jawbone—are catching on with consumers, and many researchers and companies are certain that body-worn computers will become second nature—sensing, recording, and transmitting data to and from our bodies, to networks around us" (183).

Fitbit and Jawbone offer wristbands with mobile apps that can track exercise, sleep patterns, and movement of the wearer. "Your car should know that you're tired because you didn't sleep that well, so it should be alert to that, how awake are you when you're driving, those things," said CEO Jawbone Hosain Rahman (183). "You can start to see how this Internet of me can start to work with me at the center of this device here," added Travis Bogard, Jawbone's vice president of product management and strategy (184).

Reuters reported in June 2014 that Apple was preparing to market its first wearable device in October. The Apple smartwatches would have sensors that "collect health data from blood glucose and calorie consumption to sleep activity" (185).

While the Internet of Things and the Internet of me can be tremendously helpful to us in everyday life, they can pose a real danger if our intimate details are misinterpreted, misused, or through a security breach fall into the wrong hands.

In the television show *Homeland*, a terrorist remotely caused a pacemaker to malfunction, killing the Vice President of the United States. In reality, the late security researcher Barnaby Jack told *Vice* technology reporter William Alexander in 2013 that he developed a way to hack one of those devices remotely and send it a high-voltage shock from upwards of 50 feet away (186).

The New York Times reported in June 2014 that Apple was expected to unveil software that turn our homes into WiFi-connected wonderlands where locks, lights, and appliances could all be controlled via an iPhone or iPad. "Obviously, there are lots of benefits of connected devices in the home, but there can also be complications," said Marc Rotenberg, executive director of the Electronic Privacy Information Center. "When you worry about computer viruses, you can unplug your computer. When your house gets a virus, where do you go?" (187).

16.18 Internet Addiction and Digital Detox

Black Mirror creator Charlie Brooker wrote in *The Guardian* about the dark side of our gadget addiction: "Like an addict, I check my Twitter timeline the moment I wake up. And often I wonder: is all this really good for me? For us? None of these things have been foisted upon humankind – we've merrily embraced them. But where is it all leading? If technology is a drug – and it does feel like a drug – then what, precisely, are the side-effects? This area – between delight and discomfort – is where *Black Mirror*, my new drama series, is set. The 'black mirror' of the title is the one you'll find on every wall, on every desk, in the palm of every hand: the cold, shiny screen of a TV, a monitor, a smartphone" (188).

Dave Nadig of ETF Trends explains the source of addiction, "Social media — which includes the curation algorithms of TikTok, Reddit, Robinhood, Amazon, Netflix, etc. — is designed not to do anything good for you (the consumer) but to keep you engaged on the platform you happened to launch from your phone. Nearly by definition, this leads you down a funnel into which it is very difficult to return. Once your TikTok feed is full of stock tips, it's nearly impossible to get rid of them. Once you start following /r/WallStreetBets, you're going to get the most sensational, clickbait posts bubbled to the top of your window: Go deep, Go narrow, Stay engaged. And do it in a market designed to take those few seconds of attention and execute on them" (189).

Living in Facebook Nation can turn some people into Internet addicts who experience serious problems at home, work, school, and socially. There have been tragic reports of infant deaths due to neglect by their parents who spent excessive amount of time playing computer games (190). Tell-tale signs and symptoms of Internet addiction may include (191):

- Losing track of time online.
- Having trouble completing tasks at work or home.
- Isolation from family and friends.
- Feeling guilty or defensive about your Internet use.
- Feeling a sense of euphoria while involved in Internet activities.

Tiffany Shlain, filmmaker and founder of the Webby Awards, advocates a national day of unplugging – a digital detox. Tiffany wrote in *The Huffington Post*, "Unplugging each Friday night with my family is now the day that I rushed towards each week. The 24 hours not online truly resets my soul. It has become my favorite day of the week. I feel like a better mother, wife, person on Saturdays. ... By Saturday night sundown when we go back online, we appreciate technology in this whole new way" (192).

Fortunately, there is help available for people who simply cannot unplug for even one second. In 2009, the country's first retreat center program reSTART for Internet addiction treatment was launched by the Center for Digital Technology Sustainability. The reSTART website states the following (193):

- BINGE VIEWING – Watch less. Live more.
- INTERNET – Browse less. Explore more.
- MESSAGING – Chat less. Listen more.
- MMORPG's – Raid less. Achieve more.
- SMARTPHONE USE – Text less. Connect more.

- SOCIAL MEDIA – Update less. Connect more.
- STREAMING – Broadcast less. Live more.
- TECHNOLOGY – Use less. Learn more.
- VIDEO GAMES – Play less. Accomplish more.

In 2013, the country's first inpatient treatment program for Internet addiction opened at Bradford Regional Medical Center in Pennsylvania. "I've been studying Internet addiction since 1994," said founder Dr. Kimberly Young. "When you talk about the controversy behind it, laughing it off, that's often been the case with my work. We're really behind other countries in treating this problem. China, Korea and Taiwan all have treatment centers. ... Remember, when Betty Ford first admitted she was an alcoholic, we didn't have people believing it was actually a problem until she came around and talked about her own problems with it. This is a place for people to go for help, and that we hope will help everyone around them stop taking Internet addiction so lightly" (194).

Unfortunately, the COVID-19 pandemic in 2020 further exacerbated Internet addiction among children and adults when much of the physical world was in lockdown and social distancing was strictly enforced. As people are getting vaccinated and lockdowns are being lifted, some are ready to log off social media for good. A 28-year-old resident in Rhode Island said, "After the pandemic, some personal health revelations, and 2020's political violence, I regretted sharing so much of myself—my traumas, details about my mental health, my explorations of gender, my location, my political views and ideas. I saw how these things could and probably would be used against people. It was the first time I realized online expression could potentially harm me offline, even physically. It scared me" (195).

The post-pandemic world will never be the same again. Inpatient treatment programs will likely continue at a reduced level. An interesting question is: Can an online treatment program be successful in treating Internet addiction? Similarly, can a mobile app treat smartphone addiction? Interestingly, they do exist (196), but more research needs to be conducted to evaluate their effectiveness (197).

Facebook's massive outage on October 4, 2021 also brought down Instagram and WhatsApp for some six hours, affecting billons of people worldwide. Some online entrepreneurs lost business as a result. "Not being able to have the story sale was definitely a potential financial loss. My shop would not be where it is today without Instagram. However, the outage really made me realize that Instagram cannot be my only platform for selling," said small business owner Jessica Ferrandino (198). But some Internet addicts were grateful for being temporarily unplugged. Doctoral student Lilly Logan at Abilene Christian University in Texas said, "The outage was a much-needed respite from mindless scrolling that keeps me from being productive in my studies. I completed four assignments effortlessly without the distraction. ... I realized how time-consuming, toxic, and divisive they [social media apps] are. It was a day of mental clarity." Unless you are running an online business or doing social media marketing, digital detox is highly recommended to cure Internet addiction.

References

1. **Bosker, Bianca.** Facebook's f8 Conference (LIVE BLOG): Get The Latest Facebook News. [Online] The Huffington Post, September 22, 2011. http://www.huffingtonpost.com/2011/09/22/facebook-f8-conference-live-blog-latest-news_n_975704.html.

2. **Kelly, Samantha Murphy and Duffy, Clare.** Facebook whistleblower testifies company 'is operating in the shadows, hiding its research from public scrutiny'. *CNN.* [Online] October 6, 2021. https://www.cnn.com/2021/10/05/tech/facebook-whistleblower-testify/index.html.

3. **Stelter, Brian.** How a LinkedIn message paved the way for 'The Facebook Files'. *CNN.* [Online] October 8, 2021. https://www.cnn.com/2021/10/08/media/facebook-files-jeff-horwitz-reliable-sources-podcast/index.html.

4. **Horwitz, Jeff.** The Facebook Files. *Wall Street Journal.* [Online] 2021. https://www.wsj.com/articles/the-facebook-files-11631713039.

5. **Haugen, Frances.** Statement of Frances Haugen. *United States Senate Committee on Commerce, Science and Transportation.* [Online] October 4, 2021. https://www.commerce.senate.gov/services/files/FC8A558E-824E-4914-BEDB-3A7B1190BD49.

6. **Fleishman, Glenn.** Cartoon Captures Spirit of the Internet. [Online] The New York Times, December 14, 2000. http://www.nytimes.com/2000/12/14/technology/cartoon-captures-spirit-of-the-internet.html.

7. **Ahn, Irene.** Boo Facebook Timeline. [Online] Facebook. [Cited: April 11, 2021.] http://www.facebook.com/Boo.

8. **Guildhary, Fabienne.** IBM Survey Reveals Digital Behavioral Trends for Consumers: What is your Digital Personality? [Online] IBM News Releases, April 16, 2012. http://www-03.ibm.com/press/us/en/pressrelease/37423.wss.

9. **Bower, Bruce.** No Lie! Your Facebook Profile Is the Real You. [Online] Wired, February 26, 2010. http://www.wired.com/wiredscience/2010/02/no-lie-your-facebook-profile-is-the-real-you/.

10. **Consumer Reports magazine editors.** Facebook & your privacy. Who sees the data you share on the biggest social network? [Online] Consumer Reports, June 2012. http://www.consumerreports.org/cro/magazine/2012/06/facebook-your-privacy/index.htm.

11. **Wolpert, Stuart.** Crafting your image for your 1,000 friends on Facebook or MySpace. [Online] UCLA Newsroom, November 17, 2008. http://newsroom.ucla.edu/portal/ucla/crafting-your-image-for-your-1-71910.aspx.

12. **Ryan-Mosley, Tate.** Beauty filters are changing the way young girls see themselves. [Online] MIT Technology Review, April 2, 2021. https://www.technologyreview.com/2021/04/02/1021635/beauty-filters-young-girls-augmented-reality-social-media/.

13. **Keen, Andrew.** Battle Lines Drawn as Data Becomes Oil of Digital Age. [Online] DLD (Digital Life Design), January 25, 2012. http://www.dld-conference.com/news/digital-business/battle-lines-drawn-as-data-becomes-oil-of-digital-age_aid_3097.html.

14. **The Washington Times.** Obama: Be careful what you put on Facebook. [Online] The Washington Times, September 8, 2009. http://www.washingtontimes.com/news/2009/sep/08/obama-advises-caution-what-kids-put-facebook/?page=all.

15. **Andrews, Lori.** I Know Who You Are and I Saw What You Did: Social Networks and the Death of Privacy. [Online] Free Press, January 10, 2012. http://www.nytimes.com/2012/01/29/books/review/i-know-who-you-are-and-i-saw-what-you-did-social-networks-and-the-death-of-privacy-by-lori-andrews-book-review.html?pagewanted=all&_r=0.

16. **CBSNews.** Did the Internet Kill Privacy? [Online] CBS, February 6, 2011. http://www.cbsnews.com/2100-3445_162-7323148.html.

17. **D'Zurilla, Christie.** Gilbert Gottfried fired by Aflac over Japan tsunami jokes. [Online] Los Angeles Times, March 14, 2011. http://latimesblogs.latimes.com/gossip/2011/03/gilbert-gottfried-fired-aflac-tsunami-jokes.html.

18. **TMZ Staff.** Gilbert Gottfried Shocking Japan Tsunami Jokes. [Online] TMZ, March 14, 2011. http://www.tmz.com/2011/03/14/gilbert-gottfried-japan-roasts-jokes-tsunami/.

19. **Post Staff.** Full transcript of Weiner's news conference. [Online] New York Post, June 7, 2011. http://nypost.com/2011/06/07/full-transcript-of-weiners-news-conference/.

20. **Gregory, Corinne.** The unforseen impact of online "friendships". [Online] ResumeBear, June 28, 2011. http://blog.resumebear.com/career-book-authors/the-unforseen-impact-of-online-%E2%80%9Cfriendships%E2%80%9D/.

21. **Obeidallah, Dean.** Marine's Facebook posts on Obama go too far. [Online] CNN, April 25, 2012. http://www.cnn.com/2012/04/14/opinion/obeidallah-marine-obama-facebook/index.html.

22. **Pilon, Mary.** Twitter Comment Costs Greek Athlete Spot in Olympics. [Online] The New York Times, July 25, 2012. http://www.nytimes.com/2012/07/26/sports/olympics/twitter-comment-costs-greek-athlete-spot-in-olympics.html.

23. **Gross, Doug.** Jailed Facebook teen finally getting day in court. [Online] CNN, July 3, 2013. http://www.cnn.com/2013/07/03/tech/social-media/facebook-teen-jail/index.html.

24. —. Teen in jail for months over 'sarcastic' Facebook threat. [Online] CNN, 3 2013. http://www.cnn.com/2013/07/02/tech/social-media/facebook-threat-carter/index.html.

25. **Campbell, Tiffany and Levs, Josh.** Day care workers fired over photos mocking kids on Instagram. [Online] CNN, August 21, 2013. http://www.cnn.com/2013/08/20/us/instagram-day-care-photos/index.html.

26. **Segal, Kim.** Florida university suspends fraternity over Facebook posts. [Online] CNN, August 23, 2013. http://www.cnn.com/2013/08/22/us/florida-fraternity-facebook/index.html.

27. **Willingham, A. J.** Leaked! College scandals and shocking letters. [Online] HLNtv, October 11, 2013. http://www.hlntv.com/article/2013/10/10/college-students-letters-embarrassing-scandal.

28. **Stelter, Brian.** 'Ashamed': Ex-PR exec Justine Sacco apologizes for AIDS in Africa tweet. [Online] CNN, December 22, 2013. http://www.cnn.com/2013/12/22/world/sacco-offensive-tweet/index.html.

29. **Conlon, Kevin.** Canadian teen convicted of 'sexting' photos of boyfriend's ex. [Online] CNN, January 10, 2014. http://www.cnn.com/2014/01/10/world/americas/canada-sexting-teen/index.html.

30. **D'Onfro, Jillian.** After Going On A Twitter Tirade, Former PayPal Exec Rakesh Agrawal Tells Us He's Sorry For An Experiment Gone Awry. [Online] Business Insider, May 12, 2014. http://www.businessinsider.com/ex-paypal-exec-rakesh-agrawal-interview-2014-5.

31. **Agrawal, Rakesh.** The truth behind why I left PayPal. [Online] LinkedIn, June 10, 2014. https://www.linkedin.com/today/post/article/20140610133242-247423-the-truth-behind-why-i-left-paypal?trk=tod-home-art-list-large_0.

32. **Cillizza, Chris.** How Twitter killed Neera Tanden's chances -- and why it will happen again. [Online] CNN Politics, March 3, 2021. https://www.cnn.com/2021/03/03/politics/neera-tanden-omb-biden-twitter/index.html.

33. **Flynn, Kerry.** Teen Vogue's new editor out of a job after backlash over old tweets. [Online] CNN Business, March 20, 2021. https://www.cnn.com/2021/03/18/media/alexi-mccammond-teen-vogue-out/index.html.

34. **Andrew, Scottie.** Why TikTok's chaotic 'kickbacks' took off with young people starved for company. [Online] CNN, June 2, 2021. https://www.cnn.com/2021/06/02/us/tiktok-adrians-kickback-trend-trnd/index.html.

35. **Huntington Beach PD.** Our statement regarding this past weekend's unlawful assembly incidents in #HuntingtonBeach. [Online] Twitter, May 25, 2021. https://twitter.com/HBPD_PIO/status/1397369485070258180.

36. **Damiani, Jesse.** The Curious Case Of Brad Pitt On Clubhouse. [Online] Forbes, February 16, 2021. https://www.forbes.com/sites/jessedamiani/2021/02/16/the-curious-case-of-brad-pitt-on-clubhouse/?sh=629ebd0d13ef.

37. **Hechinger, John.** College Applicants, Beware: Your Facebook Page Is Showing. [Online] The Wall Street Journal, September 8, 2008. http://online.wsj.com/article/SB122170459104151023.html#ixzz1i3OJLjmd.

38. **Kaplan Test Prep.** Facebook Checking is No Longer Unchartered Territory in College Admissions: Percentage of Admissions Officers Who Visited An Applicant's Profile On the Rise. [Online] Kaplan Test Prep, September 21, 2011. http://press.kaptest.com/press-releases/facebook-checking-is-no-longer-unchartered-territory-in-college-admissions-percentage-of-admissions-officers-who-visited-an-applicant%E2%80%99s-profile-on-the-rise.

39. **ACLU.** Your Facebook Password Should Be None of Your Boss' Business. [Online] American Civil Liberty Union, March 20, 2012. http://www.aclu.org/blog/technology-and-liberty/your-facebook-password-should-be-none-your-boss-business.

40. **Egan, Erin.** Protecting Your Passwords and Your Privacy. [Online] Facebook and Privacy, March 23, 2012. https://www.facebook.com/note.php?note_id=326598317390057.

41. **Cheng, Jacqui.** Over 3 years later, "deleted" Facebook photos are still online. [Online] CNN, February 7, 2012. http://www.cnn.com/2012/02/06/tech/social-media/deleted-facebook-photos-online/index.html.

42. **The Internet Archive.** About the Internet Archive. [Online] The Internet Archive. [Cited: April 25, 2021.] http://www.archive.org/about/about.php.

43. **Madej, Krystina and Lee, Newton.** Disney Stories: Getting to Digital. [Online] Springer Nature, October 21, 2020. https://www.springer.com/us/book/9783030427375.

44. **Gross, Doug.** Library of Congress digs into 170 billion tweets. [Online] CNN, January 7, 2013. http://www.cnn.com/2013/01/07/tech/social-media/library-congress-twitter/index.html.

45. **Raymond, Matt.** How Tweet It Is!: Library Acquires Entire Twitter Archive. [Online] U.S. Library of Congress Blog, April 14, 2010. http://blogs.loc.gov/loc/2010/04/how-tweet-it-is-library-acquires-entire-twitter-archive/.

46. **National Public Radio.** The Deleted Tweets Of Politicians Find A New Home. [Online] NPR, June 6, 2012. http://www.npr.org/2012/06/06/154432624/the-deleted-tweets-of-politicians-find-a-new-home.

47. **CNN Political Unit.** Deleted tweets spark controversy in Illinois gubernatorial race. [Online] CNN, April 24, 2014. http://politicalticker.blogs.cnn.com/2014/04/24/deleted-tweets-spark-controversy-in-illinois-gubernatorial-race/.

48. **Politwoops.** Deleted tweets from politicians. [Online] Politwoops. [Cited: October 10, 2021.] http://politwoops.sunlightfoundation.com/.

49. **Ha, Anthony.** LinkedIn's Reid Hoffman explains the brave new world of data. [Online] Venture Beat, March 15, 2011. http://venturebeat.com/2011/03/15/reid-hoffman-data-sxsw/.

50. **ACLU.** Hey! Do you use the Internet? [Online] American Civil Liberties Union. [Cited: May 12, 2012.] https://secure.aclu.org/site/SPageServer?pagename=110419_Internet_Privacy.

51. **—.** Demand Your dotRights (Privacy 2.0). [Online] American Civil Liberties Union. [Cited: May 12, 2012.] http://www.dotrights.org/education.

52. **Solon, Olivia.** Am I pretty or ugly? Louise Orwin explores this YouTube phenomenon. [Online] Wired, October 11, 2013. http://www.wired.co.uk/news/archive/2013-10/11/pretty-ugly.

53. **Mundt, Marlon P.** The Impact of Peer Social Networks on Adolescent Alcohol Use Initiation. [Online] Academic Pediatrics. Volume 11, Number 5, September/October 2011. http://www.ncbi.nlm.nih.gov/pubmed/21795133.

54. **Mehdizadeh, Soraya.** Self-Presentation 2.0: Narcissism and Self-Esteem on Facebook. [Online] Cyberpsychology, Behavior, and Social Networking. Volume 13, Number 4, August 2010. http://www.ncbi.nlm.nih.gov/pubmed/20712493.

55. **Enayati, Amanda.** Facebook: The encyclopedia of beauty? [Online] CNN, March 16, 2012. http://www.cnn.com/2012/03/16/living/beauty-social-networks/index.html.

56. **Matulef, Kevin.** Enemybook. [Online] Enemybook, July 2007. http://www.enemybook.info/.

57. **Friedman, Jaclyn and al, et.** Open Letter to Facebook. Women, Action, & the Media. [Online] WAM! Women, Action, & the Media, May 21, 2013. http://www.womenactionmedia.org/facebookaction/open-letter-to-facebook/.

58. **Gross, Doug.** Under pressure, Facebook targets sexist hate speech. [Online] CNN, May 30, 2013. http://www.cnn.com/2013/05/29/tech/social-media/facebook-hate-speech-women/index.html.

59. **Sidner, Sara and Jones, Julia.** How Instagram led to two teens' eating disorders. *CNN.* [Online] October 9, 2021. https://www.cnn.com/2021/10/09/us/instagram-eating-disorders/index.html.

60. **Hern, Alex.** Instagram apologises for promoting weight-loss content to users with eating disorders. *The Guardian.* [Online] April 15, 2021. https://www.theguardian.com/technology/2021/apr/15/instagram-apologises-for-promoting-weight-loss-content-to-users-with-eating-disorders.

61. **Bauerlein, Mark.** The Dumbest Generation: How the Digital Age Stupefies Young Americans and Jeopardizes Our Future (Or, Don't Trust Anyone Under 30). [Online] Tarcher, May 14, 2009. http://books.google.com/books/about/The_Dumbest_Generation.html?id=YKkoAAAAYAAJ.

62. **Rice, Condoleezza and Klein, Joel.** Rice, Klein: Education keeps America safe. [Online] CNN, March 20, 2012. http://www.cnn.com/2012/03/20/opinion/rice-klein-education/index.html.

63. **Lacy, Sarah.** Peter Thiel: We're in a Bubble and It's Not the Internet. It's Higher Education. [Online] TechCrunch, April 10, 2011. http://techcrunch.com/2011/04/10/peter-thiel-were-in-a-bubble-and-its-not-the-internet-its-higher-education/.

64. **Wieder, Ben.** Thiel Fellowship Pays 24 Talented Students $100,000 Not to Attend College. [Online] The Chronicle of Higher Education, May 25, 2011. http://chronicle.com/article/Thiel-Fellowship-Pays-24/127622/.

65. **Trendrr.** Social TV Has Talent. [Online] Trendrr Blog, January 25, 2012. http://blog.trendrr.com/2012/01/25/social-tv-has-talent/.

66. **Trendrr.TV.** Social TV. [Online] Trendrr. [Cited: February 6, 2012.] http://trendrr.tv/.

67. **Smith, Steve.** Facebook A Quiet Second-Screen Giant In Social TV Space? [Online] Mobile Marketing Daily, March 30, 2012. http://www.mediapost.com/publications/article/171410/facebook-a-quiet-second-screen-giant-in-social-tv.html.

68. **Carter, Bill.** Tired of Reality TV, but Still Tuning In. [Online] 2010, 13 The New York Times, September. http://www.nytimes.com/2010/09/13/business/media/13reality.html.

69. **Neff, Jack.** Move Over, 'American Idol': Walmart's the Next Reality Giant. [Online] Advertising Age, January 18, 2012. http://adage.com/article/news/move-american-idol-walmart-s-reality-giant/232178/.

70. **McNamara, Mary.** 'Real Housewives': Suicide should have scrapped Season 2. [Online] Los Angeles Times, September 5, 2011. http://latimesblogs.latimes.com/showtracker/2011/09/real-housewives-suicide-should-have-scrapped-season-2.html.

71. **Amedure, Scott.** Fatal Shooting Follows Surprise on TV Talk Show. [Online] The New York Times, March 12, 1995. http://www.nytimes.com/1995/03/12/us/fatal-shooting-follows-surprise-on-tv-talk-show.html.

72. **Nelson, David.** Meaner than fiction: Reality TV high on aggression, study shows. [Online] Brigham Young University, May 20, 2010. http://news.byu.edu/archive10-may-realitytv.aspx.

73. **Carmon, Irin.** The Exquisite Sadism Of America's Next Top Model. [Online] Jezebel, November 9, 2010. http://jezebel.com/5685443/the-exquisite-sadism-of-americas-next-top-model.

74. **Tate, Ryan.** Twitter Can't Control Rapid Growth of Its Vine. [Online] Wired, June 20, 2013. http://www.wired.com/2013/06/twitter-vine-growth/.

75. **Kushner, David.** The Six Seconds Between Love and Hate: A Vine Romance Gone Wrong. [Online] Rolling Stone, May 21, 2014. http://www.rollingstone.com/culture/news/the-six-seconds-between-love-and-hate-a-vine-romance-gone-wrong-20140521.

76. **Obeidallah, Dean.** Are we sharing too much online? [Online] CNN, August 16, 2013. http://www.cnn.com/2013/08/16/opinion/obeidallah-social-media-sharing/index.html.

77. **Sabo, Tracy and Hayes, Ashley.** Texas judge confirms video of him beating daughter, says 'I lost my temper'. [Online] CNN, November 2, 2011. http://articles.cnn.com/2011-11-02/justice/justice_texas-video-beating_1_texas-judge-disabled-daughter-video?_s=PM:JUSTICE.

78. **shoehedgie.** Judge William Adams beats daughter for using the internet. [Online] shoehedgie, October 27, 2011. http://www.youtube.com/watch?v=Wl9y3SIPt7o.

79. **Stump, Scott.** Daughter in beating video: Why I released it. [Online] MSNBC, November 3, 2011. http://today.msnbc.msn.com/id/45146961/ns/today-today_people/t/daughter-beating-video-why-i-released-it/.

80. **Carpenter, Christopher J.** Narcissism on Facebook: Self-promotional and anti-social behavior. [Online] Personality and Individual Differences. Volume 52, Issue 4, March 2012. http://www.sciencedirect.com/science/article/pii/S0191886911005332.

81. **Griggs, Brandon.** Is political comedy inherently leftist? [Online] CNN, March 10, 2012. http://www.cnn.com/2012/03/10/tech/web/sxsw-internet-comedy/index.html.

82. **Interactive Advertising Bureau.** Social: A closer look at behaviour on YouTube & Facebook. [Online] Interactive Advertising Bureau, September 3, 2010. http://static.google-usercontent.com/external_content/untrusted_dlcp/www.google.com/en/us/googleblogs/pdfs/iab_research_youtube_and_facebook_oct_2010.pdf.

83. **theofficialfacebook.** The Official Facebook Channel. [Online] Facebook, May 6, 2009. http://www.youtube.com/user/theofficialfacebook.

84. **Facebook Newsroom.** Introducing Watch, a New Platform For Shows On Facebook. [Online] Facebook, August 9, 2017. https://about.fb.com/news/2017/08/introducing-watch-a-new-platform-for-shows-on-facebook/.

85. **Shapiro, Jordan.** The 'Sex Talk' For 21st Century Parents. Forbes. [Online] Forbes, May 26, 2014. http://www.forbes.com/sites/jordanshapiro/2014/05/26/the-sex-talk-for-21st-century-parents/.

86. **Fitzgerald, Toni.** Is reality TV losing steam? Maybe so. [Online] Media Life Magazine, October 12, 2011. http://www.medialifemagazine.com/artman2/publish/Broadcastrecap_64/Is-reality-TV-losing-steam-Maybe-so-.asp.

87. **Nielsen.** Nielsen Estimates Number of U.S. Television Homes to be 114.7 Million. [Online] Nielsenwire, May 3, 2011. http://blog.nielsen.com/nielsenwire/media_entertainment/nielsen-estimates-number-of-u-s-television-homes-to-be-114-7-million/.

88. **Wood, Molly.** Top 10 Web fads. [Online] CNet, July 15, 2005. http://www.cnet.com/1990-11136_1-6268155-1.html.

89. **Gill, Steve.** Can Borat be Sued by the "I Kiss You!" Guy? [Online] Electronic News Network, November 3, 2006. http://electronicnewsnetwork.com/entertainment/borat-sued-by-mahir-cagri-201037/.

90. **Grossman, Lev.** The Beast With A Billion Eyes. [Online] Time Magazine, January 30, 2012. http://www.time.com/time/magazine/article/0,9171,2104815,00.html.

91. **Oreskovic, Alexei.** YouTube hits 4 billion daily video views. [Online] Reuters, January 23, 2012. http://www.reuters.com/article/2012/01/23/us-google-youtube-idUSTRE80M0TS20120123.

92. **YouTube.** YouTube press statistics. [Online] Google. [Cited: January 25, 2012.] http://www.youtube.com/yt/press/statistics.html.

93. **Constine, Josh.** 100 Million Americans Watch Online Video Per Day, Up 43% Since 2010 -comScore. [Online] TechCrunch, February 9, 2012. http://techcrunch.com/2012/02/09/100-million-american-watch-video/.

94. **Broadcast Engineering.** 40 billion online videos viewed by U.S. Internet users in January, says comScore. [Online] Broadcast Engineering, February 22, 2012. http://broadcastengineering.com/ott/40-billion-online-videos-US-users-January-comScore-02222012/.

95. **comScore.** 2012 U.S. Digital Future in Focus. [Online] comScore, February 9, 2012. http://www.comscore.com/Press_Events/Presentations_Whitepapers/2012/2012_US_Digital_Future_in_Focus.

96. **Pepitone, Julianne.** Americans now watch more online movies than DVDs. [Online] CNNMoney, March 22, 2012. http://money.cnn.com/2012/03/22/technology/streaming-movie-sales/index.htm.

97. **West, Chloe.** 25 YouTube stats and facts to power your 2021 marketing strategy. [Online] Sprout Social, March 18, 2021. https://sproutsocial.com/insights/youtube-stats/.

98. **Chen, Jenn.** 20 Facebook stats to guide your 2021 Facebook strategy. [Online] Sprout Social, February 17, 2021. https://sproutsocial.com/insights/facebook-stats-for-marketers/.

99. **Milian, Mark.** YouTube exec: We're heading for 'third wave' of TV. [Online] CNN, February 1, 2012. http://whatsnext.blogs.cnn.com/2012/02/01/youtube-third-wave/.

100. **Barnes, Brooks.** Disney and YouTube Make a Video Deal. [Online] The New York Times, November 6, 2011. http://www.nytimes.com/2011/11/07/business/media/disney-and-you-tube-make-a-video-deal.html.

101. **Puopolo, Joseph.** The Emergence Of The Content Creation Class. [Online] TechCruch, January 29, 2012. http://techcrunch.com/2012/01/29/the-emergence-of-the-content-creation-class/.

102. **Purcell, Kristen.** Online Video 2013. [Online] Pew Research Internet Project, October 10, 2013. http://www.pewinternet.org/2013/10/10/online-video-2013/.

103. **Cohen, Joshua.** At 26 Million YouTube Subscribers, Has The World Reached Peak PewDiePie? [Online] tubefilter, April 25, 2014. http://www.tubefilter.com/2014/04/25/pewdiepie-youtube-subscribers-peak/.

104. **PewDiePie.** https://www.youtube.com/user/PewDiePie/about. [Online] PewDiePie. [Cited: May 20, 2014.] https://www.youtube.com/user/PewDiePie/about.

105. **Adib, Desiree.** Pop Star Justin Bieber Is on the Brink of Superstardom. [Online] ABC Good Morning America, November 14, 2009. http://abcnews.go.com/GMA/Weekend/teen-pop-star-justin-bieber-discovered-youtube/story?id=9068403.

106. **Trebay, Guy.** Model Struts Path to Stardom Not on Runway, but on YouTube. [Online] The New York Times, February 13, 2012. http://www.nytimes.com/2012/02/14/us/kate-upton-uses-the-web-to-become-a-star-model.html.

107. **Tenbarge, Kat.** Sorry, Bella Poarch, this IS 'Build a B*tch'. [Online] Substack, May 16, 2021. https://kidsarentalright.substack.com/p/sorry-bella-poarch-this-is-build.

108. **Sullivan, Rory.** Eight-year-old tops YouTube list of high earners with $26 million. [Online] CNN Business, December 19, 2019. https://www.cnn.com/2019/12/19/business/highest-paid-youtuber-2019-scli-intl/index.html.

109. **Criddle, Cristina.** Social media damages teenagers' mental health, report says. [Online] BBC News, January 27, 2021. https://www.bbc.com/news/technology-55826238.

110. **Zeidler, Sari.** On YouTube, teens ask the world: Am I ugly? [Online] CNN Blogs, March 3, 2012. http://inamerica.blogs.cnn.com/2012/03/03/on-youtube-teens-ask-the-world-am-i-ugly/.

111. **Gibson, Faye.** Am I Pretty or Ugly. [Online] SmileLoveBeauty8, January 15, 2012. http://www.youtube.com/watch?v=WoyZPn6hKY4.

112. **Smith, Candace.** Teens Post 'Am I Pretty or Ugly?' Videos on YouTube. [Online] ABC News, February 23, 2012. http://abcnews.go.com/US/teens-post-insecurities-youtube-pretty-ugly-videos/story?id=15777830.

113. **Koyczan, Shane.** To This Day Project - Shane Koyczan. [Online] Shane Koyczan, February 19, 2013. http://www.youtube.com/watch?v=ltun92DfnPY.

114. —. Surviving the pain of childhood bullying. [Online] CNN, May 8, 2013. http://www.cnn.com/2013/05/08/opinion/koyczan-spoken-word-poetry/index.html.

115. **Rodger, Elliot.** Bus Monitor Karen Klein bullied by vile school children. [Online] ThinkTillDeath, June 21, 2012. http://www.youtube.com/watch?v=E12R9fMMtos.

116. **Schwartz, Alison.** Karen Klein, Bullied Bus Monitor, to Donate and Invest Her Nearly $650,000. [Online] People Magazine, June 25, 2012. http://www.people.com/people/article/0,,20606781,00.html.

117. **Elgersma, Christine.** The viral Internet stunts parents should know. [Online] CNN Health, May 24, 2017. https://www.cnn.com/2017/05/24/health/viral-youtube-challenges-partner/index.html.

118. **Karimi, Faith.** Blindfolded Utah teen crashes her car while doing the 'Bird Box' challenge. [Online] CNN, January 12, 2019. https://www.cnn.com/2019/01/12/us/utah-birdbox-challenge-crash/index.html.

119. **Toh, Michelle.** Tide Pod Challenge: YouTube is removing 'dangerous' videos. [Online] CNN Business, January 18, 2018. https://money.cnn.com/2018/01/18/technology/tide-pod-challenge-video-youtube-facebook/index.html.

120. **Warren, Christina.** Chris Brown Curses Out Twitter Critics Then Tries to Delete the Evidence. [Online] Mashable, February 14, 2012. http://mashable.com/2012/02/14/chris-brown-twitter-2/.

121. **Biddle, Sam.** "Fuck Bitches Get Leid," the Sleazy Frat Emails of Snapchat's CEO. [Online] Valley Wag, May 28, 2014. http://valleywag.gawker.com/fuck-bitches-get-leid-the-sleazy-frat-emails-of-snap-1582604137.

122. **Frier, Sarah.** Snapchat CEO 'Mortified' by Leaked Stanford Frat E-Mails. [Online] Bloomberg, May 28, 2014. http://www.bloomberg.com/news/2014-05-28/snapchat-ceo-mortified-by-leaked-stanford-frat-e-mails.html.

123. **Allday, Erin.** Nowhere to hide from the Internet. [Online] San Francisco Chronicle, November 7, 2011. http://blog.sfgate.com/cityinsider/2008/11/07/nowhere-to-hide-from-the-internet/.

124. **Goldman, David.** Tweet costs Mark Cuban $50,000. [Online] CNNMoney, January 9, 2013. http://money.cnn.com/2013/01/09/technology/social/mark-cuban-tweet-fine/index.html.

125. **Lafata, Alexia.** This Guy Tried To Group Text 32 Tinder Matches And Failed Miserably (Photos). [Online] Elite Daily, June 11, 2014. http://elitedaily.com/humor/guys-plan-to-group-text-32-tinder-matches-at-once-hilariously-backfires-photos/628423/.

126. **Dukes, Jessica.** Ladies beware? New app lets guys auto-text their girlfriends. [Online] NBC News Today, February 27, 2014. http://www.today.com/tech/ladies-beware-new-app-lets-guys-auto-text-their-girlfriends-2D12181957.

127. **Junod, Tom.** George Clooney's Rules for Living. [Online] Esquire, November 11, 2013. http://www.esquire.com/features/george-clooney-interview-1213-3.

128. **Griggs, Brandon.** Teen jailed for Facebook 'joke' is released. [Online] CNN, July 12, 2013. http://www.cnn.com/2013/07/12/tech/social-media/facebook-jailed-teen/index.html.

129. **Wang, Yang, et al.** "I regretted the minute I pressed share": A Qualitative Study of Regrets on Facebook. [Online] 2011, 20 July. http://cups.cs.cmu.edu/soups/2011/proceedings/a10_Wang.pdf.

130. **Finn, Greg.** How To Put The Facebook "Like" Button On A Site. [Online] Search Engine Land, May 25, 2010. http://searchengineland.com/how-to-put-the-facebook-like-button-on-a-site-42703.

131. **Milian, Mark and Sutter, John D.** Facebook revamps site with 'Timeline' and real-time apps. [Online] CNN, September 22, 2011. http://www.cnn.com/2011/09/22/tech/social-media/facebook-announcement-f8/index.html.

132. **McCullagh, Declan.** Facebook 'Like' button draws privacy scrutiny. [Online] CNET, June 2, 2010. http://www.cnet.com/news/facebook-like-button-draws-privacy-scrutiny/.

133. **Kosinskia, Michal, Stillwella, David and Graepelb, Thore.** Private traits and attributes are predictable from digital records of human behavior. [Online] Proceedings of the National Academy of Sciences of the United States of America, October 29, 2012. http://www.pnas.org/content/early/2013/03/06/1218772110.

134. **Marr, Bernard.** How Facebook 'Likes' Reveal Your Intimate Secrets. [Online] LinkedIn, June 13, 2013. http://www.linkedin.com/today/post/article/20130613061334-64875646-how-facebook-likes-reveal-your-intimate-secrets.

135. **Cheng, Jacqui.** Are "deleted" photos really gone from Facebook? Not always. [Online] Ars Technica, July 3, 2009. http://arstechnica.com/business/2009/07/are-those-photos-really-deleted-from-facebook-think-twice/.

136. —. "Deleted" Facebook photos still not deleted: a followup. [Online] Ars Technica, October 11, 2010. http://arstechnica.com/business/2010/10/facebook-may-be-making-strides/.

137. **Biersdorfer, J. D.** Q&A: When Facebook Marks Your Spot. [Online] The New York Times, February 13, 2012. http://gadgetwise.blogs.nytimes.com/2012/02/13/qa-when-facebook-marks-your-spot/.

138. **Pepitone, Julianne.** Facebook uses offline purchases to target ads. [Online] CNNMoney, April 11, 2013. http://money.cnn.com/2013/04/10/technology/social/facebook-offline-ad-target/.

139. **Barbaro, Michael and Zeller, Tom Jr.** A Face Is Exposed for AOL Searcher No. 4417749. [Online] The New York Times, August 9, 2006. http://www.nytimes.com/2006/08/09/technology/09aol.html.

140. **Sweeney, Latanya.** Simple Demographics Often Identify People Uniquely. [Online] Carnegie Mellon University, 2000. http://repository.cmu.edu/isr/230/.

141. **Mahmud, Jalal, Nichols, Jeffrey and Drews, Clemens.** Home Location Identification of Twitter Users. [Online] Cornell University Library, March 7, 2014. http://arxiv.org/abs/1403.2345.

142. **AVG.** Digital Birth: Welcome to the Online World. [Online] Business Wire, October 6, 2010. http://www.businesswire.com/news/home/20101006006722/en/Digital-Birth-Online-World.

143. **Sultan, Aisha and Miller, Jon.** 'Facebook parenting' is destroying our children's privacy. [Online] CNN, May 25, 2012. http://www.cnn.com/2012/05/25/opinion/sultan-miller-facebook-parenting/index.html.

144. **Phillips, Rich, Segal, Kim and Zarrella, John.** Officials: Teen commits suicide on webcam as others watch. [Online] CNN, November 21, 2008. http://www.cnn.com/2008/CRIME/11/21/webcam.suicide/.

145. **Kobayashi, Chie.** Police: Man kills himself during live internet broadcast. [Online] CNN, November 29, 2010. http://www.cnn.com/2010/WORLD/asiapcf/11/12/japan.suicide.broadcast/index.html.

146. **Cellan-Jones, Rory.** Facebook adds Samaritans suicide risk alert system. [Online] BBC News, March 7, 2011. http://www.bbc.co.uk/news/technology-12667343.

147. **Facebook.** How do I help someone who has posted suicidal content on the site? [Online] Facebook Help Center. [Cited: May 18, 2012.] http://www.facebook.com/help/?faq=216817991675637.

148. **Dickey, Megan Rose.** Facebook brings suicide prevention tools to Live and Messenger. [Online] TechCrunch, March 1, 2017. https://techcrunch.com/2017/03/01/facebook-brings-suicide-prevention-tools-to-live-and-messenger/.

149. **Manley, Martin.** Martin Manley: My Life and Death. [Online] martinmanley.org, August 15, 2013. http://martinmanley.org/suicide_preface.html.

150. **Gross, Doug.** The sportswriter who blogged his suicide. [Online] CNN, August 25, 2013. http://www.cnn.com/2013/08/23/tech/web/martin-manley-suicide-website/index.html.

151. **Kelly, Max.** Memories of Friends Departed Endure on Facebook. [Online] The Facebook Blog, October 26, 2009. http://www.facebook.com/blog.php?post=163091042130.

152. **Katayama, Lisa.** How to memorialize friends who have passed away on Facebook. [Online] BoingBoing, October 26, 2009. http://boingboing.net/2009/10/26/how-to-memorialize-f.html.

153. **Kelly, Heather.** How to post to Facebook, Twitter after you die. [Online] CNN, February 22, 2013. http://www.cnn.com/2013/02/22/tech/social-media/death-and-social-media/index.html.

154. **Coldwell, Will.** Why death is not the end of your social media life. [Online] The Guardian, February 18, 2013. http://www.theguardian.com/media/shortcuts/2013/feb/18/death-social-media-liveson-deadsocial.

155. **Tuerk, Andreas.** Plan your digital afterlife with Inactive Account Manager. [Online] Google Public Policy Blog, April 11, 2013. http://googlepublicpolicy.blogspot.com/2013/04/plan-your-digital-afterlife-with.html.

156. **USA.gov.** Write a Social Media Will. [Online] USA.gov, June 23, 2014. http://www.usa.gov/topics/money/personal-finance/wills.shtml#Write_a_Social_Media_Will.

157. **Backstrom, Lars.** Anatomy of Facebook. [Online] Facebook, November 21, 2011. https://www.facebook.com/notes/facebook-data-team/anatomy-of-facebook/10150388519243859.

158. **Cohen, Jackie.** You Don't Know One-Fifth of Your Facebook Friends. [Online] All Facebook, January 13, 2011. http://www.allfacebook.com/you-dont-know-one-fifth-of-your-facebook-friends-2011-01.

159. **Kois, Dan.** The Facebook Cleanse: Happy birthday! I'm unfriending you, stranger. [Online] Slate, May 2014. http://www.slate.com/articles/technology/future_tense/2014/05/facebook_cleanse_unfriend_strangers_on_their_birthdays.html.

160. **Kirkova, Deni.** You're breaking up with me by TEXT? Don't worry, you're not the only one being digitally dumped - most splits now happen via SMS. [Online] Mail Online, March 5, 2014. http://www.dailymail.co.uk/femail/article-2573879/Youre-breaking-TEXT-Dont-worry-youre-not-one-digitally-dumped-splits-happen-SMS.html.

161. **Morin, Ty.** Friend Request: Accepted. [Online] Kickstarter, March 26, 2013. https://www.kickstarter.com/projects/tymorin/friend-request-accepted.

162. **Slefo, George P.** Fortnite emerges as a social media platform for Gen Z. [Online] Ad Age, June 10, 2019. https://adage.com/article/digital/fortnite-emerges-social-media-platform-gen-z/2176301.

163. **Loveridge, Sam and James, Ford.** Here's how many people play Fortnite. [Online] Games Radar, March 10, 2021. https://www.gamesradar.com/how-many-people-play-fortnite/.

164. **B, Rishabh.** Fortnite We the People: Epic Games hosting screening to fight racism in America. [Online] Sportskeeda, July 4, 2020. https://www.sportskeeda.com/esports/fortnite-we-people-epic-games-hosting-screening-fight-racism-america.

165. **Allyn, Bobby.** Social Media Site Gab Is Surging, Even As Critics Blame It For Capitol Violence. [Online] NPR, January 17, 2021. https://www.npr.org/2021/01/17/957512634/social-media-site-gab-is-surging-even-as-critics-blame-it-for-capitol-violence.

166. **The FR Fintech Buzz.** Fall of Parler a boon for crypto-friendly social platforms Gab and DLive. [Online] The Financial Revolutionist, January 12, 2021. https://thefr.com/news/2021/1/18/fall-of-parler-a-boon-for-crypto-friendly-social-platforms-gab-and-dlive.

167. **Baker, Natasha.** Apps in car dashboards aim to make vehicles smarter. [Online] Reuters, March 27, 2014. http://www.reuters.com/article/2014/03/27/us-apps-autos-idUSBREA2Q10220140327.

168. **Damsky, William.** 60% of Cars to Be Internet-Ready in 5 Years. [Online] CE Outlook, July 5, 2012. http://www.ceoutlook.com/2012/07/05/60-of-cars-to-be-internet-ready-in-5-years/.

169. **Albanesius, Chloe.** Mercedes-Benz Brings Facebook, Google to the Dashboard. [Online] PC Magazine, January 10, 2012. http://www.pcmag.com/article2/0,2817,2398685,00.asp.

170. **Griggs, Brandon.** 'Augmented-reality' windshields and the future of driving. [Online] CNN, January 13, 2012. http://www.cnn.com/2012/01/13/tech/innovation/ces-future-driving/index.html.

171. **Ford Motor Company.** Ford to Showcase Roximity at 2012 CES; Encourages Developers to Innovate New App Ideas for SYNC. [Online] Ford Motor Company Online, January 6, 2012. http://www.at.ford.com/news/cn/Pages/Ford%20to%20Showcase%20Roximity%20at%20 2012%20CES;%20Encourages%20Developers%20to%20Innovate%20New%20App%20 Ideas%20for%20SYNC.aspx.

172. **Cheng, Roger.** GM: Your car's 4G data plan will start at $10 for 200MB. [Online] CNet, May 12, 2014. http://www.cnet.com/news/gm-unveils-data-plans-for-connected-cars-200mb-for-10-and-up/.

173. **Maisto, Michelle.** Nokia Announces $100 Million Connected Car Investment Fund. [Online] eWeek, May 5, 2014. http://www.eweek.com/mobile/nokia-announces-100-million-connected-car-investment-fund.html.

174. **MacManus, Richard.** Get Ready For a World of Connected Devices. [Online] ReadWriteWeb, February 3, 2012. http://www.readwriteweb.com/archives/get_ready_for_a_world_of_connected_devices.php.

175. **Virginia Tech Transportation Institute.** New data from Virginia Tech Transportation Institute provides insight into cell phone use and driving distraction. [Online] Virginia Tech News, July 29, 2009. http://www.vtnews.vt.edu/articles/2009/07/2009-571.html.

176. **Ramsey, Mike.** Don't Look Now: A Car That Tweets. As Distracted-Driving Push Fades, Auto Makers Will Let Drivers Check Facebook, Buy Movie Tickets. [Online] The Wall Street Journal, February 10, 2012. http://online.wsj.com/article/SB10001424052970203824904577213041944082370.html.

177. **Kohn, Bernard and Snyder, Andrea.** U.S. Calls for Ban on In-Car Facebook, Twitter While Driving. [Online] Bloomberg Businessweek, February 16, 2012. http://news.businessweek.com/article.asp?documentKey=1376-LZHQB31A1I4H01-68P3C92P2HL6F4L53B9P2100FB.

178. **Consumer Electronics Association.** CEA Responds to NTSB on Safe Driving Innovations. [Online] Yahoo! Finance, May 8, 2012. http://finance.yahoo.com/news/cea-responds-ntsb-safe-driving-190800191.html.

179. **Carnegie Mellon University.** Press Release: Carnegie Mellon Will Test New Internet Architecture in Vehicular Network and for Delivering Online Video. [Online] Carnegie Mellon University, May 13, 2014. http://www.cmu.edu/news/stories/archives/2014/may/may13_internetarchitecture.html.

180. **Simonite, Tom.** Startups Experiment with Ads That Know How You Drive. [Online] MIT Technology Review, May 1, 2014. http://www.technologyreview.com/news/527001/startups-experiment-with-ads-that-know-how-you-drive/.

181. **Wohlsen, Marcus.** What Google Really Gets Out of Buying Nest for $3.2 Billion. [Online] Wired, January 14, 2014. http://www.wired.com/2014/01/googles-3-billion-nest-buy-finally-make-internet-things-real-us/.

182. **Goldman, David.** Apple unveils iOS 8 and OS X Yosemite. [Online] CNNMoney, June 2, 2014. http://money.cnn.com/2014/06/02/technology/mobile/apple-wwdc-ios-8/.

183. **Metz, Rachel.** The Internet of You. [Online] MIT Technology Review, May 20, 2014. http://www.technologyreview.com/news/527386/the-internet-of-you/.

184. —. Jawbone's New Wristband Adds You to the Internet of Things. [Online] MIT Technology Review, November 13, 2013. http://www.technologyreview.com/news/521606/jawbones-new-wristband-adds-you-to-the-internet-of-things/.

185. **Reuters San Francisco Newsroom.** Apple to make 3-5 million smartwatches monthly, sales begin October: report. [Online] Reuters, June 6, 2014. http://www.reuters.com/article/2014/06/07/us-apple-smartwatches-idUSKBN0EH2AB20140607.

186. **RT.** Hacker dies days before he was to reveal how to remotely kill pacemaker patients. [Online] RT, July 26, 2013. http://rt.com/usa/hacker-pacemaker-barnaby-jack-639/.

187. **Bilton, Nick.** Intruders for the Plugged-In Home, Coming In Through the Internet. [Online] The New York Times, June 1, 2014. http://bits.blogs.nytimes.com/2014/06/01/dark-side-to-internet-of-things-hacked-homes-and-invasive-ads/.

188. **Brooker, Charlie.** Charlie Brooker: the dark side of our gadget addiction. [Online] The Guardian, December 1, 2011. https://www.theguardian.com/technology/2011/dec/01/charlie-brooker-dark-side-gadget-addiction-black-mirror.

189. **Nadig, Dave.** Semantic Density, Algos & Gamestop: This Time It's Different. [Online] ETF Trends, January 26, 2021. https://www.etftrends.com/retirement-income-channel/semantic-density-algos-gamestop-this-time-its-different/.

190. **Kwaak, Jeyup S.** Gamer Arrested After Death of Neglected Child. [Online] The Wall Street Journal, April 14, 2014. http://blogs.wsj.com/korearealtime/2014/04/14/gamer-arrested-after-death-of-neglected-child/.

191. **Saisan, Joanna, et al.** Internet & Computer Addiction. [Online] helpguilde.org, December 2013. http://www.helpguide.org/mental/internet_cybersex_addiction.htm.

192. **Shlain, Tiffany.** National Day Of Unplugging: A Digital Detox. [Online] The Huffington Post, March 23, 2012. http://www.huffingtonpost.com/tiffany-shlain/national-day-of-unplugging_b_1373842.html.

193. **reSTART.** reSTART a Sustainable Lifestyle. [Online] Center for Digital Technology Sustainability. [Cited: June 20, 2014.] http://www.netaddictionrecovery.com/the-problem/sustainable-use.html.

194. **Tinker, Ben.** Four beds ready to treat Internet addicts. [Online] CNN, September 7, 2013. http://www.cnn.com/2013/09/07/health/internet-addiction-treatment-center/index.html.

195. **Keating, Shannon.** People Are Ready To Log Off Social Media For Good. [Online] BuzzFeed News, May 20, 2021. https://www.buzzfeednews.com/article/shannonkeating/covid-delete-facebook-instagram-social-media.

196. **Goldman, Jeremy.** 6 Apps to Stop Your Smartphone Addiction. [Online] Inc., October 21, 2015. https://www.inc.com/jeremy-goldman/6-apps-to-stop-your-smartphone-addiction.html.

197. **Liu, William, et al.** Is it possible to cure Internet addiction with the Internet? *Springer.* [Online] March 2020. https://www.researchgate.net/publication/326609104_Is_it_possible_to_cure_Internet_addiction_with_the_Internet.

198. **Karimi, Faith.** The day Facebook went dark. *CNN.* [Online] October 6, 2021. https://www.cnn.com/2021/10/06/world/facebook-whatsapp-instagram-down-cec/index.html.

Chapter 17
Personal Privacy and Information Management

"Awareness is an effective weapon against many forms of identity theft."
— U.S. Federal Trade Commission (April 2007)

"As we go through our lives we create vast amounts of data. It's more than just data. It represents our actions, interests, intentions, communications, relationships, locations, behaviors and creative and consumptive efforts."
— The Locker Project (May 2011)

"I divide the entire set of Fortune Global 2000 firms into two categories: those that know they've been compromised and those that don't yet know."
— Cybersecurity Executive Dmitri Alperovitch (August 2011)

"There are only two types of companies: those that have been hacked, and those that will be. Even that is merging into one category: those that have been hacked and will be again."
— FBI Director Robert Mueller (March 2012)

"Advertising that respects privacy is not only possible, it was the standard until the growth of the Internet."
— Apple (November 2020)

"Advertising is essential to keeping the web open for everyone, but the web ecosystem is at risk if privacy practices do not keep up with changing expectations. People want assurances that their identity and information are safe as they browse the web."
— Google Product Manager Chetna Bindra (January 2021)

17.1 Personal Information for Sale

In March 2018, whistleblower Christopher Wylie disclosed that the British political consulting firm Cambridge Analytica purchased Facebook data on tens of millions of Americans without their knowledge in order to build a "psychological warfare

© Springer Science+Business Media, LLC, part of Springer Nature 2021
N. Lee, *Facebook Nation*, https://doi.org/10.1007/978-1-0716-1867-7_17

tool" on behalf of clients who intended to interfere in the 2016 U.S. presidential election in Donald Trump's favor (1).

In April 2021, LinkedIn confirmed that a database containing information scraped from around 500 million LinkedIn user profiles and other online sources were up for sale on a website popular with cybercriminals (2).

No matter how we safeguard our privacy by turning off our cell phones, avoiding the use of in-vehicle apps, deactivating Facebook accounts, opting out on all data collections, and evading Google and Bing's social searches, there are still plenty of public records that are obtainable by anyone who is willing to pay. Websites such as Intelius (whose trademark is "Live in the know") displays the age, past cities of residence, and names of the relatives on any person whom we search for. This and several other websites also sell public records including full name, date of birth, phone, address history, marriage/divorce records, property ownership, lawsuits, convictions, and other public information for a nominal fee (3).

The need-to-know maxim and the respect for personal privacy have largely been abandoned in the Internet era and commercial age. Journalists from *News of the World,* for example, paid police for information and hacked into the phone messages of celebrities, a missing 13-year-old murder victim, and the grieving families of dead soldiers (4). The illegal and immoral tactics brought down the 168-year-old tabloid *News of the World* in July 2011.

In October 2011, actress Junie Hoang sued IMDb and its parent company Amazon.com for revealing her true date of birth without her consent, thus opening her up to age discrimination. "Anyone who values their privacy and has ever given credit card information to an online company like IMDb or Amazon.com should be concerned about the outcome," Hoang said in a statement regarding IMDb illegally used her credit card information to obtain and post her age (5). Amicus curiae briefs were filed in support of Hoang by four screenwriters, Screen Actors Guild (SAG), the American Federation of Television and Radio Artists (AFTRA) and the Writers Guild of America, West (WGAW) in 2013.

In late 2011, security software company Symantec commissioned Scott Wright of Security Perspectives Inc. to conduct an experiment codenamed The Symantec Smartphone Honey Stick Project (6). In the experiment, they intentionally lost 50 smartphones in high-traffic public places in five major cities: New York City, Washington D.C., Los Angeles, San Francisco, and Ottawa, Canada. Only 50% of the people who found one of the "lost" smartphones made an attempt to return it. That statistics alone may not be too startling, but the following key findings are more disturbing (7):

- 96% of lost smartphones were accessed by the finders of the devices.
- 89% attempted to access personal mobile apps or data.
- 72% attempted to access a private photos app.
- 60% attempted to access social networking accounts and personal email.
- 53% accessed a "HR Salaries" file.
- 57% accessed a "Saved Passwords" file.

And the scariest of them all:

- 43% attempted to access an online banking app on the lost smartphone.

Andrew Grove, co-founder and former CEO of Intel Corporation, offered his thoughts on Internet privacy in an *Esquire* magazine interview reported on May 1, 2000: "Privacy is one of the biggest problems in this new electronic age. At the heart of the Internet culture is a force that wants to find out everything about you. And once it has found out everything about you and two hundred million others, that's a very valuable asset, and people will be tempted to trade and do commerce with that asset. This wasn't the information that people were thinking of when they called this the information age" (8).

While Facebook, Google, and other online businesses collect information about us and make billions of dollars from selling our data, some startup companies believe that we can better organize our own information online in a secure "data vault" and we may even be compensated for sharing that information (9). However, given the plentiful information from public records and data scraping on the web, much of our information is already available to big businesses.

17.2 Personal Information at Risk

In 2012, Facebook started switching all users to a more secure HTTPS (Hypertext Transfer Protocol Secure) connection (10). In 2014, Facebook made its debut on the Tor "dark web" for users to access its website while maintaining privacy and leaving no digital trail (11). In 2016, Facebook added support for the anonymous Tor browser on Android phones. Subsequently, more than one million people were connecting to Facebook through Tor in 2016 alone (12).

With the abundance of our digital footprint and exhaust data online, we must manage our personal data better. Although we entrust private companies and our governments to do their best to protect our private information, cybercriminals are hard at work to steal our valuable data. In May 2014, CNN reported that cybercriminals "have exposed the personal information of 110 million Americans – roughly half of the nation's adults – in the last 12 months alone" (13).

Once the genie is out of the bottle, there is no easy way to stop the dissemination of leaked or stolen information. In April 2021, hackers posted the personal information (including full name, location, birthday, email address, phone number, and relationship status) of about 533 million Facebook users on the dark web for criminals (14). Facebook said without disclosing much details, "While we can't always prevent datasets like these from re-circulating or new ones from appearing, we have a dedicated team focused on this work" (15).

Some of the high-profile data breaches between January 2007 and April 2021 include:

1. In January 2007, up to 94 million Visa and MasterCard account numbers were stolen from TJX Companies dating back to 2005 and earlier, causing more than $68 million in fraud-related losses involving Visa cards alone (16).
2. In December 2009, online games service company RockYou suffered a data breach that resulted in the exposure of over 32 million usernames and pass-

words. Adding insult to injury, RockYou stored passwords in plain text format without any encryption (17).

3. In January 2011, cybercriminals breached the database of online dating site PlentyofFish.com, exposing the personal and password information on nearly 30 million users (18).

4. In March 2011, computer and network security firm RSA suffered a massive data breach, jeopardizing the effectiveness of its SecurID system that is being used by more than 25,000 corporations and 40 million users around the world (19).

5. In April 2011, a cybercriminal stole the names, birth dates, and credit card numbers of 77 million customers on the Sony PlayStation Network (20).

6. In May 2011, cybercriminals illegally accessed 360,083 Citigroup customer accounts and withdrew $2.7 million from about 3,400 credit cards (21).

7. In December 2011, hackers affiliated with the Anonymous broke into the private intelligence analysis firm Strategic Forecasting (Stratfor) and obtained private information of about 860,000 people including former U.S. Vice President Dan Quayle, former Secretary of State Henry Kissinger, and former CIA Director Jim Woolsey. The group went on to publish the stolen emails and thousands of credit card numbers on the Internet (22).

8. From January to February 2012, cybercriminals cracked into the Global Payments administrative account and stole more than 10 million credit and debit card transaction records (23).

9. In June 2012, cybercriminals stole 6.5 million LinkedIn passwords and posted them on an online forum. LinkedIn passwords were encoded using SHA-1 - a cryptographic hash function with weak collision resistance. About half of the encrypted passwords have been decrypted and posted online (24).

10. In June 2012, online dating site eHarmony notified its customers that a "small fraction" of its user base had been compromised (25).

11. In July 2012, Yahoo! Voices was hacked, resulting in the theft of 450,000 customer usernames and passwords (26).

12. In October 2012, Barnes & Noble disclosed that a PIN pad device used by customers to swipe credit and debit cards had been compromised at 63 of its national stores located in California, Connecticut, Florida, Illinois, Massachusetts, New Jersey, New York, Pennsylvania, and Rhode Island (27).

13. In January 2013, cybercriminals accessed Twitter user data and stole the usernames, email addresses, session tokens, and encrypted/salted versions of passwords for approximately 250,000 users (28).

14. In February 2013, personal information of more than 4,000 U.S. bank executives was stolen from the Federal Reserve System by exploiting a temporary vulnerability in a website vendor product (29).

15. In March 2013, cybercriminals gained access to cloud-storage service provider Evernote's user information, including usernames, email addresses, and encrypted passwords. As a result, Evernote required all of its 50 million users to reset their passwords (30).

16. In October 2013, Adobe's chief security officer Brad Arkin disclosed that "the attackers removed from our systems certain information relating to 2.9 million

Adobe customers, including customer names, encrypted credit or debit card numbers, expiration dates, and other information relating to customer orders" (31).

17. From June to October 2013, about 1.1 million customers were impacted by a security breach of luxury retailer Neiman Marcus' payment systems due to a "sophisticated, self-concealing malware, capable of fraudulently obtaining payment card information" (32).

18. From November to December 2013, cybercriminals stole 40 million credit and debit card information as well as 70 million customers' information such as their name, address, phone number, and email address from discount retailer Target (33).

19. From May 2013 to January 2014, retailer Michaels and subsidiary Aaron Brothers were hacked. Some of their 3 million customers' credit and debit card numbers and expiration dates were compromised (34).

20. In January 2014, cyber attackers posted the account information of 4.6 million Snapchat users, making usernames and partial phone numbers available for download from the website SnapchatDB.info (35).

21. Between February and March 2014, cybercriminals gained access to eBay's corporate network and stole a database containing eBay customers' name, encrypted password, email address, physical address, phone number, and date of birth (36). The data breach potentially affected all of eBay's 148 million customers.

22. In April 2014, AOL verified that there was unauthorized access to information regarding a "significant number" of its 120 million user accounts. According to AOL, the compromised information included "AOL users' email addresses, postal addresses, address book contact information, encrypted passwords and encrypted answers to security questions that we ask when a user resets his or her password, as well as certain employee information." In addition, AOL believed that "spammers have used this contact information to send spoofed emails that appeared to come from roughly 2% of our email accounts" (37). (Two percent of 120 million is 2.4 million email accounts.)

23. In June 2014, restaurant chain P.F. Chang acknowledged that at least thousands of credit and debit card numbers were stolen in early 2014 from some of the 200+ locations in the U.S. (38).

24. In August 2014, Hold Security revealed that a Russian crime ring has stolen a massive 1.2 billion username/password combinations and more than 500 million email addresses from 420,000 websites. "Hackers did not just target U.S. companies, they targeted any website they could get, ranging from Fortune 500 companies to very small websites," said Alex Holden, founder and chief information security officer of Hold Security. "And most of these sites are still vulnerable" (39).

25. In August 2014, Apple's iCloud online data backup service might have been compromised by cybercriminals who stole and shared publicly nude selfies of Jennifer Lawrence, Kirsten Dunst, Kate Upton, Mary Elizabeth Winstead, and other celebrities. Apple claimed that the celebrity accounts "were compromised by a very targeted attack on usernames, passwords and security questions" (40).

26. Between April and September 2014, cybercriminals broke into Home Depot's in-store payments systems, siphoning payment card details from 56 million customers in the United States and Canada (41).

27. Since September 2014, hackers broke into UCLA Health System's computer network to access medical records on as many as 4.5 million patients (42).

28. In July 2015, U.S. Office of Personnel Management (OPM) reported hackers got away with sensitive information including social security numbers on 21.5 million people as well as 1.1 million fingerprints (43).

29. In November 2015, Apple removed InstaAgent from its iTunes App Store after the popular app had stolen Instagram usernames and passwords from about 500,000 users (44).

30. In December 2016, Yahoo! reported a massive data breach in August 2013 that involved 1 billion user accounts containing names, email addresses, telephone numbers, dates of birth, and MD5-hashed passwords that can be cracked (45).

31. In February 2017, CloudPets stuffed toys exposed more than 820,000 customer accounts with 2.2 million voice recordings from kids and parents (46).

32. In September 2017, Equifax revealed that its databases for 143 million people had been hacked to steal names, social security numbers, birth dates, home addresses, and drivers' license information (47).

33. In November 2017, Uber disclosed that the 2016 data breach affected some 57 million riders and drivers, exposing their names, email addresses, and phone numbers (48).

34. In August 2018, hackers gained access to 2.5 million T-Mobile customer details including billing ZIP codes, phone numbers, email addresses, and account numbers (49).

35. In July 2019, a cybercriminal was charged for breaking into a Capital One Bank server to steal 140,000 social security numbers, 1 million Canadian social insurance numbers, and 80,000 bank account numbers (50).

36. In August 2020, a ransomware attack on Carnival cruise line exposed personal information including passport numbers on more than 150,000 staff members and an undisclosed number of customers (51).

37. In April 2021, hackers posted the personal information (including full name, location, birthday, email address, phone number, and relationship status) of about 533 million Facebook users on the dark web for criminals (14).

38. In April 2021, a database containing information scraped from around 500 million LinkedIn user profiles and other online sources were up for sale on a website popular with cybercriminals (2).

39. In October 2021, an anonymous hacker leaked more than 125GB of data stolen from Twitch, including its source code and streamer payout information (52).

For every publicized data breach incident, there are probably a dozen more undisclosed security breaches. Although some organizations have come forward in reporting cyber attacks, the vast majority of companies refuse to confirm news reports of online attacks due to their fear of the stock market volatility and the loss of consumer confidence. As revealed by *The New York Times* in February 2013, the list includes the International Olympic Committee, Exxon Mobil, Baker Hughes,

Royal Dutch Shell, BP, ConocoPhillips, Chesapeake Energy, British energy giant BG Group, steel maker ArcelorMittal, and Coca-Cola (53).

Cybersecurity executive Dmitri Alperovitch wrote in a 2011 McAfee report: "I am convinced that every company in every conceivable industry with significant size and valuable intellectual property and trade secrets has been compromised (or will be shortly) with the great majority of the victims rarely discovering the intrusion or its impact. … In fact, I divide the entire set of Fortune Global 2000 firms into two categories: those that know they've been compromised and those that don't yet know" (54).

At the 2012 RSA conference in San Francisco, Federal Bureau of Investigation (FBI) director Robert Mueller said, "There are only two types of companies: those that have been hacked, and those that will be. Even that is merging into one category: those that have been hacked and will be again" (55).

17.3   Identity Theft Prevention

Stolen credit and debit cards can be replaced and the fraudulent charges reversed. But the bigger issue is identity theft or ID theft. According to Javelin Strategy and Research, more than 13.1 million Americans were victims of identity fraud in 2013; in other words, a new identity fraud victim every two seconds. The report indicated "an increase of more than 500,000 fraud victims to 13.1 million people in 2013, the second highest number since the study began. Account takeover fraud hit a new record in incidence for the second year in a row and accounted for 28 percent of all identity fraud. Additionally, fraudsters increasingly turned to eBay, PayPal and Amazon with the stolen information to make purchases. In 2013, data breaches became more damaging, with one in three people who received a data breach notification letter becoming an identity fraud victim" (56).

I was one of the identity theft victims years ago. In an attempt to find the best mortgage deal, I disclosed to several brokers my personal information including social security number, copy of my driver license, and bank statements. A few months later, an identity thief opened a new online bank account and transferred all the money from my bank to his account. I immediately reported the incident to the police and my bank reimbursed me the financial loss.

The Federal Trade Commission (FTC) advised us, "Awareness is an effective weapon against many forms of identity theft. Be aware of how information is stolen and what you can do to protect yours, monitor your personal information to uncover any problems quickly, and know what to do when you suspect your identity has been stolen" (57).

Although we can never completely eradicate identity theft, we can protect ourselves to a large extent by taking the necessary steps to deter identity thieves, detect suspicious activity, and defend against identity theft (58). Expanding on the FTC recommendations, we can:

1. Deter identity thieves by safeguarding your information:

   a. Shred financial documents and paperwork with personal information before you discard them.

   b. Sign up for paperless statements from your banks and utility companies.

   c. Do not carry your Social Security card or write your Social Security number on a check.

   d. Use hard-for-anyone-to-guess but easy-for-you-to-remember passwords with a combination of letters, numbers, and special characters.

   e. Set a passcode on your smartphone for protection.

   f. Keep the anti-virus software up-to-date on your computers.

   g. Do not access sensitive information or install any software through public WiFi or Internet connections in hotels, restaurants, and other public venues. (The FBI issued a warning on May 8, 2012 about travelers' laptops being infected with malicious software while using hotel Internet connections (59).)

   h. Opt out of pre-screened credit and insurance offers to prevent potential thieves from intercepting and accepting the offers in your name. Opting out can be done online at https://www.optoutprescreen.com/

2. Detect suspicious activity by monitoring your information:

   a. Review financial accounts and billing statements regularly.

   b. Examine your Google Account Activity for any suspicious activities with your account sign-ins, visited places, emails, web history, etc. (60).

   c. Set up Google Alerts at http://www.google.com/alerts to monitor the web 24/7 for any news and videos about you or someone with the same name as you (61). You can receive an alert once a week, once a day, or as-it-happens.

   d. Sign up for Newsle to track when your own name has come up in the news and blog posts.

   e. Obtain your free annual credit reports from TransUnion, Equifax, and Experian; and look for abnormalities or inaccuracies.

3. Defend against identity theft by proactive measures:

   a. Place a fraud alert and a credit freeze on your credit reports at TransUnion, Equifax, and Experian. Fraud alerts and credit freezes help prevent an identity thief from opening new financial accounts, applying for loans, and seeking employment in your name.

   b. Report all identity theft incidences to the police and the FTC at 1-877-ID-THEFT.

17.4 Password Protection

A 2009 article in the *Proceedings of the Human Factors and Ergonomics Society* cited a survey of 836 people about their password usage and behavior (62). The survey showed the following:

1. 18% of respondents always use the same password to access multiple computers and websites.

2. 44% of respondents use a short password (less than 8 characters).
3. 44% of respondents write their passwords down on a piece of paper or a document file.

Microsoft's security guru Jesper Johansson explained the prevalence of weak passwords: "How many have [a] password policy that says under penalty of death you shall not write down your password? I claim that is absolutely wrong. I claim that password policy should say you should write down your password. I have 68 different passwords. If I am not allowed to write any of them down, guess what I am going to do? I am going to use the same password on every one of them. Since not all systems allow good passwords, I am going to pick a really crappy one, use it everywhere and never change it" (63).

In 2012, *CNet* analyzed the most frequently used passwords that were cracked by cybercriminals in the Yahoo! Voices data breach (64). Among more than 450,000 stolen login credentials, the most common passwords in descending order of popularity were:

1. 123456
2. password
3. 111111
4. welcome
5. ninja
6. freedom
7. f*ck
8. baseball
9. superman
10. 000000
11. America
12. winner
13. starwars
14. batman
15. spiderman
16. lakers
17. maverick
18. ncc1701
19. startrek
20. ncc1701a

Surprisingly, in spite of a decade of media coverage on television and the Internet, cybersecurity experts saw to their horror that "123456" was still the most commonly used password among 2.5 million people in year 2020 (65).

One may expect that advanced computer users are better with password protection. However, *Ars Technica* revealed a disturbing observation: "Experience made a difference, as expert and advanced computer users tended to outperform the novices. But there were limits; actual network administrators, for example, didn't behave in a manner that was significantly different from an average user" (66).

Indeed, the 2012 Data Breach Investigations Report by the Verizon RISK (Response, Intelligence, Solutions, Knowledge) Team indicated that 94% of all data compromised involved servers (67). Many network administrators are simply not doing enough to prevent computer server intrusions. The SolarWinds debacle affected hundreds of major U.S. corporations and government servers in 2020. CEO Sudhakar Ramakrishna blamed an intern for the "solarwinds123" password. He said, "I believe that was a password that an intern used on one of his Github servers back in 2017, which was reported to our security team and it was immediately removed" (68). But it was too late, the damage was done.

A 2013 article in *Ars Technica* describes in detail how easy it is for cybercriminals to crack weak passwords using only free tools and resources on the Internet (69). Weak passwords include dictionary words, popular phrases, celebrity names, and strings of numbers or characters that are easy to guess.

Some security experts suggest using a secure password manager such as LastPass, 1Password, and KeePass to create a long, strong, and different password for each and every website that requires a login password. The main advantage of using a password manager is that you only need to create one strong "master" password that you can remember. The password manager would automate password generation and form filling for you. LastPass, for instance, is available as a free plugin for many popular web browsers including Internet Explorer, Firefox, Chrome, and Safari. For paid subscribers, LastPass offers additional protection such as entering your password using your mouse on a virtual screen keyboard to protect yourself from keyloggers and keysniffers.

In May 2011, however, cybercriminals breached the LastPass servers and possibly stole email addresses of users, the server salt, and the salted password hashes from the LastPass database (70). LastPass responded quickly and notified their users to change their master passwords as a precaution. The company subsequently improved their server security and rolled out PBKDF2 (Password-Based Key Derivation Function 2) using SHA-256 (a SHA-2 Secure Hash Algorithm) on their servers with a 256-bit salt utilizing 100,000 rounds.

Designed by the National Security Agency (NSA), SHA-2 is significantly better than its predecessor SHA-1 — a cryptographic hash function with weak collision resistance. In June 2012, cybercriminals stole 6.5 million LinkedIn passwords and posted them on an online forum (24). Since the LinkedIn passwords were encoded using SHA-1, about half of the encrypted passwords have been decrypted and posted online.

Two-factor authentication adds an extra layer of security to password protection by requiring users to enter a random code that is sent to their mobile device before granting access to their accounts online.

My books *Counterterrorism and Cybersecurity: Total Information Awareness* (71) and *Read Me First: Password Protection and Identity Theft Prevention (2nd Edition)* (72) detail many more stories and ideas about how to protect your valuable information and accounts online.

17.5 Password Security Questions

In the movie *Now You See Me* (2013), four illusionists were known for magically "robbing from the rich and giving to the poor" by pulling off bank heists during their live performances (73). They were able to unsuspiciously obtain the mother's maiden name and the name of the first pet from an unsuspecting victim in order to reset his back account password.

In real life, 20-year-old college student David Kernell hacked into Republican vice presidential candidate Sarah Palin's Yahoo! email account in September 2008 to look for information that would derail her campaign (74). Kernell managed to reset Palin's account password by entering her birth date and correctly answering the security question "Where did you meet your spouse?" It only took Kernell 45 minutes on Wikipedia and Google search to find the correct answer.

There is also the infamous "tinkerbell hack" that refers to Paris Hilton's T-mobile account hack (75). The attacker was able to answer Hilton's password reset security question, "What is the name of your pet?" The answer was simple: "Tinkerbell."

To prevent someone from hacking into your online account through password security questions, do not answer the online security questions straightforwardly. Instead, treat each security answer as a password or be creative in your answer. Here are some good examples:

1. Question: Where did you meet your spouse?
   Answer: lunchvtmay1980 (Meaning: During lunch at Virginia Tech in May 1980)
2. Question: What was the name of your first school?
   Answer: vanillaicecream (Meaning: Your first school reminds you of Vanilla ice cream.)
3. Question: What is your pet's name?
   Answer: squarerootofminus1 (Meaning: Since the square root of minus 1 is an imaginary number, you don't have a real pet but you may have an imaginary pet.)
4. Question: What is your pet's name?
   Answer: saturdaynightlive1979skit (Meaning: You do have a pet who reminds you of a skit in a 1979 TV show "Saturday Night Live.")

17.6 Privacy Protection

We all have dealt with annoying cold calls from telemarketers. Since 2004, the National Do Not Call Registry has allowed us to register a phone number to limit the telemarketing calls we receive (76). As for unsolicited text spam, we can reply "STOP" and forward the text to the shortcode 7726 (which spells "SPAM") (77).

Financial companies have the freedom to choose how they share our personal information. U.S. Federal law gives consumers the right to limit some but not all sharing. Federal law also requires financial companies to inform us how they collect, share, and protect our personal information.

Take the Target REDcard credit card as an example, its February 2012 privacy policy states that the types of personal information they collect and share can include: social security number, income, purchase history, payment history, credit history, and credit scores. These information may be used for their everyday business purposes, marketing purposes, joint marketing with other financial companies, affiliates' everyday business purposes, and non-affiliates to market to us. Under Federal law, consumers can limit the sharing of information for non-affiliates only by informing Target.

Some financial companies provide consumers more privacy choices than what the Federal law mandates. In February 2012, the JPMorgan Chase credit card, for instance, allowed their customers to restrict information sharing with Chase's affiliates as well as non-affiliates with whom Chase does business. Consumers can opt out the information sharing by phone, postal mail, or logging onto the Chase website.

Facebook and Google privacy policies, on the other hand, are more confusing to users than credit card agreements. A survey released in April 2012 by strategic branding firm Siegel+Gale revealed that the majority of Facebook and Google users do not fully comprehend the privacy policies and are ignorant of personal data management (78). Among the 400+ respondents, the survey found that:

1. Less than 40% of Facebook users understand how an Application Programming Interface (API) can be used to access their information on Facebook.
2. Only 15% of users know what will happen to their Facebook accounts after they delete them.
3. Just 20% of respondents know how to block outside applications and websites from accessing their information on Facebook.
4. Only 23% of Google users realize that their profile is visible to anyone online.
5. Less than 50% of Google users are aware that the same Google privacy policy applies to Google Talk, Google Maps, YouTube, and Blogger.
6. Just 38% of people realize that Google connects search activity to a user's IP address whether or not they sign into a Google account.

In February 2014, Facebook announced its $19 billion acquisition of WhatsApp, a text messaging application with 450 million users (79). Unbeknown to the general public, software developer Thijs Alkemade discovered in October 2013 that WhatsApp had a major design flaw in its cryptographic implementation that could allow attackers to decrypt intercepted messages (80). Until the security flaw is fixed, Germany's privacy regulator urges WhatsApp uses to switch to more secure messaging services such as Threema and myEnigma that employ end-to-end encryption (81).

17.7 Privacy on Facebook

1. Think twice before uploading anything to Facebook.

Even if you delete a Facebook account, the deleted photos may still be accessible through other means. The old content may be stored on Facebook servers for a month to three years or longer (82). Deleting a Facebook account does not remove the messages that you post on other people's timelines.

2. Review and set individual privacy settings carefully to control who sees your contact information, posts, and timeline, etc.

In general, the choices are public (everyone), friends of friends, friend only, and only me. The most open setting is "public (everyone)" and the most private is "only me." Facebook Help Center offers the comprehensive privacy controls by feature (83), and you can control sharing and finding you on Facebook (84).

3. Turn on the option to review tagged posts and tagged photos.

Facebook allows you to use the privacy settings to turn on the option to "review posts friends tag you in before they appear on your timeline" (85). You can also turn off "suggest photos of me to friends" in the privacy settings (86), but your friends can still tag you manually. As for tags from non-friends, Facebook automatically requires your approval before they go on your timeline.

4. Always check the privacy policy of a Facebook app before installing.

Facebook apps have access to your personal information on Facebook. The apps can keep your data even after you delete the apps (87). Do not install a Facebook app that you do not feel comfortable sharing your personal data with. Keep in mind that Facebook's "frictionless sharing" facilitates someone to find out something about you without you telling them. *Mashable* editor Lauren Hockenson offered a detail account of what to look out for with the new Facebook Open Graph (88) that enables third-party apps to integrate deeply into the Facebook experience (89). On Facebook, you can control the sharing of information with other websites and applications (90).

5. Adjust public search listing when appropriate.

Facebook by default creates a public search listing for all accounts that belong to users 18 years of age and older. If you do not want people to find your Facebook page on Google, Yahoo!, and other search engines, you can use the privacy settings to turn off "public search" (91).

6. Accept friend requests only from friends that you know.

For socializing with people other than your own friends, Facebook offers non-personal pages for building relationships with your audience and customers (92).

The categories include entertainment, artist or public figure, cause or community, brand or product, company or organization, and local business or place.

7. Use Facebook Anonymous Login to sign into third-party apps.

Facebook's Anonymous Login allows users to sign into apps without sharing their identities and personal information contained in their Facebook accounts (93).

8. Forward suspected phishing messages to Facebook at phish@fb.com.

Phishing is typically carried out by email spoofing or instant messaging that often directs users to enter details at a fake website whose look and feel are almost identical to the legitimate one. Be part of the solution protecting everyone's privacy, forward suspected phishing messages to Facebook at phish@fb.com (94).

9. Opt out of Facebook's interest-based advertising.

Facebook tracks its users even after they have logged out of the service (95). The "Do Not Track" setting in a web browser has no effect on Facebook (96). Go to Digital Advertising Alliance (http://www.aboutads.info/choices/) and opt-out of Facebook and other participating companies that are tracking your online behavior. See Chapter 4 Section 4.5 ("Facebook User Tracking Bug and Online Behavioral Tracking") for more details.

10. Follow Facebook's own advice from "3 Tips to Help Manage Privacy on Facebook".

In March 2014, Facebook sent its users an email titled "3 Tips to Help Manage Privacy on Facebook" which listed a few ways to help control what we share on Facebook:

I. Check out who can see your past posts—and limit the audience if you're not comfortable with anything.

   a. You can review the audience for your past posts in your activity log (https://m.facebook.com/home.php?_rdr)

   b. To quickly limit the audience of old posts to Friends, visit your privacy settings (https://m.facebook.com/privacy/touch/masher)

II. Consider who you're sharing with today. Each time you post a new photo, status update, link or other content, you get to set the privacy for it. Using the audience selector, you can choose one of the following:

   a. Share big ideas for anyone in the world, set the post to Public.

   b. Reserve personal pictures for the people you know the best, set the post to Friends, Close Friends or Custom.

   c. Share something with someone specific, you can also send it as a message instead of posting it.

III. To review or change who can see your stuff, any time, visit your privacy shortcuts.

17.8 Privacy on Google

1. Control personalized ads on Google search and Gmail.

Google allows you to opt out of Google search ads and Gmail ads that are personalized based on your Google search strings and email content respectively (97). While unsolicited ads can be as annoying as junk mail, the right kind of targeted ads can be beneficial to consumers however.

2. Turn off Find My Face.

Find my Face offers name tag suggestions to you and to people you know to quickly tag photos. Google+ uses the photos you are tagged in to create a model of your face. If you turn off Find my Face, your face model is deleted. However, any name tags already added are not deleted. By default, Find my Face is turned off (98).

3. Opt out of Google shared endorsements.

Pulling data from +1s and reviews, a Google+ user's name and profile photo may appear in ads across all Google products including Google Maps and Google Search. To opt out of Google shared endorsements, go to https://plus.google.com/settings/endorsements and uncheck the box next to "Based upon my activity, Google may show my name and profile photo in shared endorsements that appear in ads" (99).

4. Turn on "Do Not Track" on your Internet browser.

Much like the popular Do Not Call registry, Do Not Track gives you the choice to opt out of tracking by third-party websites, applications, and advertising networks. The Federal Trade Commission (FTC) has asked the industry for their voluntary compliance of Do Not Track. FTC chairman Jon Leibowitz said in March 2012, "Do Not Track from our perspective certainly means 'do not collect' — not 'do not advertise back. If a real Do Not Track option doesn't come to fruition by the end of the year, there will be, I don't want to say a tsunami of support for Do Not Track legislation next Congress, but certainly a lot of support" (100).

You can check to see if your Internet browser supports Do Not Track and if it has been enabled or not, by visiting http://donottrack.us/ (101). Some popular anti-virus software such as AVG has Do Not Track feature that is enabled by default. Microsoft announced in May 2012 that IE10 in Windows 8 would send the "Do Not Track" signal to web sites by default to help consumers protect their privacy (102). You may also use online tracking detection tools such as Ghostery, Disconnect, and Privacy Badger from the Electronic Frontier Foundation (EFF) to discover if you are being tracked by a website (103).

5. Accept only session cookies and block all other cookies.

Session cookies are short-lived cookies that last only as long as your browser is open. Cookies are small chunks of information that websites can put on your computer to track your activities, also known as your web history. When you create a Google Account, web history is automatically turned on (104). You can remove you web history at https://www.google.com/history, but it does not stop Google from recording your search activity. A word of caution: some websites may not work without enabling both session cookies and first-party cookies.

In March 2021, Google announced that it will stop tracking individual's web browsing for advertising purposes as its Chrome browser drops third-party cookies. Federated Learning of Cohorts (FLoC) will replace cookies. Google product manager Chetna Bindra explains, "Advertising is essential to keeping the web open for everyone, but the web ecosystem is at risk if privacy practices do not keep up with changing expectations. People want assurances that their identity and information are safe as they browse the web. … FLoC proposes a new way for businesses to reach people with relevant content and ads by clustering large groups of people with similar interests. This approach effectively hides individuals 'in the crowd' and uses on-device processing to keep a person's web history private on the browser" (105).

6. Opt out of Google's interest-based advertising.

Go to Digital Advertising Alliance (http://www.aboutads.info/choices/) and opt-out of Google and other participating companies that are tracking your online behavior. See Chapter 4 Section 4.4 ("Facebook User Tracking Bug and Online Behavioral Tracking") for more details.

7. Set up Google Alerts and send Google removal requests when necessary.

In addition to Googling yourself periodically, set up Google Alerts at http://www.google.com/alerts to monitor the web 24/7 for any news and videos about yourself (61). You can receive an alert once a week, once a day, or as-it-happens. If a Google search reveals anything inappropriate, you can send Google a request at https://www.google.com/webmasters/tools/removals to remove search links to web pages, images, and blogs for legal reasons (106). For YouTube videos, you can initiate a privacy complaint process online (107).

8. Opt out of all background check websites.

Google search indexes information on many background check websites including Intelius.com, WhitePages.com, and Spokeo.com, to name a few. To opt out, you will have to visit each and every background check website and make the request. For example, the Intelius Opt-Out page is https://www.intelius.com/optout.php A partial list of opt-out web links can be found on Reddit:

http://www.reddit.com/r/technology/comments/j1mit/how_to_remove_yourself_from_all_background_check/

9. Consider using web proxies and anonymizing software.

Since search activity is connected to a user's IP address, web proxies such as Privoxy (108) and anonymizing software like Tor (109) hide the user's real IP address. Anonymizer's Anonymous Surfing (110) is more user-friendly but their servers will have access to your original IP address. Blogger Jared Newman discussed in *Time Magazine* a list of applications and services to help you stay anonymous online: PrivacyScore, Disconnect, SafeShepherd, Cocoon, AnchorFree HotspotShield, LBE Privacy Guard, Tor, and Burn Note (111).

17.9 Privacy on Smartphones

1. Turn off location services on your Android and Apple iOS devices.

The location services function can be turned on or off in Android's setting menu. It is off by default. However, Apple, Microsoft, and RIM turn on location services by default. However, your cell phone registers its location with cell phone networks several times a minute, and this function cannot be turned off when the phone is getting a wireless signal. Moreover, each mobile user's daily movements can be used to create a unique digital fingerprint over an extended period of time (112). Therefore, it is possible to identify smartphone users by analyzing anonymous location data to look for patterns. American Civil Liberties Union reported in April 2012 that most police track phones' locations without warrants (113).

In June and July 2014, Russian soldier Alexander Sotkin posted two selfies on Instagram, being unaware that his phone logged the coordinates where the photos were taken and that location data were uploaded to the Instagram Photo Map. As a result, he inadvertently revealed that he was on the Ukrainian side during the time of conflict (114). In August 2014, *The Wall Street Journal* revealed that the revamped foursquare mobile app tracks its user's GPS coordinates even when the app is closed (115).

In case you may forget to turn off location services after using Google Maps, Prof. Janne Lindqvist at Rutgers University has developed an Android app to automatically warn you when apps are tracking your location. "Because we know how ubiquitous NSA surveillance is, this is one tool to make people aware," said Lindqvist (116).

2. Remove Carrier IQ on your Android devices.

A free Android app "Voodoo Carrier IQ Detector" can be used to detect the presence of Carrier IQ on your smartphone (117). In December 2011, Federal Bureau of Investigation director Robert Mueller testified before the US Congress, "We may obtain information that in some way Carrier IQ may have been involved with. ... [but the FBI] has neither sought nor obtained any information from Carrier IQ in any one of our investigations" (118).

3. Turn off automatic scanning for WiFi networks when you are not using WiFi.

When a smartphone is automatically scanning for WiFi networks nearby, it is continually making contact with all the WiFi routers within range. These WiFi providers can capture the ID number of your smartphone even if you do not connect to them or the WiFi is turned off. To disable WiFi scanning on an Android smartphone, uncheck "Scanning always available" option in the Advanced WiFi menu under Wireless & Networks (119).

4. Do not access unsecured websites (sites that begin with "http://") when using public WiFi.

Sites that being with "https://" are encrypted but sites with "http://" are not. Cybercriminals can intercept data transmitted to and from unencrypted websites. Security firm Immunity Inc. demonstrated the WiFi hazards with its Stalker tool that compiles a profile of a person by his online activities on Match.com, Tinder, Amazon.com, Pandora, Instagram, and other unencrypted sites (120).

5. Opt out of interest-based advertising.

You can stop companies from tracking your online behavior by opting out of interest-based advertising on your mobile devices:

a) Apple: Open iPhone Settings and go to General > Restrictions > Advertising, and then click "Limit Ad Tracking."
b) Android: Go to Google Settings > Ads > Opt Out of Interest-Based Ads, and click.
c) Windows: Go to Settings > System Applications > Advertising ID, and opt-out by setting the Advertising ID to "Off."

6. Turn off your smartphone while shopping.

U.S. retailers including American Apparel, Family Dollar, Home Depot, and Nordstrom have experimented with indoor GPS to track customers' shopping behaviors (121). Your indoor location can be tracked by either the mobile device's MAC address or Apple's iBeacon Bluetooth.

7. Remove the battery when the phone is turned off.

A cell network tower can tell your phone to fake any shutdown and stay on to record conversations through the microphone or track its GPS location (122). Removing the battery eliminates the risk of eavesdropping and location tracking.

8. Use secured apps for chatting, texting, and phone calls.

The "Reset the Net" campaign, in consultation with Electronic Frontier Foundation (EFF), published in June 2014 a Privacy Pack that recommends ChatSecure for secure chat with Google and XMPP users, TextSecure for strong protection of text messages, RedPhone for strong privacy for phone calls, and Cryptocat for chatting in secure groups (123).

9. Consider using a secure smartphone for both the caller and the receiver.

In February 2014, Blackphone was debuted at Mobile World Congress in Barcelona, Spain. "The entire reason for the phone to exist is to protect your privacy," says Phil Zimmermann, Blackphone cofounder who invented the PGP (Pretty Good Privacy) encryption system. "We are not a phone company adding a privacy feature; we are a privacy company selling a phone" (124). Blackphone includes Silent Circle apps which encrypt voice, text, and e-mail, anonymous search and private browsing tools, and secure cloud storage. "There is no such thing as a completely secure phone," forewarned Silent Circle CEO and former Navy SEAL Mike Janke. "Nothing is going to protect you from your own behavior. But out of the box, this phone does a lot of things to protect your privacy." (125)

10. Consider changing your smartphone often in order to avoid accelerometer fingerprinting.

Due to hardware imperfections of accelerometers, the raw movements of a smartphone—which can be measured without permission—can produce a unique fingerprint and allow it to be tracked over time (126). "There has been a lot of work to catch the leakage of ID information from phones," said Romit Roy Choudhury, associate professor of Electrical Engineering and Computer Science at the University of Illinois at Urbana Champaign. "We are now saying that accelerometer data going out of the phone can be treated as an ID" (127).

11. Beware of leaving sensitive data behind when you recycle your old smartphone.

When you delete a file, it is still there, just that it is no longer visible to you. U.K. mobile phone security firm BlackBelt explains, "In reality, it isn't possible for an individual to perform a full removal of personal data from any smart phone or tablet using a device's in-built factory reset or by re-flashing the operating system. This is because contemporary devices are fitted with solid state memory, which uses a technique called wear leveling to minimize data corruption and extend its lifespan by over-ruling instructions to permanently overwrite old data" (128).

BlackBelt and several other security companies offer their software solutions to effectively erase data from most handsets running a variety of operating systems (129). To ensure the destruction of top-secret digital data, the U.S. government employs companies specializing in secure data sanitization and electronics recycling to destroy hard drives, computers, monitors, phones, and other electronic equipment. "They actually shred the drives while you watch and provide a certification sheet after the process," said Scott Pearce, chief information security officer for Frederick County government (130).

Your smartphone data may also be backed up in the cloud such as Apple's iCloud, Google Drive, or Microsoft's OneDrive. As Mary Elizabeth Winstead wrote after the nude photos of her and other celebrities were stolen and leaked to the public, "Knowing those photos were deleted long ago, I can only imagine the creepy effort that went into this. Feeling for everyone who got hacked" (131). In the digital world, delete does not always delete.

In April 2021, Apple launched a new anti-tracking functionality in iOS 14.5 and iPadOS 14.5. Apple explains the rationale for anti-tracking, "Advertising that respects privacy is not only possible, it was the standard until the growth of the Internet" (132). To comply with Apple's new rules, all mobile apps must present a popup that lets users agree to or disable ad tracking. "The App Store now helps users better understand an app's privacy practices before they download the app on any Apple platform. On each app's product page, users can learn about some of the data types the app may collect, and whether that data is linked to them or used to track them. You'll need to provide information about your app's privacy practices, including the practices of third-party partners whose code you integrate into your app, in App Store Connect. This information is required to submit new apps and app updates to the App Store" (133).

17.10   Data Vault – Data is the New Oil

In normal everyday life, we need to conduct business with financial institutions, online shops, and government agencies. The Locker Project in 2011 elaborates, "As we go through our lives we create vast amounts of data. Emails, phone calls, social network posts, photos, utility bills, health monitoring devices, text messages, browsing data, purchase receipts and more are all born out of the regular course of our actions. It's more than just data. It represents our actions, interests, intentions, communications, relationships, locations, behaviors and creative and consumptive efforts" (134). The Locker Project provides open-source application programming interfaces (APIs) for developers to build applications to access and control personal data.

While Facebook, Google, and other online businesses collect information about us and make billions of dollars from selling our data, what if we can organize our own information online in a secure "data vault" so that we may even be compensated for sharing that information? (135).

A data vault is the digital counterpart of a bank vault where money, valuables, and important documents can be stored. Our individual data vault will contain the photos we take, the places we visit, the links we share, contact details for the people we communicate with, and many other personal information.

Founded by Kaliya Hamlin in June 2011, Personal Data Ecosystem Consortium brings together startup companies that are developing tools and systems for personal control over personal data. Hamlin wrote, "Privacy protections are just the tip of the iceberg; the industry of managing these assets wisely is in the process of creating new economic opportunities and is a magnet for talent and capital. … Our vision for the ecosystem is inclusive of a wide range of potential services and business models, while holding true to the core non-negotiable that people are ultimately in control of the sum of their data" (136).

Singly is one of the startups acquired by Appcelerator in August 2013. It offers an open platform where people can store their personal data after pulling it in from multiple sources such as Facebook posts, purchase histories from Amazon, past search queries from Google, and email contacts (137). Singly supports the open source The Locker Project and the new protocol TeleHash that enables lockers to connect with one another to share things (138).

Another startup – Personal – states that "small data is the new oil" as big data is rapidly becoming a commodity (139). Personal allows users to enter their personal information in structured data fields within categories ranging from banking to shopping to babysitting. "What we envisioned was effectively creating a matchmaking marketplace, and it's very predicated on online dating," said Personal's president and CEO Shane Green, "Consumers will assume the role of women, who are typically the choosier sex on dating sites, and the marketplace will employ a ranking methodology to show which deals a user is most compatible" (140).

Steve McNally, CTO at True/Slant, wrote on *Forbes* about our lives online, "All that time spent and an unprecedented level of detail about how we've spent it – and it's mostly detail others have about you but you don't see yourself" (141).

By collecting and analyzing our own digital footprint and exhaust data online, we will eventually get a more complete picture of our lives. For financial gains, we can sell the data to businesses who want us to be their customers. For personal analytics, we can use the data to help us make better life decisions and self-improvements.

17.11   Personal Analytics and Social Networks

The quantified self movement has been gaining popularity as we incorporate new technology into data acquisition on various aspects of our daily life such as caloric intake, calories burned, sleep quality, heart rate, blood-sugar level, and even mood change. Some of these personal data collected by mobile apps and wearable devices may also be uploaded to social networks.

Reports have shown that social networks can help people stay on the path to physical fitness. Social apps that track and share their fitness habits make them feel more accountable. Fitocracy, a 500 Startups accelerator program alum, is a fitness social network and online game on iPhone with almost half a million users. Canadian Virginia Champoux told CNN that Fitocracy kept her diligent about her workouts, "It is motivational and it offers me support. It's the social aspect that helps" (142).

The Nike+ sports community has more than 5 million members who share their runs and profiles with friends online. Nike's Global Digital Brand and Innovation Director Jesse Stollak said, "The Nike+ community has grown tremendously in past couple years with the addition of new products like the Nike+ GPS App and Nike+ GPS Sportwatch. We've added new features like the new Maps site, which leverages a wealth of run route data to provide recommendations. We also included the 'cheer me on' functionality inside the Nike+ GPS app, which taps into the runners' friends on Facebook for additional motivation and support. When they are running, they hear applause on top of their music when friends 'cheer' them" (143).

Martin Blinder, founder and CEO of Tictrac, spoke at the 2011 Intelligence Squared's If Conference, "We leave a data residue everywhere. ... New formats are enabling us to bring data sets together and drive compelling insights. ... What if I could compare myself to others? I could understand if certain activities in my life are normal, above average, etc. Does my daughter catch too many colds? Do I spend too much on shoes given my salary? Is my sex life normal for my age, job and location? A lot of these questions are in the back of my mind. We think about them, but we don't talk about them. The benefit of this is that we are able to improve ourselves. ... Personal analytics means we can stop lying to ourselves and start leading healthier lives, making better choices, fewer mistakes and have control over our wellbeing" (144).

Personal analytics combined with social networks provide a high-tech mechanism for self-help and self-improvement. The success in physical fitness applications is only the beginning. Apple, in partnership with Mayo Clinic, launched the "Health" app and data-sharing platform "HealthKit" in June 2014 to keep track of patients' health indicators and share the vital data with healthcare professionals (145). "If you see the glucose levels rising," said John Ward, Mayo's medical director for public affairs, "you could interact with [the patient] if they had a question, intervene appropriately, and then decrease the need for an emergency room visit or a hospital admission, which we know drives up hospital and patient costs" (146).

17.12 Community Analytics and Social Networks

Extending personal analytics to community analytics can be beneficial to the society at large. PatientsLikeMe is the largest patient social network with over 250,000 people with chronic diseases who share information about symptoms, treatments, and coping mechanisms. In April 2014, PatientsLikeMe granted the biotechnology company Genentech full access to its database for five years (147). PatientsLikeMe co-founder and chairman Jamie Heywood explained, "We envision a world where patient experience drives the way diseases are measured and medical advances are made. With Genentech we can now embark on a journey to bring together many stakeholders across healthcare and collaborate with patients in a new way" (148).

Genentech's senior vice president Bruce Cooper, M.D. concurred, "The collaboration with PatientsLikeMe will allow us to learn more from patients with serious diseases, and better integrate their insights into our decision-making. We hope our participation will encourage broader engagement of others involved in the delivery of healthcare and support a stronger voice for patients" (148).

However, there are pros and cons to community analytics. "The beauty of observational trials," said University of Pittsburgh professor Mark Roberts, "is that you can see how an intervention works in the real world" (149). But potential bias exists for any self-reported data, as Roberts warned, "What kinds of patients are willing to report their data? Is it the full range of disease? Were people who didn't do well as likely to report findings as those who did?" (149). The effectiveness of community analytics largely depends on the individuals who make up the community.

References

1. **Lapowsky, Issie.** How Cambridge Analytica Sparked the Great Privacy Awakening. [Online] Wired, March 17, 2019. https://www.wired.com/story/cambridge-analytica-facebook-privacy-awakening/.
2. **Duffy, Clare.** 500 million LinkedIn users' data is for sale on a hacker site. [Online] CNN Business, April 8, 2021. https://www.cnn.com/2021/04/08/tech/linkedin-data-scraped-hacker-site/index.html.
3. **Intelius.** Intelius Facts. [Online] Intelius. [Cited: January 25, 2012.] http://www.intelius.com/corp/intelius-facts.
4. **The Associated Press.** U.K. phone hacking leads to arrest of ex-Cameron aide. [Online] The Associated Press, July 8, 2011. http://www.cbc.ca/news/world/story/2011/07/08/phone-hacking-cameron.html.
5. **Cieply, Michael.** Actress's Suit Against IMDb for Publishing Her Actual Age Can Go to Trial. [Online] The New York Times, March 19, 2013. http://mediadecoder.blogs.nytimes.com/2013/03/19/actresss-suit-against-imdb-for-publishing-her-actual-age-can-go-to-trial/.
6. **Haley, Kevin.** Introducing the Symantec Smartphone Honey Stick Project. [Online] Symantec Official Blog, March 9, 2012. http://www.symantec.com/connect/blogs/introducing-symantec-smartphone-honey-stick-project.
7. **Symantec Corporation.** The Symantec Smartphone Honey Stick Project. [Online] Symantec Corporation, 2012. http://www.symantec.com/content/en/us/about/presskits/b-symantec-smartphone-honey-stick-project.en-us.pdf.
8. **Sager, Mike.** What I've Learned: Andy Grove. [Online] Esquire Magazine, May 1, 2000. http://www.esquire.com/features/what-ive-learned/learned-andy-grove-0500.
9. **Gross, Doug.** Manage (and make cash with?) your data online. [Online] CNN, February 27, 2012. http://www.cnn.com/2012/02/24/tech/web/owning-your-data-online/index.html.
10. **Constine, Josh.** Facebook Could Slow Down A Tiny Bit As It Starts Switching All Users To Secure HTTPS Connections. [Online] TechCrunch, November 18, 2012. http://techcrunch.com/2012/11/18/facebook-https/.
11. **pzdupe1 and pzdupe2.** You can now connect to Facebook on your phone without leaving a digital trail. [Online] Business Insider, January 19, 2016. https://www.businessinsider.com/facebook-tor-android-2016-1.
12. **Szoldra, Paul.** 1 million people are now connecting to Facebook without leaving a digital trail. [Online] Business Insider India, April 22, 2016. https://www.businessinsider.in/1-million-people-are-now-connecting-to-Facebook-without-leaving-a-digital-trail/articleshow/51948910.cms.
13. **Pagliery, Jose.** Half of American adults hacked this year. [Online] CNNMoney, May 28, 2014. http://money.cnn.com/2014/05/28/technology/security/hack-data-breach/.
14. **O'Sullivan, Donie.** Half a billion Facebook users' information posted on hacking website, cyber experts say. [Online] CNN Business, April 4, 2021. https://www.cnn.com/2021/04/04/tech/facebook-user-info-leaked/index.html.
15. **Duffy, Clare.** Facebook will not notify the 533 million users exposed in online database. [Online] CNN Business, April 9, 2021. https://www.cnn.com/2021/04/09/tech/facebook-hack-user-notification/index.html.
16. **Jewell, Mark.** TJX breach could top 94 million accounts. [Online] NBC News, October 24, 2007. http://www.msnbc.msn.com/id/21454847/ns/technology_and_science-security/t/tjx-breach-could-top-million-accounts/.
17. **Cubrilovic, Nik.** RockYou Hack: From Bad To Worse. [Online] TechCrunch, December 14, 2009. http://techcrunch.com/2009/12/14/rockyou-hack-security-myspace-facebook-passwords/.
18. **Krebs, Brian.** PlentyofFish.com Hacked, Blames Messenger. [Online] KrebsOnSecurity.com, January 31, 2011. http://krebsonsecurity.com/2011/01/plentyoffish-com-hacked-blames-messenger/.

19. **Hickins, Michael and Clark, Don.** Questions Over Break-In at Security Firm RSA. [Online] The Wall Street Journal, March 18, 2011. http://online.wsj.com/article/SB10001424052748703512404576208983743029392.html.

20. **Wingfield, Nick, Sherr, Ian and Worthen, Ben.** Hacker Raids Sony Videogame Network. [Online] The Wall Street Journal, April 27, 2011. http://online.wsj.com/article/SB10001424052748703778104576287362503776534.html.

21. **Smith, Aaron.** Citi: Millions stolen in May hack attack. [Online] CNNMoney, June 27, 2011. http://money.cnn.com/2011/06/27/technology/citi_credit_card/index.htm.

22. **Zakaria, Tabassum and Hosenball, Mark.** Stratfor Hack: Anonymous-Affiliated Hackers Publish Thousands Of Credit Card Numbers. [Online] Huffington Post, December 30, 2011. http://www.huffingtonpost.com/2011/12/30/stratfor-hack-anonymous_n_1176726.html.

23. **Acohido, Byron.** Credit card processor hit by hackers. [Online] USA Today, March 30, 2012. http://www.usatoday.com/money/industries/banking/story/2012-03-30/mastercard-security-breach/53887854/1.

24. **Goldman, David.** More than 6 million LinkedIn passwords stolen. [Online] CNNMoney, June 7, 2012. http://money.cnn.com/2012/06/06/technology/linkedin-password-hack/index.htm.

25. **eHarmony.com.** Update on Compromised Passwords. [Online] eHarmony Blog, June 6, 2012. http://www.eharmony.com/blog/2012/06/06/update-on-compromised-passwords/#.U5ynqssU914.

26. **Gross, Doug.** Yahoo hacked, 450,000 passwords posted online. [Online] CNN, July 13, 2012. http://www.cnn.com/2012/07/12/tech/web/yahoo-users-hacked/index.html.

27. **Riley, Charles.** Barnes & Noble customer data stolen. [Online] CNNMoney, October 24, 2012. http://money.cnn.com/2012/10/24/technology/barnes%2D%2Dnoble-hack/index.html.

28. **Lord, Bob.** Keeping our users secure. [Online] Twitter Blog, February 1, 2013. http://blog.twitter.com/2013/02/keeping-our-users-secure.html.

29. **Bull, Alister and Finkle, Jim.** Fed says internal site breached by hackers, no critical functions affected. [Online] Reuters, February 6, 2013. http://www.reuters.com/article/2013/02/06/net-us-usa-fed-hackers-idUSBRE91501920130206.

30. **Engberg, Dave.** Security Notice: Service-wide Password Reset. [Online] The Evernote Blog, March 2, 2013. http://blog.evernote.com/blog/2013/03/02/security-notice-service-wide-password-reset/.

31. **Arkin, Brad.** Important Customer Security Announcement. [Online] Adobe Featured Blogs, October 3, 2013. http://blogs.adobe.com/conversations/2013/10/important-customer-security-announcement.html.

32. **Wallace, Gregory.** Neiman Marcus hack hit 1.1 million customers. [Online] CNNMoney, January 23, 2014. http://money.cnn.com/2014/01/23/news/companies/neiman-marcus-hack/.

33. **Isidore, Chris.** Target: Hacking hit up to 110 million customers. [Online] CNNMoney, January 11, 2014. http://money.cnn.com/2014/01/10/news/companies/target-hacking/index.html.

34. **Lobosco, Katie.** Michaels hack hit 3 million. [Online] CNN, April 18, 2014. http://money.cnn.com/2014/04/17/news/companies/michaels-security-breach/.

35. **Gross, Doug.** Millions of accounts compromised in Snapchat hack. [Online] CNN, January 2, 2014. http://www.cnn.com/2014/01/01/tech/social-media/snapchat-hack/.

36. **eBay.** eBay Inc. To Ask eBay Users To Change Passwords. [Online] ebay inc., May 21, 2014. http://investor.ebayinc.com/releasedetail.cfm?ReleaseID=849396.

37. **AOL Mail Team.** AOL Security Update. [Online] Aol Blog, April 28, 2014. http://blog.aol.com/2014/04/28/aol-security-update/.

38. **Smith, Aaron.** P.F. Chang's confirms credit data was stolen. [Online] CNNMoney, June 13, 2014. http://money.cnn.com/2014/06/13/technology/security/pf-changs-security/index.html.

39. **Perlroth, Nicole and Gelles, David.** Russian Hackers Amass Over a Billion Internet Passwords. [Online] The New York Times, August 5, 2014. http://www.nytimes.

com/2014/08/06/technology/russian-gang-said-to-amass-more-than-a-billion-stolen-internet-credentials.html.

40. **Cooper, Charles.** Celebs, beware: Those nude selfies will be hacked and shared. [Online] CNet, September 2, 2014. http://www.cnet.com/news/the-new-price-of-celebrity-careful-before-taking-that-nudie-selfie/.

41. **Perlroth, Nicole.** Home Depot Data Breach Could Be the Largest Yet. [Online] The New York Times, September 8, 2014. http://bits.blogs.nytimes.com/2014/09/08/home-depot-confirms-that-it-was-hacked/.

42. **Terhune, Chad.** UCLA Health System data breach affects 4.5 million patients. [Online] Los Angeles Times, July 17, 2015. https://www.latimes.com/business/la-fi-ucla-medical-data-20150717-story.html.

43. **Williams, Martyn.** OPM hackers stole data on 21.5M people, including 1.1M fingerprints. [Online] Computerworld, July 9, 2015. https://www.computerworld.com/article/2946031/opm-hackers-stole-data-on-215m-people-including-11m-fingerprints.html.

44. **Pagliery, Jose.** Instagram-tracking app actually stole your password. [Online] CNN Business, November 12, 2015. https://money.cnn.com/2015/11/12/technology/instaagent-instagram/index.html.

45. **Kan, Michael.** Yahoo reports massive data breach involving 1 billion accounts. [Online] PC World, December 14, 2016. https://www.pcworld.com/article/3150670/yahoo-reports-massive-data-breach-involving-1-billion-accounts.html.

46. **Larson, Selena.** Stuffed toys leak millions of voice recordings from kids and parents. [Online] CNN Business, February 27, 2017. https://money.cnn.com/2017/02/27/technology/cloudpets-data-leak-voices-photos/index.html.

47. **Profis, Sharon.** Equifax data breach: Find out if you were one of 143 million hacked. [Online] CNet, September 11, 2017. https://www.cnet.com/how-to/equifax-data-breach-find-out-if-you-were-one-of-143-million-hacked/.

48. **Etherington, Darrell.** Uber data breach from 2016 affected 57 million riders and drivers. [Online] TechCrunch, November 21, 2017.

49. **England, R.** Hackers gain access to millions of T-Mobile customer details. [Online] Engadget, August 24, 2018. https://www.engadget.com/2018-08-24-hackers-access-millions-t-mobile-customer-details.html.

50. **McLean, Rob.** A hacker gained access to 100 million Capital One credit card applications and accounts. [Online] CNN Business, July 30, 2019. https://www.cnn.com/2019/07/29/business/capital-one-data-breach/index.html.

51. **Scroxton, Alex.** Carnival cruise lines hit by ransomware, customer data stolen. [Online] Computer Weekly, August 18, 2020. https://www.computerweekly.com/news/252487779/Carnival-cruise-lines-hit-by-ransomware-customer-data-stolen.

52. **Scullion, Chris.** The entirety of Twitch has reportedly been leaked. *Video Games Chronicle*. [Online] October 6, 2021. https://www.videogameschronicle.com/news/the-entirety-of-twitch-has-reportedly-been-leaked/.

53. **Perlroth, Nicole.** Some Victims of Online Hacking Edge Into the Light. [Online] The New York Times, February 20, 2013. http://www.nytimes.com/2013/02/21/technology/hacking-victims-edge-into-light.html.

54. **John P. Mello, Jr.** McAfee Warns of Massive 5-Year Hacking Plot. [Online] PCWorld, August 3, 2011. http://www.pcworld.com/article/237163/McAfee_Warns_of_Massive_5_Year_Hacking_Plot.html.

55. **Cowley, Stacy.** FBI Director: Cybercrime will eclipse terrorism. [Online] CNNMoney, March 2, 2012. http://money.cnn.com/2012/03/02/technology/fbi_cybersecurity/index.htm.

56. **Ozawa, Nancy and Sullivan, Lesley.** A New Identity Fraud Victim Every Two Seconds in 2013 According to Latest Javelin Strategy & Research Study. [Online] Javelin Strategy and Research, February 5, 2014. https://www.javelinstrategy.com/news/1467/92/A-New-Identity-Fraud-Victim-Every-Two-Seconds-in-2013-According-to-Latest-Javelin-Strategy-Research-Study/.

57. **Federal Trade Commission.** About Identity Theft. [Online] Federal Trade Commission, April 16, 2007. https://web.archive.org/web/20070416061102/http://www.ftc.gov/bcp/edu/microsites/idtheft/consumers/about-identity-theft.html.

58. —. Deter. Detect. Defend. Fighting Back Against Identity Theft. [Online] Federal Trade Commission. [Cited: May 14, 2012.] http://www.ftc.gov/bcp/edu/pubs/consumer/idtheft/idt01.pdf.

59. **Federal Bureau of Investigation.** Malware Installed on Travelers' Laptops Through Software Updates on Hotel Internet Connections. [Online] Federal Bureau of Investigation, May 8, 2012. http://www.fbi.gov/scams-safety/e-scams.

60. **Tuerk, Andreas.** Giving you more insight into your Google Account activity. [Online] Google Official Blog, March 28, 2012. http://googleblog.blogspot.com/2012/03/giving-you-more-insight-into-your.html#!/2012/03/giving-you-more-insight-into-your.html.

61. **Google.** What are Google Alerts? [Online] Google Alerts. [Cited: May 25, 2012.] https://support.google.com/alerts/bin/answer.py?hl=en&answer=175925.

62. **Hoonakker, Peter, Bornoe, Nis and Carayon, Pascale.** Password Authentication from a Human Factors Perspective: Results of a Survey among End-Users. [Online] Proceedings of the Human Factors and Ergonomics Society 53Rd Annual Meeting, 2009. http://www.hfes.org/web/Newsroom/HFES09-Hoonaker-CIS.pdf.

63. **Kotadia, Munir.** Microsoft security guru: Jot down your passwords. [Online] CNet, May 23, 2005. http://news.cnet.com/Microsoft-security-guru-Jot-down-your-passwords/2100-7355_3-5716590.html.

64. **Cheng, Roger and McCullagh, Declan.** Yahoo breach: Swiped passwords by the numbers. [Online] CNet, July 12, 2012. http://news.cnet.com/8301-1009_3-57470878-83/yahoo-breach-swiped-passwords-by-the-numbers/.

65. **Ebrahimji, Alisha.** Yes, people are still using '123456' and 'password' as their password. [Online] CNN, November 19, 2020. https://www.cnn.com/2020/11/19/tech/common-passwords-2020-trnd/index.html.

66. **Timmer, John.** 30 years of failure: the username/password combination. [Online] Ars Technica, October 31, 2009. http://arstechnica.com/business/2009/10/30-years-of-failure-the-user-namepassword-combination/.

67. **Verizon RISK Team.** 2012 Data Breach Investigations Report. [Online] Verizon, 2012. http://www.verizonbusiness.com/resources/reports/rp_data-breach-investigations-report-2012_en_xg.pdf.

68. **Fung, Brian and Sands, Geneva.** Former SolarWinds CEO blames intern for 'solarwinds123' password leak. [Online] CNN, January 26, 2021. https://www.cnn.com/2021/02/26/politics/solarwinds123-password-intern/index.html.

69. **Anderson, Nate.** How I became a password cracker: Cracking passwords is officially a "script kiddie" activity now. [Online] Ars Technica, March 24, 2013. http://arstechnica.com/security/2013/03/how-i-became-a-password-cracker/.

70. **The LastPass Team.** LastPass Security Notification. [Online] LastPass, May 4, 2011. http://blog.lastpass.com/2011/05/lastpass-security-notification.html.

71. **Lee, Newton.** Counterterrorism and Cybersecurity: Total Information Awareness. [Online] Springer Science+Business Media, April 30, 2013. http://www.amazon.com/Counterterrorism-Cybersecurity-Total-Information-Awareness/dp/1461472040.

72. —. Read Me First: Password Protection and Identity Theft Prevention (2nd Edition). [Online] CreateSpace Independent Publishing Platform, July 13, 2013. http://www.amazon.com/Read-Me-First-Protection-Prevention/dp/1490988874.

73. **IMDB.** Now You See Me (2013). [Online] IMDB, May 31, 2013. http://www.imdb.com/title/tt1670345/.

74. **Danchev, Dancho.** Attacker: Hacking Sarah Palin's email was easy. [Online] ZDNet, September 18, 2008. http://www.zdnet.com/blog/security/attacker-hacking-sarah-palins-email-was-easy/1939.

75. **The Mad Dog.** tinkerbell hack. [Online] Urban Dictionary, March 15, 2010. http://www.urbandictionary.com/define.php?term=tinkerbell%20hack.

76. **Federal Trade Commission.** National Do Not Call Registry. [Online] Federal Trade Commission. [Cited: May 29, 2012.] https://www.donotcall.gov/.

77. **Gahran, Amy.** Getting text spam? New service helps you report it. [Online] CNN, March 19, 2012. http://www.cnn.com/2012/03/19/tech/mobile/text-spam-gahran/index.html.

78. **Siegel+Gale.** Survey Finds Facebook and Google Privacy Policies Even More Confusing Than Credit Card Bills and Government Notices. [Online] Siegel+Gale Press Releases, April 24, 2012. http://www.siegelgale.com/media_release/survey-finds-facebook-and-google-privacy-policies-even-more-confusing-than-credit-card-bills-and-government-notices/.

79. **Ember, Sydney.** Facebook's $16 Billion Deal for WhatsApp. [Online] The New York Times, February 20, 2014. http://dealbook.nytimes.com/2014/02/20/morning-agenda-facebooks-16-billion-deal-for-whatsapp/.

80. **Alkemade, Thijs.** Piercing Through WhatsApp's Encryption. [Online] xnyhps' blog, October 8, 2013. https://blog.thijsalkema.de/blog/2013/10/08/piercing-through-whatsapp-s-encryption/.

81. **Essers, Loek.** German privacy regulator: WhatsApp users should switch to a more secure service. [Online] PC World, February 20, 2014. http://www.pcworld.com/article/2099700/whatsapp-users-should-switch-to-a-more-secure-service-german-privacy-regulator-urges.html.

82. **Cheng, Jacqui.** Over 3 years later, "deleted" Facebook photos are still online. [Online] CNN, February 7, 2012. http://www.cnn.com/2012/02/06/tech/social-media/deleted-facebook-photos-online/index.html.

83. **Facebook Privacy.** Facebook Basics. Manage Your Account. Privacy. [Online] Facebook Help Center. [Cited: May 14, 2012.] http://www.facebook.com/help/?page=187475824633454.

84. **Facebook.** Sharing and finding you on Facebook. Facebook Data Use Policy. [Online] Facebook. [Cited: May 15, 2012.] http://www.facebook.com/about/privacy/your-info-on-fb.

85. **Facebook Privacy.** How do I turn on the option to review posts and photos I'm tagged in before they appear on my profile? [Online] Facebook Help Center. [Cited: May 15, 2012.] http://www.facebook.com/help/?faq=223100381057791.

86. **Mitchell, Justin.** Making Photo Tagging Easier. [Online] The Facebook Blog, June 30, 2011. http://blog.facebook.com/blog.php?post=467145887130.

87. **Johnston, Casey.** On Facebook, deleting an app doesn't delete your data from their system. [Online] Ars Technica, May 13, 2012. http://arstechnica.com/gadgets/2012/05/on-facebook-deleting-an-app-doesnt-delete-your-data-from-their-system/.

88. **Hockenson, Lauren.** 7 Big Privacy Concerns for New Facebook and the Open Graph. [Online] Mashable, January 27, 2012. http://mashable.com/2012/01/27/facebook-privacy-open-graph/.

89. **Facebook.** Open Graph. [Online] Facebook Developers. [Cited: May 15, 2012.] https://developers.facebook.com/docs/opengraph/.

90. —. Sharing with other websites and applications. [Online] Facebook Data Use Policy. [Cited: May 15, 2012.] http://www.facebook.com/about/privacy/your-info-on-other.

91. **Facebook Privacy.** How do I prevent search engines (e.g., Google) from showing my public search listing? [Online] Facebook Help Center. [Cited: May 15, 2012.] http://www.facebook.com/help/?faq=131026496974464.

92. **Facebook.** Create a Facebook Page to build a closer relationship with your audience and customers. [Online] Facebook. [Cited: June 29, 2012.] http://www.facebook.com/pages/create.php.

93. **Spehar, Jeffrey.** The New Facebook Login and Graph API 2.0. [Online] Facebook, April 30, 2014. https://developers.facebook.com/blog/post/2014/04/30/the-new-facebook-login/.

94. **Goldman, David.** Facebook turns its users into anti-phishing detectives. [Online] CNN, August 9, 2012. http://money.cnn.com/2012/08/09/technology/facebook-phishing/index.html.

95. **Protalinski, Emil.** Facebook faces nationwide class action tracking cookie lawsuit. [Online] ZDNet, February 29, 2012. http://www.zdnet.com/blog/facebook/facebook-faces-nationwide-class-action-tracking-cookie-lawsuit/9747.

96. **Blue, Violet.** Facebook turns user tracking 'bug' into data mining 'feature' for advertisers. [Online] ZDNet, June 17, 2014. http://www.zdnet.com/facebook-turns-user-tracking-bug-into-data-mining-feature-for-advertisers-7000030603/.

97. **Google.** About personalized ads on Google Search and Gmail. [Online] Google Inside Search. [Cited: May 15, 2012.] http://support.google.com/websearch/bin/answer.py?hl=en&answer=1634057.

98. **Google+.** Find my Face. [Online] Google. [Cited: May 15, 2012.] http://support.google.com/plus/bin/answer.py?hl=en&p=name_suggest_promo&answer=2370300.

99. **Kelly, Heather.** Why your face might appear in Google ads, and how to stop it. [Online] CNN, October 11, 2013. http://www.cnn.com/2013/10/11/tech/social-media/google-plus-ads-profiles/index.html.

100. **Vega, Tanzina and Wyatt, Edward.** U.S. Agency Seeks Tougher Consumer Privacy Rules. [Online] New York Times, March 26, 2012. http://www.nytimes.com/2012/03/27/business/ftc-seeks-privacy-legislation.html.

101. **Mayer, Jonathan and Narayanan, Arvind.** Do Not Track. Universal Web Tracking Opt Out. [Online] DoNotTrack.Us. [Cited: May 15, 2012.] http://donottrack.us/.

102. **Hachamovitch, Dean.** Windows Release Preview: The Sixth IE10 Platform Preview. [Online] MSDN Blogs, May 31, 2012. http://blogs.msdn.com/b/ie/archive/2012/05/31/windows-release-preview-the-sixth-ie10-platform-preview.aspx.

103. **Chen, Hanqing.** How to Block Online Tracking. [Online] Pacific Standard, July 7, 2014. http://www.psmag.com/navigation/nature-and-technology/block-online-tracking-85243/.

104. **Google.** Google Accounts & Web History. [Online] Google. [Cited: May 16, 2012.] http://www.google.com/goodtoknow/data-on-google/web-history/.

105. **Bindra, Chetna.** Building a privacy-first future for web advertising. [Online] Google, January 25, 2021. https://blog.google/products/ads-commerce/2021-01-privacy-sandbox/.

106. **Google.** Remove content from someone else's site. [Online] Google Webmaster Tools, February 15, 2012. https://support.google.com/webmasters/bin/answer.py?hl=en&answer=1663688.

107. —. Privacy Complaint Process. [Online] YouTube. [Cited: May 27, 2012.] http://support.google.com/youtube/bin/answer.py?hl=en&answer=142443.

108. **Privoxy Developers.** Privoxy. [Online] privoxy.org. [Cited: May 15, 2012.] http://www.privoxy.org/.

109. **Tor Developers.** Tor. [Online] torproject.org. [Cited: May 15, 2012.] https://www.torproject.org/.

110. **Anonymizer Developers.** Anonymizer. [Online] anonymizer.com. [Cited: May 15, 2012.] http://www.anonymizer.com/.

111. **Newman, Jared.** 8 Tools for the Online Privacy Paranoid. [Online] TIME Magazine, May 4, 2012. http://techland.time.com/2012/05/04/8-tools-for-the-online-privacy-paranoid/.

112. **Gross, Doug.** How your movements create a GPS 'fingerprint'. [Online] CNN, March 26, 2013. http://www.cnn.com/2013/03/26/tech/mobile/mobile-gps-privacy-study/index.html.

113. **Gahran, Amy.** ACLU: Most police track phones' locations without warrants. [Online] CNN, April 3, 2012. http://www.cnn.com/2012/04/03/tech/mobile/police-phone-tracking-gahran/index.html.

114. **Segall, Laurie.** Oops! Russian soldier Instagrams himself in Ukraine. [Online] CNNMoney, August 1, 2014. http://money.cnn.com/2014/08/01/technology/social/russian-soldier-ukraine-instagram/index.html.

115. **MacMillan, Douglas.** Foursquare Now Tracks Users Even When the App Is Closed. [Online] The Wall Street Journal, August 6, 2014. http://blogs.wsj.com/digits/2014/08/06/foursquare-now-tracks-users-even-when-the-app-is-closed/.

116. **Talbot, David.** Android App Warns When You're Being Watched. [Online] MIT Technology Review, January 30, 2014. http://www.technologyreview.com/news/523981/android-app-warns-when-youre-being-watched/.

117. **Mello, John P.** Carrier IQ Test: Android App Detects Controversial Software. [Online] PC World, December 2, 2011. http://www.pcworld.com/article/245371/carrier_iq_test_android_app_detects_controversial_software.html.

118. **Vijayan, Jaikumar.** FBI never sought Carrier IQ data, director says. [Online] Computerworld, December 14, 2011. http://www.computerworld.com/s/article/9222678/FBI_never_sought_Carrier_IQ_data_director_says.

119. **Cipriani, Jason.** Stop Android 4.3 from always scanning for Wi-Fi networks. [Online] CNet, August 2, 2013. http://www.cnet.com/how-to/stop-android-4-3-from-always-scanning-for-wi-fi-networks/.

120. **Fink, Erica.** Stalker: A creepy look at you, online. [Online] CNNMoney, June 13, 2014. http://money.cnn.com/2014/06/13/technology/security/stalker/index.html.

121. **Kopytoff, Verne.** Stores Sniff Out Smartphones to Follow Shoppers. [Online] MIT Technology Review, November 12, 2013. http://www.technologyreview.com/news/520811/stores-sniff-out-smartphones-to-follow-shoppers/.

122. **Pagliery, Jose.** How the NSA can 'turn on' your phone remotely. [Online] CNNMoney, June 6, 2014. http://money.cnn.com/2014/06/06/technology/security/nsa-turn-on-phone/index.html.

123. **Fight for the Future.** Privacy Pack. [Online] Reset the Net, June 5, 2014. https://pack.resetthenet.org/.

124. **Talbot, David.** A $629 Ultrasecure Phone Aims to Protect Personal Dat. [Online] MIT Technology Review, February 24, 2014. http://www.technologyreview.com/news/524906/a-629-ultrasecure-phone-aims-to-protect-personal-data/.

125. **Szoldra, Paul.** The Smartphone Even The NSA May Have Trouble Hacking Is Coming Soon. [Online] Business Insider, June 18, 2014. http://www.businessinsider.com/silent-circle-blackphone-2014-6.

126. **Dey, Sanorita, et al.** AccelPrint: Imperfections of Accelerometers Make Smartphones Trackable. [Online] Internet Society NDSS '14, February 23–26, 2014. http://synrg.csl.illinois.edu/papers/AccelPrint_NDSS14.pdf.

127. **Talbot, David.** Now Your Phone's Tilt Sensor Can Identify You. [Online] MIT Technology Review, May 1, 2014. http://www.technologyreview.com/news/527031/now-your-phones-tilt-sensor-can-identify-you/.

128. **Guardian Professional.** Recycled mobile phones retain previous owner data. [Online] The Guardian. [Cited: May 31, 2014.] http://www.theguardian.com/media-network/partner-zone-infosecurity/mobile-phones-previous-owner-data.

129. **BlackBelt.** DataWipe. [Online] BlackBelt. [Cited: May 31, 2014.] https://www.blackbeltdefence.com/datawipe/.

130. **The Baltimore Sun.** Where digital secrets go to die. [Online] Phys.org, January 30, 2014. http://phys.org/news/2014-01-digital-secrets-die.html.

131. **Pagliery, Jose.** Naked celeb hack lesson: 'Delete' doesn't mean delete. [Online] CNNMoney, September 2, 2014. http://money.cnn.com/2014/09/02/technology/security/cloud-delete/index.html?hpt=hp_t4.

132. **Clover, Juli.** Apple Confirms Commitment to App Tracking Transparency in Letter Condemning Facebook's Data Collection [Updated]. [Online] MacRumors, November 19, 2020. https://www.macrumors.com/2020/11/19/apple-app-tracking-transparency-letter/.

133. **App Store.** App privacy details on the App Store. [Online] Apple. [Cited: April 26, 2021.] https://developer.apple.com/app-store/app-privacy-details/.

134. **Krynsky, Mark.** The Locker Project Website has Launched. [Online] Lifestream Blog, May 26, 2011. https://lifestreamblog.com/the-locker-project-website-has-launched/.

135. **Gross, Doug.** Manage (and make cash with?) your data online. [Online] CNN, February 27, 2012. http://www.cnn.com/2012/02/24/tech/web/owning-your-data-online/index.html.

136. **Hamlin, Kaliya.** What is the Personal Data Ecosystem? [Online] Personal Data Ecosystem Consortium, June 1, 2011. http://personaldataecosystem.org/category/about/.

137. **Singly.** Singly. [Online] singly.com. [Cited: August 15, 2014.] http://blog.singly.com/.

138. **Shute, Tish.** The Locker Project: data for the people. [Online] O'Reilly Radar, February 11, 2011. http://radar.oreilly.com/2011/02/singly-locker-project-telehash.html.

139. **Personal.** It's your data. Own it. [Online] personal.com. [Cited: August 15, 2014.] https://www.personal.com/our-story.

140. **Delo, Cotton.** Here's My Personal Data, Marketers. What Do I Get For it? . [Online] Advertising Age., November 28, 2011. http://adage.com/article/digital/web-data-startups-bank-consumers-controlling-data/231208/.

141. **McNally, Steve.** The Locker Project and Your Digital Wake. [Online] Forbes, June 30, 2011. http://www.forbes.com/sites/smcnally/2011/06/30/your-digital-wake/.

142. **Imam, Jareen.** Want to get fit? Pull out your phone. [Online] CNN, June 29, 2012. http://www.cnn.com/2012/06/29/tech/social-media/tech-fitness-irpt/index.html.

143. **Swallow, Erica.** How Nike Outruns the Social Media Competition. [Online] Mashable, September 22, 2011. http://mashable.com/2011/09/22/nike-social-media/.

144. **Solon, Olivia.** Personal analytics could lead to 'designed' lifestyles. [Online] Wired, November 28, 2011. http://www.wired.co.uk/news/archive/2011-11/28/martin-blinder-personal-analytics.

145. **Joh, Jae Won.** What Do Doctors Think Of Apple's HealthKit? [Online] Forbes, June 9, 2014. http://www.forbes.com/sites/quora/2014/06/09/what-do-doctors-think-of-healthkit/.

146. **Morris, Alexandra.** Why Apple Wants to Help You Track Your Health. [Online] MIT Technology Review, June 9, 2014. http://www.technologyreview.com/news/527921/why-apple-wants-to-help-you-track-your-health/.

147. **Rojahn, Susan Young.** PatientsLikeMe Gives Genentech Full Access. [Online] MIT Technology Review, April 8, 2014. http://www.technologyreview.com/view/526266/patientslikeme-gives-genentech-full-access/.

148. **PatientsLikeMe.** Genentech and PatientsLikeMe Enter Patient-Centric Research Collaboration. [Online] PatientsLikeMe Newsroom, April 7, 2014. http://news.patientslikeme.com/press-release/genentech-and-patientslikeme-enter-patient-centric-research-collaboration.

149. **Singer, Emily.** Patients' Social Network Predicts Drug Outcomes. [Online] MIT Technology Review, May 11, 2010. http://www.technologyreview.com/news/418874/patients-social-network-predicts-drug-outcomes/.

Chapter 18
Total Information Awareness in Society

"You can have data without information, but you cannot have information without data -- Daniel Keys Moran"
— Facebook Data Team (February 2008)

"I have teenage kids and [using Facebook is] the only way that you can really see what they are up to and talk to them."
— Indianapolis attorney Mark S. Zuckerberg (May 2011)

"I think that big data is going to become humanity's dashboard."
— Photographer Rick Smolan (February 2012)

"Just wait. We'll be sending you coupons for things you want before you even know you want them."
— Statistician Andrew Pole at Target (February 2012)

"The computer 'server' and the 'server' in the bar will be indistinguishable... They will both know what you want to drink before you know it yourself."
— Social critic Andrew Keen (June 2012)

"The natural flow of technology tends to move in the direction of making surveillance easier ... The ability of computers to track us doubles every eighteen months."
— PGP creator Phil Zimmermann (August 2013)

"Millions of people end romantic relationships each week, and we want to help in any way that we can."
— Facebook product manager Kelly Grimaldi (March 2016)

"[Law enforcement officials] look like they are incompetent when they say the intelligence wasn't there. It reminds us of 9/11. Here we are again. A failure to connect the dots."
— Former FBI assistant counterintelligence director Frank Figliuzzi (February 2021)

© Springer Science+Business Media, LLC, part of Springer Nature 2021
N. Lee, *Facebook Nation*, https://doi.org/10.1007/978-1-0716-1867-7_18

"Public support and understanding are essential to the FBI's success. We can't accomplish our mission if people don't believe us and trust us; our credibility can make all the difference in whether someone comes forward with a vital piece of information that could prevent crime or a terrorist attack."
– FBI Director Christopher Wray (March 2021)

"The choices being made by Facebook's leadership are a huge problem — for children, for public safety, for democracy — that is why I came forward. ... A safer, more enjoyable social media is possible."
– Former Facebook product manager Frances Haugen
(October 2021)

18.1   U.S. Capitol Riot – Free Speech vs. True Threats on Social Media

The U.S. Capitol's last breach was more than 200 years ago in August 1814 by invading British troops who set fire to the building and other landmarks during the raging war of 1812 (1). At the FBI Citizens Academy on February 23, 2021, I asked the FBI about the January 6 Capitol riot organized on social media that led to the unprecedented ban of a sitting U.S. President by all major social networks. I questioned, "According to *The Washington Post*, an FBI office in Norfolk, Virginia, issued a warning on January 5th that extremists were preparing to travel to Washington to commit violence and 'war.' Now according to fbi.gov, there are more than 830 special agents in the Washington D.C. field office. What could FBI have done in response to the Capitol riot during the four-hour insurrection on January 6th?"

A special agent assigned to the FBI Joint Terrorism Task Force (JTTF) replied, "Great question, I've heard of that report but have not had the opportunity to review. Regarding the FBI's response, or potential response, I think there would have been many different response models we could have utilized. However, I believe this was discussed during a Capitol Hearing today, and is a very hot topic. I wouldn't want to second guess any decisions which were made without having all the facts; what was passed, who received it, and what, if any, assistance was offered."

A national security special agent added, "The Washington Field Office (WFO) of the FBI is part of the whole of USG approach to the National Capitol Region (NCR). The FBI was engaged in supporting the Capitol Police in their mission."

Appearing before the House Appropriations subcommittee hearing in February 2021, U.S. Capitol Police Acting Chief Yogananda Pittman explained the ill-preparedness on the day of the riot, "It has been suggested that the department was either ignorant of or ignored critical intelligence that indicated that an attack of the magnitude that we experienced on January 6 would occur. The department was not ignorant of intelligence indicating an attack of the size and scale we encountered on the 6th. There was no such intelligence. Although we knew the likelihood for violence by extremists, no credible threat indicated that tens of thousands would attack the U.S. Capitol, nor did the intelligence received from the FBI or any other law enforcement partner indicate such a threat" (2).

Former FBI assistant counterintelligence director Frank Figliuzzi retorted that law enforcement officials "look like they are incompetent when they say the intelligence wasn't there. It reminds us of 9/11. Here we are again. A failure to connect the dots" (3).

Timing and communication method are both important factors for police preparedness (or the lack of thereof). The FBI report from the Joint Terrorism Task Force (JTTF) was emailed to Capitol Police and Washington police after business hours on January 5th. "We're talking about a report that came from the Norfolk office that was sent to email boxes," said Washington Police Acting Chief Robert Contee at a joint Senate committee hearing. "As the chief of police for the Metropolitan Police Department, I assure you that my phone is on 24 hours a day, 7 days a week, and I'm available to get a phone call from any agency that has information with respect to something of this magnitude happening in our city" (3).

The communication breakdown was compounded by the fact that the FBI never issued a Joint Intelligence Bulletin to alert other law enforcement agencies about possible Capitol violence—information that FBI intelligence analysts had gathered from social media and informants. However, the FBI refrained from sharing the full information because of First Amendment concerns (4).

At the FBI Citizens Academy, the FBI expounded its mission to "protect the American people and uphold the Constitution of the United States" (5). The First Amendment to the U.S. Constitution states: "Congress shall make no law respecting an establishment of religion, or prohibiting the free exercise thereof; or abridging the freedom of speech, or of the press; or the right of the people peaceably to assemble, and to petition the Government for a redress of grievances."

An FBI agent at the Academy emphasized the use of the word "abridging" written in the First Amendment. It means that no government agency shall curtail or put any restrictions on our right to free speech and peaceful protests. It almost seems easier for the FBI to protect the American people from international terrorism than from domestic terrorism because the federal agency can place suspects under 24/7 surveillance and disseminate intelligence about Americans linked to designated terrorist organizations such as Al Qaeda and ISIS. However, there are no designations for domestic terrorist groups in the United States.

There is a fine line between free speech and true threats. The U.S. Supreme Court defines a "true threat" as a serious communication of an intent to commit an act of unlawful violence against an individual or group. Although hate crimes are illegal, hate is not a crime in and of itself. The FBI cannot investigate individuals or hate groups (such as Ku Klux Klan, Oath Keepers, Three Percenters, and Proud Boys) based on legally protected free speech under the First Amendment. (Incidentally, the Ku Klux Klan was labeled as terrorist group by Charleston South Carolina City Council in 1999 (6); and the Proud Boys was designated as terrorist organization by the Canadian government in 2021 (7).)

In 2018, Chase Middle School student Taylor Cargile in Spokane, Washington won the Spokane Community Observance of the Holocaust essay contest (8). Her essay opens with a quote from my book *Counterterrorism and Cybersecurity* (9):

SPOKANE

Spokane Community Observance of the Holocaust essay contest, first place: 'Repeating History With Hate Speech'

UPDATED: Fri., April 6, 2018, 5:03 p.m.

By Taylor Cargile
By Chase Middle School

🐦 Twitter	f Facebook	✉ Email	⊜ Reddit

Chase Middle School student Taylor Cargile is the winner of the 2018 Spokane Community Observance of the Holocaust essay contest. (Courtesy photo)

Related topics

Spokane Community Observance of the Holocaust 2018 Art and Essay

First place essay

Newton Lee, a computer scientist and author once said, "There is a fine line between free speech and hate speech. Free speech encourages debate whereas hate speech incites violence." Lee's point was that many people confuse free speech and hate speech. Free speech was a right given to us, so we could have an opinion on controversial topics. Hate speech, however, attacks a person or group based on ethnicity, color, religion, gender or disability. We were not given the protection of freedom of speech and expression so we can bully, harass, hurt, or specifically target a group of people for the way they live. There is no question of whether hate speech is wrong or right. Hate speech and propaganda were powerful tools used to start many wars and genocides, including the Holocaust that killed almost two-thirds of the European Jewish population in 1933. Hate speech and propaganda that are used today share many similarities and differences from when they were used in the Holocaust.

Fig. 18.1 First place essay by Chase Middle School student Taylor Cargile

"Newton Lee, a computer scientist and author once said, 'There is a fine line between free speech and hate speech. Free speech encourages debate whereas hate speech incites violence.' Lee's point was that many people confuse free speech and hate speech. Free speech was a right given to us, so we could have an opinion on controversial topics. Hate speech, however, attacks a person or group based on ethnicity, color, religion, gender or disability. We were not given the protection of freedom of speech and expression so we can bully, harass, hurt, or specifically target a group of people for the way they live. There is no question of whether hate speech is wrong or right. Hate speech and propaganda were powerful tools used to start many wars and genocides, including the Holocaust that killed almost two-thirds of the European Jewish population in 1933." (See Fig. 18.1)

Without proper education and critical thinking, hate speech and propaganda perpetuate misinformation and incite violence, which led to the deadly storming of the U.S. Capitol on January 6, 2021. It was also alarming to learn that Chief of Staff Alex Ferro to Florida Congressman Carlos Gimenez overheard on the morning of January 6 the inciting statement—"We're gonna storm the FBI building"—from a man in tactical gear inside the lobby of a hotel near Capitol Hill, just hours before the insurrection (10).

On March 2, FBI Director Christopher Wray testified on Capitol Hill and adjudged "that attack, that siege was criminal behavior, plain and simple. And it's behavior that we, the FBI, view as domestic terrorism" (11).

The FBI is the lead U.S. agency responsible for investigating and preventing domestic terrorism. Yet, the lack of a domestic terrorism statute means that in order for the FBI to open an investigation, the FBI requires:

1. The existence of a potential federal violation,
2. The unlawful use of force or violence, and
3. The existence of ideological motivation.

For example, the Proud Boys leader Henry "Enrique" Tarrio was arrested in Washington D.C. on January 4, two days before the Capitol riot, not for hate speech or inciting a riot, but for the destruction of property related to burning a Black Lives Matter banner taken from a United Methodist Church as well as for the possession of high capacity firearm magazines (12).

In the absence of a domestic terrorism statute, the FBI has very little leeway in opening investigations. On April 15, FBI Director Christopher Wray testified before the House Intelligence Committee about the QAnon conspiracy. He said that the FBI arrested at least five self-identified QAnon adherents related to the January 6 attacks, but he also explained, "We're not investigating the theory in its own right. ... We focus on the violence and the federal criminal activity regardless of the inspiration. We understand QAnon to be more of a reference to a complex conspiracy theory or set of complex conspiracy theories, largely promoted online, which has sort of morphed into more of a movement. Like a lot of other conspiracy theories, the effects of Covid, anxiety social, social isolation, financial hardship ... all exacerbate people's vulnerability to those theories, and we are concerned about the potential that those things can lead to violence, and where it is an inspiration for federal crime, we're going to aggressively pursue it" (13).

In the wake of the U.S. Capitol riot, U.S. lawmakers are mulling over a new domestic terrorism statute as well as changes to Section 230 of the Communications Decency Act that provides immunity for website publishers from third-party content (14). "I believe that section 230 of the communications decency act absolutely needs attention. It needs to be reformed. It creates a shield of liability for the big social media platforms, a shield that I would suggest to you they have abused, they have utilized it to the detriment of the public," said Jonathan Greenblatt, CEO of the Anti-Defamation League (15).

How to reform section 230 is a big question mark. Social media does not incite violence. On the contrary, social media can be used to gauge public sentiments and to warn people of potential dangers. "In the days leading up to Jan. 6, I received a flood of texts from family and friends telling me to 'be safe' at the joint session," said Congressman Eric Swalwell at a joint Senate committee hearing. "They didn't have access to intelligence. But they did read the tweets from President Trump and his supporters. This was completely foreseeable" (3).

Indeed, the telltale signs were obvious. During the 2016 U.S. presidential election, Republican frontrunner Donald Trump said, "I could stand in the middle of Fifth Avenue and shoot somebody and I wouldn't lose any voters" (16). For the next four year, President Trump's rhetoric had emboldened domestic militants who eventually acted out their aggression on January 6 at the U.S. Capitol after heeding Trump's rally call to march on Congress (17).

Social media had been witnessing the brewing of violence for months before January 6th. The FBI has gathered evidence based on online chatter (11), and Congresswoman Zoe Lofgren has compiled a nearly 2,000-page report on public social media posts from members of the U.S. House of Representatives (18). For example:

1. In October, Congresswoman Marjorie Taylor Greene said in a video interview on Facebook that "If this generation doesn't stand up and defend freedom, it's gone. And once it's gone, freedom doesn't come back by itself. The only way to get your freedoms back is if it's earned with the price of blood" (19).
2. In November, Jim Arroyo of the Oath Keepers posted his two-part videos on YouTube titled "The Coming Civil War?" (20)
3. Sergeant at arms of the Proud Boys in Seattle, Ethan Nordean (aka "Rufio Panman"), asked on social media for help to buy "protective gear" and "communications equipment" in preparation for the Capitol riot. Nordean appeared in a video on Parler saying that the Proud Boys should protect the community and respond to voter fraud beliefs with "that original spirit of 1776"—a reference to the U.S. Declaration of Independence (21).
4. 18-year-old rioter Bruno Cua wrote on Parler days before the siege that "President Trump is calling us to FIGHT! It's time to take our freedom back the old fashioned way" (22).
5. Four days before the insurrection, Congressman Paul Gosar posted on Twitter that "Sedition and treason for stealing votes is appropriate" (23).
6. The day before the Capitol siege, 35-year-old QAnon adherent Ashli Babbitt tweeted, "Nothing will stop us….they can try and try and try but the storm is here and it is descending upon DC in less than 24 hours….dark to light!" (24)

Under the headline "The storming of Capitol Hill was organized on social media," *The New York Times* reported on January 7, 2021:

"On social media sites used by the far-right, such as Gab and Parler, directions on which streets to take to avoid the police and which tools to bring to help pry open doors were exchanged in comments. At least a dozen people posted about carrying guns into the halls of Congress.

Calls for violence against members of Congress and for pro-Trump movements to retake the Capitol building have been circulating online for months. Bolstered by Mr. Trump, who has courted fringe movements like QAnon and the Proud Boys, groups have openly organized on social media networks and recruited others to their cause.

At 2:24 p.m., after Mr. Trump tweeted that Mr. Pence 'didn't have the courage to do what should have been done,' dozens of messages on Gab called for those inside the Capitol building to hunt down the vice president. In videos uploaded to the channel, protesters could be heard chanting 'Where is Pence?'

As Facebook and Twitter began to crack down groups like QAnon and the Proud Boys over the summer, they slowly migrated to other sites that allowed them to openly call for violence." (25).

President Joe Biden said during his 2020 presidential campaign, "Section 230 should be revoked immediately…for Zuckerberg and other platforms. It should be revoked because it is not merely an internet company. It is propagating falsehoods they know to be false" (26). President Donald Trump also wanted to repeal Section 230 so badly that he vetoed the $740 billion defense bill in December 2020 (27). Ironically, if Section 230 had been repealed, radical Trump supporters would not have been able to utilize social media to organize the U.S. Capitol riot.

Testifying before Congress in November 2020 for a second Senate hearing, Mark Zuckerberg acknowledged, "We do have responsibilities, and it may make sense for there to be liability for some of the content that is on the platform" (28). In defense of Section 230, Zuckerberg described how Facebook's automated algorithms detect terrorist and child-exploitation content before anyone sees it.

But artificial intelligence algorithms are less than perfect, especially when company profits are factored into the equations. In October 2021, former Facebook product manager Frances Haugen testified before the U.S. Senate Subcommittee on Consumer Protection, Product Safety, and Data Security: "The choices being made by Facebook's leadership are a huge problem — for children, for public safety, for democracy — that is why I came forward. … I joined Facebook in 2019 because someone close to me was radicalized online. I felt compelled to take an active role in creating a better, less toxic Facebook. During my time at Facebook, first working as the lead product manager for Civic Misinformation and later on Counter-Espionage, I saw that Facebook repeatedly encountered conflicts between its own profits and our safety. Facebook consistently resolved those conflicts in favor of its own profits. The result has been a system that amplifies division, extremism, and polarization — and undermining societies around the world. In some cases, this dangerous online talk has led to actual violence that harms and even kills people. In other cases, their profit optimizing machine is generating self-harm and self-hate — especially for vulnerable groups, like teenage girls. … Right now, Facebook chooses what information billions of people see, shaping their perception of reality. Even those who don't use Facebook are impacted by the radicalization of people who do. A company with control over our deepest thoughts, feelings and behaviors needs real oversight" (29).

Regarding Section 230, Frances Haugen said in her testimony, "The severity of this crisis demands that we break out of previous regulatory frames. Tweaks to outdated privacy protections or changes to Section 230 will not be sufficient. The core of the issue is that no one can understand Facebook's destructive choices better than Facebook, because only Facebook gets to look under the hood. A critical starting point for effective regulation is transparency: full access to data for research not directed by Facebook. On this foundation, we can build sensible rules and standards to address consumer harms, illegal content, data protection, anticompetitive practices, algorithmic systems and more" (29).

Technology and marketing consultant Shelly Palmer asked in his blog, "Why is Pornhub doing a better job checking user identity and moderating content than Facebook, Twitter, TikTok, and almost every other social media platform? Back in December, the NYT accused Pornhub of profiting from child exploitation, revenge porn, and other illegal content (30). To its credit, Pornhub immediately banned all uploads from unverified users, blocked video downloads, and removed millions of videos from its platform (and other properties owned by its parent company). Now, to upload a video, you need to be verified by Yoti, a third-party secure digital identity company. Is there a lesson here for Big Tech? No one knows who anyone really is on Twitter. We assume that TikTok users are posting videos of themselves, but anyone can repost and revise anything on TikTok. Facebook has stricter requirements to create a profile, but it's super easy to game the system. Should Big Tech follow Pornhub's lead?" (31)

Palmer raised a good question. After all, the porn industry has standardized 8 mm films, helped win the VHS battle over Sony's Betamax, automated closed captioning, developed the first known online streaming technology, and perhaps most importantly, invented e-commerce (32). The popular anti-war slogan from the 1960's says it best: "Make love, not war."

18.2   Humanity's Dashboard in Big Data

While Mutual Assured Destruction (MAD) has helped to prevent World War III, Total Information Awareness (TIA) can offer insights into some of the biggest challenges facing humanity.

In Francis Ford Coppola's *The Godfather Part II* (1974), Michael Corleone said, "There are many things my father taught me here in this room. He taught me: keep your friends close, but your enemies closer" (33). Ironically, the biggest blows to the mafia in America have been due to the efficacious FBI infiltration. Undercover FBI agents have been able to penetrate the mafia families as wiseguys and "made men," leading to the arrests and convictions of notorious mob figures (34).

Although there are Facebook apps like "EnemyGraph" that bond like-minded haters online, in reality the real "enemies" are actually Facebook "friends" who are bullying their classmates or applying peer pressure on their weaker counterparts. School bullying has gotten so out of hand that in April 2012, 13-year-old Rachel Ehmke in Minnesota committed suicide after months of school bullying (35), and a mother sent her 17-yar-old son Darnell Young to school in Indiana armed with a stun gun for his protection against bullies. Young's mother Chelisa Grimes said, "I do not promote violence – not at all – but what is a parent to do when she has done everything that she felt she was supposed to do … at the school?" (36).

In Steven Spielberg's *Minority Report* (2002), "PreCrime" is a specialized police department that apprehends criminals based on foreknowledge provided by three psychics named "precogs" in the year 2054 (37). Although the notion of "PreCrime" is overarching Orwellian, who would not want to know if a criminal out there was planning to abduct our children or shoot up our schools?

We were appalled by the senseless massacres at Columbine High School in 1999 and at Virginia Tech in 2007. What if these atrocities could have been prevented? We were equally horrified by the kidnapping of 14-yar-old Elizabeth Smart in 2002 and of 11-year-old Jaycee Dugard, who was abducted in 1991 and held captive for

18 years. What if the abductees could have been rescued in a matter of hours or days instead of years or decades?

The answers rely heavily on the collection, interpretation, and usage of big data – the avalanche of personal data driven by social networks and other existing infrastructures. As the Facebook Data Team wrote on their official Facebook profile, "You can have data without information, but you cannot have information without data. -- Daniel Keys Moran" (38).

Indeed, the lack of electronic data could hamper police work. In early 2014, 65-year-old Philip Welsh was murdered in his home in Silver Spring, Maryland; and the case remained the only unsolved killing in Montgomery County as of May 2014 (39). Welsh had no Internet, no computer, and no cell phone. He left behind no electronic footprints.

"When people hear of big data, they think Big Brother," said Photographer Rick Smolan, co-founder of The Day in the Life photography series. "The general public and the media tend to immediately think, 'Oh, this is all invasive. People are trying to sell us stuff or spy on us, or it's the government trying to control us.' But I think that data will become one of the ways that we can finally start addressing some of the biggest challenges facing humanity – of poverty, and crime, and pollution, and overcrowding, and the use of resources, and environmental problems. Right now, I feel like the human race is like driving a car around this twisty road, and we have no idea whether our tires are inflated, how much gas we have left. We have no headlights. … It's like no dashboard in front of us. And I think that big data is going to become humanity's dashboard" (40).

Facebook nation exists in the intersection of humanities and sciences, somewhere in between the fictional worlds of *The Godfather Part II* and *Minority Report.* We saw in *Minority Report* that in 2054 computers scan human faces and display targeted advertisements to individuals as they walk down the street. It turns out that since 2010 there have been billboards in Tokyo subway stations and London bus stops that employ cameras and face recognition software to determine the gender and age of passersby. Gesture-control interfaces (41), retina scanners (42), insect robots (43), augmented-reality glasses (44), and electronic paper (45) are some of the other cutting-edge technologies that are already available today. Ericsson's human USB (46), Nokia's vibrating tattoo alerts (47), Disney's touch-sensing furniture (48), NeuroSky's mind-controlled videogames (49), and Google's self-driving cars (50) are just a few of the many new products in the works. The future is arriving sooner than we imagine.

In the age of big data, Facebook nation is progressing towards Total Information Awareness whether or not we are ready for it. A whole new world of possibilities, either good or bad, has been bestowed on us. What we opt to do or not do in this brave new world will have a significant impact on our future. In a 2013 interview, PGP (Pretty Good Privacy) creator Phil Zimmermann told *GigaOm's* Om Malik, "The natural flow of technology tends to move in the direction of making surveillance easier … The ability of computers to track us doubles every eighteen months" (51).

18.3   Ambient Awareness in Suicide Prevention

Social scientists use the term "ambient awareness" to describe the incessant online contact on Facebook, Twitter, and other social networks. Prof. Andreas Kaplan at ESCP Europe Business School in France defines ambient awareness as "awareness created through regular and constant reception, and/or exchange of information fragments through social media" (52). Clive Thompson of the *New York Times* wrote, "Ambient awareness is very much like being physically near someone and picking up on his mood through the little things he does – body language, sighs, stray comments – out of the corner of your eye" (53).

Ambient social apps and Facebook's "frictionless sharing" greatly facilitate ambient awareness among friends nearby and far away. We can find out something about others without them telling us. We can be more vigilant only by becoming more aware of people, our surroundings, and happenings around us.

Friend's awareness can save lives. Frank Warren founded PostSecret in 2004 to collect secrets mailed to him on postcards anonymously. He scans the postcards and posts them on the blog www.postsecret.com. Warren shared his testimony at the TED2012 conference, "When I posted a secret from someone who confesses to thinking about jumping from the Golden Gate Bridge, PostSecret Blog readers sprang to action creating a Facebook group page called, Please Don't Jump. They posted encouraging pictures and shared their own inspiring stories of hope. 60,000 people joined the group in 10 days. The next week the San Francisco City Council proclaimed the first annual 'Please Don't Jump Day'" (54).

The public's reaction was in sharp contrast to the bystander effect or "Genovese syndrome," named after Catherine Susan (Kitty) Genovese whose cry in the night went unanswered by 38 of her neighbors in Queens, New York, on March 13, 1964 (55). Diffusion of responsibility is a sociopsychological phenomenon whereby a person is less likely to take responsibility for an action or inaction when others are present. In 1968, John M. Darley of New York University and Bibb Latané of Columbia University performed experiments to verify their hypothesis that "the more bystanders to an emergency, the less likely, or the more slowly, any one bystander will intervene to provide aid" (56). In 2008, Mark Levine and Simon Crowther of Lancaster University conducted four new experiments, which concluded that "increasing group size inhibited intervention in a street violence scenario when bystanders were strangers but encouraged intervention when bystanders were friends" (57). The key here is "friends."

Facebook friends can make a difference in people's lives, for better or worse. In December 2009, John T. Cacioppo of University of Chicago, James H. Fowler of UC San Diego, and Nicholas A. Christakis of Harvard University showed that loneliness spreads through a contagious process in a large social network. A person is 52% more likely to be lonely if a direct connection in the social network is lonely (58). In August 2011, the National Center on Addiction and Substance Abuse at Columbia University found that teens that spend time on the social networks are likely to see images of their peers drinking or using drugs – images that could help to convince them that substance abuse is a normal, acceptable activity (59).

In January 2012, Adam D. I. Kramer from the Facebook Core Data Science Team conducted a massive psychological mood experiment on 689,003 Facebook users. Kramer and his colleagues concluded that "emotional states can be transferred to others via emotional contagion, leading people to experience the same emotions without their awareness. … Emotions expressed by friends, via online social networks, influence our own moods, constituting, to our knowledge, the first experimental evidence for massive-scale emotional contagion via social networks" (60).

On the positive side, Pew Internet Project in February 2012 released the research results by Keith N. Hampton of Rutgers University, Lauren Sessions Goulet of University of Pennsylvania, and Cameron Marlow of Facebook. The researchers combined server logs of Facebook activity with survey data to explore the structure of Facebook friendship networks and measures of social well-being. The results showed that most Facebook users receive more from their Facebook friends than they give – they receive more messages than they send, they are tagged in a photo more than they tag a friend in a photo, and their content is "liked" more often than they "like" their friend's content. Lee Rainie, Director of the Pew Internet Project, said, "This examination of people's activities in a very new realm affirms one of the oldest truths about the value of friendship: Those who are really active socially have a better shot at getting the help and emotional support they need. The Golden Rule seems to rule digital spaces, too" (61).

Sometimes help might have come too late. In September 2010, 18-year-old Rutgers University freshman Tyler Clementi killed himself after his roommate Dharun Ravi and Ravi's friend Molly Wei secretly videostreamed him kissing another man using a webcam. Clementi felt alone and helpless during the ordeals. His final message on Facebook read, "Jumping off the gw bridge sorry" (62). His friends and Ravi's apologetic text message were too late to help (63).

On Christmas Day 2010, 42-year-old Simone Back in Brighton told her 1,048 friends on Facebook: "Took all my pills, be dead soon, bye bye everyone" (64). Of the 150 online responses, one Facebook friend called her a liar, another said, "she does it all the time, takes all her pills," and yet another said, "it's her choice." No one who lived nearby contacted the police or sought her out in time to save her. Back's friend Samantha Pia Owen said, "Everyone just carried on arguing with each other on Facebook … Some of those people lived within walking distance of Simone. If one person just left their computer and went to her house, her life could have been saved. These so-called friends are a waste of air. If someone has got problems you don't go around adding to them, you don't start attacking people who are already vulnerable … Facebook should put up a flag or button so that a post can be flagged up as a suicide threat, and Facebook should be able to contact the police". (65)

While Facebook could not tell people how to choose their friends, Facebook in March 2011 added Samaritans suicide risk alert system (66). If someone is posting depressing photos or writing about killing themselves, their Facebook friends can click on the "report suicidal content" link to alert Facebook staff members who are monitoring these reports 24/7 (67). In March 2017, Facebook added suicide prevention tools in Facebook Live and Messenger so that individuals can reach out to a friend or contact a helpline. "Some might say we should cut off the livestream, but what we've learned is cutting off the stream too early could remove the opportunity for that person to receive help," said Facebook researcher Jennifer Guadagno (68).

Other social media follows suit in suicide prevention. Google provides a feature in the U.S. search engine that displays a picture of a red telephone and the National Suicide Prevention Lifeline phone number when people are searching for suicide-related topics (69). Twitter and Tumblr also allow their users to report suicidal behavior.

Surgeon General Regina Benjamin wrote on Facebook in December 2011, "The Action Alliance brings together public, private and nonprofit partners to engage every sector of society with a vision of ending the tragic experience of suicide in America. Facebook is an important part of that partnership, and I'm excited about the new initiative to augment its response to potentially suicidal members by offering the opportunity for a private chat with a trained crisis representative from the Suicide Prevention Lifeline in addition to providing the Lifeline's phone number. This service will be available to people who use Facebook in the United States and Canada. The new service enables Facebook users to report a suicidal comment they see posted by a friend to Facebook using either the Report Suicidal Content link or the report links found throughout the site. The person who posted the suicidal comment will then immediately receive an e-mail from Facebook encouraging them to call the National Suicide Prevention Lifeline 1-800-273-TALK (8255) or to click on a link to begin a confidential chat session with a crisis worker" (70).

18.4   Parental Awareness in School Bullying and Cyberbullying

CNN legal analyst and criminal defense attorney Mark O'Mara explains, "Bullying is not name calling. It's not a little harmless schoolyard razzing. Bullying is the systematic harassment of an individual with the intent to cause substantial emotional distress. It can include social ostracism, slut-shaming, extortion, sexual extortion, and more" (71). O'Mara and Florida state senator David Simmons have proposed a bill to make bullying illegal.

In April 2012, 17-year-old Darnell Young went to Arsenal Technical High School in Indianapolis with a stun gun. "I brought the stun gun 'cause I wasn't safe," said Young who was taunted and bullied for months. "I was at my wit's end. I didn't know what to do and I thought about suicide." He was kicked out of school for bringing the weapon. Young's mother Chelisa Grimes protested, "I do not promote violence – not at all – but what is a parent to do when she has done everything that she felt she was supposed to do … at the school? I think that the self-protection device is what's making the news, but the big picture is that my child is not the only one who does not feel safe at our school" (36).

It is a tragedy that some victims of school bullying took their own lives. For example, 13-year-old Rachel Ehmke in Minnesota committed suicide in April 2012 after months of bullying by her schoolmates in Kasson/Mantorville Middle School (72). A note that her parents found after her death read, "I'm fine = I wish I could tell you how I really feel," alongside a picture of a broken heart.

Cyberbullying only exacerbates the danger of bullying. Victims are constantly being stalked by bullies even after school. "As many as 25% of teenagers have experienced cyberbullying at some point," said Justin W. Patchin, Professor of Criminal Justice at the University of Wisconsin-Eau Claire (73). According to McAfee's report titled "2014 Teens and the Screen Study," cyberbullying had more than tripled in 2014 as the majority – 87% – of youth had witnessed cruel behavior online that resulted in anger and embarrassment. "Parents must discuss online activity with their children to better ensure their safety and security offline," said Michelle Dennedy, chief privacy officer at McAfee. "Whether a child is a victim or an instigator of cruel behavior such as cyberbullying, the negative behavior can deeply affect their identity and their reputation" (74).

In January 2010, 15-year-old Phoebe Prince, an immigrant from Ireland, took her own life in order to escape vicious bullying on Facebook, via text messages, and in her school. After her death, one student wrote "Done" on Facebook while another wrote that "She got what she deserved" (75). Darby O'Brien, a high school parent and friend of Prince's family, wondered why the bullies who tormented Prince were still in school. O'Brien said, "Instead of confronting the evil among us, the reality that there are bullies roaming the corridors at South Hadley High, people are blaming the victim, looking for excuses why a 15-year-old girl would do this. People are in denial" (76). The South Hadley police chief responded, "We've subpoenaed records from Facebook, we've subpoenaed web pages from Facebook, hoping to track down perpetrators of some of this criminal threatening" (77).

In September 2012, 15-year-old Audrey Pott committed suicide after being bullied by schoolmates who saw the photographs taken of her being raped by three teenage boys at the Saratoga High School in California (78). The teen rapists took photos of the attack, texting them at school, and posting them online. Pott wrote on her Facebook page, "I have a reputation for a night I don't even remember. I can't do anything to fix it. I just want this to go away. The whole school knows. I have a reputation I can never get rid of" (79).

On September 7, 2012, 15-year-old Amanda Todd published a YouTube video titled "My story: Struggling, bullying, suicide, self harm" with the description "I'm doing this to be an inspiration and to show that I can be strong" (80). Holding a stack of cards in the video, the teen showed one card after another, chronicling her long and painful journey of being a bullied victim. The last two cards read, "I have nobody … I need someone :(My name is Amanda Todd …." She struggled to survive and hoped that someone would listen. But no one did, and she took her own life one month later on October 10, 2012.

In April 2013, 17-year-old Canadian Rehtaeh Parsons killed herself after being cyberbullied for more than a year. She and her family were forced to relocate after a photo of her being raped circulated in her school and community. "She was never left alone," Leah Parsons told *CBC*. "She had to leave the community. Her friends turned against her. People harassed her. Boys she didn't know started texting her and Facebooking her asking her to have sex with them. It just never stopped" (81).

In July 2013, 14-year-old Italian Carolina Picchio jumped from her bedroom window to her death after her ex-boyfriend and his friends repeatedly bullied her via Facebook posts, online videos, and WhatsApp messages. Novara prosecutor Francesco Saluzzo said, "In the case of Carolina, it appears some of her friends, some of her relatives, asked for the removal of some of this strongly offensive content [on Facebook], and it wasn't removed – and this played a role in her decision to commit suicide" (82).

In August 2013, 14-year-old Hannah Smith hanged herself after she was bullied on the website Ask.fm where she had gone on to look for advice on the skin condition eczema. More than 15,000 people in the United Kingdom have signed an online petition urging the government to act: "Cyber-Bullying has been an ever increasing problem within the UK for a considerable amount of time with one of the biggest offenders becoming Ask.fm, a site popular amongst young people where posts can be made with confidence anonymously which has led to bullying, mental health problems and suicides as well as grooming" (83).

After 12-year-old Rebecca Sedwick leapt to her death from a water tower in September 2013, her classmate – a 14-year-old Florida girl – posted on her Facebook, "Yes IK I bullied REBECCA nd *(sic)* she killed her self *(sic)* but IDGAF" (84). The vernacular meant "I don't give a f*ck." Polk County Sheriff Grady Judd arrested the girl, but the charges were eventually dropped because bullying was not a crime.

Nova Scotia enacted a law in August 2013 allowing victims to seek protection from cyberbullying and to sue the perpetrator. "Too many young people and their families are being hurt by cyberbullies. I committed to families that the province would work with them to better protect our children and young people. Court orders, and the ability to sue, are more tools that help put a stop to this destructive behavior," said Justice Minister Ross Landry. "This sends a clear message: cyberbullying is a serious act with serious consequences. Think before you text" (85).

In September 2011, Facebook collaborated with Cartoon Network in launching the "Stop Bullying: Speak Up" social pledge application. "The Stop Bullying: Speak Up Social Pledge App is rooted in the fact that students, educators and parents have the power to stop bullying by speaking up when they see it occur," said Marne Levine, Vice President of Global Public Policy at Facebook. "The launch of this campaign reinforces our deep commitment to the safety and security of kids everywhere. By working with Time Warner, our hope is to inspire millions of people who witness bullying to take action" (86).

Bullying and cyberbullying have become such an epidemic that some schools have been going for a shock-and-awe approach by hiring The Scary Guy (a real legal name for Earl Kenneth Kaufmann) to deliver anti-bullying messages in an unconventional manner. Covered with tattoos all over his face and body, The Scary Guy pokes fun at the audience and yet gets serious about the harm of bullying. His message is to "show [kids] they have the power to make the choice to be who they want to be and not become what they see and hear around them. ... [The letters from the kids] just tell me what it's like to make a difference, to make a change -- to wake up to the idea that they don't have to live with stress and negative behavior around them" (87).

Indeed, children and teens need to learn that they are who they are and they can be what they want to be, regardless of what other people call them or how they try to hurt them. 13-year-old Faye Gibson is constantly bullied by schoolmates who call her ugly. In January 2012, Gibson made a YouTube video "Am I Pretty or Ugly" in order to get a second opinion from strangers on the Internet (88). Her mother Naomi Gibson told *ABC Good Morning America*, "I took away her Facebook and Twitter account because of bullying. She needs to stop putting herself out there. Now people are walking around asking her if she's pretty to her face. It's hurting her more in the long run, I think" (89).

Keeping children away from Facebook and Twitter may not be the right thing to do. Instead, parents should monitor their kids' Facebook messages and tweets to make sure that they are not being bullied as well as they are not bullying others. It is best for parents to "befriend" their children on Facebook, and to "follow" them on Twitter.

Indianapolis attorney Mark S. Zuckerberg was delighted when Facebook reactivated his profile after mistakenly deleting it for the reason of "false identity." Attorney Zuckerberg explained his affinity towards Facebook: "I have teenage kids and it's the only way that you can really see what they are up to and talk to them" (90).

Similarly, Anna Berry of Littleton, Colorado is connected with her 13-year-old daughter Ashley on every social network that the teen joined. Berry's rightful concern stems from her keen observation as a parent: "You would see a girl who should be on top of the world coming home and just closing herself into her bedroom" (73). Instead of being a victim, Ashley Berry founded G.I.R.L.S. Workshops (Girls Inspiring Real Leadership Skills), an interactive program for girls "to hear from anti-bullying advocate Ashley as she shares her 2-year journey as a victim of bullying and online impersonation and how she turned those experiences around to help others and now empowers young girls to be comfortable and proud with who they are" (91).

GigaOm senior writer Mathew Ingram opined that if the NSA tools were available, he probably would have used them to snoop on his kids (92). And his daughter Meaghan responded in a *GigaOm* article, "All in all, my dad's surveillance of my Internet activities has not impacted me negatively in the slightest. I don't know what my online experiences would have been like if my dad had been completely missing, or too involved in them — I do know that I appreciate what he's done for me and my sisters. In a way, it almost feels like it's a specific kind of affection: that my dad cares enough to find out what I'm doing online, but also cares enough that he trusts me to make the right decisions without hurting myself. I think that shows a level of parenting most children would be happy to have" (93).

In September 2010, SafetyWeb introduced a new subscription service for parents to help protect kids from common online dangers from sexting to cyberbullying (94). Without the parents having to monitor every post, the service automatically scours the Internet and monitors a child's online activities and immediately red-flags for the parents any and all potential threats to their child. The service goes a step further by helping parents keep tabs on their child's mobile calls and text messages. Although there is a delicate balance between children's privacy and parental awareness, a good parent should always be attentive to their children's activities and feelings – both online and offline. Rachel Ehmke's suicide note "I'm fine = I wish I could tell you how I really feel" pointed to deadly consequences of the lack of communication and parental awareness.

After all, parents play an epochal role in their children's behavior. In 1998, researchers from the University of Maryland and the National Institute of Child Health and Human Development found that "a proactive parental monitoring approach may be associated with less adolescent drinking" (95). CNN legal analyst and criminal defense attorney Mark O'Mara believes that parents should be held criminally liable for their kids' cyberbullying: "If parents are not going to assume responsibility for their children's online access on their own … I would support legislation that places legal responsibility on parents, making them liable for what the children do with the online access parents provide" (96).

Until parents step up to the challenge of responsive parenting in the digital age, legislation may be necessary to keep an eye on social media platforms. On May 10, 2021, a bipartisan coalition of 44 attorneys general[1] sent Mark Zuckerberg a letter to urge Facebook to abandon plans for a version of Instagram for kids under 13. The letter explains that the "use of social media can be detrimental to the health and well-being of children, who are not equipped to navigate the challenges of having a social media account. Further, Facebook has historically failed to protect the welfare of children on its platforms. The attorneys general have an interest in protecting our youngest citizens, and Facebook's plans to create a platform where kids under the age of 13 are encouraged to share content online is contrary to that interest" (97). Indeed, research has shown that heavy social media use is damaging teenagers' mental and emotional health (149).

Regardless of legislative intervention, parental awareness and proper education are the keys to stop bullying and cyberbullying. For instance, as a part of the five-month Aware.Prepare.Prevent (A.P.P.) campaign, the Norfolk FBI in May 2012 held a program on parental awareness on innocent images, sexting, cyberbullying, and gangs (98). FBI community outreach can move the needle.

---

[1] 44 attorneys general from Massachusetts, Nebraska, Vermont, Tennessee, Alaska, California, Connecticut, Delaware, District of Columbia, Guam, Hawaii, Idaho, Illinois, Iowa, Kansas, Kentucky, Louisiana, Maine, Maryland, Michigan, Minnesota, Mississippi, Missouri, Montana, Nevada, New Hampshire, New Jersey, New Mexico, New York, North Carolina, Northern Mariana Islands, Ohio, Oklahoma, Oregon, Puerto Rico, Rhode Island, South Carolina, South Dakota, Texas, Utah, Virginia, Washington, Wisconsin, and Wyoming.

18.5   Student Awareness in School Safety

April 16, 2007 was a truly sad day when I heard with disbelief the news about the horrific school shooting at Virginia Tech, my alma mater. 23-year-old Seung Hui Cho, an English major at Virginia Tech, murdered 32 and injured 17 students and faculty before taking his own life (99).

Although no one could have foreseen the tragedy, red flags and warning signs had been abundant for many years according to the 2007 Virginia Tech Review Panel report presented to then Virginia Governor Tim Kaine (100). In 1999 when Cho was in the 8th grade, his middle school teachers identified suicidal and homicidal ideations in his writings referencing the Columbine High School massacre that occurred on April 20th that year. The school requested his parents seek counseling for him. He received a psychiatric evaluation and was prescribed antidepressant medication.

In Fall 2005, as Cho started his junior year at Virginia Tech, his poetry professor Nikki Giovanni was concerned about violence in his writing. English Department Chair and Professor Lucinda Roy removed Cho from Giovanni's class and tutored him one-on-one with assistance from Prof. Frederick D'Aguiar. When Cho refused to go to counseling, Roy notified the Division of Student Affairs, the Cook Counseling Center, the Schiffert Health Center, the Virginia Tech police, and the College of Liberal Arts and Human Sciences.

In the winter of 2005, several female students filed reports with the Virginia Tech Police Department (VTPD) to complain about "annoying" contacts and "disturbing" instant messages from Cho. On December 13, Cho's suitemate received an instant message from Cho stating, "I might as well kill myself now." The suitemate alerted VTPD. Cho was taken to Carilion St. Albans Psychiatric Hospital for an overnight stay and mental evaluation. He was released after psychologists determined that he did not present an imminent danger to himself or others.

In Spring 2006, Cho wrote a paper in Prof. Bob Hicok's creative writing class, detailing a young man who hated the students at his school and planned to kill them and himself. In February 2007, Cho ordered his first handgun online from TGSCOM. In March, he purchased a second handgun at Roanoke Firearms. The store initiated the required background check by police, but found no record of mental health issues in the National Instant Criminal Background Check System. From March to April, Cho purchased several 10-round magazines and ammunition from eBay, Wal-Mart, and Dick's Sporting Goods.

About 7:15 in the morning of April 16, 2007, Cho entered West Ambler Johnston residence hall, a 2-minute walk from his dormitory. He shot and killed Emily Hilscher in her dormitory room after she was dropped off by her boyfriend. Resident advisor Ryan Christopher Clark went to investigate noises in Hilscher's room and was also shot.

At 9:01 a.m., Cho mailed a package at the Blacksburg post office to NBC News in New York. The package contained pictures of himself holding weapons, an

1,800-word rambling diatribe, and video recordings in which he expressed rage, resentment, and desire to get even with his oppressors.

Two hours after the first double homicide, Cho entered Norris Hall, an engineering building, at 9:15 a.m. He chained the doors shut on the three main entrances from the inside. Around 9:30 a.m., he began a shooting spree that lasted about 11 minutes. He fired 174 rounds, killing 30 and wounding 17 students and faculty. Prof. Liviu Librescu barricaded his classroom door to give his students time to escape through the windows (101). Librescu and one of his students were killed. The massacre finally ended at 9:51 a.m. when Cho shot himself in the head.

On April 19, the autopsy of Cho found no brain function abnormalities and no toxic substances, drugs, or alcohol that could explain the rampage. Furthermore, there was no evidence that he knew any of the 32 people whom he killed.

Dr. Roger Depue, a 21-year veteran of the Federal Bureau of Investigation (FBI), wrote in the Virginia Tech Review Panel report, "Experts who evaluate possible indicators that an individual is at risk of harming himself or others know to seek out many sources for clues, certain red flags that merit attention. ... When a cluster of indicators is present then the risk becomes more serious. Thus, a person who possesses firearms, is a loner, shows an interest in past shooting situations, writes stories about homicide and suicide, exhibits aberrant behavior, has talked about retribution against others, and has a history of mental illness and refuses counseling would obviously be considered a significant risk of becoming dangerous to himself or others" (102).

The report concluded, "Accurate and complete information on individuals prohibited from possessing firearms is essential to keep guns out of the wrong hands." However, privacy laws and social stigma of mental illness presented a huge obstacle in linking mental health data with criminal background check. "We need to do a much better job educating educators, [the] mental health community and law enforcement that they can, in fact, share information when a person's safety or a community's safety is in fact potentially endangered," said Health and Human Services Secretary Michael O. Leavitt after delivering the report to President George W. Bush (103).

Had Cho's mental history been added to the National Instant Criminal Background Check System, he would not have been able to purchase firearms. If school buildings had installed monitored security cameras, he might not have gotten away easily from the crime scene in West Ambler Johnston residence hall, he would not have had the time to chain the doors shut on the three main entrances of Norris Hall, and the police could have been dispatched after he fired the first few shots.

School safety is one of the topmost concerns of parents for their kids. In February 2012, community leader Morris Grifton called for video surveillance in school after two teachers were arrested for lewd acts involving pupils at Miramonte Elementary School. "We're saying enough is enough," said Grifton at a rally with angry parents. "We want cameras in the classrooms, in the hallways and around the school" (104). In August 2013, University of Maryland-Eastern Shore purchased 200 bulletproof whiteboards to offer professors and students greater protection in the event of a school shooting (105). These measures are just the tip of the iceberg.

Then Virginia Tech President Charles W. Steger hinted towards the need for better information awareness in a written statement, "The [Virginia Tech Review Panel] report unearthed the deep complexities of the issues facing college campuses today. We believe that this will further inform the national and our state discussion on the nexus between societal safety and personal freedoms" (103).

Better information awareness does not mean less personal freedoms. Feeling safe in school is a prerequisite for a conducive learning environment. Everyone should be free to express their opinions, voice their concerns, and become better informed. In the age of big data, correlating Cho's mental history and his purchase data from eBay could have alerted the authorities, mental healthcare professionals, and university counselors that he really needed psychological help.

Daniel J. Solove, John Marshall Harlan Research Professor of Law at George Washington University Law School, opines that higher education needs privacy officers and privacy/security training. Solove said, "The Family Educational Rights and Privacy Act (FERPA) and other privacy law allow for sharing of personal information about students in distress, and in many circumstances, FERPA permits schools to share the data with a student's parents. … The Department of Education issued new FERPA rules to clarify when information may be shared in a health or safety emergency. But the problem wasn't just with the FERPA rules – it was that people didn't understand them, didn't know about them, and weren't effectively trained about them. The problem also stemmed from the lack of a privacy officer whom various school officials and employees could have called to figure out what to do with the information they had. The situation at Virginia Tech can still readily happen again. That's because higher education is lagging behind other industries in at least two key privacy protections: (1) having a privacy officer; and (2) engaging in training and awareness education" (106).

The 2007 Virginia Tech shooting prompted many universities to improve their emergency notification system and procedure in compliance with the Clery Act. Signed in 1990, the Clery Act is also known as the Crime Awareness and Campus Security Act – a law enacted after 19-year-old Lehigh University freshman Jeanne Clery was raped and murdered in her dorm room in April 1986 (107).

When gunshots erupted on the Virginia Tech campus again in December 2011, the university notified all 30,000+ students within minutes via text messages, emails, the school website, Twitter, and the campus-wide public address system. "We all knew immediately after it happened not to go to campus," said Virginia Tech sophomore Abby Lorenz. "All of my roommates and I got texts and e-mails, and they've sent us multiple updates" (108). Timely notifications and crime awareness are essential to deterring violence on campus and minimizing potential causalities.

In addition to campus security, there are social apps designed for students to help one another in need. Winner of the White House "Apps Against Abuse" Technology Challenge, Circle of 6 is an iPhone app that uses GPS and pre-installed text messages to alert friends to the user's location if anything goes wrong (109). Two weeks after its launch in March 2012, Circle of 6 already had 19,000 downloads (110).

In the Spring 2012 issue of *Virginia Tech Magazine*, Alumni Distinguished Professor Emeritus William E. Snizek wrote, "During almost 40 years on the Tech faculty, I was fascinated by the graffiti I found on desktops. … On one desktop, a student wrote, 'Why do I always want to cry?' And just below that, another responded, 'I know how you feel, trust me, talk to someone'" (111).

Without someone to talk to face-to-face openly, a troubled individual may rely solely on the Internet proliferated with information, misinformation, and disinformation. It is appalling that anyone can find on the Internet detailed instructions and user guides on school shooting, a horrific act of domestic terrorism. For instance, Lolokaust's school shooting guide laden with profanity, pornography, and erroneous information was the number one search result on Google in May 2014 for the search phrase "shoot up your school." (See Fig. 18.2).

According to a 2013 study by search-targeted advertising company Chitika, the top listing in Google's organic search results receives 32.5% of the traffic, compared to 17.6% for the second position, and the traffic degrades to a mere 2.4% for the last position on the first page of Google search (112).

By February 2021, Lolokaust's school shooting guide no longer appears anywhere in the 24 pages of top Google search results for "shoot up your school." However, the site is still indexed and searchable. Google Chrome's tagline is: "The web is what you make of it" (113). The vile Lolokaust website might have a redeeming value if the Google search history – a part of user's digital footprint and exhaust data – would help identify those troubled individuals and provide them psychological counseling.

The prevalence of Facebook use also gives introverts an outlet to express their lonely feelings by reaching out to others. "By helping lonely people on the periphery of a social network," said James H. Fowler of UC San Diego and Nicholas A. Christakis of Harvard University, "we can create a protective barrier against loneliness that will keep the whole network from unraveling" (114).

Facebook and other social media platforms can serve to increase student awareness and improve school safety. In March 2012, the American Civil Liberties Union sued Minnewaska Area Middle School over a search of Facebook and email accounts of a 12-year-old, sixth-grade female student (115). Although the Minnesota middle school may have intruded on the student's privacy, the school should be commended for being proactive in the total awareness of its schoolchildren.

In September 2013, the Glendale, California school district hired a private firm – Geo Listening – to monitor and report on 14,000 middle and high school students' posts on Twitter, Facebook, and other social media for a year. Superintendent Richard Sheehan talked about some successful interventions on suicide and gun control: "We were able to save a life. It's just another avenue to open up a dialogue with parents about safety. … We had to educate the student on the dangers of guns. He was a good kid. It had a good ending" (116).

In May 2014, 17-year-old John David LaDue was arrested for planning a school massacre at Waseac High School in Minnesota. His plan was thwarted by Chelsie Shellhas and Katie Harty who alerted the police about suspicious activities at a storage locker facility. Police later found bombs, guns, pyrotechnic chemicals, and

Fig. 18.2   Google Search Results on "shoot up your school" (May 3, 2014)

attack plans in LaDue's home and storage locker. CNN's Ben Brumfield wrote, "If his Facebook page is any indicator, LaDue is partial to the dark side, and he 'likes' assault rifles… His taste in movies is dominated by blood, gore, combat and fisticuffs" (117). On the bright side of Facebook, Shellhas and Harty received many Facebook messages from people thanking them for being vigilant.

However, it is not easy to identify and help the mentally disturbed. On May 23, 2014, 22-year-old Elliot Rodger went on a killing spree in Isla Vista, California that resulted in 7 fatalities including two women outside a sorority house near the campus of UC Santa Barbara. His motivations were mainly misogyny and self-pity. Rodger frequented online discussion boards and social networks to express his frustration and hatred of women: "There is something mentally wrong with the way [women's] brains are wired. They are incapable of reason or thinking rationally. … Women are not drawn to indicators of evolutionary fitness. If they were, they'd be all over me. … The sweater I'm wearing in the picture is $500 from Neiman Marcus" (118). An online forum member known as "Dtugg" had tangled with Rodger several times in his attempt to give advice to the troubled man, but to no avail. After the tragedy, some online members emailed Dtugg saying, "God bless you" and "You truly tried."

Slate writer Brian Levinson opined that he could have been Elliot Rodger. "Many men—including me, once upon a time—know what it's like to be young, frustrated, and full of rage toward women," said Levinson. "I was just as messed up as Cho, Rodger, and Klebold. I was humiliated by my weight, which bordered on morbid obesity. I fancied myself an intellectual, but would've traded an acceptance letter to Harvard for one magical kiss from a classmate I'll call Cynthia. I was a virgin until a year after I graduated college. Klebold and Rodger had friends; Cho had a family who clearly loved him. Why did these guys pick up guns, but I never did?" (119).

In humanity, there is no one size fits all. The best we can do is to be vigilant and empathic at the same time—be more aware and more caring of the social and emotional development for all students. Thanks to the partnership with community leaders and teachers, the FBI and local police have successfully thwarted numerous school shooting plots around the country.

18.6   Crime Awareness in Video Surveillance

On the night of March 3, 1991, George Holliday was awakened in his apartment by police sirens and helicopter (120). He grabbed his camera and recorded about nine minutes of video showing four LAPD officers beating up a drunk driver and parolee named Rodney King (121). The video went viral on the national airwaves (122). On April 29, 1992, a jury acquitted the officers accused in the beating, and Los Angeles erupted in weeklong riots that left 54 people dead and $1 billion in property damage (123). The second trial of the four police offers began in February 1993. The jury found two of the officers guilty of civil rights violations, and the streets of Los Angeles remained quiet when the judge read the verdict on April 19, 1993 (124).

On May 25, 2020, 17-year-old bystander Darnella Frazier captured an incriminating video of Minneapolis police officer Derek Chauvin kneeling on George Floyd's neck for more than 9 minutes. The viral video posted on Facebook led to the murder conviction of Chauvin, the firing of three other officers at the scene, a ban on police chokeholds, and a global racial justice movement (125). Minnesota Gov. Tim Walz said, "Taking that video, I think many folks know, is maybe the only reason that Derek Chauvin will go to prison" (126). Indeed, prosecuting attorney Steve Schleicher convinced the jurors and said in his closing arguments, "This case is exactly what you thought when you saw it first, when you saw that video. It is exactly that. You can believe your eyes. … This wasn't policing. This was murder."

In some states such as Illinois, Massachusetts, and Maryland, it is illegal to record any on-duty police officer (127). Under the existing wiretapping and eavesdropping laws, all parties must consent for a recording to take place. This restriction does not apply to property owners' videotaping in their own private residences or business premises for security purposes.

There are many instances where video recordings have saved lives and brought justice:

1. In 2003, a Florida couple Jennifer and Brett Schwartz installed a nanny-cam to keep an eye on their infant daughter who seemed unsettled being around their babysitter (128). Among the hundreds of hours of video, 29-year-old babysitter Claudia Muro was seen shaking the child and slamming her to the floor. It was shocking because Muro was highly recommended by a local child care agency and she passed a series of background checks.

2. In 2010, another Florida couple noticed a black eye on one of their two children, and their nanny could not explain what happened. They installed a hidden camera, which caught the nanny swatting, slapping, and kicking an 11-month-old boy. 53-year-old nanny Jeannine Marie Campbell pleaded guilty to abuse charges (129).

3. In December 2011, Salvatore Miglino secretly recorded on his iPhone a verbal dispute with his estranged mother-in-law Cheryl Hepner. During the argument, Hepner pulled out a gun and shot Miglino. In a classic he-said, she-said, Hepner claimed self-defense; but the iPhone recording proved otherwise, and she was charged with attempted murder in the first degree (130).

4. In August 2013, Silicon Valley entrepreneur Gurbaksh Chahal was arrested and charged with hitting and kicking his girlfriend 117 times over a half-hour period. Although Chahal's victim declined to cooperate with the prosecutors, the incident was caught on film via a home surveillance system, and Chahal finally pleaded guilty to domestic violence and battery charges in April 2014 (131).

5. In October 2013, Dallas police officer Cardan Spencer fatally shot Bobby Gerald Bennett, a 52-year-old man who was mentally ill. Spencer claimed self-defense, but a video captured by a neighbor's surveillance camera showed that Bennett did not pose any threat to the police before he was shot. "Officers are not above the law," said Dallas Police Chief David Brown who fired and charged Spencer with felony aggravated assault (132).

6. In February 2021, American actress Olivia Munn posted an image and surveillance video on Twitter to ask for assistance in identifying the assailant who attacked her friend's 52-year-old mother in Queens, New York. She pleaded for help: "We're gonna find this guy. Queens, Internet, please... do your shit. 🙏@ NYPD109Pct" (133) Within 24 hours, the assailant was identified and apprehended by NYPD.

In June 2012, American professional skateboarder Tony Hawk captured in his home security camera two thieves stealing a skateboard from his car. He posted several images on Instagram asking them to return the skateboard or else he would notify the police. Hawk said, "So much of our life is recorded on video now, including the worst parts" (134).

Fixed video surveillance, aka closed-circuit television (CCTV), has long been effective in reducing and deterring crime in shopping malls, convenience stores, gas stations, parking garages, airports, banks, casinos, and other public places. Public CCTV systems have been employed extensively in cities throughout Europe, and similar systems have been deployed in some major U.S. cities.

A Long Island, New York study found that serious crimes dropped 47% after CCTV surveillance systems were installed by businesses and homeowners in 1993. There were 8,000 burglaries in 1994 compared to about 15,000 in 1975, and there were also fewer robberies in 1994 than in 1975 (135).

Researchers from UC Berkeley's Center for Information Technology Research in the Interest of Society studied the crime-deterrent effects of the San Francisco Community Safety Camera Program between January 2005 and January 2008. They found a statistically significant 22% decline in property crime occurring within 100 feet of camera locations, but no statistically significant changes in crime beyond 100 feet from the site (136).

The City of Los Angeles is a California municipality in which law enforcement monitors video surveillance cameras in real time. Researchers from USC School of Policy, Planning, and Development reported in May 2008 that there was no statistical significance in the drop of violent crimes and property crimes along Hollywood Boulevard's "Walk of Fame" (137).

Despite the mixed results based on statistical analyses, video surveillance has shown effectiveness in solving crimes and apprehending suspects:

1. For four days between December 30, 2011 and January 2, 2012, there were 52 suspicious car and building fires across Los Angeles – a city that had not seen such a rash of fires since the 1992 Rodney King riots. LAPD was able to arrest the arsonist who resembled a man seen in a surveillance video near the scene of one fire (138).
2. Police, businesses, and community associations across the U.S. have been installing AI-enabled cameras that spot and clock license plate data to help solve crimes and track down suspects. One of the surveillance-camera companies is Flock. "We started Flock to eliminate non-violent crime," said the company spokesperson Meg Heusel. "That's because 87 percent of non-violent crime goes

unsolved throughout the U.S. and that's not due to a lack of trying on the law enforcement side" (139).

3. When the anti-fraud and anti-money laundering (AML) systems identify suspicious bank transactions, it can:

- Search on transactions in the video surveillance system to find suspect's face.
- Use correlated search to identify other potential suspects aiding criminal activity.
- Use facial recognition to search across other transactions.
- Find the license plate of a vehicle when a person of interest uses a drive-up ATM.
- Export video evidence for law enforcement.

Back to the issue of police brutality: In the aftermath of the shooting death of Michael Brown in Ferguson, Missouri in August2014 followed by protests and civil unrest, a petition has gained traction calling for police to wear body cameras that capture everything in front of them while they are doing their jobs (140).

Body worn video (BWV) or wearable video camera has shown to be a promising solution. In a 2012–2013 study, half of the 54 uniformed patrol officers in Rialto, California were equipped with BWV. The Rialto PD overall had an 88% decline in complaints filed against officers, and a 60% decline in use-of-force compared with the 12 months before the study (141). "There were so many situations where it was 'he said, she said,' and juries tend to believe police officers over accused criminals," said Jay Stanley, senior policy analyst at the American Civil Liberties Union. "The technology really has the potential to level the playing field in any kind of controversy or allegation of abuse" (141).

In June 2012, *Time Magazine*'s congressional correspondent Jay Newton-Small asked the Syrian dissident Abu Ghassan whether his AK-47 or his video camera was the more powerful weapon. Ghassan replied, "My AK!" But he paused for a few seconds, and said, "Actually, if there is an Internet connection, my camera is more powerful" (142).

18.7   Community Awareness in Neighborhood Watch

San Francisco's Community Safety Camera Program was launched by then Mayor Gavin Newsom in late 2005. The program placed more than 70 non-monitored cameras in mainly high-crime areas throughout the city. Researchers from UC Berkeley's Center for Information Technology Research in the Interest of Society found that the program resulted in over 20% reduction in property crime within the view of the cameras (143). Although the cameras were less effective in providing evidence for police investigations due to their choppy video quality (low frame rate and low resolution), Newsom spokesman Nathan Ballard told reporters, "We believe these cameras have a deterrent effect on crime. The neighbors appreciate them" (144).

Apart from citywide video surveillance, Neighborhood Watch is an organized group of citizens devoted to crime and vandalism prevention within a neighborhood. The modern practice began in 1964 as a response to the rape and murder of Catherine Susan (Kitty) Genovese in Queens, New York. In 1972, the National Sheriff's Association officially launched the nationwide Neighborhood Watch program that "counts on citizens to organize themselves and work with law enforcement to keep a trained eye and ear on their communities, while demonstrating their presence at all times of day and night" (145). By 1982, 12% of the U.S. population was involved in a Neighborhood Watch.

In February 2012, neighborhood watch leader George Zimmerman fatally shot 17-year-old Trayvon Martin at a gated community in Sanford, Florida. When Zimmerman first saw Martin walking inside the community, he called police to report Martin's behavior as suspicious. Zimmerman followed Martin and confronted him. Their altercation ended with Zimmerman shooting dead Martin who was unarmed. Sanford police did not arrest Zimmerman due to Florida's controversial Stand Your Ground law (146), which states that a person may use force in self-defense when there is a reasonable belief of a threat, without an obligation to retreat first. However, public outcry resulted in the government filing charges of second-degree murder against Zimmerman in April 2012. Nevertheless, documents and evidence began to surface, making the case more complicated for the state prosecutor (147).

In March 2012, President Barack Obama addressed the Trayvon Martin shooting in personal terms: "Obviously this is a tragedy. I can only imagine what these parents are going through. When I think about this boy I think about my own kids and I think every parent in America should be able to understand why it is absolutely imperative that we investigate every aspect of this and that everybody pulls together, federal, state and local to figure out exactly how this tragedy happened. … If I had a son, he would look like Trayvon. I think they are right to expect that all of us as Americans are going to take this with the seriousness it deserves and we will get to the bottom of exactly what happened" (148).

If the gated community had installed video surveillance cameras, chances are that the truths would have been revealed or the altercation would not have occurred in the first place. In lieu of or in addition to community video cameras, homeowners can use their webcams and smartphone cameras to monitor their neighborhood on a volunteer basis.

In early 2014, there were dozens of home burglaries in the quiet residential neighborhood of Grandview, Arizona. The residents started a virtual neighborhood watch using the Nextdoor mobile app to send out detailed alerts about suspicious cars and people within a one-square-mile area. As a result, the rate of burglaries had plummeted. According to Nextdoor, over 39,000 neighborhoods across the U.S. have been using their private social network for neighborhood watch as of August 2014 (149). "Before, they didn't have these tools. It was people chit-chatting in their front yards," said Slade Grove, president of the Grandview neighborhood association. "I think it has shown the police department that we are an active neighborhood and that we are very concerned about crime" (150).

The National Sheriff's Association has been working on a mobile app that enables neighborhood watch members to share with law enforcement their GPS location and real-time video surveillance footage shot on a smartphone. "After the Trayvon Martin case in Florida, we started looking at our program," said John Thompson, chief of staff and deputy executive director of the National Sheriffs' Association. "We don't want people to get involved, and this app would pretty much stop that. You wouldn't have to get out of your car. You wouldn't have to leave your house" (150). Technology will help prevent tragedies like the Kitty Genovese murder and Trayvon Martin shooting.

Imagine taking the mobile apps further to a large-scale, big-data implementation. Before going into hibernation in March 2020, SETI@home was a distributed computing program that involved 5+ million of at-home users in the Search for Extra Terrestrial Intelligence (SETI) (151). Since its inception in 1999, SETI@home had been recycling unused CPU cycles on home computers to help analyze data collected from radio telescopes in search of signals from other intelligent worlds. Powered by IBM's World Community Grid, FightAIDS@Home is a distributed smartphone app that scientists at the Olson Laboratory and The Scripps Research Institute are tapping into the surplus power of cell phones to fight AIDS (152).

Likewise, we can envision a distributed software program "STS@home" for neighborhood watch. The artificial intelligence system analyzes live video streams from webcams and smartphones in the Search for Trespassers and Suspects (STS) in all neighborhoods. Suspicious activities automatically trigger alerts. A facial recognition feature in the software system can assist police in locating missing children, apprehending fugitives, and solving crimes nationwide. Technology exists today that uses video analytics to distill millions of hours of raw video footage into structured, searchable data (153).

About 40,000 people registered in 2012 to play Foldit, a game about protein molecules (154). These citizen scientists, with no training in science, deciphered the structure of the Mason-Pfizer monkey virus in just 10 days, solving a problem which had stumped scientists for 15 years (155). Similarly, a game about catching criminals or locating missing persons in STS@home may yield important clues even for the cold cases that are hard to crack.

To canvas Manhattan with live video feeds for the purpose of tracking pedestrian traffic, New York start-up company Placemeter is paying city residents up to $50 a month for posting a smartphone in their window (156).

Apart from all the high-tech tools and solutions, Terry Ulmer of Alpine, California, had a creative idea that honored the veterans of Pearl Harbor. In early 2014, he erected a missile launcher for the neighborhood watch sign in his front yard. "You go into neighborhoods and you see a little sign that says neighborhood watch," Ulmer told reporter Misha DiBono at Fox 5 News San Diego. "Well, this is how we roll out here in Alpine in the valley. We're the real deal! … This is the Mark 10 Twin Arm Guided Missile Launcher. The very first one was put on ships in 1959, and they ran these all the way out until the 80's" (157). (See Fig. 18.3)

Fig. 18.3 A Neighborhood Watch Missile Launcher (Courtesy of Terry Ulmer of Alpine CA and Misha DiBono at Fox 5 News San Diego)

18.8   Situational Awareness in Traffic Safety

John Leech, partner at the auditing and advisory firm KPMG, contemplated a "car-to-infrastructure" future where "traffic systems can use vehicles as sensors to quickly identify congestion and divert drivers to clearer routes, saving time and reducing emissions." Leech also proposed a "car-to-car" technology that "lets drivers spontaneously network with each other to warn of road hazards or other traffic problems" (158).

The sci-fi future may arrive sooner than we think. First, in March 2004, 15 autonomous vehicles left a starting gate in the desert outside of Barstow, California, to make history in the DARPA Grand Challenge, a first-of-its-kind race to foster the development of self-driving cars (159). Then, in June 2011, Nevada became the first state in America to pass robotic driver legislation (160). After 200,000 miles of computer-led driving without accident in freeways and service streets, Google's self-driving car passed its Nevada driver's license test with flying colors in May 2012 (161).

On May 18, 2012, journalist Peter Valdes-Dapena rode with two Google engineers in a self-driving car on a loop around several blocks in Washington D.C. He wrote about his experience on CNN, "No Google engineer taught the car that a bunch of kids on a field trip would march out in front of it at an intersection. It stopped and waited for them on its own. And no-one told it that, right after that, another car would run the four-way stop sign right in front of it. It handled that, too, avoiding a collision all on its own" (162).

Until Google's and others' self-driving cars become widely adopted, we will continue to see many drivers break traffic laws and create hazards to themselves and others. If everyone were to obey traffic safety rules, there would be no need for red light cameras installed in many busy intersections across America. A classmate of my wife was hit by a car as it was running a red traffic light. Fortunately, the classmate was not injured. The driver rushed to the pedestrian and helped her to the sidewalk. He kept apologizing and insisting that he had time to rush the yellow light. She eventually snapped out of her trance and snarled, "You obviously did not have time. The light was not yellow, it was red, and I had the right of way."

Invented in the Netherlands, red light cameras have been installed around the world (163). A 2003 study revealed that camera enforcement reduced traffic violations 40–50% (164). While there were reports of an increase in rear-end crashes following camera installation, there was a 25–30% reduction in injury crashes caused mostly by the more serious side-impact collisions.

Although there were stories about red light cameras catching cheating spouses and pot-smoking kids (165), privacy is not really an issue here because we drive on public roads and our license plates are always in plain view.

In the city of Los Angeles, I personally witness every week at least one driver ignoring a 4-way stop sign, running a red light, changing lanes without signaling, or looking totally distracted talking on the cell phone. I think to myself, "Where are the police when we need them?"

Developed by the Embedded Systems Lab at the University of California, Riverside, DuiCam is a free mobile video recorder app to empower people to report drunk drivers. A user may place a smartphone in a dashboard mount, press record to capture activity happening in front of the car, and send the license plate and GPS location to the police (166).

Akin to a police cruiser's dashboard camera, some commercial dash cams allow drivers to record in high-definition video day or night what is in front and on the sides of their vehicles. If dash cams become more prevalent, drivers will be more cautious and not endanger themselves and others on the roads because of their road rage or aggressive driving habits. Dash cams can simplify investigations of auto accident claims, and may lower auto insurance premiums for most drivers. In March 2021, an Uber driver's dash cam recorded how he was berated and coughed on by maskless passengers, leading police to identify and arrest the unruly passengers for assault and battery as well as the violation of health and safety code (167).

Some public transits including LA Metro and DART have installed the SmartDrive on-board video safety system on over 10,000 vehicles in 2013 (168). Capturing and analyzing real-world driving behavior, SmartDrive's video analysis, predictive analytics, and personalized performance program help fleets improve driving skills, save fuel, and avoid accidents. Furthermore, new Android and iOS applications such as Eco:Speed optimize GPS directions by factoring in fuel consumption, number of traffic stops, speed limits, and local traffic conditions (169).

In June 2013, Google acquired social mapping service Waze (170). Partnering with Apple, Facebook, and now Google, Waze offers real-time, user-generated mapping service as drivers vocally report traffic jam or hazardous conditions on the roads. The service had over 140 million users in 2020 (171).

Red light cameras, dash cams, on-board video safety system, automatic license plate readers, and new software applications all serve to heighten drivers' awareness, increase traffic safety, and help law enforcement in apprehending suspects.

18.9   Location Awareness in Personal Safety

Originally created by the U.S. Department of Defense (DoD) in 1973 for military applications, Global Positioning System (GPS) is a satellite-based navigation system that provides location and time information anywhere on Earth (172). On September 1, 1983, a Soviet Su-15 interceptor aircraft shot down Korean Airlines (KAL) Flight 007, killing all 269 crewmembers and passengers (173). The civilian aircraft was en route from New York City to Seoul via Anchorage when it strayed into prohibited Soviet airspace. To avoid navigational errors like that of KAL 007, President Ronald Reagan ordered the U.S. military to make GPS available for civilian use.

Researcher Amanda Lenhart at Pew Internet and American Life Project found that 75% of 12–17 year-olds owned cell phones in 2010, up from 45% in 2004 (174). Some wireless phone companies offer family locator plans for parents to keep track of their kids' whereabouts using GPS programs. Jack McArtney of Verizon Wireless spoke of VZ Navigator, "Once you locate your child on a mobile device, you can press a button and get turn-by-turn directions to that location" (175).

For young children without cell phones, there are wearable or attachable GPS tracking devices such as the Amber Alert GPS. "Our priority is child safety and security," said Carol Colombo, CEO of Amber Alert GPS. "Kids should have the freedom to be kids, to run and play and ride their bike to their friend's house. The V3 device is designed to give parents the confidence to send their children into the world, knowing they have taken the right steps to keep them safe" (176).

GPS locator is not just for child safety. Emmy Anderson of Sprint said, "We're seeing adults using it with their elderly parents, just to make sure mom or dad didn't get lost when they were driving to their doctor's appointment, that kind of thing. ... We're also seeing siblings using it, for example, if both of them are away at different colleges, and they just want to make sure the other is safe on a date" (175).

GPS also plays a role in search and rescue missions. Personal locator beacons (PLBs) have been available for satellite-aided search and rescue notification using geosynchronous and low earth orbit satellites. A more advanced system – MEOSAR (Medium Earth Orbit Search and Rescue satellites) – is adding search and rescue transponders to newer global navigation satellites including GPS (USA), GLONASS (Russia), and Galileo (ESA) (177). The GPS version is dubbed the Distress Alerting Satellite System (DASS). According to the National Aeronautics and Space

Administration (NASA) website, "NASA, in coordination with the Global Positioning System (GPS) Program Office and Sandia National Laboratories, has determined that the GPS constellation would be the best and most cost-effective MEO satellite constellation to host the search and rescue (SAR) instruments" (178).

Software companies are integrating geographic information systems (GIS) technology and social media to map people's tweets and other social media platforms with geospatial data. This pairing has been helpful in disaster response and crisis management. In the wake of the January 12th, 2010 earthquake in Haiti, a free phone number (4636) was established to allow people to text their requests for medical care, food, water, security, and shelter. According to the Mission 4636 report, "Tireless workers and volunteers translated, geolocated and categorized the messages via online crowdsourcing platforms which sorted the information by need and priority, and distributed it to various emergency responders and aid organizations. Initially, the focus was on search and rescue, but the service scaled up about one week after the earthquake to include a wide range of responses, including serious injuries, requests for fresh drinking water, security, unaccompanied children and clusters of requests for food, and even childbirths" (179).

In May 2012, researcher Laura Morris wrote in *Haiti Wired Blog*, "Not only is the ubiquity of mobile telephony globally coupled with the internet and GIS enabling the victims of crisis to become more active in their own recovery, making the delivery of aid a truly participatory process, semantic web tools such as Ushahidi are empowering the globally connected 'crowd' to engage in crisis response and support. Everywhere technology is being used in many different ways to help with disaster & conflict early-warning, management & resolution and for peacebuilding in the aftermath of crisis" (180).

To provide a certain degree of personal safety and crime deterrence, life-logging devices such as the Autographer and the Narrative Clip are clip-on cameras that continually take pictures on their own (181). Autographer, for example, automatically uploads photos and their GPS coordinates via its Bluetooth connection to an iPhone.

18.10   Information Awareness in Law Enforcement

Despite high unemployment and economic recession in 2011, the Federal Bureau of Investigation (FBI) figures showed that murder, rape, robberies, and other serious crimes have fallen to a 48-year low across the United States (182).

Facebook has been involved in promoting public awareness of crime fighting. Since December 2009, Facebook has partnered with the AMBER Alert Program (183). Named after 9-year-old Amber Hagerman who was abducted and murdered in Arlington, Texas in 1996, the AMBER (America's Missing: Broadcasting Emergency Response) Alert Program is a voluntary partnership between law-enforcement agencies, broadcasters, transportation agencies, and the wireless industry, to activate an urgent bulletin in the most serious child-abduction cases

(184). The goal of an AMBER Alert is to galvanize the entire community, adding millions of extra eyes and ears to watch, listen, and help in the safe return of the child and apprehension of the suspect (185). Since 2002, the AMBER Alert Program has been spreading internationally to Australia, Canada, France, Germany, Greece, the Netherlands, the United Kingdom, and others (186).

Law enforcement authorities in New York, Atlanta, San Diego, and Chicago have been using Facebook to gather evidence against gang members and criminals. The success of social media sleuthing has prompted the New York Police Department (NYPD) to double the size of its online investigators in October 2012.

"By capitalizing on the irresistible urge of these suspects to brag about their murderous exploits on Facebook, detectives used social media to draw a virtual map of their criminal activity over the last three years," said NYPD commissioner Raymond Kelly (187).

Donna Lieberman, executive director of the New York Civil Liberties Union, concurred with Kelly. Lieberman and said, "NYPD has the right, indeed the obligation, to pursue effective avenues for investigating criminal gang activity, and that includes using Facebook and other social media. But such methods must be closely monitored so they don't become a vehicle for entrapment or unauthorized surveillance" (187).

Social media has indeed contributed to many success stories in law enforcement:

1. To crack down on underage drinking, the La Crosse Police Department in Wisconsin created a Facebook account in 2009 under the name of "Jenny Anderson" and befriended University of Wisconsin-La Crosse college students. Many accepted the friend requests on Facebook. As a result, the police were able to obtain photos of underage drinkers and send them citations. Two of the students charged, Adam Bauer and Cassandra Stenholt, did not upload the photos themselves, but rather were tagged by friends (188).
2. 26-year-old fugitive Maxi Sopo was on the run from charges of masterminding a bank fraud in Seattle. Sopo updated his Facebook from his hiding place in Cancun, telling his friends that he was living in paradise and loving it. U.S. Secret Service agent Seth Reeg was able to track him down though one of his Facebook friends. Sopo was subsequently arrested in September 2009 (189).
3. In March 2012, detectives from the New York Police Department (NYPD) were attempting to find a shooter. The victim's brother pointed the detectives to Facebook. NYPD's Real Time Crime Center uploaded the Facebook photos into its facial recognition software, and matched them to a database of thousands of mugshots from arrest records. The police identified and arrested the shooter within a matter of days (190).
4. In May 2014, a 16-hours-old baby was kidnapped by a woman wearing a nurse's uniform in the maternity ward of a Canadian hospital in Quebec. The police asked the public for help by posting the description of the woman and her vehicle on social media. Charlène Plante spotted the photo on Facebook and recognized the woman as her former neighbor. The police arrested the kidnapper and returned the baby to her parents within hours after the baby went missing. "The

photo saved our daughter!" said Mélissa McMahon, the baby's mother. "In less than an hour, the photo was everywhere… You were more than thousands of people who shared the photo of this woman on social media. … Know that it was this that saved her, our little Victoria. Every click, every share made the difference" (191).

5. In April 2021, a woman on the online dating app Bumble contacted the FBI after her online match Robert Chapman bragged about traveling to the "District of Criminality" and storming the U.S. Capitol on January 6. She eventually told him, "We are not a match." But the FBI matched Chapman's profile picture with the body camera footage from police officers inside the Capitol (192).

Moreover, federal and local governments are increasingly using social networking sites and big data to aid law enforcement:

1. In a May 2008 memo, the U.S. Citizenship and Immigration Services (USCIS) wrote, "Social networking sites such as MySpace, Facebook, Classmates, Hi-5, and other similar sites are designed to allow people to share their creativity, pictures, and information with others. … Narcissistic tendencies in many people fuels a need to have a large group of 'friends' link to their pages and many of these people accept cyber-friends that they don't even know. This provides an excellent vantage point for FDNS [Fraud Detection and National Security] to observe the daily life of beneficiaries and petitioners who are suspected of fraudulent activities. … This social networking gives FDNS an opportunity to reveal fraud by browsing these sites to see if petitioners and beneficiaries are in a valid relationship or are attempting to deceive CIS about their relationship. Once a user posts online, they create a public record and timeline of their activities. In essence, using MySpace and other like sites is akin to doing an unannounced cyber 'site-visit' on petitioners and beneficiaries" (193).

2. In a "privacy compliance review" issued in November 2011 by the U.S. Department of Homeland Security (DHS), the DHS National Operations Center has been operating a "Social Networking/Media Capability" since June 2010. The Center regularly monitors "publicly available online forums, blogs, public websites and message boards" in order to "collect information used in providing situational awareness and establishing a common operating picture." The list of monitored sites includes household names such as Facebook, MySpace, Twitter, Hulu, YouTube, Flickr, the Drudge Report, Huffington Post, and of course WikiLeaks (194). Furthermore, CNN reported in March 2012 that DHS' surveillance program looks for "words of interest" on Facebook and Twitter posts, and triggers investigations into suspicious profiles (195).

3. Around December 2011, computer hackers were targeting the Boston police website and a police union website. Boston law enforcement contacted Twitter to obtain information about a user for an official criminal investigation. After months of court battle behind closed doors between Boston and the American Civil Liberties Union, Twitter finally complied with the court order and handed over the data from one subscriber to Boston police in March 2012 (196).

4. Police departments in New York, Los Angeles, and many other American cities have been using CompStat to monitor and reduce crime (197). Introduced in 1994 by then commissioner William Bratton of the New York City Police Department, CompStat measures crime patterns by analyzing type of crime, time of day, GPS coordinates, and demographics of suspects. The big data methodology holds police executives accountable for crime rates in the given regions of a city.

5. Police departments in the United States have been using the license plate recognition (LPR) technology to track every vehicle passing by patrol cars equipped with automatic license plate readers (198). The Los Angeles Police Department (LAPD) stores the data including the photograph, license plate number, date, time, and location for five years; and police detectives employ Palantir's data-mining tools to track and apprehend suspects. According to the Los Angeles Police Protective League (LAPPL), LPR has proven effective in solving thousands of criminal cases nationwide (199). The LPR technology and database could have saved some lives in October 2002 when John Allen Muhammad and Lee Boyd Malvo carried out sniper attacks in Virginia, Maryland, and Washington D.C. from a modified sedan.

6. In April 2014, Emilio Ferrara and fellow researchers at Indiana University Bloomington revealed an expert system that "brings together information from mobile phone records, from police databases and from the knowledge and expertise of agents themselves to recreate detailed networks behind criminal organizations" (200). The expert system is capable of discovering members who play central role and providing connection among sub-groups within a criminal organization.

7. DNA testing and genealogy companies such as 23andMe, AncestryDNA, FamilyTreeDNA, and GEDmatch have allowed law enforcement to access their PII (Personally Identifiable Information) databases in attempt to solve crimes. In one case, an alleged murderer was finally caught 40 years later because his distant cousin uploaded her DNA to a genealogy website to find out about her ancestry (201).

8. Although Google has been frowned upon for having their software automatically scan all incoming and outgoing emails (202), Gmail snooping has helped law enforcement apprehend criminals and pedophiles. In July 2014, for example, police in Texas arrested a man after he allegedly sent an email to a friend containing child pornography (203). Google, Facebook, and Microsoft use computer "algorithms to test whether the digital information encoded in images matches against the child pornography database at the National Center for Missing and Exploited Children (NCMEC)" (203).

9. In February 2021, the U.S. Justice Department had charged more than 215 people in connection with the U.S. Capitol riot, about 30 of whom were facing additional charges for attempting to destroy evidence on their social media profiles. When the FBI showed rioter Kevin Lyons a photo that he posted on Instagram, he responded, "Wow, you are pretty good. That was up for only an hour" (204).

Last but not least, the FBI encourages community involvement in law enforcement by offering Citizens Academy (CA) programs, Community Awareness Presentations (CAP), Multi-Cultural Engagement Council (MCEC), Teen Academy and Youth Academy programs, Adopt-a-School program, Junior Special Agent program, Think Before You Post campaign, Child ID app, FBI Safe Online Surfing (SOS) Internet Challenge, Don't Be a Puppet: Pull Back the Curtain on Violent Extremism interactive website, Chasing the Dragon: The Life of an Opiate Addict documentary film, and Director's Community Leadership Award (205).

Figures 18.4 and 18.5 show my graduation certificate from the FBI Citizens Academy in March 2021 and a letter from FBI Director Christopher Wray in which he wrote, "What you have learned will hopefully give you a unique insight into the successes of our organization as well as some of the challenges that we and our law enforcement partners face every day. We hope that you will share this knowledge with others, and serve as an FBI ambassador in your workplace and your community. By spreading the word, you help us to demystify the FBI and let people know the vital role our special agents, analysts, and professional staff play in protecting all people in the United States and Americans around the world. Public support and understanding are essential to the FBI's success. We can't accomplish our mission if people don't believe us and trust us; our credibility can make all the difference in whether someone comes forward with a vital piece of information that could prevent crime or a terrorist attack."

18.11 Self-Awareness in Online Dating

At the 2018 F8 Conference in San Jose, California, Mark Zuckerberg announced the launch of a new dating app. "We want Facebook to be somewhere where you can start meaningful relationships. We've designed this with privacy and safety in mind from the beginning" (206).

English professor Mark Bauerlein at Emory University accused Facebook of killing love letters. Bauerlein wrote on CNN, "Back in the old days, love wasn't social, it was private. Communication, not to mention courtship, seemed to take a long time. Genuine love is anti-social." Reporter Samuel Axon at *Mashable* agreed, "Facebook makes dating far more complicated than it used to be. … Overanalyzing [Facebook posts] will drive you crazy. … You see all the action your ex is getting. … Relationships and breakups are public. … It's a record of every relationship mistake you've made. … Other people's comments will make your date jealous" (207)

Contrary to Mark Zuckerberg's vision, Facebook not only does not cure loneliness, but it actually spreads loneliness among online friends. A December 2009 research study published in *Journal of Personality and Social Psychology* indicated that "loneliness occurs in clusters, extends up to 3 degrees of separation, is disproportionately represented at the periphery of social networks, and spreads through a contagious process. The spread of loneliness was found to be stronger than the spread of perceived social connections, stronger for friends than family members,

U.S. Department of Justice
Federal Bureau of Investigation
Indianapolis Division

Presents this certificate to

Prof. Newton Lee

on this day

March 23, 2021

*For successfully completing
the FBI Citizens Academy program
and demonstrating a commitment to the FBI mission*

_____
Special Agent in Charge

_____
Christopher A. Wray
Director

Fig. 18.4 A Certificate of Completion from the FBI Citizens Academy on March 23, 2021

U.S. Department of Justice

Federal Bureau of Investigation

Office of the Director   *Washington, D.C. 20535-0001*

March 23, 2021

Prof. Newton Lee
Federal Bureau of Investigation
Indianapolis Division

Dear Prof. Lee:

Congratulations on your graduation from the FBI Citizens Academy program. I'm grateful for your willingness to sacrifice valuable time from your work and family to learn more about the FBI and our mission.

What you have learned will hopefully give you a unique insight into the successes of our organization as well as some of the challenges that we and our law enforcement partners face every day. We hope that you will share this knowledge with others, and serve as an FBI ambassador in your workplace and your community. By spreading the word, you help us to demystify the FBI and let people know the vital role our special agents, analysts, and professional staff play in protecting all people in the United States and Americans around the world.

Public support and understanding are essential to the FBI's success. We can't accomplish our mission if people don't believe us and trust us; our credibility can make all the difference in whether someone comes forward with a vital piece of information that could prevent crime or a terrorist attack.

Beyond serving as an ambassador for the Bureau, I would ask you to do three more things as a Citizens Academy graduate. First, continue to be a role model in your community and a leader in your chosen field. Second, please recommend your peers to us for the Citizens Academy program, so even more people can benefit from this experience. And third, please join the FBI Citizens Academy Alumni Association, which promotes safer communities through community service projects with an emphasis on the FBI's mission.

Thank you for your support. We look forward to working with you in the coming years to protect our communities and our country.

Sincerely yours,

Christopher A. Wray
Director

Fig. 18.5 A Letter from FBI Director Christopher Wray on March 23, 2021

and stronger for women than for men" (208). The full network showed that participants are 52% more likely to be lonely if a person they are directly connected to (at
one degree of separation) is lonely. The size of the effect for people at two degrees
of separation (the friend of a friend) is 25% and for people at three degrees of separation (the friend of a friend of a friend) is 15%. At four degrees of separation, the
effect disappears (2%). The research results confirmed the "three degrees of influence" rule of social network contagion that has been exhibited for obesity, smoking,
and happiness.

Why do people feel lonely even when they are surrounded by hundreds of online
friends? In her 2011 book *Alone Together: Why We Expect More from Technology
and Less from Each Other* (209), MIT professor Sherry Turkle argues that people
are increasingly functioning in the society without face-to-face contact. The ubiquity of texting, emailing, and social networking has pushed people closer to their
machines and further away from each other. Dissatisfaction and alienation are often
the result of the lack of face-to-face communication.

In a 2012 survey of 425 undergraduate students at a state university in Utah,
researchers discovered that "those who have used Facebook longer agreed more that
others were happier, and agreed less that life is fair, and those spending more time
on Facebook each week agreed more that others were happier and had better lives"
(210). In other words, the more people check Facebook, the worse they feel about
their lives.

In a 2013 UK study led by the University of Birmingham, researchers found that
"increased frequency of sharing photographs of the self, regardless of the type of
target sharing the photographs, is related to a decrease in intimacy" and concluded
that frequent Facebook photo-posters "risk damaging real-life relationships" (211).

Some people put on facades when they meet people, for fear of revealing their
true selves. The online world gives them even more power to hide their real personalities and create their own alter egos, which can lead to a bigger communication
gap among friends and family. This is the same reason why some people fail to find
true love, online and offline.

Self-awareness is a prerequisite to finding one's twin soul, avoiding karmic soul
mates and codependent relationships that are painful and chaotic. "Cogito ergo
sum," said René Descartes. Chinese philosopher Zhuangzi wrote an anecdote about
himself, "Once Zhuangzi dreamt he was a butterfly, a butterfly flitting and fluttering
around, happy with himself and doing as he pleased. He didn't know he was
Zhuangzi. Suddenly he woke up and there he was, solid and unmistakable Zhuangzi.
But he didn't know if he was Zhuangzi who had dreamt he was a butterfly, or a butterfly dreaming he was Zhuangzi. Between Zhuangzi and a butterfly there must be
some distinction! This is a case of what is called the transformation of things" (212).
Indeed, we are all transforming during different stages of our life, and yesteryears
may seem like a dream.

Self-awareness also means that we genuinely know what we like and dislike in
everyday life. Couples often break up because of irreconcilable differences: After
the "honeymoon phase," a couple may begin to discover incompatible worldviews,

moral values, religious convictions, philosophy of life, and even simple things like where to shop or what to eat.

Douglas Adams wrote in *The Hitchhiker's Guide to the Galaxy*: "The History of every major Galactic Civilization tends to pass through three distinct and recognizable phases, those of Survival, Inquiry and Sophistication, otherwise known as the How, Why, and Where phases. For instance, the first phase is characterized by the question 'How can we eat?' the second by the question 'Why do we eat?' and the third by the question 'Where shall we have lunch?'" Similarly, every couple goes through three phases of relationship: Survival – How can we live together in love and harmony? Inquiry – Why do we stay together as a couple? And Sophistication – Where shall we go from here after the honeymoon phase?

MIT Technology Review reported in January 2014 that "there are 54 million single people in the U.S. and around 40 million of them have signed up with various online dating websites such as match.com and eHarmony" (213). In spite of the impressive numbers, online dating does not guarantee success in finding the perfect match. Peng Xia and fellow researchers at the University of Massachusetts Lowell analyzed 200,000 members on an online dating site and discovered that "both men and women's actual behavior differs significantly from their stated tastes and preferences which they outline when they first sign up" (214). On top of that, popular online dating site OkCupid admitted conducting experiments on users by telling them the bad matches were good matches and vice versa (215).

In Amy Webb's 2013 TED talk titled "How I hacked online dating," she said that initially she was having absolutely no luck with online dating. The dates she liked did not write her back, and her own profile attracted "crickets (and worse)." Her solution was to make a spreadsheet, prioritizing things like she was looking for somebody who was really smart, who would challenge and stimulate her, and balancing that with deal-breakers and other criteria. As a result, she had no trouble finding the man of her dream quickly (216).

Truly worthy of the Guinness World Records, my wife used a technique similar to Amy Webb's and found me through a dating website in less than one week! French poet and playwright Paul Géraldy once said, "It is the woman who chooses the man who will choose her."

One of the root causes of miscommunication is that people do not always mean what they say or do. But if we try to stay true to ourselves, online dating can be very effective. Online dating versus traditional dating is like using an electronic calculator versus an abacus. They both can give you accurate results if used properly, but one of them is obviously faster and easier in the modern age. For instance, two people who like Betty Boop cartoons can find each other using Facebook's Graph Search or other social networking sites regardless of the physical distance between them.

Is Facebook a dating site as well? Facebook's Graph Search lets users search for others by common interest, location, age, and other criteria. At a Facebook press event in January 2013, a Facebook employee stood on stage and searched for "friends of my friends who are single and living in San Francisco" (217). And in October 2013, Facebook data scientist Lars Backstrom and Cornell University professor Jon Kleinberg reported on how to identify with high accuracy a Facebook user's romantic partner from the network structure alone, given all the connections among the person's friends (218).

In addition to online searches, mobile dating services use GPS technology to allow individuals in proximity of each other to chat and meet up (219). Subscribers can use their cell phones as a homing device to find a date just a short distance away. At the 2012 South by Southwest Interactive in Austin, Texas, Highlight's founder and CEO Paul Davison introduced a new service for matching like-minded people in their immediate area. Davison told an attentive audience, "Nothing affects our happiness more than the people in our lives. But the way we find these people and bring them into our lives always has been completely random and inefficient. We don't realize how bad it is because it's always been that way. Most people walk around like ants hoping that by randomness they'll intersect paths with the person of their dreams. Sometimes it happens, but many times you'll never meet" (220). The Highlight app pulls data from the users' Facebook profiles to determine if there are matches in the physical proximity of the users.

CNN writer and producer Sarah LeTrent reported in August 2014 new dating apps created for women and Facebook friends: "Siren is an app created for women by women that puts the ladies in the driver's seat. Women control who sees their image, who can communicate with them and what type of date to pursue. ... Hinge is a matchmaking app built on finding love with a little help from friends. Users sign in through Facebook and are sent matches each day from their extended social circles. ... The Wyldfire app allows female users to invite only the men who they would want their friends to date into the dating pool. The matchmaker site likes to take things offline too by offering local meetup events for its users" (221).

Apart from mainstream dating websites such as Match.com and eHarmony, there are an increasing number of nontraditional dating sites: Survivalist Singles and PrepperDating for the doomsdayers; Kwink for health nuts, germaphobics, and nerds, to name a few (222). In June 2014, an updated Hot or Not app was re-launched to target young adults who are into causal dating. "Since 2000, the Hot or Not brand has been an inspiration behind some of the most popular platforms and products currently available to consumers including Facebook and YouTube," said Andrey Andreev, CEO of Hot or Not. "With the addition of 'Hot Lists' ... we are bringing an elevated and more exciting version of this iconic brand to a new generation of users" (223).

Some researchers have implemented facial recognition tools to help make online dating safer. In October 2013, Meitar Moscovitz (aka maymay) released "Predator Alert Tools" for OkCupid, FetLife, Facebook, and Lulu that use CreepShield's facial recognition API to scan user profile pictures against the National Sex Offender Registry (224). In December 2013, FacialNetwork.com announced the beta release of "NameTag" – the first real-time facial recognition app for Google Glass (225). The app allows Google Glass users to capture images from their live video and scan them against photos from social media, dating sites, and a database of more than 450,000 registered sex offenders.

While all dating sites are trying to find people their best matches, there is one website that informs people about who not to date: Íslendingabók (the Book of

Icelanders) enables users to avoid inbreeding by running a date's name through a genealogical database (226).

In any event, Facebook has a breakup team—part of the Facebook Compassion team—that comes to the rescue of couples who have broken up. "Millions of people end romantic relationships each week, and we want to help in any way that we can," wrote Kelly Grimaldi, product manager at Facebook App. "Not all relationships turn out the way we might initially hope. We've heard from the Facebook community that people often want to stay friends on Facebook with people who have been meaningful to them, but can find it painful to do so. They want better control over when they see this person on Facebook, streamlined ways to limit what this person might see, and easy ways to update who could see photos and posts of the two of them" (227).

18.12   Pandora's Box of Total Information Awareness

In Francis Ford Coppola's *The Godfather* (1972), Michael Corleone said, "I'll make him an offer he can't refuse" (228). Like it or not, the majority of us cannot refuse the temptation of social media and social networking services. As of 2020, Facebook family of apps had more than 3 billion monthly active users (229), Google had notched approximately 650 million daily visitors (230), and Twitter had passed 192 million daily active users (231). With the massive amount of personal data and information exchange on the Internet, Facebook nation has opened a Pandora's box of total information awareness in the age of big data. Fortunately, Pandora's box released not only evil but also hope.

On one hand, total information awareness poses a risk in personal privacy and freedom as in "Big Brother is watching us," "companies know too much about us," or "parents and friends are prying into our private lives." In May 2006, *USA Today* reported that the National Security Agency (NSA) has been secretly collecting the phone call records of tens of millions of Americans without warrants (232). In June 2013, Edward Snowden leaked to the press several top-secret NSA programs including PRISM that allows officials to collect without court orders any data including emails, chat, videos, photos, stored data, voice-over-IP, file transfers, video conferencing, logins, and online social networking details from communication providers and social networks (233).

Social critic Andrew Keen warned of future mind-reading predictive technology, "The computer 'server' and the 'server' in the bar will be indistinguishable... They will both know what you want to drink before you know it yourself" (234). And statistician Andrew Pole at the discount retailer Target said, "Just wait. We'll be sending you coupons for things you want before you even know you want them" (235).

At the CHI 2014 conference organized by ACM SIGCHI (Special Interest Group on Computer-Human Interaction) in Toronto, Canada, a fake company debuted "Quantified Toilets" in the Toronto Convention Center and other civic venues that would automatically analyze biological waste to detect a person's gender, odor,

This facility is proud to participate in the healthy building initiative.
Behaviour at these toilets is being recorded for analysis.
Access your live data at **quantifiedtoilets.com**

Quantified Toilets
Every day. Every time.

Fig. 18.6 A Quantified Toilets LLC signage at CHI 2014, Toronto, Canada

blood alcohol, drugs, pregnancy status, and infections (236). Figure 18.6 shows a signage posted in the restrooms at CHI 2014. It turned out to be a thought experiment by Matt Dalton (Simon Fraser University), Angela Gabereau (Fabule Fabrications, Inc.), Sarah Gallacher (University College London), Lisa Koeman (University College London), David Nguyen (Nokia), and Larissa Pschetz (University of Edinburgh).

Prof. Jennifer Golbeck, director of the Human-Computer Interaction Lab at the University of Maryland, wrote in *The Atlantic* about the toilet hoax and future of surveillance (237):

> This is the kind of data that public officials or marketers would love to obtain. Let's imagine a couple scenarios:
>
> - At a convention or concert, an organization could determine whether attendees have high rates of pregnant women with positive drug or alcohol tests, then use that knowledge to target public health messages to the demographic.
> - In stadiums, an organization could see which sections had higher blood alcohol levels, and even the peak levels during the game. They could market more beer to that section—or make it harder for people in that section to buy drinks. They might even sell this data to beer vendors willing to pay for such demographic information.
> - Other ideas from the Quantified Toilets website: "We use this data to streamline cleaning crew schedules, inform municipalities of the usage of resources, and help buildings and cities plan for healthier and happier citizens.

On the other hand, total information awareness creates more transparency in governments, businesses, societies, and families. Proper use of information awareness offers substantial benefits in suicide prevention, child protection, school safety, crime prevention, neighborhood watch, traffic safety, personal safety, law enforcement, and even online dating.

Upscale restaurants such as Eleven Madison Park can Google their guests to learn about their anniversaries and birthdays in order to offer more personalized services. "If I find out a guest is from Montana, and I know we have a server from there, we'll put them together," said maître d' Justin Roller (238).

The St. Regis Bora Bora Resort Googles every guest two weeks before arrival. "We actually create a little story about them – just a paragraph or so – and share that with the heads of each department at our daily NDA [next-day arrivals] meeting," said general manager Michael Schoonewagen (239). The idea is to treat every guest like a celebrity.

On December 8, 2013, 27-year-old Sanaz Nezami with severe head injuries was rushed to Marquette General Hospital in Michigan. "At the time the staff did not know anything about this young woman who came in with critical injuries," said Nurse Supervisor Gail Brandly. "I figured she was probably a student, and so I thought perhaps she would be on LinkedIn or Facebook or something like that" (240). Brandly ran her name through Google and found a resume online with her picture and a phone number through which the hospital was able to reach her relatives in Iran. Nezami's family watched her final hours from a laptop 6,000 miles away (241).

In February 2014, Pew Research Internet Project released a report on "Couples, the Internet, and Social Media" which said that "the internet, cell phones, and social media have become key actors in the life of many American couples – the 66% of adults who are married or in committed relationships. … 74% of the adult internet users who report that the internet had an impact on their marriage or partnership say the impact was positive. … 41% of 18–29 year olds in serious relationships have felt closer to their partner because of online or text message conversations" (242).

In March 2014, Tara Taylor posted a cute picture of her 3-year-old daughter Rylee on Facebook to show friends. Two of her friends replied to the picture, "Hey, I'm sure it's nothing. It's probably the lighting, but your daughter's eye is glowing and you might want to have it checked out because it's a sign there could be an issue with her eye." Taylor took her daughter to a retina specialist who diagnosed the little girl with a rare Coat's disease. Because of early detection and treatment, a complete loss of vision can be averted (thanks to Facebook photo sharing) (243).

The hope is that good will trump evil. The "precogs" in Steven Spielberg's *Minority Report* (2002) will be future artificial intelligence (AI) programs that employ biometric recognition technologies, correlate information from online and offline activities, and analyze video streams from live traffic cams, in-vehicle dash cams, ATM security cameras, Neighborhood Watch webcams, and public CCTV systems around town and in business establishments. The AI programs will help locate missing children and apprehend dangerous criminals, making our community a safer place to live.

Total information awareness affects all aspects of human lives, all levels of society, and all forms of government. As long as we are well prepared and well informed, total information awareness will prove to be more beneficial than harmful for everyone.

References

1. **Senate Historical Office.** Burning of Washington, 1814. [Online] United States Senate. [Cited: March 1, 2021.] https://www.senate.gov/artandhistory/history/common/generic/August_Burning_Washington.htm.
2. **Shabad, Rebecca.** Capitol Police chief warns extremists 'want to blow up the Capitol' when Biden addresses Congress. [Online] CBS News, February 25, 2021. https://www.nbcnews.com/politics/congress/capitol-law-enforcement-heads-detail-intelligence-failures-leading-jan-6-n1258829.
3. **Dilanian, Ken.** 'You can't just push send': 20 years after 9/11, FBI accused of intel failure before Capitol riot. [Online] CBS News, February 23, 2021. https://www.nbcnews.com/politics/national-security/you-can-t-just-push-send-20-years-after-9-n1258637.
4. **Dilanian, Ken and Ainsley, Julia.** Worried about free speech, FBI never issued intelligence bulletin about possible Capitol violence. [Online]

CBS News, January 12, 2021. https://www.nbcnews.com/news/us-news/part-due-free-speech-worries-fbi-never-issued-intel-bulletin-n1253951.

5. **FBI.** Mission & Priorities. [Online] U.S. Department of Justice. [Cited: February 28, 2021.] https://www.fbi.gov/about/mission.

6. **Editors.** Charleston council labels KKK 'terrorists' . [Online] Tulsa World, October 13, 1999. https://tulsaworld.com/archive/charleston-council-labels-kkk-terrorists/article_2bd459d8-7e31-5ccc-a97b-022e3ce13635.html.

7. —. Proud Boys: Canada labels far-right group a terrorist entity. [Online] BBC News, February 3, 2021. https://www.bbc.com/news/world-us-canada-55923485.

8. **Cargile, Taylor.** Spokane Community Observance of the Holocaust essay contest, first place: 'Repeating History With Hate Speech'. [Online] The Spokesman-Review, April 6, 2018. https://www.spokesman.com/stories/2018/apr/05/essay-contest-winner-repeating-history-with-hate-s/.

9. **Lee, Newton.** Counterterrorism and Cybersecurity: Total Information Awareness. [Online] Springer Nature, 2015. https://www.springer.com/us/book/9783319172439.

10. **Acosta, Jim.** Chief of staff for GOP lawmaker spoke to law enforcement after overhearing talk of storming FBI building on January 6. [Online] CNN, May 21, 2021. https://www.cnn.com/2021/05/21/politics/carlos-gimenez-aide-january-6/index.html.

11. **NPR Transcripts.** FBI Director Defends Agency In Testimony, Calls Jan. 6 Attack 'Domestic Terrorism'. [Online] NPR, March 2, 2021. https://www.npr.org/transcripts/972970812.

12. **Carrega, Christina, Perez, Evan and LeBlanc, Paul.** Proud Boys leader arrested for allegedly burning Black Lives Matter banner at DC church. [Online] CNN Politics, January 5, 2021. https://www.cnn.com/2021/01/04/politics/proud-boys-arrest-black-lives-matter-banner/index.html.

13. **Cohen, Zachary.** FBI director says bureau is not investigating QAnon conspiracy 'in its own right'. [Online] CNN, April 15, 2021. https://www.cnn.com/2021/04/15/politics/fbi-director-wray-qanon-threat/index.html.

14. **The 104th United States Congress.** 47 U.S. Code § 230 - Protection for private blocking and screening of offensive material. [Online] Cornell Law School, February 8, 1996. https://www.law.cornell.edu/uscode/text/47/230.

15. **Beitsch, Rebecca.** Lawmakers mull domestic terrorism statute in wake of Jan. 6 attack. [Online] The Hill, February 4, 2021. https://thehill.com/policy/national-security/537424-lawmakers-mull-domestic-terrorism-statute-in-wake-of-jan-6-attack.

16. **Reuters.** Donald Trump: 'I could shoot somebody and I wouldn't lose any voters'. [Online] The Guardian, January 24, 2016. https://www.theguardian.com/us-news/2016/jan/24/donald-trump-says-he-could-shoot-somebody-and-still-not-lose-voters.

17. **Cabral, Sam.** Capitol riots: Did Trump's words at rally incite violence? [Online] BBC News, February 14, 2021. https://www.bbc.com/news/world-us-canada-55640437.

18. **Lofgren, Zoe.** Social Media Review. [Online] U.S. House of Representatives. [Cited: March 6, 2021.] https://lofgren.house.gov/socialreview.

19. **Follman, Mark.** In a Pre-Election Video, Marjorie Taylor Greene Endorsed Political Violence. [Online] Mother Jones, January 29, 2021. https://www.motherjones.com/politics/2021/01/marjorie-taylor-greene-endorsed-political-violence-video-guns-elections-congress/.

20. **Arroyo, Jim.** The Coming Civil War? Parts 1 & 2. [Online] Prescott eNews, November 23, 2020. https://prescottenews.com/index.php/2020/11/23/the-coming-civil-war-parts-1-2/.

21. **Perez, Evan, Polantz, Katelyn and Simon, Mallory.** New charges allege Proud Boys prepped for Capitol insurrection. [Online] CNN Politics, February 3, 2021. https://www.cnn.com/2021/02/03/politics/proud-boys-indicted-capitol-riot/index.html.

22. **Temple-Raston, Dina.** Lawyers For 18-Year-Old Capitol Rioter Want Him Released To His Parents. [Online] npr, February 26, 2021. https://www.npr.org/sections/insurrection-at-the-capitol.

23. **Ghitis, Frida.** The disturbing tweets from GOPers who wouldn't accept Biden's win. [Online] CNN, March 6, 2021. https://www.cnn.com/2021/03/06/opinions/tweets-gop-zoe-lofgren-ghitis/index.html.

24. **Zadrozny,   Brandy   and   Gains,   Mosheh.** Woman   killed   in   Capitol   was Trump   supporter   who   embraced   conspiracy   theories.   [Online]   NBC News,   January   7,   2021.   https://www.nbcnews.com/news/us-news/ woman-killed-capitol-was-trump-supporter-who-embraced-conspiracy-theories-n1253285.

25. **Frenkel, Sheera.** The Storming of Capitol Hill Was Organized on Social Media. [Online] The New York Times, January 6, 2021. https://www.nytimes.com/2021/01/06/us/politics/ protesters-storm-capitol-hill-building.html.

26. **Kelly,   Makena.** Joe   Biden   wants   to   revoke   Section   230.   [Online]   The Verge,   January   17,   2020.   https://www.theverge.com/2020/1/17/21070403/ joe-biden-president-election-section-230-communications-decency-act-revoke.

27. **—.** Trump vetoes $740 billion defense bill after Section 230 complaints. [Online] The   Verge,   December   23,   2020.   https://www.theverge.com/2020/12/23/22197796/ trump-ndaa-veto-section-230-defense-bill-facebook-twitter.

28. **Fung, Brian.** Facebook and Twitter chart out different paths for Congress on internet regulation. [Online] CNN Business, November 18, 2020. https://www.cnn.com/2020/11/18/tech/ big-tech-senate-judiciary-analysis/index.html.

29. **Haugen, Frances.** Statement of Frances Haugen. *United States Senate Committee on Commerce, Science and Transportation.* [Online] October 4, 2021. https://www.commerce. senate.gov/services/files/FC8A558E-824E-4914-BEDB-3A7B1190BD49.

30. **Kristof, Nicholas.** The Children of Pornhub: Why does Canada allow this company to profit off videos of exploitation and assault? [Online] New York Times, December 4, 2020. https:// www.nytimes.com/2020/12/04/opinion/sunday/pornhub-rape-trafficking.html.

31. **Palmer, Shelly.** Porn Leads Tech Once Again. [Online] Shelly Palmer, February 4, 2021. https://www.shellypalmer.com/2021/02/porn-leads-tech-once-again/.

32. **Saint, Nick.** How Pornographers Invented E-Commerce. [Online] Business Insider, August 6, 2010.

33. **IMDb.** Memorable Quotes for The Godfather: Part II. [Online] IMDb, December 20, 1974. http://www.imdb.com/title/tt0071562/quotes.

34. **Associated Press.** Mob leaders arrested after FBI infiltration. [Online] The New York Times,   March   9,   2005.   http://www.nytimes.com/2005/03/09/world/americas/09iht-web.0309mob.html.

35. **Zhao, Emmeline.** Rachel Ehmke, 13-Year-Old Minnesota Student, Commits Suicide After Months Of Bullying. [Online] Huffington Post, May 8, 2012. http://www.huffingtonpost. com/2012/05/08/rachel-ehmke-13-year-old-_n_1501143.html.

36. **CNN Wire Staff.** Indiana mom sends son to school with stun gun to confront bullies. [Online] CNN, May 7, 2012. http://www.cnn.com/2012/05/07/us/indiana-bullied-teen/index.html.

37. **IMDb.** Minority Report. [Online] IMDb, June 21, 2002. http://www.imdb.com/title/ tt0181689/.

38. **Facebook Data Team.** Facebook Data Science. [Online] Facebook, February 12, 2008. https://www.facebook.com/data/about/.

39. **Morse, Dan.** Philip Welsh's simple life hampers search for his killer. [Online] The Washington Post,   May   6,   2014.   http://www.washingtonpost.com/local/crime/philip-welshs-simple-life-hampers-search-for-his-killer/2014/05/05/1fd20a52-cff7-11e3-a6b1-45c4dffb85a6_ story.html.

40. **Lohr, Steve.** The Age of Big Data. [Online] New York Times, February 11, 2012. https:// www.nytimes.com/2012/02/12/sunday-review/big-datas-impact-in-the-world.html.

41. **Pachal, Peter.** A 'Leap' forward in gesture-control interfaces? [Online] CNN, May 22, 2012. http://www.cnn.com/2012/05/22/tech/innovation/leap-motion-control/index.html.

42. **Steel, Emily.** How a New Police Tool for Face Recognition Works. [Online] The Wall Street Journal, July 13, 2011. http://blogs.wsj.com/digits/2011/07/13/how-a-new-police-tool-for-face-recognition-works/.

43. **Walters, Ray.** Omni-directional 6-legged insect robot can save lives, do cartwheels. [Online] Geek.com, December 14, 2011. http://www.geek.com/articles/geek-cetera/omnidirectional-insect-robot-6-legged-20111214/.

44. **Efrati, Amir.** A New Home for Computer Screens: The Face. [Online] The Wall Street Journal, May 21, 2012. http://online.wsj.com/article/SB10001424052702303610504577418181348485336.html.

45. **Toor, Amar.** LG unveils flexible plastic e-paper display, aims for European launch next month. [Online] Engadget, March 29, 2012. http://www.engadget.com/2012/03/29/lg-flexible-e-paper-display-launch/.

46. **Cheng, Roger.** Ericsson could turn you into a human USB connection next year. [Online] CNet, May 11, 2012. http://reviews.cnet.com/8301-12261_7-57433025-10356022/ericsson-could-turn-you-into-a-human-usb-connection-next-year/.

47. **BBC News.** Vibrating tattoo alerts patent filed by Nokia in US. [Online] BBC News, March 20, 2012. http://www.bbc.co.uk/news/technology-17447086.

48. **Paul, Ian.** Disney Technology Turns Everything into a Touch Device. [Online] PC World, May 7, 2012. http://www.pcworld.com/article/255124/disney_technology_turns_everything_into_a_touch_device.html.

49. **Hay, Timothy.** Mind-Controlled Videogames Become Reality. [Online] The Wall Street Journal, May 29, 2012. http://online.wsj.com/article/SB10001424052702304707604577426251091339254.html.

50. **Dvorak, John C.** Google's Revolutionary Self-Driving Car. [Online] PC Magazine, May 9, 2012. http://www.pcmag.com/article2/0,2817,2404199,00.asp.

51. **Malik, Om.** Zimmermann's Law: PGP inventor and Silent Circle co-founder Phil Zimmermann on the surveillance society. [Online] Gigaom, August 11, 2013. http://gigaom.com/2013/08/11/zimmermanns-law-pgp-inventor-and-silent-circle-co-founder-phil-zimmermann-on-the-surveillance-society/.

52. **Kaplan, Andreas M.** If you love something, let it go mobile: Mobile marketing and mobile social media 4x4. [Online] Elsevier, November 23, 2011. http://www.sciencedirect.com/science/article/pii/S0007681311001558.

53. **Thompson, Clive.** Brave New World of Digital Intimacy. [Online] The New York Time, September 5, 2008. http://www.nytimes.com/2008/09/07/magazine/07awareness-t.html?pagewanted=2.

54. **Warren, Frank.** How the world shares its secrets. [Online] CNN, April 24, 2012. http://www.cnn.com/2012/04/22/opinion/warren-post-secret/index.html.

55. **Dowd, Maureen.** 20 Years After The Murder Of Kitty Genovese, The Question Remains: Why? [Online] The New York Times, March 12, 1984. http://www.nytimes.com/1984/03/12/nyregion/20-years-after-the-murder-of-kitty-genovese-the-question-remains-why.html.

56. **Darley, John M. and Latané, Bibb.** Bystander intervention in emergencies: Diffusion of responsibility. [Online] Journal of Personality and Social Psychology 8: 377–383, 1968. http://www.ncbi.nlm.nih.gov/pubmed/5645600.

57. **Levine, M. and Crowther, S.** The responsive bystander: how social group membership and group size can encourage as well as inhibit bystander intervention. [Online] Journal of Personality and Social Psychology 95(6): 1429–1439, 2008. http://www.ncbi.nlm.nih.gov/pubmed/19025293.

58. **Cacioppo, John T., Fowler, James H. and Christakis, Nicholas A.** Alone in the crowd: The structure and spread of loneliness in a large social network. [Online] Journal of Personality and Social Psychology 97(6): 977–991, 2009. http://psycnet.apa.org/journals/psp/97/6/977/.

59. **Keilman, John and McCoppin, Robert.** Study: Teen users of Facebook, Myspace more likely to drink, use drugs. [Online] Chicago Tribune,

August   24,   2011.   http://articles.chicagotribune.com/2011-08-24/news/
ct-met-social-menace-20110824_1_social-media-teen-substance-abuse-teen-users.

60. **Kramera, Adam D. I., Guillory, Jamie E. and Hancock, Jeffrey T.** Experimental evidence of massive-scale emotional contagion through social networks. [Online] Proceedings of the National Academy of Sciences of the United States of America, October 23, 2013. http://www.pnas.org/content/111/24/8788.full.

61. **Pew Internet.** Why most Facebook users get more than they give. [Online] Pew Internet Press Release, February 3, 2012. http://www.pewinternet.org/Press-Releases/2012/Facebook-users.aspx.

62. **CNN Wire Staff.** Rutgers student's suicide reverberates 15 months later. [Online] CNN, December 12, 2011. http://www.cnn.com/2011/12/12/us/new-jersey-student-suicide/index.html.

63. **Parker, Ian.** The Story of a Suicide. [Online] The New Yorker, February 6, 2012. http://www.newyorker.com/reporting/2012/02/06/120206fa_fact_parker.

64. **Williams, Mary Elizabeth.** Can Facebook save your life? . [Online] Salon, December 14, 2011. http://www.salon.com/2011/12/14/can_facebook_save_your_life/singleton/.

65. **McVeigh, Karen.** Facebook 'friends' did not act on suicide note. [Online] The Guardian, January 5, 2011. http://www.guardian.co.uk/technology/2011/jan/05/facebook-suicide-simone-back.

66. **Cellan-Jones, Rory.** Facebook adds Samaritans suicide risk alert system. [Online] BBC News, March 7, 2011. http://www.bbc.co.uk/news/technology-12667343.

67. **Facebook.** How do I help someone who has posted suicidal content on the site? [Online] Facebook Help Center. [Cited: May 18, 2012.] http://www.facebook.com/help/?faq=216817991675637.

68. **Dickey, Megan Rose.** Facebook brings suicide prevention tools to Live and Messenger. [Online] TechCrunch, March 1, 2017. https://techcrunch.com/2017/03/01/facebook-brings-suicide-prevention-tools-to-live-and-messenger/.

69. **Codrea-Rado, Anna.** Using Social Media to Prevent Suicide. [Online] The Atlantic, April 18, 2012. http://www.theatlantic.com/health/archive/2012/04/using-social-media-to-prevent-suicide/256069/.

70. **Benjamin, Regina.** New Partnership Between Facebook and the National Suicide Prevention Lifeline. [Online] Facebook, December 13, 2011. https://www.facebook.com/notes/facebook-safety/new-partnership-between-facebook-and-the-national-suicide-prevention-lifeline/310287485658707.

71. **O'Mara, Mark.** It's time to outlaw bullying. [Online] CNN, June 3, 2014. http://www.cnn.com/2014/06/03/opinion/omara-bullying-legislation/index.html.

72. **Zhao, Emmeline.** Rachel Ehmke, 13-Year-Old Minnesota Student, Commits Suicide After Months Of Bullying. [Online] Huffington Post, May 8, 2012. http://www.huffingtonpost.com/2012/05/08/rachel-ehmke-13-year-old-_n_1501143.html.

73. **Landau, Elizabeth.** When bullying goes high-tech. [Online] CNN, April 15, 2013. http://www.cnn.com/2013/02/27/health/cyberbullying-online-bully-victims/index.html.

74. **McAfee.** Cyberbullying Triples According to New McAfee "2014 Teens and the Screen study". [Online] McAfee, June 3, 2014. http://www.mcafee.com/us/about/news/2014/q2/20140603-01.aspx.

75. **Brubaker, Elisabeth.** Anne O'Brien on the bullying her daughter suffered: "She didn't stand a chance". [Online] CNN Blogs, November 30, 2011. http://piersmorgan.blogs.cnn.com/2011/11/30/anne-obrien-on-the-bullying-her-daughter-suffered-she-didnt-stand-a-chance/.

76. **Cullen, Kevin.** The untouchable Mean Girls. [Online] Boston Globe, January 24, 2010. http://www.boston.com/news/local/massachusetts/articles/2010/01/24/the_untouchable_mean_girls/.

77. **Oliver, Kealan.** Phoebe Prince "Suicide by Bullying": Teen's Death Angers Town Asking Why Bullies Roam the Halls. [Online] CBS News, February 5, 2010. http://www.cbsnews.com/8301-504083_162-6173960-504083.html.

78. **Castillo, Mariano.** Teens accused of posting pictures of sexual assault. [Online] CNN, April 15, 2013. http://www.cnn.com/2013/04/12/justice/california-rape-arrests/index.html.

79. **Grinberg, Emanuella.** When evidence goes viral. [Online] CNN, April 16, 2013. http://www.cnn.com/2013/04/12/living/social-media-evidence-sexual-assault/index.html.

80. **Todd, Amanda.** My story: Struggling, bullying, suicide, self harm. [Online] YouTube, September 7, 2012. http://www.youtube.com/watch?v=vOHXGNx-E7E.

81. **The Huffington Post.** Rehtaeh Parsons, Canadian Girl, Dies After Suicide Attempt; Parents Allege She Was Raped By 4 Boys. [Online] The Huffington Post, April 9, 2013. http://www.huffingtonpost.com/2013/04/09/rehtaeh-parsons-girl-dies-suicide-rape-canada_n_3045033.html.

82. **Wedeman, Ben.** Facebook may face prosecution over bullied teenager's suicide in Italy. [Online] CNN, July 31, 2013. http://edition.cnn.com/2013/07/31/world/europe/italy-facebook-suicide/.

83. **Smith-Spark, Laura.** Hanna Smith suicide fuels calls for action on Ask.fm cyberbullying. [Online] CNN, August 9, 2013. http://www.cnn.com/2013/08/07/world/europe/uk-social-media-bullying/index.html.

84. **Almasy, Steve, Segal, Kim and Couwels, John.** Sheriff: Taunting post leads to arrests in Rebecca Sedwick bullying death. [Online] CNN, October 16, 2013. http://www.cnn.com/2013/10/15/justice/rebecca-sedwick-bullying-death-arrests/index.html.

85. **CBC News.** N.S. cyberbullying legislation allows victims to sue. [Online] CBC News, August 7, 2013. http://www.cbc.ca/news/canada/nova-scotia/n-s-cyberbullying-legislation-allows-victims-to-sue-1.1307338.

86. **Time Warner Inc.** Facebook and Time Warner Inc. Launch Stop Bullying: Speak Up App. [Online] Time Warner Press Releases, September 19, 2011. http://www.timewarner.com/newsroom/press-releases/2011/09/Facebook_and_Time_Warner_Inc_Launch_Stop_Bullying_Speak_Up_App_09-19-2011.php.

87. **Probst, Emily and Kaye, Randi.** Wanted: A bully to end bullying. [Online] CNN, March 31, 2012. http://www.cnn.com/2012/03/30/us/scary-guy/index.html.

88. **Gibson, Faye.** Am I Pretty or Ugly. [Online] YouTube, January 15, 2012. http://www.youtube.com/watch?v=WoyZPn6hKY4.

89. **Smith, Candace.** Teens Post 'Am I Pretty or Ugly?' Videos on YouTube. [Online] ABC News, February 23, 2012. http://abcnews.go.com/US/teens-post-insecurities-youtube-pretty-ugly-videos/story?id=15777830.

90. **Protalinski, Emil.** Facebook bans Mark Zuckerberg. [Online] ZDNet, May 11, 2011. http://www.zdnet.com/blog/facebook/facebook-bans-mark-zuckerberg/1464.

91. **Berry, Ashley.** Ashley Berry. [Online] LinkedIn. [Cited: June 20, 2014.] http://www.linkedin.com/in/ashleymichelleberry.

92. **Ingram, Mathew.** Snooping on your kids: If the NSA's tools were available, I probably would have used them. [Online] GigaOm, August 7, 2013. http://gigaom.com/2013/08/07/snooping-on-your-kids-if-the-nsas-tools-were-available-i-probably-would-have-used-them/.

93. **Ingram, Meaghan.** Snooping on your kids: How I felt about my father's online surveillance of me. [Online] GigaOm, August 12, 2013. http://gigaom.com/2013/08/12/snooping-on-your-kids-how-i-felt-about-my-fathers-online-surveillance-of-me/.

94. **SafetyWeb.** Forget Spying! SafetyWeb Offers A Smart New Way To Protect Kids Online. [Online] SafetyWeb Press Releases, September 9, 2010. http://www.safetyweb.com/forget-spying-safetyweb-offers-a-smart-new-way-to-protect-kids-online.

95. **Beck, Kenneth H., et al.** Associations between parent awareness, monitoring, enforcement and adolescent involvement with alcohol. [Online] Health Education Research 14(6): 765–775, March 26, 1998. http://her.oxfordjournals.org/content/14/6/765.full.

96. **O'Mara, Mark.** Should parents be criminally liable for kids' cyberbullying? [Online] CNN, October 20, 2013. http://www.cnn.com/2013/10/18/opinion/omara-parents-cyberbullying/index.html.

97. **National Association of Attorneys General.** Re: Facebook's Plans to Develop Instagram for Children Under the Age of 13. [Online] www.naag.org, May 10, 2021. https://1li23g1as25g1r8so11ozniw-wpengine.netdna-ssl.com/wp-content/uploads/2021/05/NAAG-Letter-to-Facebook-Final-1.pdf.

98. **FBI.** Aware.Prepare.Prevent Campaign. [Online] Federal Bureau of Investigation, May 2012. http://www.fbi.gov/norfolk/news-and-outreach/in-your-community/aware.prepare.plan-campaign.

99. **Cable News Network.** Massacre at Virginia Tech. [Online] CNN, 2007. http://www.cnn.com/SPECIALS/2007/virginiatech.shootings/.

100. **Virginia Tech Review Panel.** Mass Shootings at Virginia Tech. Report of the Virginia Tech Review Panel. Presented to Governor Kaine, Commonwealth of Virginia. [Online] Virginia.gov, August 2007. http://www.governor.virginia.gov/TempContent/techPanelReport.cfm.

101. **Virginia Tech.** Liviu Librescu. [Online] Virginia Tech, April 16, 2008. http://www.remembrance.vt.edu/biographies/librescu.html.

102. **Depue, Roger.** Red Flags, Warning Signs and Indicators. [Online] Virginia.gov, August 2007. http://www.governor.virginia.gov/tempcontent/techPanelReport-docs/28%20APPENDIX%20M%20-%20RED%20FLAGS%20WARNING%20SIGNS%20AND%20INDICATORS.pdf.

103. **CNN Special Report.** Virginia Tech report: Share mental health data. [Online] CNN, June 13, 2007. http://www.cnn.com/2007/US/06/13/virginia.tech/index.html.

104. **Hurtado, Jaqueline.** Superintendent: All of L.A. school's teachers to be replaced. [Online] CNN, February 6, 2012. http://www.cnn.com/2012/02/06/justice/california-teacher-bondage-photos/index.html.

105. **CNN Staff.** Maryland university buying bulletproof whiteboards. [Online] CNN, August 17, 2013. http://www.cnn.com/2013/08/17/us/maryland-armored-whiteboards/index.html.

106. **Solove, Daniel.** Higher Education Needs Privacy Officers and Privacy/Security Training. [Online] LinkedIn, July 9, 2013. http://www.linkedin.com/today/post/article/20130709071722-2259773-higher-education-needs-privacy-officers-and-privacy-security-training.

107. **Kassa, Jonathan.** The Jeanne Clery Act, Twenty Years Later: From Admitting to Addressing Campus Crime. Now What? [Online] Huffington Post, November 8, 2010. http://www.huffingtonpost.com/jonathan-kassa/the-jeanne-clery-act-twen_b_779989.html.

108. **Dorell, Oren.** Va. Tech's quick alerts to shootings in contrast to 2007. [Online] USA Today, December 8, 2011. http://www.usatoday.com/news/nation/story/2011-12-08/virginia-tech-shooting-swift-alerts/51750854/1.

109. **Circle of 6.** A free app that prevents violence before it happens. [Online] Circle of 6. [Cited: May 20, 2011.] http://www.circleof6app.com/.

110. **Swift, James.** New Smartphone App Aims to Prevent Date Rape. [Online] Youth Today, April 11, 2012. http://www.youthtoday.org/view_article.cfm?article_id=5236.

111. **Snizek, William E.** We Remember: The fifth anniversary of April 16. [Online] Virginia Tech Magazine, Spring 2012. http://www.vtmag.vt.edu/spring12/we-remember.html.

112. **Chitika Online Advertising Network.** The Value of Google Result Positioning. [Online] Chitika, June 7, 2013. http://chitika.com/google-positioning-value.

113. **Google Chrome.** Google Chrome Channel. [Online] YouTube. [Cited: August 16, 2014.] http://www.youtube.com/playlist?list=PL5308B2E5749D1696.

114. **Landau, Elizabeth.** Loneliness spreads in social networks. [Online] CNN, December 4, 2009. http://articles.cnn.com/2009-12-04/health/loneliness.social.network_1_loneliness-lonely-people-social-networks.

115. **CNN Wire Staff.** Minnesota girl alleges school privacy invasion. [Online] CNN, March 10, 2012. http://www.cnn.com/2012/03/10/us/minnesota-student-privacy/index.html.

116. **Martinez, Michael.** California school district hires firm to monitor students' social media. [Online] CNN, September 18, 2013. http://www.cnn.com/2013/09/14/us/california-schools-monitor-social-media/index.html.

117. **Brumfield, Ben.** Police: Woman's gut feeling thwarts planned school massacre, family murder. [Online] CNN, May 3, 2014. http://www.cnn.com/2014/05/02/justice/minnesota-attack-thwarted/index.html.

118. **Woolf, Nicky.** 'PUAhate' and 'ForeverAlone': inside Elliot Rodger's online life. [Online] The Guardian, May 30, 2014. http://www.theguardian.com/world/2014/may/30/elliot-rodger-puahate-forever-alone-reddit-forums.

119. **Levinson, Brian.** I Could Have Been Elliot Rodger. [Online] Slate, May 31, 2014. http://www.slate.com/articles/life/dispatches/2014/05/i_could_have_been_elliot_rodger_young_frustrated_and_full_of_rage_toward.single.html.

120. **Myers, Steve.** How citizen journalism has changed since George Holliday's Rodney King video. [Online] Poynter, March 3, 2011. http://www.poynter.org/latest-news/top-stories/121687/how-citizen-journalism-has-changed-since-george-hollidays-rodney-king-video/.

121. **Phillips-Sandy, Mary.** Rodney King Revisited: Meet George Holliday, the Man Who Shot the Infamous Video. [Online] AOL News, March 3, 2011. http://www.aolnews.com/2011/03/03/rodney-king-revisited-meet-george-holliday-the-man-who-shot-th/.

122. **Jmackfaragher.** Rodney King tape on national news. [Online] YouTube, November 15, 2010. http://www.youtube.com/watch?v=SW1ZDIXiuS4.

123. **Wilson, Stan.** Riot anniversary tour surveys progress and economic challenges in Los Angeles. [Online] 2012, 25 April. http://www.cnn.com/2012/04/25/us/california-post-riot/index.html.

124. **The Baltimore Sun.** Just About a Perfect Verdict. [Online] The Baltimore Sun, April 19, 1993. http://articles.baltimoresun.com/1993-04-19/news/1993109024_1_verdict-rodney-king-law-enforcement.

125. **Canon, Gabrielle.** 'I cried so hard': the teen who filmed Floyd's killing, and changed America. [Online] The Guardian, April 20, 2021. https://www.theguardian.com/us-news/2021/apr/20/darnella-frazier-george-floyd-derek-chauvin-trial-guilty-verdict.

126. **Yan, Holly.** A teen with 'a cell phone and sheer guts' is credited for Derek Chauvin's murder conviction. [Online] CNN, April 21, 2021. https://www.cnn.com/2021/04/21/us/darnella-frazier-derek-chauvin-reaction/index.html.

127. **Mcelroy, Wendy.** Are Cameras the New Guns? [Online] Gizmodo, June 2, 2010. http://gizmodo.com/5553765/are-cameras-the-new-guns.

128. **Good Moring America.** Nanny-Cam Leads to Babysitter Arrest. [Online] ABC News, October 13, 2003. http://abcnews.go.com/GMA/story?id=128269.

129. **KTLA News.** Nannycam Video Lands Sitter in Prison -- Graphic Content. [Online] KTLA, August 30, 2010. http://www.ktla.com/news/landing/ktla-nannycam-arrest,0,7859954.story.

130. **Campbell, Janie.** VIDEO: Cheryl Hepner, Angry Grandma, Shoots Son-In-Law Who Records Attack On iPhone. [Online] The Huffington Post, December 9, 2011. http://www.huffingtonpost.com/2011/12/09/video-cheryl-hepner-angry_n_1139459.html.

131. **Primack, Dan.** It's time for RadiumOne's abusive CEO to go. [Online] CNN Money, April 25, 2014. http://finance.fortune.cnn.com/2014/04/25/its-time-for-radiumone-to-fire-its-abusive-ceo/.

132. **Merchant, Nomaan.** Dallas officer who shot mentally ill man is fired. [Online] Yahoo! News, October 24, 2013. http://news.yahoo.com/dallas-officer-shot-mentally-ill-man-fired-175112193.html.

133. **@oliviamunn.** My friend's mom. [Online] Twitter, February 17, 2021. https://twitter.com/oliviamunn/status/1362084698197909508?lang=en.

134. **Zeidler, Sari.** Viral vigilantism, Tony Hawk style. [Online] CNN, June 23, 2012. http://news.blogs.cnn.com/2012/06/23/viral-vigilantism-tony-hawk-style/.

135. **Nieto, Marcus.** Public Video Surveillance: Is it an Effective Crime Prevention Tool? [Online] California Research Bureau. California State Library, June 1997. http://www.library.ca.gov/crb/97/05/crb97-005.pdf.

136. **King, Jennifer, et al.** Preliminary Findings of the Statistical Evaluation of the Crime-Deterrent Effects of The San Francisco Crime Camera Program. [Online] ACLU of Northern California, March 17, 2008. https://www.aclunc.org/issues/government_surveillance/asset_upload_file796_7024.pdf.

137. **Cameron, Aundreia, et al.** Measuring the Effects of Video Surveillance on Crime in Los Angeles. [Online] The California State Library, May 5, 2008. http://www.library.ca.gov/crb/08/08-007.pdf.

138. **CNN Wire Staff.** Man charged with arson in case of California fires. [Online] CNN, January 2, 2012. http://www.cnn.com/2012/01/02/us/california-arson/index.html.

139. **Makuch, Ben.** The AI-Enabled Cameras Surveilling Towns Across America. [Online] Vsice, March 12, 2021. https://www.vice.com/en/article/epd3yk/the-ai-enabled-cameras-surveilling-towns-across-america.

140. **Richards, Neil.** Can technology prevent another Ferguson? [Online] CNN, September 2, 2014. http://www.cnn.com/2014/09/02/opinion/richards-ferguson-cameras/index.html.

141. **Stross, Randall.** Wearing a Badge, and a Video Camera. [Online] The New York Times, April 6, 2013. http://www.nytimes.com/2013/04/07/business/wearable-video-cameras-for-police-officers.html?pagewanted=all&_r=0.

142. **CNN Editors.** Syria's 'cyber warriors' choose cameras over guns. [Online] CNN, June 14, 2012. http://globalpublicsquare.blogs.cnn.com/2012/06/14/syrias-cyber-warriors-choose-cameras-over-guns/.

143. **Center for Information Technology Research in the Interest of Society.** CITRIS study on SF public cameras released. [Online] CITRIS News, January 9, 2009. http://citris-uc.org/news/2009/01/09/citris_study_sf_public_cameras_released.

144. **Bulwa, Demian.** San Francisco security cameras' choppy video. [Online] San Francisco Chronicle, January 28, 2008. http://www.sfgate.com/cgi-bin/article.cgi?f=/c/a/2008/01/27/MN37TKH6O.DTL.

145. **National Crime Prevention Council.** Neighborhood Watch. [Online] Ncpc.org. [Cited: May 22, 2012.] http://www.ncpc.org/topics/home-and-neighborhood-safety/neighborhood-watch.

146. **Debate Club.** Are 'Stand Your Ground' Laws a Good Idea? [Online] US News and World Report. [Cited: May 22, 2012.] http://www.usnews.com/debate-club/are-stand-your-ground-laws-a-good-idea.

147. **Leger, Donna Leinwand and Dorell, Oren.** New documents show complexity of Trayvon Martin case. [Online] USA Today, May 18, 2012. http://www.usatoday.com/news/nation/story/2012-05-18/George-Zimmerman-Trayvon-Martin-police-documents/55061830/1.

148. **Deshishku, Stacia.** President Obama statement on Trayvon Martin case. [Online] White House Blogs, March 23, 2012. http://whitehouse.blogs.cnn.com/2012/03/23/president-obama-statement-on-trayvon-martin-case/.

149. **Nextdoor.** Nextdoor: The private social network for your neighborhood. [Online] Nextdoor. [Cited: August 16, 2014.] https://nextdoor.com/.

150. **Kelly, Heather.** Hyperlocal apps help residents fight crime. [Online] CNN, May 16, 2014. http://www.cnn.com/2014/05/14/tech/social-media/neighborhood-watch-apps-nextdoor/index.html.

151. **SETI@home.** SETI@home Going into Hibernation. [Online] SETI@home, March 4, 2020. https://www.seti.org/setihome-going-hibernation.

152. **Lobosco, Katie.** Fight AIDS with your smartphone. [Online] CNNMoney, August 7, 2013. http://money.cnn.com/2013/08/07/technology/innovation/aids-smartphone-app/index.html.

153. **3VR Inc.** Use Video Analytics and Data Decision Making to Grow Your Business. [Online] Digital Signage Today. [Cited: May 28, 2012.] http://www.digitalsignagetoday.com/whitepapers/4891/Use-Video-Analytics-and-Data-Decision-Making-to-Grow-Your-Business.

154. **UW Center for Game Science.** Foldit. Solve Puzzles for Science. [Online] Foldit. [Cited: May 18, 2014.] http://fold.it/portal/.

155. **Gross, Doug.** Gaming reality. Cracking the code. Turning gamers into citizen scientists. [Online] CNN, August 2012. http://www.cnn.com/interactive/2012/08/tech/gaming.series/research.html.

156. **McFarland, Mat.** Five interesting things that result from gobs of foot traffic data. [Online] The Washington Post, June 16, 2014. http://www.washingtonpost.com/blogs/innovations/wp/2014/06/16/five-interesting-things-that-result-from-gobs-of-foot-traffic-data/.

157. **DiBono, Misha.** Man outfits neighborhood watch with surface-to-air missiles. [Online] FOX 2 Now, March 26, 2014. http://fox2now.com/2014/03/26/man-outfits-neighborhood-watch-with-surface-to-air-missiles/.

158. **Leech, John.** OEMs must drive the connected car - or get left behind. [Online] AutomotiveWorld.com, February 2, 2012. http://www.automotiveworld.com/news/oems-and-markets/91682-oems-must-drive-the-connected-car-or-get-left-behind.

159. **DARPA.** The DARPA Grand Challenge: Ten Years Later. [Online] Defense Advanced Research Projects Agency, March 13, 2014. http://www.darpa.mil/NewsEvents/Releases/2014/03/13.aspx.

160. **Lee, Kevin.** Nevada Passes Robotic Driver Legislation. [Online] PC World, June 24, 2011. http://www.pcworld.com/article/231105/nevada_passes_robotic_driver_legislation.html.

161. **Paul, Ian.** Google's Self-Driving Car Licensed to Hit Nevada Streets. [Online] PC World, May 8, 2012. http://www.pcworld.com/article/255204/googles_selfdriving_car_licensed_to_hit_nevada_streets.html.

162. **Valdes-Dapena, Peter.** Thrilled and bummed by Google's self-driving car. [Online] CNNMoney, May 18, 2012. http://money.cnn.com/2012/05/17/autos/google-driverless-car/index.htm.

163. **GATSO.** GATSO Road Safety Enforcement. [Online] GATSO. [Cited: May 28, 2012.] http://www.gatso.com/road-safety-solutions/enforcement.html.

164. **Rettinga, Richard A., Fergusona, Susan A. and Hakkertb, A. Shalom.** Effects of Red Light Cameras on Violations and Crashes: A Review of the International Literature. [Online] Traffic Injury Prevention. 4(1):17–23, 2003. http://www.tandfonline.com/doi/abs/10.1080/15389580309858.

165. **Photo Enforced.** Red Light Cameras Catch Cheating Spouses & Pot Smoking Kids. [Online] Photo Enforced, October 18, 2011. http://blog.photoenforced.com/2011/10/red-light-cameras-catch-cheating.html.

166. **eslucr.** DuiCam. [Online] Google Play, January 10, 2013. https://play.google.com/store/apps/details?id=com.eslucr.duicam.

167. **CNN.** Uber driver berated and coughed on by maskless passenger. [Online] CNN Business, March 12, 2021. https://www.cnn.com/videos/business/2021/03/12/uber-driver-mask-dispute-subhakar-khadka-california-orig-llr.cnn-business/video/playlists/stories-worth-watching/.

168. **SmartDrive Systems, Inc.** SmartDrive for Transit: Seeing is Believing. [Online] SmartDrive. [Cited: May 23, 2014.] http://www.smartdrive.net/smartdrivetransit.aspx.

169. **Clarian Labs.** Eco:Speed. [Online] Clarian Labs. [Cited: May 23, 2012.] http://www.goeco-speed.com/.

170. **Goldman, David.** Google buys social mapping service Waze. [Online] CNNMoney, June 11, 2013. http://money.cnn.com/2013/06/11/technology/social/google-waze/.

171. **Graham, Jefferson.** Waze knows some new ways to make your drive better, down to which lane you should pick. [Online] USA Today, September 15, 2020. https://www.usatoday.com/story/tech/2020/09/15/traffic-waze-new-features/5793425002/.

172. **Glasscoe, Maggi.** What is GPS? [Online] NASA, August 13, 1998. http://scign.jpl.nasa.gov/learn/gps1.htm.

173. **Fischer, Benjamin B.** A Cold War Conundrum: The 1983 Soviet War Scare. [Online] U.S. Central Intelligence Agency (CIA), March 19, 2007. https://www.cia.gov/library/

center-for-the-study-of-intelligence/csi-publications/books-and-monographs/a-cold-war-conundrum/source.htm#HEADING1-12.

174. **Lenhart, Amanda.** Teens, Cell Phones and Texting. [Online] Pew Research Center Publications, April 20, 2010. http://pewresearch.org/pubs/1572/teens-cell-phones-text-messages.

175. **Choney, Suzanne.** A good find: GPS to locate the kids. [Online] 2008, 25 MSNBC, August. http://www.msnbc.msn.com/id/26318777/ns/technology_and_science-tech_and_gadgets/t/good-find-gps-locate-kids/.

176. **AT&T.** New Tracking Device Delivers Peace Of Mind To Parents. [Online] AT&T News, October 11, 2011. http://www.att.com/gen/press-room?pid=21658&cdvn=news&newsarticleid=33047&mapcode=wireless-networks-general|consumer.

177. **Reich, Jesse.** MEOSAR Overview. SAR Controllers Training 2012. [Online] United States Coast Guard, February 14–16, 2012. http://www.uscg.mil/hq/cg5/cg534/EmergencyBeacons/2012SarsatConf/Presentations/SAR2012_Feb16_MEOSAR_Overview_Reich.pdf.

178. **Morris, Christopher.** Distress Alerting Satellite System (DASS). [Online] NASA, December 22, 2008. http://searchandrescue.gsfc.nasa.gov/dass/index.html.

179. **Mission 4636.** Mission 4636 was a Haitian initiative that came together following the 2010 earthquake near Port-au-Prince. [Online] Mission 4636. [Cited: May 25, 2012.] http://www.mission4636.org/.

180. **Morris, Laura.** ICT in Conflict & Disaster Response and Peacebuilding Crowdmap. [Online] Haiti Wired Blogs, May 10, 2012. http://haitirewired.wired.com/profiles/blogs/ict-in-conflict-disaster-response-and-peacebuilding-crowdmap.

181. **Metz, Rachel.** My Life, Logged. [Online] MIT Technology Review, June 10, 2014. http://www.technologyreview.com/review/528076/my-life-logged/.

182. **McGreal, Chris.** America's serious crime rate is plunging, but why? [Online] The Guardian, August 21, 2011. http://www.guardian.co.uk/world/2011/aug/21/america-serious-crime-rate-plunging.

183. **AMBER Alert.** The AMBER Alert Program is a voluntary partnership between law-enforcement, media, transportation and others to send bulletins about child-abduction cases. [Online] Facebook, December 30, 2009. http://www.facebook.com/AMBERalert.

184. **U.S. Department of Justice.** AMBER Alert. [Online] U.S. Department of Justice. [Cited: May 24, 2012.] http://www.amberalert.gov/.

185. **FCC.** Amber Plan (America's Missing Broadcast Emergency Response). [Online] Federal Communications Commission. [Cited: May 24, 2012.] http://www.fcc.gov/guides/amber-plan-americas-missing-broadcast-emergency-response.

186. **National Center for Missing & Exploited Children.** International AMBER Alert Plans. [Online] National Center for Missing & Exploited Children. [Cited: May 24, 2012.] http://www.missingkids.com/missingkids/servlet/PageServlet?LanguageCountry=en_US&PageId=1422.

187. **Hays, Tom.** NYPD is watching Facebook to Fight Gang Bloodshed. [Online] Associated Press, October 2, 2012. http://bigstory.ap.org/article/nypd-watching-facebook-fight-gang-bloodshed.

188. **Anderson, Jonathan.** Do you know who your (Facebook) friends are? [Online] The UWM Post, December 7, 2009. http://www.uwmpost.com/2009/12/07/do-you-know-who-your-facebook-friends-are-2/.

189. **Topping, Alexandra.** Fugitive caught after updating his status on Facebook. [Online] The Guardian, October 14, 2009. http://www.guardian.co.uk/technology/2009/oct/14/mexico-fugitive-facebook-arrest.

190. **Kemp, Joe.** Police nab Queens suspect using hi-tech face-detector. [Online] New York Daily News, March 16, 2012. http://articles.nydailynews.com/2012-03-16/news/31202755_1_facial-recognition-cops-real-time-crime-center.

191. **Shoichet, Catherine E. and Cuevas, Mayra.** Kidnapped newborn found 'thanks to Facebook'. [Online] CNN, May 27, 2014. http://www.cnn.com/2014/05/27/world/canada-kidnapped-baby-facebook/index.html.

192. **Cohen, Marshall.** Capitol rioter arrested after being turned in by match on online dating app Bumble. [Online] CNN Politics, April 23, 2021. https://www.cnn.com/2021/04/23/politics/bumble-capitol-riot-robert-chapman/index.html.

193. **Lynch, Jennifer.** Applying for Citizenship? U.S. Citizenship and Immigration Wants to Be Your "Friend". [Online] Electronic Frontier Foundation, October 12, 2010. https://www.eff.org/deeplinks/2010/10/applying-citizenship-u-s-citizenship-and.

194. **Hosenball, Mark.** Homeland Security watches Twitter, social media. [Online] Reuters, January 11, 2012. http://www.reuters.com/article/2012/01/11/us-usa-homelandsecurity-websites-idUSTRE80A1RC20120111.

195. **Obeidallah, Dean.** The government is reading your tweets. [Online] CNN, March 9, 2012. http://www.cnn.com/2012/03/09/opinion/obeidallah-social-media/index.html.

196. **Ellement, John R.** Twitter gives Boston police, prosecutors data from one subscriber in criminal inquiry. [Online] Boston.com., March 1, 2012. http://www.boston.com/Boston/metrodesk/2012/03/twitter-provides-boston-police-and-suffolk-prosecutors-with-subscriber-information-for-criminal-probe/DfoELIrEBPzx4KCVbLZo8L/index.html.

197. **Weisburd, David, et al.** The Growth of Compstat in American Policing. [Online] Police Foundation, April 2004. http://www.policefoundation.org/content/growth-compstat-american-policing.

198. **Martinez, Michael.** ACLU raises privacy concerns about police technology tracking drivers. [Online] CNN, July 18, 2013. http://www.cnn.com/2013/07/17/us/aclu-license-plates-readers/index.html.

199. **LAPPL Board of Directors.** Protecting officers and the public with LPR technology. [Online] LAPPL Blog, July 11, 2013. http://lapd.com/blog/protecting_officers_and_the_public_with_lpr_technology/.

200. **Ferrara, Emilio, et al.** Detecting criminal organizations in mobile phone networks. [Online] Cornell University Library, April 3, 2014. http://arxiv.org/abs/1404.1295.

201. **Murphy, Heather.** Sooner or Later Your Cousin's DNA Is Going to Solve a Murder. [Online] The New York Times, April 25, 2019. https://www.nytimes.com/2019/04/25/us/golden-state-killer-dna.html.

202. **Rushe, Dominic.** Google: don't expect privacy when sending to Gmail. [Online] The Guardian, August 14, 2013. http://www.theguardian.com/technology/2013/aug/14/google-gmail-users-privacy-email-lawsuit.

203. **O'Toole, James.** Google snoops on Gmail to catch pedophiles. [Online] CNN, August 14, 2014. http://money.cnn.com/2014/08/14/technology/enterprise/gmail-pedophiles/.

204. **Cohen, Marshall and Murphy, Paul P.** Capitol rioters boasted on social media. Now, they're scrambling to scrub phones and pictures. [Online] CNN Politics, February 12, 2021. https://www.cnn.com/2021/02/12/politics/capitol-riot-social-media-phones/index.html.

205. **FBI.** Community Outreach. [Online] FBI.gov. [Cited: May 27, 2021.] https://www.fbi.gov/about/community-outreach.

206. **Levin, Sam.** Facebook announces dating app focused on 'meaningful relationships'. [Online] The Guardian, May 1, 2018. https://www.theguardian.com/technology/2018/may/01/facebook-dating-app-mark-zuckerberg-f8-conference.

207. **Axon, Samuel.** 5 Ways Facebook Changed Dating (For the Worse). [Online] Mashable, April 10, 2010. http://mashable.com/2010/04/10/facebook-dating/.

208. **Cacioppo, John T., Fowler, James H. and Christakis, Nicholas A.** Alone in the crowd: The structure and spread of loneliness in a large social network. [Online] Journal of Personality and Social Psychology. Vol. 97(6). pp. 977–991, January 1, 2010. http://www.ncbi.nlm.nih.gov/pmc/articles/PMC2792572/.

209. **Turkle, Sherry.** Alone Together: Why We Expect More from Technology and Less from Each Other. [Online] Basic Books, January 11, 2011. http://www.alonetogetherbook.com/.

210. **Chou, HT and Edge, N.** "They are happier and having better lives than I am": the impact of using Facebook on perceptions of others' lives. [Online] Cyberpsychology, Behavior,

and Social Networking. 15(2):117–21, February 2012. http://www.ncbi.nlm.nih.gov/pubmed/22165917.

211. **Matyszczyk, Chris.** Always posting pics on Facebook? Then you're weird, study says. [Online] CNet, August 11, 2013. http://www.cnet.com/news/always-posting-pics-on-facebook-then-youre-weird-study-says/.

212. **Wikipedia.** Zhuangzi. [Online] Wikipedia, August 7, 2011. http://en.wikipedia.org/wiki/Zhuangzi#The_butterfly_dream.

213. **arXiv.** Data Mining Reveals the Surprising Behavior of Users of Dating Websites. [Online] MIT Technology Review, January 30, 2014. http://www.technologyreview.com/view/524081/data-mining-reveals-the-surprising-behavior-of-users-of-dating-websites/.

214. **Xia, Peng, et al.** Who is Dating Whom: Characterizing User Behaviors of a Large Online Dating Site. [Online] Cornell University Library, January 22, 2014. http://arxiv.org/abs/1401.5710.

215. **Rudder, Christian.** We Experiment On Human Beings! [Online] OkCupid, July 28, 2014. http://blog.okcupid.com/index.php/we-experiment-on-human-beings/.

216. **Webb, Amy.** Amy Webb: How I hacked online dating. [Online] TED Talks, October 2, 2013. http://www.youtube.com/watch?v=d6wG_sAdP0U.

217. **Fiegerman, Seth.** How Facebook's Graph Search could disrupt online dating. [Online] CNN, January 16, 2013. http://www.cnn.com/2013/01/16/tech/social-media/facebook-graph-search-dating/index.html.

218. **Backstrom, Lars and Kleinberg, Jon.** Romantic Partnerships and the Dispersion of Social Ties: A Network Analysis of Relationship Status on Facebook. [Online] Cornell University Library, October 24, 2013. http://arxiv.org/abs/1310.6753.

219. **Kim, Ryan.** Hey, baby, want a date? New mobile dating services allow people to browse profiles via cell phone and message potential matches -- even on the spot. [Online] San Francisco Chronicle, July 23, 2005. http://www.sfgate.com/cgi-bin/article.cgi?f=/c/a/2005/07/23/BUGKMDSB4P1.DTL.

220. **Gustin, Sam.** Highlight Aims to Alert You To Like-Minded Folks in Your Immediate Vicinity. [Online] TIME Magazine, March 12, 2012. http://business.time.com/2012/03/12/sxsw-highlight-founder-aims-to-build-sixth-sense-for-mobile-web/.

221. **LeTrent, Sarah.** Siren dating app lets women call the shots. [Online] CNN, August 19, 2014. http://www.cnn.com/2014/08/19/living/siren-dating-app-for-women-relate/index.html.

222. **Ellis, Blake.** Doomsday dating sites: 'Don't face the future alone'. [Online] CNNMoney, March 29, 2012. http://money.cnn.com/2012/03/29/pf/doomsday-dating/index.htm.

223. **Petroff, Alanna.** OMG! Hot or Not is back! [Online] CNNMoney, June 17, 2014. http://money.cnn.com/2014/06/17/technology/social/hot-or-not-dating/.

224. **Moscovitz, Meitar.** Maybe Days. [Online] Meitar Moscovitz, October 14, 2013. http://days.maybemaimed.com/post/64045337134/there-are-now-four-dating-websites-that-have.

225. **McGee, Jordan.** FacialNetwork.com Announces Beta Release Of "NameTag" The First Real-Time Facial Recognition App For Google Glass. [Online] Yahoo! Finance, December 19, 2013. http://finance.yahoo.com/news/facialnetwork-com-announces-beta-release-200300439.html.

226. **Grossman, Samantha.** Icelanders Avoid Inbreeding Through Online Database. [Online] TIME Magazine, February 9, 2012. http://newsfeed.time.com/2012/02/09/icelanders-avoid-inbreeding-through-online-incest-database/.

227. **Grimaldi, Kelly, Albert, Emily and Wells, Gregory.** Designing a product to ease one of life's difficult moments. [Online] Facebook, May 5, 2021. https://www.facebook.com/notes/1100464777037193/.

228. **The Godfather.** Memorable Quotes for The Godfather. [Online] IMDb, March 24, 1972. http://www.imdb.com/title/tt0068646/quotes.

229. **Facebook Company Info.** Facebook Newsroom. [Online] Facebook. [Cited: March 1, 2021.] http://newsroom.fb.com/company-info/.

230. **Editor.** Google Statistics and Facts. [Online] Market.Us, August 21, 2020. https://market.us/statistics/web-search-engine/google/.

231. **Editors.** Twitter Statistics and Facts. [Online] Market.Us, February 12, 2021. https://market.us/statistics/social-media/twitter/.

232. **Cauley, Leslie.** NSA has massive database of Americans' phone calls. [Online] USA Today, May 11, 2006. http://www.usatoday.com/news/washington/2006-05-10-nsa_x.htm.

233. **Gidda, Mirren.** Edward Snowden and the NSA files – timeline. [Online] The Guardian, July 25, 2013. http://www.theguardian.com/world/2013/jun/23/edward-snowden-nsa-files-timeline.

234. **Keen, Andrew.** Should we fear mind-reading future tech? [Online] CNN, June 19, 2012. http://www.cnn.com/2012/06/18/tech/predictive-technology-future/index.html.

235. **Duhigg, Charles.** How Companies Learn Your Secrets. [Online] The New York Times, February 16, 2012. http://www.nytimes.com/2012/02/19/magazine/shopping-habits.html?pagewanted=all.

236. **Quantified Toilets.** Capturing toilet behaviour for real-time data and health analysis. [Online] Quantified Toilets. [Cited: May 3, 2014.] http://quantifiedtoilets.com/.

237. **Golbeck, Jennifer.** What a Toilet Hoax Can Tell Us About the Future of Surveillance. [Online] The Atlantic, April 29, 2014. http://www.theatlantic.com/technology/archive/2014/04/what-a-toilet-hoax-can-tell-us-about-the-future-of-surveillance/361408/.

238. **Sytsma, Alan.** Hardcore Coddling: How Eleven Madison Park Modernized Elite, Old-School Service. [Online] Grub Street, April 9, 2014. http://www.grubstreet.com/2014/04/eleven-madison-park-foh-staff-detailed-look.html.

239. **Lindberg, Peter Jon.** What your hotel knows about you. [Online] CNN, February 26, 2013. http://www.cnn.com/2013/02/26/travel/what-your-hotel-knows/index.html.

240. **Amani, Elahe.** Silence did not make Sanaz Nezami strong: Facing lethal immigrant domestic violence. [Online] Women News Network, December 2013. http://womennewsnetwork.net/2014/02/18/silence-did-not-make-sanaz-nezami-strong-facing-immigrant-domestic-violence/.

241. **The Associated Press.** Family watches online as Iranian woman dies in U.S. [Online] New York Daily News, January 1, 2014. http://www.nydailynews.com/news/national/family-watches-online-iranian-woman-dies-u-s-article-1.1563678.

242. **Lenhart, Amanda and Duggan, Maeve.** Couples, the Internet, and Social Media. [Online] Pew Research Internet Project, February 11, 2014. http://www.pewinternet.org/2014/02/11/couples-the-internet-and-social-media/.

243. **Moon, Melissa.** Child's Facebook Picture Leads To Diagnosis Of Rare Eye Condition. [Online] WREG, March 31, 2014. http://wreg.com/2014/03/31/childs-picture-on-facebook-leads-to-diagnosis-of-rare-eye-conditioncebo/.

Part VI
Epilogue

Chapter 19
From Total Information Awareness to 1984

"We are the nation that put cars in driveways and computers in offices; the nation of Edison and the Wright brothers; of Google and Facebook."

– President Barack Obama (January 2011)

"Our No. 1 enemy is ignorance. And I believe that is the No. 1 enemy for everyone — it's not understanding what actually is going on in the world."

– WikiLeaks founder Julian Assange (May 2011)

"Google, Facebook would not exist, had it not been for investments that we made as a country in basic science and research."

– President Barack Obama (April 2012)

"Our explicit strategy for the next several years is to focus on growing and connecting everyone in the world."

– Facebook CEO Mark Zuckerberg (February 2014)

"Today at the Facebook Communities Summit we changed our mission to focus on bringing the world closer together. … Our full mission statement is: give people the power to build community and bring the world closer together."

– Facebook CEO Mark Zuckerberg (June 2017)

"Today we're seen as a social media company. But in our DNA, we are a company that builds technology to connect people. And the metaverse is the next frontier just like social networking was when we got started."

– Facebook and Meta CEO Mark Zuckerberg (October 2021)

"Every major technological innovation propels humanity forward to the point of no return. … Instead of turning back, we must continue to innovate and push humanity towards the next point of no return. It is a good thing."

– Newton Lee

© Springer Science+Business Media, LLC, part of Springer Nature 2021
N. Lee, *Facebook Nation*, https://doi.org/10.1007/978-1-0716-1867-7_19

19.1   From Carrier Pigeons to Brave New World of Total Information Awareness

President Barack Obama, in his 2011 State of the Union Address, called America "the nation of Edison and the Wright brothers" and "of Google and Facebook" (1). On May 18, 2012 (before Alibaba's IPO in September 2014), Facebook offered the largest technology IPO in history and the third largest U.S. IPO ever, trailing only Visa in March 2008 and General Motors in November 2010 (2). Selling 421.2 million shares to raise $16 billion, Facebook had a $104.2 billion market value and was more costly than almost every company in the Standard & Poor's 500 Index (3). Former U.S. Treasury secretary Lawrence H. Summers called Facebook's offering "an American milestone" comparable to Ford and IBM's, "Many companies provide products that let people do things they've done before in better ways. Most important companies, like Ford in its day or I.B.M. in its, are those that open up whole new capabilities and permit whole new connections. Facebook is such a company" (4). However, the Facebook IPO was also one of the biggest opening flops in stock market history. The stock was down by 16.5% at the end of its first full week of trading; and it took over a year for the stock to recover.

On May 19, 2012, a day after the bumpy IPO, 28-year-old Facebook co-founder and CEO Mark Zuckerberg added a life event on his timeline: Married Priscilla Chan (5). Within a week, the wedding picture that he uploaded to Facebook had received 1.5 million "Likes" and 800 comments from his 14 million subscribers. In addition, Zuckerberg and Chan's Hungarian Sheepdog named "Beast" was also a "Public Figure" on Facebook with a respectable 575,000 "Likes," but he was far behind the Pomeranian named "Boo" who had garnered 4.4 million "Likes" in May 2012 (6).

A month prior on April 11, 2012, when a hoax spread on Twitter about Boo's death in a duck pond, Boo's owner quickly addressed the rumors on Facebook, saying, "hi friends! i heard the rumors, and i would like all my friends to know that i am happy and kickin'! i asked human if i could do a press conference to reassure everyone on camera, but she reminded me that i can't talk" (7). As Mark Twain said about his obituary mistakenly published in the *New York Journal* in May 1879, "The report of my death was an exaggeration" (8).

To some, Facebook is both a self-published tabloid and a public relations gem. To others, Facebook is a communication tool for families and friends around the world to stay in touch. From a macroscopic point of view, Facebook offers insights into public sentiments and national trends. In a microscopic view, Facebook allows people to reach out and connect on a very personal level. Zuckerberg told ABC's Robin Roberts in a 2012 interview that the idea of the organ donation initiative came to him during a dinner conversation with his then girlfriend and future wife Priscilla (9).

Increasingly for many users, Facebook has become an indispensible platform for spreading messages of anti-bullying, AMBER Alerts, organ donation, political activism, and world peace.

Whatever Facebook is or is not, the massive volume of photos, biometric data, and personally identifiable information (PII) on Facebook has raised serious privacy concerns. Some people have deactivated their Facebook for privacy reasons as well as relationship problems, job issues, or simply freeing up their time for face-to-face interpersonal connections with the people whom they really care about (10). A June 2012 survey of 1,032 Facebook users in the U.S. found that 34% of them spend less time on the site than they did half a year ago (11). There are also reports indicating that Facebook is getting "uncool" for 18 to 24 years old – a mindset tantamount to "parents turn up at the party, the party's over" (12).

The new Generation C of digital omnivores has largely accepted Facebook's norm of information sharing in lieu of the traditional norm of privacy. In January 2010, Zuckerberg told the audience at the Crunchie awards in San Francisco, "People have really gotten comfortable not only sharing more information and different kinds, but more openly and with more people. That social norm is just something that has evolved over time" (13).

At one end of the social spectrum, we have an Arizona man using carrier pigeons to communicate with his business partner in the year 2012 (14). At the other end, we have blogger Robert Scoble of Rackspace's Building 43 who said, "Facebook is good at a lot of things. It is a new kind of new media company that personalizes the media. The more Zuckerberg knows about you, the better the user experience will be. … Everybody has a freaky line. I am way over the freaky line. I want the Internet to know everything about me because that way it can really help me. In that way, Facebook is way ahead and I get more for my efforts that way" (15).

Notwithstanding privacy concerns, having our real identity rather than anonymity online has an advantage of keeping people honest and courteous in the Internet space. *Forbes Magazine* contributor Anthony Wing Kosner observed, "Instead of the anonymous trolls of the early web, Zuckerberg's social web reinforced us for being ourselves online and revealing as much (or more) about ourselves as possible. And the Facebook revolution worked. People do act more civil when their real name is attached to a comment. People do think twice (sometimes) about posting questionable photos that may come back to haunt them. And it has become much easier to find people, not only through Facebook, but LinkedIn, Google+ and other real-name networks" (16).

The same psychology applies to the offline world long before the existence of Facebook and Google. Drivers think twice about running a red traffic light when the red light camera is present at an intersection. Although red light cameras continue to be a topic of fierce debate in cities like Houston, Texas (17), reports show that there has been an overall 25–30% reduction in injury crashes at intersections following camera installation (18).

Around the world, public closed-circuit television (CCTV) systems help deter crimes in shopping malls, convenience stores, gas stations, parking garages, airports, banks, casinos, and other public places. Although the proliferation of CCTV cameras has created some unease about the erosion of civil liberties and individual human rights, the majority of people have accepted the presence of CCTV in public places.

Prof. Amitai Etzioni of George Washington University observed, "Facebook merely adds to the major inroads made by the CCTV cameras that are ubiquitous in many cities around the globe, along with surveillance satellites, tracking devices, spy malware and, most recently, drones used not for killing terrorists but for scrutinizing spaces heretofore considered private, like our backyards" (19).

Back in the 60's, Defense Advanced Research Projects Agency (DARPA) initiated and funded the research and development of Advanced Research Projects Agency Network (ARPANET) that went online in 1969. The success of ARPANET gave rise to the global commercial Internet in the 90's and the new generation of Fortune 500 companies today such as Amazon.com, Google, eBay, and Facebook.

President Barack Obama said at a campaign fundraiser in April 2012, "I believe in investing in basic research and science because I understand that all these extraordinary companies … many of them would have never been there; Google, Facebook would not exist, had it not been for investments that we made as a country in basic science and research" (20). Another good example is the talking, question-answering Siri application on Apple's iPhone (21). Siri originated from a DARPA-funded project known as PAL (Personalized Assistant that Learns) – an adaptive artificial intelligence program for data retrieval and data synthesis (22).

As if life comes full circle in the 21st century, private businesses and the ubiquity of social networks such as Facebook, Instagram, Twitter, and YouTube are creating the technologies and infrastructures necessary for the DARPA-proposed Total Information Awareness program. Facial recognition, location tracking, ambient social apps on GPS-enabled devices, Google Street View, digital footprints, and data mining are some key elements in information awareness.

WikiLeaks founder Julian Assange told RT's Laura Emmett in a May 2011 interview, "Facebook in particular is the most appalling spying machine that has ever been invented. Here we have the world's most comprehensive database about people: their relationships, their names, their addresses, their locations and their communications with each other, their relatives – all sitting within the United States, all accessible to US intelligence" (23). Assange further alleged that, "Facebook, Google, Yahoo – all these major US organizations have built-in interfaces for US intelligence. It's not a matter of serving a subpoena. They have an interface that they have developed for US intelligence to use."

Total Information Awareness requires efficient and effective data mining. On March 29, 2012, the Obama administration announced more than $200 million in funding for "Big Data Research and Development Initiative" (24). One of the beneficiaries of the initiative is Centers for Disease Control and Prevention (CDC). Using the funding, CDC runs a BioSense program to track health problems as they evolve and to safeguard the health of the American people (25).

The U.S. government has also been learning from private businesses who often share customers' data to make a profit or a future sale. Letitia Long, Director of the National Geospatial-Intelligence Agency (NGA) described the shift across the post-9/11 intelligence community as the transition from a "need-to-know" atmosphere to a "need-to-share and need-to-provide" culture. "In solving intelligence problems, including diversity of thought is essential," said Long, "[In] the Osama bin Laden operation, the intelligence community witnessed the true value of merging many thoughts and perspectives, and we must continue to replicate this kind of integration across the enterprise in the future" (26).

The quest for information awareness has also resulted in biosurveillance systems such as Argus – an artificial intelligence program that monitors foreign news reports and other open sources looking for signs that would trigger an early warning of an epidemic, nuclear accident, or environmental catastrophe. Eric Haseltine, former director of research at NSA and then associate director for science and technology at ODNI, said in a 2006 *U.S. News & World Report* interview, "I sleep a little easier at night knowing that Argus is out there" (27).

The brave new world of Total Information Awareness is a connected world that benefits individuals as well as society as a whole. Mark Zuckerberg wrote in his IPO letter in 2012, "At Facebook, we're inspired by technologies that have revolutionized how people spread and consume information. We often talk about inventions like the printing press and the television – by simply making communication more efficient, they led to a complete transformation of many important parts of society. They gave more people a voice. They encouraged progress. They changed the way society was organized. They brought us closer together. Today, our society has reached another tipping point. We live at a moment when the majority of people in the world have access to the internet or mobile phones – the raw tools necessary to start sharing what they're thinking, feeling and doing with whomever they want. Facebook aspires to build the services that give people the power to share and help them once again transform many of our core institutions and industries. There is a huge need and a huge opportunity to get everyone in the world connected, to give everyone a voice and to help transform society for the future. The scale of the technology and infrastructure that must be built is unprecedented, and we believe this is the most important problem we can focus on" (28).

But knowing that connecting people online is not enough, Facebook changed its mission in June 2017 to "focus on giving people the power to build community and bringing the world closer together" (29). Mark Zuckerberg wrote, "Our full mission statement is: give people the power to build community and bring the world closer together" (30).

19.2   George Orwell's 1984

In February 2012, a reader by the name of Helen Corey left a one-line comment on a *Wall Street Journal* report on Google's iPhone tracking, "Orwell's 1984 novel has become reality" (31). It was her response to Google and other advertising companies bypassing Apple's Safari browser settings for guarding privacy on the users' iPhones and computers (32).

In June 2013 after Edward Snowden revealed NSA's dragnet surveillance programs, sales of Orwell's 1984 novel spiked (33). One edition climbed to the top 3 spot on Amazon.com after sales jumped by almost 10,000 %.

George Orwell's novel *Nineteen Eighty-Four* (first published in 1949) (34) portrays pervasive government surveillance, incessant public mind control, disinformation, and manipulation of the past in a "Big Brother" society that is a dystopian future. It tells a terrifying story of a world without privacy. Orwell coined the terms Big Brother, doublethink, thoughtcrime, Newspeak, and memory hole that have become contemporary vernacular.

Social commentator Ed West considers George Orwell the prophet of political correctness: "Among the various characteristics of political correctness is the branding of dissident thinkers as racists, sexists or homophobes (thoughtcrime), the necessity of holding two contradictory ideas together (doublethink), and attempts to change the language to change politics (Newspeak)" (35).

CNN's Lewis Beale opines that we are living "1984" today (36). His CNN article compares Orwell's endless global war with today's war on terror, doublethink with abortion legislation, anti-sex league with abstinence-only sex education, and telescreens with websites like Facebook and the ever-present surveillance cameras.

In the year 2012, from ATMs to parking lots to shopping malls, there are approximately 30 million cameras in the world capturing 250 billion hours of raw footage annually (37). Since the 1970's, the proliferation of CCTV cameras in public places has led to some unease about the erosion of civil liberties and individual human rights, along with warnings of an Orwellian "Big Brother" culture.

In the United Kingdom, CCTV is so prevalent that some residents can expect to be captured by a camera at least 300 times a day (38). With more than 1.85 million cameras operating in the U.K. (39), the security-camera cordon surrounding London has earned the nickname of "Ring of Steel" (40). The U.K. first introduced the security measures in London's financial district in the mid-1990s during an Irish Republican Army (IRA) bombing campaign. After the terror attacks in the United States on September 11, 2011, the "Ring of Steel" was widened to include more businesses (41).

In the U.S., New York, Los Angeles, San Francisco, and Chicago are among the major cities that have implemented citywide CCTV monitoring systems. Disney theme parks, Six Flags, and other public attractions also use video surveillance systems that can see in the dark.

In January 2008, Pulitzer Prize-winner Lawrence Wright wrote in *The New Yorker*, "The fantasy worlds that Disney creates have a surprising amount in common with the ideal universe envisaged by the intelligence community, in which environments are carefully controlled and people are closely observed, and no one seems to mind" (42).

Tourists not only love to visit Disneyland but also flock to Las Vegas casinos and resorts, another fantasy world, where security cameras are in ample use. In March 2012, Mirage Resort in Las Vegas became the 50th casino to install facial recognition software as part of the surveillance suite of Visual Casino loss-reduction systems (43).

Video surveillance is not always associated with crime prevention. SceneTap, for example, allows consumers to get a real-time snapshot of 50 bars and clubs in

Chicago (44). Facial detection and "people-counting" technologies automatically inform customers about the crowd size and male-to-female ratio in each venue. Without encroaching on individual privacy, the system does not store the videos or identify the faces. SceneTap takes barhopping into the 21st century.

In the future, private citizens will join Big Brother in "watching us." An Intel-commissioned white paper in May 2012 summarized, "While the future is never certain, a future where humans are infused with mobile technology where we are part of the device, our own bodies and brains part of the technology, and where there are no barriers to pure capability, is becoming more believable by the day" (45).

We have already seen a glimpse of that future...

In 1998, Microsoft researcher Gordon Bell experimented with digitally recording as much of his life as possible for the MyLifeBits project: "Photos, letters, and memorabilia were scanned. Everything he did on his computer was captured. He wore an automatic camera, an arm-strap that logged his bio-metrics, and began recording telephone calls. This experiment, and the system they created to support it, put them at the center of a movement studying the creation and enjoyment of e-memories" (46).

In 2009, Canadian filmmaker Rob Spence called himself an "Eyeborg" when he replaced his prosthetic eye with a battery-powered, wireless video camera that records everything that he sees in real time to a computer. "In today's world, you have Facebook and camera eyes," he said. "Tomorrow, we'll have collective consciousness and the Borg. It's a collective robot consciousness. I believe that's a genuine modern concern" (47).

In 2010, controversial professor Wafaa Bilal at New York University implanted a camera in the back of his head for a yearlong art project (48). The camera snapped a picture every minute, published the image on a website, and displayed it on monitors labeled "The 3rd I" at Mathaf: Arab Museum of Modern Art in Doha, Qatar.

We may begin to wonder how many people like Gordon Bell, Rob Spence, and Wafaa Bilal are living among us. Commercially available life-logging devices such as the Autographer and the Narrative Clip are clip-on cameras that continually take pictures on their own (49). The "NameTag" app allows Google Glass users to capture images from their live video and scan them against photos from social media, dating sites, and a database of more than 450,000 registered sex offenders (50).

People have their own personal rights to take pictures and record videos in public. Dictatorship of the majority over the minority would be an encroachment on the rights of the individual and their prerogative to personal freedom. A saying commonly attributed to Benjamin Franklin goes like this, "Any society that would give up a little liberty to gain a little security will deserve neither and lose both." The question is: Did we give up any personal freedom because of public CCTV, red light cameras, Google social search, or Facebook privacy settings? The answer is: No, not really. We do not hesitate to go to public places, drive around town, search for information on Google, and socialize with friends on Facebook and other social networks.

Pete Cashmore, founder and CEO of *Mashable,* has commented that our current world is both reminiscent of George Orwell's *Nineteen Eighty-Four* and radically at odds with it. Cashmore wrote in a January 2012 CNN article, "The online world is indeed allowing our every move to be tracked, while at the same time providing a counterweight to the emergence of Big Brother. ... Unlike in Orwell's dystopian world, people today are making a conscious choice to do so. The difference between this reality and Orwell's vision is the issue of control: While his Thought Police tracked you without permission, some consumers are now comfortable with sharing their every move online" (51).

19.3   Aldous Huxley's Brave New World

Will the "Big Friend" of Facebook replace the "Big Brother" of government? Will human beings have their lives recorded from birth to death on the pages of Facebook, akin to the 2011 *Black Mirror* episode "The Entire History of You"?

In fact, some parents have been posting the sonograms of their unborn babies on Facebook (52). Some families and friends have been leaving posts on the deceased's Facebook Timeline in remembrance (53). Our future may be one step closer to Aldous Huxley's *Brave New World* (1932) rather than George Orwell's *Nineteen Eighty-Four* (1949).

Social critic Neil Postman contrasted the worlds of Orwell and Huxley in his 1985 book *Amusing Ourselves to Death: Public Discourse in the Age of Show Business.* Postman wrote, "What Orwell feared were those who would ban books. What Huxley feared was that there would be no reason to ban a book, for there would be no one who wanted to read one. Orwell feared those who would deprive us of information. Huxley feared those who would give us so much that we would be reduced to passivity and egotism. Orwell feared that the truth would be concealed from us. Huxley feared the truth would be drowned in a sea of irrelevance. Orwell feared we would become a captive culture. Huxley feared we would become a trivial culture, preoccupied with some equivalent of the feelies, the orgy porgy, and the centrifugal bumblepuppy. As Huxley remarked in *Brave New World Revisited,* the civil libertarians and rationalists who are ever on the alert to oppose tyranny 'failed to take into account man's almost infinite appetite for distractions.' In *1984,* Orwell added, 'people are controlled by inflicting pain.' In *Brave New World,* they are controlled by inflicting pleasure. In short, Orwell feared that what we fear will ruin us. Huxley feared that our desire will ruin us" (54).

What a surprise that Postman's discourse about television in the age of show business is equally applicable to the Internet and social media in the age of big data! Will an ultra-connected world with social media "likes" and crowd-sourced ratings create a dystopia akin to the 2016 *Black Mirror* episode "Nosedive"?

19.4 Point of No Return and Internet.org: "Every one of us. Everywhere. Connected."

Every major technological innovation propels humanity forward to the point of no return. Although the 1969 hit song "In the Year 2525 (Exordium et Terminus)" by Zager and Evans (55) painted a grim future of humanity being overly dependent on technology, hardly anyone today would seriously consider giving up the Internet, cell phones, automobiles, and everyday comfort and convenience. Instead of turning back, we must continue to innovate and push humanity towards the next point of no return. It is a good thing.

X PRIZE Foundation founder and CEO Peter Diamandis spoke at the TED2012 conference in February, "The future is going to be better than many of us think ... We will live in a world of abundance made possible by new technology" (56).

Time Magazine named Facebook co-founder and CEO Mark Zuckerberg its Person of the Year 2010 for connecting more than half a billion people and mapping the social relations among them, for creating a new system of exchanging information and for changing how we live our lives. *Time* summarized Facebook's mission in an idealistic description: "Facebook wants to populate the wilderness, tame the howling mob and turn the lonely, antisocial world of random chance into a friendly world, a serendipitous world. You'll be working and living inside a network of people, and you'll never have to be alone again. The Internet, and the whole world, will feel more like a family, or a college dorm, or an office where your co-workers are also your best friends" (57).

Such a grand vision is a tall order indeed. In August 2013, Facebook introduced Internet.org, a "global partnership between technology leaders, nonprofits, local communities and experts who are working together to bring the internet to the two thirds of the world's population that doesn't have it. #ConnectTheWorld" (58). The slogan is "Every one of us. Everywhere. Connected." In March, 2014, Internet.org announced Connectivity Lab at Facebook to build drones, satellites, and lasers to deliver the Internet to everyone (59). At the *MIT Technology Review*'s Digital Summit in June 2014, Facebook revealed its data diet campaign to make Facebook's apps leaner for people who have scarce bandwidth. "Our apps were crashing all the time and they maxed out their data plan in 40 minutes," said Jay Parikh, head of infrastructure at Facebook. "We now have a whole team of people focused on reducing data consumption. There's continual effort to drive data use down. ... There are three or four billion folks out there that walk around in a 2G or 3G area but may not have devices or economic standing, or don't think the Internet is valuable to them. We're working with carriers to rethink how they price and offer data plans" (60). Parikh described Internet.org as "the next phase of the company."

In a 2014 interview with *The New York Times*, Mark Zuckerberg said, "I'm focused on Internet.org and how to connect all these people. But my life is so different from the person who's going to be getting Internet in two years. One of the things that we do is ask product managers to go travel to an emerging-market country to see how people who are getting on the Internet use it. They learn the most interesting things. People ask questions like, 'It says here I'm supposed to put in my password – what's a password?' For us, that's a mind-boggling thing" (61).

"Our explicit strategy for the next several years is to focus on growing and connecting everyone in the world," Zuckerberg said (62). "They're going to use it to decide what kind of government they want, get access to healthcare for the first time ever, connect with family hundreds of miles away that they haven't seen in decades" (63).

In 2016, Facebook confirmed millimeter-wave research at Internet.org: "This work is part of the Connectivity Lab which supports the mission of Internet.org — to connect the four billion people who don't have Internet access" (64). The use of frequency bands in the 24 GHz to 100 GHz range, known as millimeter wave (mmWave), has offered benefits for 5G networks.

We will know in the future whether Facebook or a new breed of social networks will be able to connect all billions of people on Earth (65). Media theorist Douglas Rushkoff shared his optimism on CNN, "This new form of media – social networking – will not only redefine the Internet, change human relationships, create a new marketing landscape, and challenge Google, but it will now rescue and alter the economy itself. Like virtual kudzu, it will infiltrate the financial markets, creating new sorts of opportunities for this peer-to-peer 'social' economy to take root. We will all make our living playing Farmville, or designing new versions of it, or investing in companies that do" (66).

Google chairman Eric Schmidt predicted in 2013 that the entire world will be online by 2020 (67). It did not happen. Nevertheless, Facebook's Internet.org, Google-backed Geeks Without Frontiers (68), Samsung's solar-powered Internet schools in Africa (69), and other philanthropic efforts are helping to achieve the ultimate goal and to eliminate the digital divide among peoples and nations.

19.5   Privacy and E-Activism: Mesh Networks and Peer-to-Peer Social Networks

An old English proverb says, "If you can't beat them, join them." There is another saying, "If you can't beat them, join them, and then beat them."

Perhaps a decentralized Internet will create the utopia for privacy protection and personal freedom in the age of big data and total information awareness. Isaac Wilder and Charles Wyble co-founded the Free Network Foundation (FNF) in 2011 to investigate peer-to-per communications infrastructure that is resistant to government censorship and corporate influence (70). NFN deployed nine-foot-tall Freedom Towers at Occupy Wall Street in September and Occupy Austin in October 2011, in order to provide secured WiFi connectivity to activists on the ground (71).

Mesh networks have the potential to circumvent government oversight even if the Internet is being shut down. Meraka Institute in South Africa offers a do-it-yourself guide to planning and building a Freifunk based mesh network in rural areas (72). The Serval Mesh is an Android app that allows smartphones on the same WiFi network to communicate with each other like two-way radios or CB radios (73). FireChat makes use of the Multipeer Connectivity APIs in iOS 7 to enable iPhones to connect to one another directly using Bluetooth or WiFi without Internet connection (74). In September 2014, Hong Kong's young protesters were able to set up splinter protests using FireChat.

"You could have someone taking pictures and video at a protest and sharing them immediately to the mesh," said Paul Gardner-Stephen, a research fellow at Flinders University in Adelaide, Australia. "Even if that person's phone is seized, the footage has already made it to 10 other phones in the area, and then to hundreds or thousands more" (75).

As affordable computing power and data storage capacity continue to increase, we can envision a new peer-to-peer social networking application in the future that combines Skype's VoIP (voice over Internet Protocol) and Facebook's Timeline. We will not upload personal information for storage in central servers or public clouds that are subject to the exploitation by businesses. Instead, each tight-knit community of family and friends will form its own circle of peer-to-peer social network, secured from prying eyes.

Backed by America's largest home security company ADT, San Francisco-based startup Life360 offers a free mobile app that allows families to share their locations and activities with each other in a secure private network (76). Recent research on steganography allows covert communication by concealing messages among background noise like a camouflage (77). In the distant future, quantum Internet will allow the transmission of information with ultimate privacy and security using quantum teleportation which transmits data from one point to another without passing through the space in between (78).

19.6 Facebook Questions and a Google a Day

In July 2010, Facebook introduced "Facebook Questions." Akin to Yahoo! Answers, the question-and-answer feature allows users to pose their questions to the entire Facebook community (79). But by October 2012, Facebook Questions had disappeared (80).

Peace on Facebook https://www.facebook.com/peace/ posed the same question every day in the users' own language: "Do you think we will achieve world peace within 50 years?" On May 29, 2014, the answer was a minuscule 5.41% in the United States (81). So Facebook is asking the follow-up question: "How can we grow this number?"

In April 2011, Google launched "A Google a Day" trivia. User experience researcher Dan Russell wrote in the official Google blog, "As the world of information continues to explode, we hope 'A Google a Day' triggers your imagination and helps you discover all the types of questions you can ask Google – and get an answer" (82).

The "Deep Thought" supercomputer in Douglas Adams' *The Hitchhiker's Guide to the Galaxy* (first broadcasted in 1978) took seven and a half million years to compute the answer to the ultimate question of life, the universe, and everything. The answer turned out to be 42, but the ultimate question itself was unknown (83).

Billions of cybercitizens on Facebook, Google, Twitter, Yahoo!, and other social networks are giving us many different answers to every difficult question. Nevertheless, if we ask the right question, we will get the correct answer. The question is not whether Total Information Awareness (TIA) is here to stay; the real question is whether TIA is a one-way street or a two-way street.

19.7   Two-Way Street of Total Information Awareness and Metaverse

Private businesses and the ubiquity of social networks are creating the necessary technologies and infrastructures for Total Information Awareness (TIA). However, unlike the government-proposed TIA which is a rigid one-way mirror, the industry-led TIA is an evolving two-way street. Facebook, Google, YouTube, Wikipedia, Politwoops, AllGov.com, and even the controversial WikiLeaks all collect information and make it available to everyone, whether they are individuals, businesses, or government agencies. Medical patient social networks such as PatientsLikeMe share their databases with biotechnology and pharmaceutical companies to advance medical research.

There are some safety concerns about exposing too much information online, especially high value terrorist targets. According to the Federal Bureau of Investigation (FBI), the individuals who planned the attempted car bombing of Times Square on May 1, 2010 used public web cameras for reconnaissance (84).

As a precaution, Google Maps has digitally modified or blurred its satellite imagery on some landmarks including the roof of the White House, NATO air force hub serving as a retreat for the Operation Iraqi Freedom forces, Mobil Oil facilities in Buffalo New York, and even the Dutch Royal Family's Huis Ten Bosch Palace in Netherlands (85).

Not only are consumers knowingly sharing their private information with big businesses, government officials are also leaking classified information to the media and private companies for either financial gains or political purposes. In 2012, seven U.S. Navy SEALs were reprimanded for divulging classified combat gear to Electronic Arts, maker of the multiplatform game "Medal of Honor: Warfighter" (86). A string of leaks from high-ranking government officials resulted in the public airing of details about the U.S. cyberattack on Iran's nuclear centrifuge program (87), increased U.S. drone strikes against militants in Yemen (88) and Pakistan (89), and a double agent disrupting al-Qaeda's custom-fit underwear bombing plot (90).

Even President Barack Obama himself revealed on a Google+ video chat room interview in January 2012 that the U.S. conducted many drone strikes to hunt down al-Qaeda and Taliban in Pakistan (91). Some former military and intelligence officers accused Obama of disclosing clandestine operations to the public. Ex-Navy SEAL Benjamin Smith voiced his opposition to leaks, "As a citizen, it is my civic duty to tell the president to stop leaking information to the enemy. It will get Americans killed." Another former Navy SEAL Scott Taylor said of the bin Laden raid, "If you disclose how we got there, how we took down the building, what we did, how many people were there, that it's going to hinder future operations, and certainly hurt the success of those future operations" (92).

Then CIA director David Petraeus issued a statement to his employees in January 2012 about the arrest of a former Agency officer by the FBI on charges that he illegally disclosed classified information to reporters. Petraeus wrote, "Unauthorized disclosures of any sort—including information concerning the identities of other Agency officers—betray the public trust, our country, and our colleagues" (93).

On the other hand, Thomas Blanton, Director of National Security Archive at George Washington University, testified in December 2010 before the U.S. House of Representatives on the massive overclassification of the U.S. government's national security information. At the Judiciary Committee hearing on the Espionage Act and the legal and constitutional implications of WikiLeaks, Blanton said that "Actually our job as citizens is to ask questions. ... Experts believe 50% to 90% of our national security secrets could be public with little or no damage to real security" (94). He cited his findings:

> A few years back, when Rep. Christopher Shays (R-CT) asked Secretary of Defense Donald Rumsfeld's deputy for counterintelligence and security how much government information was overclassified, her answer was 50%. After the 9/11 Commission reviewed the government's most sensitive records about Osama bin Laden and Al-Qaeda, the co-chair of that commission, former Governor of New Jersey Tom Kean, commented that "three-quarters of what I read that was classified shouldn't have been" — a 75% judgment. President Reagan's National Security Council secretary Rodney McDaniel estimated in 1991 that only 10% of classification was for "legitimate protection of secrets" — so 90% unwarranted. Another data point comes from the Interagency Security Classification Appeals Panel, over the past 15 years, has overruled agency secrecy claims in whole or in part in some 65% of its cases.

WikiLeaks founder Julian Assange said in a 2011 interview, "Our No. 1 enemy is ignorance. And I believe that is the No. 1 enemy for everyone — it's not understanding what actually is going on in the world" (95). Bill Keller, former executive editor of *The Times,* opines that "the most palpable legacy of the WikiLeaks campaign for transparency is that the U.S. government is more secretive than ever" (96). U.S. Air Force Senior Airman Christopher R. Atkins wrote in his email to American filmmaker Michael Moore, "The single greatest danger to America and our way of life is ourselves. No foreign power can dictate your oppression. No foreign army can impose martial law upon us. No foreign dictator can remove the precious right that I am exercising at this moment. Militaries do not keep people free! Militaries keep us safe, but it is we citizens who ensure freedom!" (97).

Notwithstanding the potential risks of misinformation and the benefits of information sharing, the two-way street of Total Information Awareness is the road that leads to a more transparent and complete picture of ourselves, our governments, and our world. As Wikipedia's founder Jimmy Wales said, "Imagine a world in which every single person on the planet is given free access to the sum of all human knowledge" (98). Lila Tretikov, Executive Director of the Wikimedia Foundation, told *The Guardian* in her 2014 interview, "Glasnost was a phenomenal, renaissance period in the history of Russia and taught me much about importance of freedom of information. The only real way to improve conditions of civilizations is to provide open access to information for education and culture, and to be honest about the past. Otherwise we spend our lives siloed from each other and we repeat the mistakes of our grandparents" (99).

History often repeats itself. For example, World War I and World War II. But rest assured that there are many people in all walks of life—likened to military officer Stanislav Petrov (100) (101), activist Malala Yousafzai (102), and politician President Jimmy Carter (103)—who are doing everything possible to prevent World War III.

Some people may want to escape the real world at times into "metaverse"—a term coined by Neal Stephenson in his 1992 novel Snow Crash about a 3D virtual world inhabited by avatars of real people. Ernest Cline's 2011 novel *Ready Player One* and its adaption by Steven Spielberg into a 2018 blockbuster movie further popularized the term "metaverse." So much so that Facebook has changed its official company name to Meta in October 2021, and its iconic thumbs-up sign replaced by a blue infinity logo (104).

Facebook defines "metaverse" as "a set of virtual spaces where you can create and explore with other people who aren't in the same physical space as you" (105). Mark Zuckerberg explains the company's name change from Facebook to Meta: "Today we're seen as a social media company. But in our DNA, we are a company that builds technology to connect people. And the metaverse is the next frontier just like social networking was when we got started" (106).

Whether or not we embrace metaverse, humanity must learn to balance logic and emotion. Spock said in the 1982 Star Trek movie *The Wrath of Khan:* "Logic clearly dictates that the needs of the many outweigh the needs of the few." But Kirk added in the 1984 sequel *The Search for Spock:* "The needs of the one… outweigh the needs of the many." The two-way street of Total Information Awareness offers more benefits than risks in the massively connected world of Facebook Nation or Metaverse.

References

1. **Obama, Barack.** 2011 State of the Union Address. [Online] PBS, January 25, 2011. http://www.pbs.org/newshour/interactive/speeches/4/2011-state-union-address/.
2. **Pepitone, Julianne.** Facebook trading sets record IPO volume. [Online] CNNMoney, May 18, 2012. http://money.cnn.com/2012/05/18/technology/facebook-ipo-trading/index.htm.
3. **Spears, Lee and Frier, Sarah.** Facebook Advances in Public Debut After $16 Billion IPO. [Online] Bloomberg, May 18, 2012. http://www.bloomberg.com/news/2012-05-17/facebook-raises-16-billion-in-biggest-technology-ipo-on-record.html.

4. **Sengupta, Somini and Rusli, Evelyn M.** Personal Data's Value? Facebook Is Set to Find Out. [Online] The New York Times, January 31, 2012. http://www.nytimes.com/2012/02/01/technology/riding-personal-data-facebook-is-going-public.html.

5. **Zuckerberg, Mark.** Facebook Timeline. [Online] Facebook, May 19, 2012. http://www.facebook.com/zuck.

6. —. Beast. [Online] Facebook. [Cited: May 27, 2012.] http://www.facebook.com/zuck#!/beast.the.dog.

7. **Boo's owner.** Boo. [Online] Facebook, April 11, 2012. http://www.facebook.com/Boo/.

8. **Twain, Mark.** Directory of Mark Twain's maxims, quotations, and various opinions. [Online] Twainquotes.com. [Cited: May 28, 2012.] http://www.twainquotes.com/Death.html.

9. **Good Morning America.** Zuckerberg's Dinners with Girlfriend Help Spur Life-Saving Facebook Tool. [Online] ABC News, May 1, 2012. http://abcnews.go.com/blogs/headlines/2012/05/zuckerbergs-dinners-with-girlfriend-help-spur-life-saving-facebook-tool/.

10. **Imam, Jareen.** The anti-social network: Life without Facebook. [Online] CNN, May 18, 2012. http://www.cnn.com/2012/05/18/tech/social-media/facebook-deactivation-ireport/index.html.

11. **Whitney, Lance.** 1 in 3 users are tuning out Facebook. [Online] CNet, June 6, 2012. http://asia.cnet.com/1-in-3-users-are-tuning-out-facebook-62216195.htm.

12. **Mcclellan, Steve.** Is Facebook Getting Uncool for 18-24s? [Online] Adweek, November 16, 2009. http://www.adweek.com/news/technology/facebook-getting-uncool-18-24s-100908.

13. **Johnson, Bobbie.** Privacy no longer a social norm, says Facebook founder. [Online] The Guardian, January 10, 2010. http://www.theguardian.com/technology/2010/jan/11/facebook-privacy.

14. **Ellis, Blake.** Craziest tax deductions: Carrier pigeons. [Online] CNNMoney, March 9, 2012. http://money.cnn.com/galleries/2012/pf/taxes/1203/gallery.wacky-tax-deductions/.

15. **Israel, Shel.** Is Facebook Larry Page's Moby Dick? [Online] Forbes, May 3, 2012. http://www.forbes.com/sites/shelisrael/2012/05/03/is-google-larry-pages-moby-dick/2/.

16. **Kosner, Anthony Wing.** Facebook Fails Us, Why Mark Zuckerberg's Revolution Will Not Be Fully Monetized. [Online] Forbes, May 26, 2012. http://www.forbes.com/sites/anthonykosner/2012/05/26/facebook-fails-us-the-revolution-will-not-be-monetized/.

17. **Shay, Miya.** Houston City Council votes to turn off red light cameras. [Online] ABC 13, August 24, 2011. http://abclocal.go.com/ktrk/story?section=news/local&id=8323624.

18. **Rettinga, Richard A., Fergusona, Susan A. and Hakkertb, A. Shalom.** Effects of Red Light Cameras on Violations and Crashes: A Review of the International Literature. [Online] Traffic Injury Prevention. 4(1):17–23, 2003. http://www.tandfonline.com/doi/abs/10.1080/15389580309858.

19. **Etzioni, Amitai.** Despite Facebook, privacy is far from dead. [Online] CNN, May 27, 2012. http://www.cnn.com/2012/05/25/opinion/etzioni-facebook-privacy/index.html.

20. **Lucas, Fred.** Obama: 'Google, Facebook Would Not Exist' Without Government. [Online] The Washington Times, April 6, 2012. http://times247.com/articles/obama-google-facebook-would-not-exist-without-big-government.

21. **Ackerman, Spencer.** The iPhone 4S' Talking Assistant Is a Military Veteran. [Online] Wired, October 5, 2011. http://www.wired.com/dangerroom/2011/10/siri-darpa-iphone/.

22. **SRI International.** PAL (Personalized Assistant that Learns). [Online] SRI International. [Cited: May 28, 2012.] https://pal.sri.com/Plone.

23. **RT.** WikiLeaks revelations only tip of iceberg – Assange. [Online] RT News, May 2, 2011. http://www.rt.com/news/wikileaks-revelations-assange-interview/.

24. **Kalil, Tom.** Big Data is a Big Deal. [Online] The White House, March 29, 2012. http://www.whitehouse.gov/blog/2012/03/29/big-data-big-deal.

25. **CDC.** CDC BioSense Program. [Online] Centers for Disease Control and Prevention, February 8, 2012. http://www.cdc.gov/biosense/.

26. **Young, Denise.** Letitia Long: A Global Vision. Alumna leads intelligence agency in new era of collaboration. [Online] Virginia Tech Magazine, Spring 2012. http://www.vtmag.vt.edu/spring12/letitia-long.html.

27. **U.S. News & World Report.** Q&A: DNI Chief Scientist Eric Haseltine. [Online] U.S. News & World Report, November 3, 2006. http://www.usnews.com/usnews/news/articles/061103/3qahaseltine_6.htm.

28. **Facebook.** Form S-1 Registration Statement. [Online] United States Securities and Exchange Commission, February 1, 2012. http://sec.gov/Archives/edgar/data/1326801/000119312512034517/d287954ds1.htm.

29. **Zuckerberg, Mark.** Today at the Facebook Communities Summit we changed our mission to focus on bringing the world closer together. [Online] Facebook, June 22, 2017. https://www.facebook.com/zuck/posts/10154944663901634.

30. —. Bringing the World Closer Together. [Online] Facebook, June 22, 2017. https://www.facebook.com/notes/393134628500376/.

31. **Corey, Helen.** Google's iPhone Tracking. [Online] The Wall Street Journal Readers' Comments. [Cited: February 17, 2012.] http://online.wsj.com/article_email/SB10001424052970204880404577225380456599176-lMyQjAxMTAyMDEwNjExNDYyWj.html#articleTabs%3Dcomments.

32. **Angwin, Julia and Valentino-Devries, Jennifer.** Google's iPhone Tracking. [Online] The Wall Street Journal, February 17, 2012. http://online.wsj.com/article/SB10001424052970204880404577225380456599176.html.

33. **Riley, Charles.** Sales of Orwell's '1984' spike after NSA leak. [Online] CNNMoney, June 12, 2013. http://money.cnn.com/2013/06/12/news/1984-nsa-snowden/index.html.

34. **Orwell, George.** Nineteen Eighty-Four. [Online] Secker and Warburg (London), 1949. http://books.google.com/books/about/1984.html?id=yxv1LK5gyV4C.

35. **West, Ed.** George Orwell, the prophet of political correctness, does not belong to the Left. [Online] The Telegraph, August 23, 2012. http://blogs.telegraph.co.uk/news/edwest/100177627/george-orwell-the-prophet-of-political-correctness-does-not-belong-to-the-left/.

36. **Beale, Lewis.** We're living '1984' today. [Online] CNN, August 3, 2013. http://www.cnn.com/2013/08/03/opinion/beale-1984-now/index.html.

37. **3VR Inc.** Use Video Analytics and Data Decision Making to Grow Your Business. [Online] Digital Signage Today. [Cited: May 28, 2012.] http://www.digitalsignagetoday.com/whitepapers/4891/Use-Video-Analytics-and-Data-Decision-Making-to-Grow-Your-Business.

38. **Fussey, Pete.** An Interrupted Transmission? Processes of CCTV Implementation and the Impact of Human Agency, Surveillance & Society. [Online] Surveillance and Criminal Justice. 4(3): 229–256, 2007. http://www.surveillance-and-society.org.

39. **Reeve, Tom.** How many cameras in the UK? Only 1.85 million, claims ACPO lead on CCTV. [Online] Security News Desk, March 2011. http://www.securitynewsdesk.com/2011/03/01/how-many-cctv-cameras-in-the-uk/.

40. **Hope, Christopher.** 1,000 CCTV cameras to solve just one crime, Met Police admits. [Online] The Telegraph, August 25, 2009. http://www.telegraph.co.uk/news/uknews/crime/6082530/1000-CCTV-cameras-to-solve-just-one-crime-Met-Police-admits.html.

41. **BBC News.** 'Ring of steel' widened. [Online] BBC News, December 18, 2003. http://news.bbc.co.uk/2/hi/uk_news/england/london/3330771.stm.

42. **Wright, Lawrence.** The Spymaster. Can Mike McConnell fix America's intelligence community? [Online] The New Yorker, January 21, 2008. http://www.newyorker.com/reporting/2008/01/21/080121fa_fact_wright?currentPage=all.

43. **Viisage Technology, Inc.** Viisage Technology and Biometrica Systems Achieve 50th Facial Recognition Installation at Mirage Resort, Las Vegas. [Online] PR Newswire, March 29, 2012. http://www.prnewswire.com/news-releases/viisage-technology-and-biometrica-systems-achieve-50th-facial-recognition-installation-at-mirage-resort-las-vegas-73268177.html.

44. **Murph, Darren.** SceneTap app analyzes pubs and clubs in real-time, probably won't score you a Jersey Shore cameo. [Online] Engadget, June 12, 2011. http://www.engadget.com/2011/06/12/scenetap-app-analyzes-pubs-and-clubs-in-real-time-probably-won/.

45. **Goldman, David.** Intel wants to plug a smartphone into your brain. [Online] CNNMoney, May 3, 2012. http://money.cnn.com/2012/05/03/technology/smartphone-in-your-brain/index.htm.

46. **Bell, Gordon and Gemmell, Jim.** Total Recall: How the E-Memory Revolution Will Change Everything. [Online] Dutton Adult, September 17, 2009. http://books.google.com/books/about/Total_Recall.html?id=AoBdPgAACAAJ.

47. **Hornyak, Tim.** Eyeborg: Man Replaces False Eye with Bionic Camera. [Online] IEEE Spectrum, June 11, 2010. http://spectrum.ieee.org/automaton/biomedical/bionics/061110-eyeborg-bionic-eye.

48. **Orden, Erica.** His Hindsight Is 20-20. [Online] The Wall Street Journal, December 3, 2010. http://online.wsj.com/article/SB10001424052748703377504575651091530462742.html.

49. **Metz, Rachel.** My Life, Logged. [Online] MIT Technology Review, June 10, 2014. http://www.technologyreview.com/review/528076/my-life-logged/.

50. **McGee, Jordan.** FacialNetwork.com Announces Beta Release Of "NameTag" The First Real-Time Facial Recognition App For Google Glass. [Online] Yahoo! Finance, December 19, 2013. http://finance.yahoo.com/news/facialnetwork-com-announces-beta-release-200300439.html.

51. **Cashmore, Pete.** Why 2012, despite privacy fears, isn't like Orwell's 1984. [Online] CNN, January 23, 2012. http://www.cnn.com/2012/01/23/tech/social-media/web-1984-orwell-cashmore/index.html.

52. **Bartz, Andrea and Ehrlich, Brenna.** Baby-pic overload! Social media advice for parents. [Online] CNN, May 8, 2012. http://www.cnn.com/2012/05/09/tech/social-media/social-media-parents-netiquette/index.html.

53. **Kelly, Max.** Memories of Friends Departed Endure on Facebook. [Online] The Facebook Blog, October 26, 2009. http://www.facebook.com/blog.php?post=163091042130.

54. **Postman, Neil.** Amusing Ourselves to Death: Public Discourse in the Age of Show Business. [Online] Penguin, November 4, 1986. http://books.google.com/books/about/Amusing_Ourselves_to_Death.html?id=zGkhbPEjkRoC.

55. **Wikipedia.** In the Year 2525. [Online] Wikipedia. [Cited: May 11, 2014.] http://en.wikipedia.org/wiki/In_the_Year_2525.

56. **Diamandis, Peter.** The future is brighter than you think. [Online] CNN, May 6, 2012. http://www.cnn.com/2012/05/06/opinion/diamandis-abundance-innovation/index.html.

57. **Grossman, Lev.** Person of the Year 2010. Mark Zuckerberg. [Online] TIME Magazine, December 15, 2010. http://www.time.com/time/specials/packages/article/0,28804,2036683_2037183_2037185,00.html.

58. **Facebook.** Internet.org. [Online] Facebook, August 20, 2013. https://www.facebook.com/facebook/posts/10152101244851729.

59. **Internet.org.** Announcing the Connectivity Lab at Facebook. [Online] Internet.org, March 27, 2014. http://internet.org/press/announcing-the-connectivity-lab-at-facebook.

60. **Simonite, Tom.** Digital Summit: Facebook Puts Its Apps on a Data Diet as Part of a Global Internet Campaign. [Online] MIT Technology Review, June 10, 2014. http://www.technologyreview.com/news/528246/digital-summit-facebook-puts-its-apps-on-a-data-diet-as-part-of-a-global-internet/.

61. **Manjoo, Farhad.** Can Facebook Innovate? A Conversation With Mark Zuckerberg. [Online] The New York Times, April 26, 2014. http://bits.blogs.nytimes.com/2014/04/16/can-facebook-innovate-a-conversation-with-mark-zuckerberg/.

62. **Constine, Josh.** Zuck Says Ads Aren't The Way To Monetize Messaging, WhatsApp Will Prioritize Growth Not Subscriptions. [Online] TechCrunch, February 19, 2014. http://techcrunch.com/2014/02/19/whatsapp-will-monetize-later/.

63. **Griffin, John.** Mark Zuckerberg's big idea: The 'next 5 billion' people. [Online] CNNMoney, August   21,   2013.   http://money.cnn.com/2013/08/20/technology/social/facebook-zuckerberg-5-billion/index.html.

64. **Brandom, Russell.** Facebook is developing millimeter-wave networks for Internet.org. [Online] The Verge, February 9, 2016. https://www.theverge.com/2016/2/9/10951200/facebook-millimeter-wave-mesh-networks-starry.

65. **United States Census Bureau.** U.S. and World Population Clock. [Online] United States Census Bureau. [Cited: April 25, 2021.] http://www.census.gov/popclock/.

66. **Rushkoff, Douglas.** Facebook IPO's meaning: Zuckerberg faces reality. [Online] CNN, February   22,   2012.   http://www.cnn.com/2012/01/31/opinion/rushkoff-facebook-ipo/index.html.

67. **Gross, Doug.** Google boss: Entire world will be online by 2020. [Online] CNN, April 15, 2013. http://www.cnn.com/2013/04/15/tech/web/eric-schmidt-internet/index.html.

68. **Geeks Without Frontiers.** Global Vision. [Online] The Manna Energy Foundation. [Cited: June 15, 2014.] http://www.geekswf.org/vision.html.

69. **Pan, Joann.** Samsung Opens Solar-Powered Internet Schools in Africa. [Online] Mashable, November 2, 2012. http://mashable.com/2012/11/02/samsung-internet-schools/.

70. **The FNF.** We envision a world where communities build, maintain, and own their own share of the global computer network. [Online] The Free Network Foundation. [Cited: August 17, 2014.] https://thefnf.org/about/.

71. **Anderson, Brian A. and Carr, Erin Lee.** Movement aims to decentralize the Internet. [Online] CNN, March 28, 2012. http://www.cnn.com/2012/03/28/tech/web/vice-free-the-network/index.html.

72. **Meraka Institute.** DIY Mesh Guide. Wireless Africa. [Online] Meraka Institute, May 26, 2009. http://wirelessafrica.meraka.org.za/wiki/index.php/DIY_Mesh_Guide.

73. **Serval Project.** The Serval Mesh. [Online] Google Play, July 8, 2013. https://play.google.com/store/apps/details?id=org.servalproject.

74. **Simonite, Tom.** The Latest Chat App for iPhone Needs No Internet Connection. [Online] MIT Technology Review, March 28, 2014. http://www.technologyreview.com/news/525921/the-latest-chat-app-for-iphone-needs-no-internet-connection/.

75. —. Build Your Own Internet with Mobile Mesh Networking. [Online] MIT Technology Review, July 9, 2013. http://www.technologyreview.com/news/516571/build-your-own-internet-with-mobile-mesh-networking/.

76. **Chapman, Lizette.** Home Security Giant ADT Backs Startup Life360 for 'Internet of Things'. [Online] The Wall Street Journal, May 13, 2014. http://blogs.wsj.com/digits/2014/05/13/home-security-giant-adt-backs-startup-life360-for-internet-of-things/.

77. **Emerging Technology From the arXiv.** World's First Covert Communications System   with   Camouflage   Guaranteed.   [Online]   MIT   Technology Review,   May   8,   2014.   http://www.technologyreview.com/view/527186/worlds-first-covert-communications-system-with-camouflage-guaranteed/.

78. —. Diamond Teleporters Herald New Era of Quantum Routing. [Online] MIT Technology Review, April 22, 2014. http://www.technologyreview.com/view/526801/diamond-teleporters-herald-new-era-of-quantum-routing/.

79. **Ross, Blake.** Searching for Answers? Ask Facebook Questions. [Online] The Facebook Blog, July 28, 2010. http://blog.facebook.com/blog.php?post=411795942130.

80. **McGee, Matt.** Facebook Questions Is Finally Dead. [Online] Marketing Land, October 30, 2012. https://marketingland.com/facebook-questions-is-finally-dead-25474.

81. **Facebook.** Peace on Facebook. [Online] Facebook. [Cited: August 17, 2014.] https://www.facebook.com/peace/.

82. **Russell, Dan.** A trivia game where using Google is allowed. [Online] Google Official Blog, April 11, 2011. http://googleblog.blogspot.com/2011/04/trivia-game-where-using-google-is.html#!/2011/04/trivia-game-where-using-google-is.html.

83. **Adams, Douglas.** The Ultimate Hitchhiker's Guide to the Galaxy. [Online] Del Rey, April 30, 2002. http://books.google.com/books/about/The_Ultimate_Hitchhiker_s_Guide_to_the_G.html?id=a-apCPdumpsC.

84. **Mueller, Robert S. III.** Combating Threats in the Cyber World: Outsmarting Terrorists, Hackers, and Spies. [Online] Federal Bureau of Investigation, March 1, 2012. http://www.fbi.gov/news/speeches/combating-threats-in-the-cyber-world-outsmarting-terrorists-hackers-and-spies.

85. **Jackson, Nicholas.** 15 High-Profile Sites That Google Doesn't Want You to See. [Online] The Atlantic, June 21, 2011. http://www.theatlantic.com/technology/archive/2011/06/15-high-profile-sites-that-google-doesnt-want-you-to-see/240766/.

86. **Mount, Mike.** Navy SEALs punished for revealing secrets to video game maker. [Online] CNN, November 9, 2012. http://security.blogs.cnn.com/2012/11/09/navy-seals-busted-for-giving-secrets-to-make-video-game-more-real/.

87. **Sanger, David E.** Obama Order Sped Up Wave of Cyberattacks Against Iran. [Online] The New York Times, June 1, 2012. http://www.nytimes.com/2012/06/01/world/middleeast/obama-ordered-wave-of-cyberattacks-against-iran.html?pagewanted=all.

88. **Schmitt, Eric.** U.S. to Step Up Drone Strikes Inside Yemen. [Online] The New York Times, April 25, 2012. http://www.nytimes.com/2012/04/26/world/middleeast/us-to-step-up-drone-strikes-inside-yemen.html.

89. **Cloud, David S. and Rodriguez, Alex.** CIA gets nod to step up drone strikes in Pakistan. [Online] Los Angeles Times, June 8, 2012. http://articles.latimes.com/2012/jun/08/world/la-fg-pakistan-drone-surge-20120608.

90. **Shane, Scott and Schmitt, Eric.** Double Agent Disrupted Bombing Plot, U.S. Says. [Online] The New York Times, May 8, 2012. http://www.nytimes.com/2012/05/09/world/middleeast/suicide-mission-volunteer-was-double-agent-officials-say.html?pagewanted=all.

91. **Levine, Adam.** Obama admits to Pakistan drone strikes. [Online] CNN, January 30, 2012. http://security.blogs.cnn.com/2012/01/30/obama-admits-to-pakistan-drone-strikes/.

92. **McConnell, Dugald and Todd, Brian.** Former special forces officers slam Obama over leaks on bin Laden killing. [Online] CNN, August 17, 2012. http://www.cnn.com/2012/08/16/politics/former-seals-obama/index.html.

93. **Petraeus, David H.** Statement to Employees by Director of the Central Intelligence Agency David H. Petraeus on Safeguarding our Secrets. [Online] Central Intelligence Agency, January 23, 2012. https://www.cia.gov/news-information/press-releases-statements/2012-press-releases-statements/safeguarding-our-secrets.html.

94. **Blanton, Thomas.** Hearing on the Espionage Act and the Legal and Constitutional Implications of Wikileaks. [Online] Committee on the Judiciary, U.S. House of Representatives, December 16, 2010. http://www.gwu.edu/~nsarchiv/news/20101216/Blanton101216.pdf.

95. **RT.** WikiLeaks revelations only tip of iceberg – Assange. [Online] RT, May 3, 2011. http://rt.com/news/wikileaks-revelations-assange-interview/.

96. **Keller, Bill.** WikiLeaks, a Postscript. [Online] The New York Times, February 19, 2012. http://www.nytimes.com/2012/02/20/opinion/keller-wikileaks-a-postscript.html.

97. **Atkins, Christopher R.** I solemnly swear to defend the Constitution of the United States of America against all enemies, foreign and domestic. [Online] Michael Moore, January 28, 2005. http://www.michaelmoore.com/words/soldiers-letters/i-solemnly-swear-to-defend-the-constitution-of-the-united-states-of-america-against-all-enemies-foreign-and-domestic.

98. **Wales, Jimmy.** An appeal from Wikipedia founder Jimmy Wales. [Online] Wikimedia Foundation, October 30, 2010. http://wikimediafoundation.org/wiki/Appeal2/en.

99. **Kiss, Jemima and Gibbs, Samuel.** Wikipedia boss Lila Tretikov: 'Glasnost taught me much about freedom of information'. [Online] The Guardian, August 6, 2014. http://www.theguardian.com/technology/2014/aug/06/wikipedia-lila-tretikov-glasnost-freedom-of-information.

100. **Steele, Jonathan.** Cold war Soviet commander whose cool response to reports of a US missile attack was pivotal in averting nuclear war. [Online] The Guardian, October 11, 2017. https://www.theguardian.com/world/2017/oct/11/stanislav-petrov-obituary.

101. **Bennetts, Marc.** Soviet officer who averted cold war nuclear disaster dies aged 77. [Online] The Guardian, September 18, 2017. https://www.theguardian.com/world/2017/sep/18/soviet-officer-who-averted-cold-war-nuclear-disaster-dies-aged-77.

102. **NobelPrize.org.** Malala Yousafzai – Biographical. [Online] Nobel Media AB, 2014. https://www.nobelprize.org/prizes/peace/2014/yousafzai/biographical/.

103. —. The Nobel Peace Prize for 2002. [Online] Nobel Media AB, October 11, 2002. https://www.nobelprize.org/prizes/peace/2002/press-release/.

104. **Peters, Jay.** Facebook's famous thumbs-up HQ sign has been replaced with Meta. *The Verge.* [Online] October 28, 2021. https://www.theverge.com/2021/10/28/22751143/facebook-thumbs-up-like-meta-sign-global-headquarters-replaced.

105. **Facebook.** Building the Metaverse Responsibly. *Facebook Newsroom.* [Online] September 27, 2021. https://about.fb.com/news/2021/09/building-the-metaverse-responsibly/.

106. **Facebeook Reality Labs.** Mark Zuckerberg and Facebook executives share their vision for the metaverse—the next evolution of social technology, built by people like you. *Facebook.* [Online] October 28, 2021. https://www.facebook.com/watch/live/?ref=watch_permalink&v=561535698440683.

Index

Printed in the United States
by Baker & Taylor Publisher Services